Jacobean Gentleman

———————————

Portrait of Sir Edwin Sandys at Graythwaite Hall. (Courtesy of Lieutenant-Colonel G. O. Sandys and Major M. E. M. Sandys.)

Jacobean Gentleman

SIR EDWIN SANDYS, 1561–1629

Theodore K. Rabb

PRINCETON UNIVERSITY PRESS

PRINCETON, NEW JERSEY

Copyright ⓠ 1998 by Princeton University Press
Published by Princeton University Press, 41 William Street,
Princeton, New Jersey 08540
In the United Kingdom: Princeton University Press, Chichester, West Sussex

Library of Congress Cataloging-in-Publication Data

Rabb, Theodore K.
Jacobean gentleman : Sir Edwin Sandys, 1561–1629 / Theodore K.
Rabb.
p. cm.
Includes bibliographical references and index.
1. Sandys, Edwin, Sir, 1561–1629.   2. Great Britain—History—
James I, 1603–1625—Biography.   3. Great Britain—Politics and
government—1603–1625.   4. Great Britain. Parliament—
History—17th century.   5. Legislators—Great Britain—
Biography.   I. Title.
DA391.1.S3R33   1998   941.06818092—dc21   97-44316   [B]   CIP

ISBN 0-691-02694-7 (cloth : alk. paper)

This book has been composed in Caledonia

Princeton University Press books are printed on acid-free paper
and meet the guidelines for permanence and durability of the
Committee on Production Guidelines for Book Longevity of the
Council on Library Resources

http://pup.princeton.edu

Printed in the United States of America

1   3   5   7   9   10   8   6   4   2

For Tamar

_____

CONTENTS

Part Three: *Commerce and Colonization*

Part Four: *Jacobean Gentleman*

PREFACE

"I ALWAYS thought Sandys was like Ireland—the place of ultimate defeat—so many have made a start on him," Elizabeth Foster once remarked in a letter, and her reminder has haunted me during nearly forty years of interrupted attempts to complete a biography of that elusive figure. Like his colleague Bacon (though not on that august level), Sandys defies assessment because of his versatility: the biographer has to become familiar not only with the literature on religious toleration, but also with the minutiae of parliamentary procedure and the intricacies of trade and colonization in London. If one considers, in addition, the absence of personal papers and the paucity of documentation beyond his public actions, it is no wonder that historians have contented themselves with limited forays into Sandys's career. As a result, misconceptions and distortions have been legion, including such errors of fact as the creation of a twin brother for Sir Edwin or his depiction as a merchant and *not* a landowner, and such errors of interpretation as the belief that he was a tribune of the people determined to found democracy in America. Yet he also merited a 1964 *Ripley's Believe It or Not* newspaper item as "a member of the English parliament and the ancestor of 7 generations, in each of which the eldest son was elected to Parliament—it represented a continuous line of 211 years." Fine studies of certain aspects of his life, primarily his leadership of the Virginia Company, have led to no comprehensive account.

The need to roam widely has affected the writing of this book in a number of ways. It has resulted, first, in the postponement of the biography while another book, *Enterprise and Empire*, published in 1967, was completed. There seemed no way of understanding why a staid member of the English gentry, not forced to fall back on commerce as a means of making a living, should have wanted to become so involved in the world of business and colonization. Only by studying the phenomenon of gentry investment as a whole, in the context of sixteenth- and seventeenth-century London, could I satisfy myself that Sandys's efforts appeared in proper perspective.

Second, when I came to describe his role in the Jacobean House of Commons, it soon became apparent that, without private papers, one could not make sense of his public pronouncements merely by allowing them to stand on their own. It was essential to see his speeches and maneuvers in the setting of day-to-day events in Parliament. Unfortunately, with few exceptions, no detailed chronology has been established for the

Jacobean period to compare with Neale's history of the Elizabethan Commons. For all the monographs, the superb editions of diaries, the surveys by the most distinguished Stuart historians of the past century, and the recognition that this was one of the decisive acts in the drama that produced many modern notions of constitutional government, the day-to-day narrative for James I's reign has not been fundamentally recast since S. R. Gardiner outlined it over a century ago. Such narration is, of course, the oldest and most characteristic of the tasks historians undertake; few of our efforts are as fundamental as the threading together of a succession of events amidst conflicting and incomplete documentation. For the purposes of a biography I had to limit this endeavor, but Sandys was so deeply involved in most of the major issues of the time that to relate the context is often to describe the proceedings of the Commons as a whole.

Some passages in this book thus touch only indirectly on Sir Edwin's own activities; nevertheless, they are vital for an appreciation of his intentions, and they are not meant to remove him from the center of attention. In other words, there was no way to trace his career without looking more widely, raising implications and reaching conclusions that extend beyond the man himself. Indeed, my hope is that, by telling the story of the House of Commons through the eyes of the member who was its dominant figure longer than anyone else in James I's reign, I can suggest an overall perspective for the parliamentary history of the period at a level of detail that none of the recent analyses of individual sessions or issues has been able to sustain.

It will be clear that this story parts company at many points with the understanding of early Stuart politics that has been advanced for over twenty years by the so-called revisionists. We have all learned from their work, as will be apparent in these pages. But in the last few years, as criticisms have multiplied, it has become apparent that revisionism's central tenet—a depreciation of the political importance of the Commons based on the irregularity of parliamentary meetings, on the Lower House's supposed indifference to constitutional issues, on its preoccupation with local matters and devotion to consensus, and on the insignificant role of its grants—no longer stands. The pendulum has swung, and the momentous events of James's reign seem once again to resemble those that S. R. Gardiner portrayed (though cleansed by the revisionists of some of his disciples' excesses). Yet it bears emphasis that this biography, begun long before revisionism appeared, is not intended as a case study in that historiographic debate. Accordingly, I note only occasionally my departures from the recent literature. My main concern is to recapture Sandys's outlook and achievements as he might have recognized them—to throw a significant shaft of light into his world without claiming that it is the only illumination available for the general issues of his time.

A final preliminary comment about what follows may be in order. Because so many of Sandys's activities are visible only on the public stage, it is almost impossible to use the successive stages of his life as the organizing principle for the story. In an earlier version of this book I attempted to follow the progression of events, even more closely than here, from year to year. As David Harris Sacks pointed out, however, the interweaving of personal, commercial, and parliamentary business merely made each of those topics more difficult to follow. Therefore, I have basically separated them: the personal in part 1, Parliament in part 2, and Commerce in part 3. The original text is available on microfilm for those scholars interested in its details, and those seeking chronological progression may wish to read chapter 12 in this book before chapter 8, and chapter 13 before chapter 10. But it is worth emphasizing that the present structure puts the focus more on the coherences within Sandys's varied preoccupations than on the stages of his life.

The chief justification for the biography is that Sir Edwin's career reflected and often distilled so much of the intellectual, political, and economic activities of the era in which he lived. The second-level figure is often an ideal window into his age, precisely because the view is so broad. Here is someone whose life connects us to Donne and Diodati, to Southampton (and thus Shakespeare) and Sarpi, to Burghley, Bacon, and Buckingham, to Hariot and Hobbes. Moreover, Sandys's contributions to the Commons and Virginia take us beyond that justification, for they helped in no small measure to shape two of the most important developments in Stuart England. His career, in other words, bears directly on major issues of Jacobean politics and society. As its details unfold and one seeks to understand his words and actions, one could do worse than take as a guide the advice Sandys himself offered in his *Relation of the State of Religion*; though imperfectly followed, it can stand as the ideal for any biographer:

> Writers of history should know, that there is a difference between their profession and the practice of advocates. . . . The wisdom of the judge picketh the truth out of both sides, which is entire perhaps in neither.

A work that has been assembled over so many years accumulates many debts, and this one is no exception. The earliest are to Frank Craven, who suggested the subject and guided my first steps; to Menna Prestwich, my tutor at Oxford, who helped shape my view of the period; and to E. H. Harbison, who supervised the dissertation. Since that beginning, the advice of teachers and colleagues at Princeton, above all Joseph Strayer, Lawrence Stone, and Peter Lake, has remained invaluable. Equally important have been conversations and exchanges over the years with Conrad Russell, Christopher Thompson, Roy Schreiber, Linda Peck, Thomas

Kiffin, and Nicholas Tyacke. Despite the difference in our interpretations, Russell has been unfailingly generous in his comments and advice, as my footnotes testify. And they indicate, too, a special debt to Thompson: stimulating in conversation, and unstinting in the copious corrections and references he has suggested over the years. More specific help is cited in the footnotes, but I have benefited particularly from the transcripts of 1624, 1625, and 1626 diaries prepared by the Yale Center for Parliamentary History, and from the comments of Gerald Aylmer, Paul Christianson, Peter Clark, Thomas Cogswell, Esther Cope, Neil Cuddy, Richard Cust, Elizabeth Foster, William Hunt, Joel Hurstfield, Maija Jansson, Mark Kennedy, Mark Kishlansky, David Ransome, David Harris Sacks, Kevin Sharpe, Michael Young, and an anonymous reader. Like all scholars, I am also indebted to the courtesy and assistance of librarians and archivists, in my case at the Folger, Newberry, Huntington, Firestone, Houghton, and Widener libraries in the United States; at the National Library of Scotland; and in England at the British Library, the Public Records Office, the Bodleian, Queen's College Oxford, Cambridge University, Pepys, Inner and Middle Temple libraries, and various County Record Offices. Two research assistants, Carl Estabrook and Tom Webster, transcribed some essential documents on occasions when a trip to the archives proved too short; and a succession of typists labored over the drafts of a manuscript that antedated the word processor. I am grateful, too, for the encouragement of various members of the Sandys family, particularly for the hospitality my family and I were shown by Lieutenant-Colonel G. O. Sandys and his wife at Graythwaite Hall, and for the portrait of Sir Edwin which he and his son, Major M. E. M. Sandys, have provided. But only my wife has endured all the vicissitudes of this biography, steadfastly encouraging its tortoise progress while providing endless help in research, checking, reading drafts, proofreading, and indexing; she alone truly shares the pleasure at its completion. All responsibility for error remains, of course, mine alone.

ABBREVIATIONS

Note: Spellings in quotations have been modernized, except for some "th" verb endings that give a flavor of the original.

APC	*Acts of the Privy Council*
BL	British Library
CD	Wallace Notestein, F. H. Relf, and Hartley Simpson, eds., *Commons Debates 1621*, 7 vols. (New Haven, Conn., 1935)
CJ	*House of Commons Journal*
CSP	*Calendar of State Papers*
DNB	*Dictionary of National Biography*
HMC	Historical Manuscripts Commission
Kingsbury	Susan M. Kingsbury, *The Records of the Virginia Company of London*, 4 vols. (Washington, D.C., 1906–35)
LJ	*House of Lords Journal*
MCFP	Magdalene College, Cambridge: Ferrar Papers
PRO	Public Record Office
STC	*Short-Title Catalogue*

PART ONE

Early Years

Chapter I

THE SETTING AND THE MAN

THE ARCHBISHOP

Elizabeth I's reign, remembered for centuries as a golden age, had anything but an auspicious beginning. At home, religious and political confusion, compounded by a restless nobility, threatened the queen's authority. Abroad, trouble threatened from Scotland and France.[1] Particularly acute was the uncertainty over church doctrine and organization, a vital concern that was not to subside for another hundred years. Although the rejection of Roman Catholicism was decisive, within Protestantism a fierce struggle was under way between a compromising, Erastian group, led by Elizabeth herself, and enthusiastic reformers, soon to be mocked with the name Puritans, who wanted to remove every vestige of Catholic practice, from the vestments on the priest to the Virgin in the prayers. The heart of their leadership was that group of committed men who had fled to the Continent during the previous reign to escape persecution by the Catholic Mary. When these Marian exiles returned to England, however, their position was soon rendered ambivalent by their rapid elevation to a dominant place in the reestablished Church of England. Liberally endowed with bishoprics and archbishoprics, they came to represent an uneasy amalgam of reforming instinct and Establishment conservatism. For decades they, like England's elite in general, and like the upper classes of much of Europe, struggled to find compromise and resolution amidst conflicting political and religious forces.[2]

Elizabeth's first bishop of Worcester, Edwin Sandys (1517?–88), exemplified these contradictions. Born to a justice of the peace in North Lancashire, he was educated at nearby Furness Abbey and proceeded from this stronghold of monastic tradition to further education at Cambridge, a hotbed of new ideas. While working toward his doctorate in divinity, awarded in 1549, Sandys became not only an important university figure

[1] The best general account of this period is Wallace MacCaffrey, *The Shaping of the Elizabethan Regime* (Princeton, N.J., 1968).

[2] On the Elizabethan Church, see Patrick Collinson, *The Elizabethan Puritan Movement* (London, 1967) and *Archbishop Grindal, 1519–1583: The Struggle for a Reformed Church* (Berkeley, Calif., 1979). For a continental parallel to the struggles of England's upper classes, see Robert Chesler, "Crown, Lords, and God: The Establishment of Secular Authority and the Pacification of Lower Austria, 1618–1648" (Ph.D. diss., Princeton University, 1979).

(master of Catharine Hall, among other offices) but also a close friend of Martin Bucer and the reformers who congregated around the famous German theologian. Here he came into contact with such future leaders of the Elizabethan Church as Matthew Parker, Edmund Grindal, and John Aylmer, and, throwing off his earlier monastic training, he quickly emerged as one of the most ardent advocates of religious change.

Not until his late thirties, however, did he enter into a more than donnish participation in the life of the times. When the young Edward VI died in 1553, Sandys was vice-chancellor of Cambridge University. Hoping to preserve the Protestant succession, he became one of Lady Jane Grey's chief supporters, and remained stubbornly loyal to her even after the bitter end of that futile enterprise. Although as vice-chancellor he was forced to proclaim Queen Mary, he did not hesitate to deliver a violently anti-Catholic sermon a few days later. Some of his audience, taking offense, tried to unseat Sandys, and the bellicose preacher went for his dagger. Had a group of friends not restrained him, his career might well have ended then and there. As it was, his prospects were far from pleasing. He resigned the vice-chancellorship, and late in July 1553, having been arrested and brought to London, he was imprisoned in the Tower. By some process that will probably never be clear, he managed to escape and, though hunted, to flee from England to the Continent.

During his exile, spent mainly in the tolerant city of Strassburg, Sandys became well acquainted with a number of continental reformers, notably Peter Martyr. He seems to have become thoroughly confirmed in his religious radicalism, for when he returned to England in 1559, after Elizabeth's restoration of Protestantism, he emerged as one of the most outspoken critics of the new church settlement. Priestly vestments were one target of his anger; another was the laxness of his flock, which was treated to a harsh visitation when, after first refusing the see of Carlisle, Sandys finally agreed to become bishop of Worcester late in 1559. His squabbles were legion, embroiling him not only with old friends like Parker and Grindal but also with powerful laymen like the Yorkshire magnate Sir Robert Stapleton. Through all the controversies, however, he remained a major advocate of further reform. He helped revise the Anglican liturgy; he took part in the 1565 and 1572 translations of the Bible; and he led the Puritan onslaught in the Parliament of 1563. The latter was the high point of Sandys's zeal, climaxed by the preparation of two papers advocating religious reform that the House of Lords roundly rejected. Among his recommendations were the prohibition of crossing of the infant during baptism, weekly catechisms, and a procedure for acceptance into the ministry that, in the words of one commentator, looked "very much like ordination by a Swiss presbytery."[3]

[3] A. J. Carlson, "The Puritans and the Convocation of 1563," in *Action and Conviction in Early Modern Europe*, ed. Theodore K. Rabb and Jerrold E. Seigel, (Princeton, N.J., 1969),

Thereafter, following the general drift of Elizabeth's government toward a more conservative position, Sandys's fervor noticeably declined. As the middle-aged hothead mellowed with advancing years, he gradually shifted his stance amid the conflicts of his time. The former monastic schoolboy and fiery reformer became a mainstay of the Establishment, as harsh on extremists as he had once been on supporters of the status quo. It is true that he did continue for a while to help out his old friends, the Puritans, at difficult moments. In the 1570s, for example, he tried to prevent the suspension of a Puritan reader at St. Paul's and to protect some "prophesiers" in Norfolk, but on both occasions he was overruled. What is significant is that these were his last efforts on their behalf, for in 1570 he had been elevated to the bishopric of London. It was a most difficult time to hold the post, coinciding as it did with Pius V's excommunication of Elizabeth and Thomas Cartwright's influential sermons, and Sandys soon found himself acting as the chief bulwark against both Catholics and Puritans. Within a few years he was to be John Whitgift's patron and chief ally in the repression of dissent.

Various indications of the bishop's new attitudes have survived, and they all suggest that it was the threat to order in the 1570s that determined his change of heart. As he wrote to Burghley from London, "the city will never be quiet till these authors of sedition, who are now esteemed as gods, as Field, Wilcox, Cartwright, and others be removed from the city," and shortly thereafter he signed the order for Cartwright's arrest.[4] In one of his sermons he bluntly said that for "the papal stragglers, the firebrands of sedition, and the pests of the Church . . . mercy is cruel," a view that he reiterated in the preamble to his will: "Howbeit, as I do easily acknowledge our ecclesiastical policy in some points may be bettered, so do I utterly mislike even in my conscience all such rude and indigested platforms as have been more lately and boldly, than either learnedly or wisely, preferred, tending not to the reformation, but to the destruction of the Church of England."[5] It was entirely fitting, therefore, that in 1576, when

---

150. For Sandys's quarrels with his fellow bishops, see John Strype's *The Life and Acts of Matthew Parker* (London, 1711), 78–79, and *The History of the Life . . . of . . . Edmund Grindal* (London, 1710), 192, 245–247; and the works cited in note 5, below. More generally, see Joel Berlatsky, "The Social Structure of the Elizabethan Episcopate, 1558–1603" (Ph.D. diss. Northwestern University, 1970). Since the particulars are not relevant to my story, I have eschewed the fine gradations discerned by recent research within the blanket term "Puritan" and use that convenient word merely to indicate those who were seeking to reform the Elizabethan and Jacobean Church along more Calvinist lines.

[4] Quoted in J. B. Black, *The Reign of Elizabeth, 1558–1603*, 2d ed. (Oxford, 1959), 195. He was denounced by the extreme Puritans in *A friendly caveat to Bishop Sands* (1573). On the shift in attitude toward Puritans, see Collinson, *Puritan Movement*, 147–150.

[5] J. Ayre, ed., *The Sermons of Edwin Sandys, D.D.* (Cambridge, 1841), 441, 448. As he put it, quoting the Gospels, "A Kingdom divided will not endure": ibid., 139. The best sources for Sandys's life are Ayre's collection; William Archbold's biography in *DNB*, 18:772–775; the

he was about sixty years old, Sandys was elevated again, this time to the archbishopric of York. And it is not inappropriate that during his last years he was to win further fame as the chief patron of Richard Hooker.

Sandys's life embodied the oscillations of policy that characterized most of Europe from the early sixteenth through the mid-seventeenth centuries. Everywhere people were grappling with the multitude of problems spawned by the Reformation, by the growing power of central governments, and by rapid economic and social change. If Sandys at various times took positions at almost every point along the spectrum from Catholicism to Puritanism, from rebellion to repression, he was revealing only the fluctuations of his age. It is thus all the more surprising that his most famous son was so often to maintain a middle-of-the-road position amongst the opposing political and religious forces of the time.

FAMILY AND EDUCATION

On the first blank leaf of his 1574 folio Bible, still preserved at the one-room Hawkshead Grammar School in North Lancashire that he founded, the archbishop made the following entry: "Edwin Sandes was born the 9. day of december at six of the clock in the morning, in the year of our Lord God 1561." The archbishop had first married a cousin, Mary Sandys of Essex, who had given him a son, but both mother and child had died from the plague during Sandys's sojourn in Strassburg. Within a month of returning to England, he remarried, this time the daughter of a respected Kentish family, Cecily Wilford. They had a son, Samuel, in 1560, and a year later had a second child. In a curious tradition that was to be continued into the next generation, this second son received the father's name. More noteworthy was the family's eventual size: the archbishop had nine children who reached maturity and nearly fifty adult grandchildren.

The family's connections ranged throughout England's middle and upper classes. The successive godparents of the archbishop's children, for example, were of ever-higher status. The godparents of the second son came from two prominent Worcestershire families, the Russels and the Blounts, but the two youngest children were sponsored by the earls of Cumberland and Huntingdon, two lords, a countess, and a lady. Through marriage, connections were made with prominent Englishmen as different as the court-

---

biography, generously sprinkled with quotations from Fox's *Acts*, in E. S. Sandys, *History of the Family of Sandys* (Barrow-in-Furness, 1930), 33–91; I. P. Ellis, "Edwin Sandys and the Settlement of Religion in England, 1558–1588," (B.L. diss., Oxford University, 1962), and his "The Archbishop and the Usurers," *Journal of Ecclesiastical History* 21 (1970): 33–42—two references I owe to Joel Berlatsky; and Charles Sandys's notes for a biography of the archbishop in BL, Additional, 45,866. Ayre, *Sermons*, 121–125 indicates the archbishop's readiness to reprove even the queen herself.

iers Sir Francis Walsingham, Sir Humphrey Gilbert, Sir Richard Weston, and Sir Charles Cornwallis; the noble families of Devereux, Dudley, Herbert, Rich, Sandys (distant relatives), Spencer, Sydney, and Wriothesley; the powerful London merchants Sir Thomas Smythe, Sir William Cockayne, Sir Maurice Abbot, Sir John Wolstenholme, and Sir John Rivers; the future Chief Justice Sir Nicholas Hyde; various gentry families, particularly from the West Country and from Kent; and Laurence Washington, a direct ancestor of America's first president.[6]

Little Edwin was thus born into the most privileged rank of society. And he was always to move among England's political, financial, and intellectual leaders. From the start, he had the finest education the sixteenth century could offer. At the age of nine he was sent to the newly founded Merchant Taylors' School, whose headmaster, Richard Mulcaster, was perhaps the most famous humanist teacher in England. Edwin's father may have known Mulcaster from youth, because both were raised in neighboring areas of north-west England, or from Cambridge in the 1540s, when both were fellows at the university. The Sandys family also had various links with the Merchant Taylors' Company.[7] Above all, however, it must have been the excellence of the school (second only to St. Paul's, whose high master Mulcaster later became) that attracted the learned bishop of London.

What the boy learned during the next six years, until he entered Oxford,

---

[6] On the family and its connections, see the pedigrees that accompany Sandys, *Family of Sandys*, and the following volumes in the Harleian Series of Visitations of England: J. Fetherston, ed., *The Visitation of the County of Cumberland 1615* (London, 1872); W. C. Metcalfe, ed., *The Visitation of Essex* (London, 1878); J. W. Clay, ed., *The Visitation of Cambridge 1619* (London, 1897); R. Hovenden, ed., *The Visitation of Kent 1619* (London, 1898); A. R. Maddison, ed., *Lincolnshire Pedigrees*, vol. 1 (London, 1938). Also useful are J. L. Vivian, ed., *The Visitations of the County of Devon* (Exeter, 1895); T. Nash, *Collections for the History of Worcestershire*, vol. 2 (London, 1799); and the series of articles by J. H. Pleasants, "Genealogy: The Lovelace Family and Its Connections" and "Sandys of Furness Fells, Lancashire" in *Virginia Magazine of History and Biography* 28 and 29 (1920 and 1921). The best overview of the family and its background is in the chapter "Heritage" of R. B. Davis's biography of Edwin's brother, *George Sandys: Poet-Adventurer* (London, 1955). The old book by Comley Vivian, *Some Notes for a History of the Sandys Family* (London, 1907), has been superseded by these works. There are various pedigrees of the family in BL, Additional: one apparently started by Edwin's aunt Mary, the widow of Miles, in 34,307, fol. 4; others through the 1660s in 5,507, fols. 241, 242, 337; and through 1773 in 33,896, fol. 25.

[7] The archbishop's wife was the sister of a Merchant Taylor, and Edwin's sister was to marry a future master of the company. There were also connections between the school and Edwin's college at Oxford, Corpus Christi. The best source is E. P. Hart, ed., *Merchant Taylors' School Register*, 2 vols. (London, 1936). On Mulcaster, see Richard DeMolen, *Richard Mulcaster (c. 1531–1611) and Educational Reform in the Renaissance* (Nieuwkoop, 1991); Kenneth Charlton, *Education in Renaissance England* (London, 1965), 100–126 and 202–224 passim; and Joan Simon, *Education and Society in Tudor England* (Cambridge, 1966), 306, 353–354, 369, 373, 400.

would have focused on the classical humanist curriculum, laced with an emphasis on *mens sana in corpore sano* and on the English language, the two pet concerns of the headmaster.[8] Moreover, Mulcaster's special interest in public performance, the staging of masques, and singing (his charges often appeared before Elizabeth herself) may well have given Edwin solid preparation for his later proficiency as a public speaker. That he also absorbed his mentor's social opinions seems unlikely, in view of Mulcaster's distaste for merchants, the very group that Edwin was later to cultivate.[9] Yet the young man did forge strong links with Merchant Taylors that persisted long after he left. For thirty years his warmest friendship was with a schoolmate, George Cranmer, a great-nephew of Henry VIII's archbishop; and in the 1580s and 1590s Sandys lived for a few years in the house of his father's Watling Street neighbor in London, John Churchman, a master of the Merchant Taylors' Company who was closely identified with the school. In later years Edwin remained in touch with one of his most famous contemporaries, Lancelot Andrewes, though not (as far as we know) with his other famous classmate, Edmund Spenser. And, most important, the soundness of the education he received was manifest throughout his subsequent writings, speeches, and public career.[10]

For Oxford Sandys also gave evidence of long affection, a sentiment that culminated in a splendid (though unpaid) legacy of £1,500 for the establishment of a university chair of metaphysical philosophy.[11] The circumstances of his move to Oxford are clear. Edwin's father was elevated to the archbishopric in 1576; and, though his younger children were to be educated in York, there was no need to take the two oldest boys north, especially since they were approaching university age and thus would be forced to move yet again. Edwin, now fifteen years old, was undoubtedly mature enough, by the standards of the time, to be separated from his parents. Indeed, during the tumultuous years after 1570 he may not have seen

[8] See Charlton, *Education*, 102, 120. In Mulcaster's words, "I honor the Latin, but I worship the English": Richard DeMolen, "Richard Mulcaster, Elizabethan Savant" (Ph.D. diss. University of Michigan, 1970), 147.

[9] See Simon, *Education and Society*, 353–354, 369, 373. The love of singing stayed with Sandys, for he left £12 in his will to maintain a "singing man" at the Church of St. Peter in York.

[10] Another hint of further contact with the school was the enrollment at Merchant Taylors, many years later, of the son of the earl of Southampton, Edwin's close associate in the Virginia Company. On the relations with Cranmer, the Churchmans, and Andrewes, see C. J. Sisson, *The Judicious Marriage of Mr. Hooker and the Birth of the Laws of the Ecclesiastical Polity* (Cambridge, 1940).

[11] Between 1604 and 1607 Sandys also gave the Bodleian Library (with his wife) two gifts totaling £70 and helped it obtain £100 from the estate of his friend Sir Charles Danvers: Anthony à Wood, *The History and Antiquities of the University of Oxford*, vol. 2, pt. 2 (Oxford, 1796), 927–928.

much of his father, preoccupied as that worthy must have been with the demands of his sensitive position as bishop of London: troubles caused by Puritans and Papists; the excitement generated by the execution of the duke of Norfolk; and stormy sessions of Parliament. The only question may have been which university, and in particular which college, Edwin would join.

That he was not sent to his father's old university, Cambridge, at first seems surprising. But in fact the older Sandys also had many connections with Corpus Christi College at Oxford. Its president, William Cole, had been one of his companions in exile in Zürich. And its most illustrious son, John Jewel, had been among the archbishop's closest friends. Furthermore, a young fellow at the college, a twenty-three-year old by the name of Richard Hooker, was already establishing a reputation as a brilliant scholar. He had been sent to Oxford by Jewel, and when his patron had died in 1571, Sandys had become his prime benefactor. Elected a scholar as soon as the statutes allowed, Hooker became a fellow of Corpus in 1577, and was thus ready for the charge the archbishop was to give him.

Edwin entered Corpus together with his brother Samuel and his friend George Cranmer; all three matriculated on September 16, 1577.[12] During the next few years there was formed a deep friendship between Hooker, Sandys, and Cranmer that was to persist for more than two decades. Izaak Walton, Cranmer's cousin, later described the relationship as

> a sacred friendship; a friendship made up of religious principles, which increased daily by a similitude of inclinations to the same recreations and studies; a friendship elemented in youth, and in a university, free from self-ends. . . . And in this sweet, this blessed, this spiritual amity, they went on for many years . . . a friendship so sacred, that when it ended in this world, it began in the next, where it shall have no end.[13]

The "similitude of inclinations" certainly left its mark on Edwin. If any Elizabethan besides Hooker deserved the sobriquet "judicious," it was his calm and reasoned pupil. And the regard was mutual: Hooker named three

---

[12] Thomas Fowler, *The History of Corpus Christi College* (Oxford, 1893), 15. William Fulman's seventeenth-century manuscript history of the college, now at Christ Church, Oxford, refers to Edwin's stint at Corpus. On Fulman see Davis's *George Sandys*, 269–270. Davis (ibid. and 29–31) notes that two of Edwin's younger brothers and his Buckinghamshire cousin (also Edwin) attended Corpus. Other later Corpus connections for Sandys were John Spenser, president of the college; Henry Parry, bishop of Gloucester and Worcester; Sir George More the long-serving M.P.; and Henry Jacob, a Leiden Puritan who went to Virginia during the Sandys regime: Sisson, *Hooker*, 45, 47, 92 ff.; and James McConica, ed., *The Collegiate University*, vol. 3 of T. H. Aston, ed., *The History of the University of Oxford* (Oxford, 1986), 673, 684.

[13] Izaak Walton, *The Life of Mr. Richard Hooker*, ed. C. H. Dick (London, 1899), 134; for Jewel's and the elder Sandys's patronage, ibid., 130–131.

children after members of Edwin's family and made Edwin an executor of his will.[14]

Sandys remained at Oxford on and off for nearly thirteen years, taking his B.A. in 1579, at the age of seventeen, and gaining election as a fellow of Corpus that same year. Four years later he was awarded the M.A., a few months after Cranmer received his B.A. Then, until April of 1589, when Edwin for unknown reasons "did supplicate for the degree of batch. of law, but was not admitted," we hear almost nothing of his Oxford career.[15] It is not even clear whether he remained in touch with Hooker, who resigned his fellowship in the early 1580s, settled in London, and married John Churchman's daughter. According to Walton's vindictive and unfounded story, Sandys and Cranmer came to visit the newlyweds, but left in disgust at the wife's shrewish behavior toward their former teacher. More solid evidence of the continuing friendship was Archbishop Sandys's securing for Hooker the mastership of one of London's Inns of Court, the Middle Temple, in 1585; and Edwin's two-year stay at the Churchman house, accompanied by a manservant, between 1588 and 1590.[16] It was at the Temple, a few months after Edwin's failure to obtain the bachelor of law degree, that Cranmer rejoined his old friends, and the trio from Corpus was reunited.

Sandys in 1590, at the age of twenty-eight, is a shadowy figure. Solidly grounded in the classics, he had gained a mastery of Latin and Greek, and possibly some knowledge of Hebrew; all in all, he was as thoroughly educated as anyone of his day, having remained at academic institutions long after most of his contemporaries had left. Cranmer, for example, had already held a position at Court, as secretary to William Davison, Elizabeth's scapegoat for the execution of Mary Queen of Scots. For a couple of years in the mid-1580s Sandys must have been away from Oxford—he had married a Devon woman, Margaret Eveleigh, and would therefore have been barred from holding his fellowship—but he did not engage in any activity as public as Cranmer's. Of the marriage nothing is known beyond its apparently short duration. The couple had one child, Elizabeth, who was to

[14] Sisson, *Hooker*, 44. Sisson's is the best account of Hooker's links with Sandys.

[15] Fowler, *Corpus Christi*, 153–154; Anthony à Wood, *Fasti Oxonienses, or Annals of the University of Oxford*, ed. P. Bliss, 2 vols. (London, 1815–20), 212, 223, 248. For the content and structure of Oxford education in this period, see M. H. Curtis, *Oxford and Cambridge in Transition, 1558–1642* (Oxford, 1959); Hugh Kearney, *Scholars and Gentlemen: Universities and Society in Pre-Industrial Britain, 1500–1700* (London, 1970); and McConica, *Collegiate University*. Edwin's long stay at Oxford suggests he may have been headed toward a church or theological career until the 1589 "failure."

[16] Walton, *Hooker*, 139–141; Sisson, *Hooker*, 17–44, esp. 20–22, 28. (Hooker's mastership was a church living, essentially the chaplaincy of the Inn.) Sandys already knew the Churchmans as neighbors in the 1570s, as Hooker's in-laws, and as parents of William, their youngest boy, who was at Corpus from 1581 until his sudden death in 1583.

marry her own second cousin, Sir Thomas Wilford of Kent, and it was in childbirth that Margaret died in July 1588. During the same month Sandys also lost his father, but there is no record of his response to the double bereavement.[17] Yet he certainly did not languish: during the next fifteen years he married three more times.

In addition to the classics, Edwin's major qualifications were in theology and law, which rounded out his broad acquaintance with the learning of his time. His familiarity with theology was to stand him in good stead when he wrote a book on European religions a few years later, and also when he took an active role in the preparation of Hooker's masterpiece, *The Laws of the Ecclesiastical Polity*. The latter had originated in a dispute that began shortly after Hooker came to the Middle Temple. He had found himself embroiled with Walter Travers, a Puritan lecturer, and had decided to defend his position, a staunch Anglicanism, in print. Both Sandys and Cranmer made written comments on book 6 of the *Ecclesiastical Polity*, and though they may have offered suggestions for the entire work, these are the only notes that have survived. They are not particularly remarkable; Edwin, for example, seemed mainly concerned about clarity and consistency, though his suggestions of direct quotations indicated a good knowledge of the subject.[18] That the young scholar was perfectly adept at theology cannot be doubted, but it was not a skill that he was to find much use for in later life. More important, perhaps, were Hooker's interest in natural law and his belief in an organic commonwealth that was sustained by counsel and cooperation, ideas that Sandys was to develop in Parliament.

Less tangible was the influence of Edwin's study of law. Despite advanced work at Oxford and over five years at an Inn of Court, he never practiced the profession. Yet the training must have had its uses during his parliamentary career. His speeches reveal someone as well versed in legal argument as any of his colleagues, and on many issues his familiarity with precedents and expertise in hairsplitting could have qualified him as the very model of a lawyer.

FORAYS INTO POLITICS AND RELIGION

The background and formal education, in other words, were impeccable. Few young.men of the sixteenth century enjoyed so auspicious a beginning

---

[17] Clay, *Visitation of Cambridge*, 6. Elizabeth may have been brought up by relatives, because Sandys is described as being accompanied only by a manservant when he moved in with the Churchmen after Margaret's death. Edwin's mother survived the archbishop by twenty-two years; there is no evidence of her son's contacts with her, and we know only from a family pedigree (see above, note 6) that she died in 1610.

[18] Sandys's notes are printed in J. Keble's edition of Hooker's *Works*, 3d ed., 3 vols. (Oxford, 1845), 3:130–139. The originals are in the Corpus Christi College Manuscripts, no. 295.

to their lives. Yet the man himself remains elusive. Only one description survives from these years of youth and early manhood. Written by his father in 1586, it is an admiring portrayal of a learned and sober scholar, obviously intended to impress the reader, no less a personage than Lord Burghley. The archbishop's tempestuous career had continued on its erratic way, and in the 1580s he was forced to defend himself against two major attacks. First, a leading Yorkshire figure and old antagonist, Sir Robert Stapleton, contrived to have the aged prelate caught in bed with an innkeeper's wife.[19] Then the dean of York, Matthew Hutton, complained to Burghley about the archbishop's nepotism, an accusation that was richly deserved. To justify his bestowal of various offices on his sons (for Edwin, the lucrative patent for the chancellorship of the diocese of York), Sandys described the virtues of the recipients. His second son had evidently impressed Elizabeth's chief minister a few years before, when he had defended the archbishop during the embarrassing Stapleton affair, and now his father added to his praises:

> My lord, I have a son at Oxford, a master of arts of three or four years standing, and the dean [Hutton] himself will confess, that he is well learned, and hath been a student in the law (as I take it) now two years, and will in one year following be fit to proceed doctor. I must confess that having nothing else to leave him, I was content to bestow this [chancellorship] upon him and drawn thereunto by my learned and wise friends. It is he who made report unto your lordship of Sir Robert Stapleton's frivolous submission. Your lordship then liked well of him and since he hath profited in learning with the best, he is almost 25 years of age, and a great deal elder in discretion, sobriety and learning.[20]

For all the flattery, it was a shrewd assessment. The clergyman's assets it stressed (discretion, sobriety, and learning) happen also to be those that occur most readily to the modern student of Edwin's career.

---

[19] For this sordid incident and its aftermath, including blackmail, see Conyers Read, *Lord Burghley and Queen Elizabeth* (New York, 1960), 278–280. For some of the archbishop's other quarrels, see W. Page, ed., *The Victoria History of the County of York*, vol. 3 (London, 1913), 53–54. In general, see M. E. James, *English Politics and the Concept of Honour, 1485–1642* (Oxford, 1978) and Richard Cust, "Honour and Politics in Early Stuart England: The Case of Beaumont *v.* Hastings," *Past & Present*, no. 149 (1995): 57–94; and the symposium "Honour and Reputation in Early Modern England," *Transactions of the Royal Historical Society*, 6th ser. 6 (1996): 137–248.

[20] The letter, dated May 22, 1586, is printed in John Strype, *Annals of the Reformation* (Oxford, 1824), 4:597, and in Anthony à Wood, *Athenae Oxonienses*, ed. P. Bliss, 4 vols. (London, 1813–20), 2:475. See BL, Lansdowne, 50, fols. 72, 74–75. On the fights between the archbishop and Hutton, which went back to 1578, see Philip Tyler, "The Ecclesiastical Commission for the Province of York, 1561–1641" (D.Phil. diss., Oxford University, 1965), 176–177.

For the first thirty years of Sandys's life, however, there is almost no evidence on which to base an opinion. Apart from the education, the brief marriage, and the friendship with Hooker, only scraps survive. It is possible that he served as a member of Parliament during the exciting session of 1586, which was enlivened by the attack on Mary Queen of Scots and the imprisonment of Peter Wentworth, though the M.P. may have been his cousin and namesake. The election may have been determined by the earl of Leicester, because the seat was a newly enfranchised borough, Andover, which had obtained representation at the earl's request. Since Edwin's uncle Miles, a "carpetbagging" M.P. since 1563, also depended on Leicester's patronage in 1586, the seat may have been given to his son, also Edwin.[21] Sandys certainly was in the House during the much shorter and duller session of 1589, when he had a direct link to the constituency that elected him, the borough of Plympton in Devon: there was no obvious patron, and the fact that his wife was from a local family probably explains the choice. In any case, neither in 1586 nor in 1589 did he leave any mark on the record.

Our information about the now middle-aged man hardly improves during the 1590s. In fact, with the exception of the book he wrote (but did not publish) during that decade, he remains almost as indistinct as the youth at Merchant Taylors and Oxford. Not until 1604, when he reached what the times would have considered the relatively advanced age of forty-three, did he suddenly become a public figure and thus make a distinctive imprint on the historical record. In the meantime, there seems to have been only a gradual change in the pattern of his life. It was but slowly, during his thirties, that the long-time student began to apply his scholarly talents in a larger arena.

For a few years there was little hint of the change to come. Sandys entered the Middle Temple in company with Cranmer in February 1590, and thus settled further into the life of London, his adopted home.[22] The familiar faces at the Temple included his uncle Miles, treasurer of the Inn; his younger brother Thomas; two cousins; the master, Richard Hooker;

[21] J. E. Neale, *The Elizabethan House of Commons* (London, 1949), 144, 211, 224, 312. Neale calls Miles a "carpetbagger" because he served no constituency more than once in his long parliamentary career. On the likelihood that it was Miles's son, not our Edwin, who was elected in 1586, see Alan Hardin, "Edwin Sandys," in P. W. Hasler, ed., *The House of Commons, 1558–1603*, vol. 3 (London, 1981), 340. For the events of these sessions (and 1593, when Sandys was also an M.P.) see Neale, *Elizabeth I and her Parliaments, 1584–1601* (London, 1957), 103–323. Edwin's only references to this early political experience are two passing mentions in the notes on Hooker's *Ecclesiastical Polity*.

[22] See too H.A.C. Sturgess, comp., *Register of Admissions to the Honourable Society of the Middle Temple*, vol. 1 (London, 1949), 60; C. H. Hopwood, ed., *Middle Temple Records*, vol. 1 (London, 1904), 312. Given the later evidence of Sandys's familiarity with the law, he does not fit the picture of gentlemen-dilettantes in Wilfrid Prest, "Legal Education of the Gentry at the Inns of Court, 1560–1640," *Past & Present*, no. 38 (1967): 20–39.

and other relatives who were to follow in the 1590s. Hooker resigned his position in July 1591, but the close relations continued, for Sandys was deeply involved in the publication of the *Laws of the Ecclesiastical Polity*. This story, hidden in Chancery records since the seventeenth century, has now been uncovered and told in detail by Sisson.[23] For our purposes only the outline need be recounted as an indication of the continuing friendship between the two men, and of Sandys's financial generosity.

Sandys entered into a contract with the printer in January 1593, and the first four books of the *Ecclesiastical Polity* were published in that year. The fifth book appeared four years later, when Sandys was traveling abroad. In his absence, the negotiations with the printer were carried on by his brother-in-law, Nicholas Eveleigh. His outlay evidently approached £250 (a substantial sum at the time), in addition to the £30 that were paid to Hooker for his manuscript. By the time the edition was superseded in 1611, the investment had perhaps been recouped, but profit was obviously not the main purpose. Sisson's conclusion, that "Edwin Sandys saved Hooker's *Ecclesiastical Polity* from suppression [because no printer thought it would have a market], by undertaking to finance its publication" seems irrefutable.[24] But it is significant that Sandys appears to have lost interest in the work after Hooker's death. He did confer with two old colleagues from Corpus, John Spenser (Cranmer's brother-in-law) and Henry Parry, and with Hooker's great champion, Lancelot Andrewes, about the publication of the remaining books, but they were not to appear for almost fifty years. The long court case over publication rights in Chancery in 1613 and 1614, from whose records Sisson recovered the story of the book, shows Sandys, the plaintiff, defending his investment. But this was a very different kind of commitment, because he did nothing to get the work into print. The contrast suggests that his endeavors in the 1590s may have been prompted more by friendship than by devotion to Hooker's ideas.

Until 1596 Sandys's life seems to have continued in its set ways. Hooker and Cranmer, academic pursuits, family and old friends at the Temple and elsewhere in London—these were preoccupations that went back to his early teens. But some changes are apparent. It was probably during the early 1590s that he married again, the bride this time being Anne South-cote of Devon, a cousin of his first wife. According to the testimony of John Churchman's servant twenty years later, the Sandyses, accompanied by two menservants and a maidservant, lived in the Churchman house for

[23] Sisson, *Hooker*, 49–78.

[24] Ibid., 52. In 1600 £250 would have purchased approximately eleven thousand barrels of beer: Lawrence Stone, *The Crisis of the Aristocracy, 1558–1641* (Oxford, 1965), app. 24. Thomas Barnes calls anyone worth £100 a year a county "magnate," at the top of a county's elite: *Somerset 1625–1640: A County's Government During the "Personal" Rule* (Cambridge, Mass., 1961), 25.

about a year, and then departed for Yorkshire, where Anne died.[25] The reasons for the move northward are not far to seek. Edwin had been at Oxford during his father's tenure at York, but that had not prevented him from doing well out of the archbishop's blatant nepotism. When Burghley investigated these bouts of generosity in 1586, he discovered that the five Sandys boys had received twenty-six grants between them, some worth as much as £200 per annum. Edwin's four leases, all in Yorkshire, were worth £322, and in addition to these lands he had the chancellorship at York. Nor can it have been immaterial that his younger brother George, married to a wealthy ward of the archbishop worth £3,000 a year, also lived in Yorkshire.[26] With much to attract him, therefore, the Londoner, now in his early thirties, decided to set himself up as a country squire in the north.

But the change of scene did not last long. Anne died within a fairly short space of time (it may be that the tragedy was again related to childbirth, for there is no record of the couple having any children) and Edwin returned south. His affection for this second wife is evidenced by the naming of his next daughter Anne, a tribute his first and third wives did not receive until much later; his departure from Yorkshire may thus have been motivated by the wish to escape the unhappy memory of her death. Whatever the reason, he was back in London early in 1593 for a session of Parliament and also for the first long negotiations over the printing of Hooker's *Ecclesiastical Polity*. He remained in the capital, first with the Churchmen, then at the Middle Temple, until 1596.[27]

---

[25] Sisson, *Hooker*, 147: a transcript of Chancery proceedings in 1613, PRO, C.24/394/73.

[26] BL, Lansdowne, 50, fols. 74–75; R. A. Marchant, *The Church under the Law; Justice, Administration, and Discipline in the Diocese of York 1560–1640* (Cambridge, 1969), esp. 38–45; Davis, *George Sandys*, 37–39.

[27] That Sandys's stay in Yorkshire preceded the attendance at Parliament is suggested by the evidence of where he lived between 1590 and 1596 and by his parliamentary links. He stayed with the Churchmen for two years after his first wife's death in 1588; when he entered the Middle Temple early in 1590, he and George Cranmer probably lived at the Inn of Court, though we first hear of his having chambers in November 1591. The suggestion, by V. Thomas in *Notes and Queries*, 2d. ser., 11 (1861): 221–222, that they lived with Hooker has no foundation. After Anne's death Sandys stayed with the Churchmen again, this time for more than a year; in 1593 he and his uncle Miles took a lease on York House in the Strand; and in 1595 he resumed his residency in the Middle Temple. Moreover, in the 1593 Parliament he again represented the Devon borough of Plympton, this time together with Anne's kinsman Richard Southcote. He may have taken the house in the Strand, got married after the session, moved to Yorkshire, returned within a few months, and then lived with the Churchmen for over a year before moving into the Middle Temple. But Sandys, usually deliberate, is unlikely to have changed homes every few months. A wedding in 1590 or 1591 would allow more time between moves and also suggests a succession of residences (Churchmans, Temple, Yorkshire, Churchmans, Strand, Temple) with no major gaps, unlike a 1593 wedding, which would leave 1591–1593 uncertain. Sisson, *Hooker*, 147; Hopwood, *Middle Temple*, 1:312, 325, 359; PRO, SP/12/244/66.

The 1593 Parliament affords the first public glimpse of the man. Now no longer a newcomer to the House, Sandys made his first recorded speech on March 13. Considering the moderation and tolerance that were to be his hallmark in years to come, this address was hardly a foretaste of his future role. In the laconic words of the anonymous diarist, "Mr. Sands spake to the Bill for Recusants, that it might be as it went first for Recusants generally, and not restrained to Popish Recusants only: So that under this bill there might be included Brownists and Barrowists."[28] Why he should have attacked the radicals at this time—in the event, despite opposition, the wording of the bill did put "seditious sectaries" on the same footing as Catholics—is not entirely clear, but a number of possibilities present themselves. Hooker's *Ecclesiastical Polity*, whose first installment was being presented to Burghley on this very day, was a major salvo in a mounting onslaught against Puritans.[29] In other words, Sandys was already associated with the rising antiradicalism of these years. And he did have a long-standing connection, through his father, with the official Church's efforts to silence its critics. To most observers he would have been identified with Hooker and the Anglican hierarchy, and thus would have seemed an obvious spokesman for the conservative position.

But there are hints of a more direct explanation. Burghley's biographer has noted that, despite the lord treasurer's early disagreements with John Whitgift, archbishop of Canterbury, over the hounding of Puritans, he did decide to lend his support to the campaign by 1593, in the wake of Martin Marprelate's intemperance and the excesses of Peter Wentworth. Indeed, religion was the main business of that year's parliamentary session, and Burghley himself drafted the anti-Catholic bill whose ambiguous wording (as clarified by Sandys) was to embrace Protestant dissenters. It was the lord treasurer, again, who revived the bill when it seemed to have died, and who, together with Whitgift, browbeat the Lords into accepting a substitute measure, backed by the bishops, that discriminated against the Puritans alone.[30] In other words, Sandys's attempt to link Brownists and Barrowists with Catholics (the first such proposal in the debates) looks like a

---

[28] Sir Simonds D'Ewes, ed., *The Journals of all the Parliaments during the Reign of Queen Elizabeth* (London, 1682), 500. Neale, *Parliaments*, 284, attributes the speech to Edwin without proof. But there is evidence. As indicated below, Sandys spoke on this subject again on April 4; the presumption is strong that the same person spoke on the same topic. And the only other Sandys in the House, Edwin's uncle Miles, had departed for the country in the interim, on March 17 (D'Ewes, *Journals*, 502). It thus seems virtually certain that it was Edwin who delivered the March 13 speech.

[29] Sisson, *Hooker*, 64, suggests that the speech was timed to coincide with the presentation, and that the *Ecclesiastical Polity* helped sway Burghley to approve the legislation: a nice supposition, but pure speculation.

[30] Read, *Burghley*, 295–298, 444–445, esp. 488–489.

government-sponsored effort to lump together all forms of resistance to the official Church. Less than two weeks before, Whitgift's agent in the House had sent him secret reports of pro-Puritan speeches, and the archbishop may well have been the hidden mover behind Sandys's response.[31]

Edwin had even closer connections with England's primate than he did with Burghley. It is true that his father had always got on well with the lord treasurer, that he himself had had some contact with Elizabeth's chief minister in the 1580s, and that during the next decade he was to work for Burghley's son, Robert Cecil. But with Whitgift the ties were more direct. Edwin's father had been an important patron of the junior bishop, a friend from Cambridge days, and in 1581 had given Whitgift's career a considerable boost by inviting him to a small gathering to decide on policy toward the Puritans. Within two years Whitgift had become archbishop of Canterbury, and thereafter worked in tandem with his colleague from York (whose youthful radicalism was long forgotten) in the battle against the Puritans. Their twin replies to the critics of the Anglican settlement in the Parliament of 1584 demonstrated this close accord, which was exemplified again the following year, when Whitgift prevented Travers from becoming master of the Middle Temple while Sandys provided the alternative candidate, Hooker. Whitgift himself soon became one of Hooker's chief admirers, and the esteem was apparently mutual, if we can believe George Cranmer's enthusiastic letter, praising the archbishop as the restorer of discipline in the English Church, written to Hooker at about the time Edwin was delivering his maiden speech. But the best evidence for the connection comes from Sandys himself, who six years later dedicated his book on religion to Whitgift, thanking him in particular for "favour towards myself."[32]

Speaking on the government side about Separatists was his only notable activity during the session. When a new bill, "a severe measure" aimed solely at Protestant radicals, reappeared in the Commons early in April, Sandys followed Robert Cecil in supporting it.[33] And his first important committee appointment was to the body that met the following day to produce a much-amended (and softened) final version of that bill. There is

---

[31] Neale, *Parliaments*, 283. W. Speed Hill, ed., *Studies in Richard Hooker: Studies Preliminary to an Edition of his Works* (Cleveland, 1972), 132–153, links the speech to Whitgift's campaign against nonconformity, to which Hooker's *Ecclesiastical Polity* also contributed.

[32] V. J. K. Brook, *Whitgift and the English Church* (London, 1957), 61, 106–108, 148–149; Sisson, *Hooker*, passim. Cranmer's letter is printed in Hooker's *Works*, 2:598–610. Whitgift's "favour" included a letter to Hutton, the new Archbishop of York, on August 15, 1595, asking that the "good and studious" Sandys be allowed to retain his main source of income, the leases his father had given him: M. Hutton, ed., *The Correspondence of Dr. Matthew Hutton, Archbishop of York* (London, 1843), 104.

[33] D'Ewes, *Journals*, 517; Neale, *Parliaments*, 287.

no evidence, however, that he spoke again or participated in any other way in the work of the session, except for his predictable membership, as a Devon M.P., on a committee to consider Devon cloth and jersey manufacture.

For all its brevity, the involvement with court circles indicated that Sandys in his late thirties was moving, like his father before him, toward a public career. During the next ten years there were to be a number of signs that he was becoming a protégé of Cecil, and he continued to have many courtier friends. Unlike his father, however, Edwin proceeded from respectable political conformity to troublesome nonconformity. What must be emphasized in both cases, though, is that in this period, as in later periods, a change in allegiance or public stance by a member of England's "establishment" did not imply a shift in status within the ruling circles of the land. It was not a time of fixed positions, of consistency and unwavering behavior. Although for the remainder of Elizabeth's reign Sandys might have seemed destined for the role of minor courtier, in fact he was to enter upon a very different course soon after James I's succession. Yet none of his contemporaries would have considered his behavior a betrayal or disavowal of his past, just as they offered no such interpretation of his father's turnabout. Both were moving within a range of alternatives that, with few exceptions, did not divide men into mutually exclusive clusters, at least not until Charles I's reign. Political attitudes and allegiances shifted so rapidly and fluidly that opponents could be friends; stability was elusive; and for the time being almost no member of the upper levels of society, whatever his views, was likely to feel cut off from any segment of his peers.

CONTINENTAL TRAVELS

In December 1595 Sandys moved to new chambers in the Middle Temple, but five months later his rooms were taken over by his brother-in-law, Nicholas Eveleigh, and he left the Inn of Court (as far as we know) for good.[34] He was now thirty-four years old, and during the next decade the pattern of his life was to undergo a series of fundamental changes. The first was the occasion of his removal from the Middle Temple: Edwin had been asked to join the earl of Lincoln in an embassy to the landgrave of Hesse, and had been given permission by the Privy Council "afterwards to travel into other foreign parts."[35] It was not a mission of great importance,

---

[34] Hopwood, *Middle Temple*, 1:359, 364. Other estimates of Sandys's departure date are discussed in my "The Early Life of Sir Edwin Sandys and Jacobean London" (Ph.D. diss. Princeton University, 1961), 28–29n.

[35] APC, 25:496–497. His travels were cited by the Privy Council when a Yorkshireman, William Callam, brought a complaint about Edwin's northern properties before the Archbishop of York. The Council (perhaps swayed by Sandys's connection with Cecil) urged a

to judge from the limited responsibility given to Lincoln, who, though from a notable diplomatic family, was notorious for his quarrels and quickness of temper. But it was necessary to keep on good terms with leading anti-Habsburg Protestant princes in the Empire; hence the embassy, which departed heavily laden with silver and plate from Elizabeth's coffers, presumably destined for the landgrave's new baby.

The entourage left from Yarmouth in late July, passed through the Netherlands, and after two months in Germany returned home in October. By June 1597 the Privy Council was receiving requests for overdue payments from members of the retinue.[36] We have no record of Sandys's brief foray into the world of diplomacy. Since Cranmer was also on the mission, and the two friends then traveled around Europe, the assignment may have been a thinly veiled excuse for getting to the Continent, though Cranmer had had diplomatic experience in the 1580s as a member of Sir Henry Killigrew's embassy to Paris. Whatever the purpose, our first indication of their subsequent movements comes on November 6 1597, when both men (high Anglican and anti-Puritan credentials notwithstanding) registered at the Academy of Geneva. They cannot have stayed long, because by May Sandys was in Orléans, and less than a year later, in April 1599, he had finished a substantial book (of about two hundred quarto pages) that had been written in Paris. He had also spent at least a year of his continental stay, according to the internal evidence of that book and his own testimony, in Italy.[37] The registration at the Genevan Academy thus seems to have been little more than a convenience. Possibly it served the research into Europe's religious patterns that was the occasion for Sandys's

---

resolution in Edwin's favor, since he was leaving the country on royal business. See the Chancery proceedings: PRO, C.2/289/58. That the donnish Edwin may have been unworldly is apparent from his entanglement in a loan shark scheme, probably in the 1580s, that lingered into the next decade. He borrowed £50 from one William Ashenden; this rapidly escalated to £800, and it took his father's intervention with Christopher Hatton, the lord chancellor, to have the interest reduced to just £5: PRO, C.3/240/84. Sandys's disputes over money continued into James's reign: PRO, C.2/S/2/16, C.2/S/6/37, C.142/305, SP/46/62, fols. 96–98; Huntington Library, EL 385, 5974.

[36] APC, 26:8–9, 13; 27:214–215; 28:205. The ceremonial aspects of the embassy are described in Edward Monings, *The Landgrave of Hessen his princelie receiving of her Majesties Embassadour* (London, 1596), a book kindly pointed out to me by Peter Clark.

[37] For the Geneva registration, see S. Stelling-Michaud, *Le Livre du Recteur de l'academie de Genève, 1559–1878*, vol. 1 (Geneva, 1959), 126. I am most grateful to E. W. Monter for this reference. From Orléans Sandys wrote to Cecil in May 1598, mentioning that he had spent a year in Italy and the winter in Geneva; the letter is reprinted in Nicholas Tyacke, "Sir Edwin Sandys and the Cecils: A Client-Patron Relationship," *Historical Research* 64 (1991): 87–91. The best introductions to the continental traveling of this period are G. M. Trevelyan, "Wandering Englishmen in Italy," *Proceedings of the British Academy* 16 (1930): 61–84, and Boies Penrose, *Urbane Travelers 1591–1635* (Philadelphia, 1942).

tour, but it certainly did not signify a change in the religious convictions of this former and future opponent of the Calvinists.

The long-term effect of the journey is difficult to determine. It came rather late in Edwin's life, but his many comparisons between England and her continental neighbors thereafter are testimony to the usefulness of the time he spent "employed chiefly (as was from the first my principal design) viewing the State of Religion in these Western parts of the World."[38] Since this study was an extension of his theological involvements, and he promised another volume on the subject, it may be that in the late 1590s he was contemplating some sort of academic or ecclesiastical career. But such intentions (if indeed they were serious) came to nought. The second volume was never written, and Sandys had less and less to say about religion after 1599. Yet the book still provides the first sustained and detailed evidence of the man's outlook and cast of mind.

[38] Sir Edwin Sandys, *Europae Speculum, or A Relation of the State of Religion* ... (see below, chapter 2, note 1), 1.

Chapter II

WRITINGS, OUTLOOK, AND PERSONALITY

THE STATE OF RELIGION

The full title of Sandys's book, *A Relation of the State of Religion, and With What Hopes and Policies it Hath Been Framed, and is Maintained, in the Several States of These Western Parts of the World*, gives a foretaste of a somewhat heavy-handed style. The presentation is ponderous, impeded by excessive details and second thoughts, and learned and meticulous to a fault. The following is a not untypical sentence:

> But for the soldiery of this age; (a profession and exercise in old time reputed for an only School of virtue, but now inflamed with all vice and villainy; in old time such that the wisest Philosopher thought it reason sufficient why the Lacedaemonians were generally more virtuous than other Nations, because they followed the wars more; at this day a cause in all places of clean contrary effect:) these desperate Atheisms, these Spanish renouncings, and Italian blasphemings have now so prevailed in our Christian Camps, that if any restrain them he shall be upbraided as no Soldier or gallant-minded man; that the very Turks have the Christians blaspheming of CHRIST in execration, and will punish their prisoners sorely when through impatience or desperateness they burst into them; yea the Jews in their Speculations of the causes of the strange successes of the affairs of the world, assign the reason of the Turks prevailing so against the Christians, to be their blasphemies and blasphemous Oaths, which wound the ears of the very Heavens, and cry to the high throne of Justice for speedy vengeance. (161)[1]

One sentence on the page before this 185-word mammoth is a mere 111 words long. In sum, the book is anything but an easy read—the product of an academic mind concerned more with content than form.

Yet it also has the virtues of its faults. The monster sentence just quoted may seem impenetrable, but its qualities appealed to Sandys's audience: the bow to antiquity; the Christian moralizing; and above all the breadth of contemporary reference, from Turks to Spaniards, apparently based on first-hand experience. The book is a mine of information about the Conti-

---

[1] Page references in the text are to Sir Edwin Sandys, *Europae Speculum, or a Relation of the State of Religion* . . . (London, 1632). This edition, the fifth, is the earliest that is widely available. Like the fourth (1629) but not earlier editions, it is paginated and the title adds the three words *Europae Speculum, or*.

nent, and although it is not certain that Edwin observed everything he described, there is sufficient evidence of the variety of his encounters to justify the assumption that most of his comments derived from personal knowledge. The citation of the Jewish view in that sentence, for example, might seem no more than a commonplace: if one wants to berate Christians and explain the Turks' success, who can give better "neutral" testimony than the Jew? Yet this was no mere rhetorical device, because we know that Sandys tried to familiarize himself directly with Jews and Judaism. A few pages earlier, for example, he records that in Venice he was once "half threatened for no other fault than for debating with a Jew and upholding the truth of Christianity against him" (117).[2]

The descriptions of current affairs must have been a major reason for the book's eventual success. Another, undoubtedly, was the originality and insight of the assessments of continental conditions and personalities. Nothing else like this was available for Englishmen to read, and they continued to require new editions long after the events themselves had lost their immediacy. To judge by the translations, the interest was continental, too. Here one could read the opinions of Italian gentlemen and Spanish friars; learn about the excellence of Italy's hospitals and the inequality of her wealth; follow the Church's financial dealings and her connections with the Habsburgs; or discover that "at this day they ordinarily give out in Italy, that the Devil with whom [Sixtus V] had intelligence, came and fetched him away; [yet he was] in truth one of the worthiest Popes this age hath seen, and of a mind most possessed with high and honorable enterprises," (136) a judgment Sandys supported with a shrewd analysis of Sixtus' foreign policy.

The prime reason for the interest in the *Relation*, however, did not derive from its delights as a travelogue and mélange of high-class gossip. Its title gave a reasonable indication of its contents, and the few surviving contemporary notes on the book confirm that "the state of religion" really was the principal attraction. This was a unique attempt to produce an overview of religious practices and beliefs throughout western Europe. A new century was beginning, both Reformation and Counter-Reformation were well established, and Sandys was trying to show not only how things were, but also what could be expected from the future. It is these analyses that allow us our most sustained look into the man's mind.

THE ROMAN RELIGION

Having defined his task as the exposition of such matters "as may seem most necessary for our Country to be known," Sandys gave the lion's share

---

[2] See my "The Stirrings of the 1590s and the Return of the Jews to England," *Transactions of the Jewish Historical Society of England* 26 (1979): 26–33.

of his attention to Roman Catholicism (2).[3] Judaism and Greek and Russian Orthodoxy, by contrast, were treated to quick, summary descriptions. The most pressing concern, for Englishmen of this period, was Catholicism, and Sandys spent his time accordingly. A hint of how his purposes may have altered during the very process of writing emerges from his promise, at the outset, to look ahead to see "what possibility and good means of uniting at leastwise the several branches of the Reformed professors [he could find amidst] ... such bitterness of minds" (2). As it turned out, his discussion of Christian reunification came at the end of his section on Catholicism, and proceeded entirely in terms of reconciliation between Catholic and Protestant—the great issue of the day, which was far more important than differences, or hopes for unity, among Protestants alone. The Puritans' murmurings must have seemed trivial when placed in a European-wide setting. Thus, by broadening his original goal, Sandys could confront one of the burning questions of the century, and leave aside the more familiar and less momentous problems of the Protestant camp.

The 190 pages on Catholicism in the *Relation* were probably the most complete and informed survey available to English readers. Starting with a description of ceremonies, the emphasis on the Virgin, the architecture of Italian churches, the liturgy, sermons, and services, Sandys goes on to discuss individual practices like confession (which he considers sadly abused), indulgences, processions, and the rosary. Before proceeding to describe the ecclesiastical hierarchy, however, he takes an excursion into Italian daily life, which he sums up as outwardly dazzling but shot through with wickedness, mainly, it seems, because of the "filthiness of speech": a failing that he was to abhor throughout his life. As Sandys puts it, "what in some other places even a loose person would be ashamed to confess, there Priests and Friars refrain not openly to practise" (19). He accuses the clerics of dissembling and murdering almost by instinct, and seems not to have been charmed by Mediterranean ways at all (though he was soon to build one of the first Italianate country houses in England). Remarkably enough, the qualities he admired are ones that few observers would normally attribute to Italy's boisterous inhabitants: they are, he says, "a people for the most part of a grave and staid behavior, very respective [respectful] and courteous, not curious or meddling in other mens' matters, besides that ancient frugality in diet and all things not durable, which to their great ease and benefit they still retain" (19). He is similarly impressed by their

---

[3] Contemporary notes on the *Relation* concentrate largely on the descriptions of Catholic practices, the main interest of seventeenth-century English readers. See the notes by Alexander Gill, a fellow Corpus man and Mulcaster's successor as high master of St. Paul's: BL, Sloane, 3722, fols. 72–77; Edward Nicholas, a fellow Middle Templar and later secretary of state to Charles I and II: PRO, SP/14/135, fol. 61; and two unknown hands: BL, Harleian, 6383, no. 2, and Bodleian MS. Eng. th. c. 62.

quieting down during Lent, an institution whose strictness he suggests importing into England. Their nunneries, too (though not their monasteries, whose inmates would doubtless flee to Geneva if told to reform their lives), are cited as models of good behavior (unlike French nunneries) and their welfare provisions are also given high marks.

Thus far Sandys's assessment has been fairly even-handed. He clearly dislikes the honoring of the Virgin on a level with Christ; he is unhappy about the emptiness of many ceremonies; and he scoffs at those who consider Catholicism severe, arguing instead that "for a man that were desirous to save his Soul at his dying day, and yet denied his Body no wicked pleasure in his lifetime, [there is] no such Church as that of Rome, no such Country as Italy" (17). Nonetheless, he has also found much to praise, particularly a sobriety and courteousness that he evidently misses at home, and an encouragement to piety that *could* be found in some Catholic practices if only they were more faithfully followed. About the official hierarchy, however, he has few good words to say.

The analysis of the Catholics' "Ecclesiastical Government" is the meat of the book, occupying over 130 out of the 248 pages of the 1629 and 1632 editions. Here the mood changes. No longer is there a discussion of individual foibles and/or virtues; practices and beliefs take a back seat to what can only be described as the politics of religion. The emphasis is not entirely surprising, considering Sandys's familiarity with Hooker's *politique* linkage of *raison d'état* with the Anglican settlement. Moreover, the only contemporary authority Edwin mentions by name is Michel de l'Hôpital, the dean of the *politiques*. But it was one thing to see religious concord as an essential prerequisite for political harmony, a view often advanced by l'Hôpital and Hooker; it was quite another matter to treat the Church (as Sandys does) as nothing more than a political institution.

There had been hints of such an attitude before: in the writings of Marsiglio of Padua and later antipapalists, whose aim was to subordinate the authority of Rome to individual secular rulers. But even that issue was never more, at root, than a variant of the old conflict between the city of God and the city of man. And in the sixteenth century, though Reformers might have denounced the Curia as corrupt, materialistic, evil, the whore of Babylon herself, they did not go so far as to describe the Church, however depraved, as a polity structured along the lines of a territorial state. Yet that is precisely the extra step that Sandys takes. He discusses the power and structure of continental Catholicism in terms of its political and material strength. What are its resources? Its tactics? What kind of propaganda does it use? How many dedicated supporters can it count on in an emergency? How does it organize itself for maximum effectiveness? What are its relations with the various states of Europe? The questions reflect a man in transition between a theological and a political career.

Not only was an evaluation of this kind inherently fascinating (at least to

English readers, who lived in perennial unease about Catholic machinations) but it also made possible novel and concrete insights into the workings of the Church. Sandys is able to outline, in solid and believable detail, the public image that this formidable organization presented to a keen-sighted outsider. He may overdramatize occasionally: for example, in an otherwise hard-headed passage that emphasizes the importance to the pope of the sheer numbers in the religious orders, he loses plausibility as he makes his case more and more in terms of military might. The question Edwin asks himself is, "if the Papacy being reduced to any terms of extremity should resolve to put them in arms for his [sic] final refuge and succour, how many would there be?" (67). His answer, counting all priests, monks, and friars throughout the world, is the not wildly implausible estimate of a million. But it is what he does with the figure that is excessively dramatic; for he proceeds, quite seriously, to remove one-half of the million as physically unfit for warlike service, and then to discuss at great length why one should expect the remainder to be ready, at a moment's notice, for the call to arms. He even thinks they would make excellent soldiers, having had superb training in physical discomfort and adherence to discipline. After all, priests and friars have been the most brutal leaders of the Catholic League in France, and the most enthusiastic advocates of massacres—more of which, Sandys darkly warns, can be expected shortly. Nevertheless, despite occasional exaggerations like these, it is the solidity of the research and the care and sobriety of the presentation that most noticeably characterize the book. Even the forebodings about vast monkish armies and plagues of massacres gain a certain conviction from the seeming reasonableness, the citation of facts, the weighing of opposing views, by which Sandys advances his arguments.

Nor could an Englishman fail to approve of the innate anti-Catholicism that pervades the *Relation*. It is true that the shortcomings of the Roman Church are exposed without hysterical diatribes—quite the contrary: the moderation of tone not only underlines the originality of Sandys's approach, but also gives the work a power that high-pitched abuse would have lacked. Indeed, it seems likely that his restraint, so uncharacteristic of the times, created an impression of Catholic leanings that, in turn, may have led to the book's suppression when it was published. It certainly inspired George Musket to cite Sandys's book in 1623 as part of his apologia for the conversion of John King, the bishop of London, to Catholicism. But Musket was grasping for support at a time when the titles that were typical of the day were the following (all published in the same year as the *Relation*): *The Downfall of Popery*, *The Pope's Funeral*, *The Woeful Cry of Rome*, *A Declaration of Egregious Popish Impostures*, and *The Unlawfulness and Danger of Toleration of Diverse Religions in One Monarchy*.[4]

---

[4] STC, nos. 1819, 1825, 1833, 12882; E. Arber, ed., *A Transcript of the Registers of the Company of Stationers of London 1554–1640*, vol. 3 (London, 1876), 287. For many writers

Yet nobody who read the book carefully could have missed Edwin's essential anti-Catholicism or his fear of the Papacy's might. By dealing with
the Church as a political/military force, and by depicting its strengths and
weaknesses in both secular and moral terms, he makes his basic position
inescapably clear. He may find more to admire—the observation of Lent,
for example, or the custom of praying three times a day—than any right-
minded propagandist ought to admit, and he may also (to the undoubted
horror of narrow-minded Protestants) think that some Catholic practices
could be "recommended to the imitation of all worthy Christians." Moreover, he not only has praise for Sixtus V, but can actually consider the
reigning pope, Clement VIII, to be calm, competent, "devout in his way,"
humble, thrifty, successful, and, in sum, "both good Man, good Prelate,
and good Prince" (5, 151, 156). Yet the overall assessment is clearly negative: in behaving as a secular force, and in deviating from the highest moral
objectives, the Catholics, however formidable, have become proponents of
falsehood and vice.

CATHOLIC STRENGTHS AND WEAKNESSES

The analysis proceeds at various levels, with many asides, but two characteristics stand out. One is the undercurrent of hostility, despite the effort
to be even-handed. At the outset "the Roman Religion" is introduced as
the faith which, of all others, has "most manifoldly declined and degener-
ated" from Christ's original preachings. Its ceremonies are "childish," "unsavory," marked by "silliness," and productive of "disgrace and contempt."
The interesting distinction is that such belittling is reserved for the ceremonial and, in Sandys's view, "superstitious" aspects of Catholicism. He has
little quarrel with doctrines or beliefs, and even acknowledges that magnificent displays, when used to glorify God, can be beneficial: "this outward
state and glory being well disposed, doth engender, quicken, increase and
nourish, the inward reverence and respectful devotion which is due unto
so sovereign Majesty and power" (3, 9–10). Confession, too, he considers
an excellent institution. The *implementation* of these beliefs, however,is
another matter, and here he finds himself turning to words like "unsavory,"
"repugnant," "odious," and the like. Although moderation can fairly be
called his watchword—for he seems genuinely to try to live up to his
avowal, "I choose rather to commend the virtue of an enemy, than to
flatter the vice or imbecility of a friend"—the sniping at the Catholics

---

on Catholicism, a hysterical tone underlined Rome's role as Antichrist in human, and especially English, history: William Haller, *Foxe's Book of Martyrs and the Elect Nation* (London,
1963). Musket's *The Bishop of London his Legacy* (St. Omer, 1623), draws support from the
Relation on 116 and 124, citing Sandys as "a man of great eminency among us." See below,
chapter 11, notes 12, 13.

undoubtedly tilts the balance (10). The favorable adjectives are much less effusive.

A similar attempt at objectivity, which struggles in vain against an essentially negative outlook, colors the other major feature of the analysis: the construction of a pragmatic, factual account (almost Machiavellian in its unsentimentality and realism) of the Roman Church's strengths. Sandys clearly dislikes many of the Catholics' methods, but he cannot withhold a grudging admiration for their skills and achievements. Were it not for the frequent change in popes, he says, they would have mastered the world: an interpretation of their history that, like most of Sandys's views, stresses the politics of the situation as the decisive influence. For obvious reasons, though, he is appalled by the instruments that Catholics use to such great advantage. They rely on excessive "fear and restraint" for some, but allow unconscionably wide elasticity for others (such as the friars); they cynically make sure that a new believer's every "fancy may be satisfied" (once his loyalty is won); they turn popular ceremonies and attractive music into weapons of propaganda; they repress all "doubt or question"; they grant dispensations cleverly and unscrupulously; and they maintain "the ignorance of the Laity [which is] the chiefest and surest sinew of their greatness and glory." Moreover, they learn quickly from the Protestants, adopting disputations and improvements in education to noticeable effect. Their power, backed by redoubtable families and nations with vested interests in church offices, is overwhelming: they are united; they are strongest in the richest area of Europe, the south; and in the long run all the advantages seem to be on their side. Sandys concludes that the Turkish threat, the "bridle which holds in the Papacy," is the only restraint that keeps Protestantism from doom (34, 193).

This prognosis leaves little room for comforting banalities. *A Relation* does not suffer from the unrelenting gloom of a deliberate jeremiad, but the effect is no less ominous. In fact, the restraint of the prose, and the avoidance of ringing denunciations and dire exhortations, only add to the impact of the overall message—it is the down-to-earth quality of the argument, the marshaling of practical information, that makes it seem so compelling. How is one to deny the danger posed by a million clerics and friars whom the pope may enlist for a church army? What is one to do in response to the effectiveness of brilliant preachers, splendid ceremonies, or Jesuit schools? This is not just the devil and his works. It is a far tougher set of enemies: wealth, organization, and efficiency.

To hammer the point home, Sandys discusses the Catholics' ecclesiastical government not in terms of "the conduct of souls" (though he acknowledges that to be one of their aims), "but rather," in his words, "as it is addressed to the upholding of the worldly power and glory of their order, to the advancing of their part, and overthrow of their opposites, which I suppose to be the points they now chiefly respect: I think I may truly say, there was never yet state framed by man's wit in this world more powerful and forcible to work those effects; never any either more wisely contrived and plotted, or more constantly and diligently put in practice and execution." If it were not for the untruth and dishonesty of their claims, "their outward means were sufficient to subdue a whole world," because they can organize their efforts around simple and powerful dogmas that stress allegiance to the Church and utter obedience to the pope. "By this plot have their wits erected in the world a Monarchy more potent than ever any that hath been before it"—a monarchy that enjoys all the manpower it needs "without levying a soldier," while at the same time it "enricheth itself without toiling, warreth without endangering, rewardeth without spending," using colleges and friars like others use fortresses and armies, "and all these maintained at other folks' charges" (23–26).

To dismiss a portrayal of this kind as special pleading or cynicism is to miss its effectiveness, because Sandys is able to analyze *all* major features of the Catholic Church in this light. Their censorship, for example (an ironic target for an author whose book was soon to be burned by Anglicans), and their wish to keep the laity in ignorance, are political devices, designed to preserve order rather than theological purity. Similarly, although he demolishes the Church's pretensions to be the only interpreter of Christian belief (a claim that, according to Sandys, rests on a belittling of the Bible), he admits that his own criticism may be pointless, because the only purpose of the enforced orthodoxy is to bolster defenses against heretics' attacks. The driving force in Catholicism is the conquest of souls, and thus it cannot have too precise a set of beliefs, because then the intelligent Christian might actually wish to choose among the faiths. The Papacy prefers a studied vagueness of doctrine, while insisting on obedience to authority, so that "at leastwise [doubters] may be persuaded to resign up their own eyesight and to look through such spectacles as [the Romanists] temper for them"—an approach that, says Sandys, shows "them wise in policy" (34).

To forward their aims, they adjust to any demands that the faithful might have: "on the one side of the street a cloister of Virgins; on the other a sty of Courtesans . . . : This day all in Masks with all looseness and foolery: tomorrow all in Processions whipping themselves till the blood follow." And the result? "There was never yet State so well built in the world, having his ground as theirs hath in the goodwill of others" (36, 37). The popes please everyone, including other rulers who need dispensations and support. Throughout the sixteenth century, from Francis I to Philip II, princes have obtained what they want from Rome—a brilliant foreign policy. The Papacy even allows princes to ignore their own oaths, a great advantage in the struggle with Protestants, where treachery is a crucial asset. Moreover, the pontiffs have assembled the most potent body of allies imaginable: "that super-politic and irrefragable order . . . of the Jesuits" and, above all, the House of Austria (46). As for Europe's nobles, they are kept friendly with favors and offices: a system of rewards that can be adjusted quite precisely because, through confession, the Church knows what they are feeling at any given moment. Yet this policy has to be carefully watched because, if preferment were suddenly given to men who deserved it, those princes and aristocrats who hitherto "have unsheathed their swords in defense" of Rome, could turn nasty and "satisfy their greediness with the spoil of that State, whose pay they could no longer have" (55).

The members of the clergy and the orders Sandys portrays as driven by similar motives. Though he cites, at some length, such exceptions as a deeply devout and moving Capuchin preacher whose sermons he attended more than once, he regards corruption (such as the exemption from civil prosecution) and the easy life as the bonds that tie these servants to their Church. And why does the pope bother with such "vile" hangers-on? Because, of course, they form a multitude of resolute supporters, dedicated to his cause. It is the politics that counts yet again: Sandys's conclusion, built around another of his history-wide comparisons, is that "there was never yet State so well plotted in this World, or furnished with such store of instruments to employ in the service thereof" (63).

As can be expected, the Catholics do not hesitate to implement their policies with full severity. They persecute, massacre, murder Henry III, and so forth. They also adapt Protestant assets (like good preaching) to their own ends—not because they believe in the virtues of these practices, but because they are effective in winning adherents. Libels, distorted histories, and the spreading of false news are also essential to their propaganda, and give it the power it has achieved. Sobered by these discoveries, Sandys admits, in a passage that foreshadows much modern political practice, that he has had

> to mitigate my former imagination, and to deem it not impossible, that this over-politic and too wise Order may reach a note higher than our gross conceits, who think honesty the best policy, and truth the only durable armor of proof; and may find by their refined observations of experience, that news make their impression upon their first reporting, and that then if they be good, they greatly raise up the spirits . . . ; that afterwards when they happen to be controlled [refuted], mens' spirits being cold are not so sensible as before, and either little regard it, or impute it to common error and uncertainty of things. (103)

All that counts, he ruefully notes, is the immediate advantage gained from the lie, and on that score the Catholics are masters.

Censorship, according to Sandys, is perhaps the most potent instrument of all. People are kept in total ignorance of Protestantism, and some will even leave the room if the subject is raised. Both Inquisition and Index function beautifully, part of a massive effort to keep believers free of possible contamination. The effort goes to such lengths, he reports, that he himself heard Catholics express a willingness to "have censured by some means and reformed the writings of St. Paul" because the apostle was too hot-headed and zealous (116). He also cites the opinion attributed to some Jesuits (although he did not hear it himself) that Paul is dangerous reading and encourages heresy—such is the fear of Protestant emphases within the Scriptures. The censorship is so all-embracing that Sandys could not find a copy of the Catholic polemic of a great contemporary like Bellarmine, because it discussed Protestant beliefs: he failed in his search even in Venice, a republic whose relative openness he admires. Inevitably, the chief sufferers are the ordinary people, the "vulgar sort" who are allowed no chance to seek the truth for themselves, and on whose "devout, . . . humble . . . bowed knees, and hung-down heads, and beaten breasts, and lift[ed] up eyes . . . so notable a calamity" is perpetrated. Edwin's wistful phrase at the close of this analysis captures perfectly his attitude toward the Catholics' pragmatic methods: "it causeth me in generality of good desire to wish, that either the cause which they strive to maintain were better, or their policies whereby they maintain it were not so good" (124, 132).[5]

Essential to this "politic" analysis was a profound commitment to the view that religious belief could be shaped by reason. A few years later, that was exactly how Edwin approached an old friend, Sir Toby Mathew—the two of them had been named jointly in Archbishop Sandys's will to dispose of his books—to try to wean him away from the Catholicism to which he had converted. Mathew was in the Fleet Prison in 1607, and he later described Sandys's visits in terms which, though jaundiced, still ring true:

> Sir Edwin Sands came often to me, and dwelt much with me, but yet prevailed not much upon me. For though he were a man of a very great wit, and of good learning, and flowing speech, yet the tediousness of his discourse, the

---

[5] Noel Malcolm cites Sandys's condemnation of Catholic intervention in politics as evidence of the connection between Sandys and Hobbes: "Hobbes, Sandys, and the Virginia Company," *Historical Journal* 24 (1981): 297–321. The argument is convincing: Sandys, like both Hooker and Hobbes, urged strict subjection of church to state, and his link with Hobbes in the Virginia Company is irrefutable (as a recently published manuscript owned by Hobbes's patron, William Cavendish, emphasizes: below, chapter 13, note 58). But I do not see Sandys as a sophisticated natural law theorist—although natural rights served as a basic assumption from which he derived radical yet pragmatic arguments in Parliament, he showed no interest in exploring their theoretical implications: see below, chapter 4, note 69, pages 117–118, and chapter 7, note 44; and I do not see him encouraging Low Church inclinations in Virginia.

solemness of his understanding, the visible delight which he had to be extremely admired, and his resolution to reduce all religion to human reason, made me apt to fear him a little, and to like him less. One day, I remember, when he came to me, his discourse of religion was such as led me to speak of the nature of faith. Wherein, upon some question that fell between us, I resorted to a book . . . written by an Irish Jesuit [Christopher Sacrobosco's *Defensio decreti Tridentini . . . de authoritate vulgatae editionis* (Antwerp, 1604)] . . . which treats *de regula Fidei* extremely well, and shows the difference between probabilities and certainties, and between human and divine faith; the knowledge of which truths came luckily to me in these times, for Sir Edwin Sands went upon weaker grounds, and did as good as declare that he had no other kind of certainty that Christ our Lord died in Jerusalem than he had that Julius Caesar lived and governed in Rome; wherein that tract, which I had got him to read, did so unbeguile him, that it made him take the less pride in troubling himself with me afterwards.[6]

THE ISSUE OF TOLERATION

Having shown how Catholicism worked, Sandys brings his skill at reasoning to bear on the question of the Church's overall strength. The wealth both of the Papacy and of the clergy he accepts as enormous, and, having described the diplomatic maneuverings at which Rome is so adept, he offers a country-by-country survey of the continent. This is a solid, unsentimental, and essentially accurate estimate of the relative standing of Protestants and Catholics. In France, for example, he notes that the Huguenots are outnumbered twenty to one, but are able to sustain themselves because they outdo their opponents in politicking if not in religious zeal. As a disciple of Hooker, Sandys has no great respect for the French Calvinists. He regards the unexpected pacification of France, a year after the Edict of Nantes, as a fragile equilibrium at best. It would be foolish, he tells us, to predict the behavior of the French, "whose minds are so full of Quicksilver that their nimble wits would take it perhaps in dudgeon, that any should imagine they would plod on in any one tenor, with that dull constancy which their heavier mettled neighbours do use" (186).

Sandys's understanding of the disposition of Scandinavia, the German states (where he rightly emphasizes the importance of Bavaria), the Habsburgs, Italy, Iberia, France, Lorraine, Savoy, and the Netherlands, convinces him that the two sides are "in number and circuit of Territory . . . near equal" (187). This conclusion perhaps gives too much weight to what

[6] A. H. Mathew, ed., *A True Historical Relation of the Conversion of Sir Tobie Matthew to the Holy Catholic Faith; with the Antecedents and Consequences Thereof* (London, 1904), 85–88.

he considers the Protestant domination of Germany, but on the whole it is
a reasonable approximation of actual conditions. And neither camp, in his
estimate, enjoys any decisive advantages that could tip the scale in its favor.
The Catholics are richer and more unified, but they are more immediately
threatened by the Turks, and in addition their two leading powers, Spain
and France, have been weakened by foreign and civil wars. The Protestants are blessed with endurance and strength, but not unity or intelligence. How else is one to explain the enormous lead of the southerners
in establishing overseas empires? "Neither have the Northern people ever
yet for all their multitude and strength, had the honor of being founders or
possessors of any great Empire, so unequal is the combat between force
and wit, in all matters of durable and grounded establishment" (188).

Once he has established, to his own satisfaction, the even balance between the rival faiths, Sandys moves on to the major question that is the
crux of the *Relation*. "This then being so," he writes, "and that all things
considered, there falls out if not such an indifference and equality, yet at
leastwise such a proportion of strength on both sides, as bereaves the other
of hope ever by war to subdue them; . . . and since there is no appearance
of ever forcing an Unity [unless Time changes the situation] . . . ; it re-
maineth to be considered, *What* other kind of *Unity* poor *Christendom*
may hope for, whether Unity of Verity, or Unity of Charity, or Unity of
Persuasion, or Unity of Authority, or Unity of Necessity; there being so
many other kinds and causes of concord" (194). Sandys discusses this momentous issue at length (twenty-two pages), and the noble and original
sentiments he expresses justify the attention this passage has received from
modern commentators on his book.

I have assessed elsewhere the sixteenth-century literature on this topic,
and Edwin's place within that tradition. Suffice it here to say that after
eighty years of religious conflict, and thousands of pamphlets, the best
anyone could suggest was that, perhaps, with moderation and good intent,
some semblance of Christian unity could be restored. Although the finest
minds of the 1580s and 1590s—Montaigne, Bodin, Hooker—agreed with
most Europeans that a calming down of passions and hatreds was devoutly
to be wished, none of them was capable of devising practical means to that
end, and none was willing totally to abandon the chimera of a reunited
Christendom.[7] That final step Sandys, having reviewed the ideas of the day
and assessed the various possibilities, would be prepared to take.

---

[7] See below, note 11, and my "Religious Toleration during the Age of Reformation," *Politics, Religion, and Diplomacy in Early Modern Europe: Essays in Honor of De Lamar Jensen*,
ed. Malcolm Thorp and Arthur J. Slavin, Sixteenth Century Essays & Studies, vol. 27
(Kirksville, Mo., 1994), 305–319. The continuing quest for unity is broadly documented in
Gary Remer, *Humanism and the Rhetoric of Toleration* (University Park, Pa., 1996).

THE QUEST FOR UNITY

Sandys entered the discussion with the same pragmatic purposes that had informed his political interpretation of the Catholic Church. Despite the complexity, contentiousness, and recalcitrance of the issues, he was able to proceed in methodical, sober, and learned fashion through the thickets of controversy. He had informed himself of the chief positions held by his contemporaries, and his argument took the form of an analysis of each proposal, one at a time, until he gradually moved toward his own conclusions. Although he did not mention other writers by name, it is clear that he had a good knowledge of the sixteenth-century literature, and considered himself to be contributing to a long-standing debate. Indeed, Sandys seems consciously to have been seeking a new solution for the most intractable of the period's problems: the reunification of western Christianity.

The ultimate reason for the treatment of the Catholic Church as a material power becomes apparent as Edwin, having completed that analysis, turns to the possibilities of reconciliation. For he can now address himself to his predecessors' suggestions, and criticize their ideas, armed with a solid basis of evidence. It is typical of the man that he should have prepared the ground so thoroughly; there are parallels in his accumulation of nearly twenty years of parliamentary experience before assuming an important role in the House of Commons.

Sandys notes from the start that potential mediators, though present "in all Countries," are "not many in number" (194). This does not, however, weaken the common impression that, despite all the "flames of controversies," some sort of "tolerable peace" could be reestablished. The well-intentioned, he observes, still seem to believe the "possibility that [such a peace] might be wrought." They draw comfort from the demonstrable agreement of both sides on certain fundamental "touch-stones" of the Faith (rather like Erasmus' "common core" notion) and from the existence of a "multitude" of virtuous seekers of good (the people in whom moderates have placed their hopes for decades). But this "Unity of Verity"— unity coalescing around universally accepted truths—has small chance of success, in Sandys's view, because of the general eagerness to fight over subsidiary issues: "the multitude of crooked and side respects," which are the "prickles that so enfroward mens' affections." This may be the "best," the "chief," the "honourable" unity to strive for, but it is unattainable in the face of such hatreds and bitterness (195).

What, then, is left? A somewhat less ambitious unity might be the "Unity of Charity," which was one of the objectives of moderates like Erasmus and de l'Hôpital. The expectation in this case is that the "acerbity" and "poison" would finally get out of hand, "tediousness and weariness" would take over, and finally "some tolerable reconciliation" would be reached, at least to the extent of ending hostilities. Somehow, good sense would prevail; the combatants would see the futility of further struggle; and from this renewed moderation a real possibility of unity could grow (196). Taking this process one step further, Sandys describes how some observers see the two sides drawing together in recognition of their own fallibility. If the Fathers of the Church, though "nearer the times of purity" (a classic Protestant statement), occasionally erred, how much less justification is there for self-righteousness hundreds of years later. Once this admission is made, many of the stumbling blocks can be removed. The Catholics can abolish their images, their reverence of saints, "offensive Ceremonies," indulgences, and Latin services (which the pope is willing to dispense with anyhow, if necessary), and the Protestants, for their part, can "purge out that negative and contradictory humor, of thinking they are then rightest, when they are unlikest the Papacy." That may not be much of a concession, but it has to be accompanied by a recognition that much can be learned from the Catholics, and that certainty of one's own "absolute or unreproveable perfection" has to cease. The result, once again, could be a kind of "common core" unity, in which "a general and indifferent Confession and sum of Faith," a uniform (or at least "not repugnant") Liturgy, and some kind of universal church government could be created. Controversies would be left to the learned, and every man would be left alone to believe whatever nonessentials he liked (196–197, 199).

Some thoughtful observers evidently believed that the best way to reach this end was a general council which could impose, from on high, a "Unity of Authority." Sandys reports that "the sum of the discourse of that kind of people" is that the princes of Europe could easily force all sides into ending their antagonisms (200).[8] But he notes that most of the supporters of this position are Protestants, albeit "not running jump with their side in every thing," and a few moderate Catholics, hardly the power needed to move princes. More important, however, are the practical difficulties which, says Sandys, are "so great, that they draw to be next neighbors to so many impossibilities" (200–201). He wishes he could see some way of creating this "consecrated" unity, and doing so "without the ruin and subversion of either part"—a remarkable statement—but he finds the problems insuperable.

Naturally, if one side were to conquer the other, that would put a stop to all speculations. This outcome he dismisses as most unlikely, but he has no greater hope for the alternative, a new "mildness" among the antagonists, because that, too, would have to be brought about by popes and princes. The "untractableness" and authoritarianism of the Papacy remove the first

---

[8] Hooker also believed a general council could restore unity: *Works*, ed. J. Keble, 3 vols. (Oxford, 1845), 1:166–169, 477, 3:462.

from consideration. Although "there seems to be as much or more [evidence in Scripture] for the King of Spain's not erring, as there is for the Pope's," his self-certainty will never be shaken (203). He would look like a fool, and too many vested interests would be hurt, if he ever admitted the slightest fault. It should be the task of Europe's princes to make him change his ways, but "they dream of an old world, and of the heroical times, who imagine that Princes will break their sleeps for such purposes." Rulers are "brought up in the midst of their factions and flatterers, where they seldom hear truth," and indeed "the world may hold itself reasonably happy and content, if the Civil state be upheld in any tolerable terms." To expect princes to help religion is to ask too much (205).

Sandys completes this section of his analysis with a jaundiced assessment of the quality of most princes: a few may be worthy, but the failings of the majority have contributed significantly to the religious problems of the age. It may well have been the sarcasm and contempt noticeable throughout this passage, and the other unfavorable comments on royalty that appear in the *Relation*, that led to its suppression after publication. Few readers could have regarded as a harmless commonplace the following sentence: "As for great persons and Princes, of whom it was said by the Spanish Friar [?], that few went to Hell, and the reason, because they were few: it is a rare thing and happy wherever it falls out that any of them hath any true and affecting sense of those first and undoubted grounds of Religion, to what sort or sect soever it propend" (161–162).

Summing up his findings, Sandys sees "small hope" of real reform, let alone unity, especially since "the long continuance of this [religious] division [means that] both parts are formalized and settled in their oppositions." He "greatly despairs" of change, which, though "an honest-hearted desire," must be dismissed "as a cabinet discourse of speculative consideration, which practice in the world and experience doth need to rectify" (206). It is that very experience, of course, which his long tour and investigation of Catholicism is specifically designed to provide.

Only two of the possibilities in Sandys's original list of "unities" now remain: unity by "necessity" and unity by "persuasion." The first could come about only as a defense against the Turks, but he perceptively questions "whether the Turk be so fearful a Monarch as is commonly conceived" and goes on to show, at least to his own satisfaction, that the Ottoman state is incapable of mounting a real threat to the west (207). Persuasion, on the other hand, seems to be the mechanism in which both sides place their chief hopes. They expect to "eat out" their opponents gradually, winning over adherents by steady erosion. The Protestants rely on truth, the Catholics on the support of powerful princes. And there may be a real possibility that the quick-witted, conniving French could convert the "stiff" and "heavy" Germans, for Lutheranism is past its prime. But the

Catholics' real target, in Sandys's view, is England, where the only "justifiable Reformation" has taken place, retaining the apostolic succession of the episcopacy and the best ancient rites. Hence the attempted invasions, and the missions of the Jesuits Campion and Parsons. But these expectations are also chimeras; and so, since every program of reconciliation fails the tests of experience and reality, Sandys resigns himself to the inevitable: the hope for unity "must I leave and recommend to God: as being both our best and now remaining only policy" (215).[9]

The final pages of the *Relation* provide a quick summary of the behavior and teachings of the Jews, the Greek Orthodox, and the Russian Orthodox. Here again, despite his obvious disapproval of such stubborn and unredeemed believers, he tries to give a balanced picture. The longest section is on the Jews, centering around the reasons the Roman Church (to its shame) has failed to convert them to Christianity. For all his unhappiness with Judaism's rejection of Christ, he finds much to approve. Jews have "very honorable and holy" opinions about God; "very exquisite" ideas, "near unto truth," about man; moral standards that are "to be commended"; and in person seem generally to be pious, charitable, and "of singular virtue and integrity of mind" (222–227).[10]

This willingness to give even the damned their due lies at the heart of the repeated moderation of Sandys's pronouncements—a moderation visible in his very language, whose sobriety and restraint stand in strong contrast to the hysteria of his age. There is a similarly unusual quality about a cast of mind which, in its search for the concrete and the definable, could conceive of the Roman Church as a political organization. The reasoned tone, the political mode of analysis, the attention to detail, and the emphasis on tangible evidence: all these features of the *form* of his book prefigured Edwin's approach and outlook during his public career.

THE FIRST CALL FOR COEXISTENCE IN REFORMATION EUROPE

But what of the content? Why the lengthy exposition, first of Catholicism, and then, almost as a consequence, of the hopes for unity? The three principal modern commentators on the *Relation* link it to Hooker, portraying Sandys as a disciple, and placing him in a broad *politique* tradition.[11]

---

[9] Compare Hooker's sad conclusion about the prospects for reconciliation: "There is no way left but this one, 'Pray for the peace of Jerusalem.'" *Works*, 3:465. Despite this similarity of tone, Hooker's other comments on the issue show he was far less willing to accept fragmentation.

[10] Greater detail is in my "Return of the Jews."

[11] J. W. Allen, *A History of Political Thought in the Sixteenth Century* (London, 1928), 241–246 (the best available treatment); W. K. Jordan, *The Development of Religious Toleration in England from the Beginning of the English Reformation to the Death of Queen Elizabeth*

For them, his work represents a relatively minor episode in the toleration controversy of the sixteenth century, and is interesting only because of its explicit discussion of the reunification of Christianity. Within the context of their histories, each of which covers at least a century of writings on a wide variety of topics linked with toleration, their assessment is certainly appropriate. However, it misses not only those unique attributes of the *Relation* which have been outlined above, but also the book's basic purpose.

Sandys was clearly trying to do more than gather a lot of useful information for his patron Whitgift, or for his countrymen in general, though that was undoubtedly one of his aims. The centrality of the section on Christian unity has rightly been emphasized, and there can be little doubt that this was the justification and climax of the entire book. He wanted to focus systematically on what must have seemed, to a thoughtful person, the most important question of the day. During the three years of his continental journey two famous victories for reconciliation had been won: the Union of Brest-Litovsk in 1596 and the Edict of Nantes in 1598. Whether they proved to be lasting or not (and Sandys had his doubts), they did give the search for agreement a live and pressing immediacy during the last years of the sixteenth century. How likely was it that the process would continue? Might the great ideal of a reunited Christendom, to which both the tolerant and the fanatic still clung, gain a new lease on life? Did it make sense to continue hoping?

It was to this kind of question that Sandys was addressing himself, and his answer in all cases seems to have been "no." The well-intentioned could construct their arguments with the best will in the world, but wishing would not make it so. He softened the blow by recognizing occasional strengths or plausibilities in the various paths to unity that had been proposed. But he was unable to avoid the ultimate pessimistic answer: one could do nothing but pray for divine providence "to effect those things which to man's wit may seem impossible" (216). In other words, unity was not imminent, and there seemed little point in hoping for it.

For W. K. Jordan, this admission indicated that "Sandys' magnificent ideal broke down when he was obliged to discard one means of securing it

---

(Cambridge, Mass., 1932), 367–371; Joseph Lecler, *Histoire de la tolérance au siècle de la Réforme*, vol. 2 (Paris, 1955; trans. T. L. Westow, New York, 1960), 346–349. The recent Italian studies (see below, note 27) add little to these three basic accounts. A suggestive, though insufficiently documented, effort to contextualize the *Relation*—its fact-finding purpose on behalf of Whitgift, and its debts to Hooker, Botero, and "Tacitism"—is Walter Johnson's unpublished Diploma in Historical Studies thesis, "Sir Edwin Sandys and the *Relation of the State of Religion*" (Amherst College, 1989). The Botero and "Tacitism" connection is also discussed in Richard Tuck, *Philosophy and Government 1572–1651* (Cambridge, 1993), 117, 121.

after another."[12] I would argue, *per contra*, that the discarding was in fact the object of the analysis. Sandys never put forward the different theories about unity as his *own* proposals: they were views in currency at the time. As if to emphasize the distinction, Edwin added quotation marks down the entire left hand margin of each page of the section on unity when he corrected (in his own handwriting) the copy of the first edition that is now in the British Library.[13] These were other people's proposals, *not* his own; on the basis of his investigations into the state of religion, he had to conclude that they were inadequate.

On one level, therefore, the object of the book seems to have been purely negative. Sandys did the research to expose the futility of the hopes to which believers in Christian unity still clung. But the obverse of this dose of realism was positive. Once they conceded the hopelessness of reunification, Christians had to face up to a rather different situation: implicit in the abandonment of a single faith was the acceptance of a more or less permanent split. And since Sandys strongly urged that friendly contact be maintained, because disputes are "made calm by intercourse, by parley they are reconciled, by familiarity they are extinguished," he was, in effect, assembling all the ingredients for what today we would call peaceful coexistence (107).[14] To my knowledge, the *Relation* was the first book written in the wake of the Reformation which reached this position. As such, it offered the first realistic antidote to the pessimism and sense of helplessness that had intensified during eighty years of religious conflict.

REACTIONS AND READERS

It is hardly surprising that the book's qualities should have appealed both to Sandys's contemporaries and to readers ever since. The tribute by J. W.

[12] Jordan, *Religious Toleration*, 370–371.

[13] BL, C. 28f8. The quotation marks start at the page preceding sig. T and continue through the page following sig. T 2. None of the authorities on language usage in this period whom I consulted was sure when quotation marks first appeared, but all agreed, first, that such notations became fairly common later in the seventeenth century, and, second, that they always identified material attributed to another author or source.

[14] For more detailed discussion, see my "A Contribution to the Toleration Controversy of the Sixteenth Century: Sandys's 'A Relation of the State of Religion,'" in *Renaissance Studies in Honor of Hans Baron*, ed. Anthony Molho and John Tedeschi (De Kalb, Ill., 1971), 833–847. It is clear from Sandys's treatment of the question of unity (and also from the contrast highlighted in note 9, above) that there is no basis for the view that he was pursuing a Hooker-inspired agenda for Christian unification, with the Anglican Church as a model—as argued by H. R. Trevor-Roper, "The Good and Great Works of Richard Hooker," *New York Review of Books*, 24 November 1977, 48–55, esp. 51, and W. P. Haugaard, "Richard Hooker: Evidences of an Ecumenical Vision from a Twentieth-Century Perspective," *Journal of Ecumenical Studies* 24 (1987): 427–439.

Allen is far from unique: "The tolerance for which he pleaded was an attitude of mind; and its general adoption would have made legal toleration a matter of course. . . . He had gone to the root of the matter. . . . The tolerance he pleaded for remained and remains uncommon."[15] And in its own day the *Relation* aroused the interest and compliments of such diverse luminaries as Sir Henry Wotton, Paolo Sarpi, and Hugo Grotius. But the best index of the book's general reception is its publishing history.

The manuscript was printed in June 1605, six years after it had been written. By November 3, when all copies were ordered burned by the Court of High Commission, at least two editions had appeared.[16] That the need for two or more editions in less than five months indicated extraordinary popularity rather than excessive optimism or poor management is confirmed by the stature of the publisher. Valentine Simmes, a prolific printer of long standing, produced the book for Simon Waterson, who was one of London's most distinguished citizens: twice master of the Stationers' Company, with more than twenty years' experience in the book business by 1605. In 1604 alone he had produced such famous works as Spenser's *Faerie Queene*, Sidney's *Arcadia*, and the English translation of Machiavelli's *Florentine History*.[17] But none of these texts was a best-seller to compare with Sandys's *Relation*. It took popularity on the scale of the Bible, the Book of Common Prayer, or Bacon's *Essays* to merit two or more editions in less than five months at this time.

In other words, by the standards of Jacobean England, the book was a considerable success. It is impossible to know how many were printed, but one can assume that each edition consisted of at least a few hundred copies, which suggests a remarkable level of interest among buyers and readers in a very short period. Chamberlain heard a rumor that Sandys himself approved of the burning, which is probably what the author, saving face, wanted to have known. Yet if this was the truth it seems unlikely that neither a gossip as sharp-eared as Chamberlain nor anyone else was able to confirm the rumor.[18] Not until 1629, in the preface to a new edition, was the 1605 book openly denounced as "a spurious stolen Copy; in part epitomized, in part amplified, and throughout most shamefully falsified & false printed, from the Author's Original: In so much that [Sir Edwin] was infinitely wronged thereby: and as soon as it came to his knowledge, . . . he

[15] Allen, *Political Thought*, 245.

[16] Arber, *Stationers*, 3:292; N. E. McClure, ed., *The Letters of John Chamberlain*, 2 vols. (Philadelphia, 1939), 1:214: letter of November 7, 1605. The editions are STC 21715, 21716, and 21717. The revised STC puts 21717 first and 21716 second, both in 1605; it changes 21715 (a forgery of 21717) to 21717.5, of uncertain date, though no later than 1622, because of a manuscript note in the Huntington Library copy.

[17] Arber, *Stationers*, 3:269.

[18] *Chamberlain*, 1:214.

caused it . . . to be prohibited by Authority; and . . . to be deservedly burnt."[19]

More than thirty years ago, I questioned this denial and argued that there was good reason to believe that Sandys *did* want the book published in 1605. Recent research has revised the order of the early editions that the *Short Title Catalogue* proposed, and it appears that one of these was a pirated reprint of the Waterson edition. But these publications were hardly so deficient as to justify the hyperbole in the 1629 preface about a spurious, stolen, epitomized, amplified, and falsified text. The bibliographic reordering helps clarify a murky episode, but does not alter its place in Sandys's life. In particular, although the omissions and errors of 1605 included gaps of a few sentences, they lack the consistency that would support the otherwise undocumented speculation that Catholics brought out the book to embarrass Sir Edwin and the government.[20] After all, he was not averse to having the book known: he was circulating manuscript copies; he himself corrected the mistakes in one of these editions; another 1605 copy is the only one that the Sandys family has kept, from generation to generation, to this day; and a third copy was owned by Sir Edwin's cousin and son-in-law Sir Thomas Wilford.[21] Nor is it likely that a publisher of the standing of Waterson would have been involved in so shady a venture.

Then there is the question of the 1629 edition itself. Those who argue that Sandys suppressed the 1605 editions treat the 1629 preface as an

---

[19] The 1629 preface is not paginated.

[20] See my "The Editions of Sir Edwin Sandys's *Relation of the State of Religion*," *Huntington Library Quarterly* 26 (1963): 323–336. The revised order of the editions and its implications are discussed by James Ellison, "The Order of Editions of Sir Edwin Sandys's *Relation of the State of Religion*," *The Library*, 6th ser., 2 (1980): 208–211, and Peter W. M. Blayney, *The Texts of King Lear and their Origins*, vol. 1 (Cambridge, 1982), 351–352, 424–425. For the reliability of the 1629 preface, on which both these accounts depend, see below, notes 22 and 23. Just because Catholics found comfort in the *Relation* (see above, note 4) does not mean (as Ellison, "Editions," 210–211, argues) that they systematically sanitized the text: if so, why did they not remove (sig. A3 verso) Sandys's comments about "childish" and "unsavory" Catholic practices that invited "disgrace" and "contempt", or (sig. B4 recto) his attribution of "wickedness" and "beastliness" to priests and friars, and why (sig. C verso) did they remove some of his compliments about Catholic charity, including a reference to its "good order"? The excisions, none of which causes awkward syntax or noticeably interrupts the flow of the text, imply a shortage of space, not a system.

[21] Wilford's copy is now in Haigh Hall. It is described in *Bibliotheca Lindesiana*, vol. 4: *Catalogue of the Printed Books Preserved at Haigh Hall, Wigan, Co. Pal. Lancst.* (Aberdeen, 1910), 7527. Among the manuscript copies of the *Relation*, discussed in my "Editions" nearly twenty years before Ellison's article, are: Bodleian MS. e. Museo 211, which was written by Sandys's amanuensis, Hewlet, and bequeathed by Sandys to Hewlet's successor, Ralph Oxenden (see Oxenden's note at the end of the text); Queen's College Oxford MSS. 280, no. 88; Lambeth Palace Library, MS. 2007, fols. 169–203; and the magnificent version in vellum binding (possibly the presentation copy) in BL, Additional, 24,109. See also above, note 3.

accurate account of the events. But if that was the case, why was there a need to claim (probably falsely) that the 1629 edition was published in The Hague?[22] Even if not false, why take the precaution of foreign publication? If Sir Edwin was responsible for the suppression, but now wanted the book in print, why not publish openly in London? The likelihood is that Sandys (or his associates) remembered the earlier troubles, and, to strengthen the defense, insisted the 1605 editions had been unauthorized.

The best reason for accepting the 1605 publication as authentic, however, derives from the author's circumstances at the time. During the first years of the seventeenth century Sandys was moving determinedly toward a public career. As we will see, between his return from the continent in 1599 and the early days of James I's reign, he was becoming more involved in politics, primarily as one of Cecil's agents. He was trying, at a relatively advanced age, to shape a new life. And the earliest sign of his having found a distinctive role appeared in the spring of 1604 in the House of Commons, when he broke with his previous behavior and rapidly took command of those who opposed the king's wishes. Thus began his most energetic and fruitful years: a period of parliamentary leadership, of prominent involvement in England's overseas enterprises, and of personal fulfillment in the shape of twelve children. He was making a new name for himself in every sense, and the exposure for general consumption of the book he had finished a few years before was absolutely in keeping with this sudden wave of public activity.

At the same time, however, the new prominence may have given the authorities cause to suppress the *Relation*. The avowed reasons will never be known, because High Commission's records no longer exist. Nevertheless, it seems reasonable to speculate either that Sandys's obstreperous behavior in the Parliament of 1604 (not to mention his book's sarcasm about princes) encouraged the hostility of officialdom, or that his tolerant remarks about Catholics gave the Anglican hierarchy pause; after all, in the same letter that reported the burning of the *Relation*, John Chamberlain also described the discovery of a plot by one Johnson, later known as Guy Fawkes. The historian of English Arminianism, Nicholas Tyacke, has suggested that Sir Edwin may also have suffered the disfavor that was directed in the early seventeenth century toward the antipredestinarian views that were to be associated with that doctrine. There are certainly hints of a proto-Arminian position in the *Relation*, particularly in its sin-

---

[22] The suspicion that the title page of the 1629 edition falsified the place of publication is supported by the copy in Harvard University's Houghton Library, which was presented by M. Sparke (the printer of the next English editions) to his cousin Noel Sparke on April 20, 1629. The doubts derive both from the identity of the donor and from the unlikelihood that a copy could cross the North Sea and find a buyer in less than four weeks after March 25, the date when seventeenth-century Englishmen started a new year.

gling out of the doctrine of unconditional predestination as a major obstacle to Christian reunion; its moderate remarks about the papacy; and its acceptance of the potential value of such "works" as confession. Moreover, Sandys's old college, Corpus Christi, was already becoming a breeding ground of Arminianism.[23]

England's censors notwithstanding, the book's success proved to be long-term as well as immediate. Although the 1629 edition gave The Hague as place of publication, by the 1630s the atmosphere had changed sufficiently to permit three London editions, one of them reissued, between 1632 and 1638.[24] None of the reasons for the suppression still carried weight: Sandys was dead, and in any case had become reconciled with the Court in his last years; Charles I's High Church tendencies allowed more discussion of Catholicism; and Laud's ascendancy ended the disapproval of Arminianism. Ironically, the decade after Sandys's death, the 1630s, probably witnessed the high point in the reputation of his book, for his family (not to mention his friends the Ferrars) were leading lights of the Great Tew circle, and the *Relation* was approvingly quoted by Chillingworth. Significantly, there was no further edition during the Civil Wars and Interregnum, when the conditions of the 1630s were reversed, but two more did appear when the pendulum swung back again—in 1673 and 1687.[25]

Across the Channel the *Relation* also aroused considerable interest. In 1608 the future bishop of Kilmore, William Bedell, who was then chaplain

---

[23] *Chamberlain*, 1:214. On Sandys's proto-Arminianism, see Nicholas Tyacke, *Anti-Calvinists* (Oxford, 1987), 145. I am grateful to Dr. Tyacke for his comments on this issue. Later English Arminians were, of course, to draw inspiration from such associates of Sandys as Hooker, Lancelot Andrewes, and the president of Corpus, John Spenser. When, in December 1609, Sir Edwin denounced the vicar of Northbourne, Henoch Clapham, it may have been because Clapham, as a former separatist leader, espoused radical views, though Sandys's accusation, that Clapham was disorderly and drunk, also reflected a gentry concern for order (Canterbury Cathedral Library, X.11.11, fol. 119, a reference I owe to Peter Clark). On Clapham see Champlin Burrage, *The Early English Dissenters in the Light of Recent Research (1550–1641)*, vol. 1 (Cambridge, 1912), 194–200. Ironically, the 1629 preface of the *Relation* claimed that the book would distress Arminians—which may be another indication that the edition was not Sandys's doing. Finally, although the publisher's failure to obtain official approval for the book might have justified the burning of the *Relation*, it is probable that Waterson thought it unnecessary to seek the usual imprimatur from the bishop of London for an author (named for the Stationers' Company, though not on the title page) who was himself the son of a bishop of London.

[24] STC 21718 through 21722.

[25] There is also a reference to an edition of 1669 in Samuel Halkett and John Laing, eds., *Dictionary of Anonymous and Pseudonymous English Literature*, vol. 5 (London, 1929), 56, but of this I have found no other trace. For the Great Tew and Chillingworth links, see Malcolm, "Hobbes, Sandys," 310, 317–318; and Marc L. Schwarz, "Lay Anglicanism and the Crisis of the English Church in the Early Seventeenth Century," *Albion* 14 (1982): 1–17. For a midcentury Puritan reader, see M. Hunter and A. Gregory, eds., *An Astrological Diary of the Seventeenth Century: Samuel Jeake of Rye 1652–1699* (Oxford, 1988), 93.

to Sir Henry Wotton, England's ambassador to Venice, translated the book into Italian. It was eventually published at the Aldine press in 1625 as *Relatione dello stato della religione*. The reasons for the translation, described in a letter Bedell wrote in January 1609, deserve quotation, because they constitute the only substantive contemporary assessment of the work:

> It hath been considered, that to propound [religious truth] in its own naked simplicity to men ... blinded with superstition ... were but to expose it to contempt, and as it were to demand a repulse. [Venetian nobles and ecclesiastics] read gladly of discourses of policy; so as under that name if religion could be conveyed, it were like to find much better entertainment.... Agreeably whereunto it would perhaps be very convenient in our times, to convey the reproofs of the abuses and errors of the papacy in politick discourses.... In this kind there is extant already in our tongue a work so proper to that purpose, as if God had directed the pen of the author to that special end, to do him service in this place. It is the relation of Sir Edwin Sandys that I mean; which being thought fit to be translated into Italian, I undertook the work, and by God's assistance have finished it this last summer (the Fathers correcting my Errors in the Language). It hath been divided into chapters, and in the end of some of them are added some annotations.... This [Wotton] hath had on purpose to put to the press.... Some parts of it in the mean time have been shewed the principal men here, and I do believe to the Prince himself: whereof when we should have seen any Effect (and great it will be sure, if wise men's judgment be not deceived in it) then was it resolved to be put in execution.[26]

The fathers who helped Bedell were Fulgenzio Manfredi, an antipapal Franciscan who was later burned for heresy, and the famous historian of the Council of Trent, the Servite Paolo Sarpi. It was the latter who provided the notes mentioned by Bedell, which were then published in the Italian edition.[27] Sandys may have met Sarpi during his travels, but the

[26] E. S. Shuckburgh, ed., *Two Biographies of William Bedell Bishop of Kilmore with a Selection of his Letters and an Unpublished Treatise* (Cambridge, 1902), 247–248.

[27] For a good discussion of this edition, and of the translations in general, see Gaetano Cozzi, "Sir Edwin Sandys e la *Relazione dello stato della religione*," *Rivista storica italiana* 79 (1967): 1097–1121. Cozzi identifies the antipapal purposes which the book served for Sarpi. Two other Italian treatments of the *Relation* are: Corrado Vivanti's *Lotta politica e pace religiosa in Francia fra Cinque e Seicento* (Paris, 1954), which links Sandys to the irenic tradition exemplified by Isaac Casaubon; and Delio Cantimori's *Prospettive di storia ereticale italiana del Cinquecento* (Bari, 1960), which suffers from a number of errors (corrected by Cozzi) and argues that Sandys sought to restore religious unity. These writers add little to the English and French studies, and Cozzi (111) claims that Sandys's book was burned *after* the Gunpowder Plot (and thus suffered from anti-Catholic feeling) when the burning took place two days *before* November 5: see above, note 16.. On Bedell and Sarpi, see Frances Yates,

great Venetian's interest in the *Relation* is itself sufficient indication of Edwin's significance as a member of that European-wide coterie of irenic spirits which has been described as the creator, for a brief moment during the early seventeenth century, of a "distinct phase of light" amidst the darkness of Reformation and Counter-Reformation.[28] Indeed, it is indicative of the reach of this irenicism that contemporares as varied as an Irish Anglican bishop, a Servite friar, an English ambassador, and a Venetian doge appreciated the originality of Sandys's "politick" analysis of Catholicism.

Links with other members of the coterie emerge from the history of the subsequent translations of the *Relation*. When Bedell listed his own accomplishments in 1613, and mentioned his work on Sandys's book, he said that a copy of the translation was available either in Venice or in Geneva, whither it had been brought by Giovanni Diodati, the eminent Calvinist theologian. Diodati had visited Sarpi and Wotton in 1608, and had obviously discussed the *Relation* with them.[29] Over the next few years he himself translated it, this time into French, and in 1626 *two* editions of his version of *Relation de l'état de la religion* (complete with Sarpi's notes) were published in Geneva. A third edition was produced in Amsterdam fifteen years later. In the meantime, another great European figure, Hugo Grotius, had come across the book. He wrote to his brother William first in January 1637, and again two months later, suggesting the need for a Dutch edition. Whether his recommendation was followed up at the time we cannot tell, but forty years later, in 1675, a Dutch version (also including Sarpi's notes), was published at Haarlingen. The translator, listed as J. Ondaan (probably the poet Joachim Ondaan) rendered the title as *Verhael van den Staat der Religie.*[30]

"Paolo Sarpi's 'History of the Council of Trent,'" *Journal of the Warburg and Courtauld Institutes* 7 (1944): 123–143, a reference I owe to Gerald Aylmer. For further links with Wotton, see below, note 44.

[28] H. R. Trevor-Roper, "The Religious Origins of the Enlightenment," in his *Religion, the Reformation and Social Change* (London, 1967), 193–236, p. 201.

[29] Shuckburgh, *Bedell*, 254; Giovanni Diodati, *Brève Relation de mon Voyage a Venise en Septembre 1608*, ed. Eugene de Budé (Geneva, 1863). I am indebted to William Monter for this reference.

[30] Hugo Grotius, *Epistolae* (Amsterdam, 1687), 865, 866. For Ondaan see J. Melles, *Joachim Ondaan: Heraut der verdraagzaamheid, 1628–1692* (Utrecht, 1958); I owe both the identification and the reference to Herbert Rowen. No specific evidence has survived, but it is likely that Sandys also had some contact with Isaac Casaubon. Edwin just missed him in Geneva, and during the great Frenchman's English days they had good mutual friends in Henry Wotton and Lancelot Andrewes. There was a link, too, through Grotius, whom Casaubon came to know in England. It is impossible to determine whether Sandys's acquaintance stretched to other luminaries in that circle like Scaliger and de Thou, but enough has surely been shown to establish his stature as a prominent citizen of Europe's republic of letters.

Even the bare essentials of the book's history are striking: fourteen editions, two of them reissued, encompassing four languages and exciting the interest of the most celebrated leaders of Europe's intellectual life. No author could have asked for a better reception or imagined a greater success. Yet Sandys never had a "following," in any sense of that ambiguous term, mainly because nobody in the next few generations tried to pursue the kind of analysis that distinguished the *Relation*. There were travel books by the score, including one written by his brother George, and there were many pleas for religious toleration, though usually from such nonestablishment writers as John Milton and Roger Williams.[31] But no one cared to undertake a well-researched survey of western religions, to analyze religious institutions as political bodies, or to suggest that friendly coexistence might be a more practical ideal than Christian reconciliation.

Nor is there any reason that such efforts should have been taken further. If the book did help Europeans recognize that western Christianity was irrevocably split, this was a conclusion that eventually became commonplace, and the book's final edition, in the 1680s, must already have seemed rather out-of-date. The *Relation* was a tract for the times, addressing immediate religious issues but not rising above them to confront eternal values. Yet the book's pioneering qualities are undeniable, and the evidence of editions and translations makes clear that in the seventeenth century Sandys's work did strike a responsive chord.

That he was aware of his own place in the writings of the day is also clear. The reflections of Hooker and de l'Hôpital in the *Relation* leave one in no doubt as to his wide reading in contemporary religious and political literature. And the entire section on unity is a kind of critical bibliographic essay. One cannot be more precise about influences, because authors in the seventeenth century rarely felt the need to cite their sources.[32] The same held true not only for Sandys, but also for those who read his work and did not mention him by name. Nonetheless, there is no point in exaggerating the mark he made on his times. He wrote an important, often original, widely read, and much-respected book. Though blessed with distinguished admirers and a long life, the *Relation* was essentially of secondary significance: a pathbreaking, but not central, contribution to seventeenth-century literature, which is interesting mainly as a historical landmark and as a window into Sandys's mind. The qualities the book displays—broad learning, flexibility, pragmatism, political-mindedness, and

[31] George Sandys, *A Relation of a Journey begun An: Dom: 1610* (London, 1615); Roland Bainton, *The Travail of Religious Liberty* (Philadelphia, 1951), pt. 3.

[32] For example, Francis Bacon: M. R. Cohen, "The Myth about Bacon and the Inductive Method," *Scientific Monthly* 23 (1926): 504–508; F. R. Johnson, *Astronomical Thought in Renaissance England* (Baltimore, 1937), 297; R. H. Bowers, "Bacon's Spider Simile," *Journal of the History of Ideas* 17 (1956): 133–135.

reasoned moderation—persisted, with only rare lapses, throughout his subsequent public career.

GLIMPSES OF PERSONALITY AND PERSONAL LIFE

There is also evidence of Sir Edwin's personality in his second book, *Sacred Hymns, Consisting of Fifty Select Psalms of David*, published in 1615.[33] The verses were hardly masterpieces, but the fact that they were produced (in collaboration with the playwright Robert Tailor) so as "to be sung in five parts, as also to the viola, and lute or Orpharion . . . for the use of such as delight in the exercise of music" suggests a devotion to music that may have reflected the influence of his father, who had decreed that the boys at the school he founded in Hawkshead should "every day before they go to dinner . . . sing a psalm in metre." Sir Edwin's brother George similarly published *A Paraphrase upon the Psalms of David*, which implies that this was a family interest.[34]

What else can one say about this man, whose personal life has left so little mark on the record? It is only indirectly that we learn, for example, that Edwin became increasingly involved in the world of politics after he returned to England from the continent in 1599. His movements remain uncertain until 1604, but there are signs that he was an active member of Sir Robert Cecil's faction. Among his friends at court were Henry Parry, Elizabeth's personal chaplain, who was to attend the queen on her deathbed, and the Earl of Cumberland, a famous overseas adventurer who was the godfather of George Sandys, Edwin's youngest brother. He was doubtless also acquainted with many other courtiers; both Coke and Bacon, for example, had been colleagues in the House of Commons. But the great man in Elizabeth's last years was Cecil, especially after his main rival, the Earl of Essex, made his disastrous lunge for power in February 1601. That Sandys had picked the right side in that conflict and was able to keep his feet amidst a newly fluid political situation, is indicated in a letter of May 1601, written to Cecil by Matthew Hutton, now archbishop of York.

[33] The book was printed by Thomas Snodham in London. Although Sandys's name does not appear on the title page, it was confidently attributed to him by Anthony à Wood, *Athenae Oxonienses*, ed. P. Bliss, 4 vols. (London, 1813–20), 2:474, an attribution accepted by J. Holland, *The Psalmists of Britain*, vol. 1 (London, 1843), 270, on the basis of a manuscript copy in the Lambeth Palace library. Both wonder whether it might have been another Sir Edwin Sandys, since three men of that name lived in James I's reign. But one died in 1608, and the second was not knighted until 1617. The musical interests of Sir Edwin's immediate family, described below, also support this conclusion.

[34] The phrase about singing and music comes from the subtitle of the book. See, too, the reference in his father's sermons (J. Ayre, ed., *The Sermons of Edwin Sandys, D. D.* [Cambridge, 1841]), 443; and R. B. Davis, *George Sandys: Poet-Adventurer*, (London, 1955), 236–237.

Hutton had had a running fight with the Sandys family since the 1580s when, as dean of York, he had objected to the nepotism of Edwin's father. It may have been this pressure that led Edwin to resign from his sinecure, the prebendry of Wetwang, in 1602 (although he kept the lease to one of the prebendry's rectories until his death). But he was not averse to keeping up his side of the antagonism. The purpose of Hutton's letter was to counter a story that Sandys had supposedly "buzzed" in Cecil's ear about the archbishop having supported Essex in his revolt. He strenuously denied the accusation, and nothing further came of the episode; but it does indicate that Edwin was regarded as a confidant of Cecil.[35]

Another such indication was his acquisition of a manor in Kent, bestowed on him by the queen in 1601. Sandys must have had a sentimental attachment to the property, Bishops Enbrooke near Folkestone, because it had once belonged to the Cranmer family,[36] and a few months earlier the two dear friends who had linked him to that family had died: Hooker in November of 1600, and George Cranmer, killed on a military expedition in Ireland, in August. Ironically, Lancelot Andrewes had written to Henry Parry five days after Hooker's death that "Mr. Cranmer is away, happy in that he shall gain a week or two before he knows of [it]."[37]

This double blow cannot have been anything but a major turning point in Sandys's life. Suddenly two of the closest companions of his youth, intimates for thirty years, were gone, dead at forty-six and thirty-seven respectively; and he himself, almost forty years old, was well into middle age by contemporary reckonings. What intimations of mortality he glimpsed in those bereaved days of late 1600 and 1601 we will never know; but if the dramatic change in the pattern of his career during the early 1600s can be

---

[35] HMC, *Salisbury*, 11:208–209; see, too, the discussion in W. M. Wallace, *Sir Edwin Sandys and the First Parliament of James I* (Philadelphia, 1940), 2–5. Sandys also had connections on the Essex side, notably Sir Charles Danvers and Sir Thomas Wilford.

[36] E. Hasted, *The History and Topographical Survey of the County of Kent*, 12 vols. (Canterbury, 1797–1801), 8:193–194. PRO, Catalogue of Ancient Deeds, VI, C8007; C.66/1523, membranes 16–21; and E/401/1342. Edwin is listed as paying £4,180 3s. 4d. for the property (together with another property at Bishopsbourne in Yorkshire). This is a gigantic sum, so totally beyond his obvious means, and so much more than what he paid for his main residence, Northbourne, a decade later that one must assume either that the figure is a mistake or that the transaction had other dimensions that we do not know. What is clear from pages 30–31 of R. B. Outhwaite, "Who Bought Crown Lands? The Pattern of Purchases, 1589–1603," *Bulletin of the Institute of Historical Research* 44 (1971): 18–33, is that this was part of a large set of purchases made by a group of relatives (Samuel, Miles, and Edwin Sandys and Sir Thomas Wilford) in Yorkshire, Cambridgeshire, and Kent. Hasted, *County of Kent*, 3:390, says Sandys received a minor court appointment and recompense for service as castle guard at Dover at the same time, but of this there is no other record. It may be that these signs of favor were rewards for loyalty during Essex's rebellion in early 1601, but there is no evidence, apart from his Cecil connection, of Edwin playing a part in that episode.

[37] Cited in R. L. Offley, *Lancelot Andrewes* (London, 1894), 106.

taken as evidence, he must have taken a long, hard look at his past and found it wanting.[38] The almost frivolous dabblings in theology, law, politics, and the London social whirl gave way to the public activity of James I's reign, when he gained unforeseeable stature and respect as the embodiment of the views of the independent gentry in the Commons and as a leader of trade and colonization in national commercial ventures. If any time can be isolated as the beginning of that new career, it must be the last months of 1600 and the early months of 1601.

Seen in this light, the acquisition of Bishops Enbrooke must have represented a nostalgic link with a past that had now disappeared. For the move to Kent, which henceforth was to be Sandys's country residence, brought him to the county which had been both Cranmer's and, in his last years, Hooker's home. Here, too, he became a neighbor of his cousin and future Commons colleague, Dudley Digges; of other relatives, the Wilford, Lovelace, and Aucher families; and of his future merchant colleague, Sir Thomas Smythe.[39] And there was a more immediate connection as well, for it was probably around this period that he married for the third time. His new wife, Elizabeth Nevinson, came from nearby Eastrey and, though her brother Nicholas was a Londoner, it seems likely that the couple met in Kent. With Elizabeth Edwin had one child, Anne, who did not survive to

[38] Such intensive self-analysis at this stage of life has been called by Erik Erikson the "generativity" crisis, and he has described it as occurring "when a man looks at what he has generated . . . and finds it good or wanting, when his life work as part of the productivity of his time gives him some sense of being on the side of a few angels or makes him feel stagnant. All this, in turn, offers him either promise of an old age that can be faced with a sense of integrity . . . or confronts him with a sense of waste, of despair": *Young Man Luther: A Study in Psychoanalysis and History* (New York, 1958), 243. Considering both Sandys's past and his future, one can hardly imagine a better description of his feelings at around the age of thirty-nine. Other discussions of the "generativity" crisis are in Erikson's *Insight and Responsibility: Lectures on the Ethical Implications of Psychoanalytic Insight* (New York, 1964), 131; Elliott Jaques, "Death and the Mid-Life Crisis," *International Journal of Psychoanalysis* 46 (1965): 502–513; and Miles F. Shore's interesting discussion of Henry VIII at the same stage, "Henry VIII and the Crisis of Generativity," *Journal of Interdisciplinary History* 2 (1972): 359–390.

[39] Nor were these minor local figures. All were prominent Kent families, especially the Wilfords: Sir Thomas, Edwin's uncle, was a deputy lieutenant of the county from 1598 on, despite his connection with the earl of Essex, who made him a colonel in 1596. See J. J. McGurk, "Lieutenancy in Kent c. 1580–1620" (Ph.D. diss., University of London, 1971), 246. Edwin did not, however, sever all ties with Yorkshire. There was regular correspondence with tenants (some of which was handled by his wife Katherine); he had to face a complaint in Star Chamber when (as he explained it) his tenants failed to keep his property in good condition; he was owed a debt of £1,200 in the county, which in 1615 he sought to recover by giving a power of attorney to a representative (one Richard Waind); and his widow was to battle (successfully) to keep the prebendry of Wetwang in the 1630's. PRO, SP/46/62, fols. 96–99, 222–223; SP/46/63; SP/46/66, fol. 21; Star Chamber Proceedings James I, 8/16/13; BL, Egerton, 2715, fol. 192; Bodleian MS. Ashm. 181/1061; below, chapter 14, note 2.

be mentioned in her father's will. It is possible that he had to suffer through another childbirth tragedy, because by 1605 he had married again.[40] Not until he settled down with this fourth wife, Katherine, the daughter of fellow parliamentarian Sir Richard Bulkeley of Anglesey, did Sandys finally attain long-lasting domestic contentment, and he then did so with a vengeance: in the next two decades he sired twelve children.

It was when one of those pregnancies went wrong that we are afforded a unique personal glimpse of the mature Sandys. Behind the calm and reasoned public persona stood a passionately devoted family man, whose anguish became palpable when he described to Ferrar the harrowing miscarriage Katherine suffered in September 1620, a time

of the greatest dolor and anguish that I think was ever seen in any one family. About midnight my wife, being warned by her pains sent for her midwife: a good woman, and of great name; but of no skill or performance in such a case of danger. The next morning the child (being a goodly boy), lying cross in her body, through the extremity of her travail gave a sudden spring, and as was conceived (for it never moved after) at that instant died. All Friday and Saturday my poor wife continued in a painful and most uncomfortable travail, the dead child lying clear across, and no help appearing. Yet for all this they still continued me on in hope. Till on Saturday about ten of the clock at night, the midwife and women came with a lamentable outcry, that now it appeared plainly she was past their help: and therefore left it to me to provide some other means. I then sent round about for other midwives of name (which before I could not be suffered): five we had at length, some 20 miles off. Meanwhile all that night she labored unfruitfully in a continual agony, and in the greatest torment that ever woman endured, yea though she died, as all the beholders protested. But as she was a spectacle of much inconsolable misery; so was she of incredible fortitude of mind, Christian patience, and trust in God, to the admiration of all: omitting [no?] duty of one leaving the world, and no one impatient or unseemly word escaping from her. At length it pleased God, taking compassion of her [the?] lamentable estate of this family, . . . that on Sunday between four and five in the morning, there arrived a woman of skill and courage (the other hearts being daunted): who soon after her coming delivered her of her dead child; and laid her in her bed; where she continued

[40] The evidence does not allow for a precise date, but we can infer 1605 because in the 1619 visitation of Kent the couple's eldest son, Henry, was said to be thirteen years old. Presumably he was born no later than the summer of 1606, because his sister Mary was born on September 12, 1607; thus a marriage no later than mid-1605 would seem to be indicated. In any case, by the time she gave the Bodleian Library £20 in 1606, Katherine Sandys was already "the wife of Sir Edwin Sandys of London Knt." See R. Hovenden, ed., *The Visitation of Kent 1619* (London, 1898); Hasted, *Kent* (H. H. Drake's edition, London, 1886), 275; and Anthony à Wood, *The History and Antiquities of the University of Oxford* (Oxford, 1796), vol. 2, pt. 2, 928.

a whole day after with a short and thick panting, as it were for life-breath; and with little speech, and that almost inaudible.[41]

This harrowing episode took place on the estate Sandys acquired from the crown in 1611, the "moiety" of the manor of Northbourne in Kent, which became his principal residence. The land had once been owned by the Cranmer family, and was not too far from Sir Edwin's other Kent holdings. The formal grant of the property in March 1614, a month before a new Parliament met, was probably part of the Court's campaign to neutralize influential M.P.s, though it still cost Sandys the princely sum of £850. He may have been at Northbourne as long as five years earlier, but only in 1614 did he begin to construct an imposing mansion on the site.[42] Since the building was pulled down in 1750, one can only guess at its size, but a few relics and a conjectural floor plan suggest that the house had two wings, one approximately eighty feet by sixty feet, the other about fifty feet square, linked by a fifty-foot-long colonnade.[43]

If the building was on anything like this scale, even a two story structure would suggest a cost of over £5,000, possibly approaching £10,000, by comparison with some of the better-known houses of the period. And if the floor plan can be trusted, the resultant conversion of an old monastic house created one of the first Italianate villas in England, earlier even than the Queen's House that Inigo Jones designed in Greenwich. Inspired by his Italian journey (and perhaps by his friend Wotton), Sandys was making a signal contribution to the great building boom of early Stuart times. Like so many participants in that extravagant outburst, however, he undertook a burden of expenditure that he could never discharge. In the absence of information about his finances, we cannot be sure, but it seems likely that

---

[41] Letter of September 18, 1620, to John Ferrar: MCFP, Box 4, no. 971 (omitted by Kingsbury, 3:406). See also below, chapter 13, note 28.

[42] Records of the grant are in PRO, SP/14/161/120 and C66/1986/2. According to the latter document, six days earlier Sir Edwin's brother Samuel had obtained (for £700) the manor of Ombersley in Worcestershire which the family still owns. The king may have been clearing his accounts with the family at one time, or perhaps the brothers raised the necessary funds together. Either way, the coincidence lends credence to the supposition that a Court connection lay behind the transaction (for the possible influence of Carr, see below, chapter 6, note 88). Cf. Hasted, *Kent*, 9:589. The lands attached to Northbourne are described in the copy of the grant in BL, Egerton, 2396, fols. 24–25. As for the date of the move, a letter of March 1609 (PRO, SP/46/62/222) is addressed to Sandys at "his house in Kent," and he clashed with the Northbourne vicar later that year (above, note 23). Sandys was also involved in draining the land of Northbourne in 1609: Centre for Kentish Studies, S/EK/S02, pp. 159, 170, 199, 206—a reference I owe to Andrew Thrush. The first recorded letter from "Norborn" is dated March 1611: Alexander Brown, ed., *The Genesis of the United States*, vol. 1 (Boston, 1890), 461–462.

[43] The floor plan is discussed (118) and reproduced (facing p. 118) in E. S. Sandys, *History of The Family of Sandys* (Barrow-in-Furness, 1930).

the prime cause of Sir Edwin's near impoverishment in his last years was his lavish spending on real estate.[44]

Moreover, by 1608 he had also obtained a London town house on Aldersgate that he kept until his death.[45] This was one of the most fashionable streets in the city—his next-door neighbor was no less a figure than the earl of Northumberland—and it doubtless put a further drain on his finances.[46] Finally, in this accounting of real estate, it may be worth noting

[44] Lawrence Stone, *The Crisis of the Aristocracy, 1558–1641* (Oxford, 1965), 554–555. According to Sandys, *Family of Sandys*, 118, the more than one thousand acres of the estate fetched close to £30,000 when it was sold in 1795, even though the main house had been pulled down forty years earlier. The history of the estate was recounted in 1900 by its owner, Lord Northbourne: "Northbourne Court," *Archaeologia Cantiana* 24 (1900): 96–107. Hints of Sir Edwin's extraordinary outlays are his draining of the marsh around Northbourne at his own expense in 1609–11, and his purchase of £100 worth of paving stones from Amsterdam in 1621: Centre for Kentish Studies, S/EK/S02, pp. 159, 170, 199, 206, and MCFP, letter to Ferrar of October 1, 1621—references I owe to Andrew Thrush. See also the reference to "a multitude of workmen," below, chapter 13, note 28. Sandys may have conceived his fondness for the new Italian architecture even earlier than did the acknowledged English pioneer of things Palladian, Sir Henry Wotton. Wotton may have known Sandys at the Middle Temple; they had connections with Donne, Casaubon, and others in common; and Wotton's admiration for the *Relation* inspired Italian interest in the book. Both men were in Italy in the late 1590s, but it is unclear when Wotton took up his interest in the design of country houses (discussed in Yates, "Paolo Sarpi," 135–136) and whether Sir Edwin knew his work on the subject. What can safely be said is that both men belonged to the first generation of those who were to transform the English country house.

[45] One of his Yorkshire tenants wrote him there on August 15, 1608: PRO, SP/16/62/96. Located just outside the old walls, Aldersgate was a model of elegance; according to a contemporary, it "resembles an Italian street more than any other in London, by reason of the spaciousness and uniformity of buildings, and straightness thereof, with the convenient distance of the houses": cited in Peter Cunningham, *A Handbook for London* (London, 1849), 9. Among the street's inhabitants were the earls of Westmorland, Pembroke, and Shaftesbury (the latter in Inigo Jones's Thanet House) and John Milton. According to a 1595 list of gentry living in London, more had settled in Aldersgate ward than in any other: N. G. Brett-James, *The Growth of Stuart London* (London, 1935), 37. In general, see Valerie Pearl, "Change and Stability in Seventeenth-Century London," *London Journal* 5 (1979): 3–34; Steven Rappaport, *Worlds within Worlds: Structures of Life in Sixteenth-Century London* (Cambridge, 1989); I. W. Archer, *The Pursuit of Stability* (Cambridge, 1991); and M. J. Power, "East and West in Early-Modern London," in *Wealth and Power in Tudor England: Essays Presented to S. T. Bindoff*, ed. E. W. Ives et al. (London, 1978), 167–185.

[46] In February 1616 the earl rejected the city's claim to the garden of Northumberland House by asserting that it had always been considered his until "Sir Edwin Sandys stirred up the pretended title." The problem had begun when Sandys received "supposed permission" to construct a door through the wall separating the two properties and to walk in the garden. This favor, according to Northumberland, had been granted at the request of their mutual friend, Sir Charles Danvers. See the anonymous *Analytical Index to . . . Remembrancia* (London, 1878), 141. Unless the earl meant Sir John Danvers, rather than his brother Charles, this indicates that Sandys had obtained his house by 1601, for in that year Sir Charles, implicated in the plot of Northumberland's brother-in-law, the earl of Essex, was executed. Both Danvers brothers were noted horticulturalists, and the episode may suggest that Sandys and the "Wiz-

that it was a long way from Aldersgate to Westminster, and therefore Sir Edwin, like a number of M.P.s, may well have taken a pièd-a-terre in Westminster during parliamentary sessions as late evening meetings became ever more frequent. In other words, this was a man of considerable substance, whose resources as well as background and qualities of mind fitted him for the public career toward which he finally moved in his early forties.

Toward Public Life

During the final days of Elizabeth I's reign Edwin's political standing seems to have risen, because he apparently undertook one of the delicate missions through which Cecil smoothed the succession. He seems to have been in Scotland just before the old reign ended, and Anthony Wood cryptically claimed that Sandys received a knighthood from the new king "for some exemplary service which he did that prince, upon his first coming into England." At the time, he had been considered one of the Yorkshire gentry, and he was certainly still associated with Cecil. What that connection promised, though, was hard to tell, especially in this period when the collapse of Essex left only one source of patronage at court. Sandys may have hoped to be considered a foreign affairs specialist when he wrote to Cecil from Orléans about the situation in France in 1598, but if so it cannot have helped that he so confidently and mistakenly predicted a renewal of religious war within just a few weeks of the Edict of Nantes. Nor can one put much credence in the rumor, a year later, that he might be appointed ambassador to France.[47]

---

ard Earl" shared this interest. The only other link between Sir Edwin and the earl's unorthodox intellectual entourage is the involvement of the three chief luminaries of that circle, Hariot, Ralegh, and Donne, in Virginia. For this strange coterie see: M. C. Bradbrook's *The School of Night: A Study in the Literary Relationships of Sir Walter Raleigh* (Cambridge, 1936); G. R. Batho, "The Library of the Wizard Earl," *The Library* 15 (1960): 246–261; Suzanne S. Webb, "Raleigh, Hariot, and Atheism in Elizabethan and Early Stuart England," *Albion* 1 (1969): 10–18; Muriel Rukeyser, *The Traces of Thomas Hariot* (New York, 1970); and J. W. Shirley, *Thomas Harriot: A Biography* (Oxford, 1983).

[47] The quotation is from Wood, *Athenae*, 2:474. For Cecil's negotiations with James, see Joel Hurstfield, "The Succession Struggle in Late Elizabethan England," in *Elizabethan Government and Society*, ed. S. T. Bindoff et al. (London, 1961), 369–396; and Mark Nicholls, *Investigating Gunpowder Plot* (Manchester, 1991), esp. chaps. 6–10. Sandys's letter to Cecil is in Tyacke, "Sandys"; for the rumor about the French ambassadorship, see Sir Ralph Winwood, *Memorials of Affairs of State*, ed. E. Sawyer, 3 vols. (London, 1725), 2:25–26. Another token of royal esteem was Sir Edwin's appointment, in December 1603, to Queen Anne's council, which was arranging for her jointure of £5,000 a year in land. He served in this capacity as the representative of Yorkshire: BL, Additional, 38,739, fols. 104–106. This may have been a mere formality, but Neil Cuddy has suggested to me, citing evidence from Sir Herbert Croft, that Council members could profit from the position, and that the appointment may be an early indication of Sandys's connection with the earl of Southampton—a link

Though his Cecil connection promised a bright political future in government service for Sir Edwin, the reality was quite different. The bestowal of the knighthood at Charterhouse, on the edge of London, on May 11, 1603, turned out to be one of the last signs of a close identification with Court circles. And one can even question the significance of the knighthood itself, granted amidst a torrent of such awards: on the very same day, for example, the new knights included eight others who, like Sandys, were to be members of both Parliament and the Virginia Company.[48] Thus the start of James I's reign does mark a divide. If, around 1600, one can detect Sandys moving more purposefully toward a public career, it was only after 1603 that his direction became apparent: he was going to strike out as a pioneer in ways that could never have been predicted from the past behavior of this staid, respectable gentleman.

It would be convenient to assume that the change was a response to an altered political situation. After all, Edwin's first target was to be the pet project of the new monarch, James I, whose standing, unlike that of the aged heroine queen, hardly deterred criticism. He must quickly have sensed, as did many by the end of the 1604 session of Parliament, that the M.P.s had little respect for this patronizing Scotsman. Nostalgia for Elizabeth, who, despite the restlessness of younger men like Essex, was almost a legend before she died, became a growing force among Jacobean Englishmen, and the contrasting perceptions may explain why opponents of the Stuarts in the Civil War of the 1640s were older, on average, than the royalists. Thus it was not long before the relief at James's untroubled succession, with its attendant high hopes for the reign,[49] gave way to disappointment and (in some cases, such as the Puritans after the Hampton Court Conference) dismay. Small wonder, then, that an Elizabethan like Sandys should have found himself acting independently of so unprepossessing a monarch.

But that is too simple an explanation. While there can be no doubt that the course of events—the removal of Elizabeth's formidable presence, the inadequacies of her successor, the feeling that new paths might be

---

strengthened by Sir Edwin's nomination, immediately after the councillors, to the committee for Southampton's restitution in the 1604 Commons (*CJ*, 1:941). For the circle around the queen, see Linda L. Peck, *Court Patronage and Corruption in Early Stuart England* (Boston, 1990), 3, 74; and Leeds Barroll, "The Court of the First Stuart Queen," in *The Mental World of the Jacobean Court*, ed. Linda L. Peck (Cambridge, 1991), 191–208, esp. 200–203.

[48] Edmund Bowyer, John Smythe (brother of Sir Thomas), Charles Cornwallis, John Cutts, William Fleetwood, John Hanham, Valentine Knightley, and Ambrose Turville. Thomas Wenman, a Virginia adventurer, was also one of the 137 knighted that day; another 431 were dubbed on a single day two months later. On James I's effusion of dignities, see Lawrence Stone, "The Inflation of Honours, 1558–1641," *Past & Present*, no. 14 (1958): 45–70.

[49] The mood was epitomized by John Chamberlain three weeks after Elizabeth's death: "These bountiful beginnings raise all mens spirits and put them in great hopes": *Chamberlain*, 1:192.

charted—helped determine the timing and even the nature of Edwin's
new activities, his boldness and persistence (though always tempered by
the moderate's search for the middle ground) had deeper roots. For one
must never forget the remarkable strength of purpose he had developed.[50]
Here was a man who had lost three wives and at least one child; whose
father and first wife had died within days of one another; and who was to
lose at least four more children. The familiarity with death of the seventeenth century notwithstanding, this was a peculiarly cruel experience.[51] If
one adds to it the almost simultaneous and untimely deaths of his two best
friends, one can only marvel at the resilience that enabled him to begin a
difficult new career in his early forties.

And what began in 1604 was not merely an unprecedented assertiveness
in Parliament but also an unexpected role in two other areas of activity.
Between 1604 and 1606 he launched, in effect, three different careers,
each unlikely for someone of his class and background: as a leader of opposition to royal policy in the Commons, as a religious pamphleteer, and as
a prominent overseas colonizer.[52] The totality of the break with his past
suggests that the change in monarchs can have been only a part of his
inspiration. The ground had been prepared in that highly trained mind,
which, perhaps shocked into action by the deaths of Cranmer and Hooker,
was now bringing all of its determination and self-sufficiency to bear on
the search for a more distinctive role in life. The public career that ensued
was central to the shaping of two of Jacobean England's most important
preoccupations: Parliament and overseas ventures.

[50] Any attempt to understand Sandys's actions and outlook must recognize that he was
endowed with a psyche that was notably secure, resilient, and adaptable. His usual calm and
confidence were shaken in the early 1600s, but it was his essential strength, as well as his
response to external events, that enabled him to move in new directions in such different
areas, all at the same time. I am indebted to Bruce Mazlish, Fred Weinstein, and Jerrold
Seigel for discussions that have illuminated Sandys's personality during these crucial years.

[51] That the seventeenth century was more familiar with death than our own is undeniable.
But the age was by no means hardened, as the expressions of shattering grief in the Verney
letters reveal: see Ralph Verney's "afflicted and unfortunate" comments after his daughter's
death (October 10, 1647, in the Claydon House Letters), or Lady Verney's near collapse on
hearing this news (November 4, 1647, and undated letter following October 17, 1647). I am
indebted to Miriam Slater for guiding me though this huge correspondence. Cf. Alan Mac-
farlane, *The Family Life of Ralph Josselin. A Seventeenth-Century Clergyman* (Cambridge,
1970), 155–157.

[52] It is true that Sandys was not officially appointed to the Virginia Company's council until
March of 1607, but it seems appropriate to include this new venture among his 1606 initia-
tives, since he was obviously connected with the fourteen councillors named the previous
November. They at once had the king expand the council (though it took till March before
the paperwork was done), and Sandys's presence among the new members suggests that the
contacts had already been established. See below, chapter 12, note 2.

PART TWO

Parliament

Chapter III

THE "COMMONS-MAN"

NEW ROLES IN A NEW REIGN

Exactly a month after the first Parliament of the new reign assembled on March 19, 1604, Sir Edwin Sandys made a speech on James I's proposed Union between England and Scotland which transformed him from a quiet, respectable country gentleman into a leader of independent thought in the House of Commons. It was to be the decisive moment in his career, though that may not have been apparent at the time. Even more important, it marked the emergence, not just of an unexpected advocate of consultation and consent in English politics, but of a momentous new stage in the relations betwen Crown and subject. Until he retired from the House over twenty years later, Sandys was to embody the cut and thrust of that relationship, which dominated England's political development under the early Stuarts.

Viewed more broadly, one can see Sandys entering a set of pioneering ventures that were quintessentially characteristic of the new Jacobean age—an age with deep roots, of course, but distinctive in that James I's reign was a decisive stage in the shaping of English society: its art, its religion, and its literature as well as its empire and its politics. This was the time when the Palladian style swept the countryside, when a pragmatic religiosity took root, when drama and poetry enjoyed their first great golden age, when Hooker's ideas were taking hold and Hobbes's were crystalizing, when the first permanent colonies were founded, and when the structure of Parliament took a self-conscious form that was not fundamentally to be altered until the nineteenth century. In every one of these areas Sandys took a significant part. In literature this was mainly a matter of friendships (with Donne, and with playwrights through Southampton), but in the other fields it was a matter of active and often pathbreaking contributions, notably in the Commons, which became the most consequential arena for his pioneering endeavors.

Because of its wider implications for the course of English political history, no attempt to understand Sandys's unique parliamentary career can avoid addressing some of the largest issues of the age. Did the country gentry come to embrace a political and social agenda independent of the Court's? If so, how was it expressed, and how did it affect official policy? What was the role of Parliament in this story—was it primarily an adminis-

trative mechanism, or a forum for substantive debate? Did ideas and beliefs, or maneuvering and tactics, determine events? And (perhaps most
elusive of all) was there, in the long history of the relations between king
and people, a political atmosphere that was distinct or special to the Jacobean age? At the outset, therefore, to comprehend the significance of Sir
Edwin's crucial speech on the Union and its aftermath, we must take a
look at the larger context of the events of James's reign.

Government and the Gentry

England in the early seventeenth century, like all of Europe's states, was
trying to come to terms with the massive changes which had engulfed the
continent during the previous hundred years. Religious upheavals, population growth, price rises, overseas discoveries, new opportunities for trade,
and a revolution in warfare were merely the most conspicuous of the many
transformations that first challenged and then destroyed basic assumptions
and practices. A new slogan like "one king, one faith"—or, in Stuart terms,
"no bishop, no king"—would have been inconceivable and unnecessary
before the Reformation. The displacement of people, as restless travelers
left their villages and sought a better life in cities or on the road, generated
major issues of order and public policy. Economic change, opening wider
markets but also interrupting old patterns of commerce and trade, created
poverty as well as wealth. And the consequences of the gunpowder revolution extended throughout society, fashioning new industries and jobs on
the one hand, multiplying destruction and taxes on the other. Every one of
these developments proved to be a stimulus to the ever-expanding authority and responsibilities of central governments, as they attempted to settle
religion, to mitigate the effects of demographic change, and to deal with
new economic, urban, and military problems. To any thoughtful observer
in 1600, it would have been clear that these new forces were far from
assimilated or fully under control, and that the issue of the powers and
resources central governments needed to deal with them was still very
much alive.[1]

Amongst Europe's royal capitals London was perhaps unique in that
here these concerns had to be addressed in terms of long-standing and
relatively stable political traditions. Unlike the Bourbons, the Vasas, or the
Habsburgs, the Stuarts ruled over lands that had reached their borders,
and had accepted the authority of the throne, centuries before. Moreover,
the English had developed a system of political cooperation and bargaining

[1] These points are elaborated in my *The Struggle for Stability in Early Modern Europe*
(Oxford, 1974).

between center and locality, based on a high level of autonomy and responsibility for the regional unit, the county, that was unmatched elsewhere. In contrast to the magnates of France or Spain, the dominant figures of England's counties, the gentry, expected to work in close partnership with the Privy Council, the chief arm of royal government, and in turn they took it for granted that their own views would be treated seriously. Increasingly during the sixteenth century, the forum for this interchange was Parliament, especially after Henry VIII decided to rely on that institution to reform the Church.

Until the last years of Elizabeth's reign, the delicate balance between, on the one hand, the pressures driving the Crown to assert itself, and on the other, the traditional self-government of the counties, was kept in equilibrium by a parsimonious ruler who was also a genius at public relations. Lacking those qualities, neither James I nor his son was able to command the authority that, like their continental counterparts, they considered necessary in order to address the major tasks they faced, from the modernization of the navy to the relief of the growing numbers of the poor. In an age when inflation and new technology ensured that every activity, from warfare to welfare, would cost geometrically more than ever before, and when traditional means of supplying royal income were becoming ever more obsolete and inadequate, the quest for resources was the government's chief preoccupation. As a result, the interplay between money and power became the leitmotif of Stuart politics. To the proud and stingy gentry, each attempt to deal with problems in a new way, or to put the king's finances on a more secure footing, could be interpreted as an unwarranted expansion of royal authority or as an intrusion into ancient independent rights. And the Crown found itself chronically unable to persuade its landed class of the urgency—seemingly so widely accepted in other monarchies—of the need for new funds and new servants as it took on new responsibilities.

The growing self-confidence of that class, whose fears and hopes Sandys so unerringly captured, had many sources. Historians have put the gentry's behavior under a series of microscopes in recent years, and have painted them in every conceivable color, from oppressors of the people to vanguard of a capitalist future. For our purposes, however, it is worth stressing that the historiography has identified, as one of the central features of the gentry's outlook, their devotion to a sense of "magistracy"—their obligations as the overseers of their communities. They saw themselves as the guardians, not only of the people, but also of the traditions of their localities. The ideal society was distinguished by its order and harmony, which they were called upon to preserve and advance: a duty that required constant vigilance amidst the troubles and uncertainties of an age of rapid

religious, social, and economic change. Inspired by Castiglionian ideals and
Stoic models as well as Protestant theology, they emphasized sobriety, self-
restraint, and a code of honor that encouraged public service.[2]

These were the commitments that prompted the gentry to take on the
day-to-day administration of England's counties, and to do so as a kind of
class obligation. They served in their capacity as "great men," rather than
as paid Crown servants, which was the norm in the continental monarchies. And it was this voluntary work—as magistrates, as sheriffs and
justices of the peace, as agents of the Privy Council, as members of Parliament—that enabled them to develop a keen sense, not only of regional
interests, but also, from that basis, of the national welfare. They knew what
problems the country faced, and they recognized a sensible response when
they saw one. Beyond their practical outlook, moreover, was a fierce devotion to a concept of individual freedom and liberty, nurtured by common
law traditions, which was unique in Europe. For unlike the Continental
nobility, they applied these principles to all classes, with very few special
rights for themselves. If it is too much to speak of their sense of rights and
duties as an ideology, it nevertheless comprised a clear vision of politics
and society—and one that set the beliefs of the English gentry apart from
the emphasis on community privileges and aristocratic exemptions of their
Continental counterparts. When they met in Westminster, therefore, it was
their common experiences, attitudes and perspectives (formed in the cru-
cible of local administration) that bound them together as they confronted
the issues of the day. They had their own opinions as to what policies and
decisions would be widely acceptable and thus appropriate for the realm,
and they knew exactly what was meant when a Sandys spoke of their natural rights and freedoms.

Sandys as "Commons-man"

Contrary to some recent scholarly suggestions, the gentry were perfectly
capable of reaching these conclusions on their own, without prompting
from the thin layer of peers and courtiers who were their social superiors.
They were accustomed to the exercise of authority, and over the next century they made sure (with violence, when eventually it proved necessary)
that their vision of politics and society would not be ignored in the formulation of national policy.

The root of Sandys's mastery of the Commons was his advocacy of that
vision and his understanding of what the gentry, as a group, considered
logical, appropriate, lawful, and right. By tapping these feelings, and ap-

---

[2] A good introduction to this issue is A. Fletcher and J. Stevenson, eds., *Order and Disorder in Early Modern England* (Cambridge, 1985).

pealing in reasoned and moderate terms to his colleagues' deepest assumptions, he was able to shape the views of his fellow M.P.s for more than twenty years. It was because he personified their outlook so fully, and served as the engine of their demands, that he became, in the generation before Eliot, Hampden, and Pym, the first full embodiment of that peculiarly English phenomenon, the "Commons-man."

This is not to say that he was reluctant to manipulate proceedings, act the opportunist, or play the "politick" game. That much became apparent when he used the issue of the Union not only to strike a blow for what he portrayed as England's best interests, but also to enhance his stature in the House. After all, there seemed nothing intrinsically unpalatable in James's proposal; indeed, its reception by earlier speakers leaves the impression that Sandys created more of an issue than was absolutely necessary. And it may be, as we will see, that he was still acting in accordance with Cecil's wishes when he first spoke up. What is undeniable is that Sandys pursued the issue with considerable skill, quickly made it his own, and persuaded the House enthusiastically to follow his lead. Yet no vital principle seems to have been at stake, and one can hardly accuse the Crown of having made an unreasonable request. Although it may be somewhat unfair to Sir Edwin, one is left with the impression that his speech on the Union was, at least in part, the tactical device of a rather shrewd politician. The disputes over the Bucks election and Shirley's case during the first month of the session had revealed the temper of the House; now the time was ripe for an appeal to the M.P.s' prejudices and their pride—for the kind of bold move that could give a man both prominence and influence. Sandys seized the opportunity, and a major conflict between Crown and subject was born.

It has recently been suggested that conflicts like this one over the Union held little of the significance that was attributed to them by the generations of scholars, from Gardiner to Notestein, who saw events in Parliament as the seedbed of England's midcentury revolution. Such revisionism makes it impossible to explain or understand the career of an Edwin Sandys. For him, attendance at Westminster was a major event, a time when he could raise his sights from the county to the realm at large. Whether or not the money Parliament so erratically voted made much difference to royal finances; whether or not the lawmakers managed to pass many laws; whether or not deference was habitual; and whether or not quarrels in the Commons had any real impact on government; both Sandys and his colleagues took it for granted that what took place in the debates did matter. The issues they joined, the disputes they pondered, and the vision of England's welfare they expressed, all helped to form an emerging gentry political stance, committed to the belief that their standards of order and good magistracy ought to be applied to the royal gov-

ernment. In the words of a recent commentator, what was "at stake was
the very *telos* of the English polity." And it is apparent on almost every
page of the journals and diaries recording the proceedings in the Commons that, because their views were so deeply ingrained, the M.P.s felt
frustrated again and again during James's reign when they had to deal with
finance and assertions of Crown authority—a frustration that was to be
exacerbated by problems of law, taxation, and religion under Charles I. It
was certainly not their intention, as they gave vent to their disquiet, to
force England into two warring camps. But the steps they took from 1604
on, however reluctantly, were eventually to have that very outcome.[3]

Intention is crucial to this understanding of the events of the early seventeenth century. Nobody would have been more horrified than Sandys to
discover that his actions had furthered a process that led ultimately to
social and political revolution. Deeply conservative, in law as well as religion, and utterly committed, like all the gentry, to an orderly society (typified in his case by his hatred of swearing) Sir Edwin would have been
appalled by the events of the 1640s. But if history is often propelled by
unintended consequences, the English revolution exemplifies that truism,

---

[3] The quotation is from William Hunt, "Spectral Origins of the English Revolution," in
Reviving the English Revolution, ed. Geoff Eley and William Hunt (London, 1988), 309. Of
the recent literature on early Stuart political history, on Parliament, and on the outlook of the
gentry, the main works that have shaped what follows are: Conrad Russell, *Parliaments and
English Politics 1621–1629* (Oxford, 1979), and "The Nature of a Parliament in Early Stuart
England," in *Before the English Civil War*, ed. Howard Tomlinson (London, 1983), 123–150;
the critiques of his views in "Revisionism Revised: Two Perspectives on Early Stuart Parliamentary History," articles by Derek Hirst and myself, *Past & Present*, no. 92 (1981): 55–99;
the literature cited there; J. H. Hexter, "The Early Stuarts and Parliament: Old Hat and the
Nouvelle Vague," *Parliamentary History* 1 (1982): 181–215; Christopher Thompson, *Parliamentary History in the 1620s: In or Out of Perspective?* (Wivenhoe, 1986); Richard Cust and
Ann Hughes, eds., *Conflict in Early Stuart England* (London, 1989); J. H. Hexter, ed., *Parliament and Liberty: From the Reign of Elizabeth to the English Civil War* (Stanford, 1992); the
articles by Cynthia Herrup, Nicholas Tyacke, and Johann Sommerville in the "Revisionisms"
issue of *Journal of British Studies* 35 (1996): 135–194; and Peter Lake, "Retrospective: Wentworth's Political World in Revisionist and Post-Revisionist Perspective," in *The Political World
of Thomas Wentworth Earl of Strafford 1621–1641*, ed. J. F. Merritt (Cambridge, 1996),
252–283. (That Parliament can be seen not only as an arena for great debates but also as a
routine institution of government, occupied with law-making and the day-to-day business of
the realm—an approach adopted most recently by David Dean, *Law-Making and Society in
Late Elizabethan England* [Cambridge, 1996]—merely emphasizes that different historians
tell different stories. As Dean acknowledges, his treatment complements, but does not con-
tradict, Neale's emphasis on the often contested constitutional role of Parliament.) On the
gentry: C. G. A. Clay, *Economic Expansion and Social Change in England 1500–1700*, 2 vols.
(Cambridge, 1984); Keith Wrightson, *English Society 1580–1680* (London, 1982); Richard
Cust and Peter Lake, "Sir Richard Grosvenor and the Rhetoric of Magistracy," *Bulletin of the
Institute of Historical Research* 54 (1981): 40–53; Felicity Heal and Clive Holmes, *The Gentry in England and Wales, 1500–1700* (Stanford, 1994); and Fletcher and Stevenson, *Order
and Disorder*.

for we encounter it at almost every turn along the way, whether in a technicality like the transformation of a Crown mechanism, the Committee of the Whole House, into a "popular" device; in the major disputes unwittingly provoked by an agenda that may originally have come from Cecil in 1604; or, more generally, in the suspicions that increasingly greeted royal claims, even when they were perfectly straightforward and legitimate. Regardless of his intentions, therefore, one has to see Sandys's dominance of the Commons, based as it was on his ability to capture and embody gentry ideals, as an important stage in the country's political development, the next stage of which was to lead to civil war.

What is especially remarkable is that Sir Edwin was the first figure outside the government in English history to fashion an independent view of proper policy, to carry his colleagues with him, and, except for a brief stint in the Tower, to avoid retribution for his stands—the very definition of a "Commons-man." That he was always promoting policies that he and the gentry considered to be in the best interests of the realm cannot be doubted. And it is in that broad context, as one of many political leaders, usually high-minded and well-intentioned, who were struggling to devise the most appropriate means of dealing with the enormous new problems of the age, that we will most accurately understand Sandys's actions, from his first intervention on the Union until his retirement from the House over two decades later.

ALLIANCES AND LEADERSHIP

To say all this is not to imagine that anything so anachronistic as coherent parties, or even fixed political positions, were emerging in this period. In Stuart Parliaments every man could draw his own line as to the acceptable or the intolerable in royal policy; hence the different relationships with the king, at different periods, of such major figures as Coke, Strafford, and Clarendon. One Commons ally of Sandys, Sir Henry Yelverton, hastened to the king to apologize for inflammatory speeches in the 1604–10 sessions; not until he succeeded Bacon as solicitor-general in 1613 did the latter consider him "won."[4] This quite normal alternation between royal displeasure and royal favor reflected a situation by no means unique in Western history: a homogeneous "establishment" controlling social and political institutions so easily and confidently that it could tolerate wide divergences of opinions within its ranks. For a brief time in mid-seventeenth-century England the comprehensiveness and tolerance failed, but their vitality in James's reign is unmistakable.[5]

[4] On Yelverton, see Gardiner's assessment in *DNB*, 21:1231–1233.
[5] This inclusiveness has been summed up as "the clubbiness and intimacy of British political society, in which even the 'outs' stay 'in'": *New Yorker*, October 22, 1973, 176.

A central theme of the Elizabethan and Stuart periods was the struggle to assure such open receptivity for differing political views. The outburst of the Civil War apart, the main component of this process was a gradual reduction of the resort to violence to suppress dissent. As recognition of the cohesiveness of the ruling classes spread, there was a progressive withdrawal from execution, imprisonment, and exile as political weapons. But essential to this decline was the rise of an alternative: an accepted, structured form for the expression of disagreement. Not until the end of the seventeenth century did the alternative become distinct in the shape of a primitive version of the modern party system, but its origins can be traced at least to the late sixteenth century. Only under James I, however, did this development seem poised, in an equilibrium of uneasy cooperation, between the caution and punishment of Elizabethan times and the open rupture of Charles I's reign.

During this century of gestation (and especially during the unique stage represented by the rule of James I) the vital elements in the process were: the fluidity of alliances; the emergence of leaders of opinion who developed independent positions with broad appeal to gentry outside official circles; and the forging of connections among like-minded members of the Commons. The ease with which M.P.s accepted royal patronage, and the absence of consistent, clear-cut groupings, merely emphasizes how crucial (particularly in the special configuration of James's reign) was a figure like Sandys, who could capture and express the shared assumptions of his colleagues. In the end, it was this very solidarity among the gentry, the feeling that their experience entitled them to be heard when they put forward their views on the welfare of the realm, that encouraged the first steps toward the development of parties. To argue that the actions of the M.P.s, or the policies they advocated (particularly when they involved resistance to Crown wishes), must never be labeled "opposition" is to create needless confusion. Of course they were not the self-conscious and highly organized parties of future centuries; but the nature of their role is unmistakable. Even Conrad Russell, who has done so much to make us aware of the influence of court and county politics on parliamentary debates, has insisted that this form of analysis "should not replace 'government' and 'opposition' as an all-purpose explanatory tool."[6]

---

[6] *Parliamentary History* 2 (1983): 224. Later, however, Russell defined "opposition" so narrowly, and in such modern terms, that it became inapplicable to Jacobean England: "It is the first characteristic of an opposition that it represents an alternative government." *Unrevolutionary England* (London, 1990), xiv. I use the term (without the article) to describe an outlook, and specific critiques, that put various groups of M.P.s at odds with the king or his principal minister. This avoids such blanket designations as "In 1607 the opposition element in the Commons, led by Sandys . . .": Sheila Lambert, "The Clerks and Records of the House of Commons, 1600–1640," *Bulletin of the Institute of Historical Research* 43 (1970): 215–31,

As a force for change, in this as in other arenas, the religious radicals led the way. Long before James's first Parliament was dissolved, they had demonstrated that, with powerful and insistent assertions of opinion, they could have an impact on the Commons out of proportion to their numbers. And their voice, at its loudest when issuing from the lawyer Nicholas Fuller, was no less strident in 1614. But the independent-minded gentry were not far behind in seeking their ends. Many examples of their tactics, vision, and sense of purpose will be adduced, for it is in the details of debates, not in elections, that one sees the evidence of coherent groupings in the House. The kinsmen Sandys and Digges, for example, were certainly allies, but they entered the Commons in their own way. Each took electoral help wherever he could find it. If a councillor wanted to support Sandys—hoping he would serve his ends—Sir Edwin did not hesitate to accept the endorsement; but once he was in the House he was often left to his own devices. Considering that he had connections to the earl of Southampton and his kinsman Baron Sandys, both of whom followed Essex, yet at the same time had attachments to Essex's great rival Cecil; and that later he was to have links with courtiers as varied as members of the Howard clan, Carr, Cranfield, and Buckingham; it is hard to discern him having more than sporadic and informal relations with the groupings and factions that dominated the Jacobean Court.[7]

The story of these rising and falling influences at Court has long been a staple of studies of James's reign; for an understanding of Sandys's career, however, it is a background which we need consider as foreground only at certain specific moments. And, as we will see, the advantages of these connections could accrue as much to the "Commons-man" as to the courtier. Yet it is the exception, not the rule, when one needs to look to Court to explain developments in the Lower House. The day-to-day events that are the focus of the chapters that follow make it clear that, when experienced parliamentarians like Sandys, Hyde, Hollis, Alford, Owen, or Strode came to Westminster, they were able, without prompting, to renew old relation-

---

p. 216. A good assessment of the issue is Robert Zaller, "The Concept of Opposition in Early Stuart England," *Albion* 12 (1980): 211–234. For individual M.P.s I restrict myself, except when quoting other scholars, to words that Jacobeans themselves used for positions that ran counter to official policies: "popular," "patriot," "country," "oppositionist," and the like. For Sandys the word "independent" was especially apt. The quick deterioration in relations between king and subject after Charles's succession in 1625 affirms the distinctiveness of James's reign: Richard Cust, *The Forced Loan and English Politics 1626–1628* (Oxford, 1987); L. J. Reeve, *Charles I and the Road to Personal Rule* (Cambridge, 1989); and Michael Young, "Charles I and the Erosion of Trust, 1625–1628," *Albion* 22 (1990): 217–235.

[7] The occasional royal or Court favor that Sandys did enjoy was not, however, without consequence: his knighthood, his land acquisitions, the rumors of an ambassadorship and a secretaryship: see above, chapter 2, note 47, and below, chapter 6, note 88, and chapter 11, note 1.

ships, resume well-established joint efforts, work long and hard together, and do what *they* felt was best for the kingdom. New allies could rise to prominence, as did Digges in 1614 or Coke in 1621, but the presence of old hands like Fuller or Sandys ensured the continuity of developments. Again and again, these gentry, who were especially sensitive to rights, liberties, and privileges, dominated events, and they were often a more recognizable and determined grouping than the supporters of official positions.

Moreover, their purposeful and autonomous cooperation was recognized as such by contemporaries. According to one courtier, writing to Winwood in 1611, Neville had "ranged himself with those patriots that were accounted of a contrary faction to the courtiers," and it is clear that he discussed with Sandys the "undertakings" after 1610—the attempts by the Court to neutralize leading M.P.s. Bacon was more explicit. His advice to James when preparing for 1614 rested on a fundamental distinction: "That opposition which was the last Parliament to your Majesty's business, as much as was not *ex puris naturalibus* but out of party, I conceive to be now much weaker . . . and that party almost dissolved." He then proceeded to enumerate ten gentry leaders, concluding that "they cannot but find more and more the vanity of that popular course."[8] Bacon was not using the word "party" in its modern connotation: it basically meant "partisanship." But there can be no doubt that, by contrasting "party" with natural malevolence, he intended to convey an impression of coordinated tactics. Both the fluidity and the nascent organization of politics were thus readily apparent to the well-informed observer, though royal advisors still had a hard time accepting the notion that M.P.s might oppose government policies on principle or with good intent.

Yet that is precisely how Sandys's parliamentary leadership was to unfold, and by looking at the assembly through his eyes we can perceive how the institution developed. Acutely sensitive to his colleague's concerns, he was able to carry the House with him through astute advance planning (notably during brief adjournments) and through carefully structured speeches. The sentiments he espoused won favor, but so too did the moderation, the reasoned language, and the logical armature (often following numbered points) in which they were expressed. Given his ease with the forms of classical rhetoric, it is no surprise that contemporaries described Sandys as eloquent, though his persuasiveness seems to have derived pri-

---

[8] HMC, *Buccleuch*, 1:102; James Spedding, ed., *The Letters and the Life of Francis Bacon*, 7 vols. (London, 1861–74), 4:370; and, on Neville's efforts and contact with Sandys, 141–142 of Neil Cuddy, "The Conflicting Loyalties of a 'vulger counsellor': The Third Earl of Southampton, 1597–1624," in *Public Duty and Private Conscience in Seventeenth-Century England: Essays Presented to G. E. Aylmer*, ed. John Morrill et al. (Oxford, 1993), 121–150.

marily from his understanding of his audience and his ability to convey, with great clarity, views that invited assent. These skills had been developing over the years, but their sudden appearance in full maturity in 1604, when Sir Edwin was forty-two years old, invites comparison with the myth of Athena, born fully armed from the head of Zeus. And over the next two decades they were to help guide Parliament through some of the most momentous decisions of its long history.

Chapter IV

1604: THE NEW KING AND HIS "FREE SUBJECTS"

THE NEW KING

On March 19, 1604, less than a year after James I ascended the throne, the king's first Parliament assembled in Westminster. As with any commencement, this was a time of high expectations. The "great hopes" that Chamberlain had expressed within weeks of Elizabeth's death had intensified during the succeeding months. Hundreds of aspiring gentlemen had had their ambitions gratified with awards of knighthood; there were signs of an impending end to the debilitating war with Spain; and even the Puritans had renewed cause for optimism in the king's willingness to hear their case at Hampton Court. Moreover, instead of the struggle over the succession that had been so confidently predicted (with a possible Spanish candidate to lend menace to the prospect), James had inherited the Crown without a hint of disturbance. Such auspicious beginnings invited both gratitude and the promise of a harmonious reign.

There were signs of reviving discontent, however, even before Parliament met. While many, especially the merchants, welcomed the return of peace with Spain and the consequent reopening of a valuable trade, others were distressed at the abandonment of England's Protestant militancy. As for those who anticipated a return to royal favor after the change in regime, there was little but disappointment. Some of the plotters implicated with Essex, such as the earl of Southampton, were released from prison, but the only challengers to the Cecil faction at Court were Scotsmen— hardly a welcome influx. As a contemporary verse put it, juxtaposing the good feelings toward James and the ill feelings toward his countrymen:

> God save our King James and keep him from evil
> And send all such Scotchmen away to the devil;
> Or else into Scotland there still to remain
> Send home with a vengeance these Scotsmen again.[1]

---

[1] See above, chapter 2, note 49; A. J. Loomie, *Toleration and Diplomacy: The Religious Issue in Anglo-Spanish Relations, 1603–1605* (Philadelphia, 1963); Wallace Notestein, *The House of Commons 1604–1610* (New Haven, Conn., 1971), 55–60; and, for general background, ibid. and D. H. Willson's *The Privy Councillors in the House of Commons, 1604–1629* (Minneapolis, 1940). The ballad is in Folger Manuscript 452.5. I owe this reference, and other verses that will be quoted below, to an unpublished typescript collection of political

Like the xenophobes, the Puritans soon had cause to complain, too, because after Hampton Court their prospects looked more bleak than ever. And families possessed of ancient lineage were not particularly happy either, dismayed as they were at the rash of elevations that an extravagant king bestowed on his new subjects.

As James's first winter in England drew to a close, it was unclear whether the exuberant or the gloomy would prove correct. What could not be doubted was that a major change was taking place. A new dynasty was on the throne; long-standing policies were being reexamined; new advisors were gaining the monarch's ear. Inevitably, many matters besides relations with Spain or the status of the Puritans would be reassessed as the new government settled in, unencumbered by the momentum of Elizabeth's forty-five-year reign. And the critical arena for bringing these decisions to the attention of the country was obviously Parliament.

Such social shifts as the debasement of honors and the rise of the Scots had only minor effects in the long run; similarly, neither the change in foreign policy nor James's religious program (a continuation of the status quo) became more than peripherally controversial for a number of years. In Parliament, by contrast, large areas of the king's policies and outlook would be revealed. Here, more clearly than elsewhere, Englishmen could see whether the fragile equilibrium Elizabeth had maintained for most of her reign, both within her government and in her dealings with Parliament, was likely to be preserved. Even Elizabeth's talent for balancing had faltered during her last years. Could new blood assure stable relations between subjects and crown? This question, on which James's acceptance ultimately depended, could be answered only in Parliament.

All other joys and disappointments aside, therefore, it was at Westminster between March 19, and July 7, 1604, that England's broader establishment, stretching far beyond the immediate rulers of the realm, had the opportunity to decide whether the change in monarchs was for the better or the worse. Here, in three and a half months of constant contact with each other, with courtiers, and with the king himself, they could sense whether their views would be respected and whether sensible policies were likely to emerge from Whitehall. It was in his dealings with these blunt, shrewd gentry, not in his talks with Spaniards or Puritans, that

---

ballads and poems from the reign of James I by Julian Mitchell. Also helpful are the University of East Anglia M.Phil. and Ph.D. theses by R. C. Munden: "The Politics of Accession: James I and the Parliament of 1604" (1974) and "Government and Opposition: Initiative, Reform, and Politics in the House of Commons, 1597–1610" (1986), parts of which are published in his article, "James I and 'the growth of mutual distrust': King, Commons, and Reform, 1603–1604," in *Faction and Parliament: Essays on Early Stuart History*, ed. Kevin Sharpe (Oxford, 1978), 43–72.

James could ensure either that the honeymoon of his first weeks in England would continue or that it would come to an abrupt halt.

EARLY TROUBLES

The preparations for the Parliament did not augur well. Despite some electioneering, there was poor representation of officialdom in the House of Commons.[2] As a result, only two members of the inner governing circle, and rather ineffectual members at that, won election to the House: Sir John Herbert and Sir John Stanhope. Bereft of weighty, vigorous spokesmen, the King eventually had to depend on Sir Francis Bacon to advance his views. For all Bacon's skill in argument and persuasion, he still held no more than the minor office of learned counsel to the king, and he enjoyed none of the authority that had been exercised in the previous Parliament by Robert Cecil, now elevated to the peerage. It is true that, as he told James a few years later, Bacon knew exactly what a parliamentary session ought to accomplish, and personally got on well with the members. In his words, Parliaments were needed "for the supply of your estate . . . [and] for the better knitting of the hearts of your subjects unto your Majesty." Furthermore, he wrote, "I take myself to have a little skill in that region . . . [for] every man makes me believe that I was never one hour out of credit with the lower house."[3] Yet good intentions and amiable feelings were not enough to allow Bacon to dominate the House in the manner of the clusters of privy councillors who had spoken for Elizabeth.

Since the 1604 assembly continued in existence for nearly seven years, there was ample opportunity to provide Bacon with allies. And the contrast between the failings of 1604 and the determined occupation of vacated seats thereafter was striking. Of some ninety bye-elections during the life of the Parliament, eleven were won by leading courtiers or councillors.[4] Moreover, at the next general elections, in 1614, the government wielded

[2] Notestein first drew attention to the impact of the lack of officials in *The Winning of the Initiative by the House of Commons* (London, 1924), an analysis elaborated in Willson's *Privy Councillors*, esp. chap. 3. For the uneven efforts to sway elections, see Munden, "Government," 138–145; K. B. Sommers, "Court, Country and Parliament: Electoral Influences in Five English Counties, 1558–1640" (Ph.D. diss., Yale University, 1978), 77–78; and BL, Egerton, 2644, fols. 128–154—references I owe to Christopher Thompson.

[3] James Spedding, ed., *The Letters and the Life of Francis Bacon*, 7 vols. (London, 1861–74), 4:280: letter of May 31, 1612.

[4] Sir Julius Caesar, George Calvert, Sir William Cecil, John Corbett, Sir John Egerton, Sir John Fortescue, Theophilus Lord Howard of Walden, Sir James Ley, Sir Thomas Parry, Sir Thomas Vavasor and Sir Richard Weston. See further Willson, *Privy Councillors,* 104–109, and Harold Hulme, "Corrections and Additions to the Official 'Return' of Members of Parliament, 1603–04," *Bulletin of the Institute of Historical Research* 5 (1927/1928): 96–105.

its influence sharply and blatantly.[5] But this vigor came much too late. During the critical early days of 1604, to all intents and purposes Bacon was alone. The one hasty effort to redeem the situation, the attempt to replace Sir Francis Goodwin with Sir John Fortescue, chancellor of the Duchy of Lancaster, boomeranged when the Bucks election case became the first source of conflict between Commons and Crown.

If the government's election preparations were poor, its groundwork in matters of policy was little short of disastrous. The only documents containing lists of proposed legislation that have survived seem to have been written by ordinary M.P.s.[6] Although they start with such necessary measures as the recognition of James's right to the throne, they move on to standard grievances, including purveyance and monopolies, which were to cause little but trouble. Nor was there any better guidance in the royal address at the opening of the session which, far from outlining proposals for the weeks ahead, piled faux pas upon faux pas.

The first blunder was committed by the king's guard, who kept some of the Commons from hearing the speech in the Lords' chamber.[7] To make amends, James returned three days later, and gave the speech all over again. It is unlikely that the two versions were identical, however, because the monarch blithely told his audience that "I could never have leisure to think upon what I was to speak, before I came to the place where I was to speak." The result was only too apparent, as he rambled on at daunting length. Oblivious of tact, James told his audience that his way of thanking them was to pass on "the blessings, which God hath in my person bestowed upon you all." Other than recommending the union of the two kingdoms he now ruled, however, James had only a traditional injunction to offer: "beware to seek the making of too many laws."[8]

It must have been in some astonishment that the members, assembled for the purpose of making laws, withdrew from the royal presence. What a

---

[5] S. R. Gardiner, *History of England . . . 1603–1642*, 10 vols. (London, 1883–84), 2:228–229; T. L. Moir, *The Addled Parliament of 1614* (Oxford, 1958), 31–57.

[6] See Notestein, *Commons 1604–1610*, 47–54. Other papers that reveal serious preparations for Parliament, mainly by Puritans, are in BL, Sloane, 271 (esp. fol. 27) and Additional, 38,492. Nicholas Tyacke has shown that the preparations by Sir Robert Wroth, who was thought of as independent, may have been inspired by Cecil: "Wroth, Cecil and the Parliamentary Session of 1604," *Bulletin of the Institute for Historical Research* 50 (1977): 120–125. That the tactic misfired is suggested by Pauline Croft, "Wardship in the Parliament of 1604," *Parliamentary History* 2 (1983): 39–48. See, too, M. A. R. Graves, "The Common Lawyers and the Privy Council's Parliamentary Men-of-Business, 1584–1601," *Parliamentary History* 7 (1989): 192, and below, note 48.

[7] *CJ*, 141–142. This aggravating exclusion of M.P.s had also happened in 1601.

[8] Ibid. 142–146. A slightly different version of the speech is in BL, Additional, 38,139, fols. 24–26. See, too, B. R. Dunn, "Commons Debates 1603/4," 3 vols. (Ph.D. diss., Bryn Mawr College, 1987), 1:83–122.

falling off from the persuasive old queen was here! And what was next? Not for almost a month did they receive formal legislative proposals from the King;[9] in the meantime they were free to proceed as they wished. And during these fateful opening weeks the aggressive and acrimonious tone was set that persisted almost throughout James's reign. A few seemingly trivial tactical errors, and the House of Commons was able to become (and increasingly to see itself as) a forum where visions of England's welfare different from those of king or Council could be aired.

There is a natural temptation to blame the king for the difficulties that followed. He seems to have had few clear ideas about the purpose of the session, beyond the fact that it enabled his subjects to convey, respectfully, their current feelings—as had the Puritans at Hampton Court.[10] Nor was his opening speech much help. Yet there was no reason for him to have expected trouble. He was still basking in the good will of his reception in England, and in any case his relations with the Scottish Parliament hardly prepared him for the organizational efforts the English House of Commons required. James could have claimed, quite fairly, that such matters should have been foreseen by his principal minister, Cecil, who was nothing if not experienced in the ways of Parliament.[11]

But the newly created earl of Salisbury, and a fortiori all the other members of the royal entourage, may well have regarded their own positions as too ambiguous for decisive action. Who, exactly, was in control? Who would be allied with whom? And to what extent could leadership be exerted? There had hardly been time to explore such questions, let alone settle them, in the eight months between James's arrival in London and the issuance of the proclamation for a new Parliament.[12] Moreover, as the chief manager of the 1597 and 1601 sessions, Cecil had seen for himself what Neale called the "weakness . . . if compliance be a weakness" of the Commons during the last decade of Elizabeth's reign. The heroic days of the Wentworths seemed over, and Neale saw 1593 "as the hinge between

[9] The first official proposal of legislation (primarily to confirm the Union) did not come from James until April 13: *CJ*, 171. In the Lords Cecil produced "a draught conceived and dictated by His Majesty" of a bill on the Union only on April 21: BL, Additional, 48,160, fol. 9. The Venetian ambassador had claimed, the previous September, that the Crown would have a three-point program for the House; but two of those points did not appear in the government's actual proposals: *CSP, Venetian*, 10:94–95.

[10] M. H. Curtis, "The Hampton Court Conference and its Aftermath," *History*, No. 156 (1961): 1–16; P. Collinson, "The Jacobean Religious Settlement: The Hampton Court Conference," in *Before the English Civil War*, ed. Howard Tomlinson (London, 1983), 27–51.

[11] Willson, *Privy Councillors*, 103, rightly calls Cecil "the crown's parliamentary manager" in 1597 and 1601; the minister's knowledge of the House went back to 1586.

[12] Thomas M. Coakley, "Robert Cecil in Power: Elizabethan Politics in Two Reigns," in *Early Stuart Studies: Essays in Honor of David Harris Willson*, ed. H. S. Reinmuth (Minneapolis, 1970), 64–94, esp. 68 ff.

old and new." Even so insistent a "radical" leader as Nicholas Fuller "intermitted until hope dawned again with the accession of James I."[13] Under these circumstances, enhanced as they were by the joy of the new king's welcome, it might have seemed unnecessary to influence the elections. And with alliances still to work out at Court, there was no obvious seat of responsibility.

In short, the government was caught unawares too early in the reign for it to have found its bearings. And it did move to restore the situation with considerable determination once the dimensions of the problem became apparent. James was said to be anxious to secure the election of more pliant M.P.s after the 1604 session, and we have seen how successfully bye-elections were prosecuted.[14] But in the meantime the damage had been done. The relative calm since 1593, as it turned out, had not been the prelude to new harmony, but a period of waiting until Elizabeth's restraining presence was removed. And on the very first day of the session, even before the king's speech, two incidents gave a hint of what lay ahead.

Before any business could be done, every M.P. had to take the oath of allegiance. Traditionally, since the lord steward rarely performed this duty in person, twelve deputies were chosen to speed the process. As the precedent-conscious clerk of the House noted, in one of his first entries in the journal, "Privy Councillors only heretofore, and not any Members of the House of other Rank, have been made Deputies to the Lord Steward."[15] Now, however, ten mere gentry had to be chosen: the first of many innovations attributable to the election results.

When, in the next order of business, Sir John Herbert announced that the king's choice for speaker was Sir Edward Phelips, a minor legal official with twenty years' experience in the Commons but no other noticeable qualifications, the royal nomination met resistance. The clerk noted that Phelips' name was greeted with "some Silence," a certain sign of discontent. Other names were "muttered," and when the issue was put to a vote there were a few "no" votes to mar Phelips' election.[16] It can hardly have been comforting to James when, three days later, in the speaker's formal

---

[13] J. E. Neale, *Elizabeth I and Her Parliaments, 1584–1601* (London, 1957), 245, 325, 326.

[14] See the Venetian ambassador's comments in 1605 (*CSP, Venetian*, 10:268, 270) and, in general, J. K. Gruenfelder, *Influence in Early Stuart Elections* (Columbus, Ohio, 1981); Derek Hirst, "Elections and Privileges of the House of Commons in the Early Seventeenth Century," *Historical Journal* 108 (1975): 851–862; Hirst, *The Representatives of the People? Voters and Voting in England under the Early Stuarts* (Cambridge, 1975); and Mark Kishlansky, *Parliamentary Selection: Social and Political Choice in Early Modern England* (Cambridge, 1986).

[15] *CJ*, 141.

[16] Ibid. HMC, *Buccleuch*, 3:79, has a fuller account of this episode, though this diary by Sir Edward Montague (78–91) is very rarely more informative than the Journal.

reply to the royal address, Phelips spent most of his time explaining, with a patronizing air, how laws were made in England. Particularly galling must have been his emphatic argument that monarchs could confirm but not "institute" legislation—a remarkable interpretation to which Cecil gave the lie by drafting a flurry of bills. And the speaker hardly endeared himself to his sovereign when he pointed out that Elizabeth had invariably followed proper procedures and was "a true mirror to all succeeding ages."[17] That was the last thing James, perenially sensitive about his predecessor, wanted to hear.

At this stage courtiers close to the king may have begun to wonder whether they had been too sanguine about summoning a Parliament, even if its presence was essential, not only for the traditional grant of tonnage and poundage, but also for confirmation of the Union between England and Scotland. And the omens worsened after Phelips' speech. In the time left before adjournment, only three items of noteworthy business were raised, but each proved to be a seed of contention. Sir William Fleetwood, M.P. for Buckinghamshire, asked for reconsideration of Sir John Fortescue's election as the second of the county's two representatives: the beginning of a major struggle between Commons and king over jurisdiction in disputed elections. Then John Shirley, a prominent lawyer, asked for the release from prison of his kinsman Sir Thomas Shirley: the start of another drawn-out quarrel about parliamentary privilege. Finally, Sir George More, veteran of six Parliaments, proposed that the usual Committee for Privileges be appointed, and it was at once given, as its first task, the investigation of the insolent yeoman of the king's guard who had barred the way to the royal address.[18] A prickly House, already standing on its dignity, was rushing to uphold what it considered endangered rights. And the next day, March 23, the Commons moved on to an agenda of grievances proposed by Sir Robert Wroth, a veteran M.P. who, even if under instruction from Cecil, was identified with the Puritans. As we will see, the topics he proposed were picked up by a parade of ordinary members rather than Court figures.

These were not merely omens of trouble; trouble itself had arrived. After only a few hours of debate, a group of energetic members were steering the House in a direction that could only annoy the king. It may have

<hr>

[17] *CJ*, 146, 148.
[18] Ibid., 149–150. The next day the guard apologized and was pardoned. The M.P.s' awareness that something was amiss in the relations between Crown and Parliament was apparent by April 2, when Sir Thomas Lake noted that "This dissension between His Majesty and the Lower House is wonderfully talked of here": HMC, *Salisbury*, 16:50. The best account of the Committee for Privileges, on which Sandys figured prominently for two decades, is M. F. Keeler, "The Committee for Privileges of the House of Commons 1604–10 and 1614," *Parliamentary History* 13 (1994): 147–169.

been Cecil's original intention to create a program in this indirect fashion, but the result was that a few swift strokes had established a pattern for the relations between king and subject in the Commons that was never to be erased during the remainder of the reign. Thus was formed the setting, the atmosphere, in which, three and a half weeks later, Sir Edwin Sandys suddenly asserted himself. Without warning (indeed, contrary to all expectations) a new and redoubtable leader of debate, often opposed to the king's wishes, was to arise and win a commanding influence over the House. More than any other M.P., he was to ensure that the direction taken in the first days of the session would continue until its bitter end.

THE SPEECH OF APRIL 19

Sandys was elected to Parliament by the borough of Stockbridge in Hampshire. Although he had no personal links with the county, it is not hard to see how he obtained the seat. The two figures who usually controlled the borough's choices were the chancellor of the Duchy of Lancaster and the Baron Sandys, especially the latter, one of the country's greatest magnates.[19] In 1604 this tradition held, because one of the seats went to the brother of the current chancellor, Sir William Fortescue, and the other to Sir Edwin, a cousin of the baron. Lord Sandys had only just been pardoned by James I for his role in the Essex revolt, and it is not clear how much contact he had with his M.P. cousin. But there can be little doubt that he determined the result of the Stockbridge election. Sir Edwin may well have owed to Lord Sandys, too, his first introduction to a long-term associate, the earl of Southampton, a neighbor and relative by marriage of the baron and one of his fellow conspirators from the Essex days. Beyond these tenuous and tantalizing personal connections, however, there is no hint of continuity between the Essex group and those who gave Cecil and the king such trouble in the Jacobean parliaments.

During the first month of the session Sandys was not recorded as speaking from the floor of the House, though he was probably present, because he was appointed to a number of committees.[20] He must have seen the way the wind was blowing, but not until a new issue occupied the House did he intervene in the debates.

On April 11, after more than three squabbling, half-paralyzed weeks, James brought the Bucks election dispute to a close by ruling that neither Goodwin nor Fortescue would be returned for the county seat. This decision left the House with jurisdiction over elections, and on April 12 the speaker conveyed to the king the thanks of the M.P.s. The following day

---

[19] J. E. Neale, *The Elizabethan House of Commons* (London, 1949), 226–227.
[20] *CJ*, 156–157, 166, 169.

James replied: although clearly satisfied that the quarrel was at last over, he was growing impatient. The session, he told the members, was "not like to be long." and he asked for attention to those matters which "most concerned the Commonwealth." At long last, an agenda was being put forward, though it was hardly strenuous, consisting as it did of essentially two items.[21] The Union with Scotland was the business James wanted addressed, but he said he would be content with the creation of a commission to prepare for the merger, and a bill to take the crucial first step: establishing Great Britain as the name of the united kingdoms.

The House got to work at once. The next day, April 14, a committee of over one hundred (not including Sandys) conferred with the Lords, and decided to appoint commissioners to investigate the Union and arrange the details.[22] On the eighteenth a full-scale debate on the name Great Britain began, with some fourteen speakers professing themselves largely, though not entirely, in favor of the change: Sir Maurice Berkeley, in particular, raised questions of English honor and precedence, and thought the initiative should come from the Scots, while Hoskins wondered whether the Union could be made permanent. But these few doubts did not suggest that major problems lay ahead when the House adjourned, after hearing a plea for haste.[23]

The essentially favorable reception continued in the first speeches the following morning, though Fuller asked for a thorough investigation of appropriate laws and customs, and raised the fear that the poor Scots might swallow up the rich English.[24] Yet he did not object to the change of name in principle; nor did Sir Edward Hobby, an old troublemaker (though Cecil's cousin). After further support from Bacon, Francis Moore, a well-known lawyer, launched into a long defense of the proposal, refuting the eight objections he had heard to the change of name. When Sandys, following Moore, rose to address the House, he brushed aside such secondary issues and went straight to essentials. His blunt and telling speech gave the objections a weight they had not had before; with one blow he altered the complexion of the debate and brought the discussion to a new level.

[21] Ibid., 171. In one version, James suggested three items (the Union, "Commonwealth Bills," and religion), but the second was merely an umbrella for ordinary parliamentary business: Dunn, "Commons Debates," 2:352–353. On the Union see Brian Levack, "Towards a More Perfect Union: England, Scotland, and the Constitution," in *After the Reformation: Essays in Honour of J. H. Hexter,* ed. Barbara Malament (Manchester, 1980); his *The Formation of the British State: England, Scotland and the Union, 1603–1707* (Oxford, 1987); and Bruce Galloway, *The Union of England and Scotland, 1603–1608* (Edinburgh, 1986).

[22] *CJ,* 172, 173. See, too, BL, Cotton, Titus F IV, fols. 17–22, 35–85.

[23] *CJ,* 176–177, 950; Dunn, "Commons Debates," 2:410, 411.

[24] *CJ,* 177–178, 950–951 (the fullest account of Sandys's speech, discussed below). See, too, Dunn, "Commons Debates," 2:435–436; PRO, SP/14/7, fols. 145–146, 157–158; and SP/14/7/74, fol. 230.

In some ways, Sir Edwin's speech of April 19 was his true maiden address. He had not been in the Commons for over a decade, and his passing contribution in 1593 had been almost as much the government's as his own. Now, entering a new phase of his life and career, Sandys was speaking with a different, more personal voice. He was a senior member, having first sat nearly twenty years before, and he was a familiar and respected figure to his fellow M.P.s, most of whom must have known him, whether through family, Court service, London life, Inn of Court, university, or previous session of Parliament. In 1604, however, they were to hear him in a most unlikely role: as a pillar of respectability resisting the king's stated wishes.[25] Perhaps it was the very unexpectedness of his arguments (in addition to their cogency) that allowed Sandys to make so profound an impact on the House. And the immediate influence over debates that he gained was not to evaporate for twenty years.

One must assume that Sir Edwin himself was as surprised as anyone by the effect of his speech. Since the role he was to occupy in the Commons was unprecedented, he can hardly have planned the outcome. Moreover, since his opposition to the Union aroused a hostility on the part of the king that barred him from royal office for the remainder of the reign, it is difficult to doubt the ostensible purpose of the stand he took. The progression of events seems to have been that he caused a major stir, to which James himself responded when he next addressed the Commons; that Sandys's natural talents and interests then enabled to him to build on his unexpected prominence; and ultimately (because this Parliament reassembled periodically for over six more years) that his activities helped give the independent-minded gentry a substantial impact on royal policies. During the debates over the Great Contract in 1610, and again in the early 1620s, Sandys achieved a position of influence, extending beyond his prominence in the Commons, that only significant government office could have matched. That may not have been what he sought in these early days, but the rapidly changing political situation in James's reign, and the particular actions, concerns, and opportunities that it provoked, were inexorably to produce that outcome.

The contrast between Sir Edwin's crucial April 19 speech and the earlier speeches on the Union was apparent from the outset. Instead of urging a rapid conclusion, raising a few questions, or brushing off objections as unimportant, Sandys stressed the gravity of a decision to change England's name. This, he said, was "the weightiest cause, that ever came" before the

---

[25] But the contradiction should not be overdrawn. England's ruling elite was still close-knit, and Sandys had already had connections with such rival groupings as those around Leicester, Essex, and Cecil. And he had no more than rumored links with the Howards, Cecil's main opponents under James I, until 1614: see below, note 47.

Commons, and so they ought to "proceed with a leaden foot." Unlike the previous speakers, he was not worried about procedure; as in nature, he argued, one ought to look at the matter before the manner. And the moment one explored the fundamental implications of the Union, serious problems arose. For a start, he told his colleagues, one had to decide whether the change was necessary at all. It was pointless to work out details until one was sure that a basic, genuine unity (which James believed had come into being with his accession) really existed. As Sandys put it, "the ground of every name is the nature of the thing." Before going any further, therefore, they had to determine the kind of Union they wanted. To this problem, however, there was no easy solution, because (echoing the *Relation*) "in Unity [there are] many degrees," and such components as "union in commerce" and "free access" had to be considered individually.

Sandys then confronted one of the chief arguments that had been heard in favor of the Union and raised doubts about its validity. There is no denying, he admitted, that the good of King and Country are identical, but that is not to say that the country must accept whatever change the monarch seeks. "No man sits as a person, by himself. The King stands not alone." Royal wishes were not decisive on their own, especially since (and this had momentous implications) "England sits here representatively only"—that is, in ignorance of constituents' views. One had to think of the broadest possible consequences, because "as our predecessors have left us free, so let us leave our successors, without prejudice." As if these difficulties were not sufficiently intractable, Sir Edwin ended by raising a number of practical problems. Would not the change of name invalidate all current laws? Would it not undermine the reputation associated with the word "England"? And did the House, which had blithely "translated the Crown from one line to another," actually have the power to do so? Might this not require the "country's" commission? These were redoubtable challenges to James's plan, and they permitted only one conclusion: "to have things beaten in the House first, and then to send . . . to the Lords for conference."

It was a remarkable speech, not only for its daring double assault on the king's authority—the questioning of his powers when "alone" and of the transfer of his title to the throne—but also for its recourse to fundamental issues, its suggestion of the need to consult with constituents, and its effectiveness in ensuring that the bill would be delayed. So remarkable was it that one is tempted to speculate about hidden motivations. There was some suggestion at the time (echoed by the French ambassador) that Sandys was still acting for Cecil, and was in fact expressing his patron's doubts about the Union.[26] If so, the result was a classic example of the

---

[26] PRO, Baschet Transcripts, PRO 31/3/37, fols. 78, 95, 97, 105–106, 112–113 contain the French ambassador's reports of March and April which linked Cecil (apparently his main

unintended consequence, and may well have fed James's natural suspicion of the minister he had inherited from Elizabeth. Yet to regard this merely as a battle among Court factions is to apply preconceived assumptions about Jacobean politics to a situation that offers no solid evidence to support them. The campaign Sandys now waged thwarted the pet project of the king himself, and Cecil could not have associated himself with such a venture.

An alternative explanation is that Sandys, denied advancement during the governmental reshuffle at the start of the reign, and unmollified by a knighthood and an insignificant appointment to the Queen's Council, saw obstreperousness as the best route to high office. The technique was used to good effect by others in later Parliaments, most notably by the future earl of Strafford, and Sir Edwin's behavior in the 1620s implies that he would not have been averse to exchanging leadership of the "popular" cause for an appropriate place at Court. Given the career he pursued for the next twenty years, however, such short-term explanations as Cecil's patronage or ambition for office ring hollow. The most appropriate meaning for Sandys's April 19 speech is to be found in the larger movements of English political and social history. A prominent member of the gentry, concerned about the direction of royal policy, was beginning to formulate a vision of England's best course in an era of rapid change which, though sometimes related to a particular view at Court, was above all attuned to the views of his colleagues in the House; in so doing, moreover, Sandys

---

source of information) to the anti-Union forces in the Commons. On April 26 (fol. 112v.) he said members of the Council were known to "conforter et assister secrètement" the M.P.s who opposed the Union, and he had foreseen trouble much earlier (fols. 22, 65). Sandys's one clear alliance with a peer in the Union debate, however, was with a noncouncillor, the earl of Southampton: the first public chapter in a long association that may have begun because of their distant kinship through Lord Sandys; or perhaps because the older man (Sir Edwin) reputedly converted the younger from Catholicism—a possibility that gains credence from Sandys's attempt to convert Sir Toby Mathew in 1607 (see above, chapter 2, note 6); or perhaps as a result of both men being in France in 1598, when Southampton was part of Cecil's embassy to Paris. See Neil Cuddy, "Anglo-Scottish Union and the Court of James I, 1603–1625," *Transactions of the Royal Historical Society*, 5th ser., 39 (1989): 107–124, esp. 112–117; and his "The Conflicting Loyalties of a 'Vulgar Counselor': The Second Earl of Southampton, 1597–1624," in *Public Duty and Private Conscience in Seventeenth-Century England: Essays Presented to G. E. Aylmer*, ed. John Morrill et al. (Oxford, 1993), 127, 128. As indicated above, in note 25, however, and as will be clear in what follows, Sir Edwin's connections seem to me too diverse to assign him (in Cuddy's formulation) simply to "the Southampton group." Nor is Cuddy's treatment (let alone the evidence of the two men's relationship in the Virginia Company) inconsistent with the notion that Sandys was at least as much the driver as the driven. See in general, below, chapters 12 and 13; and chapters 8, note 3, and 9, notes 48–50. Cuddy's conclusions confirm a central thesis of this book: that Jacobean "politics were divided by principles," and marked by "significant and recurrent principled conflict between James and his opponents" (ibid., 145, 148).

was leading the Commons into an increasingly assertive role in the shaping of public policy.

THE UNION POSTPONED

The rebuff Sir Edwin delivered to the Union on April 19 prompted a privy councillor to enter the debate for the first time. Herbert was the next to speak, and he rather weakly countered that the good of the king and the country were together the "summa lex." Without wishing to deny the Commons the right "to debate freely, without limitation," he assured them that a Union in name and government would be "honorable, profitable, possible." This was not the speech to stem the tide, and it quickly became apparent that Sandys had changed the direction of the discussion. Three of the four principal speakers during the remainder of the day—Sir William Paddy, an East Anglian gentleman; Christopher Brooke, the lawyer and poet friend of John Donne, who had known Sandys from Yorkshire days; and Richard Martin, another lawyer—expanded on Sir Edwin's doubts, and added impetus to the momentum he had begun.[27]

The next morning mixed opinions were expressed, but the opposition to James's proposal retained its sharpness.[28] Sir Maurice Berkeley, member of a great West Country family and a leader of independent gentry sentiment for the next ten years, claimed that the House had only two alternatives: "either proceed with danger, or desist with shame."[29] There was little doubt which he preferred, and indeed the Commons showed no sign of desisting. Sandys's one contribution that day was to ask whether the adoption of a new name would require the extinction of the old. Again a privy councillor, Herbert, felt impelled to reassure the House. Indeed, he predicted that the Scots would adapt their laws and government to England's, a hint of the later notion of a "perfect" Union that might have been acceptable south of the border, but never in Scotland. When Herbert sat down the speaker brought the debate to an end by suggesting a conference with the Lords. This was agreed to, and in the meantime the committee on the Union (to which various M.P.s, including Sandys, were added) was to meet with James that very afternoon to hear his views.

On April 21, the following day, the House learned of the king's displeasure. Bacon reported the royal address, which revealed James to be surprised that the fuss had become "common alehouse talk", and ready (with a bill he himself had dictated) to lay out exactly what he sought.[30] He was particularly exercised over the "foolish" obsession (introduced by Sandys)

[27] *CJ*, 178, 951.

[28] Ibid., 179–180.

[29] Ibid., 952.

[30] Ibid., 953. See too, though with caution about details, Joel Epstein, "Francis Bacon and the Issue of the Union, 1603–1608," *Huntington Library Quarterly* 33 (1969–70): 121–132.

with names, and at times his speech was almost a point-by-point refutation of Sir Edwin. The measure he proposed would proclaim England and Scotland already united by their allegiance to a single king, create the new name of Great Britain, and appoint commissioners to prepare detailed legislation for the next session. Irritated by the Commons' scruples, James urged that they put an end to "the curious carping of some."[31]

On the twenty-third, however, both debate and carping resumed. Little new was added, for the advocates of the royal view offered nothing but vague reassurances, while their opponents voiced anxieties which mere reassurance could not allay. Although a majority of the speakers favored the Union, most urged caution and a full airing of opinions. Sandys spoke again, urging that Crown offices, as a safeguard, be restricted to Englishmen, and that Parliament remain unchanged.[32] In effect, a stalemate had descended over the issue after Sir Edwin's speech of April 19.

This situation continued for another three days, until a full week had passed without progress. In the meantime, on the twenty-fourth, a message arrived from the king that offered accommodation rather than impatience: assurances of good will and hopes that the Commons would discuss the Union freely and at length before reaching a decision. But this effort foundered on the largely aimless hostility that reappeared the following day, the twenty-fifth. This debate opened with a report from Bacon on the committee's progress. "The more we wade," he said, "the more we doubt," and he outlined thirteen main objections to the Union, starting with Sandys's question as to whether a change was necessary, and including eight doubts about the name, fears of "a deluge of Scots," and worries about precedents. The impression he left was of serious difficulty, though he did note that one particularly audacious proposal (that plans be made to preserve England's security in face of the king's project) had been rejected by the committee. The remainder of the day passed in desultory fashion, with Sandys worried about the number of commissioners, Nicholas Fuller darkly foreseeing the demise of Magna Carta, and various members exercised about the king's title.[33]

It was on April 26 that the debate reached its climax in a long and carefully reasoned speech by Sandys, delivered as soon as the subject had been raised by an independent veteran, Hobby.[34] In the guise of a review of the major issues, Sir Edwin was in fact assembling the case against the Crown and placing on record the insuperable obstacles the Union faced.

---

[31] *CJ*, 181; Dunn, "Commons Debates," 2:466–468. Neil Cuddy, citing PRO, SP/14/7/75, and Hatfield MS. 107.147, has shown that James's April 20 intervention was meant to add his authority to the bill (personal communication).

[32] *CJ*, 955.

[33] Ibid., 183–185, 957; PRO, SP/14/7/58, SP/13/7/145.

[34] *CJ*, 186–187, 958; BL, Additional, 38,139, fols. 37–38; PRO, SP/14/7/64; Dunn, "Commons Debates," 2:584–587.

He began by emphasizing the unanimity of king and Commons in seeking to advance the honor of the monarchy while preserving the rights of the House. Nevertheless, he continued, there were differences, and he reminded his colleagues that the question of whether a change was necessary could, if unanswered, put an end to the matter without further ado. All this, however, was preamble. The central portion of the speech was a detailed examination of Bacon's thirteen points, concentrating on the methods by which changes of name or unions are generally achieved. In this analysis Sandys's argument was as reasoned and pointed as any that the House had heard, and it is not difficult to understand why hardly any comments were made on the subject thereafter.

Sir Edwin began by dividing all political unions into three types: the results of marriage, election, or conquest. The case of England and Scotland was obviously of the first type, and unfortunately the precedents were not promising. "There is not any example," he said, "of any kingdoms which, though they have been united in the head, which is the person of the Prince, have held the same course in the body by union of laws, customs, privileges, and styles of honor."[35] Finding no support in precedents, he turned to reason as the only possible justification for the Union. But this, too, was a weak reed. The difficulties raised by the legal situation were themselves sufficient to deter further inquiry: "How to make laws in this new kingdom cannot well be conceived." he pointed out, "because England and Scotland severally cannot set a law to the whole, nor jointly because they are not one Parliament before they are really united."[36] Moreover, a Parliament could not undo its own work; the current session had made James king of England, and it could not now make him king of Britain. Might some clever device allow one to circumvent the obstacles? Again, not a chance. James could not stoop to the evasion of having one title at home and another abroad, because he had to present a single face to the world. A kingdom, too, was indivisible, and was incapable of carrying two names at the same time. Once the new was adopted, the old disappeared. One could not very well speak of Great Britain *viz.* England and Great Britain *viz.* Scotland. Nor was a proviso much help: Sandys dismissed as "ridiculous, that we should do a thing and say that we did not intend it."[37]

Thus far, in both argument and sarcasm, the direction of the speech was unmistakable. Now, however, to clinch the case, Sandys moved on to more

---

[35] PRO, SP/14/7/64, fol. 157. Sandys conveniently ignored Spain, though there was certainly no "perfect" union between Aragon and Castile.

[36] Ibid., fol. 158.

[37] *CJ*, 186. The attack on joint names addressed Sir Roger Aston's suggestion that there would be only an addition to the name, not a substitution: Dunn, "Commons Debates," 2:558.

treacherous ground. For he reminded the House that even if it agreed on a course of action, its legislation was always subject to interpretation. And the arbiter would be the king. Therefore any act the Commons passed had to be quite specific about safeguards, because "we do not sit here upon hopes of personal goodness, but to make real provision. If Princes had as much wisdom and goodness as God, we should need no tie."[38] In this gratuitous slap at James Sandys may well have been giving vent to the reservations about monarchy he had already expressed in the *Relation*. Yet it would have been unlike him to throw in a private aside that might have weakened his case. It is more plausible to see this as an occasion when personal inclination and rhetorical need coincided. Far from being an embarrassing diversion, the reference to the unreliability of princes went to the root of the M.P.s' fears both about the Union and about their new ruler.

After this show of boldness, the speech hammered its purpose home by outlining objections to the Union that Bacon had failed to mention. While subjects could take new oaths of allegiance, how could James retake his coronation oath, once his title was changed, "unless there were a new coronation"? What would happen to England's treaties? And what would happen to the precedence England enjoyed because of her antiquity? "A new erected kingdom," he said, in a final appeal to patriotism, "must take the latest and lowest place."[39]

Sandys never openly denounced the Union, but there could be no mistaking his intent. The proposal had been found wanting in precedent and reason, and its dangers outweighed its purported benefits. So effective were his arguments that no serious effort was made in the remainder of the session to reject his conclusions. The two speakers who immediately followed, Thomas Hedley and Richard Martin, only added to the objections, and Bacon, in the last speech of the day, seemed at wits' end. He recommended, rather lamely, that the Commons avoid objections which were too petty, too subtle, or too abstruse.[40] If this was the best the Crown's ablest representative could devise, the cause was clearly lost.

Bacon's one constructive suggestion was that a committee investigate the situation further, and when this body met it divided up its work, assigning specific topics to each member. The first item concerned arguments from reason, a subject so large that it was divided in two, with Bacon asked to explore the need for a change and Sandys the precedents.[41] Sir Edwin's prominence (as counterbalance, at the head of the list, to the Crown's chief spokesman) testified to the impact he had made on the House.

[38] *CJ*, 186.

[39] PRO, SP/14/7/64, fol. 164.

[40] *CJ*, 958; Dunn, "Commons Debates," 2:579–580, puts Martin after Sandys.

[41] *CJ*, 188.

The issue was coming to be neutralized in committee, but there was still a fairly nervous discussion with the Lords on April 28: although Bacon claimed he was only playing devil's advocate, Sandys unleashed all his precedents, and then, when Northampton, trying to reply, found himself "only repeating what [Sandys] had said," Sir Edwin devastatingly concluded that, since his precedents "were only repeated and not answered he would hold them as assented unto." This apparently (because only the opening words have survived) drew a dismissive response from Cecil, whose main task, however, was to spring a major surprise. Earlier that day, a judicial opinion had suggested that the change of name would extinguish all laws. Although Cecil did not mention it, this was doubtless why the king now distanced himself from his April 20 intervention, backed away from the name change, promised to honor England's laws, and, as Bacon reported on May 1, declared he would be satisfied with the appointment of commissioners to draw up an Act of Union after Parliament recessed.[42]

This postponement of action till the next session was confirmed the following day in a petulant message from James. Protesting his own sincerity, and complaining about the Commons' slowness on so important a matter, the king assured them again that the Union would bring them nothing but benefit. What distressed him was the M.P.s' willingness to "be transported with the curiosity of a few giddy heads."[43] He wanted them to complete their great task, because the alternative was discord and shame. James could not have conceded less gracefully. Angered by the behavior of M.P.s like Sandys, and dismayed at their influence, he resorted to a reprimand that merely encouraged further defiance.

For there should not have been another debate on the Union. The issue was tucked away in committee, and the sole remaining business was to name commissioners and draw up their instructions. The latter in fact began to emerge the following day, appropriately couched in vague language and so arranged that two of the four headings dealt with safeguards for England. The appointment of commissioners took longer, dragging on for six weeks, via endless technicalities, until the appropriate bill, laden down with provisos, finally passed on June 7. One member likened it to winter fruit, since it ripened so slowly.[44] But none of these proceedings aroused serious debate, and it was only the tactlessness of James's message on April 30 that made the M.P.s revert to the issue for another acrimonious airing.

---

[42] Ibid., 193; Dunn, "Commons Debates," 2:607–610, 625–626. Following this meeting, at which he took on both Cecil and Northampton, Sandys was apparently chased by Northampton in some anger. See below, note 47. Neil Cuddy, citing SP/14/7/49, 75, 85, has shown that the climbdown was engineered by Cecil in response to the judicial opinion (personal communication).

[43] *CJ*, 194.

[44] Ibid., 196–197, 234, 230.

One of the king's most pointed reproofs had been his assertion that "jealousy and distrust" had hampered the Commons' work. This accusation the members could not allow to pass, and on May 1 there was a long discussion of the means to give his Majesty satisfaction.[45] A succession of M.P.s offered to purge themselves, though it is revealing that every speaker stressed the purity of the House's motives. James could not have found a better way of offending his subjects. In the end, of course, their response was to appoint yet another committee. But this time the problem did not simply fade away, because the committee was packed with men who had shown themselves dissatisfied with royal proposals and were prepared to seek alternatives.[46] Their mandate was to consider how to satisfy the king: a familiar task, because the House had had to explain its actions regularly during the previous month. Yet the creation of this group was a departure, not only because of its heavily independent membership, but also because of its purpose. Unlike previous efforts of this kind, it was specifically justified on the ground that the king had been misinformed, an argument that was to assume growing importance. Moreover, the subject of the committee's deliberations, the Union, was to occupy a large part of the "Apology" drawn up a month later. It is hard to escape the conclusion that the germ of that famous constitutional statement lies in the House's irritation with James's ill-considered accusations when he realized that his pet project was being suffocated by trivialities.

As one looks back at the confrontation, however, especially with the knowledge of the Union that was to be consummated in 1707, one can easily sympathize with the king. His aim was to smooth relations between his kingdoms, not exacerbate them, and he could have been forgiven for thinking that the problems that were raised, especially the preoccupation with names, seemed largely artificial. On a number of critical occasions during his reign (notably when he supported the Great Contract in 1610 or when he pursued peace in 1604 and again after 1618) he revealed himself to be more farsighted and more concerned for the general weal than his subjects. There is no denying that the quest for the Union was another such occasion. Yet in each of these situations he so mishandled the political maneuvering that he gave his actions the appearance of blunders. Consequently, despite the justifiable allegation that his difficulties sprang from the assertiveness of a few astute M.P.s like Sandys, and that their alternative perception of England's interests often seemed more petty or oppor-

---

[45] Ibid., 194, 197.

[46] The eleven members (named ibid., 197) all spoke during the session contrary to the king's wishes. Nine are listed as "leaders" of the independent-minded M.P.s in W. W. M. Mitchell, *The Rise of the Revolutionary Party in the English House of Commons 1603–1629* (New York, 1957), 42–44, a book which, despite obvious faults (such as oversimplified labeling of political opinion), contains useful information about lesser-known parliamentarians.

tunistic than weighty, it must be said that the king's tactical shortcomings were no less to blame. He cannot be absolved for failing to see that a just cause could not triumph unaided. In Stuart politics, virtue was never more than its own reward.

Elizabeth had appreciated the need for shrewd maneuvering, and she had managed to gain her ends even when her case was weak. This was a lesson James never learned, and the Union was but the first of many casualties his policies endured. As the mistakes, particularly the intemperate speeches, flowed forth, a sensible and intelligent M.P. like Sandys, with a different vision of England's welfare, had merely to pick the right moment to sway the House, to persuade his colleagues that some dangerous innovation was intended. And success bred boldness. From the first hints of disrespect for the Crown it was but a short step to more open disregard. It was almost insolence, combined with an appeal to the M.P.s' worst feelings, that produced Sandys's last reference to the Union in the 1604 session. The issue had long been dead when, out of the blue, he made a remark whose sarcasm epitomizes both the extent of James's miscalculations and the roots of Sir Edwin's success in the House: "It hath been said that he that is against the union will be glad to come and beg it, within these forty year, on their knees, when their daughters should be married into Scotland and the Scots inhabit here."[47]

The Origins of the Free Trade and "Apology" "Issues

The Union had been the king's proposal—indeed, it was his only official request to the Commons in 1604. The beginnings of the other two matters in which Sandys became centrally involved, free trade and the "Apology," went back to the momentous first day of regular business, March 23, when the control of proceedings was left to ordinary M.P.s.

The most elaborate agenda that was put forward that day came from Sir Robert Wroth, who had not missed a session in over forty years and was sitting in his eleventh consecutive Parliament. Member of a well-known Middlesex family with wide connections in the city of London, Wroth was

[47] *CJ*, 973. The issue of the Union, the decisive break in Sandys's career, has also been seen as the crucial divide between Elizabethan and Jacobean parliaments: Conrad Russell, "English Parliaments 1593–1606: One Epoch or Two?" in *The Parliaments of Elizabethan England* ed. D. M. Dean and N. L. Jones (Oxford, 1990), 191–213. Russell suggests (207) there may have been a tenuous link between Sandys and the earl of Northampton on the Union, and quotes the earl's double pun (referring both to the Bucks election case and to Sir Edwin) that the king's hopes would founder "not on Goodwin Sands, but on Edwin Sands." But the argument between the two at the conference on April 28 suggests they had little in common: above, note 42. See, too, Linda L. Peck, "The Earl of Northampton, Merchant Grievances and the Addled Parliament of 1614," *Historical Journal* 24 (1981): 533–552, esp. 537–544.

also the most experienced Puritan in the Commons: the last of the Marian exiles. And although in Elizabeth's last years he (like Sandys) had sought favor from Cecil, he was not obviously a Crown spokeman. Consequently, even if Cecil, seeking reforms he believed would strengthen royal administration and finance, inspired the speech, that pedigree cannot have been apparent to its audience, especially since Wroth described his points as grievances. In any case, the tactic misfired, and brought a whole series of troublesome issues to the surface.[48]

Among the topics Wroth suggested (to a House startled into silence) were wardship, purveyance, monopolies, dispensations, export of ordnance, and abuses of the Exchequer and writs of entry. Other speakers expanded the list, nobody demurred, and two committes (both including Sandys) were set up to investigate the proposals.[49] It was from the exploration of two of Wroth's grievances (monopolies and wardships) that there arose the major issues with which Sandys came to be closely identified: free trade, and the quarrel over wards that led to the "Apology."

THE FREE TRADE GENTRY

Monopolies had also occupied the House in its previous two sessions, in 1597 and 1601. At stake were the special patents, granted or sold by the Crown to favored individuals, which usually bestowed a monopoly of the sale or manufacture of some commodity such as salt or playing cards. The monopolist made a handsome income by extracting license fees from the real manufacturers and retailers. Naturally, this practice was bitterly resented, and in 1604 a bill was passed to forbid its continuation. But this time the House broadened its attack, bringing under fire the holders of wider and more powerful monopolies, the overseas trading companies. Although the merchants could argue that their risks (rather than a special relationship with the monarch) entitled them to their privileges, the fact remained that their rights were restrictive, excluding from profits all but the advantaged few. And that was sufficient to draw the attention of a House bent on reform, and suspicious of special interests. If the idea of renewing the onslaught on monopolies did come from Cecil, the gesture may have been only politic, considering the events of 1597 and 1601; but very soon, in Sandys's hands, it became identified with the particular interests of the gentry.

The first sign of these expanded concerns came as the session entered

---

[48] *CJ*, 150; above, see note 6. Since consequences were often unintended, Cecil's encouragement of a proposal (e.g., when Sandys opposed the Union) was often less significant than the way M.P.s responded to it.

[49] *CJ*, 151. Another example of the link between surprise and silence is on 166, when a message from the king was received with "some amazement, and silence."

its second month, at the very time the Commons were considering the Union. On April 18 and 19 two bills were introduced, calling for "free liberty of trade" and "for the enlargement of trade" respectively. It has been suggested that they were submitted by outport merchants, the group which stood to realise the most immediate gain from a dissolution of monopolies that were largely in the hands of Londoners.[50] This is a plausible assumption, for representatives of the outports were certainly leading supporters of such legislation. But other motives were also at work, and to understand these we need to consider a wider background.

There were two types of public company in the early seventeenth century: regulated and joint-stock. Both drew their powers from royal charters which gave their members a trading monopoly in a commodity or a geographical area. Both elected officers and held meetings to decide company policy. But here the similarities ended. The regulated company, the more ancient of the two, was essentially a licensing and supervising corporation. It usually had quite stringent apprenticeship or qualification requirements, and once a merchant was admitted he had to trade according to its rules. Its main purpose was to devise and enforce its guidelines and to protect its members' monopoly. Thus success depended on the personal skill or fortune of individual traders—the company as such made neither profit nor loss. The joint-stock company, on the other hand, succeeded or failed as a totality. Originally devised to permit a group of merchants to share the financing and the risk of a venture, by the late sixteenth century it was being conceived on a much larger scale. In structure it still resembled a regulated company, but its membership was open, without apprenticeship, to anyone who had money to invest. Moreover, trade was carried on by the company as a whole, according to the judgment of its directors. Every detail, from the first proposal to the final distribution of profits, was planned and executed by the company's leaders and employees. Thus the individual member had no need for trading skills. All he had to do was pay for a share of the costs of a voyage. Then, if the venture prospered, he received a proportion of the return equivalent to his original investment.

That, of course, was the theory. In practice there was a blurring of the boundary between regulated and joint-stock ventures. The latter could be just as restrictive as the former, particularly when a tight group of merchants banded together, limiting partnerships to themselves. This was the case with the Muscovy Company, which after an expansive beginning, when its membership included leading courtiers, drifted toward exclusiveness. This trend has been described by the company's historian:

[50] Ibid., 176, 179; Astrid Friis, *Alderman Cockayne's Project and the Cloth Trade* (London, 1927), 149.

As the capital became more impermanent it seems also to have become more concentrated in the hands of fewer members of the Company. . . . When that stage was reached, as it seems to have been by at least the fifteen-nineties, the Company rather resembled a regulated company in which the entire trade was monopolized by a section of the members, who had the right to exclude from trade, not only those who were not members, but also those members who were not of the "trading company." . . . At this point the logical course was to abandon the inner monopoly by turning the company into a regulated company.[51]

The Levant Company followed a similar progression. In other words, there were joint-stock companies that acted like regulated companies and were no less exclusive. Even the East India Company was accused of such practices. Thus, to the extent that participation in a joint stock was limited, it was vulnerable to the same objection as a regulated company. In the eyes of the gentry, for whom wider opportunities in trade were identified with England's welfare, what counted was whether investment was open or closed. The exemplars of the former were the new, large joint-stock organizations, like the early Muscovy Company, which wished to raise large sums for long-distance trade and thus accepted investments from any willing subscriber. It was an extension of this freer situation that the gentry sought in 1604; and since a joint stock could be open, but a regulated undertaking could not, it was the former, *in its unrestricted form*, that they advocated.

Their intentions were confirmed by their actions. Goaded by the propaganda of brilliant publicists like Hakluyt, nearly twelve hundred gentry and nobility invested in trading and colonizing companies between 1575 and 1630—a remarkable figure, considering their traditional avoidance of the world of business.[52] Without open joint stocks the surge of interest would have been impossible. For that very reason, however, gentlemen eager to participate in these enterprises wanted as many as possible to be available for investment. With soaring rents and the early Jacobean economic boom providing them with capital, and Hakluyt and his followers giving them the motive, they sought to share in the quest for markets and empire that happened also to advance England's interests. Among the M.P.s of 1604 this sentiment seems to have been particularly strong. Some 46 percent of

[51] T. S. Willan, *The Early History of the Russia Company, 1551–1603* (Manchester, 1956), 272.

[52] Theodore K. Rabb, *Enterprise and Empire: Merchant and Gentry Investment in the Expansion of England, 1575–1630* (Cambridge, Mass., 1967), 27. They undertook business on their estates, including ventures like glassmaking, but the commerce of London drew them only when joint-stock companies offered access through investment, not direct management.

the gentry in the House had either invested in an open joint-stock company or were to do so by 1630—a percentage that was about twenty times higher than that for the gentry as a whole.[53] Little wonder, therefore, that they supported a move to challenge the restrictiveness of the regulated companies. Although joint-stock organizations also held monopolies, the target was less the privilege itself than the exclusion of those who wished to take part. A monopoly open to all investors could pass muster.

These considerations can help us make sense of the history of the Free Trade bill of 1604. Until recently the main stress has been on the role of outport hostility to London. A few other influences have received attention (the resentments of cloth-producing counties, which felt exploited by Londoners; the hopes of gentry for better careers for younger sons; and the fears that only London would benefit from peace with Spain), but these have been made subsidiary to outport ambitions.[54] Yet to rely so heavily on this one explanation, without reference to the motives and larger vision of the gentry who passed the legislation, is to miss a vital part of the story.

The composition of the committee that drew up the bill is particularly suggestive. Twenty-two M.P.s were named on April 24, and (as was often the case) the first appointee, in this case Sandys, acted as the informal chairman and reported back to the House—a responsibility that reflected his new prominence.[55] Yet Sir Edwin was no mere outport representative.

[53] Eric Kerridge, "The Movement of Rent, 1540–1640," *Economic History Review*, 2nd, ser., 6 (1953): 16–34, esp. 28–29, 34; R. H. Tawney, *The Agrarian Problem in the Sixteenth Century* (London, 1912), 115–121, 139–147, 192–200, 304–310, 403–404; Joan Thirsk, ed., *The Agrarian History of England and Wales*, vol. 4: *1500–1640* (Cambridge, 1967), 110, 161–162, 196, 199, 204–205, 211, 291–292, 435, 587, 593–685, 814–865; Rabb, *Enterprise*, 95, 27.

[54] Friis, *Cockayne's Project*, 150–151.

[55] *CJ*, 183. I first emphasized the makeup of the committee in my "Sir Edwin Sandys and the Parliament of 1604," *American Historical Review* 69 (1964): 646–670, pp. 664–665—a topic ignored in Robert Ashton's "The Parliamentary Agitation for Free Trade in the Opening Years of the Reign of James I," *Past & Present*, no. 38 (1967): 40–55, and therefore in my reply, "Free Trade and the Gentry in the Parliament of 1604," ibid., no. 40 (1968): 165–173. Yet the composition of the committee is crucial: these twenty-two men, not disgruntled outport merchants, wrote the bill. The few representatives of the provinces on the committee were outgunned by some of the most influential gentry in the House (not to mention the Londoner Sir Thomas Smythe), and there is no evidence for Ashton's claim in "Jacobean Free Trade Again," ibid., no. 43 (1969): 151–57, that parts of the report reflect "a really determined and successful effort on the part of mercantile free traders to interest gentry M.P.s in their cause" (153). In fact, Sandys describes, in the preamble to his report, a succession of merchants giving testimony who managed only to bicker among themselves (*CJ*, 218). Ashton's criticism has prompted me to modify some details of my argument, but my basic view of the gentry's motivation remains unchanged. Some gentry M.P.s may have spoken on behalf of outport constituencies, but in the main they were seeking their own ends. For a more balanced treatment of outport lobbying, see David J. Brentnall, "Regional Influences in the House of Commons 1604–10" (M.Phil. diss., University of East Anglia, 1982), 148 ff., a work

In the 1580s he had sat for the borough of Plympton, a market town near Plymouth, but that hardly made him a Devonian, for he owed the seat to the families of his first two wives, both of whom were important in the county. If anything, his commitment was to the other side, for he had lived longer in London than anywhere else in England, and his acquaintance with its merchants was extensive. Moreover, at the Middle Temple he had come into contact with a remarkable concentration of the leaders of England's overseas enterprises. Here, and in his familiarity with London's ways, was reason enough for Sandys's interest in the issue and for his appointment as head of the committee. In this case, an emphasis on outport interests reverses the truth.[56]

The second man named, the merchant prince Sir Thomas Smythe, was almost the symbol of London's power: governor of the Muscovy, East India and French companies, soon to be governor of three more. There could be no doubt as to his position, nor about the views of a third member, Sir Henry Montague, the recorder of London. The latter was subsequently to be an investor in five companies (and director of two), and he was both by office and by personal inclination moved by influences that had nothing to do with provincial jealousies.

Of the nineteen remaining members of the committee, nine were gentry who had no known outport connections, but on the other hand were to invest in joint-stock companies within the next few years. Seven of them had been closely associated with Sandys in Parliament, and probably supported both his policies and his intentions: Lawrence Hyde, Richard Martin, Sir George More, Sir Henry Neville, Sir Thomas Ridgeway, Sir William Strode, and Sir Henry Yelverton. (Two of these, moreover—Ridgeway and Strode—were related to Sir Edwin.) The other two gentry members were Sir Thomas Lake, a minor courtier, and Sir Richard Hawkins, son of Sir John Hawkins, the Armada hero. The latter was certainly a devoted Devon man, but his long personal involvement in overseas enterprise, and his subsequent activities in three companies, make one doubt that his main commitment was to the western merchants. The thirteenth member of the committee, Sir Robert Wroth, died before the major influx of gentry funds into trade, but he too cannot be linked to the outports. He had always represented Middlesex, and his sons Robert and Thomas were to invest in a number of joint-stock ventures.

At best, only seven of the twenty-two committee members can be regarded as representatives of the provinces. Five were themselves outport merchants: James Bagge, Anthony Cole, Thomas Dannett, Thomas James,

---

brought to my attention by Christopher Thompson; and Pauline Croft, "Free Trade and the House of Commons, 1605–6," *Economic History Review*, 2d ser., 28 (1975): 17–27.

[56] Rabb, *Enterprise*, 102; cf. Friis, *Cockayne's Project*, 151.

and Sir John Jeffreys. A sixth, Sir Jerome Horsey, a Buckinghamshire gentleman who sat for Bossiney, had crossed swords with the Muscovy Company in the 1580s; and the seventh, John Prowse, had been elected by Exeter. It is worth noting, though, that none of these seven was an influential figure in the Commons; they certainly did not approach the stature of a Sandys, a Wroth, or a Martin. And the last two members, Francis Moore and Sir Robert Napper, were identified neither with London nor with the provincial groups.[57]

Whatever the outports' interest in the legislation, therefore, they cannot be regarded as the driving force in the committee. Nor is it even clear that geography was all that significant. For, as David Harris Sacks has pointed out to me, there were at least two other considerations at work that the previous literature has ignored. First, both the Middle Temple in general, and six members of the committee in particular—Hyde, Martin, Montague, Moore, More, and Wroth—had been deeply involved in the anti-monopoly legislation of 1601. This had entailed a broad view of the meaning of "liberty" and the rights of property, based on Magna Carta, that emphasized the free use of labor. But it also had far-reaching implications for the gentry's emerging vision of their own liberties and rights, and their distaste for restrictions on those rights. Second, the chief victims of the "mere merchant" monopoly, particularly in the Spanish Company, were not outports or gentry, but the other tradesmen of London—grocers or vintners (for example, Sir Thomas Smythe). It was a complex coalition of interests, therefore, that sought to remove the obstacles to investment that were created by regulated or closed corporations. For the reformers, an open joint stock was the answer to the problems caused by large-scale monopolies. And their spokesman, Sandys, was able to embody the many forces that came together in support of free trade.

Sandys and the Freeing of Trade

After nearly four weeks of meetings, Sandys delivered the committee's report on May 21, and his long speech, "excellently delivered," was the manifesto of the free traders.[58] Despite its oft-noted failings—the superficiality of the economic arguments, the vagueness of the term "monopoly"—it made a strong case for the bill Sir Edwin was introducing.

Moreover, the economic arguments were not, as has been claimed, "the

[57] Although Napper, from a Dorset family, had West Country links, he left little impression on the proceedings. In addition to the named members, the citizens of all cities, the burgesses of all port towns, and the barons of the Cinque Ports were appointed to the body ex officio. But there is no evidence that those who were eligible in this way appeared at meetings or carried much weight. The named members were the prime movers.

[58] *CJ*, 976.

true reasons why the great majority of the House of Commons could accord the bill ... their warm support."[59] These were added inducements, thrown in to bolster the proposal, and their very weakness was an indication of their subordinate role and of the merchants' secondary involvement. The other failing, the absence of a definition of "monopoly," was in fact no disadvantage. This was excellent propaganda, for the imprecision allowed all M.P.s to vote against a hated form of privilege. Yet there was no uncertainty about Sandys's target. As a loose pejorative, "monopoly" denoted the restriction of a trade and its returns to fewer people than it was capable of supporting. The few could be ten, a hundred, or a thousand, but they had a monopoly if they excluded others from available profits. It was this practice that the gentry wished to terminate, and their support was won by nothing more complicated than the assertion that free trade meant an end to such "monopolies." The open joint-stock company was the panacea, and for this reason the Muscovy Company (legally a joint stock, but behaving like a regulated company) was denounced, and the East India Company, whose shares were usually available to all, was applauded.

A final criticism of the free trade bill can also be rejected. Coke later commented that the form of the bill was defective, and this view has been embellished by the claim that legal knowledge was "very feebly represented in the committee."[60] Coke's objection was merely a device for delaying the measure when the session was almost over, and can be ignored. The characterization of the committee, however, is simply untrue. Apart from Sandys's legal experience, the committee could draw on the expertise of four of the House's most distinguished lawyers (Hyde, Martin, the future Lord Chief Justice Sir Henry Montague, and Moore). On this count, few parliamentary committees were so well endowed.

The structure of Sandys's report, "penned by himself," was typical of his writings: a carefully molded and reasoned piece of rhetoric.[61] He began with a grand statement of natural right: "All free subjects are born inheritable, as to their land, so also to the free exercise of their industry, in those trades whereunto they apply themselves, and whereby they are to live." Consequently, he said, narrowing his focus to the world of commerce, it is "against the natural right and liberty of the subjects of England to restrain it [trade] into the hands of some few." England's trade, he claimed, was controlled by only two hundred men. Here was the principal grievance, and it was couched in language (an invocation of freedom, natural right, and the liberty of the subject) that refutes those who see Stuart Parlia-

[59] Friis, *Cockayne's Project*, 152.
[60] Ibid., 156. Coke's objections are in *LJ*, 2:336.
[61] *CJ*, 218. For the report, ibid., 218–221; BL, Additional, 38,139, fols. 59–62.

ments as devoid of constitutional principle or ideology. For Sandys a cause like individual liberty was a powerful ideal, which swayed the gentry precisely because it was essential to their vision of England's polity.

The speech then moved through the legal arguments (mainly a law of Henry VII which the companies' charters violated) and on to one of Sir Edwin's favorite devices, an appeal to patriotism. England was hated for its monopolies, so he claimed, by foreigners who flourished because their trade was free: a preposterous insinuation, but evidently believable in a House not blessed with much knowledge of other countries. It was here that Sandys first used the word "monopoly," and indicated that the distinction between foreign and domestic practices lay in the degree of restriction *within* the companies. The existence of companies per se, even with monopolistic privileges, was not in question.

Next came the economic analysis, buried in the middle of the speech, and hardly in the prominent position it would have occupied had it been the meat of Sandys's argument. Nor was the discrimination against outport merchants the first target. Sandys stated his belief that freedom of trade would permit a more equal distribution of wealth throughout England only after outlining other benefits of a liberalization of commerce: prices would rise because of competition among buyers; as a result, wealth would increase and industriousness would improve. The removal of restraints, Sandys claimed, would also encourage shipping and enlarge customs revenues.

Finally, as the climax of his speech, Sir Edwin presented gentry ambitions in the guise of a parent's concern for his children's welfare. "What else", he asked, "shall become of gentlemens' younger sons, who cannot live by arms, when there is [sic] no wars, and learning preferments are common to all, and mean?" Unless they were reconciled to a life as servingmen, which was a far worse fate, they had no choice but "merchandizing." In a typical aside, he added that such a career was common in foreign countries. The gentry's desire to share in trade was thus presented in its most unimpeachable form, as a matter of honor.

In fact, however, the implication that help was being sought only for helpless younger sons was particularly clever because particularly misleading. It may have had a fine ring in the ears of the M.P.s, many of whom, like Sandys himself, were younger sons. But so too were some of England's greatest merchants: Sir John Wolstenholme, to name but one. There had never been any impediment if a young man, knowing he would inherit nothing from his father, came to London in search of a fortune. He could serve an apprenticeship, learn the skills, and prosper in his own trade or in a regulated company. Every man in the House must have been aware of these opportunities, and knew that the argument could not be taken at face value. It has to be be seen, instead, as an assertion of the nonmerchant's claim to be allowed a share in profits *whether or not* he made commerce a full-time career. When Sir Edwin demanded that right, however couched, his real intentions became apparent. The plea for younger sons was a plea for the gentry.

The rest of the report consisted of replies to various defenses of restriction. James was carefully absolved from blame, because the fault lay not in the abuses of monopolies (these the king himself had denounced) but in the companies' refusal to reform. In answer to the suggestion that monopolies should be defined only as grants to a single man (which was how the complaints were framed in earlier Parliaments), Sandys elaborated on the idea that *any* unjust exclusion constituted a monopoly. As an example he cited the Merchant Adventurers, who controlled the cloth trade, and who were arousing anger at the time because they reacted to economic difficulties by buying less cloth at home. They could cause widespread hardship, he contended, only because their power remained in the hands of the few. The monopolists' claim that they helped England by keeping prices high abroad Sandys countered with the accusation that this made England unpopular among the nations. His evidence was the recent edict of the Emperor directed against the Merchant Adventurers because of this very policy, and for good measure he pointed out that high prices benefited few Englishmen.

To the companies' next defense, that there was no room for more merchants, Sir Edwin weakly responded that the end of restraint would stimulate an expansion of trading opportunities, a dubious prophecy that he justified by denouncing the current practice of having "some few overgrown men devour the wealth and make merry." But he had a simple answer to the fear that complete freedom might undermine the proper training of merchants. Whereas those who wished to could still learn the art, the untutored could take comfort from the knowledge that "at least wise men [could] adventure their stocks with other men" once restrictions were removed. This was straightforward advocacy of the open joint-stock system. As for the supposed danger that such policies would cause a great enlargement of the companies, that was exactly the aim of the legislation: the subversion of closed monopolistic practices. That there might be advantages to tight control (for instance in volatile markets) he ignored.

Sandys then returned at some length to the question of joint stocks. The companies claimed that the bill would prevent such ventures, and in rebuttal he made abundantly clear what in fact was intended. "It is true," he said, "that it is fit to trade to the East Indies in a joint stock, and so do the Hollanders [a typical reference]; this Act does therefore not forbid men to trade in a joint stock, if they list, and see it fit." What was forbidden was the insistence that, in order to trade, one had to qualify for a closed group. This was the reason the Muscovy Company came under attack, because its decisions and investment opportunities were said to be controlled by only fifteen men.

Sir Edwin's speech was now drawing to a close. He discussed a few minor points and then amplified his belief that customs revenues would benefit from liberalization. Rejecting the possibility of exemptions for the Merchant Adventurers (in recognition of their antiquity) and the Muscovy Company (because they had opened a new trade), he concluded with the hope that any defects in the bill would be remedied by future Parliaments.

Sandys had spoken for the gentry. The speech embodied their view of what was best both for themselves and for the country. Moreover, he had made his opinion of the "mere" merchants quite apparent. At the beginning of his report, he had described the committee's procedures, and in particular the five days of hearings when a stream of merchants, some of them the greatest in the land, had volunteered their testimony. Those from the provinces had complained about the restrictions imposed by the domineering Londoners, while the latter had simply squabbled among themselves, "standing stiffly for their own Company, yet repin[ing] at other Companies." In contrast to these disheartening quarrels, Sir Edwin had invoked natural rights, national welfare and prestige, and the wish of all England to share in the profits of trade. The outcome of the subsequent discussion only underlined the effectiveness of his presentation.

The measure was debated on three separate days during the next two weeks: May 31, June 4, and June 6.[62] At first the critics predominated, for on May 31 six out of the eight speakers, including Secretary Herbert and Sir Edward Montague, opposed the bill. But thereafter the tide ran with the committee. On June 4 Sandys answered Montague point by point, and at least one of the other three speakers supported him. At the final discussion, on June 6, well over half of the twelve speeches, including those by Strode, Hyde, and Sir Edwin's father-in-law Sir Richard Bulkeley, were in favor of the bill, which then passed "with great consent and applause of the House," scarcely forty of whose members dissented.[63]

Although the measure never went beyond the Lords, its passage was a significant accomplishment. And the size of the majority in the Commons demonstrated the force of Sandys's persuasiveness. For passage had been achieved despite the disapproval both of powerful London merchants and of the Crown in the person of Herbert. Although the Lords proved vulnerable to such pressure, the Lower House had revealed its receptivity to the arguments on which the committee based its case. In particular, the M.P.s had accepted Sir Edwin's argument that the bill would bring improve-

---

[62] *CJ*, pp. 229, 232, 233, 983, 985, 987.

[63] Ibid., 218. It is not always certain where each speaker stood, but the direction seems clear: Dunn, "Commons Debates," 3:979–980 and 997–1002.

ments "for the exceeding benefit of all the land."[64] What was especially remarkable was that so many gentry, with no ostensible interest in the legislation, had rallied to his side. To persuade about nine tenths of the Commons to vote with him, Sandys subtly blended their vision of national welfare with an appeal to their personal ambitions in a mélange that thoroughly demonstrated his growing ascendancy over his colleagues.

WARDSHIP

Of all the issues in which Sir Edwin became involved in 1604, wardship was at once the most eagerly addressed and the most elusive. Few practices were more distasteful to the gentry; yet few were so enshrined in impeccable legality. Despite the popularity of the cause, therefore, its pursuit took the Commons well beyond the bounds of their official jurisdiction.

Reform of the system of wardship may originally have seemed to Cecil a good way of creating a more secure source of income for the Crown. It was precisely this kind of innovative rethinking of governmental revenues and responsibilities that was characteristic of leading ministers throughout Europe in the seventeenth century. But in England it ran up against powerful traditions and resentments, and eventually all that he accomplished was to stir up an old grievance. The gentry took the offensive, and acted more daringly than they did on the Bucks election or the Union. They were now to challenge one of the monarchy's hallowed, unquestionable rights.

The grievance was perfectly understandable. For centuries England's kings had been entitled to claim as their ward any heir who was still a minor when he succeeded to lands legally held of the Crown by knight service, a category that included every significant landowner in the country. As guardian, the king could administer the ward's property, use the income as he saw fit, and marry his charge to a girl of his own choosing; or he could sell the wardship, an increasingly common practice. Under Elizabeth the Court of Wards had become a major source of royal income, and its mastership a plum office. Robert Cecil is estimated to have derived from the position some £3,000 annually during his fourteen-year tenure from 1598 to 1612.[65] And the burdens on the victims were subject to a multiplier effect, because an unscrupulous protegé of the master could buy

---

[64] *CJ*, 218.

[65] J. H. Hurstfield, *The Queen's Wards* (London, 1958); H. E. Bell, *An Introduction to the History and Records of the Court of Wards & Liveries* (Cambridge, 1953); M. J. Hawkins, ed., *Sales of Wards in Somerset 1603–1641*, Somerset Record Society, vol. 67 (Frome, 1965), introduction; Lawrence Stone, *Family and Fortune: Studies in Aristocratic Finance in the Sixteenth and Seventeenth Centuries* (Oxford, 1973), 21–22.

a guardianship and milk the estate for much more than he had paid. As a group, therefore, the unlucky families paid far more to protect their lands than the Crown received from wardships.

The gentry would have dearly liked to remove this threat to their fortunes, but they had to move cautiously. Not only was this a new grievance—when wardships had last been raised in the Commons, in 1584, thought had been given to their extension—but it clearly infringed on royal prerogatives. The M.P.s therefore acknowledged that "they esteemed it only a grief, no wrong," whose remedy they left "to the King's grace, and not to his justice."[66] Although they had no right to discuss the matter, they hoped for a show of favor from James. That the issue may have been raised by Cecil as a means of trading wardships for a regular income they had no way of knowing; hence their initial nervousness when Sir Robert Wroth suggested the subject at the beginning of the session.

Wardship had been the second item on Wroth's original agenda. Sandys was on the committee appointed to look into this grievance (as it was defined) and he was also on the successor committee that conferred with the Lords about the procedures that ought to be followed. Progress was slow, because there was much else to occupy the House during the first month of the session. The only decision that seems to have been taken by the middle of May was that they should proceed by petition rather than bill, because of the delicacy of the issue. On May 11, in the midst of a debate on another traditional irritant, purveyors, which Wroth had also raised, Sandys urged that the issue be linked with wards, but the House did not agree. Perhaps he proposed the combination because of the idea circulating at the time (probably with Cecil's blessing) that some kind of monetary composition might be offered the king as a replacement for purveyance—the crown's right to requisition supplies for the Court. This approach was soon to be tried for wardship, and in 1610 was to become the basis for a major attempt to exchange feudal rights for settled revenues, the Great Contract. For the time being, however, the motion was rejected, as was a second attempt to link purveyance and wards a few days later.[67]

Sandys finally managed to bring the issue to center stage on May 19, when, in recognition of his stature in the House, he was designated to take to the Lords four bills that had been passed by the Commons. Before departing, he asked if he could raise with the Lords the possibility of their joining together in a petition to the king for leave to discuss wardship. His colleagues agreed, and two days later the Lords replied by requesting a

[66] Neale, *Parliaments*, 91–92; *CJ*, 155. See in general Croft, "Wardship."

[67] The two proposals are in *CJ*, 207, 211. For purveyance, on which Sandys made no significant contribution until 1606, see below, chapter 5, note 13.

conference on the subject.[68] The pace was leisurely, but the Commons did not seem to be in any hurry, content to appoint a conference committee, including Sandys, to prepare reasons in favor of the petition. By May 25 Sir Edwin had taken charge, presenting the committee's proposals to the House, which officially read and debated them on the twenty-sixth.

The petition opened with a statement of Parliament's hopes: that the king would abolish not only wardship but also every feudal right, including homage, alienations, reliefs, and knight service. The request had four justifications. First, abolition of feudal dues would bring about "a restitution unto the original right of all men by the law of God and nature"—yet another declaration of the gentry's belief in individual rights, which in this case included parents' rights to decide the rearing of their children. Second, the impoverishment of His Majesty's subjects would be ended. Third, the elimination of wardship would prevent the arrangement of "forced and ill-suited marriages"—a remarkable argument for the time, though perhaps one that the quadruply wed Sandys was well fitted to appreciate. Fourth, in a far-fetched appeal which nonetheless was typical of Sir Edwin, the petition asserted that the survival of feudal rights made England an object of contempt among foreign nations.

As for the reasons that led the Commons to believe that redress would now be forthcoming, they were threefold: the ending of hostilities between England and Scotland; the king's promise to show by his actions his gratitude for the welcome he had received when he succeeded to the throne; and Parliament's offer of a perpetual revenue as compensation. The committee recommended that this last be provided by an assessment on each county according to the feudal revenues it currently paid: an offer of settled revenue in exchange for traditional obligations that turned out, after many years of struggle, to be the only way to adapt governmental finances to the problems of the age. But that was far in the future. In the meantime, the suggestion provoked argument and distrust.

There can be little doubt that the petition was Sandys's work. Not only is the style (in its carefully reasoned progression, with all arguments numbered) typical of the man, but the content reverts all too often to Sir Edwin's hobbyhorses. No other member of the House would have made the implausible reference to foreigners' contempt for England. Nor had any M.P. given signs of holding a mildly disapproving opinion of things monarchical, as had Sandys in the *Relation*. Yet this attitude is apparent thoughout the petition, especially in the sections which implied that the general belief in a natural law of original rights could be taken further, into an implication that the law took precedence over royal privileges. This is a

[68] Ibid., 215, 976, 221.

very early statement of a theory that was to have an influential life for
more than two centuries, and is a remarkable instance of Sandys breaking
new ground even as he was advancing specific arguments in the Commons.
He was making pioneering use of the notion of natural right to assert that,
although wardships were legally unimpeachable, the king had no real right
to keep them. The boldness of this proposition was recognized by the clerk
of the House, because at this point he added one of his rare footnotes to
the Journal. Original right, he wrote, could be abridged by positive law: a
mild but clear rebuke. And Sandys's demand that James grant the petition
because he had promised to reward England for his happy reception was
hardly less audacious.[69]

Such barbs were entirely in keeping with the flashes of sarcasm noticeable not only in the *Relation* but also in Sir Edwin's great speech on the
Union. The irony of kings claiming they could not err, or accepting comparisons with the wisdom of God, when their scarcity in Hell was due only
to their small number, seems never to have been far from Sandys's tongue.
His disrespect may not have been unique, but his expressions of it were.
Although the entire committee must have collaborated in the writing of
the report, Sir Edwin's imprint was the most visible, as was only to be
expected from the reporter and thus the informal head of the group. If he
was indeed assuming leadership of the Commons once again, he was doing
so at a crucial moment, because he was now persuading his colleagues to
confront a fundamental constitutional issue.

The first attempt to replace a feudal due with a settled income, to mod-
ernize England's fiscal institutions, had begun early in the session, when
the committee examining purveyance had come up with the idea (possibly
inspired by Cecil via Wroth) of offering James a fixed annual revenue to
replace this portion of his prerogative. When Sandys seized on this notion
and broadened it into a sweeping proposal to overhaul the entire structure
of royal finance, he may still have been advancing a scheme that originated
with Cecil, but now it became his own. The Lords had moved ahead cautiously, and had suggested that the obligation of homage (for which subjects compounded with cash payments) might be dealt with in the same
way as purveyance, but Sir Edwin was casting his net much more widely.[70]
What he was seeking was the abolition *in toto* of a system that relied on

[69] Ibid., 222, 226; and 227–228 for the petition. Richard Tuck, *Philosophy and Government
1572–1651* (Cambridge, 1993), 150, gives Sandys only a tangential place in the momentous
transformation of *raison d'état* theory into natural law theory (xiv); but his use of natural law
and natural rights, first in his advocacy of free trade, then in this petition, and again on
purveyance in 1606 and more generally in the 1614 Parliament (see below, chapter 5, note
21, and chapter 7, note 44) marks him as an important pioneer in the effort to apply the
theory to political and legislative action (see also above, chapter 2, note 5).
[70] *CJ*, 155.

obsolete rights to provide the Crown with money. His alternative was a more rational set of procedures for supplying governmental needs. Whatever hints there may be of Cecilian foreshadowings, this was the first clear formulation of an all-embracing solution to the persistent problem of royal revenues—a solution that was to be explored most thoroughly during the negotiations over the Great Contract in 1610, and finally adopted after the Restoration of Charles II. Thus did the gentry, exemplified by Sandys, show themselves as capable as any royal minister of addressing the greatest political problems of the age.

The immediate result, however, was as fraught with consequence as the long-term history of Sandys's proposal. Wroth confidently forecast that nothing would come of this approach (an interesting reaction from a Cecil confidant, which implies that it was no longer the minister's scheme);[71] but when, on June 1, after the Whitsun recess, Sandys reported on the conference at which the petition had been presented to the Lords, wardship was overtaken by a larger issue. He informed the House that, in introducing the document, he had stressed that if the king granted the Commons' request, it would be a great act of grace, and if not, it would be no wrong. But then had come the surprise. For in contrast to their previous enthusiasm, the Lords now gave vent to displeasure. Obviously under pressure from James, they rejected all the proposals.[72]

The one Journal of these proceedings in the Lords that has survived remarks laconically that the lord chancellor and Cecil told the Commons to forbear.[73] According to Sandys, the reproof was more dramatic. First, the Upper House chided them for their ingratitude, reminding them "what we were, in what state we were, the 12th of March was twelvemonth (two days before Elizabeth died), that we would have given half that we had, to have that we now enjoy." In return, the Commons seemed to be spending their time on nothing but privileges and grievances. The Lords then went on to refute the petition in detail. They defined, not without a touch of sarcasm, how land tenures were held, and demolished the allegation about the contempt of foreigners. Not only did other countries have similar customs, but they would be far more likely to laugh at James than to respect him if he sold his prerogative. In any case, long experience and cold figures showed that no compensation could equal the king's revenue from feudal rights.

That the effort was now identified entirely with Sandys, and divorced from any hint of an initiative by Cecil, was made clear by this rebuff. More important, the Lords' disparagement of the petition turned the Commons

[71] Ibid., 228.
[72] Ibid., 230 has Sandys's June 1 report.
[73] BL, Additional, 48,160, fol. 3.

toward a wider issue. Only two days before they had received from James himself a similar scolding, "wherein many particular actions and passages of the House were objected unto them, with taxation and blame."[74] Now their motives and maturity were being questioned yet again, this time by their own parliamentary colleagues. The gentry's tolerance for this flood of reproach was running thin, and their indignation gave their representatives the opportunity to embark on their most ambitious venture yet.

THE "APOLOGY"

When Sandys sat down after his gloomy report, the man who rose to address the House was Sir Thomas Ridgeway, a fairly active member, but a newcomer sitting in his first session who had shown little sign of "popular" sentiments. Perhaps because of the role he was about to play, Sir Thomas was to be sent to a minor post in Ireland by James after the next session, and he was thus unable to complete his one term as an M.P.[75] Nor did he have any notable distinction outside the Commons. He was a prominent Devon gentleman, sheriff of his county in 1599/1600, and in Ireland he was to become a substantial investor in English colonization, eventually acquiring the earldom of Londonderry.

It was this unexceptional figure, serving a brief stint in Parliament, who made the most daring proposal of his maiden session—suggesting, when Sandys finished his report, that, because of James's "impression of mislike of the proceedings of the House in general," the Commons should survey their past actions and justify themselves to the king.[76] Here was the proposal that gave birth to the "Apology," and Ridgeway was to take charge of the document until it reached its final form. The reason for his sudden prominence, however, takes us back, once more, to Sir Edwin Sandys.

Ridgeway was the nephew of Sandys's second wife, Anne Southcote. He was also the nephew of the wife of another leading critic of official policies in 1604, Sir William Strode.[77] All three (Ridgeway, Sandys, and Strode) had been on the committee that had conferred with the Lords about wardship the previous week. In the meantime had come the Whitsun recess, which gave the despondent committee members the time to discuss among themselves what they could do next. When, after Parliament reconvened, James treated the House to an ill-considered dosage of "taxation and blame" for its actions, his critics' opportunity became obvious. The mem-

[74] CJ, 230.

[75] Ibid., 315–316. On Ridgeway, see DNB, 16:1164–1167; for his shrievalty, Cordelia Ann Stone, "Devon and Parliament in the Early Stuart Period" (Ph.D. diss., Bryn Mawr College, 1986), 584, a reference I owe to Christopher Thompson.

[76] CJ, 230. The clerk's notes (984) indicate that Ridgeway spoke first.

[77] J. L. Vivian, ed., The Visitations of the County of Devon (Exeter, 1895), 647, 699–700.

bers were chafing under repeated royal scoldings; they had already, more than once, considered justifying themselves; and when Sandys reported the unexpected opposition of the Lords the seal was set on their frustration.

To take advantage of this moment, a spokesman not conspicuously identified with particular views took center stage to revive the recommendation that the Commons vindicate their behavior. Ridgeway performed his task admirably, and he was met by a deluge of approval that swept along the speaker himself. Since members of the committee that had drawn up the petition helped keep the flow moving, it seems likely that they had coordinated their speeches. The man who seconded Ridgeway's motion, for example, was Sir John Hollis, an independent-minded M.P. from the committee whom Bacon later singled out (together with Sandys and eight others) as a leader of opposition to royal wishes. And Strode, too, lent his weight to the discussion that followed. But these urgings were hardly needed; the House was now fully aroused, determined to clear itself "from the scandal of levity and precipitation."[78]

The anger was probably intensified by Sandys's timing. The news of the Lords' rebuff would have been irritating anyway, because it showed how futile it had been for the M.P.s to spend virtually the entire morning of May 26 discussing the petition, only to be told to forbear that very afternoon. And this recalled another annoyance, because the conference with the Lords had originally been scheduled for the previous day; not only did the Upper House postpone it at short notice, but they then asked the Commons to sit on Whit Monday—a request the Lower House refused.[79] Thus there was already cause for tension when, following the king's scolding on June 1, Sandys released the bombshell about the Lords' rejection of the wardship petition. He must have known that the predictably angry reaction would prime the M.P.s for Ridgeway's proposal.

The tactics were so successful that James seems to have become quite alarmed. Four days later he sent a message through the speaker which showed him in full retreat. He explained his harsh words as the admonition of a father, and asked that they not be taken amiss. Since there was no doubt in his mind about the loyalty and affection of the Commons, their desire for justification was alone sufficient to satisfy him. Therefore, the speaker added, the king "wisheth we would not trouble ourselves with

[78] Spedding, *Letters and Life*, IV, 370; *CJ*, 230. According to Dunn, "Commons Debates," 3:950, Speaker Phelips also supported the idea of a petition.

[79] That the Commons may already have been told to forbear on May 24 (see above, note 73) suggests the news was deliberately held back during the May 26 debate. But BL, Harleian, 767, fol. 34, and both Commons and Lords Journals make the date May 26. It was also at this time that the M.P.s were complaining to the Lords about the bishop of Bristol's book. *CJ*, 227; *LJ*, 2:305, 309; Inner Temple, Petyt MSS. 537, 12, fol. 408.

giving him satisfaction."[80] It was a naive appeal, incapable of altering the House's purpose. Not a single comment greeted the message, and preparation of the "Apology" proceeded.

Although wardship, at the special request of the speaker, was to occupy an important place in the "Apology," it was swallowed up by the much larger issue of the members' self-justification.[81] Nevertheless, Sandys's part in subsequent developments was central. The committee chosen to draw up the document was the same as the one that had handled wardship, with a few additions. Sir Edwin had been the dominant member of the earlier group, and it is unlikely that his influence diminished even though Ridgeway now took over the job of reporting to the House. Yet it is impossible to pinpoint more than a small part of the document that may have been his work. Analysis of the contents permits few solid attributions, and the handwriting of the various texts of the "Apology" that have survived, including what seem to be working texts, cannot be assigned to any of the committee members.[82] As the M.P.s hammered out the wording, they may well have been dictating to secretaries, and in that case such evidence is almost useless.

The first section that seems incontrovertibly Sandys's work is the recapitulation both of the House's discussions of wardship and of the final petition, for the language often comes straight out of the petition.[83] Similarly, the explanation of the debates on the Union repeats parts of Sandys's speeches; considering his prominence in that confrontation, there is every reason to believe that he was put in charge of his own vindication. For the rest, occasional touches suggest Sir Edwin's involvement, but no more. Near the beginning of the "Apology" there is a sentence, referring to James, that comments on the limitations of human wisdom when no adequate information is available, and this is reminiscent of Sandys's sarcasm about royal capabilities. Alike in tone is the remark that subjects would be free of worries about privileges if good kings were immortal, but unfortunately God sometimes creates hypocrites and tyrants. The whole document was in fact an implicit insult to the king, insinuating as it did that the

[80] *CJ*, 232–233.

[81] Ibid., 230.

[82] The principal manuscript versions are: Inner Temple, Petyt MSS. 537, 12, fols. 520–537; 538, 17, fols. 487–509; 538, 19, fols, 91–104; and 538, 51, fols. 76–79; BL, Lansdowne, 512, 119–132; House of Lords, Braye MSS. 67. fols. 338–356; and BL, Harleian, 2208, fols. 156–166.

[83] BL, Harleian, 2208, fols. 156–166. J. R. Tanner, ed., *Constitutional Documents of the Reign of James I, A.D. 1603–1625, with an Historical Commentary* (Cambridge, 1930), 217–230, is still the most convenient printing of the text, whose significance has withstood the criticisms of Tanner in G. R. Elton, "A High Road to Civil War?" *From the Renaissance to the Counter-Reformation: Essays in Honor of Garrett Mattingly*, ed. C. H. Carter (London 1966), 325–347, esp. 333–334.

liberties of the House had never been so "dangerously impugned"—largely, it seemed, because his Majesty had no idea how England was governed.[84] Nor can James have appreciated the repetition of the path-breaking assertion which, when first made by Sandys, had drawn a demurrer from the keeper of the official Journal: that natural rights were more basic than any laws.

The one other concrete indication of Sir Edwin's part in the "Apology" is in the section defending the Commons' discussions of religion. As we will see, his small part in these proceedings was, characteristically, to urge moderation. Since the issue had been pursued mainly by the Puritans, however, it is surprising to find the quest for moderate solutions put forward as the justification for the House's dealings with religion. "We disputed not of matters of faith and doctrine," the "Apology" claims: "our desire was peace only; and our device of unity, how this lamentable and long-lasting dissension among the ministers . . . might at length . . . be extinguished. And for the ways of this peace, we are not all addicted to our own inventions, but ready to embrace any fit way that may be offered."[85] This could almost be a passage from the *Relation*.

When the "Apology" was finally presented to the House, on June 20, the independent-minded figured prominently in the debate that followed. From the two accounts in the Journal, one can estimate the leanings of twelve speakers, only three of whom seem to have opposed the document: Bacon, the diplomat Sir Dudley Carleton, and probably Sir Edward Stafford, another diplomat.[86] Of the remaining nine whose names are mentioned, six were prominent critics of government policies, fresh from the committee that had drawn up the "Apology": Nicholas Fuller, Sir Robert Wingfield, Richard Martin, Sandys himself, Sir William Strode, and Sir John Hollis. Two other members of the committee, Sir Henry Beaumont and Sir Herbert Croft, also spoke, and the Journal notes that they supported their own motion.[87] Finally, Sir Richard Lovelace, a kinsman of

---

[84] Tanner, *Documents*, 218, 222–223. A broader assertion of Sandys's authorship of much of the "Apology" is in W. M. Wallace, *Sir Edwin Sandys and the First Parliament of James I* (Philadelphia, 1940), 70. For the problems in this attribution see my "Parliament of 1604," 659 and Notestein, *Commons 1604–1610*, 134–139.

[85] Tanner, *Documents*, 226.

[86] *CJ*, 243, 995. Elton, "High Road," 335, describes Stafford, a solid Court figure, as "probably against" the document, despite the lack of specific evidence. Yet he regards as bewildering the division (on grounds no less solidly based than Stafford's) of all seventeen speakers into pros, antis, and unknowns in my "Parliament of 1604", and repeated here. My account of Ridgeway's involvement Elton misrepresents (346); and the general shortcomings of his treatment are epitomized by the self-contradiction whereby he questions Strode's "opposition" sentiments (347) a few pages after quoting at length (335–336) the evidence (*CJ*, 248) that Strode was one of the chief shepherds of the "Apology."

[87] *CJ*, 995.

Sandys, may well have followed his lead, though this cannot be confirmed. The views of the remaining five speakers are unknown, but even if they joined Bacon, the sentiment in favor of the "Apology" must have dominated its two readings.

What happened thereafter has remained a mystery to this day. The clerk began to enter the document in the fair copy of the Journal, which he was not likely to have done had he not had some sign of approval from the House.[88] He left it unfinished, but this was a not uncommon practice at a time when long insertions were written out at leisure. Whatever the outcome, however—whether it was formally approved by the Commons or not—there can be no doubt that the document not only reflected widely held opinions but also reached the king. A presentation copy is in the British Library,[89] and Sir Robert Phelips, who as the son of the 1604 speaker ought to have known, said in 1621 that "in the first Parliament in the King's reign, the House ... *delivered* a remonstrance to the King, declaring that they had as good right to their liberties of Parliament, principally to that of speech, as to their inheritance"—an obvious reference to the section of the "Apology" that dealt with the Commons' natural rights.[90] Even more telling, "the most perfect copy" of the "Apology" in a contemporary hand (to quote the closest student of its many manuscripts) is to be found at Hatfield, among Cecil's papers. That is suggestive enough. Equally significant, a copy also reached the Upper House, for it is included in a collection of journals covering the Stuart period in the Lords' library that is the only substantial record of their proceedings during James's reign. Endorsed "to be restored to Mr. Browne of Twickenham," it doubtless belonged to John Browne, the House's clerk in Charles I's reign.[91]

But the best evidence of the document's circulation comes from James himself. His speech at the end of the session was unmistakable and pointed. "You see in how many things you did not well," he said. "The best apology-maker of you all, for all his eloquence, cannot make all good. Forsooth, a goodly matter to make apologies, when no man is by to answer."[92] To say that "this proves little enough" is to fly in the face of the obvious

---

[88] Ibid., 243.

[89] BL, Harleian, 2208, fols. 156–166—a reference I owe to Christopher Thompson.

[90] *CD*, 5:433. My italics.

[91] See the discussion of the manuscripts of the "Apology" in Dunn, "Commons Debates," 1:lxxxvii–xciii, esp. lxxxviii–lxxxix. He cites (lxxxvii) A. S. McKinley's telling point, in a Bryn Mawr master's thesis I have been unable to see ("The House of Commons: Court Councillors and Law Makers, 1603–1629"), that it is to argue from silence to suggest that the "Apology" cannot have passed the House because the last record we have is of its recommitment. If so, what then possessed the clerk to start copying it into the Journal? For the Lords' copy, see House of Lords, Braye MSS. 67, fols. 338–356.

[92] Quoted in Gardiner, *England*, 1:191.

meaning of the words. And to suggest that these comments may signify no more than the king's wish to have "a statement from the Commons" is to invite incredulity.[93] His anger at the M.P.s' proceedings reverberates in every sentence; he cannot have wanted to hear another word from them. Whether officially presented or not, therefore, the "Apology" clearly did reach him, and its framers' highest expectations were thus fulfilled. And whatever its immediate disposition, it became a beacon in the development of ideas of freedom among England's gentry during these tumultuous years. As James Spedding remarked over a century ago, although the document was "not formally placed on record," it "remains to this day a notable landmark in the progress of constitutional liberty."[94]

And that is precisely the point. Political history is not made only by government policies, enacted legislation, or majority votes. The entire House had asked its leading members to draw up a statement of parliamentary rights, and they had done so. Whether or not the resultant document was voted upon, given official consent, or formally presented, it turned out to be a ringing declaration of principle, unmistakably representative of opinions oft expressed by the M.P.s. And the views it put forward neither vanished nor remained static. Of the many ideas that shaped English history in the seventeenth century, none was more potent than the demand for rights, or "freedoms," for the subject. The conviction that rights were endangered created the "Apology," made it a milestone in the development of constitutional thought, and continued to animate the gentry for decades to come. More than anyone else, it was Sandys who had helped formulate that position, and who was to lead the M.P.s in pursuing the ideals it represented during the Parliaments of the next twenty years.

From these events, and especially from his organization of proceedings and his speeches, Sir Edwin has to be identified as the decisive influence on the session of 1604. He was the dominant figure on the wardship committee and in the Union and free trade debates, and a driving force behind

[93] Elton, "High Road," 340–341. Equally remarkable is Elton's interpretation (336) of Strode's statement of June 29 (CJ, 248)—that "such of the first committee [on the Apology] . . . as found any cause of exception . . . be commanded to attend" the next committee meeting—to mean that members of the committee "had . . . attacked the proposal in the House." Earlier historians may have made occasional errors about the documentary evidence, but they hardly took such liberties with the few texts we possess.

[94] Spedding, Letters and Life, 3:213. This judgment seems unassailable, and highlights the disservice of J. P. Kenyon, ed., The Stuart Constitution, 1603–1688: Documents and Commentary (Cambridge, 1966) in omitting the "Apology." J. H. Hexter's "The Apology," in For Veronica Wedgwood these: Studies in Seventeenth-Century History, ed. R. Ollard and P. Tudor-Craig (London, 1986), 13–44, and "Parliament, Liberty, and Freedom of Elections," in Parliament and Liberty from the Reign of Elizabeth to the English Civil War ed. Hexter (Stanford, Calif., 1992), 21–55, make the argument about the document's place in the development of ideas of freedom that I adopt here.

the "Apology"—unmatched in his audacity and unique in his ability to pilot the House through uncharted paths. It was appropriate that Sandys won from Wallace Notestein the soubriquet of "the Pym of the Jacobean Parliaments," and from Menna Prestwich the accolade that "this constitutional patriot" was "the uncrowned King of the Commons in James's reign."[95]

LEADERSHIP

As befitted his newly won prominence, Sandys served on a host of miscellaneous committees: some weighty, like the body that considered the privilege case of the bishop of Bristol's book, and some less complex, such as the groups which prepared bills against "lurking and secret" outlawries and against usury (both of which committees Sir Edwin headed).[96] He also kept in touch with the discussions of religion that were prompted by the Puritans' efforts—as James put it—to build Jerusalem overnight. Here he was usually a voice for moderation, though at one point the maneuvers of Fuller and his colleagues provoked him into an uncharacteristic assault on "the cunning of lawyers" who carried ecclessiastical issues "clear contrary to the meaning of the House."[97] Other subjects that drew his attention during these crammed four months were land reclamation in the fens, the decay of tillage, scandalous books, the London Company of Skinners, and statutes against guns. He even found time to oppose enactment of a perennial parliamentary favorite: a sumptuary law condemning "excessive apparel."[98]

It was only by constant activity, by taking an interest in a broad range of business, that a leader of the Commons established his position. Throughout the next twenty years Sandys demonstrated the importance of this kind of commitment, for he was always tireless in his dedication to the day-to-day needs of the House. Planning and organization were also vital to his success, and though we will probably never know what private meetings were held on the eve of important debates (during the Whitsun recess, for example) there is no doubt that his preparations were often extensive. Re-

---

[95] Notestein made the comment to me in the mid-1960s, and evidently repeated it to other students of the Commons; Menna Prestwich, *Cranfield: Politics and Profits under the Early Stuarts* (Oxford, 1966), 143, 142. Munden's "Government and Opposition" also emphasizes that a few members dominated the House, and he documents (29, 326) the rising frequency of Sandys's speeches.

[96] *CJ*, 230, 187, 204.

[97] Quoted in D. H. Willson, *King James VI and I* (London, 1956), 249; for Sandys's involvement, see *CJ*, 178, 199, 206, 231–232, 247, 965, and (for the comment about lawyers) 979; and Dunn, "Commons Debates," 2:678.

[98] *CJ*, 207, 225–226, 228–229, 233, 235, 990, 997, 999.

searching and writing his speeches alone must have consumed many hours. And the results were plain to see.

But the heart of Sir Edwin's appeal lay, not in his tactics or maneuvers, but in his ability to grasp and elaborate a vision of England's welfare that was close to gentry hearts. Essential to this outlook was a belief in certain principles that he came back to again and again: the concern for order; the wish to avoid such threats to tradition, stability, and England's reputation as a Union with Scotland; the need of the landed class, the guardian of national welfare in the localities, to express its views on matters of great moment; the belief in the natural rights, the liberties, of the individual; and the distaste for any restriction or burden that infringed on those rights. Every statement of these ideals, moreover, was advanced by an emphasis on their reasonableness and legality that only strengthened the House's confidence in his leadership. In all these respects Sandys showed himself the embodiment of the gentry and a true pupil of Hooker, though his mistrust of monarchy set him apart, as did his daring suggestion, when parliament next met, of a distinction between king and state.[99]

Sir Edwin put his views across with intelligence and authority. Having bided his time for the first few weeks, and sensed the House's unease at government actions—the feeling that there had arisen a king over England who knew not her laws—he moved into a dominant position among the M.P.s with remarkable speed. And he was helped by rhetorical skills, especially lucidity and reasonableness, that were his natural attributes. Sandys's speeches were conceived in simple terms, with an orderly structure whose parts were frequently numbered. He spoke logically, allowing the order of his argument to flow naturally. The content, moreover, indicates a calm delivery, which must have added considerably to the impact of his words.

But his aims were anything but subdued. James must have had Sandys often in mind during his speech at the close of the session on July 7. "I will not thank where I think no thanks due," he said. Although there were many wise men in the Commons, "where many are some must needs be idle heads, some rash, some busy informers." As a result, he told them, "you have done many things rashly."[100] Those comments alone should put paid to the notion that the principal actors regarded Stuart Parliaments as essentially harmonious occasions for doing business, or as gatherings geared largely to local issues. And it is clear that the king himself had given

[99] It has been suggested, though not convincingly, that Francis Bacon held even more radical views about the shortcomings of monarchy: Robert K. Faulkner, *Francis Bacon and the Project of Progress* (London, 1993), esp. 65–68.

[100] Quoted in Gardiner, *England*, 1:190–191. Lord Chancellor Ellesmere later described Sandys as responsible for "audacious and contemptuous speeches"; but he also called him "an eloquent and learned gent": Louis A. Knafla, *Law and Politics in Jacobean England: The Tracts of Lord Chancellor Ellesmere* (Cambridge, 1977), 257.

the House more than enough cause for its "rashness." He was vacillating and tactless, devoid of the sensitivity to the moods of the M.P.s that seemed almost innate in Elizabeth and leaders like Sandys. Eager to demonstrate his learning and exalted status, James, like Shakespeare's King John, displayed the graceless action of a heavy hand. He was simply not the man to stem the self-assertion that mounted once Elizabeth's restraining presence was removed. By the end of the Parliament there could be no doubt that his honeymoon with his subjects was over.

For Sir Edwin, these three months changed his life. The ascendancy over the Commons that he won in 1604 became the chief mark of his public career. It was to be his defining characteristic and principal legacy as he continued, for over twenty years, to guide the House through some of the most difficult and important proceedings in its history.

Chapter V

"DISSENT IS ALWAYS DISPLEASING": THE SESSIONS OF 1606 AND 1607

PARLIAMENT RETURNS

Sandys was back in Westminster for the most famous of all openings of a parliamentary session—the original Guy Fawkes Day. He seems to have been present on that November 5 because he was appointed to a committee to investigate what looked like a new regulated corporation, but within four days, as a precaution against another Gunpowder Plot, the king prorogued Parliament until the following January.[1]

The sitting that began in earnest on January 21, 1606, and lasted four months, was probably the friendliest James ever enjoyed. Relieved at their escape from disaster, the M.P.s displayed unusual benevolence. They gave the king the largest grant of money he ever received, expressed fervent loyalty, and spared no effort in pursuit of his enemies, the Catholics. Bills against recusants, Jesuits, and other "popish agents and practisers" occupied much of their attention, while grievances were discussed without quite the enthusiasm of 1604. Moreover, Cecil had prepared carefully for this session, because the king, short of money, had business to conclude.[2] The more time the Commons gave to recusants or royal needs, the less they had for grumblings and defiance.

Nevertheless, the sailing was not entirely smooth, because Sandys and other independent-minded gentry did create a few patches of turbulence. The subsidies were long delayed, while the discussions of purveyance, the focus on privileges, and the final demise of the Union aroused tensions that marred the relations of the Commons with both king and Lords. For Sandys in particular, a speech on purveyance on March 8 became the occasion for a remarkable statement about the nature of the English polity.

---

[1] *CJ*, 256.

[2] Ibid., 257; D. H. Willson, "The Earl of Salisbury and the 'Court' Party in Parliament, 1604–1610," *American Historical Review* 36 (1930–31): 274–294, pp. 277–278; Pauline Croft, "Parliamentary Preparations, September 1605: Robert Cecil, Earl of Salisbury on Free Trade and Monopolies," *Parliamentary History* 6 (1987): 127–132; the Union, a potential distraction, was deferred on May 9 (*CJ*, 307).

The Grant of Subsidies

The early days were taken up primarily with Catholics and the subsidy. Sir Edwin took little part in the first of these matters.[3] The subsidy, by contrast, elicited his full attention. James's need for money had become pressing by the time he reconvened Parliament: in mid-1606, his debts stood at more than £550,000. Cecil gave the Commons a long, though exaggerated, accounting of his requirements at conferences on February 14 and 19, by which time the machinery for action was already in place.[4] On February 10 a number of the gentry identified as "popular" during the previous session demonstrated their public-mindedness by unleashing a torrent of support for a subsidy. Sir Thomas Ridgeway took the lead, and he was followed by Berkeley, Sir Edward Montague, Strode, Hastings, Hollis, and Fuller, among others, until there was general support for a grant of two subsidies and four fifteenths. Sir Edwin joined in by noting that, although "a subsidy in time of war [was a] necessity," in peacetime it was a "matter of love, virtue, thankfulness." He even admitted that "the poverty of the land [was] as much eased as may be."[5]

Such amiability was almost unique in the Jacobean Commons. It was partly due, no doubt, to the completion of payment of the previous subsidy, voted in 1601. But relief at Parliament's escape from the Catholics' plot, and the government's vigorous countermeasures, also played their part. And one must not minimize the gentry's commitment to what they perceived as England's welfare—their readiness to endorse constructive measures, and do whatever was required to ease royal burdens, once they were convinced that relief was necessary.

Yet the suspiciousness did not disappear. After their initial show of affection and good intentions, the Commons soon found a diversion in the form of purveyance. To that dispute we will return shortly, but it should be noted that they repeatedly linked this grievance with the subject of the king's income: a continuation of the 1604 exploration of ways to exchange ancient rights for a settled revenue. Indeed, it was during a debate on purveyance that the amount finally agreed upon for the king's grant, three

---

[3] Sandys served on an antirecusant committee, and occasionally spoke on the subject (including a "comely speech"), but no legislation resulted: *CJ*, 265–266, 273, 284, 286, 288, 311; D. H. Willson, ed., *The Parliamentary Diary of Robert Bowyer, 1606–1607* (Minneapolis, 1931), 28–29, 30, 35, 89. Sandys took the Hookerian line of parliamentary authority over the Church, contrary to a future ally, Sir Robert Cotton: Kevin Sharpe, *Sir Robert Cotton 1586–1631: History and Politics in Early Modern England* (Oxford, 1979), 156.

[4] F. C. Dietz, *English Public Finance, 1558–1641* (New York, 1932), 121; *Bowyer*, 43–45, 371–375.

[5] *CJ*, 266; *Bowyer*, 31.

subsidies and six fifteenths, was first suggested.[6] On the whole, however, purveyors were a distraction, and after four weeks of squabbling the king finally decided to intervene. When he had originally heard of the proposed subsidy, on February 11, he had taken "more comfort in being King over such a people so well affected towards him than in any thing in the world." Then, on March 10, he had heard from the speaker that although there "had been many and diverse projects, . . . none [were] as yet resolved on." It was true that on the fourteenth the House had held another discussion of the subject, in which Sandys had spoken of an "act of love," though he had gone on, "in a short and eloquent speech, [to move] that the 2 subsidies and 4 fifteenths which we had willingly given should go alone and not to be tainted with any heavy or unpleasing gift," i.e. increase. But still nothing had happened, not even approval of the smaller grant of two subsidies; on March 18, therefore, James reminded the M.P.s that in their "resolutions [he] requireth expedition."[7]

Remarkably enough, considering the reception that had greeted royal messages in 1604, the Commons responded by agreeing to proceed. And, even more remarkable, they eventually decided to increase the subsidy in accordance with the Crown's wishes. This was not easily accomplished, because the decisive vote in favor of an increase to three subsidies and six fifteenths passed by the narrowest of margins: 140 to 139.[8] Cecil nevertheless chose to regard the outcome as evidence that the M.P.s had "carried themselves very lovingly and dutifully to his Majesty," though he soon discovered that it was but the fortuitous visit to the Commons of one of his friends, the prominent Suffolk landowner Sir Robert Drury, that had tilted the balance.[9] The details, however, were irrelevant; what counted was that the king would get the taxes he sought.

But the manner of payment had yet to be determined, and this aroused some dispute on March 25. Bacon, introducing the bill, suggested two payments by November 1; Sandys, per contra, asked for a postponement. Although he stressed "the cheerfulness of the giver," he thought people would best be able to pay "when the commodity is come in—after harvest." He wanted the second payment completed only a year from that Easter, and the final installment two years later (in 1609). This proposal started a long debate, and in the end the House decided, by a vote of 121 to 113, that delivery of the first two subsidies should be stretched out until

[6] Ibid., 62.

[7] Ibid., 32, 73, 81, 83; CJ, 285.

[8] Ibid., 286; Bowyer, 84–85.

[9] Ibid., 84–85 n. Bowyer noted that "they which studied to please" engineered the increased subsidy.

May 1608. The last installment of the third subsidy, for a total of £390,000, was in fact received only in 1610.[10]

Still that was not the end of the matter. On April 12 the subsidy bill had its first reading, and on the 16th its second reading, but not until May 9 did it finally pass.[11] Even then, however, it caused dispute. One veteran, Sir Anthony Cope, suggested that the discussion of grievances should be completed before action was taken on the subsidy. Other M.P.s followed his lead, and someone described their actions as "capitulation with the King." Finally it was decided that, although the bill could be approved, "the subsidy should not pass up [to the Lords] until the grievances were ready, and presented to the King." The last shot came from Sandys, who reduced the value of the subsidy by attaching a proviso that exempted England's four northernmost counties from payment. He had originally wanted to end their exemption, since they no longer had to defend a troublesome border, but they had been put to considerable expense when James entered the kingdom, and so they deserved the privilege one more time. The House agreed, and the amendment was incorporated into the bill. Thanks to Cope's motion, however, it was not sent up to the Lords until May 15, a few weeks before the House adjourned.[12] Thus ungraciously did the Commons finally grant James the money he so desperately needed.

PURVEYANCE AND THE SPEECH OF MARCH 8

The one serious confrontation between Crown and subject in 1606 was over purveyance. This was a grievance on which Sandys had made no public comment in 1604, though he had been one of the main advocates of some kind of compensation as a replacement for royal prerogatives—a proposal that had first emerged from the committee on purveyance of which he had been a member. The attempt to ban the practice had failed in 1604, but it had received special mention as an "extreme, unjust, and crying oppression" in the "Apology." Ammunition was plentiful, therefore, when the question of finding redress against purveyors was brought before the House on January 24, the fourth full day of business.[13]

---

[10] Ibid., 92; *CJ*, 289; Dietz, *Public Finance*, 121, 390. For a slightly different calculation of the figures, see below chapter 6, note 1.

[11] *CJ*, 297, 299, 307.

[12] Ibid., 307; *Bowyer*, 153, 164. This linkage of supply with grievances offers an even earlier example of the connection that Thomas Cogswell revealed in the 1620s (and which he rightly chided me for missing), in his "A Low Road to Extinction? Supply and Redress of Grievances in the Parliaments of the 1620s," *Historical Journal* 33 (1990): 283–303, 285n. See, too, below chapter 6, note 58, and chapter 10, note 18.

[13] Wallace Notestein, *The House of Commons 1604–1610*, (New Haven, Conn., 1971), 134; *Bowyer*, 6; *CJ*, 259. Pauline Croft, "Parliament, Purveyance and the City of London, 1589–

Doubtless to nobody's surprise, the man who moved consideration of this familiar grievance was the M.P. most closely associated with the issue. John Hare, a clerk of the Court of Wards, had been hounding purveyors since the 1580s, but to no avail. He had most recently exposed their corrupt dealings in 1604, and even James himself had been surprised at the peculations that were uncovered. Nevertheless, no action had been taken, as Hare now reminded the House "in a good comely speech." He had a bill prepared, he said, which he persuaded the Commons to order read the following day. This measure, which Croft argues would have brought about "the collapse of purveyance" without compensation for the king, seems to have been considered by a committee on January 29 and read for the first time on February 1. There the matter rested until February 11, when Hare reminded the House of his bill and asked if it was to "be proceeded in or to sleep." This prodding had its effect, because the Commons decided on a double course of action: not only was the bill "to be proceeded in," but the matter was to be raised in conference with the Lords so that a joint petition could be submitted to His Majesty.[14]

As with wardship in 1604, however, the Lords turned out to be the stumbling block. Hare appeared at the conference on February 14 fully armed with supporting documents and a "long and well composed" speech which he evidently delivered with some vehemence.[15] He presented in "sorrow and grief" a daunting catalogue of wickedness and abuse. But the Upper House was not of a mind to wallow in recrimination. Cecil's response was an acid reprimand. Although the king had shown the Commons love and favor, they had repaid him with an ill reward. It was James himself who had mentioned purveyors in an earlier message, "thinking there was none among you that would take on them to be Tribunes of the people," but he had obviously been mistaken. Now, instead of joy and "gratulation," the proceedings seemed to "begin with sorrow and end with misery." Cecil agreed to pass the Commons' views along to the king, yet he could not resist a parting shot: "I must say that the manner of your complaint is mixed with vinegar."[16]

1608," *Parliamentary History* 4 (1985): 9–34, seems more persuasive on this grievance than Eric Lindquist, "The King, the People and the House of Commons: The Problem of Early Jacobean Purveyance," *Historical Journal* 31 (1988): 549–570.

[14] J. E. Neale, *Elizabeth I and Her Parliaments, 1584–1601* (London, 1957), 208–209; Notestein, *Commons 1604–1610*, 32; Croft, "Purveyance," 23; *CJ*, 262; *Bowyer*, 6–7, 10–11, 16, 32–33; below, note 16.

[15] *Bowyer*, 38–41.

[16] Ibid., 41–42. Despite old obligations to Lord Burghley, Hare had long clashed with Cecil: Neale, *Parliaments*, 361. As usual, the Lords emphasized the debt the M.P.s owed James for his easy succession, while the Commons insisted that the king owed them a favor because of his reception.

The next day, the fifteenth, Hare told his colleagues what had happened, but the Lower House pressed on regardless. By February 19 a collection of articles against purveyors had been assembled (on that day alone four new ones were added) and they were sent up to the Lords. This time, however, Cecil was more conciliatory: he asked that his previous words "might be no more remembered," and cleared Hare "of all, saving of miscarriage." When this was reported to the Commons the next day, at the same time as the lord treasurer's accounting of the king's debts, the suspicious gentry, ever sensitive to their rights, swung into action. Strode opened the debate by recalling "the grievance of the country"; he was followed by Yelverton and Martin, who wanted Hare cleared and grievances remedied before a subsidy was mentioned.[17] After more discussion, Secretary Herbert reminded his colleagues of the king's wants and asked for a committee, but Sandys brought the debate back to the ill humor it retained for the rest of the day.

Harping on the treatment accorded to Hare, Sir Edwin darkly warned that "Parliament is no Parliament, if not free." Once they allowed the "precedent of a fault," it could be a "prejudice to future times." There was no point in being accommodating, because "pax, isto modo pacta, non est pax; est pactio servitutis"—a peace of that kind was the peace of servitude. He therefore moved "that Mr. Hare might be cleared by this House first, and [that] then a message [be sent] to the Lords, upon a conference, importing so much." As if that were not enough, he asked "that their Lordships would not, in future time, censure any, without the judgement of this House." These blunt recommendations ended any thought of a subsidy for a while. Even a long-time supporter of the Crown like Sir George More asked that the Commons "right" themselves, and Sir John Hollis, close to Sandys since 1604, made a motion "that the House should first be delivered from this obstruction and obloquy." On the question being put, it was resolved that Hare had not erred and that his innocence was to be conveyed to the Lords by the purveyance committee. The gentry's concerns about rights and liberties were again front and center.

There was more of the same on February 23, after which, on the twenty-fifth and twenty-sixth, the bill against purveyors was officially read. On the latter day the Lords sent a message saying they were expecting the bill, and Sandys judiciously warned that it had better be carefully framed: "if His Majesty's rights be not saved, he giveth no consent."[18] The major issue now was the question of composition: the compensation the king was to receive for the loss of his prerogative. This had been a central topic of discussion on the twenty-fifth, and it remained conspicuous as the M.P.s

---

[17] *Bowyer*, 46, 47, 48; *CJ*, 269–272 cover the debate.
[18] Ibid., 274, 275; *Bowyer*, 50–55.

anxiously sought some means of avoiding the impression that they were infringing on the king's undoubted rights—a subject of great concern both in another conference with the Lords on February 27, and in further lengthy debates on March 5, 6, and 7.[19] Opinions were sharply divided, with the independent-minded M.P.s by and large rejecting composition and official spokesmen speaking in its favor. Hare himself was against composition, as were such stalwart gentry as Fuller, Berkeley, Yelverton, and Lawrence Hyde. Bacon, on the other hand, was its chief advocate. As for James's senior councillor, Herbert, the best he could muster was an attempt to stay above the fray by assuring the M.P.s that they would doubtless be "well satisfied" if only they would "augment" their "gift" to the king. Thus the discussion continued, to and fro, through two final debates, on March 8 and 11, before the bill finally passed (apparently without provisions for compensation, which made its proposals pointless) on the 18th.[20]

Sandys's chief contribution was a long speech on the eighth that turned into a major statement about the nature of English society and government. It followed a royal message in which James tried lamely to halt criticism by saying that he himself wanted to end abuses and that he would let the law bring about a "reformation." Sir Edwin spoke "above an hour and half" in defense of the M.P.s' actions and against composition. When he finished, the latter was virtually a dead issue, and the former had led him to an extraordinary assessment of the role of gentry like himself.[21]

Admitting that he had not been a prime mover in discussions of purveyance (he had been "a hearer and no speaker"), he nevertheless wanted to remind the House that it had had "a most gracious message from the King. We may be glad of such a prince as sendeth such reports," and he hoped the Commons would respond in kind to the assurance of redress. The M.P.s had obligations both to the "country" and to the King, but what they had to avoid was "extremity": that is, "extremity of flattery to the prince [or] popularity to the state." The first provided "no assurance," and the second was "dangerous"; moreover, "of the two I hold the latter the greater" danger. The results of flattery were well known: its practitioners "spread a net for their own feet." But "popularity is won with a trifle and lost in an instant": a remarkable comment from a leader of the Commons. "Great men," he continued, "can only be populars, for from hence we

[19] Ibid., 57–67; *CJ*, 276–280.

[20] Ibid., 280–283; *Bowyer*, 70–77, 82 n; see below, note 24.

[21] Ibid., 68–72 and 70 n., which prints BL, Harleian, 6846, fol. 197, a copy of Sandys's speech by Sir Robert Harley; *CJ*, 280–281. Sandys's rejection of the notion that issues like purveyance were raised for "popularity"—to please constituents—is the only evidence for Lindquist's view (in his "Purveyance") that the bill was proposed to please the "country." The M.P.s sound genuinely concerned, and Sandys's arguments echo the themes of reform and good government that he promoted throughout his parliamentary career.

return to our private" existence. In other words, it was the people who constituted "the state" whom the M.P.s had to face all their lives, and to whom their actions would ultimately have to be true.

This was the credo of the independent gentry, forged in magistracy in their localities: a succinct self-justification and vision of a gentry state that is unique in the records of Jacobean Parliaments. For the clerk writing the official journal, it was a "protestation touching popularity": an apt evocation of the defensive connotation of "protestation." Sandys did admit that anything that harmed the head also harmed the body, but he reaffirmed his own "popularity," and the grievances from which it sprang, with the statement: "For my popularity I protest I come hither, though with a weak understanding yet with a tearful heart." The advocacy of natural rights thus led Sandys to distinguish between king and state, between government and governed. It is the clearest assertion in his career of a belief that English politics depended fundamentally on a kind of gentry democracy. Sandys bestowed on his "country" a sovereignty that was not again to be so clearly defined by an M.P. until the revolutionary 1640s.

At this point Sandys shifted the focus to purveyance. The report of the king's debts, he said, was "the heaviest news that ever came to court of Parliament." And he reached that conclusion "not out of popularity, but out of those words: fear God and honor the King." For all the "peace and tranquility" the King's succession had brought there could be no doubt that "the peace [had] much wormwood in it." A plague had replaced the war, and it "hath wasted more than a hundred years of war." As a result, poverty abounded: an amazing reversal of Sir Edwin's assurance, a month earlier, that England's poverty was "as much eased as may be."[22] Facts were adjustable to the argument of the moment, especially when the main point was to proclaim a vision of good policy and show concern for the national welfare. Yet Sandys insisted on his good will: "I speak not to hinder liberality, because speeches have gone all one way. But to lay this [poverty] in a contrary balance."

And how did this affect purveyance? It argued against composition, for Sandys bluntly noted that there could be "no such composition, as suits the easiness of the burden, and the greatness of His Majesty's wants." Nothing the M.P.s offered that was equivalent to purveyance could meet the king's needs, and they would also be setting a "dangerous" precedent: thereafter James could compound for any "oppression," thus making all lands tributary, subject to a kind of rent. This, Sandys claimed, was unlike wardship, whose composition was to be drawn only from lands already held of the king: not a very strong argument, but one that Sir Edwin had supported in 1604, which indicates how profoundly difficult the settling of royal finances had become. Sandys concluded that the bill ought to go forward, even

[22] See above, note 5.

though it seemed unlikely, after thirty-six unsuccessful laws against purveyance, that a thirty-seventh would do much good. Yet he did have a
practical suggestion for compensation, to ensure that the king "shall not
meddle with the possessions of the people"—an assertion of the in-
violability of private property that was at the heart of the gentry's world-
view.

What Sandys recommended was that the Fens be drained; though the
cost would be borne by the subject, he thought they could then be used
for the benefit of the Crown. The newly uncovered lands, he estimated,
would be worth about £40,000 a year. This suggestion (possibly inspired by
his brother Miles's interest in fen drainage) showed Sir Edwin in statesmanlike mode, trying responsibly to solve real problems. The proposal was
taken up, in the form of James abolishing purveyance once the income
reached £30,000 per annum, but the legislation was rejected later in the
session.[23]

There was some rather aimless discussion when Sandys finished, and the
following day the question of composition reappeared yet again. But no
progress was made; the bill was returned to committee; and it passed the
following week, apparently without compensation for the king.[24] But the
effort came to naught, for the legislation died in the Lords.

Sandys's contribution to the debate on purveyors may have been relatively minor as far as the issue itself was concerned, but his remarks on
March 8 deserve attention because of the general considerations he introduced. Virtually alone among the members of the Lower House, he always
seemed capable of rising above the endless details to a discussion of
broader principles: public welfare, an M.P.'s responsibilities, the inviolabil-
ity of property, and the place of purveyance (or alternatives) in the total
structure of royal finance. From the earliest days of his leadership of the
Commons, Sir Edwin recognized that it was on this plane that he could
wield his influence most effectively. Always trying to make his colleagues
aware of the wider import of their decisions, he was the voice of the gentry
in their role as governors of the realm.

THE HOUSE AND ITS PRIVILEGES

One of the features of the session of 1606 was its recurrent display of
friction between the two Houses of Parliament. Apart from the protest
(joined by Sandys) at the treatment of Hare, a fear was expressed that the

[23] *Bowyer*, 71, 157; *CJ*, 308. Lindquist rightly points out the importance of this proposal:
"Purveyance," 567–568. I owe the suggestion of the link with Miles to Mark Kennedy.

[24] *CJ*, 281–283; *Bowyer*, 73–77. No copy of the final measure has survived, but neither the
original proposal (ibid., 10–11) nor the description of the bill that passed (*CJ*, 287) mentions
composition. It thus seems plausible, albeit an argument from silence, that the bill simply
attacked purveyance.

Lords were trying to "surprise" the Commons by raising issues for which members were unprepared when they met in conferences. As a result, to the great annoyance of the peers, committees were given strictly limited authority and forbidden to exceed their instructions. The Lords, by contrast, pointedly gave their representatives full powers, and even spent entire mornings going over an issue so as "to be the better prepared" for conferences in the afternoon. The ill feeling extended even to the traditional forms of deference when Fuller denounced the custom that required the Commons to stand at conferences while the Lords sat.[25]

Despite their compliance in 1606, therefore, the M.P.s were still capable of disgruntled behavior. And even a relatively popular royal spokesman like Bacon had his difficulties. He might have shrugged off the misfortune of being caught out in a misquotation of Horace, but he cannot have appreciated the response of one independently inclined M.P., Sir John Savile, who said he had almost been convinced by one of Sir Francis's speeches until he remembered that "eloquence" is a "thief." Bacon later mused on his predicament with characteristic self-understanding: "when he doth well," he said, "no man better; when he doth ill, no man worse."[26]

Overall, it was a desultory session. The talk of purveyance led nowhere; the antagonism to Catholics had no significant consequences; and the grant of a subsidy not only took an unconscionable time in passing, but remained entangled in squabbles over grievances. Despite Sandys's energy (he was was named to more than 30 of the session's 130 committees), much committee work never reached the floor of the House, not even when the task was "to frame the grievances into a petition."[27] Nor did the bills he guided toward passage leave much mark on proceedings. He managed to put into law a statute dissolving companies of merchants trading to Spain and France, who were granted monopolies in 1604 that (despite heavy outport membership) contravened the spirit of the abortive 1604 Free Trade bill. Yet the considerable efforts this must have taken were but briefly mentioned in the Journal.[28]

---

[25] *Bowyer*, 108, 158; BL, Additional, 48,160, fol.33; *LJ*, 2:371, 378, 407; D. M. Willson, *The Privy Councillors in the House of Commons, 1604–1629* (Minneapolis, 1940), 230–231. More generally, see ibid., 225–236, and Angela Britton, "The House of Lords in English Politics 1604–1614" (D.Phil. diss., Oxford University, 1982), 54–84. The ill feeling between the two Houses seems genuine, and not merely tactical, as Lindquist, "Purveyance," 566 argues. It is true that the Lords were less touchy about their privileges: Elizabeth R. Foster, *The House of Lords 1603–1649: Structure, Procedure and the Nature of Its Business* (Chapel Hill, N.C., 1983). But they could be unpleasant to the Commons, dismissing their discomfort at conferences (in 1604, too) as the result of too many representatives being sent to meetings.

[26] *Bowyer*, 88, 120, 297.

[27] *CJ*, 300.

[28] Ibid., 304. The resultant statute was 3 Jas. 1, c. 6. The definitive account of its passage, emphasizing the combination of outport and gentry interests that brought it about, is Pauline

Much more space was given to a contretemps whose triviality seems to have been outweighed, in the judgment of the clerk of the Commons, by its overtones of breach of privilege. On February 18 Sandys reported that his coachman had been committed to Newgate Prison by Sir Robert Leigh, a justice of the peace. It turned out that in fact two of his servants, Richard Hill and William Jones, had been sent to jail. The House's sensibilities were at once aroused, and various speakers gave vent to their indignation. One of the "populars," Sir Robert Wingfield, took charge of the case for the Committee for Privileges, and by February 21 he had Leigh before the bar of the Commons. If the M.P.s were expecting an assault on their rights, they were quickly disappointed. "Sir Robert Leigh protesteth," so the Journal recorded, "it was his desire to be acquainted with Sir Edwin, because he had read of his works." Such was the price of fame! To its credit, "the house greatly laughed," and two days later found Leigh guilty but released him from the charges because of his confession.[29]

It is tantalizing to be given the details of an incident like this while silence engulfs committee proceedings. We can only guess that Sandys shepherded through the House the legislation that confirmed the title, property, and incorporation of his old college, Corpus Christi, though we do know he was prominent in the efforts, toward the end of the session, to enforce attendance by M.P.s. Matters reached such a pass that one division, on April 24, elicited only fifty-seven votes: little more than a tenth of the members. Unlike the opening of the 1604 session, when more gentry appeared than had ever been seen before, it was now becoming difficult to keep their interest. Sir Edwin was vigorous in demanding that members be "required" to appear, a usage he softened when he explained "that the word require, was no more than to desire, and so used in all the north parts where he had lived, and so observed."[30] He also defended Yelverton from a charge of disloyalty because he had recommended deliberation before the House passed the Act of Attainder against the Guy Fawkes conspirators.[31] This focus on privileges was the small change of day-to-day

---

Croft, "Free Trade and the House of Commons, 1605–6," *Economic History Review*, 2d ser., 28 (1975), 17–27. An exemption for Exeter merchant adventurers trading to France was passed later: 4 Jas. 1, c. 9. The Lords evidently caused some difficulty over the first bill, but there is no indication of the substance of their objections, except that they found the document "general and imperfect," See *LJ*, 2:412, 416, 418, 421–424. On the last page the clerk noted that the bill finally "was received with great applause." In his preparations for the session, Cecil had certainly hoped to be accommodating in this area: see Croft, "Parliamentary Preparations."

[29] *CJ*, 270, 272; *Bowyer*, 48, 50.

[30] *CJ*, 282, 300, 140 (Parliament opening), 292; *Bowyer*, 97; L. L. Shadwell, ed., *Enactments in Parliament Specially Concerning the Universities of Oxford and Cambridge*, vol. 1 (Oxford, 1912), 1:231–236 (the Corpus bill).

[31] *Bowyer*, 101.

parliamentary procedure, but it dominated this first session of 1606 because, apart from purveyance, no major issue aroused the interest of the
House.

The irritability did not escape the notice of the king, who opened the
second session of 1606 with a scolding: "There is in Parliament . . . diversity of spirits, . . . some of them more popular than profitable. . . . There
were some Tribunes of the People."[32] If the relatively amenable disposition
of the House in this session could not satisfy him, then he had even less
cause for pleasure when Parliament reassembled later that year. The
Union was once again before the assembly, and Sandys returned to the
foreground.

ASSAULTS ON THE UNION

The opening round of the final encounter on the Union was brief but
suggestive. It lasted less than a month, because when the House gathered
in late November 1606 there were only a few weeks to Christmas. Yet in
that brief time all the good will seemed to dissipate. On the fifth day of
proper business, November 24, the Lords asked for a conference on the
Union. Since the Commons had ignored the issue thus far, they decided,
before appointing a huge, hundred-man committee, that their representatives were "not to confer, but to hear what the Lords will propound, and to
report to the House." At that conference, on the twenty-sixth, the earl of
Northampton mentioned hearing that the Union might be in trouble, a
rumor that seemed confirmed by the Lower House's behavior. The Lords
were furious: they demanded that the committee be given adequate
powers, because "if all were hearers, none speakers, it would be uncomfortable; . . . by silence there was impediment in the business." After further exchanges, the Commons finally gave way on November 28.[33]

But tensions were not easing. On the twenty-seventh Fuller said he had
heard that one of the M.P.s who had been a commissioner for drawing up
the Instrument of Union had refused to sign the final document. This was
admitted by that veteran maverick, Sir Edward Hobby, who explained
"that no Commission hath been at any time called in question for his
assent or dissent; but that the major part hath overruled it, and the rest
wrapped up in silence, as it were in a void, and committed to oblivion."[34]
In other words, this was not quite the unanimous and unassailable document it was said to be. Such a revelation, coming at the very outset of the

---

[32] *CJ*, 314.

[33] Ibid., 324, 1004, 325–326. On November 22 Bowyer (189) noted that "all this day, the
Instrument of Union lay on the desk before the clerk, but not moved by any man to be read,
or dealt withal." For further background, see above, chapter 4, note 21.

[34] *CJ*, 325; *Bowyer*, 194.

debate, could only weaken the Crown's case. There followed a truculent discussion of the conference with the Lords, notable for a speech by Sandys who recommended a new procedure that was to have momentous consequences.[35]

Sir Edwin was clearly worried about conferences. Although everyone, of course, wanted "to satisfy his Majesty," there was a problem about the meetings with the Lords: "it hath been an observation that we have usually lost more by one treaty, than we have got by two battles. I pray God this be not so, and in the conference with the Lords we have rather lost ground commonly than gained." Nevertheless, "though I am not in love with conferences, yet I like of it at this time." Having said that, however, he still felt that meticulous preparation was essential. The House had to "debate thoroughly before our meeting": it had to go over everything "by points." But a normal exchange of views was impossible in a regular debate, since no member could speak more than once on a single topic. Therefore, he said, they ought to proceed "by a committee, because there a reply is admitted, which is not here." Open give and take was essential if they were to do justice to the task that lay before them. Thus was born the device of using a Committee of the Whole House to permit the free exchange of ideas, a vital step on the path toward unhampered discussion. And two days later, on November 29, Sandys's proposal became a reality when "it was resolved that a committee should be appointed to treat every afternoon, of the articles [of the union], and to report the next day what they had done.... And all the House to be present, and have free speech."[36]

At last Parliament was getting down to the business at hand. The Instrument of Union was not a complicated document, and the king might have been forgiven for expecting fairly easy passage. Only three measures were proposed: repeal of all laws expressing hostility toward the other nation, establishment of equal commercial rights for Scotsmen and Englishmen, and bestowal of a common nationality on all the king's subjects, with the one exception of those born before James assumed England's Crown (the "ante-nati") who could not hold royal office or sit in Parliament in the other country until there was such "a perfect and full accomplishment of the Union, as is mutually desired by both the realms."[37] Of the three rec-

---

[35] The debate is in ibid., 195–198; Sandys's speech is on 197–198 n.

[36] Ibid., 199. The first Lords Committee of the Whole met on December 1: *LJ*, 2:456–457. This development is a classic instance of unintended consequences, because the committee was created for official ends: Sheila Lambert, "Procedure in the House of Commons in the Early Stuart Period," *English Historical Review* 95 (1980): 763–767. Lambert subsequently recognized that Court-initiated procedures could come to serve "popular" aims: "Committees, Religion, and Parliamentary Encroachment on Royal Authority in Early Stuart England," *English Historical Review* 105 (1990): 79.

[37] *CJ*, 323. The Instrument is on 318–323.

ommendations, only the first became law; the other two faced objections virtually from the start, and eventually succumbed to the attacks of the Commons.

During the three weeks before the Christmas recess, only a few opening shots were fired. On December 4, 8, and 11 English merchants came to complain that the commercial provisions were one-sidedly advantageous to the Scots.[38] And that shrewd poser of difficult questions, Nicholas Fuller, ingenuously asked that escuage be included among the laws they intended to repeal. This ancient feudal right, which obliged the king's tenants-in-chief to supply him with troops, was hardly relevant. But, as one of Cecil's informants, Thomas Wilson, told the lord treasurer, Fuller soon "pulled off his mask and said plainly that it tended to taking away of wards." Grievances came all too easily to the Commons, and despite displays of "storm and tempest" by the Lords, there was no indication that anything concrete had been accomplished by the time the recess began on December 18.[39]

When the members assembled again, on February 10, the speaker reported that they were moving toward decisions in the area of commerce, but that a whole series of exceptions to a full union had been suggested: in particular, that as long as the Scots continued to hold a privileged position in France (as some merchants claimed), they should be treated as aliens in England. This report aroused the M.P.s' latent hostility, notably in the person of Sir Christopher Piggott, who denounced the Scots in "many words of scandal and obloquy." To the clerk's amazement, Piggott's intemperateness was not reproved.[40] Instead, other M.P.s made sure the speaker's report would not stand as the opinion of the House, and the next day Fuller bluntly denounced two of the proposals. Although he approved the repeal of hostile laws, he thought the provisions for commerce ridiculous: a man who owned two manors, one rich, one poor, did not expect both to make an equal profit. And naturalization went completely against nature: one did not "mingle two swarms of bees under one hive, upon a sudden."[41]

Objections of this kind continued to pour forth on the seventeenth,

---

[38] Ibid., 327, 1009; *Bowyer*, 203 n.

[39] Ibid., 201 n, 208 n. Wilson was suggesting that abolition of one tenant-in-chief obligation would threaten all others.

[40] *CJ*, 332–333. When the king complained, Piggott was belatedly expelled from the House and sent to the Tower: ibid., 335–336, 344. He and Hobby became the subject of a scurrilous couplet that commemorated a loud indiscretion that had stopped the House in its tracks: "Then quoth Sir Edward Hobby, well oiled with the spigot / If you fart not the union, beware of Kitt Piggott." Nottingham University MSS., PW V, 34, 36—a reference I owe to Vivienne Millenson. Other versions are in BL, Harleian, 5191, fols. 17–18, and 4931, fols. 10, 19; and Stowe 354, fol. 43. Sandys in these verses promotes "a digression" which "shall last you a whole session."

[41] *CJ*, 334–335, 1013.

eighteenth and twenieth. The one effective defender of the king was Bacon, whose citation of historical analogies and criticism of the "pittances and reckonings" of the House must have struck home. But there was no mistaking the direction of the tide. As one member put it, "the matter of the union could be compared to a bowling alley—a little rub putteth the bowl aside."[42] Sandys could thus remain quietly in the background, watching his colleagues draw toward a conclusion that he had foreshadowed in 1604.

His first known speech on the Union was given on February 23, when the House was preparing to confer with the Lords on naturalization. So many comments had been made on the subject that he thought it best to divide the various topics among different members so as to help them argue more effectively in the meeting. The House agreed, and the following day assigned specific duties to ten members of the committee. Bacon was to lead off with a preamble, and Sandys, together with Sir Roger Owen (who seems to have served as a backup), was to deal with the first issue: the "reasons and precedents, touching the moral law of nations." Sir Edwin gave this speech to the Lords on February 26 and reported it on the 28th.[43]

Taking as his point of departure the absence of precedents for the Union in common law, Sandys examined the guidance offered by the *jus gentium*, the general law of nations. And he found seven reasons to doubt that the proposed naturalization was acceptable. First, the whole trend of history was to create kingdoms that were "more distinct, more formal, more regular." When states were no more than "heaps of people," subjection was equivalent to naturalization, but this was no longer true. Second, there was the inequality of the two countries' laws: once upon a time they had been equal, but no more. Third, the consequences could not be foreseen. "Kingdoms sometimes rend and divide, and after glue again," he said. Rome herself had given birth to thirty kingdoms, while within the previous century Europe's eleven kingdoms had shrunk to six (an interesting if incomprehensible calculation). "Accidents of time do alter governments, and add unto them," which might mean automatic naturalization for all subsequent acquisitions. Fourth, Sandys noted, was another inequality: the Scots would contribute only to joint defense, while the English would continue to bear a heavier burden of taxes and impositions (customs duties) at the same time as joining in mutual defense. The fifth and sixth objections emphasized how much more England was offering, in the case

---

[42] Ibid., 336–339, 1009. Bacon's speech is on 336–337 and 1015.

[43] Ibid., 339–340, 345, 1020, 1023; T. B. Howell, ed., *State Trials*, vol. 2 (London, 1816), 563.

of a complete naturalization, than was normal in other countries. And finally, everything that prevented acceptance of the "post-nati" (born after Elizabeth's death) also excluded the ante-nati. His conclusion was "that [the Scots] are better than aliens, but not equal with natural subjects."

It was a typically magisterial report, cogent and decisive, and throughout the remainder of the session nobody really challenged the stand Sandys had taken. For a couple of days, however, the "great cause" was shunted aside as the two Houses bickered over matters of the utmost triviality. On March 4 Sir Edward Hobby had taken a message to the Lords about the scheduling of another conference. In the customary phrase, he had referred to himself as the delegate of the "knights, citizens, burgesses and barons of the Commons court of Parliament." The Upper House must have been close to the end of its tether over the delays, because it "did expostulate with him," demanding what right he had to use the words "barons" and "court." When reporting this to the Commons the next day, Hobby defended himself by saying the term "barons" came from the writs for the election of M.P.s by the Cinque Ports, which referred to the representatives as "barons." As for the House being a court, since it acted as a court of record in elections, it deserved the title. Although the Commons decided that their "dignity [and] privilege" had not been "impeached," and that it was "not fit to stand" on the word "court," they did insist on their right to "barons." The Lords, though declaring themselves "not satisfied," dropped the issue, but did smugly point out that the statute in which "barons" were mentioned was not of 9 Hen. 8, as the Commons thought, but of 6 Hen. 8.[44] There, at last, the matter rested; sanity returned, and Parliament again took up the Union.

Sandys was now clearly in control of proceedings, and over the next few days, in a succession of long speeches, he established the House's position on the complex issue of naturalization. The greatest judges in the land, including Sir Edward Coke, had delivered their opinions to the Lords on February 25, asserting that the post-nati were not aliens. From this conclusion the Commons dissented, and Sir Edwin laid out their objections in great detail when reporting on a conference with the Lords on March 7.[45] They had gone over the arguments "with great pain," he said, but could not avoid the conclusion that ante-nati and post-nati should be treated as one, that is, neither should be considered naturalized. Not only did this view go counter to the recommendation of the commissioners on the Union, but it was to be overturned in Calvin's case, the following year, when the post-nati were confirmed as full-fledged Englishmen.[46] Sir Ed-

[44] CJ, 348, 349, 1026; LJ, 2:483; Bowyer, 212–214, 217–218.
[45] Howell, State Trials, 2:567–575; LJ, 2:476; Bowyer, 218–224; CJ, 349–350, 1027–1028.
[46] Howell, State Trials, 2:575–695.

win, however, was quite unabashed in recommending "that reasons should modestly be given of our dissent in opinion from the judges."

And indeed, the justification he offered was about as modest as it could have been. One of the judges (out of eleven!) had dissented; furthermore, they had not been sitting in their official capacities in a court of justice; and, not having heard the Commons' reasons, they had spoken without examining both sides of the case. Continuing at the same petty level, he stressed that the word "naturalization" was fraught with misunderstanding and could only "be used with protestation." It seemed that Sandys was building up to a denunciation of the entire proposal, but at this point he unveiled perhaps the cleverest maneuver of his parliamentary career. Instead of chipping away at the Union, as he had since 1604, he suddenly announced that he and his colleagues wanted no part of the compromises, the "imperfect union," that the commissioners and the Lords were advocating. Rather, they sought a perfect Union. The two countries should not keep their own laws and parliaments, as the terms of the Instrument would have permitted, but should merge completely.

The brilliance of this move was that it placed the Commons beyond criticism, since they now appeared to be following the king's real wishes, "for it seemeth . . . that his Majesty desireth a perfect union." But in fact the tactic was a classic example of the good undermined by the best. Not only was Sir Edwin fully aware that such complete fusion "cannot be done in an instant" (and delay was likely to be fatal) but he demanded "that the Scottish nation be ruled by our laws, and participate all benefits with us." One side alone was to give up its institutions—obviously an impossible request. The most cunning consequence of this about-face, however, was its implications for the immediate problem of making the detailed arrangements that were required by the Instrument. "The less we yield to them by this imperfect union," Sandys said, "the more we shall draw them to the perfect, when they shall see the impediment to be in themselves." The Commons' ultimately benevolent aim thus forced them to be nasty in the short run. It would be hard to imagine a more adroit way of sabotaging the entire project.

With the House's good intentions established, the objections to the imperfect Union could pour forth: the Scots' special relationship with France, the danger of their inheriting English land while not being subject to England's laws, the likelihood of transfers of wealth across the border, the complexities of wardships held in another country, and the restrictions that would be needed on the holding of ecclesiastical, university, or legal offices. Each of these topics was assigned to a different member of the committee; between them, they presented a devastating case against the proposal. Summing up, Sandys told the Lords that the Lower House's dearest wish was to abolish the "restrictions" implicit in the Instrument, and that

the refusal to bestow "all benefits" on the Scots stemmed from the M.P.s'
fear that such generosity "may hinder them and keep them from seeking
the perfect union by us desired."[47]

The Lords asked for a week to consider these developments, and Sandys
requested, and received, the authority to discuss the Commons' position
when the Upper House made its reply on March 14. In the meantime,
there were complaints, yet again, about the discomfort of having to stand
while the peers sat, but Cecil refused to give up one of his few advantages:
if "yourselves will not oppress," he said, "or thrust one another in this
place, . . . we doubt not but you shall find more ease." He then answered
Sandys point by point, yielding almost nothing, insisting on the appropriateness of the Instrument, and leaving the perfect Union to "be
wrought by time and opportunity." He was particularly adamant on the
question of the ante-nati and post-nati: they had to be distinguished (the
former, for example, could not be justices of the peace in England) because otherwise (as everyone must have realized) no naturalization would
be possible.[48] But Sandys was equally firm. He admitted the force of the
proverb "love little, and love long"; nonetheless, if the imperfect Union
demanded by the Scots was instituted, it could not include free naturalization. "Not fit," he argued, "to grant perfect privileges of naturalization un-
limited to an unperfect union." Unless, therefore, the Lords gave them
"leave to handle the ante-nati and the post-nati both alike," the Commons
would "humbly give your Lordships audience, but not any answer" at the
conference.[49]

This infuriated the Upper House. "Putting their heads together," their
committee "did confer long." Cecil then announced that, although they
had hoped to hear from others "better able than he that had spoken" (i.e.
Sandys), they would "shut it up" until they could have a conference, not an
audience. Nor did they ever want to "meet with them who are like to take
a dissent for displeasure"—a direct reprimand to Sandys, Cecil's one-time
protégé, who had excused himself by saying he was sorry "to deliver anything displeasing to your Lordships, and dissent is always displeasing." For
all their anger, however, the peers hardly typified public opinion. To his
undoubted chagrin, Cecil soon learned that Sir Edwin's speech had won
"general commendation."[50]

Sandys's claim that he had expected the conference "to clear the wicked
imputation of the opposition of the Lower House" to the Union must have
had a rather hollow ring. Cecil's reaction, conveyed in a letter he wrote the

---

[47] *Bowyer*, 224–225; PRO, SP/14/26, fols. 88–89.
[48] *CJ*, 351, 352; *Bowyer*, 232–237.
[49] Ibid., 237–239.
[50] Ibid., 239–240.

next day, was the vain hope "that the Lower House would feel their own omissions and send to explain themselves."[51] He was afraid that they would openly declare the judges' advice on the post-nati invalid, but he was spared this open confrontation by the speaker, who conveniently fell ill that very day. In his absence the Commons could not meet, and his indisposition was diplomatically prolonged for almost two weeks.

Not until March 27 did the Lords ask that open discussion resume, emphasizing that they wanted to retain the distinction between ante-nati and post-nati, but "without prejudice or conclusion."[52] This time, however, Sandys did not need to urge his views, for his colleagues were fully prepared to thwart the Upper House. Lawrence Hyde at once argued for the perfect Union and the linkage of ante-nati and post-nati, and the next day he was supported by various M.P.s, including Sir Herbert Croft, Wingfield, and Cope. Carleton and Bacon tried to move the Commons into a more sympathetic course, but to no avail.[53] When Parliament broke up for the Easter recess on March 31, the two Houses still had not met on the Union.

James addressed the M.P.s before they departed, and as usual he expatiated upon his disappointments.[54] They had heard "long precogitate orations," he said, whereas "fewest words, with most matter, doth become best"—not a recommendation that he himself took very seriously. Because they had been long-winded, consideration of the Union had dragged out beyond all expectation, bedevilled by "many crosses, long disputations, strange questions, ... delays and curiosity." He then explained that by a perfect Union he did not mean a "confusion of all things": the law should be uniform, but many "particulars" could remain. "Every honest man desireth a perfect union; but they that say so, and admit no preparation thereto, have *mel in ore, sel in corde.*" This was a barely veiled reference to the sourness of the Commons, underlined with the comment that "after your so long talk of union, in all this long session of Parliament, you rise, without agreeing upon any particular." On the question of the ante-nati and post-nati they had been led astray by "flattering speeches" and "sophisms," when instead they ought to have relied on his justice and wisdom. Throughout the speech, which must have taken some two hours to deliver, James appealed to his audience to trust him, to put their future in his hands, to grant his honest wish, and to "cut off all vain questions." He could not have misjudged their feelings more completely; given yet another chance to establish the Union (in more than two months of meetings

---

[51] *CJ*, 1030; *Bowyer*, 240 n.
[52] *CJ*, 356.
[53] *Bowyer*, 243–251.
[54] *CJ*, 357–363.

after the Easter recess) the Commons put paid to the king's hopes once and for all.

THE END OF THE UNION

The members certainly did not flock eagerly back to London after the break: when the session reopened, on April 20, not many more than fifty appeared in the Commons.[55] Over the next week more of them drifted back, and on April 28 a major discussion of the Union was finally held. The opening speaker was Sandys, whose "long and learned speech," presented "with method, and variety of argument," laid out the case for the perfect union, now with the added justification that that was what the king had said he wanted in his March 31 speech.[56] What the M.P.s were required to do, he said, interpreting James's comments about the lack of concrete action, was to make specific preparations. Everyone (king, commissioners, Lords, Commons) was in favor of the principle, and this meant that they had to establish a single Parliament and law for both realms. It also meant that "we not need to treat of ante and post-nati, . . . nor to be troubled with assurance of performance" or the Franco-Scottish alliance. To get down to substance, they had first to pass the act abolishing hostile laws, and then to open up commerce with the Scots, at least "for a time."

Whether or not Sandys had his tongue in his cheek as he made these recommendations we will never know, but one thing is sure: he had struck a mortal blow at the entire proposal by revealing exactly what was involved in a perfect union: total naturalization, forgiveness of the French connection, and freedom of commerce. The English gentry were incapable of accepting such terms. For the next three days, however, they tossed and turned, agonizing over what to do next.[57] Some thought Sandys's suggestions worth pursuing, others dismissed them as a diversion, while yet others tried to ignore them, stressing that the House's immediate purpose ought to be to confer with the Lords about the ante-nati. One member warned that the king might not like Sir Edwin's motion, but this did not deter its advocates. The Commons were gradually becoming tied up in knots: uncertain how to proceed, they were allowing themselves to sink into paralysis.

Interestingly enough, this was but one of three occasions during the 1604–1610 Parliament when a recess was followed by a dramatic worsening of relations between subject and Crown. Both the Whitsun recess of

---

[55] *Bowyer*, 253.

[56] Ibid., 255–261; *CJ*, 365, 1035–1036; HMC, *Beaulieu: Montagu*, B.50: book 3, no. 3.

[57] *Bowyer*, 261–286; *CJ*, 265–266, 1037–1038. A record of some of these speeches, including two by Sandys, is in the Cambridgeshire Record Office (Huntingdon Branch), ddM 32/5/35: a reference I owe to Christopher Thompson.

1604 and the summer recess of 1610 had similar aftermaths. Although the lack of evidence prevents confirmation, it seems inconceivable that the M.P.s did not use these recesses to prepare the events that ensued. The days of innocent gentry coming to Westminster to hear the monarch, do his bidding, and offer advice (all with some degree of spontaneity) had given way irrevocably to a period of careful planning and organization.

Exasperated beyond endurance, James now summoned his contentious subjects to Whitehall for another tongue lashing.[58] They had misinterpreted his speech, he told them; they were using it to build "hay and stubble," and he had come "as a fire to consume and burn" such rubbish. He did not want a perfect union at all; he wanted "an absolute and full union," namely, one which would be accomplished by the three pieces of legislation the commissioners had proposed. It was "absurd" to think nothing ought to be done until the perfect union was consummated, and "idle and frivolous" to regard the arrangement he sought as imperfect. Sandys had suggested appointment of a new commission to prepare for perfection, and he rejected this prevarication out of hand. Some of the speeches had ventured so far "against duty, almost against allegiance" that he feared he might be moved "to do that, which my power may tempt me unto." One in particular had infuriated him: "that speech of 'love me little, and love me long,' was a damned speech." If he knew that much detail, James doubtless also knew that it was Sandys who had made the comment, but he named no names. "Beware of all fanatical spirits," he concluded, "all extraordinary, and colourable speeches; that there be no distractions, nor distempers, among you: that you breed not contempt to the great work so well begun, and discouragement to others, that wish well; that you tempt not the patience of your Prince."

As usual, James's bad temper was counterproductive. His outburst had come on a Saturday, May 2; it is true that on the Monday, May 4, at the speaker's urging, the bill to abolish hostile laws received its first reading; but the other two issues, commerce and naturalization, were simply never mentioned again. Instead, on May 6, during the second reading of the hostile laws bill, the Commons, offended that the king had chosen "to tax and blame the judgment, discretion, and good meaning of sundry members of the House," decided to justify themselves.[59] The speaker accordingly took to James a short but pointed document, in which he was asked not to listen to "private suggestions or reports" about M.P.s' speeches, to allow those who were "blamed or taxed" to clear themselves, and to signify that their discussions should proceed "with all liberty and freedom, and

---

[58] *CJ*, 366–368; *Bowyer*, 287–288. It was being said by May 5 that the Commons were more troublesome after the recess than before; ibid., 258 n.

[59] Ibid., 289; *CJ*, 368, 370.

without fear." The House never heard from the king, but the next day, despite Sir Edwin's concern that "clearing" was beyond his colleagues, since "judgement" had already been passed, various speakers proclaimed the innocence of the Lower House.[60] Sandys and Yelverton were specifically justified, and Sir Edwin closed the discussion with the belief that "the whole truth" would clear everyone: "Nihil est, quod male narrando non possit depravier [sic]." The wounded innocence notwithstanding, in this case even "male narrando" could not have exaggerated the destruction Sandys's speeches had caused.

The one piece of legislation on the Union that survived the disputes of late April and early May was the bill abolishing hostile laws. Even this, however, had its doubtful moments. News of troubles along the border between the two countries diverted the House's attention (at Sandys's urging) for a few days, and concern over such phraseology as "the union already begun" wasted further time. James had to send more messages to reassure the Commons and urge them along, and finally, on June 6, the bill was sent up to the Lords.[61] Dragging the legislation out of the House must have seemed like pulling teeth, yet this was the least controversial part of the three-point program outlined in the Instrument of Union. No great insight was needed to recognize the futility of pursuing the other two measures. Sandys and his colleagues had gained their ends: in Parliament James's plan for a merger of the two countries was irretrievable.

GRIEVANCES AND PROCEDURES

Preoccupied with the Union, the House found time to mention such favorite grievances as wardship and purveyance only in relation to the rights of Scotsmen.[62] But there were other opportunities for clashes with the Crown, most conspicuously when the king heard of plans for a petition against Jesuits and recusant priests and said he would not read it. Greatly exercised, the Commons started gathering precedents to show that monarchs always read their petitions, and Sandys found an instance of Elizabeth allowing them to proceed after initially forbidding a debate on the succession. In the end, however, perhaps because the Puritans who were using this petition to assault pluralism and inadequate preachers lacked the necessary strength, the M.P.s did not press the issue. That did not prevent Sir Edwin (rumors about his softness toward Catholics notwithstanding)

[60] Ibid., 370–371, 1041–1042.

[61] Ibid., 375, 377, 379, 380; *Bowyer*, 319. When the Union was finally consummated in 1707, a book celebrating the event, Ninian Wallis, *Britannia Concors*, was published in Dublin at the printshop of one Edwin Sandys.

[62] *Bowyer*, 223–224, 264 n.

from pursuing, at this very time, his own private campaign against Catholicism—his futile attempt to reconvert the imprisoned Sir Toby Mathew.[63]

The M.P.s also gave way on the one other measure with which Sandys was closely associated. At the previous session, despite government warnings that merchants would be unprotected if they traded freely, Parliament had passed a law ending the Spanish Company's monopoly and opening up commerce with Spain. Even before enactment of that statute, while the company still functioned, reports began reaching England of the ill-treatment of merchants by Spaniards. Once the monopoly was dissolved, the incidents multiplied, especially after the deterioration of relations between the two countries following the Gunpowder Plot. Not only was the Inquisition a threat to any Protestant who landed on Spanish soil, but every foreign ship was regarded as a probable pirate (as indeed many were) or as an agent of the Dutch. There were tales of atrocities, and finally the merchants turned to Parliament for help.[64] One particularly gruesome tale, embellished with torture and wanton cruelty, was chosen as exemplar, and relayed to the Commons in a petition asking for redress. The ordeal of the crew of the appropriately named vessel, the *Trial*, was duly entered in the Journal of the House on February 25, and when a committee to investigate the charges was appointed three days later, Sir Edwin, known for his familiarity with trading matters, was put in charge.[65]

The most intense stage of negotiations over the Union, followed by the Easter recess, occupied the next few weeks, but on May 13 Sandys finally reported on his committee's work.[66] The merchants' complaints, he said, revealed outrageous behavior by the Spaniards. There had been violence, confiscations, and outright thefts. Wrongs had been inflicted all over the globe, and in the space of four years the losses had amounted to "ten ships, divers mariners, and £200,000 . . . in goods." The merchants obviously deserved some kind of redress, and the committee suggested a petition to the king. It was true that the ambassador to Spain, Sir Charles Cornwallis, had complained to Philip III, but further action seemed necessary. The House concurred, and also accepted Sandys's recommendation that the Lords be asked to join in the petition.[67]

Another long delay now intervened: it was not until June 8 that the Lords replied. They finally agreed to see the petition, even though at first they had regarded it as "somewhat strange," and a conference was scheduled for June 16. In the meantime, Sandys was to "frame" the final docu-

[63] Ibid., 340; *CJ*, 384. On Mathew, see above, chapter 2, note 6.

[64] S. R. Gardiner, *History of England . . . 1604–1642*, 10 vols. (London, 1883–84), 1:342, 348–354, is the best account of the merchants' difficulties.

[65] *CJ*, 340–342, 344, 355.

[66] Ibid., 373; *Bowyer*, 292.

[67] *CJ*, 374; PRO, SP/14/27, fol. 19.

ment. On June 17, at last, Bacon reported what had happened.[68] He may well have been expecting a renewed confrontation, because he softened the acrimonious tone of the Lords' answer, and for once his tactics succeeded in heading off a nasty quarrel. The petition could not have been milder: it merely listed the merchants' grievances, and then left the manner of redress up to the king. But the government regarded any such advice as unwarranted interference. Cecil was careful not to say so in as many words, stressing that conditions were not too bad, that the king was doing all he could, and that the one measure the merchants requested (letters of mart, which would have allowed confiscation of Spanish goods as retaliation) would be ineffectual, because the English had much more to lose. Only at the end of his speech did he point out, not unkindly, that subjects had no right to meddle in foreign policy—adding, doubtless with some satisfaction, that he was nevertheless pleased to see the Commons' interest, which presumably signified their willingness to "assist" the king when foreign affairs required it. The next speaker, the earl of Northampton, showed no such restraint, and brusquely told the Lower House that their petition was insolent and beyond their competence. It was this speech that Bacon toned down—fortunately, it turned out, because after some debate the Commons decided to accept Cecil's arguments and drop the petition.[69]

The concern with petitions, precedents, and records in 1607 had one other consequence of note. On June 17 Sandys mentioned that he had found the precedent of Elizabeth allowing the House to continue a discussion she had forbidden "in the journal book of this house remaining with the clerk."[70] This information drew attention to the Commons' records, and at a committee meeting the following day, Sir Thomas Holcroft (like Sandys a recipient of favor from Cecil and one of the founders of the Virginia Company) suggested that the M.P.s ought to keep much closer control over what was entered in the Journal. His idea was taken up on the floor of the House at its next meeting, on June 19, when Wingfield, Edward Alford (another veteran "popular"), and Sandys, all precedent-conscious members, moved that "no entrance should be made by the clerk of this house of any matter which may concern the privileges of this house, nor any message or letter from his Majesty, but the same be first perused and allowed by the committee for privileges." The speaker strongly opposed this motion, but Alford and Sandys replied, and they "prevailed."

[68] *Bowyer*, 320, 293, 333–339; *CJ*, 384, 1050–1051.
[69] Ibid., 384.
[70] *Bowyer*, 340.

The clerk was thereupon ordered to bring his books for perusal by a specially designated committee the following week.[71]

A subcommittee, led by Sandys, was formed to examine the Journal, but when Sir Edwin tried to report its findings on July 1 he was rebuffed by the speaker, who insisted that subcommittees could not report directly to the House. The M.P.s agreed, an occurrence so rare that it drew from Bowyer the comment "quod mirandum."[72] The report was finally delivered on July 3, and Sandys established its importance at once: "as in this Parliament there had as many and as weighty matters come in question, as ever in any former Parliament, so it were fit, some extraordinary care and regard were had in keeping a memorial of them." His advice, therefore, was that before the next session the clerk should "perfect his journal for these three first sessions," and that nothing should "be of record, or in force" until a committee chosen for that purpose should see and "perfect" what he had written. The entire text would then have to be approved by the House. Thereafter, the Committee for Privileges was to go through the Journal every Saturday afternoon. In addition, because of "the great pains, which the clerk is to take in perfecting the said Journals," he was to be rewarded for his efforts.[73] The Commons accepted the recommendation without objection, and appropriately enough this was their final substantial action in 1607. It was appropriate, too, that Sandys, who had been chiefly responsible for torpedoing the Union, the main business of the session, should have been in charge of the last matter of moment considered by the House.

SANDYS, THE COMMONS, AND THE KING

Sir Edwin's less well-recorded activities seem to have been as numerous as ever. Although he avoided the multitude of insignificant committees, such as those which authorized sales of lands by individuals, he nevertheless managed to sit on twenty-five out of the eighty-four committees that were appointed in 1607. Some of these, such as the body that sought ways of ensuring parliamentary control over ecclesiastical regulations, or another which considered at length the decline of the armorers' trade, must have occupied him for days at a time, but there is no record of the particular

---

[71] Ibid., 343–344; Sheila Lambert, "The Clerks and Records of the House of Commons, 1600–1640," *Bulletin of the Institute of Historical Research* 43 (1970): 215–231. On Alford see R. Zaller, "Edward Alford and the Making of Country Radicalism," *Journal of British Studies* 22 (1983): 59–79.

[72] *Bowyer*, 364.

[73] Ibid., 367; *CJ*, 390, 1057.

functions he performed.[74] We do know that he was ill on February 28—the first evidence of the ailments that were increasingly to plague him during the remainder of his life—for he had to be relieved by Bacon of the responsibility of reporting to the House the proceedings in the Grand Committee, the Committee of the Whole. But he was back in action on March 2, and otherwise he seems to have been in continual attendance.[75]

Sandys's remaining interventions reveal an old Parliament man, sensitive to the dignities of the House, and constantly on the lookout for dangerous precedents or procedures. We have noted the central position he occupied when the Commons sought to justify themselves, early in May, in response to the king's displeasure over their debates on the Union. At that time one veteran advocate of official views, Sir George More, had admitted that the content of speeches was being reported to James, and that he himself "would not commend Sir Edwin Sandys." Nevertheless, he did want the speaker to ask the king to refrain from obtaining such information "for the conservation of the liberty of the House." That concern for liberty was typical of the gentry, but more controversial was More's conclusion that liberty had never been "less abridged than in this Parliament." After all, the problem of confidentiality had been troubling the Commons repeatedly, and when Sir Robert Wingfield admitted that it was he who had told the king about one speech, Sandys felt constrained to scold his colleague. Nothing could have indicated more clearly the unity of England's "Establishment"—the inextricable mingling of support and opposition on any issue—than this news, that a veteran "popular" like Wingfield had been reporting the speeches of another "popular" to James. And Sir Edwin neatly avoided blaming the king by telling Sir Robert "very modestly and in good terms" that it obviously must have been the shortcomings of his report that had caused "his Majesty . . . to be a misinterpreter."[76]

Sandys was also involved in a related issue two months later. An act of Queen Mary's time had forbidden "unlawful assemblies": in effect, dangerous gatherings of potential rioters. Its provisions remained in operation until the end of the first Parliament of each new reign, and it had to be renewed if it was to continue. A number of quite respectable gentry had been inconvenienced, however, because the act's prohibitions could be interpreted broadly, and to prevent such annoyances the committee decided not to make the act perpetual. But there was one stumbling block: the recent Midland uprising argued for continuance of the statute, and so, as a compromise, it was suggested that the law could remain in force until the end of the first session of the next Parliament. Sandys disagreed: the act

[74] Ibid., 329, 369; *Bowyer*, 323.

[75] *CJ*, 343, 345.

[76] Ibid., 1042; *Bowyer*, 370–371, 376–381. See, too, above, note 60.

caused "mischief," he said, and if it were continued at all their successors might assume that they had endorsed it. When the dispute finally came to a vote, there was a quarrel as to whether the "Ayes" or the "Noes" ought to leave the chamber, evidently because inertia or comfort worked to the advantage of those who remained. The "Ayes" demanded that privilege, but were refused, and indeed the "Noes" won the ensuing vote by a majority of seven. If the leaders of the two sides are any indication, this was a classic "official" vs. "popular" confrontation, because the "Ayes" were represented by the former solicitor-general Sir John Dodderidge, the attorney-general Sir Henry Hobart, the new solicitor Bacon, and Montague, the recorder of London, while the "Noes" followed Fuller, Sandys, Yelverton, Hyde, and Neville. In the end, therefore, the gentry did manage to have the act killed, but not without a final revelation of the House's concern about confidentiality and its determination to defend its members. In an unprecedented move, the M.P.s ordered a special procedure for counting votes with the avowed purpose of preventing official interference:

> The King's council would, upon the differing in the number of voices, have had the names of the affirmative and likewise of the negative to have been taken, but it was overruled that it should be divided by severance of persons and counting the polls and not by taking of names, which was done upon just cause, lest the names should be shown to high persons and so some particular members, which with their conscience denied the continuance, might have displeasure.[77]

The aura of suspicion was so powerful that there was even open speculation—probably justified—that the speaker's illness in late March had been deliberately prolonged. Phelips had to justify himself when he returned, assuring the House that the brief adjournment he had called right after his illness was not of his own doing, but the king's.[78] And two weeks later, when Sandys was in the midst of an attack on the stream of private bills the House was called upon to consider, he took the precaution of reminding his colleagues—and by extension, all who might hear of his action—that he could not later be held to account for what he had said in Parliament. The measure he was proposing, an act to prevent "fraud and wrongdoing in private acts of Parliament," cannot have been popular among debt-ridden landowners who would have been prevented by law from selling their property. Sir Edwin therefore recalled the precedent of Strowd's case, early in Henry VIII's reign, when an M.P. was acquitted of culpability for speeches he had made, and it was decided "that no man shall after the

---

[77] Ibid., 365–367.
[78] Ibid., 298–299; *CJ*, 376.

Parliament be called in question for his words used in Parliament."[79] That such a reminder was necessary does not speak well for the atmosphere in which business was conducted. In the event, however, nobody was called to account for their actions in Parliament—despite the clear displeasure Sandys had aroused at Court—and this suggests that gentry outspokenness and independence were gaining recognition as accepted features of the English political scene.

Sir Edwin gave special attention to only one other bill during the session, an act to restrain bullion exports and prevent Englishmen going overseas without royal licenses, which he reported to the House on June 11.[80] By then, however, he had done more than enough to make his presence felt—not only in Westminster, but also down the road in Whitehall. There is a nice little indication, in the midst of one of the rambling royal addresses, that the king was obtaining reports of Sandys's speeches. We have already noted James's awareness of Sir Edwin's "love me little, love me long" comment; but there had been a perhaps unconscious echo even earlier. On February 28, discussing the Union, Sandys commented "ab antiquo non fuit sic"; a month later, on March 31, the king remarked "ab initio non fuit sic." They interpreted the sentence differently, because Sandys regarded it as an argument against the Union, whereas his monarch emphasized the improvement inherent in a natural movement from separation towards union.[81] It may be that James was deliberately refuting Sandys, or perhaps the unwitting repetition was the result of his close attention to the speeches of his most troublesome M.P.

If the king had any doubt at the end of the 1604 session that independent-minded members of the Commons were prepared to assert their own vision of England's best interests—a doubt perhaps reinforced by the tranquility of 1606—all uncertainty must have dissolved by the summer of 1607. It is true that Cecil wrote to Cornwallis on July 15, eight days after the prorogation, of "his Majesty's having received good contentment in [Parliament's] proceedings, especially seeing so good a foundation is laid to the much desired union, by taking away already of the hostile laws." But James himself gave the lie to the earl's optimism in his closing address, which contained much "persuasion of unity and union," and an attack on "the errors of the House of Commons."[82] Cecil and the other ministers of the Crown may have decided to put on a brave front, but in fact they must

---

[79] Ibid., 381, 1050; *Bowyer*, 320–321.

[80] The bill passed four days later, only to founder in the Lords: *CJ*, 382, 383, 1051; *LJ*, 2:547.

[81] *CJ*, 345, 358.

[82] Sir Ralph Winwood, *Memorials of Affairs of State*, ed. E. Sawyer, 3 vols. (London, 1725), 2:326; *CJ*, 1057.

THE SESSIONS OF 1606 AND 1607

have heard all too often about the arguments and objections of a Sandys, a Fuller, a Wingfield, or a Yelverton.

Nor can they have entertained any real hopes for the "great cause" of the Union, the king's brainchild. Here the chief critic had been Sandys, and for that reason he must have been the object of particular resentment. With his proposal for a "perfect" Union he had persuaded the M.P.s to adopt a dissenting stance that James was helpless to counteract. All the fulminating speeches in the world could not undo the damage Sir Edwin had wrought, or change the gentry's conclusion that the measure did not serve the welfare of the realm. Sandys's decisive intervention in this crucial issue alone (by far the most important of 1607) would have entitled him to recognition as the prime moving force in the House. Taken in conjunction with his role as reporter for the Grand Committee and his contribution to a broad range of the session's business, his handling of the Union established him unmistakably both as the "Commons-man" par excellence and as the principal exponent of independent views. When he returned to the House, two and a half years later, his stature was confirmed in the most fateful of the sessions of the Stuarts' first Parliament.

Chapter VI

THE GREAT CONTRACT

Toward Contract Negotiations

Sir Edwin returned to Westminster in February 1610, as Parliament reassembled after a prorogation of nearly three years. The M.P.s had been recalled, so far as the government was concerned, for one reason and one reason alone: money. Cecil had taken over as treasurer in 1608, and had faced an appalling situation. The king's debts approached £600,000, and only by drastic measures (primarily a major extension of impositions, a type of customs duty, and sales of land) had Cecil managed to reduce the annual deficit to £160,000, but longer-range solutions now seemed essential.[1] Using as immediate justification the unexpected cost of suppressing the O'Daugherty revolt in Ireland in 1608, the treasurer laid before Parliament a two-part program: "supply" or "remuneration" in the form of subsidies which would wipe out the debt; and "support" or "revenue," a permanent arrangement for meeting both everyday needs and emergency expenses like the campaign in Ireland.[2] It was the notion of "support" that grew into the proposal known as the "Great Contract," a term that expressed the growing recognition that royal finance had become a matter of bargaining and business.

The session opened on February 9, and virtually the first piece of busi-

---

[1] F. C. Dietz, *English Public Finance, 1558–1641* (New York, 1932), 121–126. For a calculation that includes a £120,000 debt left by Elizabeth, see Robert Ashton, "Deficit Finance in the Reign of James I," *Economic History Review*, 2d ser., 10 (1957): 15–29, esp. 21, and *The Crown and the Money Market, 1603–1640* (Oxford, 1960), 37.

[2] Elizabeth R. Foster, ed., *Proceedings in Parliament 1610*, 2 vols. (New Haven, Conn., 1966), 1:3–8, 2:9–27; S. R. Gardiner, ed., *Parliamentary Debates in 1610*, Camden Society, vol. 81 (London, 1861), 1–9; The Queen's College Oxford, MS. 280, item 29 are accounts of Cecil's speech. For his role in the Contract, see Pauline Croft, ed., "A collection of several speeches and treatises of the late Lord Treasurer Cecil, and of several observations of the Lords of the Council given to King James concerning his estate and revenues in the years 1608, 1609 and 1610," *Camden Miscellany* 29 (1982): 245–317. See, too, A. G. R. Smith, "The Great Contract of 1610," in *The English Commonwealth 1547–1640: Essays in Politics and Society Presented to Joel Hurstfield*, ed. Peter Clark et al. (Leicester, 1979), 111–127, who blames "distrust between the Crown and M.P.s" for the Contract's failure; Eric Lindquist, "The Failure of the Great Contract," *Journal of Modern History* 57 (1985): 617–651, who blames the M.P.s; and Lamar M. Hill, *Bench and Bureaucracy: The Public Career of Sir Julius Caesar, 1580–1636* (Stanford, 1988), who blames the Court; responsibility for the failure now seems evenly divided.

ness was initiated by Sandys, who reminded the House of the decision it had taken, just before prorogation, to supervise the Journal. A special committee was set up, charged not only with this task (for which it was instructed to meet every Saturday afternoon) but also with privileges and elections. Sir Edwin apparently took command of this body, because he delivered its initial report on February 14, the first full day of business.[3] The borough of Lyme Regis had petitioned the Commons to order a new election because their M.P., Sir George Somers, had sailed for Virginia (he was in fact on his famous, if unintentional, journey to Bermuda). Sandys and his committee had agreed, "upon deliberation," and after some discussion their decision was upheld. The next day Sir Edwin moved the appointment of a Committee for Grievances, of which, in the words of the leading student of the 1610 session, Sandys then began an "able chairmanship."[4]

Swiftly and unmistakably, therefore, he was stamping his imprint on the session. His presence must have seemed inescapable during the next five months, because on 63 out of the 125 days of business he had something to say. And his committee work was positively Herculean—over a quarter of the nearly two hundred bodies appointed. When, on February 15, the government made its wishes known, the man it most needed to persuade was Sandys, now firmly established as the principal tactician and negotiator in the Lower House.

Over the months that followed, Sir Edwin became the first great "Commons-man" in deed as well as word. The longest-surviving Parliament since the 1530s had created a sense of familiarity, homogeneity, and purpose among its now well-acquainted members that made possible a new kind of leadership. That leadership was Sandys's, and when he became, to all intents and purposes, the nation's negotiator with the government over the Great Contract in 1610, he demonstrated the vital importance to England's polity of the unique position he had attained in Parliament, and the vision of good government that he represented,

A committee of six M.P.s heard Cecil outline the king's needs. "The branch cannot prosper and flourish," he said, "except the root be fed." The Crown's debts amounted to £300,000, and large expenses could be anticipated, particularly in Ireland, for the navy, and as a result of the Jülich-Cleves dispute. "Both money and revenue" were therefore necessary. Although he did not specify the number of subsidies that the Crown sought,

---

[3] Foster, *1610*, 2:3–4, 393; *CJ*, 392. Mary Keeler, in "The Committee for Privileges of the House of Commons 1604–10 and 1614," *Parliamentary History* 13 (1994): 165, has suggested that Sandys may have wanted this committee, filled with senior M.P.s, to become a kind of steering committee organizing the House's business, but it never did.

[4] *CJ*, 394; Foster, *1610*, 1:xv.

he did stress that "we must not look only to put the King out of debt but have sufficient supply to maintain and support his yearly and annual charge." Reporting this final part of Cecil's speech was Sandys's responsibility: having divided its work among its members, the committee had Sir Edwin present to the Commons the central issue of "retribution and ease."[5]

This section of the lord treasurer's address, Sandys told the House on February 17, he could convey "with much joy." For the ease that Cecil spoke of was "ease extraordinary." James would take care to give "a general redress of all just grievances," because he was aware that "the true scale of the King's prerogative was when [it stood] in concurrence with the public good." Since some of his actions had caused concern, he was happy to explain his intentions. The collection of all proclamations together in a single book, for instance, was merely an attempt to take "better notice . . . of those things which they command," and not a preliminary to legislation by proclamation. There were some rights, such as those of imposition and land tenures, which were inherent in the throne's prerogatives, but even these were "to be moderated." Special attention was also being given to statutes, especially penal laws, which often seemed too harsh. Cecil had even admitted that "we shall be all ill advised if we do not seek to deliver ourselves by humble petition from those burdens, whereof we cannot but complain." With this in mind, he had assured the Commons that there had never been a House of Lords so ready "to concur with you in consultation or join with you in humble requests." In return, all he asked for was freedom and openness in conferences, avoidance of "notorious delay or confusion," rejection of "precipitate remedies whatsoever we may suppose the grievance," and a decent response to James's financial requests: "that reasonable demands . . . not . . . be answered with cold supplies."

The "loving and benevolent" tone of Cecil's address, which Sandys so happily reported, was clearly designed to set the right mood for the deliberations that were to follow. This was the last major enterprise of the great minister's career, and by 1610 he must have been fully aware of the importance of first impressions. The mistakes of 1604 were not to be repeated. And yet, when his speech was debated in the Commons on February 19, problems arose almost from the first. This was just not a tractable assembly; as the difficulties mounted with each passing week, the treasurer must have regretted more and more sharply the decision to place the future of Crown finance in the hands of these defensive and truculent gentry. Although, given England's political system, he had little choice, he might have been better advised to start afresh, with new elections, and hope that the memories of the earlier sessions might have faded.

The immediate nitpicking objection in the Lower House was that sub-

---

[5] *CJ*, 396; Foster, *1610*, 2:30, 357.

sidies were usually not enacted until the end of a session, and that in any
case they proceeded "from the Commons, who will not be deprived of the
thanks for it by any motion from the Lords." More serious was the question of exactly what Cecil meant by asking for both money and revenue. A
subsidy could perhaps wipe out his Majesty's debts, but it could not serve
as "the yearly supply of the defect of his receipts, which was 46 thousand
pounds per annum."[6] The notion that there might be some kind of quid
pro quo in financial matters had not been defined very carefully at this
stage, for Cecil had not mentioned it directly in his February 15 address.
Yet it was at this very time, in February 1610, that an ordinary country
gentleman, Walter Young, living hundreds of miles away in Devon, remarked in his diary that £130,000 per year was being asked for abolition of
wardship.[7] Every M.P., therefore, must have been aware of the deal that
was in the offing, and the February 19 debate soon began to revolve
around a more familiar problem—should they deal first with the subsidy
or first with grievances? To this question Sandys had a typically reasonable
answer: "That both points may proceed equally." In particular, he wanted
"to avoid the imputation of gathering grievances in the House." But such
simple resolutions were never easy in the Jacobean Commons. The arguments went back and forth for some time, until finally it was decided to
ask the Lords to be more precise about their proposals, and also to refer to
a Committee of the Whole both "contribution and retribution."[8]

That committee, with "Sir Edwin Sandys being appointed to the chair,"
met the same afternoon, and "suits" and "grievances" soon became the
chief topic of conversation. By the time the gathering broke up, ten grievances had been specified, ranging from such old favorites as wardship,
purveyance, and ecclesiastical restraints, to newer issues like customs duties and the availability of tin and alum.[9] Over the next two days there were
further meetings to confirm this list, and also to distinguish among the
different types of grievances: some were matters of prerogative, others
were not; some caused injury, others did not; and so on. When Sandys
reported the discussions on February 21, the preliminary stage was over.
The king had already informed the House that he was "not pleased with
the delay," and his chancellor of the Exchequer, Sir Julius Caesar, a newly
elected M.P., had announced "in an angry manner" that James's wants
were so great that he needed £600,000 to erase his debts and an additional
£200,000 per year in revenue. Since the Commons, for their part, were
indulging themselves in complaints, the pattern of the exchanges over the

---

[6] Gardiner, *1610*, 9; *CJ*, 396–397.

[7] Foster, *1610*, 2:316 n.

[8] Ibid., 31; *CJ*, 396–397.

[9] Foster, *1610*, 2:358.

Contract already seemed set, even though the deliberations were less than a week old.[10]

Sir Edwin's report outlined the progress they had made. They had agreed to distinguish between injurious and noninjurious grievances, the former apparently unsupported by prerogative, the latter enjoying ancient justification. "In the first," they had concluded, "they were to deal by petition; in the other, by the way of conference and contract." This was the first mention in the Commons of the word "contract," but it was evident that the M.P.s were still not clear about Cecil's intentions. When they tried to work out what should be demanded in exchange for a grant of permanent support, "they could find nothing to pitch on," said Sandys, except the abolition of wardship, land tenures, and a few minor irritants like old debts and defective titles. The obvious next step, therefore, was to seek a conference with the Lords "for further light in particulars." And "if the Lords did not propound tenures and wardships etc., then to propound them from the House."

Led by Sandys, the Commons were groping toward a negotiating position, but they still had a long way to go. Moreover, their uncertainty was obviously a weakness, and it may have been the need to arrive quickly at a more concrete set of proposals that induced Sir Edwin to end his speech by suggesting that no grievances be accepted after the following Monday, the twenty-sixth. The House adopted this deadline, though to little purpose: nothing of consequence was raised during the five days, and thereafter grievances were accepted as before. As it happened, the next step in the investigation of the Contract had been taken in the interim, on February 24, when the two Houses met in conference and the Commons revealed, by their proposals, that their demands were beginning to crystalize.[11]

The Lords prepared for the meeting in an ill temper. Cecil reiterated that the king needed £600,000 outright, and £200,000 per year, but thought it "altogether unfit" that they should "talk with the lower House about the retribution before we receive contribution." The chancellor, Thomas Egerton, Lord Ellesmere, was more blunt—only "after [the king's] ends were satisfied, would he give way unto the petition of the Commons."[12] But Caesar immediately put paid to such notions: "without an exceedingly noble retribution," he warned, "we cannot satisfy." After some fruitless sparring, the Lords indicated that they might be more flexible than they seemed. "Offer what you will and then will we show you our reasons without prevarication," said Cecil, and he went on to assess the

[10] Ibid., 2:32, 358–359; for Sandys's report, ibid., 32, and *CJ*, 398. Hill, *Bench and Bureaucracy*, documents Caesar's role in undoing the Contract.

[11] *CJ*, 401; Foster, *1610*, 1:13–16, and 2:34–36; Gardiner, *1610*, 13–16.

[12] Foster, *1610*, 1:12–13.

various types of "retribution" the Commons sought. He had obviously seen Sandys's list of ten grievances, or something like it; to each one he had a reply, sometimes unyielding, as in the case of wardship ("the subjects pay too little") or royal rights of alienation, but sometimes conciliatory, as with homage and purveyance ("we will be suitors to his Majesty that they may be taken away"). Both committees then agreed to consult their respective Houses, cognizant of the need for more exact and substantial proposals.

On the floor of the Commons, meanwhile, the gathering of grievances continued. The same day as the conference with the Lords, the twenty-fourth, Sandys gave a long report on the latest complaints, particularly against *The Interpreter*, a book written by the Regius Professor of Civil Law at Cambridge, John Cowell, whose exaltation of prerogative and minimization of common law seemed "very unadvised and indiscreet." James eventually suppressed the book and imprisoned Cowell, but not before the Commons had become greatly exercised at such impudence. On the Contract, however, they waited three days for Sir Henry Montague's report on the conference with the Lords, and resumed debate the next day, the twenty-eighth.[13]

The situation must have seemed chaotic to most M.P.s, because they blundered about at inordinate length trying to decide what to do next. There was so little progress that a group of members attempted to close the debate, but were defeated by 160 votes to 148. Most of the speakers insisted that the Lords had misunderstood their request for information about "retribution." This had not been a hint of unwillingness to vote supplies—quite the contrary: there was "no aversion from giving at all." Their interest was to see "that both contribution and retribution went together." Consequently, they needed to know in more detail what to expect from the king, and so they settled on another message to the Lords. "In due time," they announced, they would "take consideration of" supply and "give his Majesty good satisfaction." But where annual income was concerned, they could do nothing until they had "heard from your Lordships, what course you intend in the point of tenures." With the ball thus firmly in the other House's court, the Commons could relax and await further developments.

This extended warm-up could not go on indefinitely; nevertheless, almost two weeks passed before Parliament could proceed to the next stage in the negotiations. Even as the M.P.s were deciding on their message, the Lords were hearing from Cecil that although James approved the "course we held with the Lower House," he could not tell them whether they had leave to discuss wardship until he had given the matter further consideration. Cecil relayed this message to the Commons on March 2, adding— doubtless to smooth the path ahead—that as far as he was concerned, they

---

[13] *CJ*, 399, 402–403; Foster, *1610*, 2:37–39, 48–52.

were free to investigate the Court of Wards: "I offer it to you as freely as I should a pair of gloves."[14] But official permission was not forthcoming, as Caesar and Sandys informed the House when they reported on the conference the next day. Caesar described Cecil's speech, while Sir Edwin summarized the earl of Northampton's florid address: not an easy task, for which he probably had to have a copy of the earl's text at hand. Northampton had been almost sickeningly fulsome about James's benevolence (and even about the talents of his rival, Cecil), drawing on the most improbable metaphors—countertenors, gardens, mice, and cockles, among others—to trumpet the King's qualities.[15]

These exchanges were harmless enough, for both parties to the Great Contract were marking time. On March 8 it was announced that the king had suppressed Cowell's book, and then, four days later, he finally gave his decision on wardship.[16] It would be fascinating to know what arguments Cecil put forward during these uncertain weeks, especially as this was about the last time that he was able to exert real influence over his sovereign. And indeed, it was not Cecil but Northampton who brought Parliament the news, in a simple speech to the Lords on the morning of the twelfth: "The King doubteth not but both in tenures, wards and purveyance, the Lower House will proceed as they have done in all humility, judgment, and understanding." When he gave the same message to the Commons that afternoon, however, the extravagance of phrase returned. Seas and billows, Pharaoh and Joseph, Caesar and Jonah, veins, bowels, and Fair Helen—all figured in his extravagant verbiage. But the sum of it was that they had permission to proceed, thanks to their humility, dutifulness, and "discretion, in not propounding your desires gratis, but with recompense."[17] The last impediment to open debate over the Contract was thus removed, and over the next few weeks Parliament slowly came to grips with the basic issues.

NEGOTIATIONS AND GRIEVANCES

An essential part of this formative stage of the negotiations was the collection of grievances by Sandys's committee. In the same letter in which the Venetian ambassador informed the Doge that James was permitting discussion of wardship, he reported that some sixty grievances had already accumulated. Sir Edwin had divided his colleagues into subcommittees, each of which, according to instructions issued on March 12, met from one

[14] Ibid., 1:20, 25–26.
[15] CJ, 404–405; Foster, 1610, 2:39–45.
[16] Ibid., 1:29, 2:54.
[17] Ibid., 1:34–35; 2:53–56.

until three in the afternoon and then reported to the parent committee.[18] Presumably the subsidiary groups were assigned specific subject matter, an indication of the enormous volume of business that was being generated. A week later Sandys announced that the "great committee" would "sit all day: Monday, Tuesday, Wednesday, Thursday, Friday, Saturday," and he asked "subcommittees to attend more diligently," with sessions starting at two o'clock every afternoon. By March 23 he could tell the House he needed "but one day" to organize the last phase of the investigations—"to rough-hew" the grievances. Accordingly, the subcommittees were given until the following Wednesday, March 30, to complete their findings so that the Commons could hear from Sandys shortly thereafter.[19]

Sir Edwin's commanding position in the House is amply documented by the events of these weeks. Not only was he in charge of the critical committee, but he seemed to receive almost automatic consent whenever he intervened in debate. It could be a trivial question, such as whether to pay the constable's fees in a privilege case, or a significant issue of procedure like the appropriate manner of thanking the king for permission to discuss wardship. The latter was "resolved according to Sir Edwin Sandys his project": a message was sent directly to James, but to avoid offence the Lords were informed of the action by special messenger (namely Sandys). As Sir Edwin put it, there had been "great concurrence, with great content, in all things this session, especially this matter of tenures." They ought to act graciously "because in all things we have found correspondence with their Lordships."[20] If Sandys himself was largely responsible for this smooth sailing, it was because he was now using the extraordinary control he exercised over the House to bring the influence of the independent gentry into the heart of England's government. It was an unprecedented political role, and unique in the Europe of the day.

At this stage, in mid and late March, both king and Parliament seemed in amiable mood. James delivered another oration to the Commons on the twenty-first, reiterating his good intentions and his wants, announcing the punishment of Cowell, and asking for action on a number of specific measures.[21] Although he did warn against excessive pursuit of grievances and "railing speeches," on the whole this was a moderate and conciliatory address, symptomatic of the efforts on both sides to undertake serious and fruitful negotiations on an issue that had the possibility of transforming the fiscal and legal structure of the relations between Crown and subject.

That is not to say that the collection of grievances slacked off. Sir Edwin

---

[18] *CSP, Venetian*, 9:447; *CJ*, 409.
[19] Ibid., 413, 414.
[20] Ibid., 411, 412.
[21] Foster, *1610*, 2:59–63.

remained hard at work in this business until July, coming to the House with occasional reports or queries. Even after the subcommittees completed their investigations, it took weeks of hearings to determine the final list of grievances; half of those mentioned in a paper drawn up in late April, for example, were rejected.[22] This, however, was background. The center of attention throughout these weeks was the Great Contract.

At the outset matters moved quite quickly. After only two days of debate, March 23 and 24, the Commons decided to offer the king £100,000 per year in return for the abolition of wardship. They were ignoring the remainder of Cecil's list of ten items of "retribution" so as to concentrate on this overarching grievance. The issue was thus simplified, and there was some talk at this time of king and Commons being close to agreement. Then, however, came an unfortunate delay. The Lords heard of the offer on March 29 (though the conference had been three days before), and after much debate professed themselves unable to answer without "other cogitations."[23] At this point another of Parliament's ill-fated recesses, the Easter break, intervened, and it was not until late April that the discussion resumed.

James had obviously gone through the Commons' proposal carefully and, as Attorney-General Hobart reported on April 21, was prepared to accept it in principle.[24] He did insist, however, on the "marks of sovereignty"—lands held of the Crown by knight service would not be transferred to some other form of tenure. On this he was not even to be entreated, and the Lords were as "unremovable as rocks." In other words, he would make the financial arrangement, but only if it left his "points of honor" intact. Perhaps sensing the likely objection, the king concluded by urging the House to proceed "without jealousy, without suspicion, without needless fears." Indeed, the immediate response, when the message was debated on April 23, was the concern that the Commons "could not safely contract for the tenures unless the same were wholly extinguished and destroyed in the roots."[25] The fear was that as long as the points of honor survived, wardship could always be revived.

The doubts expressed on April 23 gave the first sign that the Great Contract might face difficulty, but in the end the M.P.s accepted the king's assurances and decided to "proceed notwithstanding."[26] They now wanted confirmation of the adequacy of their offer, and also a more concrete set of proposals outlining what the king might surrender and how much he

---

[22] Foster, *1610* , 2:71–72; examples of Sandys's interventions are in *CJ*, 416.

[23] Foster, *1610*, 2:64–65, 68; 1:197–205; *CSP, Venetian*, 11:465.

[24] *CJ*, 420.

[25] Foster, *1610*, 2:70 n.

[26] Ibid., 70.

sought in return. Since the Lords seemed to be mouthpieces for James, the Commons asked for a conference to obtain the information they sought. It was at this meeting, on April 26, that the true nature of the Contract (which was far more than a simple quid pro quo over wardship) became apparent.[27]

Sandys attended the conference on April 26, and reported on it two days later, even though he was deeply enmeshed in Grievance Committee business—an indication of the energy and versatility his leadership required.[28] The main event had been a long speech "by that great Treasurer of wisdom," Cecil, with whom Sandys was now clearly working to promote the Contract. Sir Edwin had reduced the speech "into orderly parts," and if, as a result, he conveyed something that Cecil had not intended, "I shall do that which is right, for wisdom is always orderly, yea, though it neglect it, as perfection is always beautiful though it least affect it." Continuing his credo (the only time he discussed the art of public speaking directly) Sir Edwin explained, in classic rhetorical terms: "The order which I observe in this noble lord's speech was the order of a chain, which is the highest and most perfect kind of order in the world, and that within [which] the world itself is framed, each like drawing another (as depending on it) with easy motion, the former parts giving light unto the later, and the later returning strength unto the former." He then got down to the content of Cecil's remarks.

The lord treasurer had been delighted by the Commons' offer, and also by the spirit in which it had been made. He was particularly pleased that they had accepted the king's insistence on "points of honor." Unfortunately, however, that was by no means the end of the matter, and he feared either that he had misunderstood the House's meaning or that perhaps there had been "some want in himself in conveying those things to us which the King propounded." When the session opened, he reminded them, the king had asked for supply and support; what this meant, he now told them, was "that except £200,000 annually were raised to the King, above all that he now hath, it was short of [his] necessary expense, and might be dangerous." These considerations "had not brought that weight into the balance of our judgment which was expected." Put bluntly, not enough was being offered. Retribution was certainly possible in return for contribution—on the assumption that prerogatives would not be affected— but the government had in mind a totally different order of magnitude.

[27] *CJ*, 421–422; Foster, *1610*, 2:69–71.

[28] *CJ*, 419–422, documents Sandys's proliferating concern with grievances from April 18 (imposition on pepper, coal trade) to the twenty-third (ecclesiastical grievances), the twenty-fifth ("the great matter of Impositions") and the twenty-seventh (the Council in Wales, the Court of High Commission, delays in executing writs). For his report on the Contract: ibid., 422; Gardiner, *1610*, 147–152.

After all, at the beginning of Parliament, "when demand of £200,000 per annum and £600,000 was made, there was no thought (saith the King) that he should part with the wards." The offer was therefore inadequate. "Shall I flatter you (quoth his Lordship) when the Wards is too much for any thing that shall come short of the King's first demand." In other words, "unless we offered that which might give the King . . . £200,000 a year above whatsoever we defalked from him by our contract, the wards will not be had." Cecil encouraged their wish to take up purveyance and other feudal incidents, but only if, first, they did not meddle with sovereignty and, second, they made sure to offer sufficient recompense. The basic fact of life was that "the King knoweth no cause to alter his first demand," and he certainly "knew no cause to make us a lower price." The Commons could take it or leave it, but if they persisted they would have to produce a more substantial offer than £100,000 in return for the abolition of wardship.

According to most contemporary accounts, the House did not take kindly to this turn of events. The Venetian ambassador went so far as to claim that only "the members who belong to the King's party" prevented the Commons from adjourning.[29] But the debate was in fact restrained, though there was no mistaking the lack of inclination to raise the offer. Of the eighteen M.P.s who discussed Cecil's demands on May 1, none (not even the royal officers) suggested that they might comply. Strode wanted them to restrict themselves to wardship; others recommended silence; and even Sir George More said they could not go higher, because the king was demanding "double the worth." The only question seemed to be what to do next, and here Sandys had the answer that closed the debate. There was no point in remaining silent, he said, because that was not proper between House and king. They ought to indicate that it was unfair to impose new taxes on men who held no lands (and therefore were not subject to wardship), and they also ought to keep each issue separate. He suggested that a committee "pen" this message, a proposal the House accepted.[30]

There was some debate the next day, May 2, about the text of the message, and one important addition was made at the behest of Sir William Twysden, an occasionally obstreperous member from Kent, who recalled a precedent from the reign of Edward III in which the Commons consulted their constituents to "receive a resolution and authority from them"—a concern that was of growing importance to the Stuart gentry. In the end, the House's answer was threefold: "we find no just cause to vary" the offer of £100,000 for wardship; the wards were a distinct issue, because they

[29] CSP, Venetian, 11:486.
[30] CJ, 423.

affected only landowners; and it would be impossible to promise more money without betraying "the trust which so many millions of people have reposed in us." Still there was doubt as to whether so negative a reply should be given, and the issue had to be brought to a vote, which decided (by 135 to 125) that the message should be sent to the Lords.[31]

A sour note was now entering the proceedings. The Lower House was clearly upset at the unexpected escalation of royal demands, and only by great effort did it manage to respond in calm and courteous language. But it was definitely not going to make any further concessions, and on May 3, when the peers asked for a free and open conference to discuss the situation, the Commons balked. Christopher Brooke insisted that the delegates have "no such liberty—to hear what they will say, and then report nothing." More, Nathaniel Bacon, and others agreed, and it was resolved "that they have no authority to answer."[32] This decision was bound to anger the Lords, as it did; the stubbornness both symbolized and foreshadowed a deterioration in the fortunes of the Contract.

The growing uneasiness was also apparent in the Lower House's second major interest: grievances. Sandys gave another report on the subject on April 30, with "grief and grievance upon him." He delivered the eighth grievance his committee had officially accepted (proclamations) and informed the House that they were making progress on impositions, but needed help in searching out precedents. He wanted the speaker to order an examination of parliamentary records in the Tower and the archives at the Exchequer. He also sought assistance from king's counsel and from Sir Robert Cotton.[33] Sitting six days a week, his committee was building up a full head of steam, and despite some questions about the search for precedents, on May 1 nine M.P.s, including Cotton, Whitelocke, and Fuller, were given the assignment. According to one account, Sandys's charge to this committee was to examine James's claim that he could lay impositions on imports or exports without parliamentary consent. He was obviously preparing to challenge the Crown's powers in a most sensitive area, even as other concerns proliferated.[34]

The relations of the Commons with king and Lords in early May hardly boded well for the Contract. On the fourth Caesar in fact suggested breaking off negotiations because the Lower House could not offer more than £100,000 for the wards. Cecil urged further thought, but Bancroft, the archbishop of Canterbury, could not restrain himself. The king needed

[31] Ibid., 423–424; Foster, *1610*, 2:75.

[32] Ibid., 76–77, 1:227–228; *CJ*, 424; BL, Harleian, 767, fols. 117–118.

[33] *CJ*, 422; Foster, *1610*, 2:73, 365.

[34] Ibid., 74, 365; Gardiner, *1610*, 32; *CJ*, 423, 425, 426–427. New grievances included alehouse taxes and excessive fees. By May 11, the House had accepted thirteen grievances, and it must have seemed the search would never end.

money, he said, and it was up to Parliament to relieve him. Nobody could "more affect his country than I," but enough was enough. "Many there are that have fine wits yet are more in tongue than in judgment. They make long orations but ... there is nothing but froth in them." The Commons were, of course, enraged when they heard of this speech, and asked for an exact reporting of the archbishop's words. But Cecil dismissed their protest on May 7 by saying that, though "the great prelate" might have been "more lively than is usual, ... his speech ... was very suitable and fitting."[35] The contretemps was not worth blowing up any further, and it was allowed to subside. Nevertheless, the episode was further evidence of the simmering tensions that were becoming a serious impediment to constructive negotiation.

IMPOSITIONS AND FREE SPEECH

Cecil did not improve the situation when, on May 8, he used the news of Henri IV's assassination to imply that James would now need even more money. At this stage the Commons were studiously ignoring the Contract, concentrating instead on grievances. Heavyhanded pleas for money caused barely a ripple of interest. A more pressing issue, in the view of most M.P.s, was the king's prohibition (conveyed on May 11 but apparently decided a week earlier) of further discussion of impositions.[36] This announcement provoked a two-month exploration of the House's right to freedom of speech, an investigation that has become famous for a series of addresses by James Whitelocke and William Hakewill that are milestones in English constitutional history. At the time, however, the quarrel was but another distraction from Parliament's main business. There was no time to consider money matters amidst so many threats to an Englishman's liberty.

The pettiness to which the rancor could descend became apparent immediately after the royal directive was received. Sir William Twysden asked how the speaker had received the king's message, for it was well known that James was out of town. Phelips finally admitted that it had come from the Privy Council, whereupon the House issued an order denouncing this procedure and asserting its right to continue its business "as if no such message had been sent at all." Not until a full week later would the M.P.s profess themselves satisfied that the prohibition came directly from James, and that the speaker had not acted improperly. So important did they consider the issue that, according to an informed diarist, a meet-

[35] Foster, *1610* , 1:80–82, 2:77–79; *CJ*, 425.
[36] Foster, *1610*, 1:83–84, 2:81, 82, 82 n; *CJ*, 426, 427; Gardiner, *1610*, 32.

ing to discuss it attracted "more than ever I saw at any time in the House before."[37]

For some days the Commons could think of nothing but impositions and free speech. After floundering about in righteous indignation on May 18th, the M.P.s finally accepted Sandys's motion that they appoint a committee to frame a conciliatory answer to the king. The next day, however, Caesar told them that James was displeased at their persistence and forbade further discussion, and on the twenty-first a delegation was summoned to Whitehall, where the king expounded his disappointments at considerable length. Parliament had been in session fourteen weeks, but had spent less than that many days on the business for which it had been summoned. He defended impositions as an untouchable branch of his prerogative, and warned "that the more wayward you shall be I shall be the more unwilling to call you to Parliament."[38]

The following day, May 22, the issue was joined. Led by such venerable "populars" as Sir Francis Hastings, Thomas Wentworth, and Nicholas Fuller, the M.P.s chided the king for being (in Fuller's phrase) "a stranger to this government" and unaware of its laws; they insisted on their right to discuss impositions, warning darkly of the danger to all of England's laws should their purposes be thwarted. Sandys, however, brought the discussion to an end with a plea to his colleagues not to allow their suspicions to carry them away. It was usually "misreports, misadvices or errors" that led to "mistaking between us and his Majesty." They surely had no intention of impugning royal prerogatives, while for his part James was duty bound "to keep and protect all our just laws and customs." Sir Edwin seemed sanguine about the prospects for resolving the differences, and called for a committee to prepare a reply.[39]

That afternoon, using the Committee of Grievances chaired by Sandys as its forum, the House wrestled with the question of how to proceed. The Crown's side was now barely heard. Caesar was so brusque and unyielding that he made little impact. And Bacon, though more subtle and persuasive, could make no headway. After he had argued—quite admirably—that the vague boundary between royal prerogative and the subject's rights should not be too carefully defined, he was grudgingly told by Fuller that "though Mr. Solicitor's speech were full of rhetoric and art, yet it had some good substance in it." Nevertheless, when he tried to allege precedents for royal prohibitions of parliamentary discussions, he was told by "divers" that his precedents "did not match the case." Instead, it was agreed that Sandys

---

[37] *CJ*, 427; Gardiner, *1610*, 32–34; Foster, *1610*, 2:83–84, 88–96, 368–369.

[38] Ibid., 2:95–97, 100–107, 370.

[39] Sandys's advice was accepted: ibid., 2:107–110; *CJ*, 430–431.

should draw up a "petition of right" on freedom of speech. As one diarist put it, "the King's privy council, Mr. Chancellor of the Exchequer and of the Duchy [Caesar and Parry], Mr. Secretary Herbert and the learned counsel, Mr. Attorney and Solicitor [Hobart and Bacon] were appointed subcommittees [to help Sandys]; but they all went away."[40]

Sir Edwin presented the petition to the House the next day—a cogent and yet conciliatory statement of the Commons' position. No grand claims were made; indeed, Sandys was careful to insist on the M.P.s' disinclination to meddle with royal privileges: "we have no mind to impugn . . . your Highness' prerogative." Nor would the House dare "take upon us to reverse" the crucial Exchequer decision justifying imposition, Bate's case. All they wanted was "to know the reasons, whereupon the same was grounded." And the king on his side had to acknowledge their right to discuss matters which "do properly concern the subject," particularly since there was "a general conceit" that the precedent of Bate's case might "be extended much farther, even to the utter ruin of the ancient liberty of this kingdom, and of your subjects' right of propriety of their lands and goods." They wanted to look at the new impositions so as to remove "all cause of fears and jealousies from the loyal hearts of your subjects." Once they had permission, they could "cheerfully pass on to your Majesty's business, from which this stop hath by diversion so long witheld us."[41]

It was an astute series of arguments, focused on a high-minded concern for liberties, and rendered well-nigh irresistible by the moderate and reasonable language in which it was couched. Not only did Sandys's petition give little cause for offense (James found it "more reasonable than 'twas reported to him") but it brought about a quite remarkable accommodation. As Caesar announced on the twenty-fifth, the king was ready to give way completely. The Commons had permission to discuss impositions, and indeed the previous royal message, it was now claimed, had not been intended as a prohibition but only as a request "to forbear till we heard his further pleasure . . . he being then 70 miles from us." James became positively mawkish in expressing his hopes for the future: "he said he could not think any of this House misliked his person; and when he looked upon all our faces he did not think any of us would deny to support his estate." The Commons were delighted, and when Sandys informed them that grievances and impositions were to be discussed again that afternoon, they accepted Hobart's recommendation that support be placed on the agenda

    [40] Foster, 1610, 2:110–112; Gardiner, 1610, 36–41.
    [41] CJ, 431–432; PRO, SP/14/54, fols. 75–76; Pauline Croft, "Fresh Light on Bate's Case," Historical Journal 30 (1987): 523–539.

too. Moreover, their main accomplishment during the afternoon session was the preparation of six measures to ensure the king's safety.[42]

On the next day, May 26, normal business resumed, with grievances and the Contract again the center of attention. Sandys reported on the previous afternoon's work and assured the Commons that the search for precedents on impositions was proceeding. He also urged that they await a proposal from the Lords before going into the matter of support. As it happened, one of their committee was in fact receiving such proposals from Cecil that very afternoon. According to the treasurer, the difference between their offer and the king's demand was £140,000. The wards were worth £40,000 a year; since they were willing to give £100,000, that was an excess of £60,000. But James needed an excess of £200,000. He was willing, however, "to fall from that demand"; and "if he fall you should rise." The stage was being set for some nitty-gritty bargaining, but for that purpose, according to Cecil, a free and open conference was essential.[43]

As usual, this suggestion aroused doubts in the Lower House, but Sir Edwin had the perfect compromise. They could have a free conference, he said, but only "upon grounds." They had to have the "heads [i.e., subjects] set down." Although an open exchange was "the best kind" of conference, it was not likely to be fruitful "without discussing." In other words, careful preparation was necessary. As Sandys put it, there were "three sorts of conferences"—those in which everyone offered "his own opinion without direction from the House, wherein the House received often great disadvantage"; those in which no answer was given, "which is rather an audience or meeting than a conference"; and those in which the House decided "first to debate and resolve, and then to divide to certain men their parts." It was the last approach that he advocated. The House agreed, and set aside May 30, following Whitsun, as the first of many sessions when the M.P.s would organize their views.[44] The discussions were to take up almost a month, because it was not until June 25 that the next conference with the Lords on the Contract took place. During the intervening weeks the session's major items of business began to assume their final shape.

GRIEVANCES, SUBSIDIES, AND AGREEMENT ON THE CONTRACT

The next few days were taken up by a brief Whitsun recess, by the ceremony creating James's eldest son, Henry, prince of Wales, and by the subsequent administration of an oath of allegiance to all members of Parlia-

---

[42] Foster, *1610*, 2:115–119; Gardiner, *1610*, 41–42; *CJ*, 433.
[43] Ibid.; Foster, *1610*, 2:120–124.
[44] *CJ*, 434; Gardiner, *1610*, 45–46.

ment. On June 9, however, major business resumed with a report by
Sandys on the progress of the grievances.[45] Three complaints had now resulted in bills for the House to consider; another, dealing with excommunication, was imminent; and the search for precedents on impositions
was well under way, with a chance that it might end the following week.
Two days later, however, Sandys was being distracted by yet another task.

The Lords had asked for a conference to impart a message from the
king. At this news the M.P.s had become extraordinarily upset, and indeed
had made Sandys go off to compose an official order of the House stating
that, if the king's message had been intended for them, they were not to
receive it via the Lords. If, however, it had been delivered to the Upper
House originally, they would deign to hear what James had said. After this
display of sound and fury the delegates went off to the Lords, only to hear
that the king was thinking of ending the session, that his needs were
mounting, and that although he would not mind leaving the Contract "suspended till we meet next Parliament," he did want a subsidy in the meantime. In Cecil's sarcastic words, "I hope you have not forgotten this word,
supply, support. Many understand not what it is."[46]

James's request was not transmitted to the House until June 13th. In the
meantime, on the twelfth, Sandys reported on various privilege matters
and also informed his colleagues that the search for precedents was turning up "no such use" of impositions in earlier times. The next two days
were set aside for a debate on the subsidy, but the House was becoming
less amenable.[47] Nineteen M.P.s had their say on the thirteenth, ten of
whom opposed the immediate granting of a subsidy; even Sir George
More, a veteran Crown spokesman, suggested that they "grant a subsidy,
or two, and stay it, until the grievances be ready in the King's hands." The
following day, Caesar reported a promise from James to listen to all grievances, but this had little effect. Twenty-six members now unburdened
themselves, and the tide ran at least nineteen to seven against the recommendation that they set aside grievances so as to concentrate on a subsidy.
There was no thought of refusing the money. The only issue was the timing of a grant, and on this subject the Commons were resolute even
against Bacon, despite his care not to "blast the affections of this House
with elaborate speech."

Nevertheless, Sir Edwin tried a compromise. The country was fully prepared to pay, he said, but it was very important not to put the issue of
timing to a vote. "If carried" by "three or four voices," he warned, "disre-
putation" would ensue; and "if not carried, a worse sound." Once again, as

[45] CJ, 436.

[46] Foster, 1610, 2:133–141, 133 n; Gardiner, 1610, 50–55.

[47] CJ, 437–439; Foster, 1610, 2:141–148; Gardiner, 1610, 55–58.

in 1606, he was emphasizing the opinion of the "country." But his middle ground was rejected, and the House voted not to proceed with the subsidy. Whereupon that old firebrand, Martin, declared that "this is the fairest day, that ever he saw in Parliament." But Sir Edwin, still hopeful that something concrete could be achieved, managed to salvage something from the debate by persuading the House to approve a mild message to the king. This at least averted an outburst of royal fury and a possible instant dissolution. Making the concession seem to be more than it was, Sandys had the message say: "though this supply be deferred for a time, yet the purpose of the House is to set all other business aside and principally to intend his supply and the subjects' grievances."

In fact, of course, the subsidy was simply shunted aside while grievances (and later the Contract) occupied the Commons. Sandys reported progress on some minor matters on June 15, after which Sir Herbert Croft suggested not only that consideration of impositions be speeded up but also that discussions of the Contract resume. Accordingly, Sandys announced the next day that the precedents were being gathered at full speed (a new group was sent to look at the Port Books) and that the committee would report again within a week. As for the Contract, a message was sent to the Lords on the eighteenth requesting a conference so that new "Heads of Retribution" could be added to the list of disposable royal rights and the total price could be revealed. On the nineteenth Sir Edwin reported that there had been delays in the search for imposition precedents, but that the debate would take place the following Friday, June 22. Meanwhile, the House's lawyers were to prepare a preamble for the petition of grievances.[48]

Still matters did not move as expected. The Lords finally agreed to a conference on the Contract, but it was not to take place until the twenty-sixth. And Sir Edwin explained that the examination of precedents was becoming a mountainous task. As he told the House on the twenty-second, they had already looked at eighty-six records, and it seemed better "to insist upon those they had [seen], than to stay the business." Hinting at what was to come, he explained that "though they had made diligent search, [no impositions had ever] been laid, save only by Queen Mary upon French commodities," and even these "were taken away the first year of Queen Elizabeth." Later that day, he delivered four more grievances, which were added to the Commons' petition.[49]

On June 23 the M.P.s at last heard the results of the deliberations on impositions. Fuller was the spokesman, and his massive speech, replete

[48] *CJ*, 440, 441; Foster, *1610*, 2:149 n.

[49] Ibid., 442–443; Gardiner, *1610*, 58–61 (Fuller's June 23 list of precedents); Foster, *1610*, 2:372 (the quotations). Sandys was right about the French commodities, but another imposition, on cloth, was not taken away, a point I owe to Conrad Russell.

with references to the Bible, to Bracton, and to more than twenty-five precedents, including his own pleading in the recent Monopolies Case, *Darcy* vs. *Allen*, denounced arbitrary impositions as "against the laws of the realm." He was met by "a great silence" that was characteristic of the House at its most concerned. Sir Dudley Carleton and Sir Henry Montague did try to defend the practice, but they were beaten back, and within a few days the Commons were moving toward the preparation of a petition.[50]

With grievances thus rumbling in the background, the House turned once more to the Contract. (It is revealing that the subsidy bill, on which the M.P.s had promised simultaneous action, was not to receive its first reading until July 13.)[51] The conference with the Lords took place on June 26, and Sandys reported the proceedings the following day. Despite some haggling, the outlines of the proposed exchange were clear: in addition to the abolition of wardship, purveyance, and debts more than twenty years old, there were to be seven concessions by the king, mainly in the area of landholding and the working of the law. In return, the king wanted £220,000, which was £140,000 more than the value of wardship and purveyance alone. The Commons, in response, indicated that they did "not think it fit to lay a greater burden upon land than £100,000 per annum."[52]

There the matter rested for nearly three weeks. In the meantime, the House devoted itself to impositions and the petition for grievances. Sandys was in charge of the proceedings almost without cease. He took the chair whenever the Commons constituted themselves into a Committee of the Whole, and then had to deliver the report when they resumed their normal sitting. On July 3 he seems to have been leaping back and forth from his seat, and with better records we would doubtless find him resembling a jack-in-the-box on other days of business as well.[53] He was orchestrating the debates throughout this period, and the burdens he shouldered can have left him no time to prepare his own contributions. Although he had organized the assault on impositions, therefore, he himself did not speak during the climactic debates between June 28 and July 2, notable mainly for William Hakewill's famous speech, a stirring appeal for the subject's liberties that, in the version printed in 1641, must have lasted well over three hours.[54] Not until July 3 did the M.P.s at last agree to put together a

[50] Ibid., 152–165; *CJ*, 443; Gardiner, *1610*, 61–66.
[51] *CJ*, 449.
[52] Ibid., 444; Foster, *1610*, 1:117–120, 2:167–169; Gardiner, *1610*, 121–123.
[53] *CJ*, 445; Foster, *1610*, 2:249.
[54] Ibid., 170–248; Gardiner, *1610*, 66–120, for the debates of June 28 and 29 and July 2. On the constitutional issues raised by James's March 21 speech and these debates, see Paul Christianson, "Royal and Parliamentary Voices on the Ancient Constitution, c. 1604–1621," in *The Mental World of the Jacobean Court*, ed. Linda L. Peck (Cambridge, 1991), 71–95, and

petition, which, when rejected by the king, was elevated into a bill on July 12. Moving with exceptional speed, the Commons managed in five days to pass the bill, which prohibited impositions unless approved by Parliament, "without any negative voice." That the measure progressed no further than a first reading in the Lords does not detract from its significance as a manifestation of the growing differences between subjects and king.[55]

Nor can the members have been pleased by the outcome of the next major item of business, the presentation of their grievances. Sandys and his committee had finally organized what must have been a titanic load of paperwork into two petitions, which were presented to the king on July 7: one, ecclesiastical, requested sterner measures against Jesuits and priests, reinstatement of deprived ministers, an end to pluralities, and greater care in excommunication; the other, temporal, was more extensive, and complained about proclamations, legal abuses, and various impositions and taxes.[56] But James gave the M.P.s little satisfaction.

When he replied, on July 10, he accepted two of the Commons' lesser demands, but rejected their pleas against impositions and procrastinated on all the remaining questions. On most issues he was on fairly firm ground; in dealing with impositions, however, he resorted to evasion: "If I have done wrong, blame the Lord Treasurer who told me that I might impose." And indeed, Cecil himself defended the impositions in considerable detail. Concerned that a vital source of Crown revenue was at stake, he even took the unusual step of arranging an evening meeting at his home in Hyde Park with eight leading M.P.s, mostly supporters of the Contract, in an apparent effort to change their minds. Sandys was among the eight, all of whom were at once suspected by their colleagues as "plotters" of some kind. But the encounter brought Cecil no discernible benefit, because the bill prohibiting impositions, which James (somewhat disingenuously) declared himself "content" to receive, proceeded to rapid passage.[57]

Having disposed of grievances, the M.P.s had no choice but to return to the subsidy and the Contract. Caesar reopened the discussion on the eleventh, and soon the House became embroiled in a dispute over the number of subsidies and the relevance of fifteenths. Sandys reminded his colleagues of the exemption of the northern counties, which was accepted, and then argued against fifteenths: "if it were in regard of war, then a

---

"Ancient Constitutions in the Age of Sir Edward Coke and John Selden," in *The Roots of Liberty: Magna Carta, Ancient Constitution, and the Anglo-American Tradition of Rule of Law*, ed. Ellis Sandoz (Columbia, Mo., 1993), 89–146.

[55] Gardiner, *1610*, 120; Foster, *1610*, 2:249–250, 276, 283 n, 410–412; *CJ*, 449–450; *LJ*, 2:639, 646.

[56] Foster, *1610*, 2:253–271. Every objectionable proclamation was specified.

[57] Ibid., 2:273–275, 274 n; 1:129–134; Gardiner, *1610*, 153–162.

fifteen; if in any other regard, of magnificence [i.e., James's personal needs], then no fifteen." But this time Sir Edwin lost. The House took a vote, and decided, 149 to 129, to grant a fifteenth. But when the king's supporters tried to make it two fifteenths they were defeated, 145 to 130. And despite some proposals that went as high as three subsidies, only one was granted. There was again disagreement over the timing of the payments, but eventually the M.P.s resolved to stretch out their obligations until the following May. There was also some talk of having Parliament supervise the disbursements; this was not taken any further, however, and the bill had its first reading two days later. It passed on July 16.[58]

The session, already over five months old, was not likely to continue much longer (it was in fact prorogued a week after the subsidy passed). The one major item of business still on the agenda was the Contract, and the House devoted most of its remaining time to the thorny question of funding. On July 13 Sandys reported that his committee had decided to offer either a tax of 2d. on each pound's worth of land per annum, or else £180,000 (£60,000 less than demanded by Cecil) for wardship, purveyance, and a number of lesser royal exactions. The first idea was disliked, which facilitated agreement on the £180,000. Not many M.P.s were left at Westminster (one division attracted only thirty votes) but the survivors nevertheless arranged a conference to discuss the Contract with the Lords on July 16 and 17, Sandys's assignment being the haggling over price.[59]

It was on the seventeenth, too, that James announced that he would agree to £200,000 as a final compromise, and would yield all but three of the "retributions" the House had sought. The Commons accepted this offer by a majority of about sixty, but with the implicit condition that they had to consult with their constituents before making final arrangements. Sandys, in particular, emphasized this provision in his speeches during the two-day conference with the Lords. "Public contracts had always respect unto the public good," he proclaimed, "and we come not for a few but for the kingdom." He was also pointed about guarantees for the future: "there must be security on both sides, from him that buys, from him that sells."[60] Nevertheless, despite jabs from both sides that came perilously close to terminating the discussions in an uproar, an uneasy cordiality did endure.

And when Sandys came back on the nineteenth with the news that the Commons had agreed to £200,000, Cecil must have felt that the long or-

---

[58] *CJ*, 448–450; Foster *1610*, 2:278. This is another instance of the linkage between grievances and the Commons' power of the purse that is discussed above, chapter 5, note 12.

[59] Foster, *1610*, 2:277; *CJ*, 449, 450. Sandys at this time also prepared a letter (never sent) to reprimand the universities, whose officials had insulted the House.

[60] Foster, *1610*, 2:283–284, 1:141–143; *CJ*, 449, 451. For the state of Contract negotiations, see John Pory's July 17 letter in Sir Ralph Winwood, *Memorials of Affairs of State*, ed. E. Sawyer, 3 vols. (London, 1725), 3:193–194, and BL, Harleian, 767, fols. 131–132.

deal had been justified. "Finis coronavit actionem," he rejoiced. But there were still problems. The contract "with the whole kingdom" might seem settled, said Sandys, but too many M.P.s (including the lawyers) had departed to "make a final end of the business." Quite simply, "to think now of [arrangements for] a levy, the time is too short." Cecil belittled the possible remaining difficulties: "I cannot see any cause to break this contract" even though no bill had passed.[61] The essential agreement could await confirmation at the next session; for now, the main obstacles had been overcome.

With business winding down, Sandys concentrated on tying up loose ends. He proposed a raise for the clerk of the House for "his pains," and gave some thought to the information the M.P.s would bring to their constituents.[62] On the twentieth, for instance, he moved "that copies of the articles [of the Contract] may go into every country [i.e., county]." These he "set down in writing," and had the House approve them. Although the manner of the levy was left open, the very fact that an annual tax of £200,000 was being contemplated had to be brought to the attention of landowners in their "several counties." Sandys conveyed an account of these proceedings to the Lords in one final conference, on July 21. He was delighted the Contract had been decided, he said, particularly since so little else had been accomplished: "as we now shall bring great contentment unto the people, so had we broken off without agreeing how could we have given an account to those whom we represent, having sit [sic] so long and brought forth nothing worthy so grave a senate."[63]

Even though Sandys was alone in asserting its centrality to the English political system, the growing emphasis on the need to consult the Commons' constituents was one of the most remarkable features of the 1604–10 Parliament. The M.P.s not only considered their business more weighty than ever before, but felt that their actions were shaping England's polity. Sandys emphasized for the Lords that "we will carry down copies of this contract," so that there could be no mistake about the further consultation that would be taking place. He proclaimed himself confident, moreover, that his neighbors would derive "comfort" from the news that "where we

---

[61] Foster, *1610*, 1:154–156.

[62] *CJ*, 452. I owe to Conrad Russell the suggestion that generosity to the clerk may have served both parliamentary self-esteem and the M.P.s' need for solid help when researching their precedents; Sandys himself was to be grateful for the clerk's assistance in 1614 when he sought to recall the 1610 grievances.

[63] Ibid., 453; Foster, *1610*, 2:291–292, 1:159–161; *LJ*, 2:660–662. On the issue of consulting with constituents, see David J. Brentnall, "Regional Influences in the House of Commons 1604–10 (M. Phil. diss., University of East Anglia, 1982), passim. He concludes (59) that the Commons fought harder against Crown influence in James's first Parliament than in the 1620s.

had wont to bring them word of the making of new laws, now the time in this session hath been spent in grievances and matter of support."[64]

Sandys's one other set of comments to the Lords dealt with the subsidy. He expatiated on England's poverty as justification for the grant of a mere one fifteenth, and then concluded by extolling the country's generosity. "For the time to come his Majesty will have a support little inferior unto any king in Christendom, for Louis the XIth, King of France [140 years before!] had not above 4 hundred thousand pounds per annum." Quite apart from its indifference to inflation (a fatal flaw in all discussions of the Contract) this was nonsense, and Cecil sharply replied: "I can show you it was 10 hundred thousand pounds."[65] The treasurer's nerves must have been getting frayed by the smugness of his former protégé; predictably, he had nothing but negative answers to the new grievances.

The last debate of the session took place on the twenty-third, the day of prorogation. The House was still concerned about its grievances, and indeed that afternoon the king was to devote his closing address to a point-by-point rejection of every one of their complaints. But Sandys obviously saw a momentous agreement in the offing, a major transformation of England's fiscal and legal structure, and so he convinced the M.P.s not to pursue these matters any further, nor to press James for some sort of guarantee for the Contract. His persuasiveness on these tender issues revealed the power he had achieved as arbiter of the House—a position reflected by the supreme accolade he received when the suspicious M.P.s allowed him "to propound according to his own direction" at a conference with the Lords.[66] Now virtually negotiating on a one-to-one basis with Cecil, Sir Edwin was maneuvering the Commons toward acceptance of terms that, as Caesar was soon to show, were lopsidedly favorable to England's gentry. First, however, the "country" was to have its say, and the decision it formed over the next three months, together with the government's second thoughts, spelled the end of the project. Once again, a recess was to thwart the chance for harmony between king and Parliament, and on this occasion the consequences prevented genuine reform for half a century.

[64] Foster, *1610*, 1:160.

[65] Ibid., 1:161–163. Both Sandys and Cecil may have known Commines' history of Louis XI's reign; otherwise, as William Hunt pointed out to me, the reference would be inexplicable.

[66] *CJ*, 453–454; *LJ*, 2:658–660; Foster, *1610*, 2:294–295. Another example of the respect he had won was the House's dismissal of a petition against Sir Edwin's continued holding of one of his father's nepotist grants, the valuable prebendry of Osbaldwick, near York, whose lease price had been £100 in Elizabeth's reign: Sir William Dugdale, *Monasticon Anglicanum*, vol. 6 (London, 1830), 1174 n. Although some pending legislation on episcopal grants was clearly in Sandys's interest, the Commons eschewed their customary stand against special privileges in his case: *CJ*, 450; Foster, *1610*, 2:323–324.

The Contract Collapses

The talk that decisive summer must have flowed fast and furious, as the country embarked on a process of political discussion and consultation unique in the Europe of the day. We have little evidence about what was said, but the tenor was doubtless captured by Sir Thomas Beaumont, a Leicestershire gentleman and a future viscount, who summarized the gentry's concerns when Parliament reassembled:

> When I went home into my country, I did (according to the trust reposed by them in me) acquaint them with what we had done, and withal required their advice, telling them the sum offered and withal that some gratuity must come. Their answer was they were glad that the sunshine of his Majesty's favor should come so far as to reach them. But they pressed me particularly to tell them whether the impositions, which were resolved in parliament to be unlawful, were determined by the King to be laid down; and then they said so as the levy might be in a reasonable manner, which they hoped should not be all upon land and all our grievances drawn in together into the contract, they would be willing to give £200,000 a year and also give some present supply.[67]

The response elsewhere must have been similar; if even an inland county like Leicestershire placed so much stress on impositions, despite good intentions, then the Contract was probably in trouble.

Nor were the obstacles coming from one side alone. James had never abandoned his suspicions of Cecil, and the minister's rivals at Court were more than happy to see his project flounder. The Howards, for example, may have been against the arrangement from the start. Their leader, Northampton, was conspicuously silent on the subject in the House of Lords, as were his relatives, Charles, Thomas, and William. Both in early March and in mid-November the earl exhorted the Commons to grant money, but each time he emphasized subsidies rather than the Contract, managing to ignore the issue in November amidst two hours of florid oratory. That neither Chancellor Ellesmere nor the earl of Dunbar was reconciled to the king surrendering prerogatives merely added to the forces arrayed against Cecil.[68] Thus was one of the most farsighted of the vast reform projects devised by great ministers in seventeenth-century Europe—worthy of comparison with the schemes of Oxenstierna, Richelieu, and Olivares—to be brought to nothing in the Court politics that swirled

---

[67] Ibid., 2:318. Sir John Hollis reported similar comments in Nottinghamshire: *CSP, Domestic, 1603–1610*, 633.

[68] On Northampton, see Foster, *1610*, 1:22–23, 259–275; on the jockeying at Court in general, Neil Cuddy, *Bedchamber, Parliaments and Politics in the Reign of James I* (forthcoming), chap. 6.

around a weak king. Cecil's tragedy was that he served James I rather than Henri IV.

The critical blow came from Caesar. The chancellor of the Exchequer owed his rise in royal service to the Cecils, but he also had loyalties to Dunbar and others in the Council. And his position as second-in-command at the Treasury made him well placed to assess the advantages and disadvantages of the Contract. This he did in a long memorandum dated August 17, 1610, which, while suggesting that the Contract might be good value for the subject, gave no such hope to the king.[69] His argument proved decisive as reports of the demise of the Contract spread in midsummer. Bishop Goodman, for example, attributed the change in fortune to the dying words of an unnamed lord, who warned James, presumably in the summer of 1610, never to give up the wards. According to Gardiner, it was in "late 1610" that the king finally lost patience with his minister—a shift in royal favor that was apparent to a minor courtier, John More, by December 1, when he described Cecil as short of temper and unhappy, adding that James now blamed the treasurer for the failure of the Contract. Echoing rumors that had been circulating for months, More intimated that His Majesty's new tactic was to win over individual M.P.s.[70]

If this open break was public knowledge by November, the inner Court circle must have seen it coming months before, as Goodman implied. The mortal wound Caesar dealt the Contract in mid-August, therefore, was as much a symptom as a cause of Cecil's decline. The crucial memorandum was in the form of a dialogue, with "C," obviously Caesar, arguing against the Contract and prevailing. Although some of his criticisms were damaging—for example, the disclosure that £200,000 exceeded the king's losses only by £85,000, not by £120,000, because the minor rights that were to be surrendered (in addition to wardship and purveyance) produced £35,000 a year—others were pure fantasy. Caesar's case rested on the prediction that the king could solve his fiscal predicament, in the absence of the Contract,

[69] Gardiner, 1610, 164–179. Cuddy, Bedchamber, chap. 6, nn. 125–135, identifies a second draft and documents Caesar's divided loyalties; he may also have had a connection through his godfather, the earl of Arundel, to the Howards.

[70] Godfrey Goodman, The Court of King James the First, vol. 1 (London, 1839), 40–41; S. R. Gardiner, History of England . . . 1603–1642, 10 vols. (1883–84), 2:109; Winwood, Memorials, 3:235–236. The only candidate for Goodman's deathbed scene is George Home, earl of Dunbar, a confidant of James who returned to London from Scotland in September 1610 and died at Whitehall four months later. Goodman, often imprecise, may have confused the timing, and shifted both advice and dying a few months earlier: he claims Dunbar brought the warning to the king at a time when the earl was in fact still in Scotland. Despite his inaccuracies, Goodman had a real feel for James's Court; thus, although the story is marred by errors, the reality it represents—the changing atmosphere at Court—should not be dismissed.

by raising the additional £85,000 from the very branches of the prerogative the Commons were seeking to abolish; that he could balance his budget with a little restraint and further use of his feudal rights; and that he could wipe out his £600,000 debt with subsidies, fees, and higher rents. These rosy expectations contrast vividly with the disaster that in fact overtook royal finances in succeeding years, and grew worse until Cranfield restored some semblance of order to a shattered budget. But the chimera was enough to satisfy James. As soon as Parliament gathered, in mid-October, it was clear that neither side was serious about further negotiation.

It is not easy to follow the events of that autumn, because the Commons' Journal has not survived. But there seems no reason to doubt the impression that the Lower House devoted little of the six-week session to substantive business. Between October 16 and 25 not a thing was done, at first for no apparent reason, then because the speaker was ill, and finally because there was "so small a number there (for there were not 100)."[71] At last, on the afternoon of the twenty-fifth, a delegation went to the Lords to hear where matters stood on the Contract. "I must tell you," said Cecil, "that we have perused the memorial [prepared by Sandys on July 20], and to tell you no news we find it imperfect." The choice of phrase reveals both the minister's personal frustrations and the widespread recognition of the Contract's imminent collapse. But he pressed on valiantly. Nothing had been settled, he noted, and he urged the Commons to try immediately to turn their memorial into some kind of definite offer. "The longer you are about it," he complained, "the more will the King's affection kindle against the contract."[72] The kindling had obviously begun, and even Cecil seemed halfhearted in urging his project.

Bacon reported the speech on October 27, whereupon a veteran "popular," Sir Maurice Berkeley, rose to ask whether it was "the want of company" or "somewhat else" that made them "so backward in this business." His answer was unambiguous. "To speak plainly, I think that [somewhat else] is the cause" that they were "more cold in the business than [they] were in the end of the last session." And what was it that was holding them back? "I wish that the first thing we do be to call for the King's answer to our grievances and if we find the answers satisfactory we may then with cheerfulness go on with the contract." Obviously James's responses in July had not been satisfactory. Fuller seconded the motion, and despite More's protests it carried the day.[73] Now the M.P.s had another excuse for delay, especially since the Lords went into recess for a week on October 30.

---

[71] Foster, *1610*, 2:295–296.
[72] Ibid., 2:297–302.
[73] Ibid., 2:302–305.

On the thirty-first, however, James summoned them to Whitehall to tell them they had one last chance to deliver or depart. He was obviously well informed about their discussions, because he pointedly remarked: "whether our slackness proceeded from want of company or from any humor stirring amongst ourselves, ourselves best knew." He angrily dismissed their request to hear once more his response to their grievances: "to require this again is *actum agere*, to tread upon my feet." All they now had to do was to "resolve upon the giving me an answer affirmative or negative to your memorial." As usual, James's exhortations only served to distract the Commons yet further. For two days, November 2 and 3, they debated whether they ought to send some kind of reply so as "to clear some mistaking which it seemed the King had apprehended of the House." Eventually they decided to forbear, and to return to their memorial on November 6.[74]

But November 6 produced the bombshell from the king that put paid to the Contract once and for all. He told them, first, "that 'twas never his intention, much less his agreement, to proceed in the contract finally, except he should receive as well supply as support." In other words, an annual revenue was not enough: he needed, in addition, an outright grant of £500,000. Moreover, the yearly income had to exceed what he surrendered by £200,000.[75] When the M.P.s came to discuss this message on November 7, they noted that the king's terms excluded any abatement of impositions. Christopher Brooke's response was that, although they could perhaps provide the £500,000 with three subsidies and six fifteenths, the situation would be fraught with danger unless impositions were abolished: "if the King wanted (as 'twas said and he believed) 'twas to be feared if he could not take with the right hand, he would take it with the left." Put bluntly, "if we shall not clear the point of impositions, better it were the King should impose alone than we and the King too." It was at this point that Beaumont reported the conversations in his county, and concluded: "upon these terms it is impossible for us to deal for it, and though it be a fair fruit, 'tis out of our reach." More of the same followed from other members, until, called to decide whether the contract should proceed, "the whole House (I think not 5 voices excepted) answered, No."[76]

To this point there had been no sign of Sir Edwin Sandys. Yet he seems to have been in Westminster on the decisive days of November 6 and 7,

---

[74] Ibid., 2:308–312.

[75] Ibid., 2:313–316; Gardiner, *1610*, 128. The progression of events makes it difficult to accuse the Commons of wrecking the Contract; and Croft, "A collection," passim, demonstrates that it had been Cecil's project. Neither point, however, is inconsistent with Cecil's continuing (though perhaps reduced) enjoyment of James's favor after 1610: Eric Lindquist, "The Last Years of the First Earl of Salisbury, 1610–1612," *Albion* 18 (1986): 23–41.

[76] Foster, *1610*, 2:317–319; Gardiner, *1610*, 129–131, says the final decision was reached "una voce."

because on the eighth he took charge of preparing the House's answer to the king—not a responsibility he could have undertaken had he been absent during the discussion of the royal message. Perhaps he remained silent because he could not add to his colleagues' arguments, or because he could not bring himself either to assault or to defend a project that he had been identified with and which, just a few months before, had given his views such prominence in the highest reaches of the government. A final possibility is that his absence was due to another illness. By the eighth, however, his presence was once more unavoidable.

The speaker thought that a committee could prepare the Commons' reply to the king. But Sandys suggested that "it was a matter of too great weight for a few to take upon them at the first, without the direction of the House." He therefore suggested a Committee of the Whole. The M.P.s agreed, and appointed Sir Edwin to the chair. At first there was talk of offering James reasons for their decision, but then Fuller, seconded by Sir Edward Montague, cut off the prospect of a lengthy discussion with the crisp recommendation "that we make a short answer to declare our resolution without yielding any reason at all." The House approved, Sandys left the chair to report the decision, and he and Bacon were designated to write the official reply. Both the notes and the final text have survived, and they underline the emphasis on simplicity. Carefully avoiding any imputations against the king's behavior, the Commons thanked the king for letting them discuss wardship and then, without further ado, terminated the negotiation: "We have resolved that we cannot proceed in the contract."[77]

That was that. It merely remained for James, in reply, to confirm: "the bargain is at an end." This he did on November 14; yet he had by no means given up on taxes. "Now ye are only returned where you began," he told them; therefore "his Majesty leaves you to think how you will think fit to supply him." As it happened, within a week he was to consider dissolving the assembly. But for the time being the search for money went on. The Lords asked for a conference the same afternoon, and both Cecil and Northampton again asked for subsidies. The treasurer even listed eight grievances that he thought both Houses were agreed on.[78] It was to no avail. There was some talk of subsidies for the next two days, but then another distraction arose.

Perhaps because he really could not understand his subjects' reasoning, or perhaps because he thought he could apply some pressure, James called thirty of the M.P.s to Whitehall on the afternoon of November 16. The

---

[77] Foster, *1610*, 2:320–321; the M.P.s stressed that their conclusion was reached "according to this Your Majesty's declaration"—presumably the message of November 6: ibid., 2:322–323; Gardiner, *1610*, 131.

[78] Foster, *1610*, 2:327, 329–330, 1:259–275; *CSP, Domestic, 1603–1610*, 644.

main question he asked was whether they believed he had genuinely in-curred large debts. Nobody denied it, but still they responded by discuss-ing grievances: prohibitions against preachers, proclamations, the jurisdic-tion of the Council of Wales, and impositions. The latter issue devolved on Sandys, who "spake to the King in justification of the proceedings of the lower House," apparently emphasizing "the poverty of the people." Caesar regarded this entire conference as breeding "contempt in the inferior to-wards the superior," but its immediate consequence was anger in the Com-mons.[79]

James justified himself even before objections could be raised. In a mes-sage delivered the following day, the seventeenth, he adjourned the House for four days so as to give himself time to write a longer message, and he said he had summoned the M.P.s "only to confer with them as private men," not "for anything that they had spoken in Parliament." He simply wanted "to make them see how unwilling he would be to suffer anything to be mistaken that may have passed heretofore." But the Commons were not to be diverted from their sensitivity to breaches of privilege. Although another message was awaiting them when they returned to Westminster on the twenty-first, they ignored it for two days. Instead, they wallowed in denunciations of the episode at Whitehall (with some of the thirty, includ-ing Sandys, joining in the attacks), and finally drew up an order forbidding M.P.s to discuss "any matter depending in consultation in this House" with either king or Lords except with the express approval of the House.[80]

With that accomplished, they could return to the better humor that James's November 21 message was designed to elicit. He had apparently thought further about the four grievances the thirty M.P.s had raised. Ac-cordingly, he professed himself willing to receive a bill restraining future impositions; he protested that he had never intended the Council of Wales to cause injustice; and he promised further action on prohibitions and proclamations. Thus mollified, the House returned to a consideration of relief for the king on November 23. But this debate soon deteriorated into denunciation of the Scots as the cause of the "continual and remedyless leak" in the royal budget. Hearing that there might be a petition against the Scots, James adjourned Parliament on the twenty-fourth, this time for five days. Only seven members turned up on the twenty-ninth, however, and they were promptly adjourned for a further week. The comedy finally came to an end on December 6, when Parliament was formally prorogued. Three weeks later, on the last day of the year, the assembly whose sittings had begun amid such hope nearly seven years before was finally dissolved.[81]

[79] Foster, 1610, 2:337–338, 348 n.
[80] Ibid., 2:339–340, 342–343, 391–392.
[81] Ibid., 2:340–341, 343–345, 345 n, 347–349.

POST MORTEMS

James did not hide his disappointment. Even his proclamation of dissolution indicated that the Parliament had not lived up to his expectations. It had gone on too long, he said, and had to end "for many good considerations, known to himself." This was taken as a reprimand by the anonymous author of the only defense of a Parliament published in James's reign.[82] The Commons, in his view, were "covertly traduced"; to avoid the appearance of blaming the king, however, he argued that the proclamation, which used "his Majesty" instead of the customary "We," could not have been written by James himself. And to prove the fruitfulness of the session, he printed a speech delivered by Fuller on November 23, in the midst of a debate on further subsidies, that stressed the country's poverty, the persistence of ecclesiastical abuses, and the great efforts the House had made to achieve reforms. "As we had care of the church," Fuller had asserted, "so had we care of the commonwealth," particularly in regard to impositions, purveyance, and wardship. If the remedies were not forthcoming, it was not the M.P.s' fault. In Fuller's words, "if way had been as well given by others, as it was made by us, I say by others whom these things concerned as deeply as ourselves, many abuses had been reformed, that are not now, and much good done."[83] The pamphleteer then listed eighteen abuses the House had sought to terminate through the Contract, and printed the various petitions of grievances that had been submitted.

That the Parliament aroused sufficient high feeling to provoke a publication of this kind is not entirely surprising. Both Puritans who hoped for further reforms and gentry who anticipated an end to feudal dues had expected much from the sessions of 1610. But their optimism was ill placed, and they doubtless ended up as frustrated as the king. Looking for a scapegoat, James saw only Cecil. More than ten years later he still harped on the theme. His first Parliament failed, he claimed, because he "was frustrated by the underhand practices of some, by whom he was misled, trusting upon their experience, himself being but then a stranger to the government." That was a travesty of the facts—and a confession of ignorance that James would angrily have rejected both in 1604 and in 1610. Yet at the time he was hardly less unfair to his minister. "I have found," he wrote, "that by the perturbations of your mind, you have bro-

[82] Ibid., 2:348–349; James F. Larkin and Paul L. Hughes, eds., *Stuart Royal Proclamations*, vol. 1 (Oxford, 1973), 257–258; *A Record of some worthy proceedings in the Honorable, wise, and faithful House of Commons in the Parliament holden in the year 1611.* The British Library and STC catalogues list this work as published in Amsterdam in 1611, not 1641, as suggested by Foster, *1610*, 2:344 n, and Walter Scott, ed., *Somers Tracts*, 2d ed., vol. 2 (London, 1809), 148.

[83] Foster, *1610*, 2:405–410.

ken forth in more passionate and strange discourses these last two sessions of Parliament than ever you were wont to do, wherein for pity of your great burden I forbear to admonish you." It was all Cecil's fault, or at the very least the fault of misguided M.P.s. When he opened the next Parliament, in 1614, James complained of the "polluted eyes" of some members, and the "misunderstandings" that had sabotaged the 1610 sessions. He grumbled (not inappropriately) that the entire Parliament "began with trouble."[84]

Yet the king's simplistic analyses ignored the real undercurrents of the age. It was as foolish to assume that his difficulties with the Commons were anyone's "fault" as it was to believe that stern lectures would inspire easy compliance. Toward the end of the assembly's life, it is true, the members seemed capable of little but hunting for grievances, and James's anger, laced with accusations of treason, was understandable. So, too, was Ellesmere's charge that the M.P.s "did not so much endeavor to seek remedy and reformation of mischiefs or inconveniences in the commonweal as to quarrel and impeach his Majesty's prerogative, and his regal jurisdiction, power and authority."[85]

Nevertheless, it is obvious that both the king and his councillors misjudged the temper of England's legislators. That Cecil, in November of 1610, could still have been urging patience, and expecting "better issue" and imminent changes in "mood" and "humor," signals only the ebbing of a great minister's once formidable powers.[86] The assurance, even the impatience, of the M.P.s cries out from every page of their proceedings. This was a House of Commons that felt it knew the country's needs: what policies were required, what freedoms had to be defended, what problems had to be solved, and what measures and cures were necessary. If the monarch had to change his ways, the members did not hesitate to tell him so, despite the disarray this caused in the body politic by dividing its head from its members. When James shielded an abuse with his prerogative, they persisted until they won the right to breach the shield; and they used the Crown's need for money with telling effect. The author of the anonymous pamphlet of 1611 may have exaggerated in asserting that no assembly had ever had "greater zeal for the ease and freedom of the subjects than the late House had," but six years of meetings had crystalized this particular Lower House into a redoubtable force.[87] It had blocked Union with Scotland, given the King lecture after lecture, accumulated grievances beyond all previous bounds, streamlined its own proceedings, and entered into

[84] *CD*, 5:429; Foster, *1610*, 2:346 n; BL, Additional, 41,613, folss. 262, 265, 266.
[85] Foster, *1610*, 1:279–280; Gardiner, *1610*, 146 n.
[86] Ibid.
[87] Foster, *1610*, 2:349 n.

tough negotiations over the Contract that often made it seem the equal of the Crown.

THE ROLE OF SIR EDWIN SANDYS

One man above all others had been responsible for the new vigor of the Commons: Sir Edwin Sandys. After taking command of three critical issues in the first session of the Parliament, he had become the Commons' chief spokesman on most of the major subjects they dealt with thereafter. More closely identified with opposition to the Union than any other member, he was also instrumental in the preparation of the "Apology" and the guiding light in most subsequent investigations of grievance. He was always, moreover, the perfect "Commons-man." He threw himself into the dreary routines of day-to-day business with unflagging energy, and he consistently took the lead in seeking better procedures for conducting the House's affairs. The decisive part he played in the creation of the Committee of the Whole and in the improvement of the official Journal was as fraught with implications for the future as many of his more substantive recommendations.

Yet it was primarily as the embodiment of independent gentry concerns that he gained and retained his prominence. Able to raise the broadest considerations when addressing major issues (for instance, in the debate on purveyance in 1606) Sir Edwin was also adept in the kind of detailed bargaining that was often essential in swaying the House. It is impossible to trace all the work that went into his preparations, the careful maneuvering that must have preceded his activities on the floor of the Commons; but there can be no doubt that the level of his commitment to parliamentary business required almost day-and-night attention during a session. If Sandys's public actions are any indication of his private concerns and undertakings, then he emerges as a man who, once he sensed his ability to shape the Commons' agenda, determined to advance his vision of good government, to attack abuses, and to defend the privileges of Parliament and subject at every turn. In these objectives he was entirely in tune with his colleagues, and for that reason more than any other he was able to gain his remarkable ascendancy in the House. If at times he resorted to what seems like petty obstructionism, that, too, merely reflected the predilections of his fellow M.P.s, though it was never (as some, including James himself, thought) the prime aim of the independent gentry.

To say that Sir Edwin often embodied the qualities and aspirations of the assembly in which he sat is not, however, to ascribe monolithic unity to the more than four hundred disparate M.P.s. They could achieve broad levels of agreement, but there was little cohesion, let alone strict conformity, even among small groups of like-minded members. His credentials as a "popular" notwithstanding, Sandys was not immune to the accusation of betraying the House at the meeting with Cecil in Hyde Park in July 1610. There is no reason, therefore, given the evidence we have, to suggest the emergence of some entity that significantly foreshadowed the parties of the late seventeenth century. Stuart gentry were not incapable of creating such structures (the Puritans, with their contacts in Court and country, their planning for Parliament, their program of reform, and their coordinated leadership under Nicholas Fuller, possessed the preliminary attributes of a party) but none with broad aims is observable in the meetings of 1604–10. The long duration of the Parliament allowed Sandys and his cohorts to refine their preparations and also their appreciation of the concerns their colleagues shared, but they pursued their goals through a shifting congeries of alliances, not as a party, but as a lobby: as a constantly changing pressure group that relied on argument, maneuver, and contacts at Court, rather than disciplined organization, to win acceptance of its views.

An important corollary to that conclusion is the weakness of aristocratic influence on the events of 1604–10. Although the absence of senior officials in the House was the Court's most serious problem, James and his ministers also failed to create the body of clients that had formerly marked the Commons. The days of the great Elizabethan patrons like Leicester and Bedford were over, and despite his domination of the Lords, particularly in 1610, Cecil never assembled a group of effective agents in the Commons; indeed, the blurring of coalitions and lines of power after Elizabeth's death may have weakened the old patronage system and prevented the creation of clusters of aristocratic protégés. In 1614 the Howards were able to make their weight felt, and in the 1620s Southampton and, above all, Buckingham and Pembroke were able to gather significant sets of adherents. But in the first Stuart parliament there was no such assemblage, a situation which, like the paucity of privy councillors, helped strengthen the Lower House's growing immunity to outside pressure. Even the Puritans seemed to be free of the nobility's direction; the shots were being called, not by a Leicester or a Bedford, but by commoners like Fuller. And the power of the peers was never to be the same again.

That there were rumors of Sandys being sent as ambassador to Brussels in 1611 (which suggests a rapprochement with Cecil) does not imply that he subordinated himself to the minister. Nor can one see any of his connections in James's reign—whether with Cecil, Southampton, Carr, or the Howards—as the origin of the courses he pursued; these were alliances that reinforced rather than inspired his actions. Thus, when Sir Edwin linked up with Southampton in 1621, he acted as an equal, not a dependent; he and Digges allied themselves with Buckingham in 1624 as much for the advantage of the Commons as for the benefit of the duke; two years later, Eliot went his own way despite the awesome power of his patron, Buckingham; and there is evidence that the Lords followed the Commons' lead in 1628 over the Petition of Right.[88] The sessions of 1604–10 were therefore an important stage in the Lower House's movement toward a position of partnership with king and aristocracy (a position they briefly held during the Contract negotiations in 1610) because, even though Crown and nobles soon sought to reassert their influence, they never erased the effects of that first withdrawal. Having had a taste of increased autonomy, of their ability to put forward their own vision of the welfare of the realm, the gentry M.P.s were assuming an independent position in the polity of England.

And Sandys was the epitome of the change. Capable of infuriating the old mentor, Cecil, whose spokesman he had been in 1593, he was unmistakably his own man, making connections where *he* chose. When he took a stand or acted in concert with other M.P.s the decision was his, not that of a peer to whom he felt beholden. Sir Edwin had found his metier, and his rise to prominence was a microcosm of the process whereby the Commons as a whole moved toward a new, self-contained authority. His mounting confidence provided a gauge of the growth of those qualities in the House at large, and for the rest of the reign he remained both the symbol and the vanguard of the M.P.s' powers.

[88] On the ambassadorship, see HMC *Downshire*, 3:146, 180, 226—a reference I owe to Neil Cuddy. Cuddy has suggested that Sandys may also have forged a link with another major Court figure, Sir Robert Carr, who was helping Southampton at this time and may have enabled Sandys to obtain Northbourne (which further undermines any notion of clients loyal to a single patron): P. R. Seddon, ed., *The Letters of John Holles 1587–1637*, vol. 1, Thoroton Society Record Series, vol. 31 (Nottingham, 1975), 74. On Eliot, J. N. Ball, "The Parliamentary Career of Sir John Eliot, 1624–1629" (Ph.D. diss., Cambridge University, 1953), 93–125, and "Sir John Eliot at the Oxford Parliament, 1625," *Bulletin of the Institute of Historical Research* 28 (1955): 113–127; on Lords and Commons in 1628, J. S. Flemion, "The Struggle for the Petition of Right in the House of Lords: The Study of an Opposition Party Victory," *Journal of Modern History* 45 (1973): 193–210.

Chapter VII

"NOT MANY ARGUMENTS, BUT STRONG":
THE ADDLED PARLIAMENT

PREPARATIONS FOR PARLIAMENT

The new Parliament that brought Sandys back to Westminster in 1614 was called because James was again desperately short of money, this time to the tune of some £600,000, approaching a record for the reign.[1] It was not a decision he reached easily: the argument in the Privy Council was fierce, and even the staunchest advocates of subsidies as the key to solvency admitted that the temper of the Commons was highly doubtful.[2] But there seemed no better way to reduce the deficit. Moreover, remembering the consequences of neglect in 1604, the Court could make extensive preparations. But those who opposed the calling of Parliament could also prepare. Northampton in particular had been contemptuous of the Commons in 1610, wanted no Parliament, and, as the most weighty figure at Court after the death of Cecil, could ensure that the proceedings encountered difficulty at every turn. Having made his own prophecy come true, he could pose as the only advisor who had foreseen parliamentary behavior accurately.[3] Thus did the success of Parliament, and the newly perceived means of influencing its deliberations, become a pawn in the factional battle for James's favor.

But the groundwork that was laid for the new meeting was not merely a reflection of Court politics. Two veterans of the 1604–10 sessions, Sir Henry Neville and Sir Francis Bacon, sent the king memoranda advising

---

[1] According to F. C. Dietz, *English Public Finance, 1558–1641* (New York, 1932), 149, 161, James's debts rose from £500,000 in 1612 to £700,000 in 1615. Robert Ashton, "Deficit Finance in the Reign of James I," *Economic History Review*, 2d ser., 10 (1957): 23, which gives similar figures, suggests that the annual deficit in this period may have been as high as £160,000. The debt may therefore have been even larger than £600,000 on the eve of Parliament.

[2] T. L. Moir, *The Addled Parliament of 1614* (Oxford, 1958), chap. 2.

[3] D. H. Willson, *King James VI and I* (London, 1956), 334–335, 348–349; Neil Cuddy, *Bedchamber, Parliaments, and Politics in the Reign of James I* (forthcoming), chap. 6. Northampton's nephew Suffolk, by contrast, sought a Parliament; his appointment as treasurer in July 1614, following his uncle's death, continued the Howards' disastrous control over royal finance.

him on prospects only partially in the hope of private gain.[4] Both men believed their extensive experience of day-to-day maneuvering unimpeded by strong Crown leadership in 1604–10 enabled them to recommend effective parliamentary tactics. Bacon rightly claimed: "I take myself to have a little skill in that region."[5] And the chief necessity was careful planning. The new political situation required a new intensity of preparation. Both general and partisan considerations, therefore, demanded electioneering. The interventions that ensued took place on so unprecedented a scale, and attitudes and practices contrasted so sharply with the lackadaisical approach of 1604, that for the first time "undertaking"—the acceptance by M.P.s of instructions from powerful patrons who arranged their election—became an issue in the House of Commons.[6]

Yet it is not clear that the Court's efforts had tangible effect, beyond arousing the Commons' ire. Despite the formulation of an elaborate legislative program, much encouraged by Bacon, and despite the pressing need for funds, royal views were more weakly heard in 1614 than in 1604. For all the influx of government officials—they apparently constituted over a third of the House—the king's wishes were pathetically represented.[7] Partly this was due to the inexperience of Sir Ralph Winwood, newly ap-

---

[4] Two versions of Bacon's advice are in James Spedding, ed., *The Letters and the Life of Francis Bacon*, 7 vols. (London, 1861–74), 4:365–373. Neville's recommendations are in BL, Cotton, Titus F IV, fols. 344, 346, 351–352, and PRO, SP/14/74/44–46. See, too, Spedding, *Letters and Life*, 363–365, 373–378; Gardiner, *History of England . . . 1603–1642*, 10 vols. (London, 1883–84), 2:201–206; and Moir, *Addled Parliament*, 11–23. Cuddy, *Bedchamber*, links Neville's efforts with factions at Court.

[5] Spedding, *Letters and Life*, 4:280.

[6] On the electioneering see Moir, *Addled Parliament*, 30–54. The distinction between "packing" and "undertaking" is explored in Clayton Roberts and Duncan Owen, "The Parliamentary Undertaking of 1614," *English Historical Review*, 93 (1978), 481–498. See, too, Linda L. Peck, *Northampton: Patronage and Policy at the Court of James I* (London, 1982), 174; Maija Jansson, ed., *Proceedings in Parliament 1614* (Philadelphia, 1988), xxiii–xxiv (henceforth *Proceedings 1614*); and, on Jacobean elections in general, Robert Ruigh, *The Parliament of 1624: Politics and Foreign Policy* (Cambridge, Mass., 1971), 43–148; J. K. Gruenfelder, *Influence in Early Stuart Elections* (Columbus, Ohio, 1981); Derek Hirst, "Elections and Privileges of the House of Commons in the Early Seventeenth Century," *Historical Journal* 108 (1975): 851–862; Hirst, *The Representatives of the People? Voters and Voting in England under the Early Stuarts* (Cambridge, 1975); Mark Kishlansky, *Parliamentary Selection: Social and Political Choice in Early Modern England* (Cambridge, 1986); and V. J. Hodges, "The Electoral Influence of the Aristocracy, 1604–41" (Ph.D. thesis, Columbia University, 1977). The role of Somerset, Suffolk, Pembroke and Southampton in the "undertaking" is analysed in Cuddy, *Bedchamber*.

[7] Spedding, *Letters and Life*, 5:14–18, lists fifty-seven proposed bills. Some (e.g., to clarify penal laws: *CJ*, 470) were introduced, but there was no evidence of a purposeful Court campaign to implement a legislative program, and most proposals, such as an unexplained "act for the better plantation of Virginia," remained in limbo: Moir, *Addled Parliament*, 45–57.

pointed secretary of state and the Crown's most senior spokesman, who was sitting in his first and only Parliament. Equally crippling, however, was the lack of unity among courtiers.[8] Both Caesar and Bacon, who may have resented playing supporting roles, conspicuously refrained from entering into partnership with Winwood, and lesser courtiers showed few signs of cohesion: most remained silent, and they did not use their numbers to pack committees or dominate voting. It makes no more sense to speak of a body of members working for the king in 1614 than in 1604–10.

Reinforcing this disarray was the determination of a number of powerful figures at Court, notably Northampton, that the session not succeed. The ally of the earl in the Commons was a hitherto second-echelon "popular," John Hoskins, who had made a name for himself only by his contentious-ness. One scholar has called him "the most radical member" of the 1610 Parliament, and in 1614 he was so obstreperous that both he and the agent of Northampton who egged him on, Sir Charles Cornwallis, earned them-selves a year's imprisonment in the Tower for their pains.[9]

As for Sandys, he owed his election to Northampton's rivals—an indica-tion he was expected to help the session succeed. With the support of his cousin, Sir Dudley Digges, a leading Kentish landowner, and Sir Robert Mansell, treasurer of the navy and a protégé of Nottingham (a Howard but opposed to Northampton), he stood for Kent's county seat together with a veteran Puritan, Sir John Scott, but they had no chance against two power-ful county figures, Sir Peter Manwood and Sir Thomas Walsingham. Scott's nephew, Thomas, indicated the forces at work when he remarked that at least one freeholder had been threatened because "laboring as he does for Sir Edwin Sandys he is too busy in state matters and will hear of it."[10] As

---

[8] Moir, *Addled Parliament*, 167–168, describes the disarray. A foretaste of Winwood's inex-perience was the "great silence" on the first day of business before he remembered to rise and propose Crew as speaker: *Proceedings 1614*, 12.

[9] Margaret Judson, *The Crisis of the Constitution: An Essay in Constitutional and Political Thought in England, 1603–1645* (New Brunswick, N.J., 1949), 305; Moir, *Addled Parliament*, 140, 145–146. Moir's linkage of Hoskins with Northampton has been questioned by Peck, *Northampton*, 208–210, who treats Hoskins, like many M.P.s, as an independent figure, not programmed from above. She sees Northampton's power waning in 1614, and regards him as only one of a number who sought to undo the session, but her exoneration of the earl seems to go too far. In particular, there is reason to doubt Moir's interpretation (which she appar-ently accepts) that the House was "unruly from the beginning" (ibid., 208), and that therefore one need not seek outside forces to explain the session's failure. Even if he was not the power he once was, Northampton's damaging influence, attested to by various contemporaries (ibid., 210), seems incontrovertible, though other outsiders, including James, certainly also contrib-uted to the "addling."

[10] Moir, *Addled Parliament*, 31. Mansell owed his navy position to his distant relative, Charles Howard, earl of Nottingham, who was lord admiral and a cousin of Northampton. Symptomatic of the gentry's shifting alliances was Mansell's very different view of Sandys in 1621: see below, chapter 9, note 49. Thomas Scott's diary: Centre for Kentish Studies, U951

an alternative, Sandys was recommended to Rochester both by Mansell and by James's favorite, the earl of Somerset (another rival of Northampton). The townsmen could hardly refuse, but the mayor did ask whether Sir Edwin had been elected elsewhere, in which case they might use the seat for another candidate. Their new M.P. replied, disingenuously, that he could "not be so injurious . . . to your city . . . as to admit any thought of reversing or altering that election." He rode up to Rochester, had himself sworn in as a freeman of the borough, and moved smartly on to the Commons.[11]

Yet the efforts to influence elections had little concrete effect. For the individual acts of patronage were not followed, once Parliament assembled, by attempts to redeem the debt: to use the beneficiaries to advance the patron's wishes. The irrelevance of the electioneering is symbolized by Northampton's staunchest adherent, Hoskins, who was chosen by Hereford (as he had been in 1604) because of his family's status in Herefordshire, not because of the intervention of a great courtier.

Compared to the difficulty of discerning a Crown or courtier faction in the House, it is well-nigh impossible to distinguish a coherent cluster of independent-minded M.P.s. Only occasional parallel purposes united such bedfellows as the Puritan Fuller, the Parliament-man Sandys, and the troublemaker Hoskins. Although some groups of M.P.s did embody specific causes (like the Puritans on ecclesiastical reform), usually individual leaders like Sandys shaped their colleagues' perception of significant issues. This was why Bacon, that veteran observer, argued that a new Parliament would not be unruly because (so he vainly hoped) ten leading "populars" would no longer advance their independent views. "Yelverton is won," he wrote; "Sandys is fallen off; Crew and Hyde stand to be sergeants; Brooke is dead; Nevill hath hopes; Berkeley I think will be respective; Martin hath money in his purse; Dudley Digges and Hollis are yours."

Z16/1, item 3, and Bodleian Library, Ballard MSS. 61, fol. 88. I owe these references to Peter Clark, whose "Thomas Scott and the Growth of Urban Opposition to the Early Stuart Regime," *Historical Journal* 21 (1978): 1–26, is an essential assessment.

[11] Staffordshire Record Office, D 593 (Leveson Papers) S/4/60/11, 13. My attention was brought to these documents by Terence Hartley. On Kentish politics see Peter Clark, *English Provincial Society from the Reformation to the Revolution: Religion, Politics, and Society in Kent, 1500–1640* (Hassocks, Sussex, 1977). Sandys was also returned by Hindon in Wiltshire, probably thanks to the earl of Pembroke, an ally of Southampton, an associate of Sandys in the Virginia Company, and Northampton's principal opponent in the Privy Council: Moir, *Addled Parliament*, 185; Brian O'Farrell, "The Third Earl of Pembroke's 'Connection,' Electoral Power, and Parliamentary Influence in the Early Seventeenth Century," an unpublished paper based on his Ph.D. dissertation (University of California at Los Angeles, 1966) that is to appear in revised form in his *Sidney's Heir: William Herbert, Third Earl of Pembroke, 1580–1630*; and J. R. Bailey, "A Biography of William Herbert, Third Earl of Pembroke, 1580–1630" (Ph.D. diss., Birmingham University, 1961).

Despite the extraordinary inaccuracy of this assessment, Bacon's comments are a clear tribute to the power that M.P.s could exercise in early Stuart politics when they worked together to articulate and pursue a convincing gentry agenda on significant issues.[12]

WHY WAS THE 1614 PARLIAMENT ADDLED?

The central question about the 1614 Parliament concerns its place in the development of the institution following the remarkable events of 1604–10. Would the attempts at cooperation have better success, or would the suspicions intensify? Clearly, given the Parliament's nickname, the outcome was the latter. Which leads to the further question: to what extent were the "populars" responsible for that outcome? In what follows we will see that leaders like Sandys continued to exercise essential control over the House; that in many respects there was a continuity from 1610 that extended beyond 1614; and that the sharpening of confrontation was as much, if not more, the work of Court circles as of M.P.s.[13]

That there were furious debates and a final unpleasant showdown cannot be doubted. Moreover, as Moir points out, there was a brief quarrel between Digges and Sandys, and there were occasions when the "populars" did not have their way. But these features of 1614 were not unprecedented, and Maija Jansson's conclusion about Sandys's organization of the assault on impositions is impeccable: "there can be no room for argument about lack of leadership here."[14] It is especially in the debates on impositions that we see the gentry who dominated the House promoting (as

[12] Spedding, *Letters and Life*, 4:370. Cuddy, *Bedchamber*, argues that Somerset had been cultivating the group since 1611. Bacon mistakenly dismissed Sandys, Hyde, and Hollis; killed Brooke fifteen years early; and included Digges, who had been new and quiet in Parliament in 1610, but was now disaffected because he had not succeeded Winwood as ambassador at The Hague: Thomas Kiffin, "Sir Dudley Digges: A Study in Early Stuart Politics" (Ph.D. diss., New York University, 1972), 48–51; Moir, *Addled Parliament*, 19.

[13] Moir, *Addled Parliament*, 59, argues that the "opposition leaders" were disunited, and that therefore the House was chaotic and "ungovernable" (ibid., 133, 164–165, 168–169). Yet he gives more examples of Sandys and his associates intervening decisively in debates than of their failures (ibid., 101, 111, 124–126, 142). Moreover, (ibid., 60) Moir's argument that the disunity derived from a lack of "experienced leaders in the House" flies in the face of Sandys's and Fuller's long leadership, and contradicts his conclusion (ibid., 159): "The Addled Parliament was not [an] isolated event. . . . the continuity of development was unbroken."

[14] Ibid., 132–133. Moir stresses the "opposition's" irresponsibility and its strained, "crabbed" arguments, despite the evidence of its logical and constructive efforts: contrast ibid., 164, 168 with 103, 124–126, 130. For Jansson's more convincing view, see *Proceedings 1614*, xxix. Moir dismisses as a "bitter speech" (115) Sandys's famous statement of the king's contractual obligations to his subjects, which Judson calls "extreme" but still part of a theory of "contract within the state" that was compatible with Sandys's insistence on deference to the Crown: Judson, *Crisis of the Constitution*, 19, 305–306.

before) their vision of good government. Despite the distraction of the "undertaking," and the fraying of tempers at the end of the session, they were developing the themes and tactics that had crystalized between 1606 and 1610.

The major change lay elsewhere: in the king's refusal to outwait the complaining. There was a hint of what was to come when the second session of 1610 was dissolved after seven and a half weeks; in 1614 James hung on a little longer, for nine weeks. But in both cases the ultimate sterility of the meeting, as measured by legislative output, was the result of royal impatience. Of the two sessions, it was in fact the 1610 gathering that showed the greater apathy, repeatedly going into recess, failing to meet, and leaving behind no official record of its acts, though it did produce five bills, four of which became law. By contrast, the atmosphere of commitment and engagement in 1614—the sense of dedication to parliamentary duties—was unmistakable, and betokened the M.P.s.' readiness to come to grips with the major issues facing the government and the country. What rendered their deliberations fruitless was the king's refusal to mark time, to compromise, until the Commons could delay a subsidy no longer. Even in the friendly days of 1606 almost four months of debates elapsed before a subsidy bill was finally sent up to the Lords, and in 1610 the delay was five months. The one law that the Addled Parliament did pass, with commendable dispatch, was a bill naturalizing James's new son-in-law, the luckless Frederick of the Palatinate. For his part James offered concessions on long-standing issues of landholding and legal procedure that had been part of the Contract and had kept progress alive through the worst patches of discontent.[15] But he was not willing to wait the extra weeks to maneuver and stay in the fight until the subsidies grudgingly appeared, nor to discuss the impositions that were crucial to his income.

Only one explanation for the failure of royal policy is possible: the change in the King's advisors. Although both Bacon and James blamed Cecil for the shortcomings of the 1604–10 Parliament, even suggesting that he was responsible for the campaigns of the "populars," they missed the truth.[16] For the ascendancy of the Howards was an unmitigated disaster, particularly in the dealings with Parliament. The difference was already noticeable in the second session of 1610, when Cecil's influence was waning; by 1614 there was no mistaking the transformation. It was North-

---

[15] Moir, *Addled Parliament*, 97; Spedding, *Letters and Life*, 5:15–16; *CJ*, 470.

[16] Spedding, *Letters and Life*, 4:371; 5:30 reveals the origin of James's elliptical reference, in 1614, to servants of his who had "bred . . . ill affection" between king and Parliament in 1610: HMC, *Hastings*, 4:234. Bacon could be startlingly myopic when he allowed partisan venom to distort his view of Cecil: Spedding, *Letters and Life*, 4:280, 313 n; Willson, *James VI & I*, 269, 335. Neville also blamed Cecil: BL, Cotton, Titus F IV, fol. 349—a reference I owe to Neil Cuddy.

ampton himself, combining with the Spanish ambassador, who guided James to the premature, ill-advised dissolution.[17] The responsibility for the "addling" of the Parliament rested squarely on the Crown.

ELECTIONS, UNDERTAKERS, AND GRIEVANCES

There were four issues that aroused significant interest during the session of 1614: elections and undertaking, the subsidy, impositions, and the intemperate defense of royal prerogative by the bishop of Lincoln. All but the first were familiar sparks for debate, and the course of the discussions was not substantially different than it had been in 1610. There was the same reluctant acceptance of the need for taxes, the same outrage over impositions, and the same anger when a member of the Upper House implicitly limited the Commons' area of competence. Nor were the remarks about the new issue, elections and undertaking, dissimilar in tone from the comments that had greeted the Bucks election case in 1604 or other manifestations of Court interference in parliamentary proceedings. And the final constant was the prominence of Sandys, as usual carrying the main burden of major committee appointments and chairmanships, frequently deciding debates by his interventions, and balancing his emphasis on moderation with a suspicion of Crown policies and a passionate commitment to the rights of the Commons and the liberties of the subject.

The problem of elections and undertakers arose on the very first day of business, April 8. There was concern both at Court interference in elections and at the presence of a leading judicial officer, the attorney-general (Bacon) in the House. The anxieties were linked by Fuller, who feared the "mixture . . . of both bodies," the blurring of distinctions between Lords and Commons, through the presence of Bacon and the election of undertakers. As the hue and cry gathered force, committees were appointed to investigate the attorney-general's position and to consider privileges. Sandys was named to both groups, and at once put these specific concerns in a larger context by emphasizing how they all came under the mandate of the Privilege Committee. Its task, he said, was central to their deliberations: to examine "the liberties of the House" in the broadest terms. The first liberty that had "to be preserved, as our lives," was "freedom of election." His own quest for a seat notwithstanding, he stressed that, if elections were "pressed by power, fear, etc., [they were] not free." (The other two liberties were the M.P.s' personal privileges and their freedom of speech.)[18]

---

[17] Moir, *Addled Parliament*, 140.

[18] J. P. Cooper, ed., *Wentworth Papers 1597–1628*, Camden Society, 4th ser., vol. 12 (London, 1973), 64–66; *CJ*, 456–460; *Proceedings 1614*, 30–36, 52–58. The question about the

In focusing so early on this issue, Sandys was setting a tone that Jansson has seen as crucial to this Parliament—its preoccupation with privilege. She has argued that, at times, the Commons seemed less concerned with the substance of an issue than with the effect it might have on their liberties. In her words, "The success of the assembly of 1614 lay in the experience gained in learning to manage itself. What was important was . . . what the members learned . . . about the nature of the institution of parliament." And, just as Sandys, on the last full day of the 1614 session, was to link privilege to procedure, so, she notes, Charles I himself was to admit, in 1629, that the growing assertiveness of the Commons had derived from their endeavors "to extend their privileges."[19] It was precisely this strategy that Sandys was following when, after the establishment of the Privilege Committee, he asked for the creation of another committee, charged with the task not only of deciding which statutes should continue in force and which "pernicious" laws ought to be allowed to expire, but also of hearing all petitions of grievances that did not "impeach the King's honor [or] profit." Fuller seconded the motion, and the Grievance Committee—in this session as before, the formal means whereby the Commons attacked governmental abuses—came into being, appropriately chaired by Sandys.

In other words, Sir Edwin was playing the elder statesman. Refraining from entering into the details of disputes, he determined to establish regular procedures for further discussion. He laid down the general principles that had to guide his colleagues, including the necessity of guarding their privileges and the important caution that the king heard their petitions "as a body politic, and not natural." The very large number of new M.P.s— over 55 percent of the House, more than in any assembly since 1584— must have realized that Sandys's speech was their introduction to the underlying aims and methods of parliamentary business, and were vital to its success. They must have sensed, too, that Sir Edwin was beginning to formulate an agenda, and was taking little notice of the three proposals put forward in the king's opening address: the subsidy, anti-Catholic legislation, and confirmation of the succession rights of the grandchildren born to James by his daughter and the elector palatine.[20] Instead, privileges, elections and grievances held center stage. Even religion—which had obviously been suggested by the king, despite his current pro-Spanish sentiments, because it would appeal to most M.P.s—was brushed aside. The impression was that the Commons and their leaders, not official spokes-

---

attorney general was whether he should serve, like a judge, as an advisor to the Lords. Despite powerful arguments, he was excluded on the eleventh, though Bacon himself was allowed to retain his seat.

[19] *Proceedings 1614*, xxxiv–xxxv.

[20] Theodore K. Rabb, *Enterprise and Empire: Merchant and Gentry Investment in the Expansion of England, 1575–1630* (Cambridge, Mass., 1967) 94.; HMC, *Hastings*, 4:230–234.

men or the Lords, were calling the tune. As the session progressed, that impression was confirmed when the Lords came increasingly to react to events in the Lower House rather than to initiate developments.

By the end of the third full day of debate, April 11, the preliminary issues—Bacon and disputed elections—had been dealt with. Sandys had intervened decisively on the ninth to settle long arguments about sheriffs and mayors who returned themselves for Parliament, and on the eleventh he had spoken again about procedures: no bill should have a second reading till 8:30 or a third reading till after 9:00, and no motion was to be passed until discussed by a committee, where it could be debated back and forth.[21] With the concession to late risers and the technicalities settled, Sandys could move on to more substantive issues. Little more than a week remained before the Easter recess, but in that period he and his colleagues prepared the course that lay ahead.

The official agenda was laid out by a message from the king, reported on the eleventh. This effort at magnanimity disavowed the undertakers, urged the grant of subsidies, and in return promised relief from purveyors and offered bills of grace to correct abuses in the legal system that had been central to the Contract. None of these matters got very far, however, not even purveyance—an issue whose intractability seems to have deterred further inquiry. Instead, the debate of the following day, after focusing on the subsidy and the bills of grace (with the usual protestations of loyalty, tempered by a wish to see grievances settled) was diverted into the issue of the undertakers and rumblings about ecclesiastical courts and freedom of speech. One recommendation was universal: the need to move slowly, a sentiment which Sandys summed up toward the end of the day in a speech that put the House's inclinations in a nutshell.[22]

Starting with the king's desire to have "the love of his people," Sir Edwin ingenuously recalled a speech by Sir Walter Mildmay that had argued against an "extraordinary number of subsidies" by saying that if the M.P.s gave "his Majesty their hearts . . . then their purses would be his."[23] More concretely, he followed up a suggestion by Crew (either Thomas or Richard, both country gentry) that they ought to consult with their constituents before committing themselves. Thus had a device first used on a great occasion, the decision over the Union, become a mechanical response to normal business. But by these means the question of the subsidy could be deferred until after Easter, as Sandys proposed. He wanted time, too, for

---

[21] *CJ*, 457, 458. Sir Edwin also obtained a new parliamentary seat for Durham.

[22] Ibid., 458–459, 461–463; *Proceedings 1614*, 48–52, 68–69; HMC, *Hastings*, 4:239–241; Moir, *Addled Parliament*, 89–90.

[23] Probably his 1589 speech on the subsidy: J. E. Neale, *Elizabeth I and Her Parliaments, 1584–1601* (London, 1957), 204–205.

the purpose of "clearing of the suspicion of undertaking," and he made an important distinction: "not packing of a Parliament, for nobles to write letters to them to whom they [are] bound in love; but [it is packing] to press with letters, or by fear, etc." Clearly, it was going to be impossible to determine which type of letter had been sent in each individual case (he thus gained a convenient escape hatch for himself), and he sought to divert the House's anger to more productive ends. The distaste for undertaking, he claimed, could become an instrument for silencing those who slandered the Commons, a grave problem in the previous session. He therefore asked for a message to the king stating that they were "grieved, that divers of the most worthy members of the last and this Parliament, should be so unthankfully dealt with, as to be traduced as undertakers, till their own actions discover them. . . . Great wrong done the last Parliament, by misreporting the speeches of many members of this House." Sir Edwin was hoping the obsession with undertakers might excuse his ill treatment in 1610, and he was also playing for time so that grievances could be more fully explored. The latter succeeded: all action was postponed.

During the seven remaining days of business before the recess a number of fairly straightforward matters were cleared up. More importantly, a bill against impositions received two readings and incited heated denunciations similar to those of 1610, with Fuller again in the lead. Sandys was evidently spending most of his time chairing the committees for privileges and petitions (the latter taking charge of grievances). He reported on the fifteenth that a search was in progress to determine which grievances from the last Parliament were still outstanding, and that this had revealed the need to take better care of the Journal in future. He also warned that some petitions had been too audacious, which was dangerous. M.P.s had learned the need for caution: "then more bold, now more wary" in producing petitions "against the King himself, for reforming some things in himself." He suggested, therefore, that they have "the party's name torn off" petitions so that nobody would be held responsible for a demand that was taken amiss.[24] This constant worry about Court reprisals is one of the most notable features of the 1614 session, and it was amply justified after the dissolution.

Sandys also made some other procedural recommendations, an interest that increasingly marked him as the repository of wisdom about the business of the Commons who had to keep his colleagues aware that the liberties of the House rested on procedures and privileges. But his main work

---

[24] Cooper, *Wentworth*, 66–73; *CJ*, 461, 464–467, 469–471; HMC, *Hastings*, 4:242–243; *Proceedings 1614*, 85–86. Among the "opposition" men who kept the debate at high temperature were Berkeley, Whitelocke, Owen, and Digges. Yet the House did get business done: it terminated the patent for the newly formed company of merchants trading to France and entitled the elector palatine's children to the royal succession.

was substantive. When he reported again from the Committee for Grievances, on the last day before the recess, the tearing off of names became
official policy, and he placed before the M.P.s the earliest of a series of
grievances that were to become steadily more numerous. He persuaded
the House to condemn the French Company as "a plain monopoly," and
he served notice that there would be assaults on "a pregnant monopoly" of
glassmaking and "a surreptitious patent" for making iron.[25] As the M.P.s
departed for Easter, they must have noted that they had hardly heard from
Court spokesmen.

THE DISGRACE OF A PRIVY COUNCILLOR

The nearly two weeks of recess proved decisive, in 1614 as in earlier years,
for the outcome of a parliamentary session. Sandys probably spent the
time working on grievances and impositions, his prime responsibilities
both before April 20 and after May 2. He doubtless remained in London,
because it would hardly have been worth the time and trouble of a journey
to Northbourne. Other M.P.s such as Digges may well have remained in
the city, too, and one can assume that they coordinated their plans for the
coming debates. But the principal machinations of the recess apparently
involved Northampton and his allies. The outburst over undertakers that
exploded on the day the session resumed seems to have been largely their
work, though the chief instigator, Sir Roger Owen, was probably his own
man: a prominent Shropshire gentleman, returned for the county, who had
revealed a hot temper in previous Parliaments. Moir has nevertheless argued convincingly that it was the Howards who were behind the leaks of
information that sustained this diversion of the House's attention, while
Northampton's spokesman, Hoskins, helped keep the fires alive.[26] If so, the
planning must have been done during the Easter holiday.

And it was done to telling effect. Despite a convincing counterattack by
Bacon, a declaration by the king clearing the House of any imputation of
undertaking, and an almost total lack of evidence, the Commons managed
to sustain a high level of indignation on the basis of rumors and the discovery of Neville's advice to James about calling a Parliament. When the issue
finally evaporated after a climactic debate on May 14, it was obvious that
the M.P.s had been chasing a phantom, but one whose emotional impact
(because of its challenge to their very independence) was such that members had even come to blows. Sandys finally intervened on this last day,
dismissing as unproved the one remaining accusation of undertaking, hav-

---

[25] Ibid., 116–117; *CJ*, 468, 469. Typical of Sandys's procedural acumen was his ensuring that
details of each day's committee meetings be posted in the morning by the clerk.

[26] Moir, *Addled Parliament*, 97–98, 108–109.

ing to do with the county election in Huntingdon, and absolving his friend Sir Henry Neville from wrongdoing. Indeed, no reading of Neville's paper could suggest that, for all his recommendations of ways to improve relations between king and Parliament, he was offering advice that was either improper or devious. Sir Edwin's only question was why Neville had left impositions out of his survey of issues; as he recalled, Sir Henry had told him that impositions presented too many difficulties, but in fact the revival of this issue may have been Sir Edwin's way of asserting the bona fides of the leaders of the House: their willingness to tackle difficult grievances, and not merely offer a subsidy in return for the bills of grace. This shift, together with Sandys's admission that the eagerness to vote subsidies at the very beginning of the session had convinced him that "there was undertaking," signalled the end of the upheaval. That the House soon calmed down, and dropped the issue, was renewed testimony to the influence he exercised over his colleagues. Owen made one last effort, but his support had disappeared.[27]

The one case of electoral tampering that was proved beyond a doubt, however, was of momentous significance. It concerned a privy councillor, Sir Thomas Parry, who, as chancellor of the Duchy of Lancaster, had extensive electoral patronage throughout England. One of his fiefs was the borough of Stockbridge, which had returned Sandys to the previous Parliament. In 1614 there were no obvious candidates, and Parry, a leading courtier for nearly twenty years, intervened on behalf of another courtier, Sir Walter Cope, and a Hampshire friend, Sir Henry Wallop, in the crudest fashion. When threats and an arrest were of no avail, he altered the results fraudulently. Why the electors remained obstinately loyal to their own choices—Sir Richard Gifford, and an unknown St. John (possibly Henry who, like Gifford, was a virtually invisible M.P. in the 1620s)—is a mystery, but the heavy-handedness of Parry was plain. The contrast between his menacing admonitions and the low-keyed approach of other "great" men (possibly because he felt that his power was of a lesser order) was unavoidable. The evidence was presented on May 9, and a well-concerted rush of denunciations, led by Hobby, Digges, and Sir Alexander St. John (presumably a relative), ensued. It continued the next day, joined not only by Parry's subordinate, William Fanshawe, the auditor of the duchy, but by such reliable "populars" as Brooke, Owen, and a rising new figure of independent views, Robert Phelips, the son of the 1604 speaker, who

[27] Ibid., 97–108; *CJ*, 470–471, 477–480, 485; HMC, *Portland*, 9:132–133; *Proceedings 1614*, 139–144, 153–154, 241, 246–256. It is telling that, on this same day, Neville was absolved of blame for advising the king about calling a new Parliament when he insisted that he had merely been seeking ways of avoiding dissension between king and subject—a claim which a reading of the "Advice" confirms.

entered the attack on both days. The defense, hesitantly undertaken by
More and Bacon, consisted mainly of pleas for mercy. The following day,
the eleventh, Parry was expelled from the House, and at the Commons'
request James removed him from office and from the Privy Council.[28] Although he was partially restored to favor the next year, he died in 1616 in
semi-disgrace.

Sandys's role in this quick explosion of parliamentary power was on the
side of severity. When word came on the eleventh that James planned to
suspend Parry from the Privy Council, a number of M.P.s advocated a
show of compassion. Even Alford, a staunch "country" member, suggested
that unless they could persuade the king to relent, the punishment would
seem so great that no other electoral miscreants would be pursued. But
Sandys would have no talk of mercy. It was true, he said on the eleventh,
that in the previous Parliament Sir Christopher Piggott had described expulsion from the Commons as a "judgment greater to him than if they
struck off his head." And he noted "how much greater" it was "where a
Councillor was thus sentenced." Nevertheless, he moved for a message to
the king in which they would express themselves "doubly satisfied: 1. With
the censure in this House; and then with his Majesty's message, for a
further punishment." The point of Sandys's tactic, which won immediate
acceptance, was to prevent an appeal for leniency, and leave further punishment entirely to the king.[29] There could be no minimizing of malfeasance by a Crown servant, especially when it infringed on the liberties of
the subject. Thus was struck the first of the increasingly formidable blows
whereby the Commons destroyed a series of powerful ministers, ultimately
forcing the leaders of the government to see themselves as responsible to
Parliament.

IMPOSITIONS

Sir Edwin's main preoccupation during the recess, however, had been with
impositions and grievances in general. On May 4, the third day of resumed
debate, he represented the Committee on Grievances in asking that the
patent for the manufacture of glass be declared a monopoly and dissolved.
The following day, after a brief contretemps over whether he could speak
before the subsidy was considered, he reported from the Committee on
Impositions. He explained that a petition against impositions in the last
Parliament had met no success, that the precedents demanded parliamen-

---

[28] *CJ*, 477–481; HMC, *Portland*, 9:132.
[29] *CJ*, 480–481. One account (*Proceedings 1614*, 209) quotes Sandys as asking for no further punishment by the king; the Journal, citing Sandys's fondness for numbered points,
seems more convincing.

tary consent for such exactions (because otherwise all Englishmen were "bondmen"), that impositions were supposed to be a response to need and temporary at best, and that his committee suggested "that the supply might stay till this determined." Advance knowledge of this final recommendation was obviously the occasion of the contretemps that preceded the speech, and it became the main ground of contention immediately thereafter. But the momentum in Sandys's favor was sustained by Fuller, by Brooke, and by a learned discourse from Whitelocke. When a lawyer, Leonard Bawtrey, appearing in his only session, declared that the king alone could allow the M.P.s to defer consideration of the subsidy, he was hissed.[30]

Finally Sandys took charge, persuading his colleagues in reasonable terms that their best course was to move to a conference with the Lords on impositions. This had been discussed in committee, partly to enable the many new members to familiarize themselves with the issue so that they would not have to accept previous conclusions "by an implicit faith."[31] The "populars," determined to remove a burden from the subject without much thought for its fiscal implications, were sweeping the Commons toward the same outcome as in 1610, and the conference was simply the next step toward a confrontation with the king. Their determination was also the undoing of the subsidy. Once the conference with the Lords had been decided on, there was no avoiding a discussion of supply, but Alford at once suggested deferral. Sir Thomas Lake, a month-old privy councillor, objected, but again it was Sandys who decided the issue. He wanted the House "not to have one negative" against the subsidy, he said. For there had never been any dissent under Elizabeth, and only "one or two odd voices" in the last Parliament. It was "not honorable" that they should vote now "with so many negative voices," especially as the issue had never been decided so early in a session except in time of war. What he wanted was for "honorable persons" to inform the king that they did intend to vote a subsidy eventually. Seconded by Hakewill, this was the ingenious proposal, saving appearances but granting nothing, that carried the day.[32]

[30] Ibid., 155–156, 158–159; *CJ*, 472–474; Cooper, *Wentworth*, 73–76. The contretemps arose when the speaker apparently ruled that the subsidy had to precede Sandys's report. Sir Edwin said that members had to give way to the speaker, but then—if one can trust the record—Sandys's old Yorkshire neighbor Sir John Savile reprimanded the speaker, and Brooke and Digges persuaded the M.P.s that impositions should precede the subsidy. The veteran Sir Herbert Croft thought the House resembled a cockpit during this quarrel.

[31] *CJ*, 473–474. They were "to proceed both by bill and petition": Cooper, *Wentworth*, 75.

[32] *CJ*, 474. Winwood responded to Sandys's assertion that subsidies were discussed early in a session only in an emergency, when Hannibal was *ad portas*, by claiming the presence of Aquila (presumably Aquilius Regulus, the famous informer) and the Trojan horse (Catholics?) *intra portas*. Such resort to conspiracy did the Crown little good, and underscores Winwood's ineffectiveness.

For the next week undertakers took up nearly all of the House's time, but on May 12 Sandys brought the M.P.s' attention back to impositions with a major speech, the report of the committee that was preparing for the conference with the Lords.[33] Stressing one of his favorite themes, he began by asserting that their aim was "to inform his Majesty's understanding of the subject's right against impositions; which [had been] wronged by misinformation." James surely did not want to balance his own profit against his subjects' rights, because all of them, not just merchants, were hurt by the higher prices. This was "the way to ruin any commonwealth," and therefore the M.P.s wanted the Lords to join in the petition. Only when their minds were thus eased could they achieve sufficient "affection and plenitude of liberality" to "proceed to the King's supply, the first end of this Parliament"—a protestation of good intent that the courtiers in Sandys's audience must have found hard to take at face value.

In the conference with the Lords "one selected person" was to be charged with the preamble, consisting of two "matters in fact": that impositions had proliferated under James (reaching a total of 1,360), and that the House had expressed the unanimous opinion, after a search of precedents, that the king could impose only with consent of Parliament. Although the king had answered all their other petitions in 1610, he had ignored this one because it had come from a single House, and therefore, Sir Edwin explained, they needed the Lords to join them. The first point, however, was probably the crucial one: impositions were a threat to traditional rights precisely because they were multiplying. For the many among the gentry who believed that an orderly realm depended on precedent and custom, it was the innovation of a proliferation of impositions that made them appear so dangerous.

Sandys then went through the nine topics around which the petition was to be organized, each assigned to a different member of the committee. They were to start with the facts, including the lack of precedents ("his Majesty hath departed from all his ancestors"), the current proliferation, the permanence of the new impositions, and the absence of genuine justi-

[33] Ibid., 481–482. "The several points that were given in charge by the Lower House to some principal gentlemen . . . to have conference with the Lords . . . about . . . Impositions . . . 1614": Huntington Library, HA Parliamentary Papers, is printed in *Proceedings 1614*, 223–227—a fair copy written within a week of the speech, for it incorporates the assignments given to Digges and Sir Samuel Sandys, but not the decision, on the nineteenth, to remove Sir Samuel: *CJ*, 482, 490. Whitelocke cited 1,100 impositions, and Wentworth put the number at 1,330 (Cooper, *Wentworth*, 67, 75), but I use the Hastings figure (1,360) on the assumption that Sandys would have wanted the situation to sound as bad as possible. In the account in HMC, *De L'Isle and Dudley*, 5:176–178, Sandys is quoted (176) as emphasizing that "An Act of Parliament in the affirmative cannot be withstood nor countermanded by the King."

fication such as war. These issues were assigned to Bacon, "whose fidelity and ability have been well proved the last Parliament." Sandys himself undertook "matters of state," including "the fundamental policy of this Kingdom": a recognition of his ability to articulate an independent gentry vision of England's welfare. And the search for precedents, which would allow the M.P.s to assess impositions in light of common law, was divided, by period, among five lawyers: Thomas Crew, Whitelocke, Wentworth, Hoskins, and Nicholas Hyde. They were to show that Englishmen "gave more than ever was demanded" when kings avoided impositions! The response to the Exchequer decision in Bate's case was given to another three lawyers, including Hakewill, who had thought the Crown position strong but had become, "by search and study" of the records, "a convert, upon sight of precedents."

The inconvenience to merchants and to "every man's liberty" was also on the agenda (the responsibility of Digges and Sir Edwin's brother Sir Samuel Sandys), as was a rebuttal to James's claim that other kings imposed. Owen was to handle this latter topic, focusing on the supposed reliance on the consent of subjects and Estates in foreign lands. It is hard to tell whether this total misreading of Continental procedures, put forward in the year of the last meeting of the French Estates General before 1789, was merely uninformed or deliberately misleading. Sandys was on no firmer ground in his claim that the barons of the Exchequer had no right to decide so far-reaching a case, though as justification he did make a famous constitutional distinction: "some cases are above common courts and fit only for this high court, for no King will set his Crown nor subject his liberty upon the judgment of any common court."

The most remarkable part of Sir Edwin's speech was its coda. The M.P.s, he said, "required" five "qualities" in their deliberations. First was sincerity and truth. Second was cogency: "not many arguments, but strong." Third came "mutual aid": the seekers of precedents had to work in tandem with the merchants. The fourth (the need for "secrecy," which revived the old worry over the Court's reaction) was described in military terms, as though the House were off to battle. They were "to deliver out no copies. Truth, going to war, must be armed"—a quite remarkable prescription, born in the atmosphere of recrimination of late 1610 and the hysteria over undertakers in 1614.[34] By contrast, the last recommendation, unanimity, was unexceptionable.

Although there was still to be a continuing search for precedents, Sandys's magisterial address left no room for argument. The response indi-

---

[34] The Hastings version has Truth "put on armor" even though it is often "strongest when it is most naked," and adds a military touch to Sandys's insistence on strength: "reasons without weight do weaken any cause, as cowards do an army."

cated the totality of the leadership's control of the Commons: "the course reported [was] agreed, upon the question."[35] The assault on impositions was to be renewed, and it was up to the Lords to decide whether to join the Lower House.

It was this question that produced the first unambiguous evidence that the motive force in Parliament now emanated from the Commons. In the one major issue involving both Houses thus far, the initiative lay entirely with the gentry; the peers merely responded. Even more revealing, the Lords had discussed little of real consequence in over four weeks of meetings. Although there were antagonisms aplenty within the membership (primarily the anti-Spaniards Pembroke, Southampton, and Archbishop Abbot against the pro-Spaniard Howards) nothing of moment had been argued. Most of their business, in fact, had concerned either minor matters of privilege such as the arrest of servants or pro forma actions like the never-ending naturalizations of prominent Scotsmen. There had been some talk about land tenures, but it had been couched in muted tones that contrasted sharply with the lively feelings aroused by impositions.[36]

And the central issue, when the Lords met as a Committee of the Whole on May 21, was not whether they were for or against impositions, but whether they should confer with the Commons.[37] That this question was no more than a surrogate for the real disagreement (over the legality of impositions) does not lessen the significance of the Lords' decision to pose the problem in these terms. Moreover, the particular point on which the defenders of impositions took their stand was the need for prior consultation with the judges. It was as if they were reluctant to come to the showdown unless they had the backing of irreproachable authorities. But the chief proponent of this argument, Ellesmere, the lord chancellor, supported by Abbot, could not overcome the combined objections of Southampton, St. John, and Rich. As the diarist remarked, at the end of the day "all the committee took it for granted we were resolved to meet with" the Commons.[38]

But the "official" group was not so easily defeated. When Ellesmere made his report from the Committee of the Whole to the House on the twenty-third, he blithely announced that "all of my Lordships considered a conference to be unfit as yet." A few had wanted one, but had had no ideas about time, place, etc., and so it was an unresolved *res integra*. Thereupon

---

[35] *CJ*, 482. The message to the Lords had to be ironed out two more times before Winwood went to ask for a conference on the nineteenth: ibid., 486, 490.

[36] HMC, *Hastings*, 4:244–246.

[37] Ibid., 249–251; *LJ*, 2:705–706; Elizabeth R. Foster, *The House of Lords 1603–1649: Structure, Procedure and the Nature of Its Business* (Chapel Hill, N.C., 1983), chap. 7, esp. 128.

[38] HMC, *Hastings*, 4:251.

the argument resumed, with the bishops and the privy councillors joining Ellesmere, while Southampton, Rich, St. John, and Saye sought to accommodate the Lower House. This time, however, the Howard group, obviously sensing another good means of subverting the session, was better organized, and the motion to consult the judges won by nine votes—carried, according to the diarist, by "the Lords of the Council and Bishops." The judges were no help, however. Six were present; they went off to consult for half an hour, and then Coke, lord chief justice of the King's Bench, gave a "short and undigested speech" of at least another half an hour that evaded the issue entirely. Anyone who removes a genuine royal prerogative "should show too much popularity," he said, but if it is "against law," then it could be approved only by "perjury . . . baseness and flattery."[39] In other words, the judges refused to commit themselves.

The next day, the twenty-fourth, there was nothing for it but to discuss what had now become the most serious subject of the session: whether to meet with the Commons or not. The defense of impositions had become a secondary worry; more important was the doubt that the peers could negotiate successfully with their colleagues, and the fear that the conference would put paid to the hope James had expressed in his opening address that this would be a Parliament of love. The Lower House had taken such firm control over the direction of events that the Lords could find refuge only in evasion. Despite giving the longest speech of the day, therefore, Southampton pleaded in vain for a conference. Even an agonizingly uncertain Pembroke opposed him. The *coup de grâce* was delivered by Ellesmere, who ended the debate by informing the members that James's wish was that nothing touching the prerogative be discussed without the express approval of the Privy Council. The refusal of the conference was accordingly conveyed to the Commons on the twenty-sixth, but when they replied, two days later, they caught the Upper House off balance again with a new and grave complaint that had emerged out of the debate over impositions.[40]

The M.P.s had returned to the subject on May 18 when, sitting as a Committee of the Whole with Sandys in the chair, they had learned that the principal lawyers of the House, and the king's counsel, "concluded . . . that the king could not impose on any thing within the land."[41] The discussion continued on the nineteenth, and then, on the twenty-first, the Commons slipped into yet another debate on impositions. They had just passed

[39] Ibid., 251–257; *LJ*, 2:706.

[40] HMC, *Hastings*, 4:257–264; *LJ*, 2:707; *CJ*, 498; see below, 195–199.

[41] *CJ*, 490; *Proceedings 1614*, 285–288; *CD*, 7:642. In 1621 Sir Robert Phelips recalled (ibid., 5:227) that "it was agreed by the King's counsel here that the King could not impose without the consent of the people."

a bill that repealed an act of Henry VIII creating broad royal powers over Wales and the Marches. As Sandys noted, "a Parliament cannot give liberty to the King to make laws." But the next speaker, William Jones, a lawyer (probably the later chief justice of Ireland), made the analogy between this resistance to arbitrary government and the resistance to an arbitrary levying of impositions. The subject seemed to be preying on members' minds, and this reference unleashed yet another outpouring.[42] Most of the discussion involved elusive interpretations of Continental practices, but one extreme speech, by Thomas Wentworth, citing Daniel and Ezekiel on the destruction of tax-raising tyrants, revealed the emotion that the issue had aroused. Sandys's contribution was milder; nevertheless, he, like Wentworth, stepped far enough onto dangerous ground to expose himself to the Court's displeasure.

THE ASSAULT ON TYRANTS

Sir Edwin's speech was a response to the argument that arbitrary impositions were common on the Continent, put forward by two knowledgeable courtier-diplomats, Winwood and Sandys's friend Sir Henry Wotton (who was briefly in disgrace for his famous "ambassadors are sent to lie abroad" comment, and was currying favor with the King). Wotton had said that "successive" princes (like James) could impose, whereas elective ones could not; Winwood emphasized that prerogative, not law, was the basis of the right. One king, Sandys said, presumably referring to France, had received nearly £15 million from taxes on salt. Moreover, "the king of France, and the rest of the imposing princes, do also make laws": a clear and dire warning to every Englishman. With an uncharacteristic touch of recklessness, Sir Edwin then justified his view by asserting a bold constitutional interpretation: "no successive king" existed, he argued, "but first elected." This "election [was] double: of person, and care; but both come in by consent of the people, and with reciprocal conditions between King and people." To underline his statement he added "that a King, by conquest, may also (when power [is adequate]) be expelled." James's beloved divine right was here unequivocally rejected. And Sandys rejected, too, the belief that foreign examples could determine the English case. Nevertheless, he concluded, Owen had been assigned to look into this topic, and he should be asked to bring his sources and authorities into the House, a motion that the M.P.s accepted.

For one diarist, the rejection of foreign precedents was Sandys's most decisive contribution, and indeed his comments did put an end to this

---

[42] For the debate and Sandys's speech, discussed below, see *Proceedings 1614*, 293, 314; *CJ*, 492–493; *CD*, 7:644

rather dubious line of reasoning. But for other observers, and for posterity, the most sensational part of the speech was the discussion of the people's rights and the direct challenge to the king himself. According to two independent reports, which there is no reason to doubt, Sir Edwin concluded his speech by quoting the tenth satire of Juvenal (lines 112 and 113):

Ad generum Cereris sine caede et vulnere pauci
Descenderunt reges, et sicca morte tyranni.

In other words, few kings and tyrants go to their grave without violence and bloodshed (one reporter substituted "sanguine" for "vulnere"), or by a natural death. Taken in conjunction with the jaundiced view of princes in the *Relation*, this citation suggests that Sandys was not immune to a subversive view of monarchical authority that was highly unusual among the Englishmen, not to mention the gentry, of his day. One diarist even had him making his accusation of tyranny more directly: "so do our impositions daily increase in England as it is come to be almost a tyrannical government in England."[43] Contemporary Frenchmen during the civil wars, or Dutchmen struggling against the king of Spain, might have taken such a stand; but from a widely respected member of England's Parliament it was little short of shocking. Especially startling must have been the realization that the boldness came, not from a Puritan carried away by zeal, but from a solid and impeccable country gentleman. It was one thing for Wentworth to quote Daniel (11:20): "Then shall stand up . . . a raiser of taxes in the glory of the kingdom; but within a few days he shall be destroyed," or a similar passage from Ezekiel (45:9). It was quite another for a moderate, scholarly leader of the Commons to quote incendiary verses from Juvenal.

One can hardly take this brief flash of fire as indicative either of the fundamentals of Sandys's political outlook or of the constitutional philosophy of the Commons. Members did occasionally get carried away with themselves, as we saw in the Parliament of 1604–10. Yet it would be equally mistaken to ignore these eruptions. Sir Edwin's speech was more than the "bitter" aberration dismissed by both Chamberlain and Moir.[44]

---

[43] *Proceedings 1614*, 316; Chamberlain, (N. E. McClure, ed., *The Letters of John Chamberlain*, 2 vols. [Philadelphia, 1939], 1:533), uses "sanguine." There was apparently much comment on the Juvenal quotation and what Sir John Hollis called the "speech of elective and successive kings": HMC, *Portland*, 9:138. The Venetian ambassador emphasized the references to elected kings, especially as the speech was received "with a certain amount of applause": *CSP, Venetian, 1613–1615*, 138. Jansson (introduction to *Proceedings 1614*) notes that foreigners were watching events in this Parliament closely, which may have prompted Sandys's lengthy comparison of English and Continental practices.

[44] *Chamberlain*, 1:533; Moir, *Addled Parliament*, 115. Conrad Russell dismisses Sandys's place in English political thought as the product of what he learned from Hooker: *The Addled Parliament of 1614: The Limits of Revision* (Reading, 1992), 8—an essay that downplays the M.P.s' constitutional concerns because (like Burke?) they argued against, rather than for,

And, though Judson is certainly right to place it (together with similar tremors) in a broad context of "unity between king and people," this interpretation underrates the real concern out of which such bursts of anger grew.[45] It was the very sense of unity within England's ruling stratum that made its constituents so sensitive to what they regarded as breaches of the consensus: the derelictions from the "reciprocal conditions" that Sandys stressed. Many of them had long felt that James was inadequately informed about the procedures and conventions whereby the country was ruled. The influx of Scots and the new efforts to raise money, particularly the unprecedented expansion of impositions, only heightened the suspicion, which was then exacerbated by the growing influence of Spain, the Court scandals, and the noticeably poor administrative skills that characterized the Howards' ascendancy. There was a genuine wellspring of unease, therefore, to stimulate the talk of consent and tyrants, and it was only intensified by the dread specter the gentry always conjured up when they considered impositions: the threat to the sanctity of private property. Sandys may not have been seeking drastic action; yet the fact that such unrestrained language could bubble to the surface, disturbing his perennially moderate demeanor, reveals the tension that was beginning to undermine the unanimity of Jacobean society.[46]

---

change (18). More nuanced is Noel Malcolm, "Hobbes, Sandys, and the Virginia Company," *Historical Journal* 24 (1981): 312, which sees Sir Edwin as a sophisticated advocate of natural law, an explorer of subtle differences between ethical and religious knowledge who influenced Hobbes. Sandys had already made significant use of natural law theory in 1604 (above, chapter 4, note 69), but his arguments had practical, political purposes. Their inadequacies as statements of theory explain his absence from Richard Tuck's *Natural Rights Theories: Their Origin and Development* (Cambridge, 1979).

[45] Judson, *Crisis of the Constitution*, 305–306; J. P. Sommerville, *Politics and Ideology in England, 1603–1640* (London, 1986), 79, 138–141. See, too, Robert Zaller, "Legitimation and Delegitimation in Early Modern Europe: The Case of England," *History of European Ideas* 10 (1989): 641–665; and C. C. Weston and J. F. Greenberg, *Subjects and Sovereigns: The Grand Controversy over Legal Sovereignty in Stuart England* (Cambridge, 1981). On the revisionist criticisms of these general assessments of Stuart political theory—e.g., Glenn Burgess, *The Politics of the Ancient Constitution: An Introduction to English Political Thought, 1603–1642* (University Park, Pa., 1992)—see J. P. Sommerville, "English and European Political Ideas in the Early Seventeenth Century: Revisionism and the Case of Absolutism," *Journal of British Studies* 36 (1996): 168–194, and the review by W. B. Robison in *Sixteenth Century Journal* 36 (1995): 187. Sandys may have quoted Juvenal to warn James *not* to be tyrannical with impositions, but that is not how it reads.

[46] When Chamberlain described courtiers undergoing "the fiery trial of this Parliament," and his correspondent Sir Dudley Carleton referred to "so skittish a jade of the mutineers' corner" in the Commons (before they knew of the House's proceedings), they signaled their awareness of a dissonance that had not existed before: *Chamberlain*, 1:523; Maurice Lee, ed., *Dudley Carleton to John Chamberlain, 1603–1624: Jacobean Letters* (New Brunswick, N.J., 1972), 161. Sommerville rightly emphasizes the concern for property, and especially the debates over impositions, as central to early Stuart ideas about the liberty of the subject: *Politics*

Beyond revealing the temper of the Commons, however, the debates on impositions had taken the M.P.s further than they had been on May 12, when they had decided to approach the Lords. It was evident that major events were in the offing, and the sessions seem to have been very well attended—a minor bill on the twenty-third, for example, evoked 334 votes in one division.[47] On the twenty-fifth, the day before the Upper House responded, the pent-up frustrations, far from satisfied by the disgrace of Parry and the sporadic expressions of ill feeling, finally found their outlet.

Noli Me Tangere

The previous Saturday, May 21, the very first speech in the Lords to greet Winwood's request for a conference on impositions had been delivered by Richard Neile, bishop of Lincoln. A fierce defender of royal authority, he had revealed his colors in his maiden speech in the House four years earlier. He had then been the newly created bishop of Rochester, and, recalling his oath of allegiance, he had denounced a bill reducing the monarch's power to appoint canons as a measure that would "bring his prerogative in question"; he had called James "as wise and as learned a king as ever was in this Christian world." When impositions were questioned in 1614, therefore, he was on his feet telling his colleagues: "My Lords, I think it a dangerous thing for us to confer with them about the point of impositions. For it is a *Noli me tangere*, and none that have either taken the Oath of Supremacy or Allegiance may do it with a good conscience. . . . In this conference we should not confer about a flower, but strike at the root of the imperial Crown." Neile's recommendation displays the relentless loyalty that was eventually to take him to the archbishopric of York, and the poor syntax that recalled his failures as a student.[48] Yet for the ill-intentioned in the Upper House, and the rawly sensitive in the Lower, the speech was the occasion for vitriol.

The Commons heard of Neile's remarks from Henry Mervin, later Sir Henry, an inconspicuous M.P. both in 1614 and in 1621. As in the case of Ridgeway and the "Apology" in 1604, it was a relative unknown who launched a major investigation. This time, however, the strings were not pulled by Sandys and his cohorts. Mervin was in the administration of the navy, a future admiral, and a protégé of Nottingham, the lord high admiral of England. It is difficult to conceive of another source for the information and encouragement that led Mervin to inform the M.P.s that "one" had

---

and Ideology, 151–160. It may also be, as Neil Cuddy suggested to me, that Sandys was willing to go overboard to demonstrate that he had not been tarnished by the undertaking.

[47] *CJ*, 493.

[48] Elizabeth R. Foster, ed., *Proceedings in Parliament 1610*, 2 vols. (New Haven, Conn., 1967), 1:101–102; HMC, *Hastings*, 4:249; *DNB*, 14:171–173.

accused them of striking "at the root of the Crown—at the Crown itself."
And the response was immediate. Phelips elaborated on the news by
claiming that they had been accused of "mutiny and sedition." Warning the
Lords that the Commons could treat them equally badly, he demanded a
petition against "any traducer of this House." The angry expostulations
seem to have continued for about six hours, sped along by the usual band
of "populars"—Phelips, Strode, Hoskins, Digges, Alford, Hobby, Brooke,
Berkeley, and Owen. To hedge against counter-attack, Wentworth was
cleared for his citation of Daniel, and then, after invocations of precedents
(notably Cowell's book) and proposals for action, the standard solution was
reached: a committee.[49]

Fast work was evidently demanded, because the report was the first
item on the agenda the next day, divided between Hakewill and Sandys.[50]
Hakewill described what Neile had said, stressing the *noli me tangere*, and
he announced that the committee had decided to complain both to the
Lords and to the king. Moreover, they suggested that the House "forbear"
to engage in any other business till they had heard from the king. Sandys
then elaborated at about twice the length of his co-reporter. Using words
he had previously reserved for the Union, he claimed that the issue was "as
weighty as any [that] ever came here." But, in a characteristic recommendation, he urged his colleagues "to sever passion from judgment." This was
an academic issue: to whom did one complain when a lord made "a scandalous speech"? The precedents were problematic, and if they went
straight to the king Neile might defend himself by saying, "he meant not
those words of England, but of Bohemia." Were it a matter of treason or
felony, they would have to appeal to James; in this case, however, where
"words of scandal . . . may make sedition between the two Houses," the
responsibility lay with the House in which the fault occurred. Thus the
Commons had dealt with Piggott in 1607 and the Lords with Montague in
1604. Therefore "this House can challenge no liberty further than the
Lords." Indeed, if they were to appeal to James and he were to punish
Neile, "the Lords will take it ill." Not only might the Commons "make a
division between the Lords and the King," but there was also danger of a
"breach between the two Houses." Consequently, the best course would
be caution, and dealings directly with the Lords. They had to exercise
"great care," so that if there was a quarrel "the fault not to be ours."

This was Sandys at his most statesmanlike—preserving a principle with-

[49] *CJ*, 496–498; *Proceedings 1614*, 339, 348. That it took about six hours is apparent from
Brooke's comment, about halfway through (*CJ*, 497), that the original news from Mervin had
come three hours earlier; this prompts the *very* rough estimate that one and a half hours of
debate produced one column in the printed Journal.

[50] *CJ*, 498; *CD*, 7:645–646; *Proceedings 1614*, 361–364.

out causing offence—but it was not easy to impose so reasoned a course on an impassioned House, even though he received the support of Digges, Berkeley, and Hakewill, the latter admitting that he had been "converted" to an approach to the Lords. Slowly but surely, the gentry's leaders managed to regain control. They brought a fiery outburst by Owen to a halt, and eventually, using the device of a committee, they had the House agree, first, to complain only to the Lords, and, second, to cease all business until they had a response. The "forbearance" was the more difficult achievement, but still won approval from the committee by thirty votes to fourteen.[51] It was in the midst of these deliberations that the news arrived that the peers refused to discuss impositions.

THE COMMONS OUT OF CONTROL?

At this point, with less than two weeks remaining before James's angry dissolution of Parliament, one might justifiably regard the Commons as completely out of control. Their assault against impositions had met a stone wall; they had verged on hysteria about the bishop of Lincoln; and they had virtually adjourned themselves, refusing to consider other business until the *noli me tangere* affair was settled. This last decision had drawn immediate reprimands both from the speaker and from James, who insisted that only the king had the right to prorogue a session, and that "forbearance" (a word that James professed himself "full of" three days after it was first used) was tantamount to an illegal "cessation." The House thus seemed to be entering dangerous legal territory—though nobody mentioned the fact that the Lords often adjourned themselves for days at a time, and had done so with impunity in the autumn of 1610—and there was renewed concern that "misinformation" would do the members serious harm in the eyes of the king. Tensions were high enough to lead Sandys and Digges, "who have hitherto agreed like sworn brethren," to quarrel in public.[52]

But the moments of bad temper and hot-headed words were exceptional, short-lived, and not significantly more frequent than they had been between 1604 and 1610. Moreover, the recalcitrance of the Lords over impositions, news of which might have been expected to arouse considerable fury, coming as it did in the midst of the debate over the bishop of Lincoln, merely convinced the Commons to proceed on their own. Another meeting was ordered on May 31, five days after the Lords' message, and on June 4, in a session held despite the speaker's absence with a sup-

---

[51] *CJ*, 498–499; HMC, *Portland*, 9:133.
[52] *CJ*, 499, 503; *CD*, 7:647; HMC, *Portland*, 9:133–134; *Proceedings 1614*, 398; *Chamberlain*, 1:536.

posed case of mumps (a politic illness that again recalled the tactics of 1604–10), the M.P.s decided to tell the king that they "could proceed with nothing effectually . . . unless his Majesty was pleased to give in the impositions lately laid without example, huge in number and proportion." Sir Robert Phelips correctly believed that the issue of impositions "was the breach" of the 1614 session.[53] And yet, while the linkage of subsidies to a single grievance was provocative, it seems clear that a conciliatory message from James would have allowed business to proceed.

It is also clear that the familiar leaders of the House were in command throughout these proceedings. The spokesman in the first discussions with the Lords over Neile was Hobby, a veteran of the campaigns of 1604–10, and when, on May 30, the Upper House sent its initial response—a refusal to take action on a complaint that was based on rumor—it was a succession of "populars," concluding with Sandys, who persuaded their colleagues that they should not denounce the peers to the king, but should return to the Lords with a request for a copy of the speech in writing. When the House accepted this moderate course, it appointed Sir Edwin to head the inevitable committee to draft the message. And his ascendancy persisted amid some of the most crowded sessions the Commons had ever witnessed. Doubtless drawn by the momentous happenings, 439 M.P.s packed the House on June 3—an extraordinary 95 percent turnout.[54] It is well to remember, too, that the entire controversy over Neile centered, not on his view that Parliament had no right to discuss impositions, but on his characterization of their proposal as seditious. Self-defense, not aggression, was their motivating force.

Nor must one forget that the Commons had good reason for anger in the total immovability of the Lords. There can be little doubt that Neile uttered the words attributed to him; yet his colleagues steadfastly refused to make amends. And Sandys and his friends must have had plenty of information from their contacts in the Upper House to justify their sense of outrage. Although yet another long debate, on May 31, indicated that the peers' support of the bishop had eroded, they still accepted his tearful statement, "I never spoke the words."[55] When the Lords passed this information along, suggesting that the issue could now be laid to rest, the Commons had obviously been painted into a corner. Their one other recourse was blocked two days earlier when a message from James commended them for "wishing to clear themselves from the imputation" of sedition, but advised them "not [to] meddle with the words." It is hardly surprising,

[53] *CJ*, 503; HMC, *Portland*, 9:136; *CD*, 7:651–652; 5:227.
[54] *CJ*, 499–502; HMC, *Portland*, 9:133, 135, 136; *CD*, 7:646–648; HMC, *Hastings*, 4:267.
[55] Ibid., 273–277; *LJ*, 2:711, 713. The tears were much emphasized: *CJ*, 504; HMC, *Portland*, 9:135; *CD*, 7:649.

therefore, that they then launched an obviously malicious investigation of Neile's protection of a Catholic recusant, a crude but effective witch-hunt that eventually did get the bishop into some trouble with the king.[56]

Again and again, the M.P.s found themselves embroiled in controversies that were scarcely of their own making. With the exception of the brief "forbearance," however, regular business continued throughout the second half of May and the early days of June. Sandys's Committee of Grievances kept meeting and deciding on action on a variety of issues, including problems the previous Parliament supposedly had solved, which were investigated in orderly fashion, as was a new grievance, the creation of the order of baronets.[57] Even religion was treated calmly. A bill to improve observance of the Sabbath progressed uneventfully, as did legislation to improve the income of ecclesiastical livings so as to prevent nonresidence. Indeed, Sandys's contribution to this discussion was to have the problem—"Many benefices very small; things very dear"—aired at a meeting with colleagues from the Lords, the bishops.[58]

Nor were the Commons especially vexed by a privilege case that could have seemed analogous to Neile's. On May 17 Richard Martin, a distinguished lawyer and former "popular" known for his "slippery tongue," brought the House a plea for support of the Virginia Company. In honor of the occasion, the earl of Southampton, Lord De la Warr, and Lord Sheffield, all prominent members of the company, came to hear the speech.[59] Carried away by his audience, and perhaps remembering his days as a "popular" in previous Parliaments, Martin moved on from his sober account of the Virginia enterprise and its need for parliamentary help to a rambling discourse on the nature and failings of the House of Commons. He told them how to proceed, chided them for their slowness, and, surveying his juniors, asserted that "nature is . . . inverted, seeing young men enact laws to govern their fathers." Despite the members' natural anger, however, they accepted Sandys's plea for moderation and merely censured the apologetic Martin, while complimenting him on his advocacy of Virginia.[60]

[56] *CJ*, 501, 505–506; *CD*, 7:650–651.

[57] *CJ*, 484, 491, 492 (new monopolies: "as in a garden, clean weeded, weeds next year"), 494 (baronets, an issue that led Sandys to suggest tearing the proposer's name off a *bill*, because of possible retaliation by the Crown).

[58] Ibid., 482; HMC, *Hastings*, 4:265–267, 278–280.

[59] *CJ*, 487–488; *Chamberlain*, 1:531; ibid., 525, for the "slippery tongue."

[60] Alexander Brown, *The Genesis of the United States*, 2 vols. (Boston, 1890), 2:694; *CJ*, 489; *Proceedings 1614*, 275–279, 284–288; one diarist notes (278) that Sandys made the decisive plea for leniency for Martin. A more serious privilege case, when two M.P.s tried to restrain Owen's excesses on undertaking by pulling him out of his chair during a committee meeting, also ended with a reprimand: ibid., 483; HMC, *Portland*, 9:132.

During the last week or so of the session, the atmosphere of orderly procedure did begin to disintegrate. But it is clear that the Commons were as much sinned against as sinning. Above all, the Howards' machinations were having more effect. Volatile issues could justify extreme speeches, and so Northampton's protégé, Hoskins, ranted against the Court Scots and even mentioned the Sicilian Vespers in a tirade on June 3.[61] Moreover, it was Northampton himself who urged the untimely dissolution upon the king.

Faced by the deafness to their pleas, the M.P.s became increasingly helpless and shrill. But they were assuredly not responsible for the deteriorating situation. Indeed, their restraint was remarkable throughout the last days of May. Deeply disturbed, for example, that the speaker had shown James their book of orders so that he could see the phrase about "forbearance" for himself, they nevertheless merely "excepted against" the action, even though such tale-bearing to the monarch aroused their deepest anxieties about the privileges of the House.[62] And for all the unsatisfactoriness of the Lords' response about Bishop Neile on May 30, the Commons did end the "forbearance" when the reply arrived. As for the extraordinary exclusion of "all the King's servants" from a committee to meet James on May 28, this did not prevent courtiers and officials of various degrees from comprising a fifth of the committee.[63]

Close to the very end, therefore, the Commons remained accommodating, in no way out of control, still following the guidance of the "populars," and still taking care of routine business. The chief problem lay less in their behavior than in the indifference and hostility they generated. Many observers realized that unprecedented animosities had become visible on all sides during the last days of the session.[64] In hindsight, we can see that the conflicts, largely provoked by Court and Lords, and long remembered, only emphasized the divergences in the views of the kingdom's best interests that were appearing among the leaders of English society.

THE DISSOLUTION

The denouement was swift and dramatic. James's message of May 29 reminded the Commons of "the great and important business" that lay be-

[61] Ibid., 138; *CJ*, 506; *Chamberlain*, 1:538.

[62] *CJ*, 500; HMC, *Portland*, 9:134. The record is full of apprehensions about reports to the king and misinformation about M.P.s during these last two weeks of the session.

[63] Moir, *Addled Parliament*, 128, calls the exclusion a "significant step," but his own lists (ibid., 187 ff.) identify Goodwin, Hatton, Hobby, Horsey, Savile, Smith, and Strode (eight out of forty—see *CJ*, 501) as royal servants, which weakens his point, regardless of whether some of them behaved as "populars." The committee also included More, whom Moir (ibid., 32) describes as "the most active royal supporter in this parliament."

[64] *CSP, Venetian, 1613–1615*, 121–122, 133–135; James Whitelocke, *Liber Famelicus, of Sir James Whitelocke*, ed. John Bruce, Camden Society, 1st ser., 70 (London, 1858), 41; *Chamberlain*, 1:533–541, passim.

fore them, and warned that the "nimble lawyers . . . searching out precedents" might provoke him to similar action for a contrary purpose. Four
days later, when the M.P.s had been sitting for exactly a month since the
recess, and Neile was still uppermost in their minds, the king made his
intentions quite clear. He gave them one more week. Parliament was to be
dissolved on June 9 "unless we concluded to give him an effectual supply."[65]
It was in response to this message that Hoskins made his inflammatory
Sicilian Vespers speech, but the debate does not otherwise give the impression of vehement or destructive reaction. The first to comment was
that staunch supporter of the king, More, who professed himself perplexed
at the situation, because if they did not proceed in their deliberations over
impositions "the commonwealth will receive the prejudice." Another courtier, Sir Thomas Roe, feared that this might be the dissolution "of all Parliaments," and like More asked for a committee to prepare a reply. This was
the course taken, after much talk which included suggestions of subsidies
as well as reminders of impositions and the profligacy of the Court. It was
not as heated a response as the message might have provoked, coming as it
did amidst a busy morning that included first readings of six bills.[66]

But James was now determined to press the issue. Quite gratuitously, he
had Winwood and Lake tell the House, as it assembled to devise a reply,
"that he coveted no answer from us; if we did not the one, he would do the
other." Despite such contemptuous treatment—after all, it was unprecedented for the Commons not to reply to a royal message, just as it had
been unprecedented for the Lords to refuse them a conference—the
M.P.s behaved with noteworthy restraint. They drew up their message,
pointing out the impasse that had been reached: they could not back down
over arbitrary impositions, which seemed so contrary to law, and thus they
needed some satisfaction from the king before they could proceed to a
subsidy that they were quite willing to grant. James, by contrast, was adamant, bolstered by the encouragement he was receiving from the Spanish
ambassador Gondomar and from Northampton. It was on the next day,
Saturday June 4, that the speaker, doubtless under royal orders, claimed to
be suffering from the mumps, an illness whose miraculous disappearance
two days later excited no comment presumably because nobody had
thought it real in the first place. And the message was sent to the king
nonetheless.[67]

The last two days of the meeting witnessed a major effort by all sides in
the Commons to resolve the stalemate: to obtain, on the one hand, a conciliatory gesture on impositions from James, and on the other, a subsidy
from Parliament. The king assured the M.P.s in yet another message that

[65] CJ, 501; HMC, Portland, 9:136; CD, 7:651.
[66] HMC, Portland, 9:136; CJ, 505–506.
[67] HMC, Portland, 9:136–137; CD, 7:651–652; Moir, Addled Parliament, 139–140.

he had not meant "to prescribe" what they should do, but that he was now bent on dissolution.[68] Fearing for its members, the House cleared Hoskins of wrongdoing, and then concentrated on ways to remain in session so that both impositions and subsidy might be settled. Winwood and the speaker himself urged a new approach to James, but after "a long and an intricate dispute" it was again Sandys who came up with the suggestion around which the M.P.s coalesced.

He realized, he said, how grave the situation was. Giving a subsidy now, he felt, would mean that "no man could know his right and property in his own goods." The grievance of impositions had first to be redressed, for "the main liberty of the people is engaged in this question." Accordingly, he spoke from his conscience, "as though he were dying," to find a way of preserving both "the liberty of the House [and] . . . the liberty of the kingdom." His recommendation was "an overture or proposition by which he thought to reconcile both the extremes, preserve the liberty of the subject and satisfy the king." Precedents and the examples of hated foreign Kings, he said, demanded the abolition of impositions, and "in granting now a subsidy [the Commons] might imply an assent to impose in future ages." Nevertheless, an orderly way of dealing with the matter was surely possible, and he proposed a bold and original means of resolving the dispute. Since Parliament's consent would establish the king's right forever, why did he not come to an open session at which both Houses would deliberate together and pronounce upon the justice of impositions?[69]

After much discussion, Sir Edwin's proposal was accepted as the perfect resolution of the House's dilemma. He was asked to produce a written text, accompanied by four M.P.s who were to make it "milder and sweeter" (yet another sign of their wish for accommodation), and they approved the final version the next day, June 7, the last of the session. All that was asked of the king was a letter signifying he would attend such a meeting of the two Houses. And the intention was to accompany the request with a grant of a subsidy, about as convincing a peace offer as Parliament could make. The members were in the midst of a discussion of the size of the subsidy, and the best way to approve it, when word came that the ceremony of dissolution was under way in the Upper House.[70]

That the rapid ending of the session was as exceptional and disturbing as

[68] *CD*, 7:652; HMC, *Portland*, 9:137.

[69] Ibid.; *CD*, 7:652–654; *Proceedings 1614*, 426–435. The Venetian ambassador reported Sandys's proposal to the Doge: *CSP, Venetian, 1613–1615*, 138.

[70] HMC, *Portland*, 9:137–138; *CD*, 7:654–656; *Proceedings 1614*, 442–444. So bad were relations that a prominent courtier, Sir Thomas Lake, proposed a security to ensure that James came to the joint meeting; Sandys reassured him that a "royal letter" would be "sufficient." Conrad Russell has speculated plausibly that this was mischief-making, since Lake was associated with the Howards.

anything that happened in 1614 is clear from the reactions it aroused. Chamberlain, though showing little sympathy for the "roaring boys" of the Commons, admitted that the dismissal was peremptory, and Lord Chancellor Ellesmere said that he "himself scarce understood" why there had been so sudden a dissolution. In the Commons, of course, there was "much distraction that a Parliament should be broken up so abruptly"— two days earlier than James's own deadline of June 9—but it is noteworthy that there were still considerable efforts, particularly by leading courtiers in both Houses, to prolong the session.[71] Only the determination of the king and a few around him wrecked the efforts at reconciliation that were widely supported during the decisive first week of June.

To make his intentions absolutely unmistakable, James was vindictive toward an unprecedented number of M.P.s after the session was over. In the commission dissolving the assembly he had said that "quod quidem Parliamentum tantummodo fuit inchoatum," he was decreeing that it was "nullum Parliamentum." Despite the passage of the bill for the succession of the elector palatine's children, the bill for the continuance of statutes had not become law, and only by declaring the Parliament nonexistent could much important legislation remain in effect. Perhaps because of this declaration, James and his advisers may have felt that conventions of free speech (which presumably took effect solely in a "real" Parliament) did not apply, and they could subject their more outspoken critics to unparalleled hounding. Hoskins, recognized by most, including Chamberlain, as the lynchpin of "a plot . . . to overthrow all orderly proceedings," was sent to the Tower, along with four non-M.P.s who had acted as intermediaries with Northampton.[72] Also committed to the Tower were Wentworth, for his speech on Ezekiel and Daniel; Sir Walter Chute, who had denounced the profiteering from impositions rather too fervently; and Christopher Neville, the son of a peer, who had been too liberal in unburdening himself of grievances on the day of Hoskins's notorious outburst, June 3. Furthermore, all the members who had received an assignment in Sandys's May 12 report about impositions were ordered to bring their papers to White-

---

[71] *Chamberlain*, 1:537–538; *LJ*, 2:715; *CD*, 7:654. Winwood, Caesar, More, and Speaker Crew in the Commons, and Ellesmere, Suffolk, Southampton, and others in the Lords, all tried to postpone the dissolution: ibid., 653; *CJ*, 505–506; HMC, *Portland*, 9:137; HMC, *Hastings*, 4:280–281. In Whitelocke's words (*Liber Famelicus*, 41), "people were very sorry for" the manner of the dissolution.

[72] *LJ*, 2:717; *Chamberlain*, 1:540. Chamberlain implies Sandys may have been part of the plot: his sentence begins with Sir Edwin's acquittal, continues "though upon examination . . . there was a plot discovered," and goes on to explain Hoskins' imprisonment. But no other evidence supports this implication, and close reading of Chamberlain's more-than-two-hundred-words-long sentence confirms that the juxtaposition is merely a product of elaborate Jacobean syntax. For Sir Edwin's restraint and discharge, see PRO, PC 2–27, fols. 170, 183.

hall. The offending documents were burned, as were other official papers, and these investigators of precedents (except for Bacon) were ordered not to leave London. Thus eight more M.P.s (Montague, Sandys, Thomas Crew, Whitelocke, Owen, Hakewill, Digges, and Nicholas Hyde) suffered the consequences of royal displeasure. And at least three others (Sir John Savile, Sir Edward Giles, and Sir James Perrot) joined the group who were confined to London—as it turned out, only for a month—or were subjected to minor reprisals such as temporary removal from the rolls of justices of the peace.[73]

THE BEGINNINGS OF POLITICAL DIVISION

At least twenty people, therefore, including sixteen M.P.s, suffered some sort of punishment as a result of their activities in Parliament. The members' fear that they might be entering into an adversary relationship with the Crown that required secrecy, names torn from documents, and similar measures, seemed confirmed. The showing of their records to the king, and the "secret intelligence" that was making its way to the Lords, must have suggested to the leaders of the Lower House that in future advice, criticism, and even attempts at accommodation might be harder to sustain.[74] After all, despite their toppling of a privy councillor, their challenge to Crown authority had always been strictly limited. They had not asked for Parry's dismissal; they had wanted only a reprimand for Neile; they had searched for a compromise on impositions; and, for all the divisiveness of the undertaker issue, they had not allowed it to wreck their proceedings. At worst, some members had been guilty of ill-considered speeches. Considering the tensions, even these had been relatively rare. Certainly their actions had not been so much more egregious than in previous sessions as

---

[73] Ibid.; HMC, *Portland*, 9:138–139. Whitelocke, *Liber Famelicus*, 41–43, adds Montague's name, and suggests that Sir Edwin's brother Sir Samuel Sandys (one of the original May 12 group, later excused) was also summoned to Whitehall, though this account was written some time after Parliament ended. The contrast between 1614 and 1610 (when James seemed just as angry at the M.P.s) is striking. After the 1610 dissolution, Lewknor, Fuller, Wentworth, and Hoskins were merely admonished by Cecil, and the Privy Council persuaded James not to imprison Wentworth, though Whitelocke claimed that his commitment to the Fleet after a 1613 Chancery case was punishment for his conduct in the 1610 Commons: Foster, *1610*, 2:344 n; *DNB*, 20:1178; Whitelocke, *Liber Famelicus*, 34–37. That these M.P.s were not a united group is suggested by the Chancery case Sandys brought against Perrot around this time over an unpaid loan: Huntington Library, EL 5974—a reference I owe to Neil Cuddy.

[74] HMC, *Hastings*, 4:134; *CJ*, 500. Sir Samuel Sandys's rebuke to the speaker for passing on information about the House's activities came in the context of "more bones [having been] cast in this Parliament, to divert the good proceedings of the House, than in all the Parliaments he [had] known" in thirty years (ibid.). The Commons leadership clearly thought it knew who was responsible for the "addling."

to warrant the reaction of the king and the Lords, except for the fact that, with Cecil removed, the hard-liners were in command.

The consequent anxiety about England's freedoms, expressed in Roe's fear for "all Parliaments," in Sandys's uncharacteristically provocative quotation of Juvenal, and (more typically) in his consistent emphasis on the liberties of the subject, was exacerbated by the burst of revenge after the dissolution, which must have convinced many M.P.s that in future they would have to organize much more carefully when pursuing their aims. Despite the control over the Commons exercised by Sandys and his friends (Sir Edwin alone spoke on two out of every three days of debate, and sat on over 50 percent of the House's committees, including nearly all important ones), James had thwarted their power from without.

Yet the fears proved unwarranted, at least in James's reign. The next time Parliament met—after a seven-year gap which merely confirmed the validity of the M.P.s' concerns—such measures as careful coordination with the Lords, the enlistment of a redoubtable new ally, Sir Edward Coke, and a frontal assault on the Court itself, ensured that the process under way until 1614 would in fact continue. At that Parliament, and its successor, the new ascendancy forged by Sandys and the other independent gentry would have a real effect on the government of England. Rather than signaling the arrival of the divisions of Charles I's reign, therefore, the Parliament of 1614 was no more than a diversion from lines of development that stretched from the 1604 to the 1624 sessions; indeed, the very resumption of previous trends when the M.P.s next assembled highlights the distinctively adaptable nature of political relations during the reign of James I.

That, however, is an assessment of the significance of 1614 that holds true only within the context of this single reign (and, not coincidentally, of Sandys's career). A wider perspective gives 1614 a very different meaning. For in the long run, the shocks of the 1610s—scandal at Court, mismanagement by the Howards, the influence of Gondomar, the rise of Buckingham, and the shoddy vengeance visited upon Ralegh (whose execution turned an unpopular egoist into a national hero)—provided the first major impetus toward the dissolution of the unity of England's ruling elite. And none of these events had a greater impact than the 1614 Parliament. Problems may have been expected, but the king's overreaction aroused uneasiness even among conservative courtiers like Ellesmere and Roe. This was simply not the way England was run. Elizabeth at her most impatient, and James himself in previous years, had never been so intolerant or demanding. And the Court was to reap the whirlwind in 1621.

How Sandys took all these events we can only speculate, but he can have been in no doubt as to the potential seriousness of his own position. He had been the dominant figure in the Commons—in one recent view, his "influence was obviously paramount throughout"—and hence, despite his repeated urging of moderation, he could be considered responsible for much of its behavior. Worse still, "his speech of elective and successive kings, and his rehearsing two verses in Juvenal" had attracted sufficiently wide attention to merit a special Court investigation. Chamberlain's sardonic guess was that Sir Edwin "so demeaned himself that he was dismissed without taint or touch," though his restriction to London belied that conclusion. A less jaundiced observer, the Reverend Thomas Lorkin, thought Sandys "in some danger," but able to present "so good an interpretation" of what he had said that he was "presently dismissed."[75] The truth probably lies somewhere between the two, because, as we shall see, Sandys in his waning years could be as anxious for favor as any aspiring courtier. But he was also experienced at persuasion, and doubtless was able to convince his questioners, all of whom probably knew him quite well, that he intended no disrespect. The homogeneity of that broad "Establishment" (suspect though it was in James's eyes) was still intact, and Sir Edwin, as one of its most respected lights, had some room for maneuver.

In the context of a divided Court and an often uncertain king, therefore, Sandys was able to create an ultimately tolerated "independent" stance that was to be his most notable contribution to the structure of English politics. And yet, his visibility and cogency in leading "popular" causes were driving him increasingly toward open confrontation with the servants of the Crown. There had been no hint of such a cleavage ten years before, even amidst the exchanges that led to the "Apology" or the abandonment of the Union. The first sign of real strain had appeared in the fall of 1610, when, ironically, both James and the Commons were in agreement about the futility of the Great Contract. But they had reached that agreement by almost diametrically opposite routes. It was not just that the king wanted more money, while the M.P.s wanted to give him less; James was worried about how his government could be financed at a time when the Commons were beginning to doubt that government's responsiveness. The decline of Cecil was crucial in this regard, because he was the last of the great Elizabethan statesmen who had as much respect in Parliament as at Court. By 1614, with Cecil gone, the parting of ways was clear, and it was emphasized by the issue that emerged as the center of attention. For the Cecils, father and son, had developed two instruments in particular to support the proliferating royal government: wardship and customs duties. The former was essential for the patronage system, the latter for crown income, of which it formed easily the largest part. And, as Burghley had enlarged

---

[75] Kiffin, "Digges," 69; above, note 43; *Chamberlain*, 1:540; Thomas Birch, *The Court and Times of James I*, vol. 1 (London, 1848), 1:324. Whitelocke (*Liber Famelicus*, 43) says Sir Edwin, like Savile, was "dismissed upon bonds."

wardship by leaps and bounds, so Cecil had multiplied the income from customs. The first was the vain target of the 1604 and 1610 sessions of Parliament; the second of 1614.

Though contemporaries never spoke of them in quite such terms, these two campaigns, both orchestrated by Sandys and his allies, represented a basic attempt to turn the clock back, to remove the vital supports fashioned by two shrewd ministers for an enlarged central government.[76] The law may have been on the king's side, as he pointed out when he threatened to search out his own precedents, but the gentry obviously regarded the vastly expanded use of these traditional devices as a change in kind, not merely degree. If their words are to be believed—which surely they must—then what concerned them in this change was not so much the amount of money involved as the threat it posed to the traditional liberties of the subject. Seen in this light, the chief failure of the Cecils was their inability to convince the country, not only that the funds were needed, but also that they could be raised without infringing on traditional freedoms. By 1614, the first attacks on the methods they advocated had been blunted, but in the 1620s the House was to seek different targets and approaches in considering royal finance until, in Charles I's reign, customs again came to the fore.

What this first phase of the encounter revealed was that the assumed (and often practiced) unity of England's "Establishment" was beginning to fade. The House of Commons was now lost to the Crown. Individual courtiers, even a dominant one like Buckingham, could make alliances with the commons' leadership, but no longer as an equal, let alone as a controlling force. The independent gentry, led by Sandys and his allies, were in command of Parliament, and on major policy issues they were now shaping events, not merely reacting to them. A very long and tortuous path had to be traversed before the elite divided in two, as it did to some extent in 1629, and openly in 1640. But in the mounting distrust and bad temper

---

[76] A notable point of contact among the leaders of the House was the Middle Temple (which also linked promoters of overseas enterprise: Rabb, *Enterprise*, 102 n). In addition to Sandys, Sir Edward Giles, John Hoskins, Nicholas Hyde, Sir Henry Montague, Sir James Perrott, Sir John Savile, and James Whitelocke were all members of the Inn (as were such past and future colleagues of Sandys as Richard Martin, John Selden, Edward Hyde, and John Pym). As was noted above (p. 92) the Middle Temple had been particularly associated with the attack on monopolies in 1601. Now, more than a decade later, almost half of those reprimanded or punished after the 1614 Parliament were connected through the Middle Temple—an association that may have been relevant yet again when, in 1633, the Inn sponsored a famous antiroyalist masque: Stephen Orgel and Roy Strong, *Inigo Jones: The Theatre of the Stuart Court*, 2 vols. (London, 1973), 1:64–66; 2:537–565. A study of the Inn in this period might therefore yield interesting results, particularly since it was also connected to the circle around Prince Henry through his attorney, Thomas Stephens: Whitelocke, *Liber Famelicus*, 31.

of the autumn of 1610 and the spring of 1614, the first steps were taken. Two distinct views of the way England ought to be governed were beginning to crystalize; though the process was to undergo short periods of remission, on the fundamental question—whether the gentry were to have a powerful say in government—the antagonisms were essentially incompatible, and a resolution could be reached only after decades of struggle.

Chapter VIII

THE PARLIAMENT OF 1621:
HARMONY AND HARD WORK, FEBRUARY TO APRIL

Friends and Election to Parliament

The Parliament of 1621 opened with Sandys apparently in command of his future. Well established in Kent, and a major force in the colonization of Virginia, he also could regard three of the most important men below Buckingham at Court as friends. Lionel Cranfield, soon to be lord treasurer, and already master of the wards and a privy councillor, was someone he had come to know during the 1610s. They had contacts in the 1614 Parliament and in the East India and Virginia companies, where they worked together in 1618. Cranfield seems to have been the godfather of Sandys's youngest son, Francis, who was born between 1614 and 1619, since Sir Edwin told Sir Lionel "your little Francis is well" in September 1619.[1] The same letter mentions Cranfield's "good love and favor" to the writer, and their having spent time together in the capital. It ends with a punning salutation unique in Sandys's surviving correspondence—a touch of frivolity that suggests an easy relationship: "So Sir, I betake you to the happy tuition of the highest."[2]

Southampton, another new privy councillor, was as intimate a colleague as Sir Edwin had during this period, and they were to work as partners in

---

[1] "Lord Sackville's Papers Respecting Virginia, 1613–1831," *American Historical Review* 27 (1922): 498, printing Sackville MSS., ON 6206. Godfathers were not necessarily close friends, because both sides sought mutual advantage. By 1619 Cranfield had not reached his later eminence, but he must have seemed a good choice, both because of his considerable position at Court (from 1613) and because of his great wealth. Yet personal links must also have been important; otherwise, there would have been no reason for the connection. And even if the phrase "your little Francis" does not denote formal godfatherhood, it does imply a special relationship between the childless, middle-aged merchant-courtier and Sandys's baby. For the age of Francis, see R. Hovenden, ed., *The Visitation of Kent, 1619* (London, 1898), 148. He was at least the eighth child born since 1606 (as Sandys's seventh son, with at least one girl born in the interim); but he could not have been later than the twelfth child, for Sandys had no more than five daughters (the complication arises because girls are numbered separately from boys in the records). And "little Francis" implies that he was born close to 1619. See also below, p. 391.

[2] "Lord Sackville's Papers," 498–499. The pun gives meaning to the convoluted way of saying "God bless you": Sandys linked lessons from heaven with the education of noble minors because the latter was Cranfield's responsibility as master of the wards.

Parliament.[3] Sir Robert Naunton, secretary of state, was the third of these prominent friends. He probably first met Sandys upon entering the Commons in 1606; by 1629 he was close enough to serve as an executor of the latter's will. And in the late 1610s he served as a vital conduit to Court, especially to his great patron, Buckingham, from whom in May 1620 he undertook to win support for Sandys's reelection as treasurer of the Virginia Company. "Here," wrote Sir Robert "is . . . Sir Edwin Sandys his letter to your Lordship, in reducing whom into His Majesty's favor and good opinion you shall do God and His Majesty's service and yourself a great deal of honor, if I can judge anything aright or have any instinct of my duty and respect to God, His Majesty, and your Lordship."[4] Sir Edwin indeed wrote to Buckingham, defending his administration of the Virginia Company. Moreover, another powerful privy councillor close to the king, Viscount Doncaster, was also supporting him during this period.[5] In the end, these advocacies proved fruitless where the Virginia treasureship was concerned (see below, pp. 349–350), but the efforts did show that he retained contacts in high places despite his role as a parliamentary "popular." It is true that on the eve of the new Parliament Naunton was briefly disgraced for indiscreet remarks to the French ambassador about the dowry for James's daughter.[6] Nevertheless, he retained the secretaryship in token fashion for over two years; he was yet to be master of the wards; he remained on good terms with Buckingham; and he continued to be a consequential friend.

As Sandys prepared for the new Parliament, therefore, his advantages seemed enviable: a reputation for good sense and astute leadership, combined with unparalleled influence in the Commons and prominent connections at Court. Even the manner of his election may have gratified Sir Edwin, for he won the seat in opposition to his Virginia Company rival, the powerful Sir Thomas Smythe. The tactic that apparently won the election

---

[3] See above, chapter 4, note 26, and below, pages 262–263. The relationship may have started in the 1590s because they had mutual friends in the Danvers, and common kinship in Sir Edwin's distant relative Lord Sandys, Southampton's Hampshire neighbor who was connected to him via Mabel Sandys, the earl's aunt. We cannot judge the warmth of the friendship, because the main evidence comes from the trading companies they both joined. By the late 1610s, however, they were acting closely together in the Virginia Company and keeping in constant touch with one another.

[4] BL, Harleian, 1581, fol. 111. The standard biography is Roy E. Schreiber, *The Political Career of Sir Robert Naunton, 1589–1635* (London, 1981).

[5] Kingsbury, 3:294–296 (printing PRO, CO/1/1/164); ibid., 59, 216 show that Doncaster, one of James's oldest Scottish associates, joined the Virginia Company during Sandys's regime, that Sandys was "beholden" to him, and that he may have visited Northbourne.

[6] The story is told in S. R. Gardiner, *History of England . . . 1603–1642*, 10 vols. (London, 1882–84), 3:391. Confined by the king, Naunton had to excuse himself from the seat in the Commons to which he had been elected, and so inform the House: *CD*, IV, 18.

was his linking of Smythe with the East India Company and its monopoly—an effective maneuver in Sandwich, an outport that held an ancient grudge against Londoners, though it is likely that the proximity of Northbourne to Sandwich was equally decisive.[7] Sandys was the local "great man," whereas Smythe's house, Sutton-at-Home, was near Gravesend, on the other side of the county.

Yet Sir Edwin also had to resort to fierce electioneering. He enlisted the support of Thomas Gookin, a leading citizen of Sandwich, who solicited the moderate vote; outport sentiments added to his backers; and on the Puritan wing (the "rabble of schismatical sectaries with whom that town aboundeth," according to one observer) he had support from Thomas Brewer, an English organizer of the voyage of the Pilgrims (whom Sandys had helped), and one of whose letters was found among Sandys's effects when he was examined by the Privy Council a few months later. The election itself was apparently tumultuous, with the mayor finally unable to resist the overwhelming sentiment in Sandys's favor.[8]

PREPARATIONS FOR PARLIAMENT AND THE LEADERS OF THE HOUSE

The Parliament had been called, once again, to raise money. James's son-in-law, Frederick the Winter King, had been driven from Bohemia, and Spain's armies were about to occupy his hereditary lands in the Palatinate. To mollify the outrage of his subjects, to counter the impression that all of Protestantism was in danger, and to lend plausibility to his diplomacy against the Habsburgs, James had to threaten a military response, which meant that he needed to raise funds. First he tried to obtain voluntary contributions, but when that effort failed another assemblage of M.P.s became inevitable. The seven years of Crown independence (eleven if one reckons since the previous subsidy), which had been made possible by Cranfield's belt tightening, were drawing to an end. As Charles I was to discover at the end of another, far more dramatic eleven-year period, the

[7] See below, chapter 12, notes 31 and 44; and chapter 13, note 37.

[8] PRO, SP/14/119/11, printed in *CD*, 7:567–570; William Bradford, *Of Plymouth Plantation 1620–1647*, ed. S. E. Morison (New York, 1953), 43; Edward Nicholas, *Proceedings and Debates of the House of Commons, In 1620 and 1621*, 2 vols.(Oxford, 1766), 2:370–371. Robert Zaller, *The Parliament of 1621: A Study in Constitutional Conflict* (Berkeley, 1971), 29. Sandys's prominence in the county was clear from his appointment as Sheriff of Kent in 1615, and as a commissioner to examine disputed customs payments in Dover in 1617: PRO, *Lists and Indexes*, no. 9: *List of Sheriffs for England and Wales* (New York, 1963), 69, and SP/14/93/142, fols. 337–338. The election was disputed, but the Commons decided for him on March 22: *CJ*, 568. The electioneering gives the lie to Sir Edwin's later claim, when he sought to be excused from the Commons so as to attend to Virginia, that he had been "chosen by a borough against his will": *CD*, 4:26. He could also have sat for a Yorkshire seat: *CD*, 7:567.

huge costs of seventeenth-century war, whatever the level of involvement, were the sure undoing of financial autonomy.

Both James and his lord chancellor, Bacon (newly dubbed Viscount St. Albans), were by now old hands at preparing for Parliament. The lessons of 1604 had not been forgotten; accordingly, considerable pains were taken to get ready for the meeting, especially to tone down the appearance of prerogative financial expedients. And the detailed planning was much more sophisticated than the heavy-handed "undertaking" of 1614, with a special commission set up, headed by Bacon, that included four other ex-M.P.s: two judges (Hobart and Montague), the previous speaker (Crew), and Sir Edward Coke. Apart from setting the mechanism for summoning Parliament into motion, the commission suggested that reform of justice and patents of monopoly were likely to be major topics of concern. Cranfield thought that the decay of trade and the need for an end to abuses at Court were potential issues. For all the deliberations, though, nothing concrete emerged from these assessments, and even the attempt to place privy councillors in the Commons succeeded only after intense efforts.

As for the the councillors themselves, they displayed the same fluidity of attitudes and alliances as a Sandys or a Phelips. The different views of England's welfare that were visible in the consideration of the Great Contract in 1610 had become more clear-cut by 1621, and they caused divisions both among royal servants and among ordinary M.P.s. Thus, a position might crystalize, but those who held it were not always predictable. Calvert, Naunton's fellow secretary of state, took a consistent stand as the king's most direct spokesman. But his two chief councillor colleagues, Coke and Cranfield, followed more independent paths. They worked hard for Crown interests such as subsidies, of course, but their activities also went beyond these "official" commitments to particular interests of their own. If, as a result of the latter, they sometimes joined in the hunt for grievances, and were applauded by the M.P.s for their pains, this reflected, not an inclination to "switch sides," but their special concerns—for Cranfield, the wish to improve finances and revive trade; for Coke, the obsession with correctness and precision in law.

The latter deserves further comment, because he loomed like a colossus over the House's proceedings. The former chief justice of the King's Bench, dismissed by James in 1616 for decisions contrary to royal wishes, had not been disgraced for long. In 1617 he had returned to the Privy Council, and his renewed prominence at Court casts doubt on the traditional view that Coke, smarting at his disgrace, took vengeance by leading the opponents of the Crown at the 1621 session. Rather, Coke was the legal scholar to end all legal scholars, and it was his erudition and his commitment to the power of precedent that animated his pronouncements on constitutional issues. That he was also intensely ambitious merely complicates the picture. The twin pulls of royal favor and the common law blur any attempt to place him in some well-defined camp.

For it is clear that Coke was not engaged in some scheme to implement an elaborate ideal of England's constitutional structure. He was no visionary, just a hard-working, earthbound lawyer and politician. He held carefully conceived, even pedantic, views about the applications of England's legal traditions—which he knew more thoroughly than any of his contemporaries—but he was far from set in his opinions about the issues of the day.[9] A pragmatic sense of what was politically unwise tempered his positions again and again—for instance, his refusal to support a petition for extensive immunities to enlarge the freedom of speech. The most thorough student of Coke as M.P., Stephen White, has contrasted the positions he took in the House with the much stronger claims he made in the *Fourth Institute*, and has argued persuasively that "Coke lacked the kind of coherent judicial philosophy attributed to him by historians; . . . in 1621 and 1624 at least, his views on constitutional issues were controlled to a considerable degree by political circumstances."[10]

Coke loved reeling off precedents and legal statistics. But his conclusions did not always point in the same direction. As White notes, he could support the House's authority over disputed elections but urge restraint over freedom of speech. That is why "his speeches . . . are marked by apparent vacillation and inconsistency." Sir Edward, White argues, defended the House's rights *not* "as a crusader for parliamentary privilege, but rather as a lawyer . . . anxious to establish and clarify uncertain points of law and procedure, or as a Parliamentary tactician who sought political advantage through legal argument."[11]

The oscillations that took Coke back and forth between a sober conciliar position and a more "popular" stand meant that he lent weight, rather than set the pace, in debates. He certainly became a powerful resource for the "patriot" leaders of the Commons, such as Sandys, but it is as a resource

[9] Justifying the attack on the non-M.P. Floyd, for instance, he noted: "When [I] was Speaker [in 1593], one that was no member justified his fact [actions] in the House and was committed to the Tower." When Sandys pointed out that such cases were in the Lords' jurisdiction, Coke backed down: "if we have erred a little, yet it is but an error." *CD*, 5:133, 6:127–128, 3:183.

[10] Stephen D. White, "Sir Edward Coke in the Parliaments of 1621 and 1624: Parliament, the Law, and the Economy" (Ph.D. diss., Harvard University, 1972), 44, 6. A similar assessment appears on p. 22 of his *Sir Edward Coke and "The Grievances of the Commonwealth," 1621–1628* (Chapel Hill, N.C., 1979). Cf. Zaller, *1621*, 53: Coke "dared to arrogate to himself the function of setting the English constitution to rights."

[11] White, "Coke," 6–85 passim, esp. 15–18, 46–49, 76–77, 80, 83–84. The quotations are on 43 and 50. On foreign policy, Coke both backed the Commons' rights *and* wavered (ibid., 80, 83–84). There are equivalent passages in White's *Coke*, 166–183. On Coke's precedents and statistics, see *CD*, 2:265–266 and notes.

that his part is best understood. Although he held the floor longer than any other M.P. (he takes up eight columns in the index to Notestein, Relf, and Simpson's edition of the 1621 diaries, whereas Sandys and Cranfield manage no more than three each), his interventions leave the impression that he was not a prime mover. Coke was the heavy artillery trundled up to deliver the precedents and the technical arguments once the direction of debate was decided; he did not create the issues. While greatly bolstering campaigns for redress of grievance, he did not formulate them. For the initiative one must look elsewhere, to the veteran M.P.s.

As in earlier Parliaments, these gentry had the advantage of being able to fill out the meager agenda offered by the Crown. With his councillors divided, the sole proposal James deigned to lay before the House in his opening address was the request for subsidies. His debts were now over £750,000, and so, after rehearsing the problems of Bohemia, he requested "the help of his subjects." The absence of other proposals (emphasized by James's insistence that one perennial favorite, religion, did not merit further discussion) once again opened the way for those who had very different ideas about the problems England faced and how they could be solved.[12]

Moreover, in 1621 these old hands had a strong claim to authority because, as in 1614, there was a notably high turnover. Over 53 percent of the M.P.s were new, the eighth Parliament in a row in which the proportion was 46 percent or higher, though only the third since 1586 in which it exceeded 53 percent.[13] Only Sir George More, now approaching his seventieth year, had a longer attendance record than Sandys. Surrounded by novices, Sir Edwin had a breadth of experience that was bound to command respect; and since the turnover dropped strikingly during the remainder of the 1620s (40 percent in 1624, and around 26 percent in the first three Parliaments of Charles I) the events of 1621 had a major influence on the crucial developments of the rest of the decade. It is not too far-fetched to suggest that Sandys and his allies, notably Phelips, Alford, and Giles, all veterans of the 1614 confrontation, were now setting examples for the generation that would lead Parliament (and the king) into the Civil War.

---

[12] For the preparations and elections, see Zaller, *1621*, 19–30, and Menna Prestwich, *Cranfield: Politics and Profits under the Early Stuarts* (Oxford, 1966), 286–290; for James's debts, R. H. Tawney, *Business and Politics under James I: Lionel Cranfield as Merchant and Minister* (Cambridge, 1958), 301–302; for his speech at the opening of Parliament, *CD*, 5:425–429 (the quotation is on 427). On attitudes to Bohemia, see my "English Readers and the Revolt in Bohemia, 1619–1622," in *Aharon M. K. Rabinowicz Jubilee Volume*, ed. Moshe Aberbach (Jerusalem, 1996), 152–175.

[13] Theodore K. Rabb, *Enterprise and Empire: Merchant and Gentry Investment in the Expansion of England, 1575–1630* (Cambridge, Mass., 1967), 94. The figures for the remainder of the 1620s, given below, come from the same source.

Nor could there be any remaining doubts in 1621 that the leaders of the independent gentry were meeting together and plotting tactics. In his opening speech, James referred to "the underhand practices of some" who had misled him, and to the undertakers of 1614, "which in number being twelve, would undertake to guide the whole House."[14] Nobody had nailed down that accusation before, but in 1621, as Sir Anthony Ashley informed Buckingham, it was well known that "your adversaries continue their meetings and conferences here in Holborn," the home of the earl of Southampton.[15] During the privy councillors' interrogations of Southampton and Sandys during the summer, a major charge, clearly well founded, was that the two colleagues had coordinated their tactics. As Cranfield put it: "the Earl in lieu of his fellow councillors consorted himself during the time of the Parliament with those young Lords in the Upper and those knights and the burgesses in the Lower House which were most stirring and active to cross the general proceedings and to asperse and infame the present government."[16] There seems little reason to question the assumption which the later interrogators took for granted: that the two friends, Sandys and Southampton, were the heart of a well-planned effort which, starting with the peacefulness of the early weeks of the session (when the potentially wrecking issue of impositions was avoided), soon determined many of the day-to-day events in the two Houses. The "patriot" faction was coming to be less of a fluid, constantly shifting series of alliances, and more of a definable and conscious grouping.

The burning issues that dominated the session—finance, foreign affairs, and religion—could not have caused this change on their own, because the transformation was as much a matter of personal relations as of ideology. In fact, the essential catalyst was the evidence of extraordinary corruption at Court in the 1610s (notably the dreadful Somerset and Lake scandals, the disgracing of Parry, and the Star Chamber trial of the earl of Suffolk for embezzlement), evidence that was dramatically enlarged by the fall of Bacon in 1621 and the behavior of Buckingham over the succeeding years. One could no longer quite see England's elite as a homogeneous body of friends, relations, and connections; a section of it, attached to the Court, seemed to be drifting beyond acceptable standards of conduct, and the response of another section, critical of the Court, was to begin to form a distinct group. The end result of this process, which gathered momentum during the 1620s, was the destruction of the flexible, imprecise differentiations in which Sir Edwin thrived. There was still a long way to go: in 1621 Coke and Southampton, both privy councillors, were able to straddle the

---

[14] *CD*, 5:429.
[15] Quoted in Prestwich, *Cranfield*, 325.
[16] *CD*, 7:616.

vague boundary with ease, and Sandys was to do so in 1624. Nevertheless, the momentum was undermining the homogeneity of England's "Establishment," and with it the feasibility of the kind of independent yet influential stance that was the unique achievement of Sandys's career.

FREE SPEECH, SUBSIDIES, ABUSES, AND THE MANAGEMENT OF THE HOUSE

As in the previous Parliaments, Sandys gave major attention to the two issues that had become his specialties, grievances and trade. But his presence was also felt—despite the division of labor whereby leading M.P.s, notably Coke and Phelips, undertook distinct responsibilities—in the other concerns of these early weeks: free speech, subsidies, and abuses at Court. Increasingly, moreover, Sandys had to work to maintain the smooth flow of business that was essential to legislative progress.

Free Speech

Although initially Sandys asked to be excused from the House so as to attend to Virginia—a request that was curtly denied: "Virginia [was] not to keep him from England"—he soon joined in the session's opening contretemps over free speech.[17] Both James and Bacon in their opening addresses had voiced disapproval of "immoderate" talk in Parliament. This prompted a demand, by Sir Edward Giles and Phelips in "dovetailed" speeches, for the traditional petition for free speech, which gained urgency from memories of the aftermath of the 1614 session. And Sandys became involved at once, being named on February 5 to the committee that was to draw up the petition.[18]

The issue was first debated in a Committee of the Whole House four days later, and by then Sir Edwin was playing a central role, for he alone of the leaders of the committee had been present when the exemplary case they chose to illustrate the meaning and limits of the House's freedom had unfolded: Christopher Piggott's expulsion from the House in 1607. Piggott had vilified all Scotsmen; the M.P.s had done nothing about it; and James, furious, had told the Privy Council to examine the miscreant. Whereat the Commons, insisting that their members were within their jurisdiction, had expelled him and sent him briefly to the Tower. With the punishments meted out after the dissolution in 1614 now very much on the M.P.s'

[17] Ibid., 2:26 n., 28, 6:351; Nicholas, *Debates*, 1:15–16; *CJ*, 510. Joseph Mead's suggestion (*CD*, 2:28 n.) that Sandys was afraid to join the House seems far-fetched. Sandys and his brother Samuel made the plausible excuse that urgent Virginia business was intervening.

[18] *CD*, 5:426–429, for James and Bacon; *CJ*, 508, for the free speech proposals; Zaller, *1621*, 37, 41–44; *CD*, 2:26 n. for the committee appointment.

minds, Piggott's case seemed a useful means of drawing the delicate line between the House's rights and the king's powers.[19]

But the petition brought in on February 9—a simple statement citing Piggott's case, and claiming that a member was subject to proceedings only if the House acted against him—was rejected as giving inadequate protection to either king or Commons. Sandys accepted the criticism, and (as his prominence warranted) responded on behalf of the committee. "A man must speak with favor that discovers errors," he said. The trouble was that the House had not given the committee very good instructions: "parvus error in principio est magnus in fine." Respect had to be maintained for the king, because although "every man is to speak freely according to his conscience, no man can have any conscience to speak against the King." In avuncular fashion, he set the tone for novice colleagues, and his request for more precise instructions was accepted.[20]

The full-dress debate that ensued, on February 12, took up almost an entire day. More than twenty-five members spoke, with Coke laying out grand principles, and Sandys delivering an agonized examination of the varied issues that lay before them. "I never spoke with less assurance," he began, and admitted that he was "much perplexed." The dilemma was that they were "loth to lose the fundamental privileges of parliament and loth to give just offence to the King." The precedents from Elizabeth's reign (whom he recalled with a warmth—"a terror to her enemies"—and an implicit contrast to James that were hardly tactful) were not really conclusive, for she had punished extreme speeches "which tended to a combustion." Therefore they needed a bill defining free speech that would "remove imputation from his Majesty and wrong from the subject," guard against "misinformation of his Majesty," and protect members after Parliaments. Sandys's kinsman Strode agreed, but urged a petition as well, and it was this double onslaught that the Commons adopted.[21]

Although Strode described Sir Edwin as "eloquent," Wallace Notestein rightly questioned the description. Sandys, he wrote, "was a keeper of common sense, a voice of sweet reasonableness, whose thoughts were stated clearly and barely, a man . . . of policy rather than words." The February 12 speech was a perfect example, for it reduced a vexatious issue into assimilable parts, and came up with specific recommendations the House could follow. It created a consensus and guided the Commons by

[19] The story is in Gardiner, *England*, 1:330–331, and see *CD*, 4:17.

[20] Ibid., 37–38 describes the debate; Sandys's speech is on 38; see also 2:53. His scolding of both House and committee for taking up a difficult subject without sufficient forethought was about as strong a reproof as Sandys gave his fellow M.P.s.

[21] The fullest account of the debate is in *CJ*, 517–518; Sandys's speech is on 518; see, too, the accounts in *CD*, 2:60, 4:40; and Nicholas, *Debates*, 1:32.

invoking the best interests of subject, Parliament, and the realm. Swiftly
convinced, the M.P.s named a committee to draw up the petition and bill.[22]

Neither was produced, for a few days later James sent Calvert (who
doubtless warned the king what was brewing) a letter which allayed the
House's fears. None of his acts or speeches, he wrote, should be construed
"to lessen, or diminish, the lawful and free liberty of speech, which apper-
tains unto the House of Commons." It was the official reassurance that had
been missing thus far, and the M.P.s gratefully dropped the subject.[23] The
irony, of course, was that the behavior and treatment of Sandys himself
were to be sources of dispute when, after the summer recess, this issue
developed into a major confrontation. And when, in 1624, freedom of
speech was expanded by the king, his action was a kind of reparation: the
completion of a cycle in which Sir Edwin had played a crucial part.

Subsidies

On the afternoon of February 15, the day Calvert produced James's letter,
the Commons took up the subject that had brought them all together:
money. Sir George More opened the proceedings by reminding the M.P.s
of the parlous situation on the Continent, but special pleading was not
really necessary. The Crown had a popular cause to justify subsidies, for a
change, and the usual grumbles were muted. There were worries about
the amounts James needed, but the suggestion by Sir Edwin's friend Christopher Brooke of two subsidies was accepted, and Sandys himself removed
the last difficulties.[24]

There had been concern about the grant of fifteenths that usually accompanied subsidies, for these were regressive taxes, hardest on the poor.
Moreover, the question of whether two subsidies could support a war was
never answered. Yet Sir Edwin brought the debate to an end with one of
the decisive speeches that were his trademark. "I am against fifteens because they are upon the poorer sort who already have no money to traffic.
My motion therefore is (in regard that this is no proportion for the regaining of the Palatinate, and therefore instead of terrifying our enemies it will
but hearten them) that these two subsidies proceed as a present of love to
the King without any other consideration." In other words, everyone was
happy, and the diarist could conclude the debate with the usual formula
after a Sandys motion: "which was agreed."[25]

[22] *CD*, 2:61; *CJ*, 518.

[23] *CD*, 7:575–576 and 5:462–463; see Harold Hulme, "The Winning of Freedom of Speech
by the House of Commons," *American Historical Review* 41 (1956): 825–853.

[24] The fullest accounts of the debate are in *CD*, 2:84–91, 4:56–59. See, too, Zaller, *1621*,
47–49. The subject had first been raised on February 5: *CJ*, 508–509.

[25] Sandys's speech is in *CD*, 2:91.

The king had received his first grant of taxation by Parliament in over a decade. By any standard, it was a notable moment, but it was even more notable for its speed, coming as it did without a linkage to grievances—the stumbling block that had wrecked the previous Parliament. The change was caused not only by the dismay at events in the Empire, but by the conciliatory tone of Coke and Cranfield. Both privy councillors showed a serious interest in reform, and spoke in support of the redress of grievances. With such encouragement, the House could vote the subsidies, confident that its other interests would be pursued.[26]

Abuses at Court

The first of the grievances that provoked high feelings was the granting of special patents to individuals. Cranfield had originally suggested the topic, because the practice hindered his efforts to reduce government expenses. Not only did patentees misuse their privileges, but they siphoned off revenue the Crown badly needed. Two particularly obnoxious examples were Sir Giles Mompesson, who had the right to issue the licenses every inn needed to remain in business, and Sir Francis Michell, who had the same power in the licensing of alehouses (where a lowering of standards could promote drunkenness).[27]

Michell was quickly dealt with. On February 21, the Committee for Grievances, chaired by Coke, declared the patent a grievance. Sir Francis responded by taking refuge in royal prerogative, a tactical blunder that enraged the Commons, who dispatched him to the Tower.[28] Although there is no record of Sandys taking part in these proceedings, either in committee or on the floor of the House, that merely indicates how much more active he was than even the journals and diaries reveal, because Michell had no doubt that Sir Edwin masterminded the entire affair:

[26] Popular unhappiness at the disasters of 1620 is treated in Walter Schumacher, "Vox Populi: The Thirty Years' War in English Pamphlets and Newspapers" (Ph.D. diss., Princeton University, 1975). Zaller, 1621, 49–50, discusses the reforming bent of Coke and Cranfield, and their resultant popularity in the Commons.

[27] The fullest discussion of the general issues is Elizabeth R. Foster, "The Procedure of the House of Commons against Patents and Monopolies, 1621–1624," in Conflict in Stuart England: Essays in Honor of Wallace Notestein, ed. W.A. Aiken and Basil D. Henning (London, 1960), 57–85. For the legal issues in the Commons' proceedings against Mompesson and Michell, see Colin G. C. Tite, Impeachment and Parliamentary Judicature in Early Stuart England (London, 1974), chaps. 4 and 5, passim; and William R. Stacy, "Impeachment, Attainder, and the 'Revival' of Parliamentary Judicature under the Early Stuarts," Parliamentary History 11 (1992): 40–56.

[28] Tite, Impeachment, 91, summarizes the case; the proceedings are in CD, 5:482–486, 6:259–262, 2:127–132.

There was much muttering and some aspersions cast upon me . . . and three
stood up more violent and adding fuel to the fire made a flame. And one more
bitter than those who spoke before him threw down as it were his gauntlet
against all comers, which none of my valiant friends took up. . . . Sir Edwin
Sandys that old make-bate had formerly for many days before whispered in
the ears of diverse the most populars, and some great ones of the higher
House, what wrong I had done him in his particular about letting a thief go
that robbed his house; which he never yet dared bring to the question. All this
while I gave my attendance at the door, hearing them within very loud. At last
came out Sir Edward Sackville and [said] . . . Dudley Digges hath paid you an
hour together. I never heard any man as paid. . . . [He laid] on me many bitter
aspersions and detractions with such an assured boldness and confidence as if
he and I (that never spoke one word to each other) had been bedfellows from
our cradle.

Michell concluded that "In the Commons House of Parliament I had diverse professed adversaries, whereof Sir Edwin Sandys and all the friends
he could make were not the least."[29]

Michell could connect Digges and Sandys easily, and also guess why a
man he never met could be so vehement against him. But regardless of the
truth of his explanation of his troubles (and it is obviously self-serving), it
reveals how influential Sandys was thought to be in Parliament, even when
he did not speak on an issue. Michell could later derive satisfaction from
knowing that both Coke and Phelips (his other enemies) spent longer in
the Tower than he did, but he found no such solace in Sir Edwin's career.[30]

Mompesson's case was more dramatic. Within little more than a month
after it was first raised, on February 19, the awesome power of parliamentary judicature had been revived, after centuries of disuse; the culprit himself had escaped into exile, had been outlawed, and had been stripped of
his knighthood and his seat in the House; and the investigation had expanded into an onslaught against two of the greatest men at Court, Buckingham and Bacon. Such were the possibilities when the Committee for
Grievances unleashed its full armory.[31]

During the opening rounds, as William Noy, a veteran lawyer, and Coke
slowly built the case, Sandys's only interventions were procedural: having
the full House confirm that Mompesson's patent was a grievance, and asking that Noy and Hakewill search the records in the Tower for precedents
for a committee (to which he was appointed) that was deciding whether

[29] Ibid., 2:129 n., 6:264 n. Digges and Sackville were close colleagues of Sandys—the former a cousin and neighbor in Kent, the latter a major supporter in the Virginia Company at
this very time. For the burglary, see Kingsbury, 3:416.
[30] CD, 2:130 n.
[31] Ibid., 4:78–81.

the M.P.s should consult the Lords about the next steps.[32] Knowing that an investigation of Mompesson's affairs could lead to prominent figures, including Buckingham, who had been involved in bestowing patents, the courtiers in the Lords played for time when, on February 28, the Commons decided to approach the Upper House. Bacon adjourned the Lords for two days just before the M.P.s' message arrived, and when they reconvened Mompesson had escaped to the Continent, perhaps with the connivance of Buckingham. Sandys, upset by the sudden adjournment, had sought the reason, and his engagement with the issue deepened when he urged the Commons to approach the Lords as soon as they reassembled.[33] "The Matter [is] of great weight," he said; it could "hew at the roots of the tree of the kingdom." They had to tell "the Lords that, searching into the Grievances, they had found one, of so a nature and of so high a strain, both against King and kingdom, as never the like." It was a tone that the House at once adopted.[34]

Mompesson's escape redoubled the Commons' determination, not only to punish the culprit (eventually with outlawry and loss of knighthood), but also to track down those at Court who had granted him his rights. The latter focused attention on the so called referees: the courtiers who verified the legality of patents and advised the king to approve them. It was this investigation that brought them to Buckingham's door, and also began the downfall of Bacon who, as lord chancellor, was the most important of the referees. Sandys, in charge of a subcommittee of the Grievance Committee that screened petitions, had already heard the first complaint against Bacon on March 2. Sir Edwin had dismissed the petition as a product of "loosa fantasia," but it was an ominous tremor, not only because Mompesson's case was rousing strong emotions but also because the precedent for the process of impeachment was being established.[35]

Sandys was now taking a larger role in the Mompesson case, as one of eleven M.P.s charged with preparing the indictment that was to be presented to the Lords on March 8. This became a difficult responsibility, because the eleven were not chosen until the sixth, and only on that day

[32] Ibid., 6:253. The debate is in ibid., 2:145–147, 4:110–111; and in *CJ*, 530. The latter lists twenty-two members on the committee; cf. Tite, *Impeachment*, 95.

[33] *CJ*, 532; Tite, *Impeachment*, 97–98. Sandys was seconded by Southampton's friend Sir John Jephson: *CJ*, 533. On Jephson, see: *CD*, 6:113, and C. C. Stopes, *The Life of Henry, Third Earl of Southampton* (Cambridge, 1922), 406–409.

[34] *CJ*, 533.

[35] The connection to Buckingham came from the former M.P. Sir Henry Yelverton, now attorney-general but in the Tower, having run afoul of Buckingham. He told the M.P.s that Mompesson also had a patent to license the manufacture of gold and silver thread—a patent he had secured through Buckingham's brother Sir Edward Villiers: Tite, *Impeachment*, 99, and Zaller, *1621*, 63–64. The complaint against Bacon, by Caleb Morley, a clergyman, involved a presentation to a benefice that proved to be legal: *CD*, 6:276, 278, 5:21, 268.

were they told that they also had to identify the referees. Indeed, the delegates were later reproached because, except for Coke, they barely mentioned the referees. Even Sandys did not escape criticism, although he had the most difficult and ill-defined of the eleven M.P.s' tasks.[36]

Sir Edwin had been absent from the House as the eleven were being chosen; he had returned just as the process ended, and immediately questioned his particular commission. The others all had specific tasks—an introduction (Digges), the specific patents and illegalities (Hakewill, Noy, Coke, and six others), and precedents and a conclusion (Coke)—while he had been "thought fittest" for a combination of "Aggravation, Amplification, and Advice for Punishment." He argued that "Aggravation" (the elaboration of the seriousness of Mompesson's crimes) belonged together with the individual grievances, and that he should merely summarize and advise on punishment. After discussion, his responsibilities were redefined and put to the question as "Aggravation, Amplification, or Recollection," which required a division that the "Yeas" won by 188 to 169—a sizeable vote. What the fuss was about is difficult to tell, though it may be that the vagueness of having "to recollect what shall be omitted by any and to aggravate the whole" raised doubts. In the end, though, this large responsibility "was imposed upon Sir Edwin Sandys," and he had to prepare a long address.[37]

Although weighty tasks were not new to Sandys, he was an odd choice for "Aggravation," because his instincts were always to moderate extremes. Alone among the reporters to the Lords, he began his statement by saying "I take no delight in accusing any man." Nonetheless, he continued, he had to defend "the honor of the King, the justice of the kingdom, and the livelihood and liberty of the subject." James, who, "among many other . . . virtues, is famous for his wisdom and justice," had been wronged by an act of *lesa maiestas*. Due procedure had also suffered, because the regulation of alehouses belonged to justices of the peace, whom Mompesson had usurped, and whom he alone could not replace. Moreover, the burden of the fees the patentee extracted was particularly hard on the poor. It was avarice that had driven Mompesson, and this in turn had reflected on the king. "His Majesty's Treasury is in the hearts of his subjects. How can it

---

[36] Frances H. Relf, ed., *Notes of the Debates in the House of Lords . . . 1621, 1625, 1628*, Camden Society, 3d ser., vol. 42 (London, 1929), 11. Coke's suggestion that the referees be named (connections were made that afternoon with two brothers of Buckingham) cemented his role as a "popular," according to Chamberlain: *CJ*, 540–542; *CD*, 2:198 n.

[37] *CJ*, 540 and 541; *CD*, 2:171, 4:126. "Aggravation" is an elusive word: it could imply a rhetorical "intensification of the accusation," a stress on the seriousness of the crimes, or a concern with the sufferings the crimes caused. No one meaning is particularly supported by the content of the speech, though "the seriousness of the crimes" seems closest. I wish to thank Nicholas Tyacke for a most useful discussion of these interpretations.

then be profitable for his Majesty when . . . the hearts of his subjects shall be alienated by such vexations and injurious projects?"[38] This conclusion was as close as Sandys came to mentioning the referees, and although the speech was a typical performance—carefully organized, with numbers for the different points, and liberally sprinkled with Latin quotations and similes from Greek mythology—the omission of the referees aroused the displeasure of a House that wanted to move on from Mompesson to larger grievances.

Coke, who had performed as instructed, defended his colleagues the next morning. They could easily add the referees, he said, in another conference with the Lords. In the meantime, everyone had performed admirably; Sandys, like the rest, "did also well." Sir Edwin then defended himself, repeating the main points of his speech, explaining that there seemed no appropriate place for the referees, and vehemently rejecting a suggestion by Phelips that the spokesmen were awed by "the greatness" of the referees' status. As the diarist noted, "he was not afraid of the puff of any wind nor the frown of any cloud"; few men in the Commons could make such a claim, and Sandys was to prove it before this Parliament came to a close. He was at once "acquitted by the House," and that ended the matter.[39] Moreover, the damage had been done, for James came to the Lords the next day and disassociated himself from the wrongdoing. This gave Buckingham some difficult moments, but it was a disaster for Bacon. He had lost the shield of royal prerogative just as the Commons were launching the attack on official corruption that was to bring him down.[40]

Sandys's final intervention in the Mompesson case, on March 16, showed that his influence, even in opposition to other leading M.P.s, was undimmed. The Lords had asked that five M.P.s testify against Mompesson under oath. The denunciations of this request portrayed it as an insult to the Commons and as a dark plot to cause trouble between the Houses. Coke and Noy lent legal weight to the rejection, but gradually the torrent began to change direction. One of the five, Sir Francis Fane, said he would not mind taking an oath, and Sir Humphrey May, chancellor of the duchy of Lancaster, and Digges thought it could be permitted. In fact, a refusal might have jeopardized the newly developing case against Bacon, which

[38] The fullest version of the speech is in *CD*, 2:191–193.

[39] *CJ*, 546–547; the main target of the criticism was the speaker, Thomas Richardson, a lawyer closely connected with Bacon, who had suddenly adjourned the meeting when the eleven met to discuss their speeches: Zaller, *1621*, 28, 66; Sandys's remarks and clearance are in *CD*, 4:139, 5:285, 6:47.

[40] Ibid., 6:48–49, 382–383; Relf, *Lords*, 12–15. The best discussions of corruption in Jacobean government are Joel Hurstfield, "Political Corruption in Modern England: the Historian's Problem," *History* 52 (1967): 16–34; and Linda L. Peck, *Court Patronage and Corruption in Early Stuart England* (Boston, 1990).

required M.P.s as witnesses. But it was Sandys who made the major speech that finally decided the issue.[41]

The brunt of his argument was a direct refutation of the two major assertions on which Noy and Coke had rested their case. Noy had claimed that Mompesson had been judged by the House, and that therefore sworn depositions cast doubt on the judgment. Sandys replied: "Whether this be judged or not, I think not. . . . It is true we have judged it to be a grievance. But we brought this to the Lords not only to know whether it be so in their opinion but that it may also be punished." And since "the question before the Lords is of the punishment, which may reach to life, . . . God forbid they should proceed with an implicit faith of the examinations taken by us without oath." Coke's contention had been that the Commons were judges, and judges could not be sworn as witnesses. To that Sandys had a simple response: "they send to us to give evidence, but not as judges": that is, not "in the quality of judges but of witnesses." And he concluded with a typically reasonable recommendation:

> We have seen two of the joyfullest days that ever were in Parliament. The one in the ready, free and joyful presenting of the subsidies to his Majesty and his reciprocal love and kindness to us [in expressing willingness to remedy grievances]. The other in the happy conjunction of both Houses. I will not think that this is a bone of contention cast in among us. I pray god we make it not a bone. They have no means, they say, to direct their judgements. Let us therefore signify unto them that we hope that they have no intent to break our privileges. Therefore, observing our ancient liberties, we are content to yield to them.

It was a masterly appeal, couched in terms that almost always swayed the House, and it marked the reassertion of Sandys's presence after a fairly quiet period. As it happened, it had not been a good day for Coke. He had been rude to Alford, for which he had been reproved for thinking "himself so great, as to oppress any member of this House with his greatness." Now he tried to maintain his views on the oaths, even though Sir Edwin had argued "understandingly," but the momentum had swung against him. Attempts at delay were rejected, and permission for the oaths was given. As Chamberlain remarked, "Sir Edwin Sandys turned the tide and brought them all about."[42] His success ensured that good relations with the Lords (essential now that the Mompesson and Bacon cases were nearing resolution) remained intact.

---

[41] *CD*, 2:234, 4:163, 5:47; *CJ*, 557–558.

[42] Ibid., 557, 558; *CD*, 2:235 n. He made a similar case for direct testimony five days later, when he asked that patents be examined to see who the referee had been. He hoped to shift blame from Naunton, who had been accused (correctly) of being a referee, but who might not have been mentioned in the patents: *CJ*, 566.

Managing the House

In perceiving that strategic advantage outweighed the tactical benefits to be gained from niceties of privilege, Sir Edwin revealed his uniquely expert eye for parliamentary affairs and also his understanding that cooperation with the Lords (especially against Mompesson and Bacon) was giving the Commons more leverage than in any previous Jacobean session. He displayed the same concern when, on the same day, he led the way in gaining approval for a request from the Lords for delivery of two agents of Mompesson whom the Commons had in custody. And a little more than a week later, on the twenty-sixth, when news arrived that the Upper House was passing judgment on Mompesson, Sandys again promoted cooperation by asking his colleagues to "show our liking thereof." The harmony was so remarkable that Treasurer Mandeville declared it to be "such as no precedent can parallel." When the king, moreover, abolished the patent of inns and concurred in the sentence on Mompesson, there was almost an orgy of good feeling. "It is comfort to us all," exclaimed the speaker when James came to Westminster to bask in the general happiness on March 27, "and to every one joy and great rejoicing of heart, to see those mists, that in the other Parliaments darkened the sun of our sovereign, to clear so and so to break up to us that we can so behold nothing in your Majesty but a very fair heaven and wonderful grace."[43]

And yet these expressions of good will did not mask the struggles that were now intensifying. The attack on Bacon, which both Cranfield and Coke favored, harmed the Court not only by exacerbating its internal splits, but also by baring standards of conduct that were genuinely shocking to the parliamentarians. On March 14 Sandys's committee handling petitions of grievance passed damaging complaints by Aubrey and Egerton to the committee investigating abuses in courts of justice—the main anti-Baconian forum—and it is possible that at this stage Sandys joined the assault because of his connection with Cranfield, one of the chancellor's most bitter enemies. Southampton's prominence when the case came before the Lords, and Phelips's chairmanship of the abuses of justice committee, also suggest that this group of co-workers was as responsible as Coke for Bacon's destruction.[44]

These developments were not reinforcing the joint satisfaction among Commons, Lords, and king that was prompted by the subsidy, the condemnation of Mompesson, and the termination of the patent for the li-

[43] Ibid., 557 , 576; Relf, *Lords*, 46–47; *CD*, 6:387, 388. It was in Sandys's interest to maintain harmonious relations for another reason: his alliance with Southampton worked most effectively when coordination was easy.

[44] Ibid., 4:155–156; Nicholas *Debates*, 1:157.

censing of inns. Yet, as Sandys knew, if Parliament was to have results, its
work required a balance between the need for harmony on the one hand,
and the concern over grievances on the other. Thus, with petitions pouring
into his grievance subcommittee, Sandys had to ask on March 12 that
further subcommittees be allowed to handle each petition, with power to
dismiss "with rebuke" those that were scandalous, while passing others on
to the larger Grievance Committee or appropriate courts.[45]

Nor was there likely to be agreement about another measure: the bill
drawn up by Coke that prohibited the granting of further monopolies. It
was first suggested by Digges on March 5, and although hasty composition
led to flaws, by the nineteenth Sandys was already urging a third reading.
At this debate, on the twentieth, further objections were raised, and
Sandys himself answered the main concern—whether the king's right to
suspend a law was being infringed: "The Committee never meddled with
the King's power to dispense with any penal law; but to transfer this regal
power to another, that hath not a regal mind." He denied that the Crown
would lose either prerogative or profit; the act was aimed only at patentees. With that clarified in a final revision, the bill was engrossed on
March 26. Soon, however, Court pressure defeated the bill in the Lords: as
clear an indicator of the continuing tensions as Bacon's impeachment.[46]

Yet Sandys's hurrying along of the monopolies bill was not mere griev-
ance-chasing. Like many of his interventions to shape debate, it was evidence of the need to manage the House's proceedings. This had been his
role in 1614, and it was a crucial responsibility, because if the House's
business was to be completed, effective management was as essential as
harmony in getting laws actually passed and grievances actually remedied.
Sandys now had persuasive cohorts (Phelips, Coke, and others), but his
leadership in this area was unmatched.

On the March 24, for example, shortly before the House was due to
adjourn for the Easter recess, he clarified for the M.P.s exactly how they
could prevent pending bills and investigations from lapsing during the
three-week break. The numbered points were trotted out, and the tasks
precisely defined: six bills were to be worked on, and both the Grievance
and the Trade committees were to meet.[47] The House followed Sandys's

[45] *CJ*, 550, 578.

[46] *CD*, 2:167, 210, 266; *CJ*, 553, 563, 564. Another bill not to the king's liking, which Sandys
was largely responsible for getting through the House, repealed the arbitrary powers granted
Henry VIII in Wales: ibid., 551.

[47] *CJ*, 572; *CD*, 4:191. Sandys's attention to privileges and procedure was evident in his
insistence that Oxford be named before Cambridge in the subsidy bill (a subject that
prompted a rare but predictable disagreement with Southampton): ibid., 144, 5:34; Relf,
Lords, 28; also in his ensuring, as M.P. for Sandwich, that the same bill retained the usual tax
exemptions for the Cinque Ports and Berwick: *CJ*, 530; *CD*, 4:146–147; and in his successful

recommendations exactly. And on the twenty-seventh, just before the adjournment, Sir Edwin made sure the M.P.s fully understood the accommodating speech the king had made in the Lords the previous day, commending the Lower House, and assuring them he would have abolished all grievous patents if he had known about them. Sandys rebuked Coke for reporting the speech, because he "had no direction from the House to make the report," but he did not want the gist to be lost because of the procedural nicety that the king had not been addressing them. "The King's speech," he noted, "did for the most part concern us," even though delivered to the Lords. "Praises in the face," he continued, "are subject to misconstruction; but this in our absence is a great blessing." Sandys boiled down the speech to James's appreciation of the House's work and his promise to remove abuses, and he suggested it would be appropriate if, on their own, they thanked the king, which they did that afternoon. The final act before this generally contented adjournment was thus the work of a reassertive Sandys who, after a quiet start, was roaming across the gamut of Commons business, managing day-to-day affairs, and in general resuming his central place in Parliament.[48]

TRADE AND VIRGINIA

For all his other concerns, Sir Edwin's main preoccupation during these first ten weeks of the four-month session was a committee devoted to problems of foreign trade. England was in an economic depression, with its crucial clothmaking industry languishing and unemployment high; and, more personally for Sandys, the Virginia Company's trade was under threat from both Spain and rival entrepreneurs.

Sir Edwin had remained quiet when, early in the session, one of Virginia's sources of income, a lottery, was dissolved as an example of private

---

promotion of Pontefract, near his Yorkshire lands, to the status of a borough entitled to representation in the Commons: *CJ*, 572. He had also obtained a seat for Durham in 1614 (see above, chapter 7, note 21). These last efforts are put in context by Norman Ball, "Representation in the English House of Commons: The New Boroughs, 1485–1640," *Parliaments, Estates and Representatives* 15 (1995): 117–124. Other examples of Sandys's work in matters of procedure are in *CD*, 2:45, 209, 3:20; *CJ*, 548, 567, 578, 579. A more personal hobbyhorse was a March speech denouncing swearing—a favorite cause of the order-loving gentry: Joan Kent, "Attitudes of Members of the House of Commons to the Regulation of 'Personal Conduct' in Late Elizabethan and Early Stuart England," *Bulletin of the Institute of Historical Research* 46 (1973): 41–71.

[48] *CD*, 4:205–206; *CJ*, 576–577; Zaller, *1621*, 85–86. Sandys worked throughout the recess, raising practical considerations about legislation against Catholics; encouraging the collection of grievances; and helping lower lighthouse fees. When the House reconvened, on April 17, he made the decisive recommendation for a bill on iron ordnance: *CD*, 2:273, 279, 284, 285; *CJ*, 578.

benefit derived from a royal proclamation—a grievance he obviously could not bring himself to defend.[49] But on February 26, two days after the House finished with the lottery, he stirred himself, and brought to the fore much larger issues of England's trade and prosperity. Cranfield had proposed at least three times that the Commons investigate the causes of "decay of money," but not until Sir Edwin intervened on the twenty-sixth did this concern become a central theme of the M.P.s' debates. Urging formation of a committee to explore all sides of the problem, and outlining the main topics it ought to pursue, he delivered what was one of the formative speeches of the session, initiating a series of activities that were to occupy the M.P.s for the remainder of the Parliament. The resultant committee, chaired by Cranfield, became the main interest of its real creator, Sandys.[50]

Sir Edwin explained that he had not been present when, in the speech opening Parliament, the king had "commended one thing of singular importance to our consideration, which was the cause of the want and decay of money and what remedies may be had for the same." The "necessity," Sandys said, was "pressing," because the poor, the farmers, and the clothiers were the chief sufferers. Since "fairs and markets stand still," the worst might happen to "the gentleman and nobleman," let alone "the merchant and tradesman." And Sandys felt he could "contribute somewhat both to the discovery of the causes and the remedies."

That was the first part of the speech, and it prompted merchant M.P.s, Coke, Calvert, and others to enlarge on the seriousness of the situation and its causes. However, it was the second part of Sandys's speech (delivered when he was asked to "speak his knowledge") that offered an analysis of the situation and proposals for action. He had the advantage, by this time, that he had heard various theories and could indulge in his favorite exercise of summarizing where the House stood. The result was that he was able to reassert the primacy on trade matters that had been his niche in the Commons since 1604. Even in the presence of a prominent financial expert like Cranfield, it was to him that the M.P.s looked for "knowledge"

[49] The lottery was increasingly regarded as a questionable means of raising money, even within the Virginia Company (despite the £8,000 annual income it generated). When Coke denounced royal proclamations for private benefit, this was an early casualty: James suppressed all lotteries on March 8. Robert C. Johnson, "The Lotteries of the Virginia Company, 1612–1621," *Virginia Magazine of History and Biography* 74 (1966): 259–292, esp. 287–292; *CD*, 2:118–119, 140–141, 6:7–8; *APC, 1619–1621*, 359; and James F. Larkin and Paul L. Hughes, eds., *Stuart Royal Proclamations*, vol. 1 (Oxford, 1973), 500–502.

[50] Zaller, *1621*, 50; the best versions of the speech and the debate described below are in *CJ*, 527; *CD*, 2:137–139, 4:104–106, 5:490–493; Nicholas, *Debates*, 1:95–97. Cranfield's chairmanship is revealed by his role as reporter (e.g., *CD*, 5:287). For the lord treasurer's perspective on the trade debates and his quarrels with Sandys in 1621, see Prestwich, *Cranfield*, chapter 7.

as they grappled with the great depression that they acknowledged as England's most serious problem in 1621.

There had been "much spoken, that he intended," Sandys remarked, but it reduced itself to "three general heads: 1, first, the not importing of money; 2, the exporting of it; 3, the consumption and wasting of it within the land." This encapsulated the hypotheses that had been put forward, ranging from inadequate minting of money and the importation of French wines and Irish beef to the making of too many gold and silver ornaments and the export of bullion by the East India Company. But the most notorious culprit, in his view, was Spanish tobacco. For "the wellhead from whence [bullion] must come is the West Indies, from thence it floweth into Spain, and from thence in our countries." At one time £100,000 a year had come from Spain to England, buying cloth and merchandise. Now the Spaniards were doing better by the exchange, and had a surplus of £20,000. Why? Because Englishmen "bring home, instead of money, tobacco," and the Spaniards can amuse themselves by saying, when a laden English ship arrives, "we shall have all this for smoke." Other countries refused to import goods until all native production was consumed—French and Spanish wine, for example. The obvious conclusion was that the King should "initiate the wisdom of other nations" by restricting his subjects to "tobacco [grown] in England or [brought] from Virginia and the [Somers] Islands." Although Sandys added that imports of grain were equally reprehensible, he had brilliantly linked the great issue of the day to a problem peculiar to Virginia.[51]

And he did the same with another Virginia concern, the effort by Sir Ferdinando Gorges to control the fishing off the New England coast from which the colonists hoped to profit. "The money drawn out of Spain for the overplus of our commodities," he said, was "increased by a new fishing discovered on the North coast of Virginia, having ever been 100,000 by year, but is [now] intercepted by the way by merchants trading into other countries." Although fishing had less potential than tobacco for the Virginians, Sandys was using his stature in trade matters to help the colony in any way he could.[52]

---

[51] With the lottery gone, Virginia's one remaining asset, tobacco, needed all the advantages it could get. Yet the previous summer the king had sold the tobacco farm (the right to import tobacco) to a syndicate that profited mainly from Spanish tobacco, and James enhanced the grant by restricting Virginian and Bermudan exports to well below their production in 1619: W. F. Craven, *Dissolution of the Virginia Company: The Failure of a Colonial Experiment* (New York, 1932), 227–229. Sandys used the trade debate to portray the tobacco farm as perpetrating all three of the prime transgressions on the Commons' blacklist: it was a monopoly, bestowed by patent; it aided the ravager of the Palatinate, Spain; and it accentuated England's crippling trade depression.

[52] *CD*, 2:139 n–140 n. The fisheries off Cape Cod had become a matter of dispute a year

This multipronged campaign continued the next day, when Sandys was the most active speaker at the first meeting of the Committee on Trade. The dangers of a poor balance of trade, the need for mercantilist protection, and the problems of tobacco and fishing were his main themes. "We have no mines of gold at home," he told his colleagues; but that was no reason to act cravenly. Catholic leaders forbade trade with heretics, and England should do likewise, accepting tobacco only from places "which are under the protection of our King." He moved that imports of Spanish tobacco be prohibited, and at the end of the day his motion was renewed by Phelips. The committee's only resolution was to accept Sandys's view that the imports from Spain were a "cause of the want of money."[53]

Sir Edwin's continued dominance of the committee was apparent when it made its first report to the House on March 13. His motion brought the matter back on the agenda and led to merchants being summoned as witnesses. And even though Cranfield, as chairman, delivered the report, it was heavily influenced by Sandys's comments of February 26 and 27. Over twenty causes of the decay of money had been assembled, but everything could be reduced to three heads, as had been done "by a worthy member of this House," namely Sandys. Cranfield followed Sir Edwin's summary exactly, and ended by saying that Spanish tobacco had been the first cause of the decline. The House accepted this conclusion in a formal resolution "without one negative," and there the matter rested for the time being.[54]

This outcome was a considerable triumph for Sandys, for he had managed to persuade both the committee and the House to endorse his own aims. The committee was now to consider free trade, another of his pet subjects, and much of its work henceforth was to be in subcommittees which he often dominated. Despite Cranfield's chairmanship of the overall committee, control of its work was slipping into other hands, and it was pursuing special interests as well as the grand objectives that he had in mind. In contrast to the Crown minister, who sought thorough inquiries into the *facts* of imports and exports, Sandys was in tune with the M.P.s' less informed assumptions and fears, and the result was predictable:

---

earlier, when the northern (Plymouth) half of the twin Virginia companies, established in 1606, was revived by Gorges, a Devon man whom Sandys had known at least since the time of the Essex affair. Gorges received a patent to settle New England in 1620, and insisted, at a Virginia Company meeting, that each company had to fish within its own waters. The Privy Council ruled that each group could fish in the other's waters only for the "sustentation" of colonists, and it was this decision that Sandys sought to overturn by raising questions about free fishing and the legality of Gorges' grant. See R. A. Preston, *Gorges of Plymouth Fort* (Toronto, 1953), 166–177.

[53] *CD*, 2:213–214, 4:112–113, 5:524–529; Nicholas, *Debates*, 1:104–105. Unlike Phelips, Sandys did not want to abolish the tobacco farm—merely to reorient it away from Spain and toward Virginia: *CD*, 4:113.

[54] *CJ*, 551–552; *CD*, 2:212–214, 4:149–150, 5:294.

Cranfield pressed for an impartial inquiry based on the customs figures, but found he was blocked by the diversionary theme of tobacco. . . . Sandys swept the committee for the decay of money. Cranfield's plea as chairman that the general problem of an adverse balance of £270,000 should be debated could not divert members of the committee from chasing the hare of Spanish tobacco. . . . The tobacco episode illustrates how difficult it was for Cranfield to force a general programme on committees swayed by vested interests, while it also drove the first wedge between Cranfield and the Commons.[55]

There is little doubt that Cranfield's disillusionment with Parliament as a means of reform began with his experiences in the Committee on Trade. Sir Edwin, by contrast, maintained his efforts unflaggingly.[56] And when, on March 28, a recess began, the momentum of his activities accelerated.

As in previous Jacobean sessions of Parliament, this period, when only a few of the most determined M.P.s remained at work, helped shape the period that followed. In the Lords, the charges were being accumulated that would bring about Bacon's disgrace; and a number of observers, James among them, now realized that an avalanche of grievances was about to descend from M.P.s "greedy to snatch at accusations."[57] Cranfield's drift toward stolid representation of the king's views, and away from his cooperation when he still hoped for reform, was symptomatic of the change of mood in the month of April. And the fulcrum around which the transformation revolved was the three-week recess that lasted until April 17.

It was certainly the time when Sandys's exertions on the Trade Committee intensified, for on April 10 he delivered an enormous report outlining progress to date. The uniting concern was the liberalization of trade, but this had many aspects. It required, first, that the tradesmen of great cities such as London maintain a distinction between a merchant, who engaged in foreign commerce, and a dealer in goods at home, such as a vintner. A man could be one or the other, but not both, for "shopkeepers" were "not brought up in" the "merchandizing" business, and therefore did poorly. Such combinations were permitted only in the outports, whose subordinate position in the economy prevented specialization. A second necessity

[55] Prestwich, *Cranfield*, 309–310.

[56] On March 23 Sandys attended an examination of the Spanish merchants who were importing the notorious tobacco. And on March 26 he first showed his support for the Cinque Ports (among them his own constituency of Sandwich), who soon submitted a petition for free trade: *CD*, 5:319, 2:364; *CJ*, 573.

[57] Ibid., 5:86. Chamberlain had similar views: N. E. McClure, ed., *The Letters of John Chamberlain*, 2 vols. (Philadelphia, 1939), 2:363. James lost some of the M.P.s' good will at the start of the recess, when he unexpectedly drew his sword and knighted the speaker, Thomas Richardson, about whom the Commons had been complaining regularly. The honor looked suspiciously like a reward for such unpopular actions as his sudden departure in the middle of the debate about the referees a few weeks earlier. *CD*, 2:273.

was strict adherence to manufacturing standards to stop an alarming slide in cloth exports caused, he claimed, by poor production and the follies of the "new draperies," Cockayne's project. A bill to this effect was to be introduced. Third was the thorn of Spanish tobacco which, despite protests by the farmers that it was worth only £30,000, was branded a stimulus to Spain's economy that harmed Virginia. "It was advised to banish all tobacco not growing in the King's dominions." Sandys darkly warned that the two chief importers of the Spanish crop (named by Cranfield) were "patentees and malefactors, who have much abused this kingdom; and that they have more monopolies besides." He concluded by noting the problem of obtaining refunds for customs duties on reexported goods and the burden of high customs duties in general, both of which diminished trade.[58]

His principal target was Spain, because the dread enemy was a sure means of arousing emotions favorable to his cause. But he still had the problem of the 1604 treaty between the two nations, whose ninth article explicitly proclaimed freedom of commerce. When the treaty was read at the next meeting of the committee, on the thirteenth, Sandys explained that the ninth article was not all that it seemed. James had prohibited importation of Spanish pepper; the Lords had forbidden export of ordnance to Spain; and Catholic books, which were surely "contained in free commerce," could not be brought into England. If the Spaniards' mistreatment and pillage of English merchants had not caused a breach of the treaty, he asked, why should the cessation of tobacco imports have such an effect? A merchant named John Fletcher had been interrogated by the committee about his mistreatment in Spain, and this evidence permitted Sandys to wax indignant: "It is no news to have ... Englishmen thus abused in Spain, and their goods taken away: that those who were of the first Parliament in the King's time know, that it was then complained of, that the King of Spain's officers had taken away ... the value of two hundred thousand pounds." The rest was easy. "Hereupon," reported John Pym, "the committee delivered their opinion that tobacco might be restrained without breach of the league."[59]

On this busy day the committee also heard the Merchant Adventurers' and Eastland Company's reasons for the decline of trade; asked other companies to give similar reports; received the Cinque Ports' petition for free trade and referred it to the full House; and discussed at length the impounding, at the request of Gondomar, the Spanish ambassador, of some

---

[58] Ibid., 2:285–290, 4:216–218; and Nicholas, *Debates*, 1:237–240. Cranfield might have made concessions on customs, including perhaps abolishing impositions, but the prospect faded as the trade committee became increasingly involved with tobacco and the great trading companies: Prestwich, *Cranfield*, 312.

[59] Nicholas, *Debates*, 1:252; *CD*, 2:293–294, 4:288.

tobacco that Roger North had brought back from an expedition to Guiana. North petitioned Parliament for help, and Sandys jumped to the rescue. "If they were intruders or invaders," he admitted, "they have no right to the tobacco." But the Spaniards had a claim only if they could prove prior settlement of the area, "for by the law of nations anybody may make use of a desolate country whereof nobody is in possession." Alexander VI's division of the world between Spain and Portugal meant nothing, because if that act were recognized as valid, "then the Spaniard will have, by the same title, both Virginia and the Bermudas." Since the English were "the occupiers," they had "a good title and claim." The committee agreed, but it is unclear whether the Commons had a part in the return of the impounded tobacco to North three months later.[60]

The day that the full House resumed meeting, April 17, saw Sandys working at full steam. He spoke four different times during the morning, including comments on Cranfield's report about trade—which itself merely repeated what Sir Lionel described as Sandys's report on the decay of trade. Cranfield went through the recommendations put forward in committee point by point, and Sir Edwin added that complaints about trading companies referred mainly to the Spanish merchants. He also said that Cranfield had left out one matter, the committee's view that tobacco should be kept at eight shillings a pound, because the cheapness would deter smugglers. Unlike the prohibition of Spanish imports, however, this was Sandys's own project, and Cranfield responded not only by correcting his colleague but also by opposing such limits as invitations to retaliation by other countries.[61]

That afternoon, when the House had constituted itself as a Committee of the Whole, there was some murmuring about the slow pace of progress on trade. To speed things along, Sandys suggested that seven different subcommittees hear the seven trading companies that wished to testify, but the M.P.s insisted on just one—which Sandys henceforth chaired, thus retaining control of proceedings. Although he now had an enormous workload, he moved ahead as quickly as possible, spending the afternoon of the twenty-first in a mammoth session with the companies, listening to the familiar self-serving theories of at least six mercantile groups. Three days later, he attended an attack on the Muscovy Company, and yet the following morning managed to summarize for the House the proceedings thus far.[62]

---

[60] James had also imprisoned North for infringing on Spanish interests, but apparently released him unexpectedly: *CD*, 2:223–225, 228–229, 4:224–225; Nicholas, *Debates*, 1:250–251; *APC, 1621–1623*, 26–27.

[61] *CJ*, 578–579. Coke, too, was unhelpful, calling the proclamations forbidding tobacco plantations in England (which helped the Virginia Company) illegal.

[62] *CD*, 3:3–4, 45–50, 73–74, 6:99; *CJ*, 591. Barrington mentions the Merchant Adventurers,

At the same time, he was maintaining the momentum of the Virginia issues, tobacco and fishing. The full-dress debate on tobacco imports had taken place on the eighteenth, introduced by one of the seventy-nine members of the Virginia Company in the House (over 15 percent of the M.P.s), William Lord Cavendish, heir to the Earldom of Devonshire, and among Sandys's closest associates. Samuel Sandys followed, asking for approval of the committee's recommendation that foreign imports be banned. Coke argued for a proper bill, but Sandys, like his brother, asked merely for a resolution of the full House. When Cranfield raised the treaty again, Digges countered by saying that no treaty was worth £100,000 a year, while Sandys and Phelips reiterated that the Spaniards themselves banned some goods. Sir Edwin also reassured the merchants that trade with Virginia would be conducted openly and freely. Over twenty more speakers had their say, most of them supporters of the company, and when Cranfield argued for a total ban the House disagreed: "Upon question, importation of all foreign tobacco fit to be barred; not one negative." The diarist added: "that of Virginia, or of any of the King's dominions, is not held foreign."[63]

Sandys now moved on to a bill, which was ready for its first reading five days later. To allay the objections of the tobacco farmers, he postponed implementation until October 1, when their patent expired, but thereafter, for seven years, there was to be tobacco imported only from Virginia and Bermuda. At the second reading, on May 3, Sir Edwin astutely added that the profits would go toward building hospitals and colleges in Virginia; he accepted a few minor amendments, assured the M.P.s that Virginia was seeking other means of livelihood such as iron and silk, had the bill engrossed on the sixteenth, and on May 25 shepherded it through a third reading to final passage.[64] The measure then died in the Lords, but it did serve Virginia, because when James renewed the tobacco farm with a new syndicate in December, he allowed the patentees to import only sixty-thousand pounds' weight of Spanish tobacco a year, whereas tobacco from the colonies was left unrestricted.[65] This reversed the situation as it had been before Parliament met, and the following year the company itself gained control of all tobacco importation.

---

the Eastland, Muscovy, French, and East India companies, and the Barbary merchants at the April 21 hearing, but the debate on the afternoon of the seventeenth suggests that a seventh, probably the Levant Company, was also present—possibly in the person of Maurice Abbot, who spoke briefly.

[63] *CJ*, 581–582; *CD*, 3:7–12, 5:76–78; and Nicholas, *Debates*, 1:269–271, describe the debate; the diarist's comment is Nicholas's (271). The figures on Virginia Company members in the House are in my *Enterprise*, 94, 128.

[64] *CD*, 2:309–310, 341, 371, 3:50, 232–234, 305, 4:332–333, 5:170; Nicholas, *Debates*, 1:296–297; *CJ*, 622, 627.

[65] Craven, *Dissolution*, 230.

For the fisheries bill, which Sandys also pursued after the recess, he got powerful support from allies in the outports, especially the West Country. This measure was brought in from Sandys's committee as soon as the Commons reconvened, on April 17, by John Glanville, a lawyer closely tied to Plymouth and connected to the Virginia Company through his brother, Sir Francis, also an M.P. At the second reading, on the twenty-fifth, Sandys stressed the grievances of the Virginians, who had sunk £100,000 into their colony, against the New Englanders and Gorges, who had done nothing. The northern fishing, he said, was "far better than that of Newfoundland," and likely to bring England the talismanic figure of "£100,000 per annum . . . in coin." This the Virginians could achieve without costing the nation anything, all the while stimulating shipping and earning Spanish silver. It was "pitiful" that the king's subjects were kept from the fishing banks by the New England patent while Dutchmen and Frenchmen took full advantage of the opportunities—a typical Sandys argument. The only solution was to open up both fishing and shore rights (so that sailors could land to repair ships and dry fish). Backed by outport merchants who also sought such liberties off Newfoundland, Sir Edwin gained the House's approval for the appointment of a committee (which he was to head) to prepare the final bill.[66]

The one caution came from Calvert, who had been involved in East India, Virginia, and Irish ventures for more than a decade and was about to found a new American colony. He raised a constitutional issue: Parliament's jurisdiction over colonies that were the king's direct possessions, by right of conquest, and thus not subject to the laws of England. Brooke replied that an act of Parliament held greater force in law than a royal patent, and Sandys noted that in their charters the colonies were said to be held of the King's manor of East Greenwich, which "may be bound by the parliament." The argument was fraught with danger for the colonizers, because James was apparently thinking of ways of implementing the powers he claimed. If Gondomar's prediction that the Virginia Company "would prove a seminary for a seditious parliament" might seem to be coming true, then the remedy might be the kind of interventionism that the colony had largely escaped thus far. The warnings were in the air, but for the time being they were dismissed, and the fishing bill moved ahead.[67]

[66] *CD*, 2:294, 320–321; *CJ*, 591–592; Nicholas, *Debates*, 1:318–319. See, too, Preston, *Gorges*, 177–181, and "Fishing and Plantation: New England in the Parliament of 1621," *American Historical Review* 45 (1939): 29–43.

[67] *CJ*, 591–592; *CD*, 2:321; Nicholas, *Debates*, 1:319. On James's interest in the colonies as conquests, annexed to the Crown but not subject to England's laws, see John T. Juricek, "English Claims in North America to 1660: A Study in Legal and Constitutional History" (Ph.D. diss., University of Chicago, 1970), esp. chap. 9. Gondomar's remark is quoted in Prestwich, *Cranfield*, 305.

Like the tobacco bill, it was delayed by the press of business at the end of April, but on May 16 the committee heard John Guy, a leader of the Newfoundland colony, and Gorges offer spirited objections. They made little headway, however, against the Virginia adventurers on the committee, one of whom, John Smith, smugly described their own enterprise as "A company that undergoes all care, labor, and charges out of their private [purses] for a general end and public good of the commonwealth, who can never look for any benefit by dividend. . . . Considering the benefit which Virginia promises, . . . [we] conclude that since this bill aims . . . [to] help . . . that plantation, that it is a good bill and wish it to pass for a law."[68]

Swamped with business, Sir Edwin left chairmanship of the committee to Christopher Earle, a member of the Virginia Company who brought the bill before the Commons on May 24. Despite renewed concerns from Guy and Calvert, Sandys carried the day with a simple appeal: "this bill restrains only such as restrain our own countrymen, and give liberty to strangers (who give most [money] for their booths [on shore]) to fish." Even Sir Edward Giles, a member of Gorges' Council for New England, was moved to declare it "as good as any bill in this House whatsoever." The Commons ordered it engrossed, and, despite Sandys's absence in the fall session, it was to pass, with Gorges also given some nasty moments when the M.P.s examined his patent as a possible grievance. As with the tobacco bill, the legislation did not get through the Lords, but it did delay Gorges' enforcement of his rights. Moreover, the exception that allowed Jamestown fishing and shore privileges for its "sustentation" created an unmeasurable loophole. Although the Virginians never became seriously interested in fishing, Sandys had managed, once again, to link the colony with his cause, free trade.[69]

THE FREE TRADE BILL

That central issue—the heart of the efforts of 1621, and an echo of the legislation he had steered through the House in 1604—displayed fully Sir Edwin's mastery of the Commons. Although the 1621 bill for free trade went no further than its second reading, it did enable Sandys to strengthen his alliance with the outports and also to shape national policy indirectly. Just as the government's actions on tobacco and fishing, later in 1621, reflected the influence of parliamentary events, so too did its decision to investigate and seek ways to relieve the economic depression.

[68] *CD*, 5:378–379. The quotation is from 379.

[69] Ibid., 5:386, 3:297–298, 4:367–368; and Nicholas, *Debates*, 2:97, describe the May 24 debate. For the actions in the fall, see *CD*, 2:482–483, 3:408–409. The Privy Council's order of June 18, 1621, is printed in Kingsbury, 3:459–460. For the effects of the delay on Gorges, see Preston, *Gorges*, 184 ff.

The causes of the difficulties the country endured in the 1620s remain shadowy to this day, though economic historians have identified three prime culprits: the Cockayne project, whose offspring, the so-called "new draperies," converted Englishmen's thriving exports of unfinished cloths into unsellable finished cloth; the disruption of trade by fighting on the Continent; and the consequences of wild coinage debasements and inflation in the Germany of the Thirty Years' War.[70] Only the first of these was clearly perceived by contemporaries, whose anger was therefore directed primarily at the Merchant Adventurers, the company that had controlled England's cloth trade for centuries. In the Commons this sentiment was powerfully abetted by the outport merchants who (though often Merchant Adventurers themselves) felt that chartered companies were, in general, devices for the subjugation of the provinces by London.

Sandys's major speech of February 26 set the bill in motion. As he saw it, a central reason for England's problems was defined by the very description of her terrible condition. If we were to look at the poor, he said,

> we should find, that they had the inheritance of their hands taken from them through monopolies and restraint of commerce, insomuch that in one place there were 200 looms laid down, and each loom would have set on work 40 persons; these men by these means turned out of their inheritance, which is their trades, and to seek new, which is not only pitiful but fearful, lest, as in Germany, it should cause *Bellum Rusticum*.

The trade and textile monopolists, in other words, might soon be provoking serious domestic conflict, and they, above all, had to be curbed.[71]

On March 2 the bill to free trade had its first reading. Ten days later Sandys reminded the M.P.s that the poverty of his constituents, the Cinque Ports, stemmed from "the restraint of free trade," and the next day he finally got his colleagues to summon merchants for hearings. By the seventeenth the first complaints against the Merchant Adventurers had appeared, an attack that gathered steam on the twentieth, during a debate that aired new grievances about the Cockayne project as well as also old ones about the difficulty of becoming a Merchant Adventurer, the woes of the outports, and the freedom practiced in other countries. When the recess approached, Sandys made sure, in his speech of March 24, that the issue was included in the agenda that was to be pursued over the next few

---

[70] Astrid Friis, *Alderman Cockayne's Project and the Cloth Trade* (London, 1927); J. D. Gould, "The Trade Depression of the Early 1620's," *Economic History Review*, 2d ser., 7 (1954): 81–90; Barry E. Supple, *Commercial Crisis and Change in England, 1600–1642* (Cambridge, 1959).

[71] *CD*, 2:137, 5:490.

weeks; among the M.P.s' tasks, he said, was further work on the "26 heads; scarce one finished" that had been prepared for the free trade bill.[72]

As we have seen, the recess was when Sir Edwin took control of the principal trade matters before the House. Although Cranfield remained the chairman of the parent grand committee, the subcommittees on tobacco, fishing, and free trade were now under Sandys's wing. Thus, when he summarized what had been accomplished thus far, on April 10, he covered all these topics, but his theme was the liberalization of trade. Even the request for customs reform served to build free trade into an emotional issue. As in 1604, it was the appeal, rather than the precision, of the arguments that counted.[73]

The last three weeks of April were Sandys's busiest time on the trade committee. He heard testimony from the Merchant Adventurers four times between April 13 and 30; he listened to the views of the leading London companies on the sixteenth and twenty-first; and he sat through complaints about the Muscovy Company in another session on the twenty-fourth. All of this must have seemed like a replay of the investigation of 1604, when the great companies had "repined at others" while "standing stiffly" for themselves. If the outports thought that the Londoners were to blame for the depression, each set of the capital's merchants had other scapegoats, preferably the dastardly policies of foreigners.[74]

Finally, on April 28, the bill received its second reading. Despite worries about the king's prerogative in granting charters (and the pointed observation that a grant of liberty in trade was inconsistent with the restraint on tobacco) the measure apparently had overwhelming support. The outport M.P.s demanded the abolition of the London companies' privileges, and there were even suggestions that members of those companies should not be permitted to attend committee discussions.[75] Despite the determination to continue the investigation, however, little more was heard about the bill. Inundated by pressing concerns on all sides, the Commons apparently could not find the time to see the legislation through to passage.

Some spin-off measures did receive attention, notably the petition from the Cinque Ports to have their trade freed of domination by the Merchant Adventurers, which Sandys brought to the fore on May 14. Sir Edwin reminded the Commons of the parlous state of French Protestantism and invoked the fearful dangers of an invasion from the south—against which, of course, the Cinque Ports were the principal defence even though their

---

[72] Ibid., 6:23, 56, 72, 4:175–177; *CJ*, 551, 572.

[73] See above, note 58.

[74] *CD*, 4:228, 3:45–46, 2:325–326, 5:357, 7:593–596, on the Merchant Adventurers; ibid., 4:228–231, 254, 3:45–50, for the other companies.

[75] Ibid., 3:105–107, 4:271–273.

trade "hath been of late taken from them utterly, [and therefore] they are all like to quit the ports."[76] This aroused a number of members. William Towerson, one of the Merchant Adventurers' leaders, begged to let his side be heard, but he was swept aside by outport M.P.s, backed by Coke, who demanded that a committee examining the Merchant Adventurers' charter speed up its work. This flouted the will of the king, who had told the House on May 3 that the Merchant Adventurers "are not like mushrooms and new patentees start[ed] up yesterday," and had urged caution. James's intervention, however, merely prompted questions about the company's misbehavior in having "disclosed the treaties [discussions] of the House." These quarrels continued on May 16 and 24, and on the twenty-eighth the charter committee was ordered to report two days later.[77] By then, though, the session was on the point of adjournment, and this final splutter proved to be the last echo of the legislation to free trade.

As with the tobacco and fishing bills, however, the failure of the measure in Parliament did not prevent action elsewhere. In June Cranfield forced the Merchant Adventurers to admit the Cinque Ports and other outports into the "new draperies" trade freely. And the creation of a commission on trade, later that year, set in motion the most comprehensive inquiry into economic conditions the government had ever undertaken. Sandys was by then in such poor standing with the Court that there was no chance of his being appointed to the commission, though the inclusion of his relatively inexperienced brother Samuel may have been an implicit recognition of the value of his views. Moreover, the work he and his colleagues did was doubtless a vital stimulus to the inquiry.

Nor were these the only issues generated by the trade depression on which Sandys made his mark, or the only topics that enabled him to use the House to promote Virginia. On April 30, for instance, he squashed a bill that sought to curb migration to the cities by the many people, forced to move by economic difficulty, who had no trade or little property. If either town or country had to have the poor, Sir Edwin said, he opted for the towns, where there was more work to do. In any case, one should not restrain the charitable impulse. And, although "this is like the turning of a sick man from one side of the bed to the other: the malady still remains," one had to recognize the cause—monopolies, since without free trade "the poor cannot be employed." He therefore had a suggestion. "I would move that the poor that cannot be set on work may be sent to Virginia. Never

---

[76] A bill to free trade into France was read on May 3; and the trade committee was requested on May 7 to add the Staplers' privileges to its considerations: Ibid., 3:147, 190, 245; Nicholas, *Debates*, 2:66; *CJ*, 620. The Cinque Ports' petition is in *CD*, 7:593–596.

[77] For the debate on the fourteenth, see ibid., 3:245–246, 4:338–339; Nicholas, *Debates*, 2:66–67; and *CJ*, 620; for subsequent events, *CD*, 3:276–277, 300–301, 337.

was there a fairer gate opened to a nation to disburden itself nor better means, by reason of the abundance of people, to advance such a plantation." As if that effort were not enough, Sandys also spoke, later that same day, to moderate the penalties in a bill to prohibit the export of wool.[78]

In these last days of April, as Sandys's interventions multiplied, it was becoming apparent that the volume of business was overwhelming the House. On April 26 there was a major debate about where to go next, and a committee "for disposing of business," suggested by Sir Edwin, met to survey the proposals that were pending. He also had the M.P.s continue the work of the subcommittees that had met during the recess, even though his "disposing of business" committee discovered, that afternoon, that over sixty bills were at various stages of deliberation. Of the fifteen that were then chosen to have precedence, three had to do with cloth, and four of the others were Coke's monopolies bill and Sandys's bills for free trade, tobacco, and fishing. Such precedence was obviously no guarantee of passage, but it did reveal the influence that Sandys had achieved.[79]

In a pattern that paralleled the events of 1604, it had been trade, as much as any other issue, that had brought Sir Edwin to the forefront. He had not been a central figure in the early days of the session: a quiet beginning, once more like 1604. But in the recess, as so often, he had taken the reins in his hands, and had emerged after the adjournment in control of a great deal of business. He had spoken on the floor thirty-seven times during the seven weeks he had been in attendance before the recess, from February 7 to March 27. Yet he spoke twenty-three times in just two weeks between the reconvening of the House on April 17 and the end of the month: over double his earlier rate. And he was to maintain an even faster pace in May: fifty-one speeches in little more than four weeks (numbers which, given the diarists' likely inaccuracy, are probably minima). This was what it took to be the "Commons-man" par excellence.

[78] Ibid., 5:113–114, 355, 2:332, 4:274–275. Exercising his trademark moderation, Sandys said the proposed penalty, the loss of life and goods, was too harsh. He urged a "pecuniary" punishment, with a share for the informer. His view eventually prevailed after he had left the House: the bill was allowed to die "because sanguinary." He may have been protecting his outport constituents, because Towerson later noted that the bill would prevent exports from the Cinque Ports as well as London: ibid., 2:395. For the debate, ibid., 4:275–276, 5:114–115, 226–227; Nicholas, *Debates*, 1:353; and *CJ*, 597.

[79] *CJ*, 592–594; *CD*, 3:92–96, 4:260–264.

Chapter IX

THE PARLIAMENT OF 1621:
DESCENT INTO CONFLICT, MAY TO DECEMBER

STIRRINGS OF CONFLICT: THE FLOYD CASE

If, at the end of April 1621, there seemed reason to believe that the three-month-old parliamentary session would be productive and effective, the month of May put an end to such hopes, and revived the suspicions and conflicts of 1614. As in 1614 (and even as early as 1610), Sandys was the most conspicuous seeker of order, harmony, and progress amidst the discord. He wanted to get on with the great business of the realm, and he used all his influence to moderate his colleagues' eruptions. But in the end he, too, was to succumb to the high emotion that swept through Parliament.

The first outburst was prefigured on April 30, when the House heard that a prisoner in the Fleet, a Catholic lawyer named Edward Floyd, had maligned the king's unfortunate daughter and son-in-law shortly after the defeat of their Bohemian adventure at the Battle of the White Mountain. Floyd was reported to have said: "Tut, good man palsgrave and goodie palsgrave, I have as much right—or any man of England—to the kingdom of Bohemia as he." These "base words" caused trouble for the warden of the Fleet, who failed to act against the miscreant, and prompted dismay at the horrendous conditions that were discovered in the prison cells, but they unleashed hysteria at Floyd himself.[1]

The immediate reaction of the M.P.s was uncertainty about what to do, and about their jurisdiction in the matter. Sandys tried to give them guidance: the "words of malice and scorn, goodman palsgrave, etc," he said, had to give them offence, and therefore—choosing his phrasing carefully—he recommended that the House "begin the punishment here." It is the word "begin" that is crucial, for this implied that the final sentence might have to be delivered elsewhere—a distinction that soon became the crux of the issue. In a case having nothing to do with an M.P. or a public grievance, the Commons were entitled at most to the role of accuser; the Lords alone were able to mete out punishment.[2]

By the following day, however, having heard Floyd and his accuser di-

---

[1] *CJ*, 597; *CD*, 2, 157–158, 5:116–117.
[2] Ibid., 4:278, 5:117; *CJ*, 597.

rectly, the Commons were ready to do their worst. Suggestions for punishment cascaded forth, and Sandys was carried along in the momentum, albeit reluctantly. "A good cause does sometimes breed a bad precedent," he warned, noting that there was "much difficulty in this cause" and that their actions would be "censured in a great part of the Christian world" as religious persecution. He did not want Floyd to be made a martyr, and he hoped the punishment could "avoid cruelty" and measures inappropriate to a gentleman. Yet he did agree that Floyd's contempt should be met with contempt: the pillory, a backward ride on an ass with his offences proclaimed on a sheet of paper, and a fine—exactly the combination the Commons decided upon. Worried about the disruptive potential of the case, however, he forgot his advice of the previous day and suggested that they not "interrupt the business of the Lords, who are now full of business, by sending of Floyd thither." This may have shown good intent, and Sandys's links to proceedings in the Upper House, but it was also poor advice—a rare occurrence, which he later tried to disavow.[3]

For the M.P.s were now overstepping their bounds, and the next day the reproof came from James, who thanked them for their zeal but halted their proceedings because (a) they had acted without his approval, (b) they had censured a man not sitting in Parliament, and (c) they had not allowed Floyd due process. Sandys saw the justice of these arguments, and backpedalled. "Quod inconsulto fecimus consulto revocamus," he said, admitting that the Commons had acted inadvisedly. They could still "come off fairly," because the speaker had not yet signed their orders and therefore nothing was official. Theirs was an "error amoris to the young princess." And he added, somewhat lamely, that "though I said not so yesterday, my opinion was first to have preferred it to the Lords and to have acquainted the King with it, being his prisoner." He now wanted to stop the sheriff carrying out the punishment, and instead to approach the Lords.

But Coke argued against retreat. The difference between the two men emerges sharply from this debate: Sandys the compromiser, the moderator, the politician, versus the relentless, blinkered lawyer. Coke had not even been present at the previous day's debate, but he was ready to pour forth the precedents nonetheless. Hammering away at a favorite theme, he reminded the Commons that they were a court of record and therefore holders of judicature in some cases. They should press ahead, leave the sheriff alone, and merely acquaint the Lords with their opinion. Significantly, the committee that was appointed to decide what to do included Sandys but not Coke.[4]

[3] Ibid., 600–602; Edward Nicholas, *Proceedings and Debates of the House of Commons, In 1620 and 1621*, 2 vols. (Oxford, 1766), 1:373; *CD*, 3:120–128, 5:128–130.
[4] Ibid., 3:134–143; *CJ*, 603–604, give the details of the debate. Having backed Sandys's

The House's better instincts may have led it to endorse, at least temporarily, the calm that Sir Edwin represented. He had already urged restraint with wrongdoers during the session, most recently a few days earlier, when the judge Sir John Bennett, a Kentish friend, had been accused of corruption. Coke, also a friend of Bennett, had rejected leniency, but Sandys had asked for "humanity to be used towards all, how great the delinquents whatsoever." It was this moderating influence that held the flood in check, at least for a while.[5]

That Sandys needed all his persuasive powers was clear from the debate on Floyd that continued at full blast in the afternoon of May 2, despite Noy's warning: "I do not find that of foreign matters [we] can give judgement."[6] This identified both what was impermissible in the M.P.s' actions and the source of their frustration. Bohemia and the deteriorating relations with the Habsburgs, especially Spain, were the burning questions of the day, the cause of the money shortage that had brought them to Westminster in the first place. And yet, forbidden to discuss foreign policy, they had to watch silently as Digby's futile continental diplomacy ran its course, while James vainly hoped for a peaceful resolution. Floyd gave them the excuse to show their pent-up feelings about international Catholicism, but Noy showed them that the evasion could not work.

With all roads blocked, the M.P.s' strategy shifted. Instead of vainly as-

---

recommendations for punishment on May 1, Cranfield now questioned Coke's arguments (and precedents) for allowing the House to judge the case. Growing short-tempered, he was soon to quarrel openly with Coke and Sandys, for he was beginning to realise the ambiguity of his support for the Commons' claims. His repudiation, on May 2, of views he had expressed the previous day was the result of someone at Court showing him precedents that denied the House's right to judge Floyd. Cranfield conformed; Coke did not.

[5] Sandys had also tried (unsuccessfully) to prevent the House expelling Sir John Leeds for forgetting to take the oath of allegiance—possibly a relative of the Sir Thomas Leeds who was a tenant of Sir Edwin and a Virginia adventurer. In Bennett's case Sandys was supported by Digges, another friend. Coke's relentless severity was reflected in a popular doggerel about Bacon's fall:

> Into thy past life see thou look,
> For if thy faults grow common,
> Thou soon wilt find a nimble cook,
> Slice rashers from thy gammon.

In the end, Bennett lost his seat and served a term in the Tower, but then the M.P.s lost interest in him: *CJ*, 517, 584, 587, 588; *CD*, 2:54–55, 314, 3:31, 58, 5:92, 340–341; Nicholas, *Debates*, 1:284; PRO, SP/46/62/96, 97, 222 (Leeds); BL, Additional, 22,118, fol. 38—the doggerel, as cited by Julian Mitchell, typescript collection of political ballads and poems from the reign of James I.

[6] One diarist quoted Noy as saying he "knows not how we can judge" of "foreign business," which could have meant either nonparliamentary or Continental affairs, or both, an ambiguity pointed out to me by Stephen White and Mark Kennedy: *CJ*, 603; *CD*, 5:132, 3:136–137.

serting their rights, they decided to petition the king to let them have their way anyhow, though Coke still truculently affirmed their right to judge Floyd and asked the king to confirm their decision.[7] James seemed to have little comfort for them. He commended their good intentions, though not their haste, but he rejected their shaky precedents, calling their "reason . . . so large a thing as that a man knows not where to pitch"; warned them about challenging his "omnipotency"; and stressed the dangers of "erecting a judicature which is not known how far it may reach"—a comment that showed James's shrewdness as well as his tactlessness. Nevertheless, he did agree to consider their petition, and he promised to act against Floyd.[8]

The next day, May 4, cracks appeared in this accommodation, because James, unsure without due process that Floyd was indeed guilty, asked that the case be sent to the Lords, who had undoubted powers of judicature, and who could administer the oaths necessary to a proper investigation. The Commons agreed, only to become embroiled in a confrontation with the Lords that the anti-Buckingham peers (notably Southampton, Sheffield, and Saye and Sele), now in full cry, sought to resolve so as to avoid diversions from their main purpose. Helped by the leading M.P.s who were in direct touch with them—Sandys, for instance, with Southampton—they managed to avoid an angry quarrel that could have crippled all parliamentary business.[9]

When Pembroke, no friend of Buckingham, first told the Lords about the Commons' treatment of Floyd, on May 5, his tone was significant. He began by commending "the concurrence between the Commons and the Lords," and although he agreed that the Commons could do no more than make a complaint in a judicial matter, he asked his colleagues "not to aggravate against" the Lower House. Instead, he "moved for a conference with them in the kindest fashion and manner." Seconded by Pembroke's ally Archbishop Abbot, this proposal was accepted, with Southampton making sure the M.P.s would know what the Lords had heard, so that they could "come prepared," and Saye and Sele urging that the message "be such as may not distaste them."[10]

Although the Commons recognized the message as the friendly attempt to avoid quarrels that it was, their self-righteousness got the better of

---

[7] The Commons' assurance may have been reinforced when, before going to see James, they attended the pronouncement of the sentence on Bacon (the next day they heard the sentence on Michell): *CJ*, 603–606; *LJ*, 3:106, 108; S. R. Gardiner, ed., *Notes of the Debates in the House of Lords . . . 1621*, Camden Society, vol. 103 (London, 1870) (henceforth *Lords*), 64, 65.

[8] *CD*, 2:342–343, 3:155–158.

[9] *CJ*, 607–609; *Lords*, 3–90, passim; Robert Zaller, *The Parliament of 1621: A Study in Constitutional Conflict* (Berkeley, 1971), 116–124.

[10] *Lords*, 66.

them. Sir Edwin's brother Samuel, abetted by Coke, urged the M.P.s not to retreat, and it took some effort by Sandys and Alford to persuade them even to meet with the Upper House. The Lords wanted to be accommodating, Sandys said, and they would not question the Commons' rights. But the real question was whether Floyd fell within their jurisdiction. That was very doubtful: "a wise man says men never fall out about matter plain but controversial, therefore philosophers do but not arithmeticians." There was nothing to be gained by making a fuss, and he wanted them merely to explain how the matter had come to their attention (accidentally, through the warden of the Fleet) and then indicate how, despite the lack of precedents, reason had led them to censure Floyd. This was not, of course, the "flying and unbounded reason which has no limit" that the king had correctly dismissed, but "grounded reason," straight out of the old maxim, "deficiente lege currendum ad rationem naturalem," which encouraged reason when laws were deficient. After this "bare narration" matters could be left in the Lords' hands.[11]

Unfortunately, the conference did not unfold as he had wished. Sir Samuel, after starting with apologies and describing what had happened, ended by claiming a "possessory right" of judgment for the Lower House. Mandeville, a former chief justice, asked for precedents for this claim, which Coke failed to produce in a verbose speech about the Commons as a court of record. Mandeville noted that no "precedent of your possessory right" had been forthcoming and it was left to Sandys to try to smooth things over. Repeating the speech he had given the M.P.s earlier, he emphasized that they had done only what the king would have done, and had never meant to encroach on the Lords' privileges. Coke admitted it was "but an error," yet, unable to control himself, argued with Pembroke over who had what rights. It was small wonder that the Lords went away "unsatisfied"— or that Sheffield, trying to repair the breach, told his colleagues that most M.P.s "did disavow the most part what Sir Edward Coke spoke."[12]

Sheffield must have had good information, because the Commons were eventually to rebuke Coke. But not just yet. The Lords' dissatisfaction had not subsided two days later, on the seventh, and they asked the Commons to explain what Coke had meant by his arguments about a court of record. So suspicious were they of Coke that the official report of the conference referred to Coke's "alleged precedents." But Southampton worked hard to restrain his colleagues' dismay, and he finally persuaded them to have the differences handled by small subcommittees.[13]

---

[11] *CJ*, 610; *CD*, 3:173–179 (Sandys's speech on 177), 5:145; Nicholas, *Debates*, 2:28.

[12] Ibid., 2:32; *CD*, 3:179–184, 5:147; *Lords*, 67. Sheffield also worked closely with Southampton and Sandys in the Virginia Company.

[13] *Lord*, 67–71; the conference report (69) mistakes Edwin for Samuel Sandys.

The news that the Lords wanted further discussion evoked defiant talk from the M.P.s, and demands that precedents be gathered to justify their behavior. It was Sandys, again, who tried to hold them back. In words reminiscent of what Abbot and Southampton were saying in the Lords, he stressed the widespread joy caused by the "unity . . . between the Houses and us and the King." The last thing they wanted was a breach; "let us therefore raise no new questions nor produce new precedents." After all, the Lords had questioned only whether Floyd came under their competence. "Questions engender questions," he warned, "and so ends in strife." They could preserve their honor and defend their punishment of Floyd, but they did not have to claim that the case established a precedent. Coordinating with Southampton, he urged that subcommittees from both Houses be allowed to deal with the matter.[14]

The following day, before meeting the Lords, the Commons discussed their next moves in a debate that Sandys and his cohorts were able at last to control. Digges began by asking that careful instructions be given to their representatives. He was seconded by Sir Henry Widdrington, who, together with his in-law William Mallory (a neighbor of Sandys from Yorkshire days), was to lead the attempt, that autumn, to find out why Sir Edwin was punished after the first session of Parliament. Then Phelips hammered away at the theme of "maintaining love and unity with the Lords," endorsing Sandys's idea of subcommittees. He was followed by Sir Edwin himself, who noted that they had had little time to prepare for the last conference, which probably explained the "great mistaking" that had taken place. Here, following Sheffield's line, he specifically blamed Coke for stirring up precedents when none was needed. To remedy the situation, he proposed to tell the Lords "that this allegation of precedents was but collateral," for he believed "this will take away a great part of the difference betwixt the Lords and us." They were to offer no new arguments, and were to explain their position as a product of reason which, however, was their own and would "never be used as a precedent to draw judicature to us." He repeated the wish for a subcommittee, which was endorsed, again, by Digges. The Commons Journal struck the leitmotiv of the House's proceedings when it summed up: "Mr. Alford concurs with Sir Robert Phelips, Sir Edwin Sandys, Sir Dudley Digges."[15]

---

[14] *CJ*, 612; *CD*, 3:192; Nicholas, *Debates*, 2:36. Zaller, *1621*, 113, cites Sandys proposing the subcommittees on the eighth, the day after the Lords, as evidence of coordination between Sandys and Southampton. But Sir Edwin's May 7 speech indicates that he had joined forces with the earl *before* the debate in either House—possibly on the Sunday after the conference on the fifth.

[15] *CJ*, 613; *CD*, 3:204–205; Nicholas, *Debates*, 2:44. Sandys's closeness to Phelips emerges from this speech: "The gentleman that last spoke [Phelips] . . . is like a string that, being struck, moves harmony in an instrument far off. He moves the thought of my heart." *CD*,

At this point, however, the tensions burst through. Sandys had implied in his speech that Coke had gone to such length to prove the House a court of record because someone had asked for the precedents. That someone was Cranfield, who on May 1 had asked Coke to produce the precedents for a claim of judicature "so the power of the House might not be so puzzled as it is by infinite doubts." But Sir Lionel's patience was wearing thin. A few days after his May 1 request he had quarreled bitterly with Coke, and now, a week later, he was not going to let Sandys even imply that he had somehow been responsible for Coke's mistakes. "I was secretly charged," he complained, "to have said this House was no court of record"; in fact, he had hoped they *could* "prove themselves a court of record. I suffer because I said that I had heard such an objection, . . . [and I wanted] the House prepared." As for his accuser, the threat was unmistakable: "I will in due time call them into account for it"—or, in another version, "he should feel it afterwards."[16]

Cranfield's target was obviously Sandys, who immediately replied: "It pleased this honorable person to deliver somewhat in the clouds that touches upon me. . . . We argued pro and con, and it is not fit to question anything afterward. . . . I spake as an honest man and so I will defend it. . . . It is a sign of weakness and declination of our fame when we stumble at every straw."[17] This was a cool, careful, and correct response, which succeeded in ending both the altercation and the distraction. Yet it was also an ominous foretaste of what lay ahead. The relationship between the two men was deteriorating, and at the end of the session (little more than three weeks away) Cranfield was to sharpen his threats and see to it that they were implemented.

For the time being, after some desultory debate, the House agreed to be as accommodating as possible, and chose Sandys to be the reporter of events. Significantly, Coke was not listed as one of the eleven M.P.s permitted to talk at the conference with the Lords. The Upper House was also moving toward "a gentle ending," prodded by Abbot and Sheffield. Abbot opened the conference by urging compromise; Cranfield responded in kind; and subcommittees were chosen to work out a final face-saving formula. As Sandys put it in his report to the Commons, everyone had taken "great joy in the union of the two Houses"; as a result, the Lords were not going to press the matter, but instead "desired reconciliation." Coke took over the writing of the actual text, and he tried to keep some

---

5:155. Widdrington's sister had married the brother of Mallory, whose home near Ripon was close to Sandys's Yorkshire lands.

[16] *CD*, 3:206; 2:355 for Cranfield's speech; ibid., 3:127, for his May 1 speech requesting the precedents. See, too, *CJ*, 614.

[17] *CD*, 3:206–207.

rights for the Commons, an effort that provoked a quarrel with Cranfield that went on for two days. But the Lords seemed happy to acknowledge that the Floyd case would create no precedent, and they themselves punished him even more harshly than had the Commons. With that done, Sandys ended the affair by making sure the M.P.s expressed their "liking" for the Lords' "readiness to accommodation." Cranfield's fight with Coke, meanwhile, gave both Phelips and Sandys a chance to scold Cranfield again for being so troublesome.[18]

If the Floyd affair had any significance for Sandys, beyond the opportunity it gave him to exercise his moderation on his colleagues, to maintain smooth relations with the Lords, and to confirm his unique standing in the House, it was in the rupture of his friendship with Cranfield. They had been on different sides before (notably on the issue of Virginian tobacco) but now a personal animosity appeared that Sir Edwin should have been careful to avoid.

MOUNTING DISORDER

It was during these early days of May, as the Floyd affair unsettled relations among M.P.s and between the Houses, that one could see on the horizon the ill-tempered end of the session—so different in tone from the cooperation and accomplishment that had marked proceedings during its early weeks. Increasingly since the recess that had ended in mid-April, it had taken all of Sandys's powers (and those of his allies) to keep business moving and to suppress disruptive diversions. The urge to root out abuses, punish corruption, and remedy grievances; the proliferation of bills, committees, and hearings; and the sensitivities of proud M.P.s (exacerbated by Coke's often blinkered interventions) generated collision rather than compromise, and finally wrecked the chance for productive legislation.

So susceptible was the House to these diversions that it even got itself entangled in that most distracting of topics, Ireland. The parlous conditions there were yet another way of attacking corruption by Buckingham, which explains why a friend of Southampton, Sir John Jephson (a privy councillor in Ireland), was the M.P. who brought up the subject in late April. This was a prerogative matter, however, over which the House had no jurisdiction (Coke's incendiary claims to the contrary notwithstanding). James did not insist on this, but he told them that he was fully informed

---

[18] Ibid., 3:207–211, 229–232, 237–240, 4:334, 5:162; and *CJ*, 614, 618–619, 621, cover the events in the Commons and at the conference. *Lords*, 74–75, 85; and *LJ*, 3:113, 116, 119, deal with proceedings in the Lords.

about Ireland (by Buckingham), that problems should have been raised with him, not in the House, and that nothing further ought to be done.[19]

As usual, the slightest hint of constraint from above got the House exercised about what Alford called "a dangerous precedent." Even Sandys, though he had no obvious expertise, elaborated on Jephson's grim picture, emphasizing, during a long debate on April 30, that Catholic advances meant there was "scarce one Protestant for 100 there were before" among the Irish. And yet he wanted to make sure the M.P.s' enthusiasms did not get out of hand. If they wanted to take the subject further, they had to seek permission from James—which was what the House agreed to do, after Digges, Seymour, Phelips, Giles, Mallory, and Widdrington had all endorsed Sandys's views. Sir Edwin drew up their petition; James declared himself satisfied, though he needled them for talking about it at such length; and the subject was not raised again.

One reason that Sandys had played his customary role of keeping the House on an even keel was that he knew, by early May, that the Lords' campaign against Buckingham was faltering.[20] This may also have been why, together with his brother Samuel, Sackville, and Digges, he tried to smooth over yet another distraction, prompted by the same animosity, on May 2: the effort, led by Mallory and Coke, to keep Buckingham's brother, Sir Edward Villiers (newly home from the Netherlands), from taking his seat in the Commons because he was under investigation as a referee. Sir Samuel Sandys specifically deplored the M.P.s' irritability: "I am sorry that we have so many unhappy diversions; daily we are diverted by motions rather springing from passion than judgement. . . . Let us leave these fruitless questions." And Sir Edwin picked up elegantly where his brother had left off: "I join with him in grief that grieves most to see us thus interrupted by particular business and hindered from the private." In the end, Villiers waited until the Lords cleared him, but both Sandys brothers had seen that the Commons were in effect wasting their time.[21]

Self-defense, however, was another matter. Phelips mentioned "that Sir E. Villiers himself threatened diverse with perpetual imprisonment," a reminder of the aftermath of the 1614 Parliament and, like Cranfield's highhandedness, a portent of deteriorating relations with the Court. Jephson

---

[19] *CJ*, 593, 597; *CD*, 5:118–119.

[20] Even a non-M.P. (labeled 'B' in *CD*, but identified by Mark Kennedy as Robert Horne) knew that "the Marquis Buckingham is aimed at" in the Irish grievances. The assault collapsed when the star witness, Yelverton, insulted the king; nevertheless, the government again responded to a failed Commons initiative, for James appointed a commission to look into Irish grievances: *CJ*, 597–598; *CD*, 5:119–121, 3:119, 6:396; *Lords*, 42–53; Zaller, *1621*, 116–124.

[21] *CD*, 3:130–134; Zaller, *1621*, 124–125.

had encouraged this uneasiness when he complained of being "traduced" to the king for his remarks on Ireland, and a message from James on May 1 seemed merely to confirm the Commons' suspicions. They had been examining the sale of honors, including baronetcies, and had focused on a Knighthood of the Bath for which Sir George Marshall had demanded payment. Calvert informed the Commons that James had heard what they were up to; that they had permission to proceed against Marshall; but that they could go no further on the baronets or another of their issues, reform of the office of justice of the peace.[22]

The response to this development was outrage at the excellence of the king's information about the House's proceedings, and Sandys now called for action. "Since so many mis-informations have been [sent] to the King, whereby so great ill offices are done," he said, "I desire that there may be an order entered that Mr. Speaker may go to the King, as the mouth of the House, . . . to inform the King the truth." Alford, oblivious to the dangers of insolence, wanted "to move the King that there may not be so many interpositions, which interrupt the business of the House very much." Although nothing emerged from a committee that was to reply to James, suggest how precedents could be used to guarantee confidentiality, and recommend ways of correcting the king when he was misinformed, its composition (a solid phalanx of grievance hunters and leaders of debate, including Coke, Sandys, Alford, Digges, Phelips, and Widdrington) was indicative of the growing suspicion of James's attitudes toward Parliament.[23]

And indeed, during the remaining month of the session very little was accomplished, except for the discovery of new grievances. Sandys did keep trying to turn the House's energies toward constructive ends,[24] and in particular used his knowledge of Continental Catholicism to aid efforts to deal more strictly with recusants. On May 4, for instance, he warned that "The excess of recusants is such as may threaten the Crown," because the number of Jesuits and priests in England had doubled since Elizabeth's reign. The seminaries of France and the Netherlands were especially dangerous: St. Omer alone "had in it 7 score gentlemen's sons," who tended to "converse most with the best sort and win gentlemen"—a worrisome prospect, since "the converting of one gentleman is more worth than 20 poor coun-

---

[22] CD, 3:133, 111–115, 4:280, 5:106–107.

[23] Ibid., 3:12; CJ, 599.

[24] His concerns during these weeks encompassed much of the House's business: a bill to restrain official informers, an urging of caution in denunciations of Chancery, various trade bills, new grievances like Sir Robert Mansell's patent to license the manufacture of glass, and unauthorized exceptions added to the monopolies bill: Nicholas, Debates, 1:277–278, 348; CJ, 582; CD, 3:108, 5:111–112, 7:632, 4:352–355; and, on the monopolies bill, ibid., 3:198, 235–236, 4:318; Nicholas, Debates, 2:40–41; and Stephen D. White, Sir Edward Coke and "The Grievances of the Commonwealth," 1621–1628 (Chapel Hill, N.C., 1979), 128–135.

try people." He therefore wanted attendance at the seminaries banned, and on May 15 he produced a list of the relevant institutions, from Salamanca to Louvain. Carried away, he even suggested that James might negotiate the closing of Spain's seminaries, an implausible notion that so undermined his normal levelheadedness that he justified it with an even more implausible notion: "Kings often desire to be importuned to that which they desire to do."[25]

Although Sandys was trying to sustain the momentum of the session, there were endless details to be dealt with on the subject of the economy alone, from amendments to the trade bill to ideas for new legislation. Early in May, for instance, Sir Edwin argued for a ban on imports of Irish cattle, on the grounds that some regions might have to suffer for the good of the kingdom as a whole, yet he convincingly opposed a ban on corn imports because it would have hurt English merchants. As for other topics, he twice had to persuade the M.P.s not to become involved in the problems of parliamentary representation in specific constituencies, and he even had to deal with such trivia as the disposition of a trunk of Floyd's papers.

He was trying to hurry the House's work along because he knew the Commons could ill afford the luxury of leisurely investigations. In a message on May 4, James had told them to "consider alas how the time and heat of the year must necessarily call you away shortly into your several countries [counties]," and this was clearly not idle rhetoric. Sandys's ability to bring a debate to a close therefore took on special urgency. After half a morning spent on ways of dealing with the warden of the Fleet, for instance, it took but one speech from Sir Edwin to convince the Commons what to do: send the complaints back to the committee, which would provide six examples for each piece of misconduct; the warden would reply, and the House would give its judgment. There was not to be time for all this, but Sandys had at least freed the docket for other business.[26]

A similar aimlessness had settled on the Lords. Thus it was only after much urging that they acted against the bishop of Llandaff, whom the Commons had accused of corruption at the same time as they indicted Bacon. Sandys greeted the news by asking the Commons to "thank the Lords for their good correspondence with us and respect of us, and send

<hr />

[25] *CJ*, 607; Nicholas, *Debates*, 2:18–19; *CD*, 3:161–162, 268–269, 2:344, 5:140.

[26] *CD*, 3:304, 214, 323, 285, 287, 173, 158, 275–276; *CJ*, 615, 617, 624, 623; Nicholas, *Debates*, 2:83. For other intimations that the session was ending, see Zaller, *1621*, 125, who also gives excellent examples (216–217) of the way the burden of business was overwhelming the M.P.s. The most ridiculous of the detours began at a meeting of the committee on the glass patent when Sir Charles Morison, reciting ribald verses about glasses and asses, referred to judges riding on asses. Coke's son Clement, sitting next to him, hit Morison, and this led to royal intervention, most of a morning's debate, committee meetings, and over a week of distraction: *CJ*, 615–616; *CD*, 3:188, 215–219, 230, 248–249, 4:345–346.

many thanks for it."[27] This may have been an effort to revive cooperation in the face of adjournment, but by then it was too late. Much of the House's business remained hopelessly incomplete, and it now looked as though some of the members might be held accountable for words they had spoken in Parliament.

The chaotic denouement that followed, with James proroguing the assembly until November, raises the question of why, despite the efforts of Sandys and other leading M.P.s, the relatively ordered structure of events disintegrated. It may be that the Commons' extraordinary success in curbing governmental excess, despite reprimands and attempts to limit their actions, emboldened them in their pursuit of grievances and abuses and their defense of their privileges and rights. Nor was it insignificant that they were strongly abetted by two privy councillors, particularly Coke who, lacking Cranfield's instinctive orderliness, bears considerable responsibility for the M.P.s' obstreperousness. At times Sandys and his allies found Coke the main obstacle, rather than the heavy artillery, as they tried to maintain the flow of productive business.

It must also be remembered that the fall of Bacon was a traumatic moment in Jacobean history. No previous revelation had brought malfeasance so close to the heart of England's hallowed institutions. Coming as it did when many of the gentry were beginning to appreciate the implications of the rise of Buckingham (against whom much of the 1621 agitation was directed), the scandal must have intensified the M.P.s' sense that the Court was stepping beyond accepted bounds of proper conduct. Dismayed by genuine crises in the economy and on the Continent, they found little comfort in the sorry state of domestic politics. And it was their easy vexatiousness, the lack of discipline, that finally undermined Sandys's desperate efforts, in May 1621, to bring concrete, practical results out of the parliamentary session. The old forms of leadership were fruitless as an impatient king and an irritable House hastened the approach of an angry adjournment.

THE END OF THE SESSION

The final act was precipitated by the very bill against recusants that Sandys had so stirringly championed. Such hostile measures endangered James's delicate negotiations with Spain, and he thus had good reason to send the assembly home for the summer.[28] Calvert brought the news on May 28: with over three months of sittings completed, "the session shall not long continue." The reasons ranged from the season to the needs of local gov-

---

[27] Ibid., 3:356, 4:416–417, 5:201–202.
[28] Zaller, *1621*, 133.

ernment, and James wanted the final presentation of grievances the following Sunday, just six days away. Though the news was not unexpected, the M.P.s were as usual not prepared for it.[29]

A cacophony of suggestions flowed forth as to how they should spend their remaining time, from assembling grievances to organizing work for the summer or passing a few more bills. Coke was particularly unhappy that they had granted two subsidies but "have nothing yet to carry with us into the country."[30] It took Sir Edwin to restore a degree of order. Echoing Calvert's view that "before this Parliament [there had been] a misunderstanding of some difference between the King and us, [but] the effects have proved the contrary," he brought the discussion back to a sense that something *had* been accomplished. "As it was our great care that there might be a perfect union between both Houses and between us and the King," he reminded the M.P.s, "we should desire this still, and that it may appear." This last, the appearance, was very important, for "the eyes and cries of all the land are upon us." It was true, he admitted, that "the hope deferred is the fainting of the heart; but since it must, let us consider how we may spend our little time left for the session well." Having accepted the king's will, they should try to pass any pending bills that required only one more reading, "debate how we may best report in the country our employments here," and stress that "most [of the session's work had been] for their [the country's] content and the King's honor." To get down to business at once, Sandys suggested that they reconvene after the fast-approaching dinner hour, a procedure which the House immediately accepted.[31]

The mood soured over dinner. The first speaker (probably Giles) set the tone by saying "there never was so great a grievance as the King's message." Samuel Sandys lamented that "his Majesty should have such bad counsel," and complained that "if we be sent home thus, . . . we shall be sure of so much shame as will hardly be borne. The last Parliament we gave nothing, now we have given two subsidies and carry home nothing"— a succinct statement of the country gentleman's view of the quid pro quo that constituted a Parliament. Amidst the suggestions that followed, the only practical idea came from Thomas Crew, a veteran M.P., who advised a joint petition with the Lords for continuation of the session.[32] Even Sir

[29] *CJ*, 629; *CD*, 3:325–326.

[30] Ibid., 326–329; *CJ*, 629.

[31] Ibid.; *CD*, 3:329. Nicholas noted that Sandys "would have all those bills, that are engrossed, read and passed before the recess; because otherwise, at our next meeting, which is not like to be till all-hallowtide, they will seem strange and new to us": *Debates*, 2:113. In fact, a number of bills passed quickly in November; the fishing bill, for instance, sailed through despite the absence of its chief mover, Sandys.

[32] *CD*, 3:329–334, 2:399–401, 4:384–386; 1:22 identifies Giles as the likely first speaker.

Edwin drifted into the delusion that "the message might be mistaken, for the King does not know that we have so much business" still to complete. With a few more weeks, and their willingness, "notwithstanding the weather, to sit for the service of his Majesty and the kingdom," they would "finish many particular business for the honor of the King, the satisfaction of the country, the general good." However hollow this sounded after more than three months, the M.P.s did finally resolve to follow Crew's recommendation and ask the Lords for a joint petition.[33]

These efforts, however, were futile, for the next day they heard from the Lords that the king "determinately" intended to adjourn Parliament the following Monday. Prince Charles himself warned their representatives, at a meeting in the Lords, "not to stir any more in it." "But we all cry, to the House," noted one observer as the meeting ended, and John Pym observed that back in the Commons "the discontent of the House could hardly be restrained." Some (including Sandys, who was carried away, albeit temporarily, by the general outrage) shouted "Rise, Rise," so that they would not have to answer the Lords. Despite pleas for moderation, the anger persisted, culminating in a sharp quarrel between the M.P.s and the speaker. When Sandys, regaining his composure, arose for a major speech, he not only gave voice to the emotion sweeping his colleagues, but also, more characteristically, restored a sense of direction to the proceedings.[34]

"Passions," he observed, "are ill councillors." And yet, "that the House was full of passion was evident, and of two the most restless passions, fear and grief." The causes, which were clear, made him, though "never a coward, . . . never more afraid." Feeding the very hysteria that he had decried, he rehearsed the reasons that "all things in the country are out of frame." True religion was being rooted out in Bohemia, the Palatinate, and France. "It was a misery," he reminded them, "to see so many of all sorts of French [Huguenot refugees] in Westminster Hall as we came through yesterday, fled from their country for religion. We are next door to them. But our gates, our port towns, are forsaken, . . . there is not one man in them worth £300." After this segue, he could lament that "Trade is decayed, cattle bear no price." Moreover, "If trade, markets, and fairs are at a stand, farmers cannot pay their rents, want must needs cost disorders, breach of covenant and confusion." As for the origin of these catastrophes, it was obvious that "by monopolies, trade is brought into a few men's hands, which as they were gotten, so are they maintained by corruption." And the consequences were clear: "I had rather speak now than betray my country with silence; if

---

[33] Ibid., 3:333, 2:400; Nicholas, *Debates*, 2:115.

[34] *CJ*, 630; *CD*, 2:405–406, 3:344–346, 4:390–391. Alford had the temerity to suggest that even dissolutions had to wait "when we have things in the forge of moment till they were finished": ibid., 4:340.

ploughs be rested, cattle unsold, grazing decay, trade perish, what will follow but confusion?" Despite the gravity of the situation, however, "there is no news or message of redress." If the M.P.s returned home empty-handed, "what satisfaction shall we give the country, seeing we are sur-charged with grief?" He too, he admitted, had been "one of those that were of the opinion to rise, and so is still," but he wanted them not to act precipitously, and he suggested that they defer answering the Lords till the next morning; in the meantime, "by ourselves we might advise this night what to do," a call for the kind of extraparliamentary discussion that the Privy Council was to condemn at the end of the session. Phelips seconded Sandys, and the House accepted the suggestion.[35]

This speech, for all its disparagement of passion and the cool appro-priateness of its conclusion, was the closest Sir Edwin ever came to dema-goguery. His dismay at the condition of the country was undeniably genu-ine, and his frustration at the prospect of the session ending fruitlessly, despite far more time than the M.P.s had had in 1614, must have been acute. The chaos of these last days was coloring all the proceedings, and although Sandys did not participate in the discussion when it continued the next day, the House followed his mood into ever deeper despair. Phe-lips gave perhaps the most extraordinary speech of the entire Parliament—a confession, almost a credo, that must have been deeply moving: "I know not whether I shall ever speak within these walls again; therefore I will now make you partakers of those thoughts I brought in at those doors and will by the grace of God carry out whenever I go." He told the Commons what many of them doubtless felt: "I resolved this Parliament would be the only means of our redress." Since that was not to be, there was no alterna-tive but to acquiesce. He ended sadly: "I have offered you, Mr. Speaker, my heart, as a poor member of the House who may happily never return again."[36] Nobody who reads this speech can doubt the centrality to En-gland's well-being that the gentry assigned to Parliament.

The helplessness encouraged the fears that Phelips had already raised about actions against members after the adjournment. Some, such as Giles, urged caution perhaps for this very reason. Others, however, pressed on regardless. "Some ill members," proclaimed Sir Edward Cecil, "have shortened this session. . . . I think someone has cast a bone twixt us and the King." Cranfield, by contrast, suggested that a lot of fuss was being made over nothing. The people who were causing the trouble, in his view, were the bearers of all kinds of "misinformation" about the problems of the economy (an unmistakable reference to Sandys and his outport allies). Parliament had had plenty of time to complete its work, and ought to

---

[35] Ibid., 2:406, 3:345, 4:390–391; Nicholas, *Debates*, 2:121–122.
[36] *CD*, 3:347–349.

disperse as it began, in amity with the king.[37] It was this kind of haughty dismissal of the Commons' fears that provoked a major outburst on the following day, the thirty-first.

The debate that morning was as aimless and unhappy as before until Delbridge, an outport merchant, seized an opportunity to renew the worries about commerce, and audaciously proposed that all trade be freed of restraint until the next session, an idea he supported with more statistics about the collapse of the economy. This was too much for Cranfield. He had already told the M.P.s that trade was not so badly off; now he produced his own statistics, from customs receipts, to indicate that "trade is as great as ever." Should one blame the king, he asked, because France had a civil war that hampered *some* trade? There was no reason to do anything until the next session, when more accurate figures would be available.[38]

Sandys was not going to let Cranfield dismiss the issue that easily. "The King has been abused by misinformation," he said, but there was no way now "to satisfy the country." Therefore, they had to tell the king "the true estate of all things" in "a true remonstrance of the state of the kingdom," and when they got home they would have "to make fair weather to maintain content[ment]." How else could they "promise avoiding discontent? Poverty reigns and will . . . cause it." They had no time for grievances or for issues like Sabbath observance, swearing, or Welsh butter—what were these "to a man in want?" Consequently, priority had to be given to bills like the monopolies bill that touched on the safety and well-being of the country. If these could not pass, "let us leave them all till our next meeting." And he concluded with a thinly disguised warning: "if we bring [the common people] so slender comfort as these poor bills, we make their discontents and dislike of their miserable fortunes reflect upon the higher powers." The disclaimer, "which God forbid," hardly lessened the force of his prediction.[39]

Sandys used these arguments to suggest, a little later, that the Commons ought to decide, for want of a better alternative, to pass no more bills at all. By convoluted reasoning, he even claimed that this course would bring honor to the king and the House, and satisfy the people, because it would offer a promise that they were not going to rest after passing so few bills, but intended to pass many more. It is more than possible that the entire performance was an exercise in sarcasm, but for Cranfield it was the final, intolerable impudence. Abandoning his statesmanly facade, he turned on Sandys. "We have to deal with a wise King," he reminded the M.P.s, "one

[37] Ibid., 3:355, 357, 363, 364.

[38] *CJ*, 632–634; *CD*, 3:372–374.

[39] Ibid., 3:374, 2:416, 5:190; *CJ*, 633. John Smith of Nibley thought this a "most excellently" fashioned speech: ibid,, 5:391.

that can apprehend quickly when he is abused." The menace was clear. "Sir Edwin Sandys is mistaken, for it cannot be (as he says) for the honor of the King that we shall refuse to pass any bills, when as His Majesty, at our request, has yielded [agreed] to pass bills." Nor, he continued, could it "be for the reputation of this House to be so inconstant, as first to desire to pass bills, and then to desire not to pass bills." As his rebuttal of Sandys continued, Cecil interrupted him to announce that Cranfield was the man who, abandoning his previous good offices, was now doing the House "ill service by misinformations" to the King. Cranfield was asserting "that that which we have intended for the honor of the King is only to delude and abuse the King," and he was trying "to tax the whole House." He was obviously the person who was "in such manner" misinforming the King, "since here openly our speeches and intentions are wrested to the worst construction."[40]

What exactly happened after Cranfield was interrupted is not clear. The Journal says that there was "some heat" between Cranfield, Sandys, Delbridge, and Sir Peter Heyman, a friend of Sandys and fellow Cinque Ports representative. The one speech of which we have a record is Sir Edwin's, and it certainly held nothing back. "That gentleman presses too much quickness in reproving," he scolded; "Let every man that comes in here lay down his greatness at the door, and so the meanest lay down his meanness. They that tittle the King with informations, let us not think they do discreetly, nor suffer any to be taxed here." After all, said Sir Edwin, Calvert himself had told them that the king expected no more bills. Yet it was the threat of retribution—already raised by Cranfield earlier in May—that was particularly on Sandys's mind. Two M.P.s had been specifically absolved of wrongdoing by the House for statements that had landed them in trouble at Court: Jephson for his speech about Ireland, and Sir Francis Seymour for an attack on Viscount Mandeville. Exception had also been taken in official circles to Sir Samuel Sandys's activities, and Sir Edwin wanted such retaliation stopped. His criticism of the adjournment, he told the House, had been taken as a criticism of the Privy Council which had ordered it, and "at a committee it was said he slandered the Council;" he "therefore desired to pass the judgement of the House that he might not be questioned after the Parliament, as his brother was threatened to be."[41]

In Pym's view, this "was the occasion of discontent between [Cranfield and Sandys] which had greater effects after the adjournment," an opinion there is no reason to doubt, and which Sandys himself obviously shared. Even though both antagonists agreed that they had been expressing mere

[40] Ibid., 3:175, 375–376; Nicholas, *Debates*, 2:141–142.

[41] *CJ*, 634; *CD*, 3:376, 4:399; Nicholas, *Debates*, 2:142–143. Others had been cleared earlier in May: *CD*, 3:225–228, 5:197.

opinions, and "difference in opinion should not dissever our affections," the damage had been done. Significantly, Sandys started the morning's business the next day, June 1, by proposing an order of the House to ensure that all members' privileges would remain in force after the adjournment. Supported by Hakewill, Digges, Phelips, and Coke, he got the order approved. His only other comment on the first was to confirm that there would be regular meetings of a committee that was assigned (in vain) to meet during the summer under Phelips' chairmanship.[42] But the next day he returned to the theme of absolution from wrongdoing.

The subject seems to have been planned carefully in advance. It was not introduced by Sandys himself, but by one of his allies from the western outports, Sir Walter Earle. "The King has given us liberty of speech," he said, and "because some tax has been made upon Sir Edwin Sandys his speeches, [he asked] to have him cleared, or condemned, by question in this House." Earle apparently named Cranfield as the one for whom the offence still rankled, and Sir Edwin then made a truculent defence. "We are all in passions," he said, "but I will make no apology but justify myself." He had heard that "some words of his have been misconstrued, and that out of the House"—presumably at Court. Since he knew by "sound intelligence" that his words had "been excepted much against," and "that there is notice taken, and misinformation made" of his speeches, he wanted to explain himself. He had indeed cried "rise, rise," he admitted, but only "desiring, passion might be avoided, and not speak till next morning, that passion were over": an entirely plausible version of his behavior. As for his comment that "the trade of the kingdom was swallowed up by monopolies," that had been spoken "suddenly, and passionately, out of sorrow." He knew of specific cases where the statement was true, having received information both in the House and "from the lord" [Southampton?], and he was prepared to name names. In any case, "his desire was rather to look forward to the reformation of the disorders than backwards to the punishment of the persons." Nor did he regret his unhappiness about the state of religion, expressed in the phrase "no man ought to be patient in suspicion of heresy," even though this was a "hasty reply made to an honorable person," namely, Cranfield.

Having outlined some of his possible misdemeanors, he moved on to the question of whether he had "laid a charge upon the King." In this instance "I was taxed by his [Cranfield's] saying that we had to do with a wise King. Answer, so I think too and did ever." As for having been "taxed to say the whole kingdom was out of frame, I think I erred not much, for we want money." He had not meant "to include in that general [statement] other parts of government," for had he not once remarked on the admirable

---

[42] Ibid., 4:399, 3:384; Nicholas, *Debates*, 2:143; *CJ*, 634.

absence of complaints against common law (as opposed to Chancery) judges? As for the "great want of money," that subject had been broached at the "special recommendation" of the king; therefore he had not "slandered His Majesty's government" when he had given his own catalogue of England's economic woes, which, for good measure, he now repeated. Above all, "he was much troubled" by the absence of any measures "whereupon to ground a reformation," and it had been "in that grief" that he had spoken perhaps ill-advised words about not "palliating with the King." If he had urged the Commons to tell James only the sad truth about the state of the realm, why, "ex falsis bonis nascuntur vera mala." He had "labored in vain and spent my strength in vain" through sixteen weeks of small accomplishment. But, "whether we meet or meet not, if any cross accident should hinder us," his conscience was clear that he had always worked in the public interest and for God's glory.

After this extraordinary catalogue, carefully researched so as to unearth any remarks that might cause offence, he asked to be cleared of all evil imputations. In so doing, he may have hedged himself about on every side, but at the same time he had provided those who were hostile toward him with a thorough bill of indictment. Not even his detractors, consulting the clerk's journal (as they were to do) could have drawn up so complete a collection of accusations. Although effective at the time, the speech, by indicating the full extent of his questionable comments, may have given ammunition to those who later sought to punish him.

For the immediate situation, however, it accomplished exactly what Sir Edwin wished. He had asked for the judgement of the House, and Alford moved that he be cleared. By the unanimous vote of a packed Commons, although "none of the 6 councillors" was present, "Sir Edwin Sandys [was absolved] from letting fall any word against the King or this House or any member in it that gives just offence."[43]

Sandys's last speech of the session, that afternoon, was an attempt to spread some sweetness and light, but it did not lessen his problems. James, trying to be conciliatory, had offered to postpone for two weeks the adjournment that was now only two days away. Without the postponement, the meeting that day, a Saturday, was likely to be the last opportunity for the conduct of business; they could not sit on Sunday, and the adjourn-

---

[43] Ibid., 635–636; *CD*, 2:421–422, 3:389–391, 4:405–407, 6:186–187; Nicholas, *Debates*, 2:151–152. The use of the clerk's Journal is confirmed by the examination of Sandys's friend Mallory in January 1622. The last item reads: "was told by one of the Lords that if I had been as careful to look to the clerk as I was to the Speaker [whom Mallory repeatedly reprimanded] many things had been known that now comes to light." Conrad Russell, "The Examination of Mr. Mallory after the Parliament of 1621," *Bulletin of the Institute of Historical Research* 50 (1977): 125–132, transcribing Somerset Record Office, Phelips manuscripts, DD/PH/216/11.

ment ceremonies on Monday the fourth would leave no time for serious work. Some M.P.s were at first inclined to accept the postponement so as to get down to a flurry of bill passing. But the majority disagreed. Phelips pointed out that in two weeks they could accomplish very little; that it was better for their privileges if they themselves ordered their own adjournment; and that a cooling-off period might allow them to reassemble "more . . . lovingly." Sandys followed, oozing flattery, and adding justifications for immediate adjournment that were to irritate James. The king's "gracious offer," he said, "was made to the Lords, but the fruit of it no doubt the King's intention was equally meant to us." He therefore wanted the M.P.s to stress "humble thanks to his Majesty, for his grace and favor to both Houses of Parliament." They could then explain their decision to adjourn right away—in two weeks "we cannot do the good that we desire"—and thank the Lords for "the great correspondency" and love between the Houses. By adjourning themselves in response to the king's commission, he reminded the M.P.s, they were not prejudicing their privileges; moreover, they could justify their action by stressing that it was taken in obedience to the king.[44]

None of this reasoning moved James. The Lords received the Commons' decision without comment, but James dismissed their explanation as "childish, because we could not do all, therefore we would do nothing." He had hoped for "a happy Parliament," and the two subsidies and the "brave endeavors" to discover abuses had been to his liking. "He was still satisfied in the good affection of the House." The M.P.s ought to consider, therefore, "what diverted us." Certainly the Privy Council thought it knew whom to blame, as the Commons must have realized, because the potential targets of displeasure (notably Coke, Phelips, and Sandys) were left out of the group of twenty-four M.P.s who went to Greenwich on the Sunday to present grievances to the King.[45] On no other occasion of such importance were all three missing, and one must conclude that this was an attempt to keep a low profile. But the rancor of the Court was not to be diverted. Exactly two weeks after Sir Edwin's last speech in the 1621 Parliament the long arm of the king reached out.

SANDYS UNDER ARREST

The arrest of Sandys on June 16 has the semblance of mystery only because the Commons were so unsuccessful when they tried to determine the reasons for his detention five months later. That he was placed in the custody of the sheriff of London, secretly examined over a number of days, and finally released after five unpleasant weeks, everyone knew. But the

---

[44] Nicholas, *Debates*, 2:159; *CJ*, 637; *CD*, 3:398, 401–402, 4:409–410.
[45] *Ibid.*, 3:403–404, 4:414; *CJ*, 637.

reluctance of the House—and of Sandys himself, who was so daunted by his imprisonment and his subsequent restriction to his home in Kent that he kept away from Parliament during the second session—to make public the reasons for his punishment, because of the danger of confrontation with the king, has encouraged speculation. Possible reasons have included his work in the Virginia Company, his connections with religious extremists, the anger he aroused in Gondomar with his attacks on recusant seminaries, the displeasure of Buckingham or Lepton—almost anything but the obvious, and clearly correct, explanation that he was suffering for his boldness in Parliament.[46]

The proof is available in the questions asked of him at his examination. They began with his actions during the last chaotic days of the session, and particularly with his emotional speech on May 28:

> 1. What conference he had at any time, and with whom, touching a petition to be made to the King, by the Parliament, for the long continuance thereof, after his Majesty had signified to the Houses his purpose of dissolving thereof; and, where he dined that day the message was brought?
>
> 2. What conference he had, and with whom, either by word, message, or writing, concerning a charge offered by the King to the Houses, by the mouth of the Lord Treasurer, whether they would have a cessation of it by selecting some few bills to be passed, such as his Majesty should like of, or an adjournment to some other time?[47]

That the major issue was the trouble caused when James announced the adjournment and when he offered a postponement is readily apparent. What is equally unmistakable is that Sandys's contacts with other M.P.s outside of Parliament were regarded as crucial to the organization of proceedings in the House. Those dinners that seemed to crystalize the mood of the Commons were of particular interest, and not inappropriately, because the souring of the M.P.s' mood between the morning and afternoon of the twenty-eighth had been dramatic. Nor was this troublesome plotting confined to the Commons, as the next question indicated:

> 3. What conference he had, and with which of the Lords, at any time, in the Committee Chamber of the Upper House?

[46] The implausible notion of Sandys being connected with the Brownists arises only because of this question at his inquisition; for the Virginia hypothesis, see Thomas Kiffin, "Sir Dudley Digges: A Study in Early Stuart Politics" (Ph.D. diss., New York University, 1972), 164; for Gondomar, Zaller, *1621*, 133. Conrad Russell, *Parliaments and English Politics, 1621–1629* (Oxford, 1979), 122–140, passim, links Buckingham to the vindictive John Lepton, a patentee attacked in this Parliament, who helped mount the assault on M.P.s in 1621; this connection might have added to Sandys's difficulties, because in 1616 he had had a nasty dispute with Lepton, whom he had taken to court over a long-standing and unpaid loan: Huntington Library, EL 385 and 5974—a reference I owe to Neil Cuddy.

[47] See Nicholas, *Debates*, 2:370–371, for these and the later questions, cited below.

This inquiry highlighted the links between Sandys and Southampton, who was imprisoned at the same time, and for essentially the same reasons.

In Southampton's examination, the five questions he was first asked were directed to this issue: whether there was disloyalty to be detected in the actions, near the end of Parliament, both of himself and "in the Lower House of some very near him"; whether they had met "to hinder the King's ends" during the Easter recess; whether he had directed Commoners' activities; whether they had joined together to stop bills passing at the end; and whether they had thought of sending part of the subsidies to James's daughter, Elizabeth of Bohemia. Southampton denied everything, stressing parliamentary privilege wherever he could, and Sandys doubtless did the same, even though he told the Virginia Company on June 9, a week before they were arrested, that they had "had conferences for many hours together"—at which they doubtless discussed more than the appointment of a new governor of the colony, the ostensible reason for their meeting.[48]

That these friends talked about parliamentary affairs would seem incontrovertible. Southampton's one admission was that he had heard Jephson speak of the Irish business "before, at his own house," which was tantamount to saying they had discussed it. Considering that this issue was known to have been directed at Buckingham, that Southampton was leading the assault against Buckingham at the time, and that even Sandys spoke about Irish matters (surprisingly, for he rarely addressed subjects he knew little about), the conclusion that prior planning had taken place was not difficult to reach.

The nature of the relationship between the two men is harder to define. Sir Robert Mansell, who had reason to hate Sandys for having had his glass patent condemned as a grievance (after he had supported him in the 1614 election), regarded Sir Edwin as the evil influence: "I did ever assure myself that that busy head would never be the author of any good to that Lord." And Southampton's role as a "front" for Sandys in the Virginia Company would support that view. On the other hand, the interrogators' questions reveal that the king (and his advisers) saw Southampton as the one giving instructions, and no less would have been expected of a peer of the realm and a privy councillor.[49] Cranfield, whose advice to the king about the questions that were asked of Southampton marks him as a major instigator of the inquiry, and whose clashes with Sandys must have hardened his resolve, also wrote as if the earl had led the way when "he consorted himself during the time of the Parliament with those young lords in the Upper and those knights and burgesses in the Lower House which

[48] Ibid., 367–370; Kingsbury, 1:478; BL, Harleian, 161, fols. 39–40.
[49] BL, Additional, 36,455, fol. 187 (a reference I owe to David Hebb); Zaller, 1621, 140; and on Mansell, above, chapter 7, note 10.

were most stirring and active to cross the general proceedings and to asperse and infame the present government." Yet Cranfield was aware of Sandys's independence, for he added that "the Earl cannot be forced to make good the indiscretions of his friends." He even admitted that these friends' "affected miscarriage" may have been their own, and stressed that he was primarily interested in why Southampton did not stop them. The implication that the earl might thus have been able to control the M.P.s was, of course, inconsistent with Cranfield's acknowledgment of their autonomy, and he justified it, rather lamely, by arguing that it was "impossible that those tongues should be silent under his roof which talked so licentiously in a more public theatre." As for Cranfield's claim "that scarce one speech concerning any public grievance . . . was uttered in Parliament by any other man than some bosom friend or ordinary guest at the least of the said Earl," this patent exaggeration was no proof that the ideas came from Southampton.[50]

The truth probably lies somewhere in the middle. Sandys and Southampton were distant kin and colleagues who had worked long and hard together in a variety of pursuits. Their collaboration went back at least to the Union debates of 1604, but it was by no means a one-way street. Sir Edwin was the older by twelve years; he may have helped convert the younger man from Catholicism; and in the Virginia Company he clearly took the lead. For all the deference the knight undoubtedly gave the earl, their partnership suggests a relationship more equal than not. And in the Commons most of Sandys's activity in 1621 has antecedents that stretch back throughout the Jacobean period, through alliances with peers and fellow-M.P.s that reflect his own predilections rather than theirs. As will be apparent in 1624, when he worked closely with great courtiers, it is crucial to remember the consistency with which this quintessential "commonsman" pursued his vision of parliamentary privilege, individual freedom, and the welfare of the realm. His connections at different times with the likes of Cecil, Southampton, and Buckingham enhanced rather than determined the agendas he pursued in the House.

The remaining questions in Sir Edwin's interrogation had to do with foreign policy:

4. What conference he had, and with whom, touching a benevolence to the Lady Elizabeth?

5. What conference he had with the Baron Dour [Dohna?] at any time, and in what places, and to what purpose?

6. What conference he had at any time concerning the match with Spain, and with whom he had discourse thereof, as he remembers?

[50] *CD*, 7:617–619. My discussion of Cranfield's inconsistency derives from comments by Mark Kennedy.

These questions are the only record of such activity in foreign affairs by Sandys. His friend Mallory may have supported the benevolence for Elizabeth, but there is no evidence of his own involvement.[51] If the fifth question refers to the Palatine ambassador Achatius Dohna, who visited England in 1619, it may be that Sandys (like other enemies of Spain) promised him help, but on this, as on the Spanish match, he made no known comment.

The interrogation was apparently repeated, and on "the two last days" two questions were added following a search of Sandys's papers at his home. From comments in the Commons later that year it emerges that the man who conducted the search was probably Sir Henry Spiller, an M.P. and a prominent official of the Exchequer, who had been under suspicion for abusing his office in 1614 and 1621. What he found cast doubts on Sir Edwin's religious beliefs:

1. Upon a letter found in his closet from one Mr. Brewer, living at Amsterdam, he was demanded, when he had received it? what answer he had made to it? and of his correspondence with the Brownists?

2. Upon a meditation found in his closet, begun to be penned by him, touching the power of God, something was therein spoken of the Kings of the earth, judges, magistrates, masters of families, and of their power and right, which he was willed to explain.

For a man whose maiden speech in Parliament had been an attack on Brownists, the first question must have seemed ironic. And he doubtless answered it by explaining the circumstances of the correspondence: the expedition of the Pilgrims. But the second question frustrates the biographer. No such meditation has survived, and although one can guess that Sandys expressed highly independent religious and political views, probably having to do with order, authority, and the individual (there are hints of them in his speeches, in the *Relation,* and in his will) it would be idle to speculate on what Spiller found. That Sir Edwin was charged neither with heresy nor with treason is sufficient to indicate that, though unorthodox, his views cannot have been impermissible. And if his interrogation in 1614 is any guide, he probably resorted to enough evasion and feigned innocence to satisfy his inquisitors.

DISILLUSION AND DISSOLUTION

On July 20, just under five weeks after his arrest, Sandys was released from the custody of Edward Allen, the sheriff, and ordered by the Privy Council to "remain confined to his said house [at Northbourne] and within five

[51] Ibid., 3:96–97; *CJ,* 594.

miles compass of the same until further order be given by his Majesty."
The agent of his release appears to have been the newly appointed lord
keeper, Bishop Williams, who persuaded James at the same time to pardon
Naunton and also prominent prisoners like Yelverton, Floyd, John Selden
(not an M.P., but a legal advisor to the Commons on impeachment and to
Sir Edwin in the Virginia Company), and Sandys's London neighbor, the
earl of Northumberland. Had Ralegh lived that long, he might well have
been freed, too. Sir Edwin was released even from his restriction to Northbourne on November 6, nicely in time for the reassembly of Parliament
eight days later. For the time being, however, the aged warrior, nearing his
sixtieth birthday, had lost the stomach for the parliamentary fight. Indeed,
he may have regretted his enforced absence from Virginia business more
than his exile from the Commons. On November 21 the Company heard
"that he would ere long be here," and although he did not appear at an
official meeting until January 30, he was certainly in London by early December, when some M.P.s came to discuss the reasons for his imprisonment.[52]

What they found must have been a dispiriting sight. The doubts raised
by both Sandys and Phelips in late May and early June as to whether they
would ever speak in Parliament again, and their admission, when James
offered them an extra two weeks, that little was likely to be achieved,
testify as much to their disillusion with events in the Commons as to their
fears of royal retribution. A session that had begun with such high hopes
had come apart in May. The control a leader like Sandys had been able to
exert, the ability he had shown in focusing the House on a few major
issues, had come to nought in the anarchy after the Easter recess. The
appointment of the "committee for disposing business" in the last week of
April was new for the Commons, and a disturbing omen. That the priorities the committee laid down were soon ignored only reinforced the chaos,
and Sandys's admission that two additional weeks of sitting would accomplish nothing merely confirmed his helplessness.

It may be that he was also distressed by the collapse of effective cooperation with the Lords in the last days of April. That was when the campaign
against Buckingham fell apart, and when Sandys, though still working with

[52] *APC, 1621–1623*, 23, 80; Zaller, *1621*, 141 (see 221, n. 128, and PRO, SP/14/122/350, for
the rumor that Sandys might be sent to Ireland in September); Kingsbury, 1:558, 584. On
Selden and his connections with Sandys, see David Berkowitz, *John Selden's Formative Years*
(Washington, D.C., 1988), 55–58, 60–62, and more generally, Paul Christianson, "Young John
Selden and the Ancient Constitution, ca. 1610–18" *Proceedings of the American Philosophical
Society* 128 (1984): 271–315, and his unpublished paper "John Selden and the Dispute over
English Liberties in the 1620s." The distance between Selden's (and Grotius's) theoretical
explorations of natural law and Sandys's more practical bent emerges clearly from Richard
Tuck, *Natural Rights Theories: Their Origin and Development* (Cambridge, 1979).

Southampton on Jephson and Floyd, was unable to forestall the death of some twenty bills (including the tobacco bill) that the House had sent the Lords, mainly in late April and early May. There was thus more than enough reason for Sandys to feel, even without prompting (or, possibly, a prohibition from taking his seat), that there was nothing left for him to do in Parliament.

I would argue that it was this gloomy atmosphere, rather than seditious comments about the king (which are all too easy to assume), that greeted the representatives of the House when they came to see Sandys in early December. It had taken a while for them to be dispatched, but his old Yorkshire friend Mallory (aided by his relative Widdrington) made sure that Sir Edwin's absence would not pass unnoticed. On the very first day of the new session, November 20, Mallory mentioned that he "misses Sir Edwin Sandys," and "moves we may know what is become of him." It was a moment fraught with political implications, as Richard Spencer (Sir Edwin's future son-in-law and a new M.P.) recognized when he wrote later that day to a Northamptonshire friend, Sir John Isham: "Tomorrow the house is called and then without doubt we shall fall upon Sir Edwin Sands his imprisonment, purposive to maintain the liberties of parliament, or to live quietly in our countries." Doubtless because of such ominous speculations, the answer came swiftly. On the morrow the speaker read a letter he had received from Sandys, who explained that "he wanted health, and had done these six weeks, and so long kept his chamber. He besought them that they would be pleased to dispense with his absence until God should restore him better health."[53] A reasonable excuse; but, as subsequent events showed, a prevarication.

The problem returned on November 23, two days later, when Wentworth urged the members to get down to business and pass some bills by Christmas. Alford replied by saying that they were "pinioned." They dared not talk about foreign affairs or religion, because these might be matters of state that rendered M.P.s liable to imprisonment, since James was being fed all sorts of misinformation about speeches in the Commons. Calvert professed outraged innocence. What was Alford afraid of? And why had he been so rude about the king, who would not like such impertinence? As for "imprisonment, I know not what he means; and no man has been threatened with it for speaking anything here nor touched for it." To be kind, this was an equivocation; to be blunt, a lie. Alford was not satisfied: Sandys had been cleared by the Commons, he reminded them, and concluded "I have discharged my conscience." Digges, doubtless aware that Sandys was hoping to avoid a fuss, tried to calm things down, though he

---

[53] *CJ*, 641; *CD*, 3:410,412, 5:206; Spencer's letter is in Northamptonshire Record Office, Isham of Lamport Collection, I.C. 155: a reference I owe to Richard Cust.

admitted that, "since Sir Edwin Sandys has been named, if it were for Parliament business, we have cause to be touched." And Mallory would not let go. "The gentleman that first spoke [Alford] . . . moved well," he said; things *were* misreported to the king. Moreover, since they had cleared Sandys, but his letter mentioned confinement, Mallory wanted the letter read again, for until he knew "the cause of his imprisonment" he would boycott House business.

In the face of further efforts to move on, Sir Robert Crane, normally a quiet member, insisted that the matter be cleared up, since "there is a murmur abroad, that he was committed for Parliament business." When, in response, Calvert made his equivocation more explicit—"Sir Edwin Sandys was not committed for anything said or done in Parliament"— Nicholas laconically remarked, to himself: "But the House will scarce believe [Calvert], but thinks he equivocates; and some say, they are not yet satisfied Sir Edwin Sandys was not committed for Parliament business."[54]

And the concern would not die. On November 26, in what may have been an oblique reference to Sir Edwin, Digges opened an audacious debate on foreign affairs by hoping that his speech could thread a narrow path, like a place he knew at sea that was threatened by "sands of the one side and the rocks of the other." And the next day the questions were unmistakable. Sir Peter Heyman asked for news of Sandys, and demanded an account from Spiller, who had searched the imprisoned man's study. This effort was stifled by the speaker, who ruled it a dead issue, but on December 1 the determination to uncover further information triumphed.[55]

The instigator was Sir William Spencer. Like Crane, he was not a prominent M.P., but he was the son-in-law of the earl of Southampton. Spencer bluntly denied that Calvert, "a party in the commitment," could give adequate satisfaction, and insisted on having the truth from Sandys directly. Mallory seconded him: the imprisonment was "notorious throughout the kingdom," he said, and he wanted the House to tell the king of "our grief for this breach of our privilege." If the M.P.s did not defend their privileges, "we deserve to be hanged." He suggested that they either summon

[54] *CD*, 3:433–438; Nicholas, *Debates*, 2:200. That Calvert knew the truth is clear from his letter the previous June to Digby, when he reported that Southampton and Sandys were detained because they were "upon very violent presumptions supposed (during the time of this Parliament) to have been too busy and industrious, to trouble his Majesty's service and affairs both at home and abroad": BL, Additional, 36,445, fol. 152, a reference I owe to Christopher Thompson.

[55] *CD*, 2:445, 3:458–459. I owe to Conrad Russell the suggestion that Digges's reference to "sands" may have been intended as a pun. Christopher Thompson's unpublished paper "The Reaction of the House of Commons in November and December, 1621 to the Confinement of Sir Edwin Sandys" demonstrates that the House was eager, not reluctant, to take up the issue.

Sir Edwin before them or obtain a direct report from him. Sir Humphrey May, the chancellor of the Duchy of Lancaster, tried to head off the demands by requesting that they leave the king's secret "apprehensions" alone, particularly since Sandys had been found innocent. But Phelips neatly prevented suppression of the issue by agreeing that Calvert had probably been right; they ought to interview Sir Edwin merely for confirmation. Although Sir Samuel Sandys (clearly reflecting his brother's wishes) tried to stop them, the Commons finally decided to send Mallory and Heyman to interview Sandys.[56]

Perhaps because he had heard of these events, Sir Edwin was already telling Ferrar on December 3 that he had decided to return to London. He sounded resigned: his absence, he said, "hath been just and necessary." Yet he was not reconciled to those who had brought the troubles upon him. His friends, he wrote, had not forsaken him, "though [he was] frowned upon by so great persons. And I would that to frown on me were the worst they meant me. But God forgive the wrongdoers, and receive those that are wronged into his protection."[57] The timing of the journey may indicate that Sir Edwin was a party to the provocative investigation the Commons were now launching.

For it was obvious that Mallory, Heyman, and Spencer were not fishing innocently in the dark; they had a fairly good idea of what they were likely to find. All three had close contacts with Sandys (Mallory from Yorkshire, Heyman as a fellow representative from Sandwich, and Spencer through Southampton). They must have heard about the substance of Sir Edwin's interrogation, and they were determined to bring the truth to light. At this juncture, unfortunately, there intervenes the most frustrating of the many lacunae in our spotty record of Sandys's career: the total lack of information about what he, Mallory, and Heyman discussed "by the fire side" at his London home "at ten of clock at night, the servants being put out and but [the three of them] there." The written report Heyman brought to the Commons was ordered destroyed, and no copy has survived. Both Mallory and Heyman suffered for their actions after the session, in company with Coke, Phelips, Hakewill, and Digges, which indicates how seriously their brief venture was taken.[58]

It seems plausible that Sandys told them that the interrogation had indeed concerned his activities in the House; he thus directly contradicted Calvert, and indirectly the king himself. Like the Commons, however, who had the report burned, he may not have wanted to press this blatant breach of parliamentary privilege. His disillusionment, and his own

---

[56] Ibid., 2:483–486, 5:227–228, 6:218–219; *CJ*, 654.
[57] MCFP, Box 7, no. 975.
[58] Russell, "Mallory."

brother's wish for postponement, suggest no less. As he must have expected, the king's reaction to the very investigation was swift and unambiguous: a message to the Commons on December 4 that the imprisonment was "not for any misdemeanor of his in Parliament." Sandys could tell friends that James himself was prepared to lie, but he could not say so in public. That Mallory and Heyman's report contained such inflammatory evidence appears likely, given the burning of the document. Above all, however, the episode underlines the despair Sandys, together with many of his colleagues, must have felt about the future of Parliament.

Despite Sir Edwin's efforts to remain inconspicuous, he still contributed, albeit indirectly, to the uproar that brought the Parliament to an end. For James had gone on in his December 4 message to claim that, had he wanted to confine Sandys for words spoken in the Commons, he regarded himself "very free and able to punish any man's misdemeanors in Parliament." This, together with his prohibition of discussions of the Spanish match, caused a commotion that did not die down until the assembly was dissolved on December 19.[59] Even the "true remonstrance" the M.P.s produced to justify themselves (which enraged James into one of his few violent acts off the hunting field, the ripping of a page from the Commons' Journal) harked back to Sandys's original suggestion of such a statement in the dying days of the spring session.

Sir Edwin's distant presence must have been felt to the bitter end of the Parliament. When the immediate response to the king's letter was the suggestion that no business be done until the privilege issue was settled, Digges reminded the House that *"rise, rise,* were fearful words." And Phelips's sarcasm, on the day after the king's message, caught perfectly the tone of this catastrophic autumn session: "How fortunate we have been in our meeting; that we blanched the business of Sir Edwin Sandys, we gave two subsidies so freely as we never did before; to the end we did this was to the glory of God and stability of the kingdom." Almost the last action of the House before it departed was to order that "the paper, brought by Sir Peter Heyman, about Sir Edwin Sandys, shall be burned by him."[60]

It may be that Sandys expected, during that melancholy autumn, that his voice would not be heard again on national affairs, and that the role of the "Commons-man" and the independent gentry he represented was over. What he could not have guessed was that the bleak prospects of 1621, with Cranfield turned against him, Southampton in disfavor, and his own imprisonment, were to be transformed, in 1624, into the high point of Jacobean political development and his own parliamentary career.

[59] Nicholas, *Debates*, 2:277. The angry debate that followed is in *CD*, 5:232–234.
[60] Ibid., 6:224 (italics in original), 2:500; *CJ*, 669. See too BL, Egerton, 2651, a reference I owe to Christopher Thompson.

Chapter X

THE M.P. VICTORIOUS:
BUCKINGHAM AND THE PARLIAMENT OF 1624

THE DISTINCTIVENESS OF THE 1624 PARLIAMENT

The Parliament that met in February 1624 was a thoroughly experienced assembly. Less than 40 percent of the members of the Commons were new to the House: the lowest proportion in memory, certainly since early in Elizabeth's reign.[1] And these M.P.s continued essentially together for the remaining three Parliaments of the 1620s; indeed, the new men in 1625, 1626, and 1628 represented only a quarter of each House. To the extent that it was during the sessions of 1624–28 that the leaders of the Long Parliament won their legislative spurs, it would be difficult to exaggerate the importance of these meetings in establishing the attitudes and expectations that were to foreshadow revolution when the Commons reassembled in 1640.

Seen in that context, 1624 takes on a major yet ironic significance. From the perspective of James's reign and Sandys's career alone, it appears as the climax to two decades of political development; within the larger framework of all early Stuart Parliaments, however, it turns out to have been the great exception. As a result, the hopes and assumptions that it misleadingly provoked became remarkably persistent. The legacy of 1624, which Prince Charles was largely responsible for creating, was to haunt him for over twenty years, and in the long run it was to help shape a new view of the place of Parliament in the government of England.

Among those who descended on Westminster that February, Sir Edwin held a unique position. His memory of proceedings at Westminster now went back almost forty years; only one colleague, Sir George More, had enjoyed longer and more consistent service, and only one other, Sir John Savile, had entered the House at the same time as Sandys, though he had been elected fewer times. None of the speakers who dominated debates could equal Sandys in his familiarity with the ways of the House. None embodied so clearly the growing influence of the independent gentry, or was identified so closely with the correspondingly rising status of the Commons. And none could have been regarded so distinctly as the mentor of

[1] Theodore K. Rabb, *Enterprise and Empire: Merchant and Gentry Investment in the Expansion of England, 1575–1630* (Cambridge, Mass., 1967), 94.

the new generation of leaders that was being forged in the mid- and late 1620s.

The opportunity to occupy this crucial position was given Sandys by events entirely outside his control. Deeply suspected by the king, and humiliated by the collapse of the Virginia Company, he would normally have been kept out of the Commons, and even if allowed to sit, he might well have found his former stature compromised by the revelations from Virginia (see below, chapter 13). The circumstances which unexpectedly allowed him to undertake the last and most important of his major roles in Parliament, and to attain a level of effectiveness that had eluded him for twenty years, derived from the fiasco of the Spanish match. That story, related in comprehensive detail by Gardiner, and reviewed most recently by Robert Ruigh and Thomas Cogswell, need not detain us at any length.[2] Suffice it to recall that, following the collapse of their futile negotiations in Madrid, Prince Charles and his new ally, the Duke of Buckingham, were determined to reverse England's policy of friendship with the Habsburgs. The instrument they chose for the task was Parliament, likely to be anti-Spanish, and the proper forum for canceling existing treaties as a prelude to a declaration of war.

The idea of summoning a new assembly was already being reported in October 1623, shortly after the prince's return, and by mid-December agreement had been wrung from a reluctant king and a divided Privy Council. One of James's conditions was apparently the dispatch of Coke and Sandys, the two principal irritants, to Ireland. But even here Buckingham and Charles won the final round. Coke prepared very slowly to depart; Sandys also delayed; since they had not left by the time they were elected, they were allowed to take their seats. The prince and the duke wanted the full support of the House, and were prepared to ally themselves with the leaders of the Commons to gain their ends.[3] Hence the smoothing of Sandys's path; and hence the extraordinarily harmonious and effective session that ensued.

The elections themselves were a harbinger of events to come. Sandys stood for a major seat, that of his county, Kent. He was perhaps not as

---

[2] S. R. Gardiner, *History of England . . . 1603–1642*, 10 vols. (London, 1883–84), 5:1–214; Robert E. Ruigh, *The Parliament of 1624: Politics and Foreign Policy* (Cambridge, Mass., 1971), 16–42; Thomas Cogswell, *The Blessed Revolution: English Politics and the Coming of War, 1621–1624* (Cambridge, 1989), and "England and the Spanish Match," in *Conflict in Early Stuart England: Studies in Religion and Politics, 1603–1642* ed. Richard Cust and Ann Hughes (London, 1989), 107–133.

[3] Ruigh, *1624*, 34–35, 74 n. When summoned by the Privy Council (*APC, 1623–1625*, 156–157), Sandys on January 8 cited illness as the reason for delay. His "weakness still continuing," he had to stay at Northbourne to avoid "a great infection of mortality" from smallpox and purple ague in nearby Sandwich: PRO, SP/14/158/14.

great a local figure as his opponent and kinsman, Digges, but once again
the tactics of denunciation that had worked with Sir Thomas Smythe apparently brought success. In Chamberlain's words, Sandys's supporters
cried out against the other candidates, saying "[Sir Nicholas] Tufton was a
papist and Digges a royalist." Whether such accusations alone could have
swayed the electors is doubtful, especially as Tufton was in fact elected,
and Sir Edwin was not even present. But Digges did have to look elsewhere (to Tewkesbury) and by the end of January Chamberlain could report that Sandys had made his peace at Court "with promise of all manner
of conformity."[4]

This was by no means the whole story. Sir Edwin had hardly acted the
cautious outcast, fearful of his place, during the election. In addition to his
own campaign, he doubtless intervened in Sandwich, where he was known
to be "beloved of the Sandwich rabble"; and he also meddled in two other
nearby towns, Dover and Canterbury. This was not the behavior of a man
excluded from politics by Court disfavor. Nor can his own account of the
election, in a letter to John Ferrar, be taken entirely at face value. Although he starts by warning that the events "may raise some envy against
me," he continues with a modesty that tests credulity:

> On Wednesday last I was advertised by some of my friends that the writ for
> choice of the knight of the shire, was come to the Sheriff the day before; and
> that the Monday ensuing was the County Court day. The next day, being
> Thursday, came divers to me, desiring me that I would stand for the place;
> and presuming so much of the love of the country, that though other worthy
> gentlemen had solicited for it many weeks before, and though the time was
> short, and the place and election far off (thirty miles and upwards) and in the
> midst of their friends; yet that all these disadvantages, and some others not-
> withstanding, the country would in the election express their love towards me
> more than ordinary, my answer was to this effect, that I was full of that ser-
> vice: And as for standing for any place, by way of suit or request, I never had
> done it since I was seventy years of age: besides other allegations, which to be
> brief I pass over. Notwithstanding it pleased the gentlemen and others my
> neighbours, to set the matter on foot without my standing for it: saying that if I
> were chosen, being a freeholder, I could not refuse it: and within less than
> three days, there went out of this neglected part of the Shire, (me being far
> off) about six hundred horse of freeholders, as they were esteemed. [At the
> election, a large number called for Tufton and Digges jointly.] But the rest of
> the assembly, concurring all upon my name only, without any other (for they

---

[4] N. E. McClure, ed., *The Letters of John Chamberlain*, 2 vols., (Philadelphia, 1939) 2:540,
543. Yet the Venetian ambassador reported on January 26 that someone "whom I reported
the King detested, named Sans, has been elected by a county, and thus the seeds of dissension are possibly being sown": *CSP, Venetian, 1623–1625*, 201.

had no directions . . .) and those exceeding the former troop by many hundreds as they were esteemed, the choice fell in fine on Sir Nicholas Tufton and myself.

In fact, by the time he wrote this, on January 12, 1624, Sandys must have known that Buckingham and Charles were working to ensure his place in the Commons so that he could help them obtain speedy parliamentary action against Spain. But he relished the honor of the county seat, and soon demonstrated to the duke and prince that an alliance with "popular" leaders produced much better results than their largely unsuccessful attempts to create a friendly House through electoral influence alone.[5]

The consequences of the new partnership between Court and Commons were as remarkable as they were unprecedented. The most visible outcome was the increase in the number of bills that became law. In 1614 none had even reached the Lords. In 1621 eighty-one had been passed, but only two had become law so that the subsidy could be collected. In 1624, by contrast, over one hundred were passed, of which thirty-eight became public statutes, and about the same number were signed by the king as private bills: a staggering success rate of over 70 percent. The decisive feature of the 1624 Parliament that marked it as the climax of developments since 1604 (and thus, in the long term, as the great exception of the age) was that at least half of the public statutes that now received royal approval had originally been introduced and passed in 1621 or in earlier sessions, but had never before received James's consent.[6]

This was the miracle that the partnership between prince and people could create, yet the cooperation proved to be as unique as the flurry of statutes. At no other time in early Stuart England was the particular situation of 1624 repeated; contrary to the fondest wishes of those who marveled at this "happiest" of Parliaments, the precedents for legislative effi-

[5] Ruigh, *1624*, 135, and chaps. 2 and 3, passim; *CSP, Domestic, 1623–1625*, 165; PRO, SP/14/161, fols. 178–179; MCFP, Box 11, no. 986; and, for his connection with Tufton, below, chapter 12, note 54.

[6] Among the 1624 public statutes, the following chapters had been introduced in the 1621 Parliament, if not before: nos. 1, 2, 3, 4, 6, 7, 8, 9, 10, 11, 12, 13, 14, 15, 16, 17, 18, 19, 20, 21, 22, 23, 24, 25, 26, 29, 31, and 32. A number of private bills—e.g., concerning Alice Dudley, Stephen Leisure, and Stepney—had also been considered in 1621. The three principal non-taxation measures passed by the next Parliament (1 Chas. 1, c. 1, 3, and 4) originated in 1624, but passed the Commons too late for enactment. See *LJ*, 2:427–430. I have benefited from Mark Kennedy's comments and corrections throughout this chapter, beginning with this complex area, since bill counting is hardly straightforward (there are discrepancies, for example, between the Parliament Roll and the *Statutes of the Realm*), and the numbers are subject to revision. Conrad Russell, *Parliaments and English Politics, 1621–1629* (Oxford, 1979), 190 outlines the problems of defining and counting public bills. Yet it is worth noting that not since the 1540s had a single Parliament enacted so many new laws; even the fruitful session of 1604 passed only seventy-two statutes.

ciency and the acceptance of Commons proposals that it seemed to establish were not followed. The resultant misinterpretation of the special circumstances of 1624 created a burden for Charles I from which he could never struggle free.

BUCKINGHAM AND THE COMMONS

The evidence of Sandys's accommodation with Buckingham is inescapable. Chamberlain's belief that now he really was an "undertaker" (the dirty word from 1614) is amply confirmed. One indication was Sir Edwin's unlikely endorsement of the controversial measure that allowed Buckingham to take over York House; more telling was the support that the duke gave the Sandys family in subsequent elections. He urged Sandwich to elect young Henry in 1625 (to no avail, despite glowing remarks about his father's virtues and concern for the town's welfare) and he recommended Sir Edwin himself, also unsuccessfully, in 1628. There can be no doubt that an accommodation was forged in 1624 between the royal favorite and the erstwhile target of royal displeasure.[7]

What is less obvious is the balance of benefit in the arrangement. Since the initiative unmistakably came from Buckingham and Charles, and they achieved their anti-Spanish purposes, as well as their secondary objective, the disgrace of Cranfield, it is easy to conclude that from their point of view the deal was entirely successful. But did they really gain that much? The Commons scarcely needed major concessions to adopt anti-Spanish policies. Nor was the toppling of Cranfield a one-sided campaign; plenty of M.P.s, notably Sandys himself, were eager for such a fray, and there had been no need for collusion to bring down Bacon. Indeed, the lord chancellor's disgrace smoothed the way, both in precedent and in experience, for the assault on the lord treasurer. The one undoubted gain that Buckingham could cite was the passage of a subsidy bill. But Conrad Russell has recently demonstrated the relatively small contribution of subsidies to

---

[7] *Chamberlain*, 2:549; *CJ*, 797; Nicholas, *1624*, fol. 243 (see note 9, below); note 59, below; BL, Additional, Misc. Correspondence, SA/ZB2, nos. 102, 103; PRO, SP/16/95/67. The evidence that Charles and Buckingham, as well as James, had shown distaste for Sandys is in Cogswell, *Revolution*, 146.

A cryptic reference by Sandys on November 22, 1623 (Kingsbury, 4:405) may be the first evidence of his link with the duke. Sir Edwin, in deep trouble over Virginia at the time, disguised names in this letter. Thus Sir Thomas Smythe is probably "the Knight at Fanchurch" who lived nearby; "H.H." could be Smythe's protégé Humphrey Handford. Perhaps, therefore, "my friend G.B. than whom I thought I could have none more assured" is G[eorge, duke of] B[uckingham]. The only other "G.B." whose good opinion Sandys cherished in late 1623 was Gabriel Barbour, but since his name appeared twice in the same letter, it is unlikely that he was the person whom the initials disguised.

royal revenues, and in any case the Commons' side of the balance seems far to outweigh these victories.[8]

The statistics of bills previously frustrated but now passed into law are indication enough of the extent of the House's gains during 1624. The release of a long and frustrating logjam must be counted as a significant reason this could be called the "happiest" of Parliaments. Moreover, the confirmation of the power to destroy royal ministers; the acceptance, after twenty years' effort, of a reasonably effective Monopolies Act; and the endorsement of free speech in foreign affairs; were all signal advances for the Commons. In no single Parliament until the Civil War did they move so far, and on so many fronts, simultaneously. In legislative output, in the securing of privileges, and in the remedy of grievances (despite the many that were dismissed, as they had been for twenty years), 1624 was a land-mark session. It is therefore difficult to escape the conclusion that the M.P.s were the principal beneficiaries of the accommodation with Buck-ingham. Rather than merely yielding to the Court at the first sign of favor, Sandys and his colleagues seem to have taken shrewd advantage of the situation that developed in the wake of the collapse of the Spanish match, and used it to bring into reality a significant part of the vision of England's best interests that Sir Edwin had been proclaiming for twenty years.

SPAIN

James opened the session on February 19 with an anxious speech that suggested how weak he felt. He protested "that never any king was more beloved of his people," but his dominant metaphor offered less certainty. Comparing Crown-Parliament relations to the kinship between a husband and a wife, he justified discussion of the "secret" matter of his son's mar-riage as a family affair. But he could not avoid the less happy aspects of matrimony, and he ended rather cheerlessly by defending himself against the "jealousies" of his supposedly loving subjects. One image in particular strikes the biographer of Sandys. In an age so fond of punning, and so aware of verbal linkages, was it mere coincidence that James described his desire for a successful Parliament as being greater than the desire for wa-ter of "a king . . . in the sandy deserts"?[9]

Sir Edwin's presence is not confirmed until the third day of business, February 25, when he spoke on a recusants bill. He had been appointed to

---

[8] Conrad Russell, "Parliamentary History in Perspective 1604–1629," *History* 61 (1976): 1–27.

[9] PRO, SP/14/166/2. Written by Edward Nicholas, and cited here as Nicholas, *1624*, this is the most complete diary of the session. In BL, Additional, 18,597, fol. 4—a diary by Sir Walter Erle (henceforth Erle, *1624*)—the king rejects the image of himself as a "soldier in a dry, sandy wilderness."

no committees on the first two days, and had not spoken on his specialties, the decay of trade, the abuse of monopolies, and free fishing in America, on the 24th, which suggests a late arrival. Since he had missed a Virginia Company meeting at the beginning of the month, he was probably still in the country, and his age and sporadic ill health may have required a slow journey—hence a tardy appearance at Westminster.

Once in the Commons, however, Sandys lost little time in shaping the House's affairs. He may have missed the important conference with the Lords on the twenty-fourth, when Buckingham told the sad tale of the mission to Madrid, but he was soon at the heart of the Commons' consideration of the Spanish treaties, and by the afternoon of the twenty-sixth he was taking his usual lead on trade (now as chairman of the Trade Committee), examining monopolies, wool exports, American fishing, and the like.[10] These two items of business, Spain and trade, the latter of which evolved into the proceedings against Cranfield, took up more of the House's time than any other subjects. Since Sandys was centrally involved in both areas, one can again distill the nature of a parliamentary session through his contributions to the debates.

In his address, James had announced that "the principal cause" for the summoning of Parliament was the need to consider policy toward Spain. Wasting no time, the Lords invited the Commons to a conference on February 24 to hear Buckingham's report on recent negotiations. The issues were simple, and England's more hostile course could be discerned in the comments of the duke, Secretary Calvert, and Prince Charles himself. At this point James was still undecided about a breach with the Habsburgs, but his son and favorite minister were determined to gain revenge for the failure of the Spanish match. Having electioneered and allied with leading M.P.s, they now presented a one-sided case that left no room for uncertainty.[11]

The central issue, as the story unfolded before the two Houses, had been whether the Spaniards would assure the return of the Palatinate (half of which their troops had occupied) to James's son-in-law, the Elector Frederick, before Prince Charles's marriage to the Infanta proceeded, and whether the English in turn would have to grant some toleration to Catho-

---

[10] *CJ*, 671–673; Kingsbury, 2:512; Nicholas, *1624*, fols. 8–20, 25–28. Sandys's likely absence before February 25 is confirmed by the failure to name him to the committee which examined the clerk's journal (a particular concern of his), an omission rectified two weeks later: *CJ*, 673, 683.

[11] Ibid., 670, 672; Erle, *1624*, fols. 1–6, 14; Nicholas, *1624*, fols. 8–20. For background see Cogswell, *Revolution*, pts. 1 and 2, and his "Spanish Match"; S. L. Adams, "Foreign Policy and the Parliaments of 1621 and 1624," in *Faction and Parliament: Essays on Early Stuart History*, ed. Kevin Sharpe (Oxford, 1978), 139–171; and Mark E. Kennedy, "Legislation, Foreign Policy, and the 'Proper Business' of the Parliament of 1624," *Albion* 23 (1991): 41–60.

lics. One of the targets of Buckingham's account was the Earl of Bristol, England's ambassador, who had remained loyal to James's own wishes and had tried to ease the strains in the relationship with Spain. But the main targets were Philip IV and Olivares. Despite disingenuous evasions like "if I speak like an Englishman and the truth, I should be thought malicious," Buckingham left no doubt about the villainy of the Spaniards. "In their conceits they have already swallowed the world," he said, and recounted a string of dishonesties, including Olivares' supposed offer to let Charles spend the night with the Infanta, "if not as his wife yet as his mistress." The question before Parliament was whether James should accept Philip IV's promise to intercede with Emperor Ferdinand over the Palatinate as sufficient inducement to conclude the marriage. In case anyone was still uncertain, Buckingham threw in a final tidbit: he had just heard that all English ships in Spanish ports had been confiscated.

Sandys was in the Commons on February 27, when this tale was recounted by the official reporters of the conference, Chancellor of the Exchequer Weston and Secretary Cottington, because he joined the privy councillors, Coke, Phelips, Digges, and other senior M.P.s on a committee, created after the report was finished, to respond to the information that the Spanish ambassador had demanded Buckingham's head for insulting Philip IV in his address to Parliament. The committee was to exonerate the favorite, and served to tighten the bond between House and minister.[12]

Thereafter, events moved smoothly toward the conclusion Buckingham sought. At the major debate on March 1 sentiment ran in the predictable direction as M.P.s demanded an end to negotiations both for the marriage and for the restoration of the Palatinate. Sir John Eliot even asked the House to advise James "to set forth his own fleet to prevent the King [of] Spain's armada"—the first suggestion that more than stalled treaties were at stake. After some uncertainty about how to proceed, Digges recommended a meeting of the House as a Committee of the Whole in the afternoon, to give them the opportunity of free debate. Characteristically, though, it was Sandys who had the last word, and set the tone for the afternoon's deliberations. People such as Eliot had been looking beyond the immediate issue, and Sir Edwin suggested that, in accordance with James's request, they should concentrate solely on the treaties themselves, "and not, as yet, to meddle with the consequences." It was important that they not only give their opinion in favor of the breach, but also (again a characteristic touch) draw up the *reasons* for their advice. One can almost sense the numbered list forming in Sandys's mind.[13]

[12] *CJ*, 720–722; BL, Harleian, 1219, fol. 148 (an example of the cooperation between Buckingham and Sandys).

[13] *CJ*, 676; Nicholas *1624*, fols. 35 (Eliot), 37 (Sandys); MCFP, Box 11, no. 1433 (unfoli-

At the Committee of the Whole that afternoon, it was Sandys himself who took the chair, while the speaker remained at his side. Before him the notables of the House, including Digges and Phelips, expatiated on the reasons for breaking off both treaties with Spain. Christopher Brooke, mindful of the need for specifics, listed four justifications, and by the time his colleagues had finished there were at least a dozen, ranging from Brooke's concern about discomfiting the Dutch to Sir George Cheke's suspicion that the request for toleration of English Catholics proved Spain's intention "to make a rebellion here." The Commons' determination mounted steadily until the speaker returned to his chair so that Sandys could officially report the outcome of the afternoon's discussion: a unanimous recommendation to break off the treaties, with a small committee (as Sir Edwin suggested) to draw up the reasons.[14]

That committee had about as redoubtable a membership as the House could muster, including four of the principal courtier M.P.s (Chancellor Weston, Secretary Calvert, Chancellor of the Duchy May, and Solicitor Heath), Coke, Phelips, and Digges. Yet it was Sandys who remained in the central role, delivering the next day a report that bears all the marks of his work. They had decided to emphasize five reasons for the breach: (1) Spain's "continual connivancy of religion" on behalf of English Catholics; (2) Spanish help in enlarging England's "popish faction" during the negotiations; (3) the deceit practiced in "deluding his Majesty" and using the time to "oppress the protestant party elsewhere"; (4) the assault on the Palatinate, and the attempt to have its heir (James's grandson) raised at the Emperor's Catholic court; and (5) the "small respect" shown to Charles in Madrid, including the attempt to convert him.[15]

This report won enthusiastic approval, though a lengthy discussion ensued about how to proceed in conjunction with the Lords. Eventually six members of the same committee were, in essence, given power to come to an agreement and discuss preparation of a final document for the king. According to one diary, Sandys was asked to report the results to the House (perhaps because his clarity was preferred to Coke's prolixity), but in the event Coke did the honors at his usual length. Full agreement had been reached; yet since the Lords had offered four somewhat different reasons, a joint committee was to devise the final declaration to the king.

---

ated), where Sandys says "he had in Italy heard Embassies and Treaties called the Spaniard's own weapon, at which he would ever fox us"; Houghton Library, MS. English 980 (diary of Sir William Spring: henceforth Spring, *1624*), 41–61; *The Holles Account of Proceedings in the House of Commons in 1624*, ed. Christopher Thompson (Orsett, Essex, 1985), 13.

[14] *CJ*, 724–725; Nicholas *1624*, fols. 38–39.

[15] Ibid., fols. 40–41; MCFP, Box 11, no. 1433, where Sandys contrasts the Spaniards' promotion of Catholicism with the toleration of Huguenots by Henri IV, who had not "any truer subjects than they."

On these further developments Digges and Phelips were asked to report. It looked as though Sandys was drifting into the background, but on March 4, when the Digges/Phelips reports were given, he came to the fore again.[16]

By now Parliament's conclusions and reasoning were being set down in writing. A huge amount of information about Anglo-Spanish negotiations had been presented, and there was obviously no problem about documenting their advice to the king. Nevertheless, Sandys felt that one point was still not sufficiently clear. It had been revealed that Philip IV had promised the Papacy to take up arms against England if James refused to grant toleration to English Catholics. Although this came under the heading of the first reason for breaking off the treaties, Sir Edwin felt that the implications had not been sufficiently elaborated in Parliament's document: namely, that such an undertaking by the Habsburg "would draw an immediate dependency of all the Catholics of this kingdom upon the King of Spain." Even the Huguenots, he said, felt allegiance only to the king of France. Such interference by Philip was intolerable, and deserved citation in the Commons' advice to James. The M.P.s agreed, and asked Sir Edwin to write appropriate language for the document. He was now back at the vanguard of the issue, for later in the debate he was appointed the House's "penman" (presumably, the drafter of the final text) at the afternoon conference with the Lords, and asked to report the results the next day. At that conference he was to be on top form, as young Dudley Carleton waspishly reported to his uncle, Sir Dudley: "Sir Edwin Sandys . . . in a speech he made . . . by way of amplifying those reasons went beyond all expectation of his abilities."[17]

Back at the center of developments, and perhaps overconfident about his ability to sway his colleagues, Sandys now became involved in a misguided attempt to push the Commons along faster than they were prepared to go. The entire episode was out of character, because one of the leitmotifs of his career (epitomized by his overthrow of fifteenths in 1621) was his insistence on the shortcomings of England's economy, his hesitance

---

[16] Nicholas, *1624*, fols. 41–44 (naming Sandys as reporter); *CJ*, 724–726, has the committee to name the reporter, which may be why Coke was chosen.

[17] Ibid., 728; Nicholas, *1624*, fol. 47; Spring, *1624*, 90; PRO, SP/14/160/33 and 1017; and Nicholas Ferrar's diary, as printed in D. R. Ransome, ed., "The Parliamentary Papers of Nicholas Ferrar 1624," *Camden Miscellany*, vol. 33 (Cambridge, 1996), 5–104, esp. 52 (Phelips noting that Sandys's report was received "with exceeding commendation and applause" in the Lords) and 53 (Sandys saying the Huguenots had "no manner of dependence . . . in any other prince than in their own king"). Spring warns readers against taking a diarist's record too literally. Next to a speech by Digges he comments: "Whosoever shall read this I wish them to know that I took short notes of his speech and may much wrong it both for the manner of the delivery and for the matter, because I could not either follow his method nor note all the matters as he laid them down: these are but private notes for my own memory" (55).

about granting more taxes than the nation could afford, and his relegation of other commitments to second place behind economic issues. Now, however, he was being swept along in the anti-Spanish campaign by his new ally, Buckingham, and by his old friend Southampton, a veteran enemy of Spain. The results doubtless taught him not to abandon his usual instincts.

What happened was that he used the vehicle of his March 5 report on the conference with the Lords not merely to convey the text of the final document (which was happily accepted), but also to announce a motion made by the conferees to promise James financial support in case war broke out with Spain. This uncalled-for expansion of the committee's original mandate met instant rebuff in the Commons. They had been perfectly willing to accept five additional reasons suggested by the Lords (all instances of Spanish treachery) as well as the specific wording Sandys and the lord chamberlain had devised for the document. But they balked when a new idea was introduced at the very end of Sir Edwin's report. "Lord of Southampton had made an objection," he said, that the king's response to Parliament's recommendation might be to ask "what assistance" would be available if the termination of negotiations led to "a breach with Spain, and a war." The Lords had therefore prepared an answer: "In the pursuit of this advice, we will assist His Majesty with our persons and fortunes."[18]

Given Sandys's usual concern about England's poverty, his acquiescence in this proposal is unexpected. And yet he *had* intervened decisively on behalf of the two subsidies voted in the previous Parliament; the mover of this new motion was his old friend Southampton; and he knew that in 1621 similar expressions of support had been made out of anxiety for the Palatinate. But the Commons would have nothing to do with it. Sandys himself had said they should restrict themselves to the king's request for advice about the treaties, and, as Alford and Phelips quickly pointed out, there was no need to anticipate a hypothetical situation, to make "a kind of engagement" where none was required, or to breach the ancient precedent that motions for supply originated in the Commons, not the Lords. In the absence of specifics, the M.P.s were not going to make a general promise. Mallory, Sir Edwin's champion in 1621, even suggested that those who exceeded their instructions at conferences with the Lords ought to be ex-

---

[18] *CJ*, 677, 729; Nicholas, *1624*, fols. 48–49; Spring, *1624*, 81–84. MCFP, Box 11, no. 1433, does not quote the "persons and fortunes" phrase, but stresses that, without funds, the breach of the treaties would be seen abroad as an empty gesture. Sandys here lays down two conditions for the supply: it had to be raised "in a Parliamentary way, to avoid the imposing of Benevolences and other kinds of Contributions," and it assumed the king would respond by "relieving of grievances and taking off burdens"—as clear a linkage between grievance and supply as one finds in a Jacobean Parliament (see above, chapter 5, note 12, and chapter 6, note 58). Buckingham tried to persuade James to respond to the "persons and fortunes" promise, and an offer of six subsidies, by renouncing the treaties: BL, Harleian, 6987, f. 200.

pelled from the House. The vehemence quickly persuaded Sandys of the magnitude of the blunder, and he told his colleagues that he wished "this question . . . had not been delivered here." Since it had been, however, he wanted to point out that he had merely reported on events at the conference, that the language was no stronger than the offer of support to James in 1621, that neither then nor now were they committed to anything, and that the king would doubtless follow "a parliamentary course" if he sought further funds.

As if to reassert his well-known credentials, Sandys ended his speech of apology by reverting to his more usual concern for the kingdom's poverty: he was sure that, in return for new supply, "his Majesty will give way for the passing of such laws as shall enable his subjects to undergo the charge of this business"—in other words, provide some form of economic relief, though of course where it was to come from Sandys was in no position to say. After renewed objections, Sir Edwin suggested that the offending statement be removed from the advice to the king, whereupon "by a voice" the House excused the committee as "discreet men" and accepted his suggestion to have the discussion "cease without further debate." The document was approved, and a committee chosen to attend the king that afternoon.[19]

The king's response was to demand cash in hand before he would break with Spain, though he did agree that, if money were forthcoming, the funds could be supervised by parliamentary treasurers and restricted to fortifying the realm and Ireland, outfitting a fleet, and helping the Dutch. There the matter rested for a week while the House busied itself with trade, monopolies, and other legislation, but on March 11 the question that had given Sandys trouble on the fifth resurfaced, and in a much more difficult context. The king's response to Parliament's advice (in essence: if they were serious, would they take the next step?) had been reported on the eighth, and on the eleventh Chancellor Weston reiterated the position bluntly: if the breach of the treaties led to war, James would need more money. His expenses in connection with the defense of the realm and negotiations with Spain exceeded the income he had received by almost £300,000. How were these debts to be met, and funds raised for a possible war?[20] The king was asking the question that Southampton and Sandys had

---

[19] Nicholas, *1624*, fols. 48–52; Spring, *1624*, 81–89; *CJ*, 677, 728–729. Sandys's omission from the committee was doubtless a slap on the wrist for the "persons and fortunes" blunder. For the worry that the offer of supply might emanate from the Lords see *Sir Nathaniel Rich's Diary of Proceedings in the House of Commons in 1624*, ed. Christopher Thompson (Wivenhoe, Essex, 1985), 41; for Parliament's "Advice" to the King, *LJ*, 3:250. Sandys put the House's reasons into the Commons' records: *CJ*, 678.

[20] Nicholas, *1624*, fols. 65–66; *LJ*, 3:256. Sir Heneage Finch reported the king's speech (*CJ*, 679), but Weston's reiteration of its central point brought the subject to the fore.

hypothesized, and it became central to the remaining days of debate. If Charles, Buckingham, and their allies wanted war, James was saying, they had to know what that implied. It may have been helpful to Buckingham's cause at this point that Sandys had already raised the matter of support, because the objections in the first discussion had been to procedure, not to supply itself. Thus the lack of argument over the *principle* of aid might induce M.P.s to assume that the House was in favor of subsidies.

Nor would the assumption have been mistaken. Perhaps because they had already been forced to think about the aftermath of the breach of the treaties, the M.P.s did not try to evade the dilemma James placed before them. Rudyard, protégé of the anti-Spanish Pembroke, urged his colleagues, as soon as Weston finished, to follow through on their advice. He knew they could prevaricate ("we may blow up this House with gunpowder with our own breath"), but if they failed in their responsibilities this would "be the last of parliaments." Preparations for war had to go forward. Others agreed, with only few variations, and even Coke was so carried away that he asserted England "never thrived so well as when it had wars with Spain."

Still it was Sandys who made the central speech of the day. Taking his usual middle position, he urged that both haste and delay be avoided, for it was important to establish the justice of a war. But he also pointed out that this was easy to demonstrate, because a wrong had been done, and in the absence of restitution war was just. He then endorsed and—reviving the wording that had got him in trouble on March 5—gave form to the proposal that carried the rest of the discussion: they should tell James "that in pursuit of our advice we will . . . assist his Majesty with our persons and fortunes." Although he could not resist mentioning the redress of grievances, he admitted this was not the time to raise them. Rather, they should join the Lords in this venture (again an echo of the events of March 5), ignoring the procedural infraction so as to show a united face to England's enemies.[21]

Matters did not go quite as smoothly as Sir Edwin might have wished, because the issues of a just war and of joining with the Lords were postponed. James wanted a response on the question of supply before he would commit himself to war, and there was understandable nervousness about the linkage between the two. The Commons therefore decided on two resolutions: first, that they would not declare themselves on the issue of war because the king had not "propounded" his intentions; and second,

---

[21] Nicholas, *1624*, fols. 67–71. John Pym (Northamptonshire Record Office, Finch-Hatton MS. 50, henceforth Pym, *1624*), fols. 25–26, says Sandys cited the motion Southampton had made in the Lords. Sandys's emphasis on the justness of the war is especially clear in Sir Thomas Holland's version: Bodleian Library, Tanner MS. 392, fol. 45.

following Sandys, that they would "assist him with our persons and abilities," though with two qualifications. They would assist "in a parliamentary manner"—that is, through normal tax-granting procedures—and they would do so only when he had declared the treaties dissolved. In other words, they were shifting responsibility for the next move back to James. The Lords were anxiously debating royal intentions at this very time, and both Houses agreed to join in a conference that afternoon to hear Prince Charles explain matters further.[22]

What he had to say was so welcome to M.P.s of all persuasions (whether enemies of Spain, opponents of war, or foes of taxation) that he provoked one of the few rapturous outpourings of self-congratulatory harmony in a Jacobean Parliament. Hoping to speed the Commons to demand the breaking-off of the treaties, and even war, the prince assured them there was no rush for funds: the king's estate could be taken care of in time. For the present, James certainly loved his Parliaments, and had no intention of living without them once he had sufficient supply. All that was needed was a quick resolution, a view that evoked a torrent of joy the next morning, when the speech was reported back to the House. Charles probably received more compliments on that March 12, and evoked more visions of political contentment, than on any other day of his life. A fulsome message of thanks was prepared, with Sandys's participation, and the M.P.s promised each other they would move ahead in demanding quickly the breach of the treaties.[23]

As usual, the honeymoon did not last long. The Commons, the Lords, Buckingham, Charles, and much of the Privy Council may have been united, but James had different ideas. Meeting a delegation from both Houses two days later, on March 14, he told them bluntly that the money had to come first, the policy second: unless he had the major sum of six subsidies and twelve fifteenths, he could not declare war. Promises were insufficient.[24]

The fourteenth was a Sunday. Because of the need to confer with the Lords, and other delays while Charles and Buckingham maneuvered at Court to soften the blow, the Commons did not get a report of the king's speech until the following Wednesday, the seventeenth. The news was in the air, however, and attempts were under way to cool possibly heated tempers. Thus, when the M.P.s heard the report on the seventeenth, they found it accompanied by reassurance from Charles that if they satisfied the

[22] Nicholas, 1624, fol. 71; S. R. Gardiner, ed., Notes of the Debates of the House of Lords, 1624 and 1626, Camden Society, n.s. 24 (London, 1879), 23–31.

[23] Nicholas, 1624, fols. 72–76; CJ, 683–684; LJ, 3:257–258. Sir Humphrey May said he had "never rejoiced so much in any Parliament."

[24] Erle, 1624, fols. 83–86; LJ, 3:265–266. One of the subsidies and two of the fifteenths were to be an annual grant to pay off royal debts.

king, the treaties would be revoked, and by a suggestion that they study copies of the speech before starting the debate. The decisive two-day consideration of the issue, therefore, did not begin until the nineteenth.

On the first day about forty members spoke, including such luminaries as Coke and Secretary Conway, and old "Commons-men" like Alford and Digges. Not one opposed the royal demand directly, though there were many questions: could the country bear so many subsidies, would £300,000 be enough, might it be wise to find out how the money was to be used, how would one convince the country, and so forth. The day ended in some confusion, with a score of proposals, talk of a committee, and uncertainty about how to proceed.[25]

Sandys cannot have had much rest that evening, because he was the first to speak the next morning, and his address bore signs of careful preparation, as well as coordination with his allies among the Buckingham forces. It also revealed that he had lost none of his mastery of the House. Laying out the issues in his usual numbered headings, he created an orderly agenda for the rest of the debate, and helped bring it to the speedy conclusion that Buckingham sought. By contrast with the previous day, when the members had given what seemed a series of set speeches, paying little attention to one another, Sir Edwin was trying to shape his colleagues' views into a coherent agenda. Capturing what the M.P.s felt was always at the heart of his ability to sway the House.[26]

He took for granted that money would be offered. It had become a matter of both honor and necessity. Therefore they ought to concentrate on how and how much. Laying out five essential topics in his usual numbered heads, he wanted his colleagues to define: first, what would be accomplished (here he repeated James's listing of the defense of the realm and Ireland, outfitting the fleet, and helping the Dutch); second, the cost; third, the means, not restricted to subsidies and fifteenths; fourth, the method of disbursement; and fifth, the form of the message to the king, to make sure the commitment was solely for one year. All the speakers accepted this as the agenda for the day, and shortly afterwards Sandys took the chair so that the M.P.s could debate as a Committee of the Whole.[27]

The discussion soon centered on the amount to be offered, which eventually was settled, at the suggestion of Coke and Phelips, at three subsidies and three fifteenths. Diversions began when the purpose of the grant and its supervision came under consideration, but Sandys intervened to end the confusion. Taking pen in hand, he framed the question, put it to his colleagues, and obtained a unanimous vote in favor of three subsidies and

---

[25] *CJ*, 738, 740–744, Nicholas, *1624*, fols. 89–95.
[26] Ibid., fol. 96; Spring, *1624*, 140; Erle, *1624*, fol. 98; *CJ*, 744.
[27] Ibid.

three fifteenths, to be paid after the breaking-off of the treaties with Spain, in order to defend the realm and Ireland, assist the Netherlands and other allies, and refurbish the navy.[28] A few details were then tidied up—Selden and Cotton were to examine precedents for the commission that was to supervise disbursement of the taxes, and a date of one year from the breach of the treaties was set for payment of the grant—before the issue was brought adroitly to a close.

Buckingham's aims had been admirably served. He himself had been absolved by Parliament for speaking irreverently of the king of Spain; he had elicited the demand for the breach of the treaties; and, thanks to Sandys and his cohorts, he had managed to surmount the monetary obstacle James had raised, for even the Commons' offer of half of what had been sought was enough to move the king to assent. Sir Edwin himself reported the wording of the final message on March 22, and he shepherded the text through amendments and discussions with the Lords later that day. To the end, despite worries about the country's ability to pay, he kept his bargain with Buckingham, and remained essential (alongside Phelips, Digges, and Rudyard) to the passage of the request for the breaking-off of the Spanish treaties and the offer of the accompanying subsidy. It was thus only fitting that he should have been the bearer, on the 25th, of the tidings that dispatches were being sent to inform the king of Spain that "on the petition and advice of his subjects in Parliament," James was declaring the treaties dissolved. The king wanted a full account of the proceedings that had led to this outcome, and at Coke's motion Sandys was named to the august six-man committee that drew up the report—joining Pembroke and his friend Southampton from the Lords and Secretaries Calvert and Conway and Chancellor Weston from the Commons.[29]

When Parliament reconvened after the Easter recess on April 1, this focus of Sandys's attention was no longer central to the proceedings. He did report from the Lords the news that Buckingham had been present when the message was sent to Spain; that preparations for war seemed under way; and that money was still a concern. But the M.P.s took their time voting the subsidy, for they remained unconvinced of the king's commitment to breaking with Spain. Not until the news was unequivocal (on the seventeenth) did they start action. Even the prince had not been able to move them when, on the tenth, he related that James had told the Spanish ambassador he would renounce the treaties "upon the humble

[28] Nicholas, *1624*, fols. 96–104; *CJ*, 744; Spring, *1624*, 150. On the importance of the Council of War which supervised the financing of the conflict with Spain over the next two years, see Michael B. Young, "Revisionism and the Council of War, 1624–1626," *Parliamentary History* 8 (1989): 1–27; and, more generally, his "Buckingham, War and Parliament: Revisionism Gone Too Far," *Parliamentary History* 4 (1985): 45–70.

[29] *CJ*, 745–746, 750; Nicholas, *1624*, fols. 109–110; *LJ*, 3:275.

Advice, both of the Lords and Commons assembled in Parliament; [for] he did never hear, nor read, that any King had ever refused the Advice of his people, given in Parliament."[30]

Such disingenuousness had hovered over much of the deliberations. Everyone knew Charles and Buckingham were out to avenge a humiliation, but even James, who had had the greatest doubts, felt unable to do more than hold up the momentum temporarily with his request for funds. He was not well, and he understood that his son and minister had Parliament firmly on their side. Pacifier and mediator that he was, he acceded. But he cannot have been happy to see that old thorn Sandys still at the center of the mischief. Nobody had done more to ensure that the Commons adhered to the agenda whereby Spain's enemies brought about the change in foreign policy. And despite the presence of six privy councillors in the House, it was Sandys who not only took charge of the final debates but who conveyed to the Commons on April 17 (following a conference with the Lords) the text of the King's decisive letter to Philip IV. James, said Sandys, had stressed the advice of Parliament in his letter, repeating the phrase about never refusing such advice. He had informed England's allies of the decision, and had already begun military preparations.

That Sandys "made his report of all this . . . so punctually and clearly as begot much admiration" can have added only gall to James's feelings.[31] Far from languishing in Ireland, Sir Edwin had assumed his usual dominance of the House. He had drawn on his extraordinary influence to coordinate Buckingham's campaign in the Commons, and the very smoothness with which it had progressed may have made it harder for James to resist. To the very end of their relationship, Sandys was asserting his mastery of Parliament in a manner that was less than congenial to the king. And his second major effort in 1624, the investigation of the economy, which began to turn toward Cranfield almost as soon as the Spanish question was settled, can only have soured him further in the eyes of his weary monarch.

THE ECONOMY

Since 1604, Sandys had been the acknowledged arbiter of questions relating to trade or the economy in the Commons. The leitmotif of his activities for twenty years had been the removal of restraints on commerce (primarily by powerful regulated companies) and the relief of economic distress.

---

[30] *CJ*, 751, 761, The heavy-handed cultivation of the Commons received a much noticed boost from Prince Charles, who urged that the House be named *before* the Lords in the subsidy message, because it had originated the subsidy—as the precedent-conscious Sandys reported on March 22: ibid., 746; Nicholas, *1624*, fol. 106.

[31] Ibid., fols. 161–163; *CJ*, 769–770; PRO, SP/14/163/2.

The latter had been central to his concerns in 1621, as a major depression tightened its grip on the country. But that Parliament, despite its assault on the Merchant Adventurers, had had little effect. Not until 1622 had the Privy Council become sufficiently alarmed to appoint a special committee, and then a permanent commission, to investigate the nation's economic problems. Sandys, still suspect, had been excluded from membership, but the appointment of his brother, Sir Samuel, might have been an acknowledgment of the importance, even if indirect, of Sir Edwin's expertise. Eventually, the commission (and in turn the Privy Council) was to accept recommendations from the Commons in 1624. Thus on this issue, too, Sandys was at last to influence government policy.

The historian of the depression of the 1620s, Barry Supple, has concluded that by early 1624 the worst was over. But he also notes that people did not seem aware of the amelioration until 1625.[32] Parliament therefore met with a sense of greater urgency than in 1621, for three more years had passed, and no end seemed in sight to the distress in England's commerce, particularly in its vital cloth industry. For Sandys, as always, the central problem was the restraint of trade, especially the Merchant Adventurers' monopoly (his chief target in 1621) and other governmental exactions and regulations. If the latter eventually provided the opening for the attack on Cranfield, all the better, because the Virginia Company, collapsing about him as Parliament opened, had to be avenged. But the grievances were weighty in and of themselves, and little time was lost in bringing them onto the Commons' agenda.

One of the very first bills introduced in the House was aimed at one of Sir Edwin's old bugbears, Sir Ferdinando Gorges' patent for fishing in New England waters. The issue had drawn attention in 1621 when, on the last day of the session, Parliament had petitioned the king to free fishing. But Gorges' right to the patent, which restricted the Virginia settlers as well as West Country fishermen, had been reconfirmed in September 1621 and again in November 1622. The question was raised in 1624 on February 25, the first day Sandys was in the House, and it doubtless had his support, combining as it did his distaste for restraint on trade, his attachment to outport demands, and his representation of Virginia.[33]

By the next afternoon, the first of many, Sandys was presiding over a meeting of the Committee on Trade. The establishment of the committee had been approved before Sandys was even in the House, on February 24,

---

[32] Barry E. Supple, *Commercial Crisis and Change in England, 1600–1642* (Cambridge, 1959), 96–99.

[33] *CJ*, 673; Nicholas, *1624*, fol. 20. The Dartmouth merchant William Neale immediately complained that five ships were being detained in Plymouth harbour for having infringed on Gorges' rights (ibid., fol. 21). For the patent, see *APC, 1621–1623*, 51, 340.

in response to Coke's evocation of England's sorry economic condition. Yet by the time the committee met, Sir Edwin was well in command; as a contemporary observed, for this "business he always had the chair."[34] The Monopolies Act, an echo of the 1621 proposal, soon had its own committee, but the Trade Committee remained the gathering place for a multitude of grievances.

In addition to further complaints about Gorges, the meeting of the twenty-sixth heard a major assault on monopolies and impositions by Sir John Eliot, and an endless cataloguing of the reasons for the depression—or, in the terms these legislators instinctively used, of those who were to blame for it. Riots of clothing workers in 1622 had led to the government commission investigating the economy, and the Commons committee hoped to hear its conclusions. In the meantime, current theories were rehearsed by various speakers, ranging from monopolies and taxes to interlopers, the policies of the Merchant Adventurers and the East India Company, and government interference. Sandys extracted a structure from this list of bogeymen when he summarized the allegations as "three principal causes of the decay of trade . . . : 1) the overburthening of trade; 2) the monopolizing of trade or restraining of trade; 3) the want of money which is by transporting of our coin and the importation which so much exceeds the exportation." The second, easily embodied, became the main focus of attention, with the Merchant Adventurers as the prime target.[35]

Sandys reported the discussion of the twenty-sixth to the full House on March 4, and made several requests to advance the committee's business: that they be allowed to meet on Tuesday as well as Thursday afternoons; that Cranfield be asked to report on the committee's work in 1621, when he had been in the chair; and that a bill to forbid the export of wool (a perfect example of the M.P.s' scapegoating) be given speedy attention.[36] And Sandys linked the work on trade with the foreign policy issue that was before the House: his committee, he said, was trying "to enable the subject" to come up with the "great supply" that seemed a "probable" result of the breach of the Spanish treaties. As the different strands of England's economic problems continued to exercise the M.P.s, however, the emphasis turned increasingly toward the restraint of trade. At its March 9

[34] CJ, 672; PRO, SP/14/163/2. On Sandys's chief ally in the monopolies legislation, see Barbara Malament, "The 'Economic Liberalism' of Sir Edward Coke," Yale Law Journal 76 (1967): 1321–1358; and Stephen D. White, Sir Edward Coke and "The Grievances of the Commonwealth," 1621–1628 (Chapel Hill, N.C., 1979), 115–141.

[35] Nicholas, 1624, fols. 25–28. The interest in Gorges receded as the much bigger prize of the Merchant Adventurers came to the fore. Coke's Grievances Committee took up the issue, and included it in the petition of grievances; a bill to overturn Gorges' patent passed the House but died in the Lords.

[36] CJ, 728; Nicholas 1624, fol. 47.

meeting, for instance, the committee heard a multitude of complaints directed at the Merchant Adventurers and the Eastland Company (which controlled trade with the Baltic), and Sandys got the House to require the two companies to bring in their patents and whatever restraining orders they had issued on the basis of those patents. Three days later the Merchant Adventurers were told to bring in all their account books and the court books recording their meetings. At the same time, Edmund Nicholson, the holder of the patent for the pretermitted custom, a new duty on cloth exports, was ordered to produce his patent.[37] The attack on restrainers of trade was taking shape.

These were the days when the discussion of the treaties with Spain was reaching its climax, but that did not divert Sandys's committee. Before the major foreign policy debate on March 19, Sir Edwin got in a report of the current trade investigations, and obtained a series of orders to help him broaden his inquiries: four merchants from every London company were to attend the committee, give their views on the economy, and explain why they opposed the freeing of trade; customs officials were to provide figures on exports and imports; the mint master was to account for the state of coinage; and the Merchant Adventurers were again ordered to bring in their books. These examinations occupied the following week, before the Easter recess, and advanced the bills to free foreign trade, to reestablish an old rival of the Merchant Adventurers, the Merchants of the Staple, and to reduce customs fees. It was only natural, therefore, when the House reassembled on April 1, and began discussing trade, that Sandys should have been asked to report the committee's findings thus far.[38]

The April 1 discussion had begun with Sir Edwin asking for legislation (like a bill that had been suggested in 1621) to stop towns using their charters to raise impositions, or customs duties. When he was then asked for a report from his committee, Coke launched into a disquisition on the cause of England's economic ills; this was politely referred to the committee, and the next day the M.P.s settled down to hear Sandys's enormous report, which took up almost the entire morning.[39] In his usual way, he had his subject matter clearly laid out, with numbered heads. There were, he said, six indications of "the badness of trade," all taken from the cloth

[37] Ibid., fols. 55–56, 80; CJ, 732, 736. Cf. Russell, Parliaments, 199 n., where it is suggested that the pretermitted custom was not mentioned until a week later, March 20. There is no evidence that the attack on the custom led to the attack on the Merchant Adventurers (cf. ibid., 60); the chronology, particularly if the 1621 background is recalled, goes the other way: the new duty was seen as a restraint partly because the great restrainers, the Merchant Adventurers, had agreed to pay it.

[38] Nicholas, 1624, fol. 89; CJ, 740, 747, 749.

[39] Ibid., 751–753; Spring, 1624, 167–168; PRO, SP/14/164, fols. 86, 309, and 14/165, fols. 34, 343.

industry, which suffered from fewer clothiers, poorer materials, falling prices, lack of sales, a decline of exports (by one-third), and a rise in imports (also of a third). The causes were threefold: "1) Restraint of Trade; 2) Over-burthening of Trade; 3) Want of Money." The first two were related, but he placed all his emphasis on the "burthens" which, like the indicators, totaled six items. Three of these, customs duties, tonnage and poundage, and impositions by royal prerogative, could not be touched. But three could be remedied, and these were the chief targets of his report: excessive fees by customs officers, the Merchant Adventurers' charges on their fellow merchants, and some newly created impositions. The bulk of Sir Edwin's report was devoted to the last two matters. He must have been on his feet for something like two hours, and it was his careful accumulation of particulars that gave force to his indictment.

The heart of the Merchant Adventurers' culpability lay in the new patent they had received, more than six years earlier, after the collapse of the Cockayne project. This gave them such complete control of the cloth trade that they had "officers in every port." The result was a steady rise in the imposition they were allowed to levy on the trade, which Sandys estimated to amount to no "less than a 100,000" pounds, a gigantic sum. He wanted the company's accounts examined, and (a sign of new tactics) he wished to know who had approved the patent. Both requests for permission to proceed were approved by the House, but the latter, which raised the issue of a culprit, was crucial, for it signaled the start of an assault on Court referees of patents that was to help bring down Cranfield.

When linked to the sixth of Sir Edwin's "burthens," new impositions, the quest for a miscreant turned inevitably against the treasurer. There were three new impositions, Sandys said, amounting to "60,000 pounds of new Charge to the subject." The first, the pretermitted custom on cloth, had already been raised, and was to be pursued with the patentee, Edmund Nicholson. The other two could be traced directly to Cranfield: on wine, and on grocery as a "composition" for purveyance. Cranfield had rather weakly excused himself by saying that the new book of rates which contained the impositions had been "misprinted: these charges never intended." The wine imposition, moreover, had been intended to support James's unfortunate daughter, and the grocery composition had been intended only for London. Sandys chillingly pointed out that the book was printed by authority; that the wine imposition made no reference to Princess Elizabeth, but was "made perpetual, and no time limited"; and that the grocery composition was laid "upon the outports." The raising of the impositions had been riddled by abuses, and Sir Edwin left their remedy "to the wisdom of the House." But his larger intentions were unmistakable: if unrelieved, these burdens would "tend to the utter destruction of the kingdom"; if they were removed, the consequent surge in trade would more than compensate the king for any revenue lost from canceled impositions.

Weston, chancellor of the exchequer, tried a halfhearted defense of Cranfield, but it must have been apparent to everyone in the House on that April 2 that the scapegoat had been found. Although some of the M.P.s may already have had an inkling of the more serious charge of bribery that was to be raised three days later, this was the decisive moment when the treasurer was first "touched." For Sandys it must have been particularly satisfying to have lit the first warning light, to have set in motion the assault that was to destroy Cranfield. The work on the Spanish treaties was essentially complete, and he had been able to devote the recess to preparing for the major business that lay ahead. That this should have consisted of the attack on Cranfield doubtless reflected Buckingham's wishes, and the duke's help was to be essential to the success of the effort. But Sandys was no stalking horse. There was not a man in England at this moment who had more reason to wish the treasurer ill, none who could have brought more passion and personal commitment to the task. As Sir Edwin saw it, this former friend had been responsible both for his humiliation and imprisonment in 1621, and for the dissolution of his beloved Virginia Company. With the latter process now reaching its climax, Sandys's eagerness for revenge was at a peak; and his animus toward Cranfield was only reinforced by his longstanding pursuit of public grievances. It gives insufficient weight to the Commons' potent indictment to slight the Lower House's contribution to the downfall of the lord treasurer. And it distorts the emotions of the time to call the impeachment Buckingham's sole responsibility. Neither Coke and Phelips, who were to prepare the central charges of bribery, nor Sandys, investigating that old grievance, impositions, were mere agents; their dismay and determination were at least equally responsible for toppling one of James's most able ministers.[40]

It may be, moreover, that Cranfield himself shared this interpretation of the events. On April 5, he told the Lords that there was "a dangerous plot, conspiracy, and combination against him." When called to explain, on April 9, because he could have been understood to be accusing one of his colleagues in the Lords, he strongly denied any such imputation. The reference, he said, was not to any member of the Upper House, a statement that has been dismissed as an evasion, because Cranfield would not have dared name Buckingham openly.[41] Perhaps so, but the the case for evasion is pure conjecture, and it is no less plausible to take Cranfield's words at

---

[40] This view of Sandys's centrality is shared by Menna Prestwich, *Cranfield: Politics and Profits under the Early Stuarts* (Oxford, 1966), 442, 455, 467. Cf. Russell, *Parliaments*, 198, 201.

[41] *LJ*, 3:296; cf. Russell, *Parliaments*, 200.

face value: to assume that the speaker meant what he said. After all, Cranfield had not been cautious in making an enemy of Buckingham in the first place. More to the point, he may have had good reason to know that the conspirators were not in the Lords, because, as we shall see, he was fully aware by April 9 of how ominously Coke, Phelips, and Sandys were uncovering his misdemeanors. It testifies merely to Cranfield's shrewdness if we take literally his implication that the Commons were the source of the danger. Only three years earlier, the initiative that toppled Bacon had been theirs alone. If they now had powerful help that did not make them any less the prime foe.

From April 2, Sandys's two major interests (Cranfield and trade) diverged to some extent, but he sustained the pressure on both fronts, while at the same time continuing the mopping-up on foreign policy. Although both his major activities took up an enormous amount of time, the results, and the means by which they were achieved, can be summarized fairly quickly.

The Destruction of Cranfield

The fullest immediate attention was directed at the lord treasurer, whose case was moved swiftly and expertly through the House. On April 5 Sir Miles Fleetwood, an official in the Court of Wards under Cranfield, presented the charges of bribery and misuse of authority that were to be the core of the campaign against the minister. After much hand-wringing by the M.P.s, notably Phelips and Coke, Sandys cautioned that "every man is presumed to be innocent, till he be proved otherwise." Although he made a quick jab at the misuse of authority, on the whole he kept to this high-minded theme, urging quick investigation of the charges by the Committee on Grievances, because "this will fly over town, and receive diverse constructions." He also insisted that the treasurer or his representative have the right to attend the investigation—a profession of rectitude that made Sandys's own assault so devastating when it came.[42]

During the following week, under the tutelage of Coke and Phelips, a detailed set of charges against Cranfield was prepared. Sandys's only contribution was indirect, a reference to impositions on wine and groceries in the course of a Trade Committee report on April 9. Although Cranfield denied it, these impositions were apparently connected to the lord treasurer, because a leading customs official, Abraham Jacob (currently under questioning about excessive fees), had produced a letter showing that the composition for grocery was being levied under the lord treasurer's warrant. This was the root of a "grievous" burden on the subject, but for the

---

[42] *CJ*, 755.

time being Sir Edwin "delivered no opinion concerning these things."[43] He was setting the scene for his most impassioned speech in this Parliament, three days later, on April 12.

The House had followed Sandys's cue: sensing another serious charge against Cranfield, the M.P.s had responded to Sir Edwin's April 9 trade report by launching an investigation into "who advised the King, and first projected, the issuing out of the authority, concerning this new imposition on wine, sugar, and grocery." They were careful to say they were not re-opening the debate about impositions. The anger was over *new* levies, and it was sure to be aimed, under Sandys's adroit guidance, at Cranfield. As Chamberlain noted the next day, the "matters brought against [Cranfield] hitherto," namely the bribery, "might pass uncensured"; but his haughtiness, his plotting at Court, and his "projects and devices to raise money by the impoverishing of the realm" were his undoing.[44] This was the view Sandys hammered home in his April 12 speech.

Reporting on behalf of those who had investigated the origins of the new impositions, Sir Edwin allowed himself no restraint. There was no doubt, he said, that the new levy on wines originated with the lord treasurer, and that it had been viciously collected: one merchant was told "that unless he would pay the £3 on a tun he should rot in prison." Sandys not only denounced the new impositions, and the manner of their enforcement, but added a deadly twist by making Cranfield a knowing culprit in the impoverishment of England. After all, he had been a member of the 1621 Parliament, which had reached the conclusion that "a principal cause of the decay of trade hath been the overburdening thereof by a multitude of charges," and yet he had added more. The merchant complaints were damning enough, but Sir Edwin intensified them with one of the few emotional pleas of his parliamentary career: "I would willingly suppress all acerbity of speech, which is the breeder of no good blood, but I am commanded contrary in the anguish of [the merchants'] souls and sense of their toil and poverty. They compared the suffering under his Lordship's rigor to the Israelites' brick making in Egypt." That Sandys could resort to such excess was testimony to the strength of his feelings against Cranfield. And the rhetoric worked. Later that day, after the Commons had brushed aside the lord treasurer's quite plausible refutation of the bribery accusation, the new impositions were added to the bill of indictment that a committee was to prepare for the Lords.[45]

[43] Nicholas, *1624*, fols. 128–129; Spring, *1624*, 194; *CJ*, 759.

[44] Ibid., 762; *Chamberlain*, 2:553.

[45] Nicholas, *1624*, fols. 142–143, 147; Spring, *1624*, 206–207; Erle, *1624*, fol. 132; *CJ*, 763, 764; PRO, SP/14/162/49/1 and 14/163/2. That afternoon, after the Grievances Committee discussed Cranfield's sins, Sandys estimated that, on the sugar imposition alone, £4,000 had been "gained to the Lord Treasurer . . . with so much loss to the King." (Erle, *1624*, fol. 135.)

Three days later, on April 15 (less than two weeks after Sandys had unleashed the first threat against Cranfield) the formal indictment was ready. Coke took control of the issues of bribery and malfeasance at the Court of Wards. Sandys took responsibility for the new impositions, though his additions to his brief made his speech the main focus of the House's discussion of the three sets of charges. Before laying out the case, however, Sir Edwin exonerated those whom Cranfield could have claimed as partners in guilt. And the sobriety of tone (in marked contrast to the heated rhetoric of April 12) was a great strength, because the M.P.s had to be careful to offend neither king nor Council, both of whom were deliberately cleared of involvement. James could have argued that impositions were part of his prerogative; the indictment therefore excluded that issue, calling Cranfield's exactions "impositions laid upon impositions," and thus not impositions but "oppression." The Council was freed of blame because Cranfield "was the first propounder of the laying of these oppressions," and it had merely accepted the lord treasurer's supposedly expert advice.

But there was no doubt about the minister's own, deliberate guilt. He had been chosen as chairman of the Committee on Trade by the 1621 Parliament specifically "for the ease and bettering of trade, which his Lordship said he would make his masterpiece." That appointment, to a leadership position Sandys had monopolized, may have rankled, because Sir Edwin turned it cruelly against Cranfield who, he argued, "made no other use thereof but only to devise how he might lay new impositions on merchandises." That was the only low blow in an otherwise straightforward summary of the consequences of the new "oppressions": some merchants "undone," others ready to abandon trade, and all certain they could double their business if the impositions were removed. The ensuing discussion consisted mainly of anger at Cranfield, though it was felt that Sandys had insufficient proof of Cranfield's "aggravations": his responsibility for the "breach" of the previous Parliament. This charge was dropped, but the "oppressions" remained, and the indictment was accepted for forwarding to the Lords.[46]

From that point onward, the destruction of Cranfield was out of the Commons' hands. When Sandys actually presented the charges to the Lords, however, he made some significant changes in the text he had delivered to the Lower House. In the first place, he excused himself with classically feigned reluctance: he was "undesirous of any such employment," because "he had rather defend the innocent than discover the culpable." Yet he was forced to obey the Commons' wishes. Indeed, when he came to the passage where he regretted his "acerbity of speech," he justified himself, not by citing the merchants' anguish and his own emotions, but rather

[46] Nicholas, *1624*. fols. 152–156; Spring, *1624*, 221–226.

by stressing that "the Commons had commanded him to speak." Echoing Chamberlain's judgement, Sandys put prime emphasis on "the want of measure and moderation most men complain of in this great personage." He may have twisted the knife into Cranfield purposely, recalling their quarrel in 1621 about M.P.s in exalted positions; and he ended his indictment on this theme, quoting Ecclesiastes: "If thou seest the oppression of the poor, . . . marvel not at it; for he that is higher than the highest regardeth."[47]

Sandys's friend Southampton, also aggrieved at the fate of the Virginia Company, took a notably prominent part in Cranfield's prosecution, and Sir Edwin himself added a final thrust: in the midst of the lord treasurer's trial he brought from the Commons another charge, the levying of an imposition on hops. Although none of Sandys's accusations appeared in the final verdict against the minister, since the bribes Coke and Phelips documented were the chief cause of his undoing, there is no question that the process which led to the discovery of these bribes (notably in Cranfield's dealings with the wine trade) began with Sir Edwin.

Like others at the time, James vainly warned that the hunting "after other men's lives" was a dangerous pastime, likely to rebound on those who encouraged it. And Cranfield in his final defense, though weakly claiming that he was opposed to all impositions except the two in which he had been involved, rightly traced the root of his troubles, not to his malfeasance, but to "the King's necessity and want of money."[48] From the time of the Great Contract, it had been clear that the Stuarts' means were inadequate to the expanded scale of government in seventeenth-century England. Cranfield was, quite simply, a martyr to the cause that enmeshed his sovereign: the search for new ways to finance the running of a country. The very problems caused by the painful adjustments to a new fiscal situation made an effective reformer like himself, whose activities earned him many enemies, all too vulnerable to the assault by Buckingham and Sandys.

FREEDOM OF TRADE

Sir Edwin may have used his Trade Committee to bring up questions about impositions, and to turn its investigations into an emotional attack on Cranfield's "overburdenings," but its concerns were diverted only temporarily into the campaign against the lord treasurer. The uncovering of ex-

---

[47] Earle, *1624*, fol. 143; *LJ*, 3:309–310. It is possible the quotation was a final twist of the knife, since references to the "highest" and "greatest" are a repeated theme in Sandys's relationship with Cranfield: from the punning salutation in the early letter, when they were still friends, to the first dark moments in the 1621 Commons.

[48] Ibid., 335, 344, 378, 380–381.

cessive charges and restraints in the economy continued after the Easter recess as it had before, and during the remaining weeks of Parliament Sandys put the capstone on his twenty years of investigation into England's trade.

The main target was the Merchant Adventurers, whose books were ordered brought for inspection on April 8. The same order had been issued in 1621, but had been blocked by the king. Now, thanks to Buckingham's intervention, Sandys had his way, and the inspection proceeded. By April 13, however, the inquiry had been diverted into an assault on the pretermitted custom on cloth, a new duty imposed in 1618, which the Merchant Adventurers had been paying. The patentee, Edmund Nicholson, had been questioned, and Sir Edwin's report of the findings did not stint the denunciations: Weymouth merchants had had to pay the equivalent of over four subsidies the previous year; the exaction was "like letting blood of a body that is in a consumption." The harm to trade was unmistakable, but the Commons were now on tricky legal ground. Justification for the levy was drawn from the grant of tonnage and poundage, a matter that could not be too far pursued, entailing as it did questions about the royal prerogative. The same hesitation had restrained the recent Trade Commission, which, though clearly unhappy about the pretermitted custom, had left it alone for fear of encroaching on the prerogative. For the time being, therefore, Nicholson was asked to bring in his patent, but the House agreed to hear legal arguments on behalf of royal privilege.[49] In the event, Noy and Coke demonstrated, with precedents by the gross, that tonnage and poundage was irrelevant, but the House's leisurely pace was to save Nicholson from its wrath. Not until May 19 did he finally deliver up his patent, which then vanished into a committee of lawyers. The M.P.s did manage to condemn the custom, add it to their list of grievances, and request punishment for the patentee, but to no effect. Almost their last decision on the final day they met, May 29, was to return uncondemned patents to their patentees, among whom must have been a relieved Edmund Nicholson.[50]

---

[49] *CJ*, 754, 758, 764–765; Pym, *1624*, fols. 67–69; Spring, *1624*, 212–214; Erle, *1624*, fols. 135–136. The pretermitted custom occupied the Committee for Trade on April 6 (Nicholas, *1624*, fols. 115–117) and the House on April 16 (*CJ*, 768–769). The fullest accounts are Astrid Friis, *Alderman Cockayne's Project and the Cloth Trade* (London, 1927), esp. chap. 6, and Supple, *Crisis*, who estimates (61) that taxes and duties increased the price of shortcloths "by as much as £2"; this suggests Sandys was right to focus on the issue as a cause of economic difficulty. On the free trade legislation in general, see Robert Brenner, *Merchants and Revolution: Commercial Change, Political Conflict, and London's Overseas Traders, 1550–1653* (Cambridge, 1993), 212–217.

[50] *CJ*, 693, 778, 707, 798. The petition of grievances sought punishment for Nicholson in vain.

On the larger issue of restraint of trade, Sandys's efforts were not without reward. His prime targets, the regulated companies, did not get off as easily as Nicholson. By April 23, when Sandys reported to the House, a long line of companies had been called before his committee; he was eventually to examine trade to most parts of the world, from Spain to the East Indies. The investigations must have continued just about every afternoon during April, whenever time could be found from such pressing matters as the Spanish treaties or the attack on Cranfield. But about the main concern, the Merchant Adventurers, Sandys could report on the twenty-third.[51]

Sir Edwin's economic policy throughout his years in Parliament was two-fold: to open trading companies to anyone who wished to join them, and to reduce as far as possible the duties and impositions that raised prices and hampered the marketplace. Both aims were aspects of his commitment to the notion that, the less it was restricted, the more trade would flourish. For his own urgent purposes, when the viability of the Virginia Company was threatened, he abandoned these principles, placing his hopes on a tobacco monopoly to save a struggling enterprise. But even here he might have claimed consistency, pointing to the newness of the Jamestown venture as justification for special support: a distinction that the Monopolies Act of this very Parliament was to enshrine in a statute that allowed exceptions for new inventions. The basic themes he had sounded since 1604 were thus heard at full volume by the Trade Committee of 1624.

The difficulty Sandys ran into was a conflict between his two aims as they applied to the Merchant Adventurers. The company acknowledged that it did not permit easy access, for it could hardly deny the dozens of complaints against its arbitrary actions and impositions from the outports and other sectors of the cloth industry. But the directors for their part pointed not only to the many duties they themselves suffered under, but also to foreign discrimination, notably the special duties imposed on their cloths in the Netherlands. The result was that there was not enough trade to go round. In principle, they liked the privileges granted by the Crown to patentees, and the pretermitted customs, no better than did the Commons; indeed, said Sandys, "they much complain." To ease conditions, therefore, they offered a deal. They would open their membership for a fee, even though "1800 of their company" could find no trade, but in return they wanted their charter confirmed, support against competing merchants, and relief from duties, officers' fees, and other levies on the cloth trade.

This proposal was taken seriously, but Sir Edwin thought it important to stress that the squabbles among different merchant groups had to be resolved, that the impositions the Merchant Adventurers themselves raised

---

[51] Erle, *1624*, fols. 156–158; *CJ*, 689, 773.

were impermissible, and that their own patent had to be considered a grievance. Nevertheless, he did agree that the House ought to try to reduce the duties, stop abuses in general (for instance, in the dyeing industry, which he was investigating), and in particular examine the activities of the alnager, an official who collected fees for inspecting cloth. It looked as though the Merchant Adventurers could be left in business if the various restrictions were removed, and Sandys therefore had a special twelve-man committee appointed (including himself, Calvert, Cavendish, and Digges) to negotiate the issues with the company.[52]

The discussions continued almost to the very end of the parliamentary session. A first report, given at great length by Sandys on April 30, indicated that the M.P.s were sympathetic to the company's wish to reduce customs duties, and were willing to raise them as grievances before the king. But they were adamantly opposed to the company's own impositions and to its exclusiveness. Trade in finished cloth had to be opened up, and in unfinished cloth the Merchant Adventurers could have only the first purchase rights: if they did not buy goods from producers within six weeks, any merchant could do so. The M.P.s accepted the recommendations on impositions and finished cloths, but wanted to discuss the Merchant Adventurers' control over the export of finished cloth more fully. This they did on May 5 and 10 when, despite warnings about the danger of undermining all regulation of trade, Sandys and others insisted that at least some reform was needed. Without wishing to dissolve the company, Sir Edwin said, he felt that "the Merchant Adventurers have so gotten trade into their own hands that it resteth much in rectifying of them to amend trade." The Commons agreed, and voted to open up the trade in finished cloth. The following week, on May 19, the other elements of Sandys's recommendations were accepted: the six-week advantage for the company in unfinished cloth, and a petition to James against the company's patent, foreign impositions, and various fees and duties. Sir Edwin and Nicholas Ferrar were to draw up the petition.[53]

The result, in the words of Astrid Friis, was that the issue "was preferred with such energy [by the Commons] that the King and Councillors . . . dared not neglect it." The Commission for Trade was ordered to negotiate reforms with the company, and in July they were put into effect by order of the Privy Council. The trade was opened to any merchant who paid the appropriate fee, and although the reduction of duties was more promised

---

[52] Ibid. (and 771 on the dyers).

[53] Ibid., 695, 698–699, 702, 706, 778, 783–784, 787, 791; Nicholas, *1624*, fol. 192. Sandys and Ferrar also combined on the clothworkers and alnager petitions, which suggests they may have worked together on the entire petition of trade grievances at the end of the session: *CJ*, 709.

than implemented, the Merchant Adventurers' own impositions were reduced. As Friis sums it up, "That the Merchant Adventurers voluntarily consented to all these concessions shows that the perpetual attacks in Parliament which were now backed up by the Government, as well as their stagnating trade, had made them meek."[54] In other words, twenty years of effort by Sandys now bore fruit, thanks to the arrangement with Buckingham. Trade was by no means free, but it was certainly freer than before.

By the time of the decision to proceed by petition, little more than a week remained in the session. The M.P.s had heard on May 4 that the king intended to prorogue them on the twenty-second, and on the nineteenth Sir Edwin (having ensured that the major committees on grievances, justice, and trade would have their progress approved by the House) took to the Lords a request for further time, justified by the efforts given to the subsidy and "the great business of trade now in hand." The Lords interceded with Prince Charles, and (this being 1624) succeeded: Parliament was given an extra week, which Sandys managed to put to good use.[55]

Sir Edwin gave the last hectic days almost completely over to trade. He did help with some details concerning Cranfield, and in completing charges against Thomas Anyan (the president of his old college, Corpus Christi, and soon to be chaplain to Charles I), whose offences ranged from financial malfeasance to "unnatural lust with some tavern boys." But his chief endeavor was to put before the Commons the trade abuses he had been investigating. A major culprit, the alnager, was condemned, and a series of companies—the Eastland, the Ginny and Binny (trading to Africa), the Turkey, and the Spanish—were marked either as guilty or as victims of various abuses. The first two excluded people from trade, the third was subject to unwarranted impositions, and the Spanish merchants were importing the tobacco that hurt the Virginia Company. There were also difficulties concerning clothworkers and customs farmers, and a duty on wine known as prisage. All had to be included in the petition of grievances, and only a frantic scramble enabled the M.P.s to complete the document by the time the king had them attend him with their grievances on May 28.[56]

---

[54] Friis, *Cockayne's Project*, 429–431. Sir Francis Nethersole said Sandys's pursuit had given "the last deadly strike to the Merchant Adventurers": PRO, SP/14/661/165.

[55] *CJ*, 706, 707, 790, 791; Nicholas, *1624*, fols. 190–191, 208–210. In Sandys's words, "unless there be some addition of time for our sitting we shall have an exclusion instead of a conclusion" (ibid., fol. 208).

[56] *CJ*, 707–715, esp. 714 (Cranfield), 707, 713 (Anyan), 709 (alnager), 710 (companies), 711 (other grievances), 713 (audience with the king); Erle, *1624*, fols. 187 (Anyan), 191–195 (trade). Sandys called "the universities and their discipline much corrupted," and Anyan "a notorious and incorrigible offender." He also took on dozens of other matters: the brief assault on impositions; fees charged by boroughs; bankruptcy; corn exports; the East India

Trade also spilled over into Coke's Committee on Grievances. When, on May 26, eleven grievances were accepted by the House, they included Gorges' fishing patent and the Staplers Company's misuse of its patent. The latter appeared so late it could not be included among the thirteen items presented to the king, but it did indicate that the removal of restraints on trade had also concerned Coke's committee. Sandys followed Coke with a list almost as long: nine subjects, all of which were presented to the king on a separate roll on May 28. The consequences of these efforts were perhaps more general than specific: as J.P. Cooper put it, "a number of informed and acceptable compromises on economic policy between government and Commons." As he noted, the Commission for Trade took the grievances seriously, and the result was a set of actions (including acceptance of the monopolies bill, regulation of the Merchant Adventurers and the cloth trade, restraint in patents, and measures dealing with foreign tobacco and the export of wool) that suggest the harmony of 1624 had more effect in economic than in political affairs. For the good will did not extend to James himself, who used the occasion of the presentation of the petition to complain, as he often had before, about the "Tribunitian orators among you."[57]

GAINS, LOSSES, AND AFTERMATH

The acceptance, at least to some degree, of Sandys's long-standing economic program was a major consequence of his "undertaking" agreement with Buckingham in 1624—an outcome that only strengthens the conclusion that the balance of benefits in the arrangement was fairly even. The destruction of Cranfield, the passage of so many old bills, and the impact of the trade grievances—these were notable victories for the Commons, for which little price was paid. Rather than seeing the deal with Buckingham as "a major blow to back-bench 'country' sentiment," therefore, one must see the events of 1624 as an enormous achievement for the

---

Company's patent; the monopolies bill; Gorges' fishing patent; Coke's Grievances Committee, on which he sat; collection of the subsidy; recusants; House concerns like the journal, constituencies, elections, and privileges; private bills; and the shaping of proceedings as messenger to the Lords, teller of votes, reporter of conferences, and penner of documents: *CJ*, 751, 787, 709, 793, 744, 695, 692, 777, 674, 688, 719, 690, 708, 762, 788, 792, 696, 781, 680, 731, 683, 734, 697, 725, 720, 674, 718, 756; Nicholas, *1624*, fols. 137, 82, 173, 176, 21, 115, 118, 180. See too Cogswell, *Revolution*, 161.

[57] *CJ*, 711–712, 714, 797; Nicholas, *1624*, fols. 242–243 and 228–229; Northamptonshire Record Office, Montague Papers, 26, fol. 21. On the tobacco grievance: Spring, *1624*, fol. 226; J. P. Cooper, "The Fall of the Stuart Monarchy," chap. 8 in *The New Cambridge Modern History*, vol. 4 (Cambridge, 1970), 551–552. Although the Commons wanted the monopolies bill to apply to both companies and individuals, the Lords restricted it to the latter.

Jacobean "patriots". The duke and prince certainly gained significantly, but there was advantage to both sides. It is only by viewing the developments from the perspective of the Court, rather than in the context of twenty years of Commons history, that the benefits appear one-sided.[58]

It is true that both Phelips and Sandys played a rather unseemly role in the confirmation, by 168 to 143 votes, of Buckingham's possession of York House. "Never bishop of York did yet receive any benefit or profit of this House," Sandys said disingenuously, and his opinion, as the son of an archbishop, undoubtedly helped Buckingham carry the day.[59] If that was the only position Sir Edwin had to take against his conscience, then the cost of the duke's support was trivial by comparison with its dividends.

On Virginia, however, the alliance with duke and prince proved fruitless. Sir Edwin did manage to secure for the colony the vital monopoly of tobacco imports, a concession he gained as a result of pleas by both the Commons and (orchestrated by Sandys) the settlers in Jamestown. That monopoly was not only to save the settlement, but was to turn it at last into a highly profitable enterprise. Ironically, the joyous news that it had been approved reached the company at its very last recorded meeting, on June 7; it thus proved to be Sir Edwin's farewell gift to Virginia. For the final desperate attempt to use the Commons, and their anger at Cranfield, as a means of preventing the dissolution of the company, had been blocked by James himself. On April 21 the company had approved a petition to the Commons asking for help against the machinations which Cranfield, "out of his private and most unjust ends," had devised to destroy the colony, deceive the king, ruin England's trade, and endanger the liberty of all Englishmen. James got wind of this approach, and a week later wrote to the speaker forbidding the M.P.s "to trouble themselves with those matters." It was too late for Buckingham or Charles to help, the Commons accepted the royal command, and the Virginia Company's last hope was gone.[60]

Whether Sandys would have exchanged all the legislative successes, especially on trade, plus the destruction of Cranfield, for the preservation of the Virginia Company, one can only speculate. The last agonies of his cherished project must have made the spring and summer of 1624 a painful time. And yet the company had been a major commitment for only five years. By contrast, the accomplishments of 1624 marked the climax of a

[58] Cogswell, *Revolution*, 150.

[59] *CJ*, 797; Nicholas, *1624*, fols. 235–236; Esther S. Cope, "The Bishops and Parliamentary Politics in Early Stuart England," *Parliamentary History* 9 (1990): 8. In addition to his father's ex officio connection with the site, Sir Edwin himself had taken a lease on York House (see above, chapter 1, note 27).

[60] Kingsbury, 2:540, 526–528, 4:477–478; PRO, SP/14/164/46/3; *CJ*, 691, 694.

twenty-year parliamentary effort. Whether or not the pleasure outweighed the sadness, as the best and worst of spring seasons in Sir Edwin's long public career came to an end, he may have seen that the Virginia loss (particularly since the colony itself had been saved) was outshone by the triumph of the Commons.

It is true that, despite the huge outpouring of legislation, he was still worried about what remained undone, since it was "a great dishonour to this House, to dismiss so many suitors and attendants without any satisfaction"—as if the clamor of petitioners could ever have been satisfied. Nevertheless, his prominence and his successes in the House, and his commitment to the belief that Parliament was the great remedy for Englishmen's ills, made it seem likely that he would be one of the parliamentary treasurers appointed to supervise the collection and distribution of the 1624 subsidy. But he put paid to that idea by saying that he "had rather be sent to the Tower or pay £500 than to be one of the treasurers." He predicted that the position would make him "obnoxious to the displeasure of the King," and would force him to spend all summer in London, a consideration that led finally to the appointment of London merchants.[61]

If Sir Edwin in the summer of 1624 entertained the belief that his partnership with Charles and Buckingham might lead to major royal office, he may have drawn hope from the king's approval, given in August, for his membership in the Academy Royal, an institution similar to Sir Robert Cotton's defunct Society of Antiquaries that was being organized by Edmund Bolton to oversee the writing of history in England.[62] For the weary and possibly ailing James seemed to have little fight left in him to resist the demands of his son and his favorite. He did not prevent the autumn marriage treaty with France which, in order to give Charles his revenge against Spain, offered concessions on Catholicism that Parliament (which had expected to be consulted) could never have allowed. That betrayal began the erosion of the alliance between prince and Commons, a process that accelerated as it became clear that their petitions of grievance prompted little but indifference. Very soon they were to realise how exceptional and misleading the events of 1624 had been.

But those problems lay in the future. During the months of the prince's and the duke's ascendancy, Sir Edwin's hopes of favor must have been high, and they must have peaked in March 1625, when James died. The silence of the records about his whereabouts and activities after June 1624 suddenly gives way to new speculations. Surely one of the beneficiaries of

[61] *CJ*, 730, 766, 780, 783, 694, 779; Nicholas, *1624*, fols. 54, 205, 216.

[62] David Berkowitz, *John Selden's Formative Years* (Washington, D.C., 1988), 80–82. The academy, which Berkowitz sees as a potential arm of censorship, was prevented from coming into being by the death of its chief patron, James himself, the following year.

the new reign of Charles I would be Sandys, that capable and experienced ally. In the event, though, the expectations (if Sir Edwin ever allowed himself to share them) proved unfounded. With the death of James I, Sandys's public career, so closely associated with the first Stuart reign, faded rapidly into the shadows of old age and decline.

Chapter XI

FAREWELL TO PARLIAMENT

THE END OF AN ERA

The death of James I marked the end of an era in English political life. Despite his shifting relationship with the Commons, he had managed his relations with his subjects with more than a little success. When he felt he had to back down, as in the impeachment of Bacon or the breaking-off of the treaties with Spain, he did so with reasonable grace. But he also got his own way on dozens of issues, such as peace abroad, because when crucial moments arrived he did not allow his high-flown notions of royal power to determine his actions. Even a pet project like the Union was allowed to die when it ran into major difficulties. James did not forget troublemakers like Sandys, but he was no remorseless enemy, and he managed to maintain respect and equilibrium in dealing with those who felt the country's policies were mistaken.

That the balance—the sense of contact, of large areas of compromise— did not long survive the succession of his son is the best indication of why 1625 marked the end of an era. As the linkages began to fray, confrontation soon replaced argument, and eventually civil war replaced domestic peace. James's balance was not the same as Elizabeth's, and perhaps Charles's was bound to differ again. But the situation under James was no mere transition. This was an authentic stage in the relations between the Crown and the political nation, pregnant with implications to be sure, but distinct and fruitful nevertheless: a unique period of nascent cooperation between government and subject that made possible (as the reigns before and after James did not) Sandys's remarkable career. There was to be a leap in kind, not degree, when England's "Establishment," hitherto held together in endless permutations, disintegrated into hostile camps. Much of the fault must be laid on Charles, and to the degree that the signs of trouble began to mount early in his reign, it seems appropriate to consider the start of his rule as a major political landmark. In 1625 one passes from the lively, disputatious, aggressive, but still homogeneous politics of the first Stuart to the bitter, resentful, and vindictive politics of the second.

It might have seemed that Sandys was perfectly placed to benefit from the change in monarchs. The evidence of Buckingham's support in the elections of 1625, 1626, and 1628 suggests that his connection with the duke remained in force. And there was a brief rumor early in Charles's reign that Sandys would be named secretary of state.[1] But it was not to be. Instead, the last four years of his life, from 1625 to 1629, saw the virtual eclipse of Sir Edwin's public career. The Virginia Company was gone, and in the Commons he contented himself with an occasional speech on one of his trademark issues, such as the economy or religion, and memberships but not major chairmanships of committees. As "Father" of the House in 1626, with the longest memory of sessions of any M.P., he was doubtless consulted about procedures and precedents. Those who now led the way, like Digges and Eliot, had seen him perform, and doubtless had learned their tactics from him. But they hardly needed his help, and on many central concerns he might have been less than helpful—when his kinsman Digges, for example, headed the campaign to impeach Buckingham. These were twilight years for Sandys—partly, perhaps because of fading health; perhaps, too, because the growing polarization of the Commons was uncongenial to his determinedly reasoned outlook; and possibly because the association with Buckingham reduced his status in the House.

The Parliament of 1625

There were still to be three Parliaments in Sandys's lifetime: in 1625, 1626, and 1628. In each one he had difficulty finding a seat, and the surest indication that his career was over was his failure to win a place in the Commons in 1628, despite pressure from Buckingham on the borough of Sandwich. These elections were not as stormy as the one in 1624, but Sir Edwin found little support in Kent. If Chamberlain is to be believed, he lost the county in 1625 by a margin of three to one, despite an uncharacteristic harangue—a "speech none of the wisest"—and much caviling at the sheriff's bias. He also failed in Sandwich and Maidstone. The most authoritative student of the elections of the 1620s has implied that Sandys may have given promises to his neighbors about taxation in order to win a seat. But the evidence—an obscure suggestion that Sir Edwin's 1625 support in Kent vanished the following year because he broke his promise and endorsed a subsidy early in the 1625 session—is curious in light of the feeble support that he did receive. Since only a quarter of the electorate voted for Sandys, one can doubt how important his promises to a few nonconstituents were a year later.[2]

---

[1] N. E. McClure, ed., *The Letters of John Chamberlain* (Philadelphia, 1939), 2:613.

[2] Ibid., 615, 617; Derek Hirst, *The Representatives of the People? Voters and Voting in England under the Early Stuarts* (Cambridge, 1975), 174, citing Bodleian MS. Rawl. A. 346, fol. 233: Thomas Scott's account of the 1626 Kent election, partially published in G. D. Scull, *Dorothea Scott* (Oxford, 1883), 131–143. Scott describes Digges's effort to prevent Sandys (a juggler, a fool, and a knave) from being elected—probably in retaliation for his own loss in 1624. Scott says Sandys "deserted and even betrayed us and our freehold contrary to his own

In any case, not only was Sir Edwin rebuffed in Kent, but his son, despite a letter from Buckingham, had no luck in his neighboring borough of Sandwich. Even a letter from Dorset had no effect on the Kentish electors. In the end Sir Edwin had to rely on Sir Robert Killigrew, a former associate in the Virginia Company and an acolyte of Buckingham, who had influence in the faraway Cornish borough of Penryn. As Thomas Scott, who had been as unsuccessful as Sandys in standing for Kent in 1625, put it, "Sir Edwin Sandys had never seen Penryn, nor knew the name of it, he told me, nor was a freeman there, nor chosen there; but by Sir Robert Killigrew, at London; who, for that purpose, or to put in some other, if Sir Edwin had sped elsewhere, brought up a blank in his pocket." It was not the most glorious of routes into the Commons, but it worked in 1625 and again in 1626, when even a recommendation to Buckingham to pack the Kent electorate with navy men proved futile. Then, in 1628, Sandys tried for Sandwich himself. "I thought good to tender my service unto you," he wrote. And Buckingham added his support: "you will have just cause to thank me for recommending him." But the mayor, for all his efforts, had to report nervously that the nomination "bred such a distraction, that we could have no power over" the burgesses. Sir Edwin's parliamentary career was over.[3]

That it was coming to an end was apparent not only on the hustings, but in the House itself. As the historian of John Eliot's parliamentary career noted, Sandys was remarkably quiet in 1625. He was even more so in 1626, but there seems little political meaning in the change, though Ball has suggested that Sandys, despite his reluctance to return to the "popular" cause, hesitated to support royal policy, and thus presumably sat on the fence, while Russell has characterized him simply as "Buckingham's ally."[4] What seems more likely is that he was finding the daily give-and-take less

---

engagement and handwriting"(142), which could refer to the subsidy, though the allusion is unclear. People may have been upset that Sir Edwin missed the 1625 Oxford session entirely—thus "deserting" them and giving their freeholds inadequate representation. See Richard Cust, "Politics and the Electorate in the 1620s," in *Conflict in Early Stuart England: Studies in Religion and Politics, 1603–1642* ed. Richard Cust and Ann Hughes (London, 1989), 134–167, esp. 152–154, 161–162.

[3] BL, Additional, 37,619, fol. 11 (Buckingham for Sandys's son); BL, Stowe, 743, fol. 64 (Dorset); Centre for Kentish Studies, Thomas Scott MSS., fol. 19, and Sandwich MSS., Misc. Correspondence, SA/ZB2, nos. 102 and 103 (Sandys and Buckingham to Sandwich mayor); Scull, *Scott*, 127 (the call for "all those of the navy to be there"); PRO, SP/16/18, fols. 28, 60, and 16/95, fol. 67. Sandys himself wrote in support of his "friends and kinsmen" Sir Thomas Finch and Sir Edward Dering for the county seats in 1628: Centre for Kentish Studies, U.350, C.2/18, a reference I owe to Peter Salt.

[4] J. N. Ball, "The Parliamentary Career of Sir John Eliot, 1624–1629" (Ph.D. diss., Cambridge University, 1953), 76; Conrad Russell, *Parliaments and English Politics, 1621–1629* (Oxford, 1979), 248.

congenial as antagonisms rose, and that he was getting old and tired. A more complex interpretation risks becoming an argument from silence.

Still, some of the old spirit and the old interests continued to animate Sandys. The 1625 Parliament was convened on June 18, amidst fear of plague, which may explain why there is no sign of Sir Edwin until the 23rd, when he was appointed to four committees, including one on recusants that was to become his main interest.[5] This narrow focus reflects his receding commitment to the House's affairs, though his work on religion did play a significant part in the session.

The state of religion had been raised in Charles's opening address, responding to demands "for the restraint of Priests and Jesuits." On the second full day of business, June 23, the Commons appointed a committee, from which there emerged an assignment to Sandys and Pym to draw up a petition "concerning religion." The choice of these two men created a fine historical coincidence; a pairing of the old with the new, the Commons leaders of past and future. And there could hardly have been a less likely combination: Sandys the staid middle-of-the-roader, the conservative but irenic friend of Hooker and Pilgrims alike, inclined to order and orderliness, suspicious of Calvin and perhaps a proto-Arminian, working in conjunction with his more radical and Puritanical young colleague, a future leader of revolution. Sandys's and Pym's petition stands as the last landmark of a Jacobean era that had been notable for comprehensiveness despite difference, for argument within unity—qualities of its religious as well as its political life. It was a final combined assault on a common enemy, the Catholics, through reforms that were still acceptable to a broad spectrum of Protestant opinion. That it was the end of the era became clear when, on the very day Pym was assigned to prepare the petition, he sparked an anti-Arminian explosion that forced the antagonisms within Protestantism into open hostility.[6]

The petition itself is very much Sir Edwin's handiwork. It was he who first suggested the structure it ought to take and the topics it ought to cover. Moreover, the final document is divided into the complex series of numbered points—six reasons for the rise of popery, and two types of remedy, one under six heads and the second under fourteen—that was Sandys's hallmark.[7] Also close to his heart would have been the attacks on the influence of foreign Catholics that opened the petition, and the use of

[5] Russell, *Parliamentary*, 205–206, 213–214, 219; HMC, *Manuscripts of the House of Lords*, n.s. 11 (Henceforth *HL*), 181, 183, 184, 186. See too G. A. Harrison, "Innovation and Precedent: A Procedural Reappraisal of the 1625 Parliament," *English Historical Review* 102 (1987), 31–62.

[6] S. R. Gardiner, ed., *Debates in the House of Commons in 1625*, Camden Society, n.s., vol. 6 (London, 1873), 4, 12, 18.

[7] Ibid., 18–25; *HL*, 205, 206.

Corpus's president, Dr. Anyan, a target in 1624, as the exemplar of the decline of godliness at the universities. Beyond these obvious signatures, it is likely that the emphasis on the failings of education as a cause of the decline in the Anglican Church reflected Sandys's views, just as the stress on nonresidencies and pluralities (of which Sir Edwin and his family had been guilty) probably came from Pym. The wish for more effective execution of the laws against recusancy was an old hobbyhorse of Sir Edwin's (though shared by most M.P.s), and it became the heart of the petition. The document rang the alarm about the rising confidence of the recusants; it pointed to plausible reasons for weakness in the English Church; and it suggested appropriately stern measures of repression to resolve an alarming problem. The overall moderation not only reflects Sandys's participation, but suggests the breadth of agreement about major religious issues that was still apparent in 1625. Both the writers, and the House as a whole, could unite over the remedies for the problem, in terms of education, better conditions for ministers, and greater severity against Catholics. Such agreement about solutions, let alone about the nature of the difficulty, was not to be much in evidence during subsequent months and years.

A few of the details of the petition were eventually amended, but in all essentials Sandys's and Pym's document passed the House. It was forwarded to the king, and eventually received a favorable reception from him, though not until the Oxford session, when Sir Edwin was no longer present.[8] By then, however, the Commons were enmeshed in the disputes over Arminianism and the request for further subsidies that were to bring the entire Parliament to an acrimonious end. Sir Edwin had thus played a major role in an important episode which was to fade in significance only because relations between king and Commons deteriorated so rapidly.

A good part of Sandys's other activities in this session also had to do with religion in some form. He took part in the effort to have a public fast proclaimed, and he was considered for the chairmanship of the Committee of the Whole on Religion when objections were raised to Sir Robert Heath's being chairman, because he was solicitor-general and thus a servant of the king. That Sandys allowed his name to be put forward against Heath, and remained in contention during a quarrel that "distracted" the House, suggests that he was no mere ally of Buckingham or anyone else at Court.[9]

Heath won the day, but Sir Edwin remained involved in the issue, helping draw up the final recusant petition and two other bills dealing with religion. And he gave an alarming report about priests and Jesuits more

[8] Gardiner, *1625*, 69, 95.

[9] *CJ*, 799, 851; Russell, *Parliaments*, 239; *CJ*, 851; HMC, *Cowper*, 1:271; Gardiner, *1625*, 26.

than doubling in number since Elizabeth's death.[10] Yet after this first week of full, even strenuous activity—not unlike his contributions to earlier Parliaments—Sandys faded from the scene, and did so just when he might have needed to be particularly alert in his own defense. For an anti-Arminian campaign was gathering strength, and one knowledgeable colleague thought Sir Edwin might find himself tainted by the assault. The comment is not without its ambiguities, but John Pym's first reference in his Commons diary to Richard Montague (of whose Arminianism he was to be the most persistent and best-informed assailant) described Montague's offending book as an attempt to reconcile Catholics and Protestants, and continued, "Another book printed of the conversion of the late Bishop of London and dispersed, wherein Sir Ed. Sandes is likewise touched."[11]

The precise meaning of that remark cannot be determined, but a few of its implications can be disentangled. The book on the bishop of London, John King, who was rumored to have converted to Catholicism on his deathbed, was George Musket's *The Bishop of London his Legacy*.[12] This effort to demonstrate the superiority of Roman traditions, and their appeal to Anglicans, drew on a large body of Protestant writings, from Luther onward, to make its case. Since Musket's aim was to find passages complimentary to Catholicism, Sandys's *Relation* was an obvious source, and indeed he came up with two quotations to bolster his own views. This was hardly a major part of Musket's tome, which drew far more heavily on authorities of greater note, such as Hooker and Bishop Jewel. Yet Sandys was certainly included, and even praised—as "a man of great eminency among us" and, more surprisingly, as "a great master in Israel." The quoted passages were fairly trivial: a critique of Protestant exaggerations about Catholic practices, and a suggestion that charity would allow Protestants to find some parts of Catholicism "singular helps for increase of godliness and devotion."[13] Yet there is no question that these comments fairly reflected Sir Edwin's outlook, and that he did provide grist for an apologist's mill. Although he was not actually cited in the major book at issue, Montague's *Apello Caesarem*, Pym was by no means unfair to suggest the linkage by his use of the word "likewise." Montague drew heavily on Sandys's close friend Hooker, and Sandys's own views were sufficiently similar to warrant at least an implicit connection.

What, then, is one to conclude from this tantalizing reference? Was Pym indicating the means whereby he hoped to arouse the anger of a fellow M.P., with whom he was at that very time preparing the petition on reli-

---

[10] *HL*, 26.

[11] Gardiner, *1625*, 26.

[12] Published in St. Omer in 1623.

[13] George Musket, *The Bishop of London his Legacy* (St. Omer, 1623), 116–117, 124.

gion? Did the two discuss the references to the *Relation*, and did Pym think he might win a powerful colleague to the anti-Arminian side? The use of the word "touched" might imply that the book brought opprobrium on Sandys or that Pym had doubts about his fellow M.P.; either way, at a time of rising anger at Arminians, it could have provided another reason for Sir Edwin's withdrawal from center stage. His one speech on the subject was certainly on Montague's behalf, defending him against a charge of contempt of Parliament. This arose from the accusation that *Appello Caesarem* had been published without the approval of the archbishop of Canterbury, even though the archbishop had, at Parliament's behest, reprimanded Montague for an earlier book. Sandys pointed out that this might have given the archbishop cause for action, but could hardly be construed as contempt of Parliament, since the House had not been in touch with Montague directly. This view, accepted by the Commons, shows that Sandys was not loath to defend the Arminian, or any less able than before to influence his colleagues.[14]

As in the past, Sir Edwin was trying to moderate extremist zeal, but as the case unfolded, demonstrating the speed of change in England's religious situation, he may have concluded that he had no stomach for such a fight. If, as seems plausible, he was to miss the second session because of ill health—he was to be absent for this reason for a long part of the 1626 Parliament as well—he may already have been feeling the strain. A week of activity at his old pace may have taken a toll, and thereafter he faded from view. If Pym's notation reflected a hope that Sir Edwin might join a campaign against the Arminians who had "touched" his reputation, he was soon disappointed as it became apparent that Sandys's irenicism was unchanged, and that in any case his energies were not up to the hard toil of parliamentary leadership.

Sir Edwin also spent time on financial affairs. The subsidy, trade, and the economy did not become major issues until the Oxford session, but he was involved in all of them during the brief period he was in the House.[15] He joined in the subsidy discussion on June 30, though not as the Crown supporter that the Kent electors supposedly considered him. He agreed with the many who felt that two subsidies and no fifteenths were sufficient, and he even suggested that the payments be stretched out into the following year. The latter idea was picked up by other speakers, and accepted in the final resolution. This was barely more than "a derisory sum," as Russell calls it, and contrasts Sandys with his electoral patron Killigrew, who sought four fifteenths.[16]

[14] *CJ*, 805; Gardiner, *1625*, 52–53.

[15] *HL*, 184, 198, 199, 200.

[16] Ibid., 197; Gardiner, *1625*, 32; Russell, *Parliaments*, 225. Sandys suggested the second

Sir Edwin also raised questions about Charles's accounting for the 1624 subsidy. He gave the official report to the House on July 1, the day after the new subsidy was voted, and he led the objections to one aspect of the accounts. Instead of paying for the troops raised in each locality out of the subsidy, as the 1624 act had required, the government had raised additional local military rates. "In the County of Kent," said Sandys, it had "levied half a subsidy" for this purpose, above and beyond what it should have obtained. This classic defense of county privilege became an increasingly important concern, but again only after Sir Edwin's withdrawal from the House.[17]

Finally, it was Sandys who brought up the subject of impositions. He was given his regular task of looking into hindrances to trade, and the first large instance that arose was the impost on wines. Outport merchants had petitioned against it, asserting it was raised without their consent. They were not bound by London merchants, they said, and in any case were subject only to parliamentary legislation. Sir Edwin recalled that the imposition had been a grievance against Cranfield, and urged that it be condemned again by the Commons. When it was, the complaint was rejected by Charles, who claimed that the proceeds supported his sister, the queen of Bohemia. But by then the damage had been done. As Russell has shown, it was the question of impositions that drifted inexorably into the much larger quarrel over customs in 1625: the issue of tonnage and poundage. But once again, though Sandys had taken a crucial part at the beginning, he was no longer in the House when the affair reached its climax.[18]

Indeed, after July 1 (just eight days after he first appeared in the parliamentary record) Sir Edwin essentially vanished from notice. It had been quite a hectic period, not unlike the opening days of earlier Parliaments. But this time his work came to an end just as he was gathering steam. He may well have been in the Commons on July 4 to hear Charles's lengthy replies to the petitions of grievance of 1624, and have been pleased by the positive response to the request to ban foreign tobacco, which was to prove the salvation of Virginia. But his only other recorded intervention was his support, on July 9, for a suggestion by the Lords to allow the prisoners in the Fleet habeas corpus so as to escape the plague.[19]

---

subsidy be paid the following February. Cf. Russell, who interprets this to mean that Sandys expected the House to vote more after Christmas (ibid., 226).

[17] Gardiner, *1625*, 35–36; *HL*, 199; *CJ*, 804; Russell, *Parliaments*, 223.

[18] *HL*, 200–201; Gardiner, *1625*, 35–36, 62; *CJ*, 804, 807; Russell, *Parliaments*, 228 and n. Sandys was on the committee that drew up the preamble to the tonnage and poundage bill, but there is no other evidence of his involvement: *CJ*, 804.

[19] Gardiner, *1625*, 37–41, 65. His one other assignment was on the committee for continuation of statutes: *CJ*, 804.

Sir Edwin did not turn up for the August session, though it is recorded that he was admitted to the House on the first day despite not having taken Communion: a reference that must be incorrect, given the absence of any other mention of Sandys. Charles had already "heard the House was very thin" in London in July, and perhaps Sir Edwin was among the many who wished to escape the plague.[20] Yet it seems unlikely that, having traveled to Westminster and taken an active role until July 9, he would then have developed a belated fear of the plague. One has to assume that he simply no longer had the energy to enter the lists as the stirring debates of July 1625 unfolded. And his silence in 1626 was directly linked to illness. That final Parliament of his long career felt his presence only slightly more than had his first Parliament, forty years before.

THE PARLIAMENT OF 1626

The great business of the Parliament of 1626 was the attempt to destroy Buckingham. As in 1625, there is no evidence of Sandys trying to curry favor with the duke, despite the latter's electoral patronage. It is true that he spoke only four times on the issue, yet his silence has to be attributed to his failing strength, not to political motivations. For even though his few interventions were hardly defenses of Buckingham, the minister's electoral support continued in 1628, and Sir Edwin remained in touch with the Court immediately after the Parliament. The inherent cohesiveness of England's "Establishment" still seemed intact. What is also interesting is that, as in 1625, Sandys started the session off strongly (we have evidence of energetic action, including his one important speech, in the first five days he was in the House) but then faded away. The pattern once again suggests easy fatigue.

The House had been sitting for three weeks when Sandys first appeared in its records. It had already spent a great deal of time on matters close to his heart, especially religion and trade, and also on Buckingham's detention of a French ship, the *St. Peter*, on suspicion that it was trading with Spain: the issue that the pro-French faction was to use to start the assault on Buckingham. Sir Edwin made his impact the moment he finally appeared. It was the morning of February 27, and the House, lumping its grievances together, was discussing the "evil causes" of the kingdom's ills, a thinly veiled reference to Buckingham. After some debate, Sandys provided the focus that he had so often given to his colleagues' meanderings. "Who runs into the remedy . . . without knowing the . . . cause?" he asked. The first issue, he said, was "Diminution of the kingdom—reputation, honour, and strength: in reputation by our great loss—ships lost—strength by the loss

---

[20] Ibid., 809, 807.

of our men." The second issue, an old favorite, was "stopping of the trade of the kingdom." Ball has rightly pointed out that these charges could include almost anything, but they were crucial because they set the stage for "a full-scale attack on Buckingham under the cover of the investigation of impersonal grievances." Sandys had set the tone for the House as of old. After little more debate, it was "Resolved that the diminution of the kingdom in reputation honour and strength is one of the evils and the stopping of trade at home and abroad another general evil."[21]

Having given shape to the debate (though probably more to reiterate old themes and give order to the discussions than deliberately to betray his patron), Sir Edwin made only minor contributions to further developments. He seems to have been absent from the House for most of March: that is, after just one week's work, as in 1625. Then, on April 1, he spoke twice about procedures, which suggests that this remained his chief interest as the House pursued the duke. He gave uneasy consent to the use of common fame as grounds for an accusation; he discussed the precedents for the granting of patents; and he powerfully supported the Commons' right to continue the assault despite a prohibition from the king. Charles forbade the attacks on Buckingham in a message on March 29. In the debate that followed the M.P.s, especially Eliot and Noy, turned on the duke, but it was Sir Edwin who brought the discussion to a firm conclusion with a crisp statement of privilege: "It is a clear and undoubted and by examples both ancient and modern . . . confirmed privilege of parliament to complain of any subject whatsoever, that is taxed for public grievances." Although this was again an intervention about procedure, the ensuing remonstrance justified the continuing deliberations by quoting Sandys almost verbatim. It is because Sir Edwin was acting primarily in defense of the House's rights, not in pursuit of Buckingham, that he was able to remain in close contact with the duke's fellow minister, Sir John Coke, the secretary of state, and send him a copy of a Commons committee report right after the session ended.[22]

Another month then passed with few hints of Sir Edwin's presence. On May 3 and 8 he made procedural suggestions of little moment to the deliberations about Buckingham. On the twelfth he gave one of his clarifying speeches, which, as so often in the past, ended a debate. Digges and Eliot had just been imprisoned for their speeches against Buckingham, and the M.P.s were set to prepare another remonstrance. Sandys, however, wanted

---

[21] Russell, *Parliaments*, 278 ff.; Cambridge University Library MSS., Dd 12, 20, fol. 52 (Bulstrode Whitelocke's diary: henceforth Whitelocke, *1626*); Ball, "Eliot," 147.

[22] Whitelocke, *1626*, 21, fol. 119. Sandys sent the committee report to Coke from Aldersgate on June 17, two days after Parliament was dissolved: HMC, *Cowper*, 1:271—a reference I owe to Christopher Thompson.

to make sure it had a logical structure: "The first part of wisdom is to propound a good end and the second part the means to attain unto the end. Our ends are two in this case: to give the King satisfaction, and to get satisfaction to ourselves for the breach of our liberties. In matters where objections are plain I think it wisdom to anticipate the answer."[23] Only by saving the king's as well as the House's face did it indeed prove possible to secure the release of the two M.P.s.

Sandys's final parliamentary speech was on this subject. It came, after another long absence due to illness and the Whitsun recess, on June 12, just three days before Parliament was dissolved. And, ironically for the old "popular," this last Commons address has been interpreted as one more futile plea, by a member of the Buckingham alliance, for subsidies. But it was by no means one-sided. The subject was yet another remonstrance about Buckingham, though there was uncertainty whether to proceed with the subsidy first. Sandys offered a typical compromise. He suggested that the M.P.s insert into the remonstrance a clause "that in confidence of reformation in that great grievance we have begun with the bill [of subsidy] and given it a first reading." He urged the House to give the reading the next day, when the remonstrance would be submitted, and he clearly was hoping that both House and king would recognize the clause as a quid pro quo. Perhaps this can be seen as a maneuver to achieve progress on the subsidy, but if so, it certainly also entailed redress against Buckingham. In any case, as must have been clear by then, the assembly was in its last hours, and therefore, whatever its merits or purposes, Sandys's last proposal was scarcely a major boost for the subsidy. There was a rumor after the session that he "and other caterpillars of the commonwealth" had suggested levying a subsidy anyway, without a vote, but that the "project" had vanished "(like sal insipians)" when the king decided in favor of nonparliamentary methods. That there could have been a fabrication like this, linking Sir Edwin and Charles I in a travesty of their opposing views of the centrality of Parliament, indicates how far beyond his own electorate the fear had spread that the old "Commons-man" had betrayed his principles.[24]

Sandys had certainly spoken in favor of a subsidy on two occasions during late April. It had not, however, been unalloyed support. On the nine-

[23] Whitelocke, *1626*, 21, fols. 176, 182; 22, fol. 11; HMC, *Thirtieth Report*, pt. 7: *Lonsdale*, 14 (the Lowther diary: henceforth Lowther, *1626*); Russell, *Parliaments*, 306–307.

[24] Whitelocke, *1626*, 22, fol. 55; cf. Russell, *Parliaments*, 308 and Ball, "Eliot," 207. The "caterpillars" comment is from a newsletter of June 30: BL, Harleian, 390, fol. 83; "sal insipians" from the Reverend Joseph Mead's letter of July 26, ibid., fol. 99—a manuscript brought to my attention by Christopher Thompson, as was Harleian 383, where a letter of July 6, 1626, by Sir Edwin's fellow Middle Templar, Simonds D'Ewes (fol. 39) sums up the old parliamentarian's declining powers: "no man hath lost more of himself than Sir Edwin Sandes."

teenth he had agreed with Digges that the matter ought to be postponed for six days while the House discussed Buckingham. At the same time he had spoken of the country as this "not very rich island," and had called three subsidies (the minimum the king needed) a matter of difficulty because of the handling of earlier subsidies. He knew about this directly, because he had been sitting on the committee which was still looking into the accounts of the war commissioners for the 1624 subsidies. Sandys did not deny that money was needed for war, that the king had used "gracious language," and that he hoped "in the end we [will] all agree" to provide the money for "the good of our country." Yet it was surely not mere tactics, but rather a reiteration of concerns that he had advanced for two decades, when he also urged the M.P.s to "hold on our course—our grievances, especially . . . those that have brought the Kingdom into this distress." On April 25 Sir Edwin seemed more straightforwardly in favor of the grant, but he was still thinking of ways to lessen its impact. He opposed the raising of the rate at which the tax was paid, and supported setting minimum payments for knights and lords. What worried him was that the subsidies were not raising as much as they had in Elizabeth's time. Limits were being reached, "for we cannot exceed utmost." And impositions, above all, were responsible for the poverty. In other words, grievances were not forgotten, and even this support for the subsidy was grudging at best—full of concerns that give the lie to the rumor that he advocated extraparliamentary taxation.[25]

These brief interventions hardly amounted to a large role in the House's deliberations. In 1626, as in 1625, a quick start had been followed by a fade into the background. This was a much longer meeting, and Sandys did make sporadic appearances, but for long stretches he was probably not in the House. We know for certain that he was ill in mid-May, when the Commons sent Barrington to obtain written confirmation of his illness. It may also be that, after his opening spurt, when he made two speeches and was appointed to four committees in the space of four days, his assignments fell off because he was not regularly present. He was appointed to only four more committees during the entire session. Sir Edwin also spoke briefly on March 1 on procedure (pointing out, as befitted a veteran member, that no M.P. could speak twice in a debate) and on June 3 on the punishment of a fellow member. The latter, his penultimate speech in Parliament, showed that the old spirit of moderation had not died. Like his

---

[25] Whitelocke, *1626*, 21, fols. 143–144, 162–163; Lowther, *1626*, 7; the latter dates the debate April 26, but *CJ*, 49, confirms Whitelocke's April 25. For the rumors, see above, note 24. Sandys dutifully paid his taxes in Charles's early years: PRO, E.401/2586/83 (£25 for the forced loan, a reference I owe to Conrad Russell), and E.179/128/617, 623, and 624 (£28, £24, and £24 for the subsidies).

last speech, nine days later, this one sought compromise. His later suggestions (about the subsidy) were to prove futile, but his recommendation of
June 3 carried the House as in days gone by.[26]

The M.P. in trouble was a Mr. Moore, who had rather too bluntly raised
the issue of liberty that was now becoming ever more salient in the con-
sciousness of M.P.s. He had expressed, more frankly than he should have,
the fear of tyranny and the implicit warning to the king that was increasingly on his colleagues' minds. It was essential, he had said, that we "must
continue free, if the King would keep his Kingdom." In the debate that
followed, there was some question as to whether Moore ought to be expelled from the House and then handed over to the king for punishment.
Sandys thought otherwise. "Those things that are here offensive are common in books," he noted, and he warned his colleagues, with a quotation
from Isaiah, against laying "a snare for a man by the slip of the tongue."
His offense had been no worse than that, and there was no need to expel
him or expose him to the king's wrath. A brief (and probably fairly comfortable) spell in the Tower, "which is our place," would be quite enough.
First Pym and then the House as a whole agreed.[27] Sir Edwin's temperate
voice had swayed Parliament for the last time.

[26] *CJ*, 860, 826, 828, 829, 851, 857, 865; Whitelocke, *1626*, 21, fol. 52 and 22, fol. 35. Two of
his committees concerned recusants: one on the public fast, the other involving his old friend
Toby Mathew, whom he had failed to convert from Catholicism in 1607 (above, chapter 2,
note 6); three were procedural; and two were financial. It was the report on the fast that
Sandys sent Coke after the Parliament (above, note 22). Appropriately, his last official commission was to seek out recusants in Kent in 1627: PRO, SP/16/85/55.

[27] *CJ*, 866. Of the two Moores in the House, this was probably Poynings, a Surrey M.P.,
recently admitted to the Inner Temple, and a grandson of the veteran Sir George More. This
well-known Londoner (later to become a baronet) might have had more interest in liberty
than the alternative candidate, an obscure Hampshire member named John Moore. See *Surrey Archaeological Collections* 14 (1899): 27. Sandys's reference to the antimonarchical comments in books was also a nice touch, considering his own tendencies in the *Relation*.

PART THREE

Commerce and Colonization

Chapter XII

OVERSEAS VENTURES

The Interest in Overseas Enterprise

Parliament was by far the most important of Sir Edwin's public preoccupations during the first decade of the seventeenth century, but it was not the only indication of his broadening horizons. For it was at this very time that he was also entering the worlds of trade and colonization.

After a number of preliminary explorations, a small group of entrepreneurs had managed to obtain letters patent from the king on April 10, 1606, to explore the possibilities of a settlement in Virginia. Evidently able to gain access to Cecil, who had his own interests in overseas ventures, they were given control over all the land that now covers the northern half of the east coast of the United States.[1] Among these first promoters, Sandys may have known Richard Hakluyt at the Middle Temple, and Thomas Hanham from the Parliaments of 1586–93, but they were hardly close associates. The following year, however, his fortunes became intertwined with the enterprise they were trying to launch.

Seven months after the issuance of the original patent, James decided to appoint a council, consisting of weighty and responsible subjects, to supervise the colonization. Accordingly, fourteen prominent knights and merchants were designated councillors in a set of articles issued on November 20, 1606. Most were closely connected with the Court, and all but three were sitting in the Commons at the time. Sandys must have been a familiar figure to them—even to Sir Ferdinando Gorges who, though not in Parliament in 1606, had been Sir Edwin's colleague as an M.P. in 1593 and had probably known him, as a Devon man, through his first two wives. It was not surprising, therefore, that when the council asked the king to enlarge their number because they were too few, lived too far apart, and could not assemble a "competent number . . . together for consultation," Sandys—virtually a Londoner, and known for his interest in trade—was among the twenty-six gentry added to the group.[2]

The ordinance naming the new members of the council was issued on March 9, 1607. That this was a deliberate effort to give political weight and

---

[1] Alexander Brown, *The Genesis of the United States*, 2 vols. (Boston, 1890), 1:36–42, 52–63. See, too, BL, Additional, 12, 496, fols. 448–449.

[2] Brown, *Genesis*, 1:65–75, 91–95.

influence to the Virginia enterprise is clear. Relations with Spain were deteriorating, anti-Spanish merchants' complaints were intensifying, and James was preparing to receive a delegation from the rebellious Dutch. Moreover, Cecil was about to tell Parliament that the treaty of 1604 had left the status of North America ambiguous. Thus the ordinance of 1607, even more openly than the 1606 articles, seems to have been an admission of government interest in Virginia.[3] To the November 1606 group, which had included the solicitor-general of England, Dodderidge, and the lieutenant of the Tower, Sir William Wade, there were now added the distinguished diplomat and tutor to Prince Henry, Sir Thomas Challoner; another experienced diplomat, Sir Henry Neville; courtiers like Sir Fulke Grevill, Sir Robert Mansell, and Sir Thomas Smith, clerk of the Privy Council; and important gentry like Sir Maurice Berkeley, Sir Thomas Roe, Sir Oliver Cromwell, and Sandys. Many of them had also been involved in expeditions against Spain—Neville and Mansell won their knighthoods at Cadiz, Sir Richard Hawkins had fought the Armada, and Sir John Scott and Sir Edward Michelborne had been in the Azores voyage with Essex. The message for the Spaniards must have been unmistakable.

More than half of the new councillors were M.P.s in 1606, and all but eight of them sat in the Commons at some point in their lives. Most were likely to have known each other, and all seem to have been nominated primarily for political reasons because, with the exception of Sandys, not one became a major investor or active participant in the colonization of Virginia and New England. For Sir Edwin, however, it was the beginning of a long and often agonizing involvement in the worlds of commerce and overseas settlement.

We do not know how closely he participated in the events of the early years of the Jamestown colony, but it has been suggested that he, together with Bacon, drew up the next document in which he is mentioned, the second charter, issued on May 23, 1609.[4] These new letters patent strongly reinforced the impression of an official undertaking. Not only did they name over twenty members of the aristocracy, and nearly a hundred knights, as members of the company, but they listed the greatest figures of the land—Cecil himself, his brother Thomas, and the earls of Suffolk, Southampton, and Pembroke. There were now more than 650 members, who between them had subscribed at least £10,000 to support the colony. Sandys had joined in the fund-raising, which evidently took place under

---

[3] D. H. Willson, ed., *The Parliamentary Diary of Robert Bowyer, 1606–1607* (Minneapolis, 1931), 336: speech of June 17, 1607.

[4] Brown, *Genesis*, 1:208–237. For Sandys's authorship see 207. The account of the founding of the Virginia Company in Roy Strong, *Henry, Prince of Wales and England's Lost Renaissance* (London, 1986), 47, 61–62, 178, emphasizes Prince Henry's interest (and thus possibly that of his close follower Southampton) in the venture.

lofty auspices—one of the planning meetings, so we are told, was held at the house of Cecil's brother Thomas, the earl of Exeter. Very few documents from these years have survived, however, and it is not until 1611 that we again find Sandys signing company letters in his capacity as a councillor.[5] The chief administrator of the colony's affairs at this time was Sir Thomas Smythe, the merchant prince, from whom Sir Edwin doubtless acquired an understanding of the world of sailors, ships, and supplies that he cannot have gained from his experiences as a Londoner or as an M.P. investigating trade.

Yet it was presumably these last two qualifications that drew him into activities that still must have seemed remote to most members of his class. Sandys in his forties seems to have been a man looking for challenges—a man who, after an utterly conventional youth and early middle age, suddenly decided to try his hand at unusual and even dangerous undertakings. Given security by a solid and happy home life, he used his talents in ways that he probably would have considered unimaginable a few years before. And his success in the Commons may have encouraged him to venture into new fields. For his membership of the council did not remain a formality; he built it into a major part of his life. Sandys in his forties and fifties gives an impression of striving, of breaking new ground, that lent both excitement and significance to his work, and colored his activities for the remainder of his life.

What was it that drew him to commerce and colonization? One influence was his familiarity with London since childhood. The city was not, as it was for many country gentlemen, a place to be visited sporadically and briefly. Indeed, his town house on Aldersgate enabled Sir Edwin to maintain constant contact with the metropolis and with a circle of acquaintances that extended to almost every major group in the city: courtiers, lawyers, intellectuals, and merchants. It was not entirely a break with his past, therefore, when, in the second half of the 1610s, a mercantile venture, the Virginia colony, became his chief public activity.

But the level of his commitment was certainly unique. Although his friend the earl of Southampton participated in more ventures than Sandys, and succeeded him as treasurer of the Virginia Company, he never gave these efforts the devoted and concentrated service we see in Sir Edwin. Even the earl's assumption of the chief office in the Virginia Company "was merely," in the words of the standard account, "a screen behind

---

[5] Brown, *Genesis*, 1:206. The evidence of Sandys's fund-raising is his signature (the first to survive) as a council member on a letter to Plymouth requesting support for the company in February 1609: ibid., 238–240. His request for a subscription from Sir Ralph Winwood is of uncertain date: Kingsbury, 3:31–32. But he did sign two letters (Brown, *Genesis*, 1:461–465) on behalf of the company in 1611. The first proposal of a lottery for Virginia, submitted to the Privy Council in February 1612, may also have involved Sandys: MCFP, Box 1, no. 1566.

which Sandys continued to direct the work of the company."[6] Sir Edwin was unarguably the member of the gentry most closely involved with business in Jacobean London—not in number of undertakings, but in intensity of effort. He was associated with Virginia from its earliest days, serving as an active director from at least 1609; he was also a member of the East India Company from 1611, and a founder of the Bermuda Company. But it was the quality of his memberships, not their number, that distinguished him. He ran one of the largest companies, the Virginia, for six years, if not day by day (that was largely the responsibility of his friends the Ferrars) then at least through general supervision and the establishment of policy. No other nonmerchant took on such a responsibility.[7] Nor was any other nonmerchant (except his cousin Digges, a protégé of the powerful Sir Thomas Smythe) elected to a full-fledged directorship of the East India Company, as he was in 1621, or seriously considered a potential governor, as he also was a few years later. In other words, Sandys achieved a position in the world of commerce that no other gentleman equaled. He gave, not merely money, but time, and attained a prominence unique among members of the landed class.

Perhaps Sir Edwin was better equipped for this role than his peers. After all, he was always the M.P. most closely identified with trade issues in the House of Commons. But that is still not enough of an explanation. We must recall, first, that he was part of a remarkably broad movement among the gentry of the time. Various courtiers and aristocrats throughout the sixteenth century had shown a keen interest in maritime undertakings. The interest may date as far back as the reign of Henry VII, and it gathered momentum during the reign of Elizabeth, abetted by leaders of the stature of Burghley and Walsingham. The aim, in addition to the obvious hope for windfall profits, was to further national policies. A constant preoccupation was the use of the New World either as a convenient repository for dissident religious groups (Catholic as well as Separatist) or as a strategic base in the struggle against Spain. Both aims could be served simultaneously, as could such national concerns as protecting England's fisheries and seeking materials (like dyes) for the cloth industry.[8]

---

[6] W. F. Craven, *Dissolution of the Virginia Company: The Failure of a Colonial Experiment* (New York, 1932), 145.

[7] Robert Rich, second Earl of Warwick, probably had the largest investment of a nonmerchant in overseas enterprise at the time, and in some areas (such as the New England Council) he pursued broad concerns, but his major efforts of the 1620s (in Bermuda and privateering) differed from those of Sandys or Southampton in that he was not involved in the management of public, large-scale undertakings: until the Providence Island project, his ventures were mainly private quests for personal profit.

[8] David B. Quinn, *England and the Discovery of America, 1481–1620* (New York, 1973), passim.

These larger, noncommercial considerations bear stressing, because they provide a link that helps explain the large number of M.P.s who invested in colonization companies. Naturally, all of these men were seeking financial gain, but that motive alone would hardly have drawn them to overseas enterprise in particular. They would have been far better off (except for a few, unpredictable periods of the East India Company's history) if they had put their capital into land. That they persisted is a tribute to their public-mindedness and to the propaganda that appealed to this very quality. The insistence of Hakluyt and all the pamphleteers on the benefit to the commonwealth of maritime ventures, and on the poor showing of England by comparison with southern nations, reveals how strongly such sentiments appealed to the leaders of English society. Sandys himself drew the comparison in his first recorded comment on the quest for colonies:

> The Kingdoms and States of the Romish part, are not only in riches, . . . by greater opportunity to traffic to all parts of the world, by manifold degrees superior to their Northern adversaries, but also in fineness and subtlety of wit. . . . Neither have the Northern people ever yet for all their multitude and strength, had the honour of being founders or possessors of any great Empire, so unequal is the combat between force and wit, in all matters of durable and grounded establishment.[9]

The sense of purpose that arose from this perception of English weakness, and from the hope for remedy, was a major force propelling the landed classes into commercial and colonial ventures.

Like their Continental equivalents, the gentry had an instinctive distrust of the business world. In 1604, just two years before the establishment of the Virginia Company, Sandys's cousin Sir Dudley Digges summed up the prevailing attitude when he wrote: "to play the merchants was only for gentlemen of Florence, Venice or the like." Since Digges had little but contempt for Continental Europeans, the drift of his remarks was unmistakable.[10] Yet Sir Dudley himself was soon to become a prominent figure in various overseas undertakings, notably the East India Company, and eventually he was to be an investor ranking in importance perhaps only behind Warwick, Sandys, and Southampton among the gentry of James I's reign. What overcame this resistance was the call of public service. Without the sense that they were performing a vital duty for the benefit of the nation,

---

[9] Sir Edwin Sandys, *Europae Speculum, or a Relation of the State of Religion* . . . (London, 1632), 187–188.

[10] *Four Paradoxes, or Politique Discourses* (London, 1604), 79. The crucial distinction for Digges is between urban patricians (who can play the merchant) and landowners like himself; the imminent participation of England's gentry in the merchant's world is thus all the more remarkable. See Thomas Kiffin, "Sir Dudley Digges: A Study in Early Stuart Politics" (Ph.D. diss., New York University, 1972), 23.

that this was part of the sense of responsibility they had been cultivating for so long, it is highly doubtful that the gentry's participation (unique among Europe's landed classes) would have been forthcoming. And the intensification of their efforts in the late 1610s may well have been a response to the widely perceived worsening of England's economic situation.

The best indication of the connection between a commitment to public obligations and support for overseas efforts is the remarkable proportion of 53 percent who also sat in Parliament among the gentry and peers who invested in a voyage or company between 1575 and 1630.[11] There is little doubt that the nearly twelve hundred lords, knights, and gentlemen who took part in these undertakings were the most public-minded men of their class. They were following the lead set in Elizabeth's reign by a few courtiers, whose determination to promote the general well-being of the country by this means is beyond question. The motives of the Jacobean gentry were essentially the same, and considering that their help was essential to the survival of the Virginia and Massachusetts colonies, they succeeded beyond all expectation. It is not surprising that when the group that yearned most acutely to "improve" the country, the Puritans, sought a mechanism for gathering together, they should have thought of a colonizing company.[12]

If this motivation was so important to the leadership of the class as a whole, it was all the more decisive in Sandys's case. For the events we have been following in the last few chapters reveal him to have been par excellence the M.P. driven by a broad vision of England's welfare. To a greater degree than any other member, he worked tirelessly for those causes that he, and his fellow gentry, regarded as essential for the welfare of the realm, whether in defence of liberties or in pursuit of more orderly government. He had no set program, as did the Puritans; instead, he was able to achieve a preeminent influence among his colleagues for the very reason that his proposals so unmistakably upheld (and almost embodied) what

[11] Theodore K. Rabb, *Enterprise and Empire: Merchant and Gentry Investment in the Expansion of England, 1575–1630* (Cambridge, Mass., 1967), 93.

[12] The classic work, A. P. Newton, *The Colonising Activities of the English Puritans: The Last Phase of the Elizabethan Struggle with Spain* (New Haven, Conn., 1914), has been superseded by K. O. Kupperman, *Providence Island, 1630–1641: The Other Puritan Colony* (Cambridge, 1993). See, too, Christopher Thompson, "The Origins of the Politics of the Parliamentary Middle Group, 1625–1629," *Transactions of the Royal Historical Society*, 5th ser., 22 (1972): 71–86, esp. 86. The only evidence for Alexander Brown's interpretation—that Sandys, frustrated at home, sought to advance democracy in America—is the warning the Spanish ambassador Gondomar is said to have given James: that Virginia "would prove a seminary for a seditious parliament" (Menna Prestwich, *Cranfield: Politics and Profits under the Early Stuarts* (Oxford, 1966), 305). Yet it is worth noting that, when the company was collapsing, Sandys's supporters accused Smythe of arbitrary rule, in contrast to their own commitment to representation. See below, chapter 13, note 58.

they regarded as the "common weal." His repeated references to the contempt England might arouse among foreigners (an argument a Puritan would never have used); his wary and staunch defence of the privileges and importance of the Commons; his identification with issues, such as freedom of trade and distrust of the Scots, that seemingly united everyone in the House for the sake of the public good; and his constant citation of general principles, especially natural rights, in support of his views—all combined to mark Sir Edwin as a personification of his class's commitment to the welfare of the realm, and thus as a natural leader of the most exciting new effort to advance that welfare, colonial enterprise.

But was the high-mindedness real? To a large degree it was. Sandys was certainly hoping for personal gain from his investments, and in the tobacco contract he had a chance to profit handsomely. Moreover, he was probably feeling the financial strain of his ambitious house building by the late 1610s, at the very time that he became most deeply involved in commerce. The need to recoup must have been strong, and his failure resulted in serious indebtedness when he died ten years later. If this were the whole story, however, Sir Edwin's actions would be inexplicable. The critical defect in the "profiteering" hypothesis is that Sandys ran the Virginia Company for three years before he gained control of the tobacco contract. Until that coup, which he could not have foreseen, Virginia was anything but a source of income. By shouldering the unending problems of colonization, Sir Edwin was taking on one of the least rewarding (though also one of the most important) responsibilities in Jacobean England.

As in Parliament, so in the Virginia Company, it is difficult to avoid accepting Sandys's own professions of intent. He may well have been disingenuous at times, and he was undoubtedly adept at political maneuvering. Furthermore, when he was battling to retain control over the company and prolong its existence during its grim last years, he resorted to deceit, slander, and other improprieties without remorse. But he was then in a very different situation, when high hopes had been crushed by mismanagement and harsh reality, and his only aim was self-justification. It would be grossly unfair to tar his early ideals with the brush of his later failings. None of our information from 1618, 1619, or 1620 suggests that it would be appropriate to discount all, or even a goodly number, of the claims he made when seeking the treasurership (in effect, the governorship) of the Virginia Company.

Indeed, the prima facie evidence supports Sir Edwin's contention that, despite a growing population, the colony was weak and its treasury exhausted when he and his associates took "the matter anew in hand, and at their private charge" tried to put new life into the enterprise by broadening its economic base and increasing its population. Sandys's assertion that he was "grieved to see this great action fall to nothing" deserves to be taken at face value, as does his insistence (in a private letter to his friend the earl of Southampton, where he was surely not dissembling) that, though Governor Yeardley had offered to serve them in their private plantation, which "were a matter of much benefit: . . . the well carrying of the public is of more importance." Nor was the contrasting picture of Smythe's activities that he drew for the marquess of Buckingham in 1620 entirely disingenuous: "the disheartening of all adventurers and perpetual keeping down of the plantation that it might not prosper; and on the other side . . . the enriching of themselves." Even so hostile a witness as Nathaniel Butler, who denounced Sandys's factionalism and politicking in the Somers Island Company, admitted that the criticism of Smythe was led by "such as were thought and esteemed to be of great integrity and judgement; and a prime one among the rest was Sir Edwin Sandys."[13]

It is all too easy to pour a dampening cynicism over idealistic aims. In this instance, however, the public record should be sufficient to still the censorious. Sir Edwin would hardly have gained ascendancy in the Commons and the Virginia Company if those who heard him and knew him had not considered him public-spirited. In sum, there is no reason to doubt what he said, that he wanted to control the company so that the "great action" would not "fall to nothing." England's strategic foothold in America, on which so many hopes of emulating Spain rested, had to be kept alive. Independent, and with a high sense of the duties and responsibilities of the gentry, Sandys was seeking out another public trust.

THE TAKEOVER OF THE VIRGINIA COMPANY

In the case of Virginia, this conclusion seems inescapable. Here Sandys's sense of public duty and national needs had free rein, and he threw himself with dauntless energy into a difficult, frustrating, and ultimately futile endeavor. Despite his advanced age, he struggled for five years with the problems of sustaining the settlement at Jamestown. Inexperienced in day-to-day commercial affairs, and hounded by not unjustified criticism, he nevertheless persevered in a thankless task, determined to make England's vital colony flourish. He may often have been misguided, and toward the end of his tenure his behavior was shabby, but one cannot denigrate the

---

[13] Kingsbury, 1:350, 3:217, 295; Craven, *Dissolution*, 143–144 n.; *The Historye of Bermudaes or Summer Islands*, ed. J. H. Lefroy, Hakluyt Society, 1st ser., vol. 65 (London, 1882), 128. The latter's hostility to Sandys (e.g., 246) strengthens the usual (though not definitive) attribution of the book to Nathaniel Butler, governor of the Bermuda colony from 1619 to 1622, and a client of the earls of Warwick. See W. F. Craven, *An Introduction to the History of Bermuda* (Williamsburg, Va., 1938), 45–46, 119, 141; and Butler's papers in BL, Sloane, 750 and 758, a reference I owe to Christopher Thompson. A less sympathetic assessment is in Prestwich, *Cranfield*, 306–309.

high-mindedness of his aims and hopes. If this one commitment is Sandys's best remembered endeavor, that is not entirely unfair, because his leadership of the Virginia Company reveals him both at his best and at his worst.

Craven has assessed the history of the company, and of Sandys's part in its development, with such lucidity, judiciousness, and completeness, that the details need not be repeated in the following pages. Instead, we can take a more general look at his contribution to American colonization. As in Parliament, the record is by no means complete, but one can gauge in outline what Sir Edwin aimed to do and what he accomplished.

By the mid-1610s the main problem bedeviling the settlers at Jamestown was the paucity of numbers which, exacerbated by a lack of clear commercial purpose, threatened their ability to survive.[14] At the heart of their difficulties was their failure, after a decade in the New World, to establish a solid economic base that could guarantee their continued existence. Neither gold nor spices, the traditional supporters of Europeans overseas, were available, and the glowing descriptions in propaganda tracts of a fertile land, saturated with exotic products, must have sounded hollow to the colonists, frequently on the verge of starvation, as they surveyed their swampy domain. With investment drying up at home because of the lack of dividends, and with no profitable commodities in sight, the company could keep itself afloat only with stopgap measures.

The first was the sale of the island of Bermuda (for £12,000) to a syndicate of leading Virginia investors who incorporated themselves into a separate organization, governed by Smythe, which in effect remained a subgroup within the parent company. Another device was a large-scale lottery, licensed by the Crown in 1612, which raised about £8,000 a year thereafter. But still there seemed no way to attract new investors; if anything, financial prospects diminished as the earliest colonists completed their contracted seven years of labor, received their reward in land, and left the company's service so as to cultivate their own property. The supplies that had to be sent to Virginia were a constant drain, which took the organization's debts above £3,000 by the end of the decade, and to ensure continued shipments Smythe tried another remedy in 1616: a separate "Magazine," controlled by himself and a few close associates, which turned the provisioning of Jamestown into a private enterprise, run for profit. In the

[14] Edmund S. Morgan, "The Labor Problem at Jamestown, 1607–18," *American Historical Review* 76 (1971): 595–611, emphasizes poor work habits, but as Karen Kupperman pointed out to me, the more fundamental problem was the company's expectation that its profits would come from the Indian trade, and the slowness of its realization that the colony's future lay with land distribution and the harvesting of tobacco. She has put the picture of the colonists in a less negative light than Morgan in her "Apathy and Death in Early Jamestown," *Journal of American History* 66 (1979): 24–40, and "Fear of Hot Climates in the Anglo-American Colonial Experience," *William and Mary Quarterly*, 3d ser., 41 (1984): 213–240.

same year he also devised a new stimulus for investors, inspired by the Bermuda adventurers, who had divided up their island into individual plantations and were beginning to harvest the first lucrative product of an English American colony: tobacco. Smythe simply applied their example to Virginia. He issued dividends in land instead of money, encouraged the formation of plantations, and did all he could to stimulate the raising of tobacco. The latter was facilitated by the Magazine, which was the sole intermediary for exports from Jamestown. Smythe used this monopoly to insist on tobacco production, and the results were spectacular: twenty-three hundred pounds were exported in the 1614–15 fiscal year, but in the booming twelve months that ended at Michaelmas 1617 ships from Virginia and Bermuda carried to London just under fifty thousand pounds.[15]

The significant feature of the reforms of 1616, apart from their initial success, is that they shifted almost all economic activity into private hands. Their effect was thus to reinforce the virtually moribund state of the company as a whole. Naturally, such consequences provoked discontent among those who sought more than profit, let alone the many small investors who had watched both high hopes and capital dissipate. Both groups considered further restorative action necessary, and they found their champion in Sandys.

Sir Edwin had been participating in the enterprise sporadically for over a decade, and like so many gentry at the time, he doubtless regarded it as a kind of public duty, appropriate service for a prominent country gentleman with connections in London. Why, then, the sharpened concern in the late 1610s? The most plausible explanation, given what we know about Sandys's career in general, and about his later actions as head of the company in particular, is that he became genuinely fearful of a total collapse of the venture. Craven calls the years from 1615 to 1618 the "low ebb" of its fortunes, a time when a tiny band maintained a precarious foothold in

[15] Kingsbury, 3:48 for the Bermuda sale; ibid., 1:216, for the debt; Craven, *Dissolution*, 39, 44–45, 48, 150, and Christopher Thompson, "The Earl of Warwick and the Virginia Company 1619–1622" (unpublished manuscript), for Bermuda, the lottery, the Magazine, the land distribution, and the encouragement of tobacco; p. 526 of "Lord Sackville's Papers Respecting Virginia, 1613–1631," *American Historical Review* 27 (1922): 493–538, 738–765, for the tobacco exports; and, for the lottery, above, note 5, and Robert C. Johnson, "The Lotteries of the Virginia Company, 1612–1621," *Virginia Magazine of History and Biography* 74 (1966): 259–292. Craven, *History of Bermuda*, 70–155, demonstrates that the model for the shift in emphasis from public to private interests was the Bermuda colony, where the reliance on profit-making private plantations enabled the island's population to grow at a time when Jamestown was struggling to survive. See in general W. R. Scott, *The Constitution and Finance of English, Scottish and Irish Joint-Stock Companies to 1720*, vol. 2 (Cambridge, 1910), 246–289; Craven, *The Virginia Company of London, 1606–1624* (Williamsburg, Va., 1957), 29 ff., and Charles M. Andrews, *The Colonial Period of American History*, vol. 1 (New Haven, Conn., 1934), 112–155.

America and bankruptcy loomed at home.[16] As we have seen, the company was no longer able even to supply Jamestown, and the private, profit-making Magazine had had to take over this function. It was possibly the contrast between the profits Smythe and his son-in-law, Robert Johnson, were making from the Magazine, and the mounting debts of the company as a whole, that finally spurred Sandys to action. That was precisely the contrast he drew for Buckingham in his 1620 letter: a concern that he took seriously, for he later limited the Magazine's profits and eventually dissolved the partnership.[17]

The first sign of Sandys's major new interest emerged from the land distributions of 1616. He and Southampton already owned significant plantations in Bermuda, and in 1618 they extended their investment into Virginia. A number of other groups also sent out settlers that year, but these two sponsored by far the largest wave of emigration. In April 1618 the colony was reduced to about four hundred inhabitants, almost as low as it had been since its beginnings, and less than half its previous largest size; within a year, however, because of the private plantations, the population reached close to one thousand. Half of these fresh Virginians (310 to be precise) had crossed the Atlantic under the patronage of Sandys and Southampton, and it is from this effort in the spring and summer of 1618 (perhaps inspired by the success of the Bermuda plantations) that one can date Sir Edwin's assumption of a leading role in the colonization of the New World.[18]

As yet there was no hint that his efforts were in any way displeasing to Smythe. Rather, it was in conjunction with the treasurer (or at least with his tacit support) that in 1618 Sandys threw himself into the task of reviving Virginia's fortunes. Arranging for the dispatch of 310 settlers in the

---

[16] Craven, *Dissolution*, 33.

[17] See above, note 15; Craven, *Dissolution*, 33–34, 51; Thompson, "Warwick"; and Kingsbury, 1:238, 293, 3:519–520. Sandys may, however, have written to Buckingham in some pique, because when he revived the Magazine to supply the colony, it lost money consistently. Edmund S. Morgan, "The First American Boom: Virginia 1618–1630," *William and Mary Quarterly*, 3d ser., 28 (1971): 169–198, esp. 181 ff. demonstrates that the Magazine encountered difficulties precisely because Sandys helped Jamestown's population grow, and it became worth the while of private traders to compete with the company in supporting the colonists. Under Smythe, by contrast, when there were too few settlers to attract interlopers, the Magazine suffered no losses; as Thompson, "Warwick," notes, the restriction of Magazine profits to 25 percent suggests they had been higher.

[18] Kingsbury, 1:350. The lowest estimate for April 1619 is seven hundred (ibid., 3:537) an unlikely figure, for it implies Sandys and Southampton were responsible for the entire growth. One must remember that Sir Edwin was, in addition, "one of the principal Bermuda adventurers," and presumably was sending letters to the island at this time, too; Craven, *History of Bermuda*, 155 n. Other indications of his growing interest in the company in 1617 are in MCFP, Box 2, nos. 960A, 1607, 1611.

course of one year was a herculean undertaking, and it must have absorbed much of his energy. This was especially so in that Sir Edwin was determined to diversify Jamestown's agriculture. Whether because of a moral repugnance that was quite common at the time, or because he believed (mistakenly) that economic advantage demanded it, Sandys repeatedly denounced the concentration on tobacco. So complete was the dependence on a single crop that even food supply was neglected, and one of Sir Edwin's proudest moments after less than a year in office was a report from Virginia about "the plenty of corn that God this year hath blessed them with, the like never happened since the English was there planted."[19] Tobacco production continued to increase, of course, and Sir Edwin himself joined in the profit-making, but in the early stages of his plantation his insistence on diversification can only have made the struggle harder.

Sandys's sudden prominence in this overseas commerce was not entirely surprising, for it came at a time when his work on the home front had been growing steadily, though quietly, for some two years. The low point of the company's history, 1616, had apparently coincided with his awakening to the inadequacy of his previous efforts. In that year he became an "assistant" (the equivalent of a director) and at once began to take his duties seriously; by December 1616 he had joined an attempt to extend the lottery, and the following year he became deeply involved in the preliminary negotiations with the Pilgrim Fathers.[20]

This story, too, has been fully recounted, and need not be repeated here. Suffice it to say that Sandys was clearly the pivotal figure in the discussions. Of all the leaders of the Virginia enterprise, he was the one with the closest personal links to the Leyden Puritans, both through his brother Samuel and because the most important elder of the congregation, William Brewster, has been a close friend of Sir Edwin's old schoolmate George Cranmer.[21] His encouragement of the Pilgrims was as enthusiastic as it was not because of some new and unexpected preference for "the Genevan way" but because they fitted so perfectly into his hopes for a rapid increase in the Virginia population. That context is quite sufficient to explain his strenuous efforts to obtain approval for the settlement. And his contacts at Court proved vital to the success of the enterprise, because the company's approach to the Privy Council and the king was made through

[19] Kingsbury, 1:310.

[20] Alexander Brown, The First Republic in America (Boston, 1898), 242–243, mistakenly defines "assistant" as assistant to Smythe. See also ibid., 244.

[21] Ibid., 252, 263. Our chief source for the negotiations between the Pilgrims and the Virginia Company is William Bradford, Of Plymouth Plantation 1620–1647, ed. S. E. Morison (New York, 1953). For Sandys's role, see pp. 29 n, 30–31 (his letter to the Leyden group in November 1617), 60 n, and 356 (Robert Cushman's opinion that "things will go well in Virginia" with Sir Edwin in charge of the company).

another of Sandys's friends, Sir Robert Naunton, the secretary of state as of January 1618. Throughout the long preparations Sir Edwin remained the company's spokesman. He wrote the official letter of November 1617 encouraging the Pilgrims to pursue their idea of emigrating; he met their agent to discuss strategy after a company meeting in February 1618; and he brought that agent to the next meeting a week later.[22] Smythe had undoubtedly given his approval at the outset, but most of the work was done by Sandys—not only because of his personal connections, but also because of his commitment to the policy of boosting Virginia's population.

Sir Edwin's growing prominence may also have become possible because Smythe's health was declining: the latter cited his "weakness of body" as the reason for resigning the governorships of the East India and Bermuda companies in 1621. Yet Smythe was only three years older than Sandys, he remained prominent in both companies, and he did not shrink from a difficult election to Parliament in 1621. Sir Edwin's determination, rather than Smythe's abdication, was the main reason for the shifting balance in the Virginia Company.[23]

Unfortunately, it was not entirely in good feeling that the final changeover took place. As Sandys assumed a larger role, he began to move in directions that were bound to make relations difficult. Soon after his reappointment as assistant in 1618, he and his cronies, Sir John Danvers and the earl of Southampton, met together and agreed to start pressing for an audit of the company's books—a request that was inevitable once there was real interest in seeing the colony continue, and thus in finding out why it had not prospered thus far, but equally inevitably a cause of resentment between the old and new guards. Both Sandys and Danvers were appointed auditors, but so were others not of their coterie: John Wroth, who was the son of Sandys's former parliamentary colleague, Sir Robert Wroth, but who later was one of Sir Edwin's chief critics in the company; and two merchants, Anthony Abdy and Maurice Abbot, who were close associates of

---

[22] Brown, *First Republic*, 263–264. Brown's view (251), shared by many historians of the Virginia colony, that Sandys's patronage of the Pilgrims was motivated by a fondness for Geneva, was decisively refuted by Craven (see below, note 60), and is also contradicted by the evidence we have seen of his proto-Arminianism. For Sandys's relationship with Naunton, see above, chapter 8, note 4.

[23] Ibid., 242–243, and Brown, *Genesis*, 2:1014, where he notes that Smythe's doctor, Henry Atkins, was admitted to the East India Company gratis for attending the governor during 1615. Yet Sandys's doctor was admitted for the same reason at about the same time (see below, note 40); moreover, Smythe's attempt to be excused from the governorship in 1614 "on account of his . . . age and health" contrasts with his acceptance of reelection despite competition from four other candidates. His eventual resignation because of "weakness" in 1621 suggests that the first episode was not as ominous as Brown implies, especially since he did not complain of ill health again until 1621; CSP, *East Indies*, *1513–1616*, 302, and *1617–1621*, 435.

Smythe. Whatever the sentiments of the group, its inquiry soon managed to give the treasurer considerable offence, as Butler perceived:

> These auditors falling closely to their business, even at the very first [did] procure and give many disgusts to Sir Thomas Smith. He took it ill that they held not their meetings at his house in Phillpott-lane, as others had formerly used; he believed they meant him no good by their so earnest requires for all old books of account; and to have them delivered into their hands, and left with them during their audit; but the point that especially galled was, that some of the auditors (and chiefly Sir Edwin Sandys) made it their ordinary and frequent use, to lament openly in the courts, that unless they were attended, more freely informed, and a truer correspondence practiced, it would prove altogether impossible for them to attain to any perfect account; nay they sticked not to say in plain terms, that instead of these fair and equal dealings which they expected, they found nothing but courses and endeavors daily put upon them which aimed only (as far as they could perceive) to breed delay and intricateness, and to enwrap them in all obscurities. To which charge and imputations, howsoever, Sir Thomas Smith's answer in public was only, that these conceived difficulties and complaints seemed rather to arise from the want of experience and from insufficiencies of the most part of the auditors, and especially the leading men (wherein he was well known to aim at Sir Edwin Sandys), than any other just cause whatsoever; yet such a heart-burning and separation of affections (not to say spleen and malice) ensued thereupon betwixt them, as for ever after, it was easily discerned and even generally observed, that the most of their motions and propositions tended more to cross and snub one another, than to procure any fair and good effects; as rather looking after who it was that spoke than what it was was spoken; and to such a height of heat these distempers became inflamed within a very short time, that all their meetings and consultations seemed rather cockpits than courts.[24]

Thereafter it was but a small step, in Butler's opinion, to Sandys's candidacy for the treasurership.

Yet the progression was not quite so simple, and certainly not so poisonous. Long after his displacement, Smythe continued to host Virginia Company meetings, and it is inconceivable that Sandys could later have been elected a director of the East India Company over Smythe's opposition. Furthermore, it is clear that the two men were cooperating closely throughout 1618 in formulating a series of sweeping reforms for the Jamestown colony. If, as seems likely, these documents were primarily Sandys's work, it is nevertheless well to remember that the reorganization could not have been accomplished without the treasurer's agreement. The

[24] *Bermudaes*, 128–129.

process whereby Sir Edwin replaced Smythe was hardly a one-dimensional struggle between single-minded antagonists; it was a complex transition, often marked by reciprocal support on both sides.

The argument for Sandys's prominence in the authorship of the reforms is textual and circumstantial. In the first place, the few documents of this period whose writers are identified (such as a draft description of the Company's officers and their duties) were drawn up by a committee of five, among whom Sir Edwin was not only the first named but also the senior figure with legal training. And when the description of the officers reached the position of auditor, "it [was] referred to Sir Edwin Sandys to propound such rules as he holds fit to be observed in the execution of that office, for that he hath been long acquainted with it."[25] Beyond this straightforward comment lies the implication that Sandys was not only the moving force of the committee, but actually wrote on his own some of the fuller version of the report that it subsequently produced. His expertise in the law and in drafting legislation bears stressing, because as the only member so thoroughly qualified on this committee, which also drew up a constitution for the company at home and for the colony in Virginia, he must have taken the central role in producing what were essentially legal documents. Moreover, the final version of the regulations included the provision for a secret ballot which helped him win the treasurership, and the entire set of provisions was eventually published during his administration: circumstances that strengthen the case for Sandys's involvement.[26]

Where the most famous of the documents of 1618 are concerned (the new rules for land distribution and the economy; and the instructions for the colony's political reorganization, climaxing in the momentous stipulation that a "general assembly," including "two burgesses out of every town, hundred, and other particular plantation" had to meet at least once a year) Sir Edwin's hand is much in evidence. Both are legal documents. They end with the affixing of the company's seal, and the recitation of the date according to the standard legal formula.[27] And the legal training is apparent in such phrases as: "To all people to whom these presents shall come [to] be seen or heard, the Treasurer, Council and Company . . . send greeting.

---

[25] Kingsbury, 3:139, 143. The other member of the committee who apparently had legal training was Sir Nathaniel Rich. There is also a draft of suggestions for regularizing the date of elections in Sir Edwin's hand in MCFP, Box 3, no. 1562, fol. 3.

[26] Peter Force, ed., *Tracts and Other Papers, Relating Principally to the Origin, Settlement, and Progress of the Colonies in North America*, vol. 3 (Washington, 1844), no. 6; Craven, *Dissolution*, 86. It is significant that the regulations limited the treasurer to three terms in office, and forbade the election of a governor of another company, except the Bermuda— provisions obviously aimed at Smythe: Kingsbury, 3:141; Craven, *Company of London*, 42.

[27] Kingsbury, 3:109, 483, 484. As Craven has shown (*Dissolution*, 73–74), the surviving 1621 document incorporates the instructions of 1618.

Know ye that we the said Treasurer . . .''; or "We therefore, the said Treasurer and Company, upon a solemn treaty and resolution and with the advice, consent and assent of his Majesty's Council here of Virginia . . .'' The repeated references to the king's ultimate authority are also suggestive: just the sort of defensive wording that Sandys would have been careful to include. And the instruction to stop "the excessive applying of tobacco" clearly reflects his particular hobbyhorse; two years later he was still denouncing the colonists' "overweening esteem of their darling tobacco."[28]

Yet it is the overall intent of these documents that provides the most telling argument for Sir Edwin's authorship. The first group of instructions paved the way for the rapid growth of private plantations; encouraged would-be settlers; made provision for the economic interests of the company as a totality; and assured the colony's administrators of an independent income from public lands so as to avoid heavy taxation. The second established a moderate form of representative government. Both sets of aims were identified more closely with Sandys than with any other leader of the company. The first was the heart of his policy for restoring Jamestown's fortunes by enticing new inhabitants, achieving company profits (and thus perhaps dividends), and making local conditions as unburdensome as possible; the second established a government that promoted these aims, including procedures that he was uniquely qualified to advocate and assess.

It seems inconceivable that he was anything but the moving force behind the formulation and adoption of the reforms. And it is significant that seven years later, when he and his supporters drew up a catalogue of the benefits they had brought to Virginia, they stressed the consequences of the 1618 reforms as their most important contribution. Previously there had been but four hundred colonists, "very many of them in want" and "utterly destitute"; plantations were few, "poorly housed," and "ill fortified"; there was "no commodity . . . save tobacco"; and the people "suffered under martial law" and "a most extorting Governor." By 1621, in contrast, the Virginians, their provisions, and their housing had multiplied, not to mention that the "manner of building [was] much bettered"; new products and plantations were prospering; "the bloody laws being silenced,

---

[28] Kingsbury, 3:98, 99, 482–484; for the comments on tobacco see ibid., 504, and Craven, *Dissolution*, 50. Yet Sir Edwin was able to adjust to the realities of the situation. Twenty months before his "darling tobacco" sarcasm, he had joined his friend Lionel Cranfield in assuring the Company's tobacco market (by banning native English production) in return for higher customs duties: Kingsbury, 1:290–292, and Andrews, *Colonial Period*, 1:152–157. Sandys's subsequent fight for the tobacco monopoly and free fishing is described as essential to the survival of the venture in Ronald M. Berger, "Sir Edwin Sandys and the Virginia Company of London, 1618–1621" (M.A. thesis, University of Wisconsin, 1966).

... their government [was] ordered like to that of this kingdom"; officials were financially supported so that they did "not need to prey upon the people"; and the planters had "the liberty of a general assembly."[29] For all the one-sidedness of this tabulation (and the limitation of the "liberty" it trumpeted to a privileged few while the majority toiled in servitude), the transformation it depicts was real enough, and deserves to be regarded as one of Sandys's most enlightened and impressive achievements.

One other circumstance suggests the extent to which Sir Edwin was coming to dominate the company even before he took office as treasurer. The choice of Sir George Yeardley as the new governor, charged with the task of implementing the reforms of 1618, appears to have put into office a man closer to Sandys than to Smythe. In fact, Smythe was reported to be "highly offended" with Yeardley shortly before the governor left for Virginia (he apparently thought the latter's knighthood undeserved), and Sir Edwin himself "labored and effected a reconciliation." But this did not last long. Soon "Sir Thomas . . . renewed his former displeasure," and in response Yeardley conceived "a violent resolution of quitting his place," feeling unable "to serve under his control, whose hatred . . . was strong, as to break through the . . . bonds of a public reconciliation." It was this discontent that had led Yeardley to propose himself as the manager of Sandys's and Southampton's plantation. In the letter making the offer, moreover, he indicated how deeply he felt himself indebted to Sir Edwin: "perceiving your constant affection still to remain towards me, as well in the great travail and pains you take for defending, upholding, and maintaining my reputation and credit, as also for the good advice, counsel, and directions I do receive from you. . . . I may not omit first to give thanks unto God who hath raised me so worthy a friend . . . whereby I may in some measure deserve your so great kindness showed me, meanwhile I return unto you unfeigned thanks."[30] This was written before Yeardley knew that his patron had been elected treasurer, and reveals not only that he was Sandys's protégé, but that he was already receiving instructions from Sir Edwin. Smythe's anger was thus doubtless fed by a natural resentment of the man who had not only spearheaded the demand for an audit, and had assumed a major role in the reorganization of the company, but had now also "taken over" the colony's governor.

These, then, were the steps (partly in cooperation with his predecessor,

[29] Kingsbury, 4:520–523. The parallels with events in Bermuda, and the lessons in economics and government that the two colonies learned from one another, are analyzed in Craven, *History of Bermuda*, passim. Unfortunately, the Bermuda records are too sparse to provide details of Sandys's activities, but his influence was presumably similar to what it was in the Virginia Company.

[30] Kingsbury, 3:216, 217, and 118, 119.

partly amid friction) whereby Sandys moved to take control of the Virginia Company. Even though he may have had the best of intentions throughout, and been genuinely concerned to revive a flagging enterprise, his actions were bound to cause bad feeling. Relations were certainly strained, but there does not seem to have been a total break between the two men for at least a year; indeed, it is worth noting that the traditional insistence on a dichotomy between a united "Smythe party" and a monolithic "Sandys party" seems as overdrawn a description of an essentially homogeneous "Establishment" as is the concentration on antipathies between "Court" and "Country" members of the Commons.[31] It obviously did not help matters that at the same time as the Virginia Company takeover, Sandys was also involved in attempted conquests of the Bermuda and East India companies. In the latter he was to fail, while at the Bermuda election "Smythe was continued in his governorship of the Company, contrary to the expectation, as it was thought, of Sir Edwin Sandys, who verily looked to have had that also." Considering that more than 94 percent of the Bermuda voters were also members of the Virginia Company, and that the leaderships of the two organizations were well-nigh indistinguishable, this outcome suggests that the two "parties" were anything but solid or irreconcilable, especially in view of the simultaneous appointment of Nathaniel Butler, the candidate of Sandys's ally Warwick, as governor of the Bermuda colony.[32]

Yet 1619 was still the end of an era, not least because Smythe now began to lose interest in Virginia. And the absence of the great merchant's support and capital was to be one of the weightiest of the handicaps which burdened Sandys in the years that followed. His alliance with Warwick was small compensation, because that adventurous nobleman had no patience for the kind of investments in agriculture, transportation, and supplies that the change of policy required. By winning the battle, Sir Edwin increased the likelihood that he would lose the war.

---

[31] The differences between Sandys and Smythe in the 1619–21 period were colored and exaggerated by those who were looking for antecedents of the major quarrels of 1621–24. The talk of "conspiracy and faction," and of Sandys as a "chief mover, and principal backer of . . . impudent backbiters" (*Bermudaes*, 246–247) may be appropriate for the later stages of the dispute, but it does not fit what we know about the early days of his Virginia Company leadership. The famous depiction of the court meetings as "Cock-pits" (Craven, *Dissolution*, 141) dates from late 1620, when it began to correspond to reality, though this, too, was probably an exaggeration. In October 1619 Sandys was still saying (apparently sincerely, in a private letter to Ferrar) that his deputy ought to withdraw from a meeting rather than let potential quarrels break out, for he did not want "the public good or justice . . . oppressed by faction": Kingsbury, 3:224. The quarrels over the audit described by Robert Cushman in 1619 (Bradford, *Plymouth*, 356) were sporadic, and at this stage did not cause open rupture.

[32] *Bermudaes*, 131; Rabb, *Enterprise*, 108.

RELATIONS WITH SMYTHE AND WARWICK

Election day in the Virginia Company, April 28, 1619, passed quite smoothly.[33] The General Court's first action was to approve the document Sandys had worked on, describing the officers' duties. Smythe then announced that he had labored in the company's behalf for twelve years, but because of his new appointment to the Commission for the Navy he no longer had the time to continue as treasurer. Accordingly, he declined to stand for reelection, and Sir Edwin easily won, gaining fifty-nine out of the hundred votes cast, the remainder being divided among two friends of Smythe. At the same time, his friend John Ferrar, the son of a well-known London merchant, defeated Alderman Robert Johnson, Smythe's friend, for the post of deputy treasurer. But the sixteen directors who were chosen immediately thereafter were not conspicuously adherents of either side. One or two, such as Thomas Keightley, were new directors and identified with Sandys; others, such as Ralph Gore, were old associates of Smythe, or, as in the case of William Palmer, major critics of Sandys in subsequent years. Their only noticeable common characteristics were, first, that most were members of the Bermuda Company (which was reelecting Smythe at this very time) and nearly half of them were Grocers. The latter seems to have had little significance, since both Smythe and the Ferrars were members of another livery company, the Skinners.[34]

The auditors, elected next, were a different matter. They were clearly pro-Sandys, which may be one reason that Smythe's parting request to the company was that they do him the favor of having "his account . . . with all speed audited, that before he dies, he might see the same cleared." This was not to be, and for years Sandys vainly attempted to settle on a figure; Smythe, in return, was to demand that three of his own auditors join the investigation, and he claimed that he, not the company, was owed hundreds of pounds.[35] The quarrel was never satisfactorily resolved, and thus the pattern set in the year before Sandys took over the treasurership persisted: the two men could work together in many important areas, but the audit always drove them apart. The other side of this ambivalent relationship was confirmed by the last item of major business on that election day,

[33] Kingsbury, 1:211–214. Significantly, this court, held at Smythe's house, is the first one whose minutes have survived. As in the Commons, Sandys appreciated the importance of keeping a written record.

[34] The new directors are listed in ibid., 213. Brief biographies of most of them are in Brown, *Genesis*, 2:842 ff. The possibility that Ferrar appealed to Sandys because, although from a well-known family, he had yet to make his way in the world, and would thus be an amenable yet reputable partner, is suggested by David A. Smith, "Mr. Deputy Ferrar and the Virginia Company, 1619–1622" (unpublished manuscript).

[35] Craven, *Dissolution*, 106–117; Thompson, "Warwick."

when Sandys generously proposed a gift of twenty shares to Smythe as thanks for his efforts in "so great a business."

Sandys's capture of the company was not entirely surprising. He had been moving into a dominant position during the previous year, and had probably done more than Smythe in 1618 to inject new life into the sagging enterprise: a show of concern that undoubtedly enhanced his appeal to the small investors, whose crucial votes were susceptible anyway to Sandys's skill in politicking and public speaking. All that he needed for a complete takeover was the support of a powerful figure like Robert Rich, earl of Warwick; when that was forthcoming as a result of a quarrel between Warwick and Smythe, a joint effort was easy to arrange. The earl's main concern in the spring of 1619 was to replace Daniel Tucker, the Smythe-approved governor of Bermuda, who had imprisoned a member of the Rich family. Sandys provided himself with a bargaining counter for the negotiations by proposing his brother George as a candidate for the governorship, thus making it a three-way race and endangering the chances of Warwick's candidate, Nathaniel Butler. The quid pro quo that followed was that Sir Edwin removed his brother's name and helped get Butler elected, while Warwick delivered the votes in the Virginia Company.[36] Smythe obviously saw that was coming, and used the rather transparent excuse of the Navy Commission to avoid a confrontation. Yet it would be unfair to regard his withdrawal as involuntary. With the exception of doubts about the audit, he may have been quite willing to allow Sandys to succeed him in this faltering venture, and to give the rising star of the company a chance to implement his new proposals. After all, when Sir Edwin tried the same approach in the Bermuda and East India companies, both of which were prosperous organizations, Smythe repulsed him quite easily. Perhaps for these later elections he had more time to organize the votes, but that does not seem likely in view of Butler's successful campaign to become governor of the Bermuda colony. Rather more plausible is the conclusion that Smythe supposedly "lost" an election only when he was not too deter-

---

[36] *Bermudaes*, 130–132; Craven, *Dissolution*, 83–87, and *History of Bermuda*, 119–120. There was a fourth candidate, too, but the real alternative to Butler was George Sandys, whose hand was strengthened because "a fast and sure kinsman" of his, Captain Miles Kendall, was already the acting governor of the colony (ibid., 42, 120). The link with Kendall is obscure: he may have been the "Kendall" who married Dorothy, the daughter of Sir Edwin's older cousin and namesake from Buckinghamshire; or his name may reflect origins in the town of Kendall, a few miles from the ancestral Sandys estates in Westmorland, where several members of the family had marital connections. Moreover, Miles was an unusually common Sandys name (the aforementioned Dorothy, for example, had a grandfather, brother, and cousin called Miles). And the captain may also have been related to the ill-fated Captain George Kendall, a distant kinsman of Sandys who was executed in Jamestown in 1607: Philip L. Barbour, *The Three Worlds of Captain John Smith* (Boston, 1964), 104, 153–154. To simplify, I use "Warwick" to refer to Robert Rich, the second earl of Warwick, though he did not succeed to the earldom until March 1619.

mined to win. His refusal to oppose Sandys in the Virginia Company is thus a good indication that he approved, even if only tacitly, of his successor.

That is not to say that Sandys was able to maintain good relations with Smythe and Warwick indefinitely. The former, though increasingly angry over the audit, still allowed an occasional Virginia Company meeting in his house in succeeding years, but eventually he broke openly with the new administration.[37] And with Warwick the cordiality did not survive much longer. In an episode similar to one that had embroiled him with the East India Company (see below, note 50), Rich found himself denounced by the Virginians in 1620 for a privateering expedition which, by preying on Spanish shipping in the Atlantic and Caribbean, threatened to arouse the Spaniards (and, through Ambassador Gondomar, James himself) against the colony that had given the privateers shelter. The company may have freed itself from subordination to a royal council in its 1609 and 1612 charters, but its independence still rested on royal benevolence, and Sandys obviously felt he could not risk its future by defending Warwick and his friends, though he may have regretted the decision bitterly when, three years later, a still angry Warwick became the nemesis who helped destroy the company.[38]

Within a matter of months, therefore, Sir Edwin had lost some of his support among the Virginia adventurers. Nevertheless, he did manage to retain the loyalty of a majority of the shareholders throughout the organization's remaining five years of existence, and for the first two of those years, until the spring of 1621, he reached the apex of this particular phase of his career. This was the period when he was at the height of his powers in the Commons, and when Virginian affairs were running most strongly in his favor.

THE EAST INDIA COMPANY

It may have been that Sir Edwin was feeling his oats, because this was also the very period when he sought to extend his commercial involvements

---

[37] Meetings on July 13, 1619, and March 18, 1620, were at his house; the latter was a committee meeting on the tobacco monopoly attended not only by Smythe himself but also by his chief supporters, such as Alderman Johnson: Kingsbury, 1:243, 327.

[38] Craven, *Dissolution*, 127–140. Thompson, "Warwick" suggests the earl made the break complete in the summer of 1620 by selling his Virginia land and withdrawing from company affairs. Yet he was still interested enough to attend a General Court in June 1621, a full year after Smythe's last appearance at a Company meeting. Kingsbury, 1:382, 486. One cannot, of course, argue from silence and date the final severance of either man's ties to Virginia on grounds of his absence from courts; yet mid-1620 and mid-1621 seem plausible estimates for Smythe and Warwick, respectively.

beyond Virginia and Bermuda to the Far East. And here, too, he found himself in conflict with the ubiquitous Sir Thomas Smythe.

It was possibly as early as 1609 that Sandys joined the East India Company. The exact date of his admission is not known, but he may well have been one of the "other Lords, knights, and gentlemen" who were admitted together with the earl of Southampton (a likely companion for Sandys) in 1609. He was certainly a member by March 1613, when he and the earl of Pembroke asked the company to permit postponed payment of their contribution to the current joint stock because their rents were not yet due— a request the directors granted to "so worthy a gentleman, whom they do honor and respect."[39]

For the next six years Sandys gave the company only sporadic attention, such as sponsoring the membership of a doctor, Theodore Gulston, whom he credited with saving his life. The company admitted him in 1614 because they esteemed "Sir Edwin a very good gentleman who hath deserved well of the Commonwealth, and worthy to be respected," and also "for the love they bear unto him."[40]

These protestations notwithstanding, there is no record of Sir Edwin's investments in the East India Company, though they may have exceeded £1,000, his approximate eventual outlay for Virginia. In general, he left little mark on the record. He twice attended a General Court in November 1618, but his only link to the proceedings came when his cousin Sir Dudley Digges bought a carpet at an auction of goods from the East. In March of the following year both he and Digges joined a committee to explore a possible merger with the Muscovy Company. He participated in the early deliberations for a week or so, and then again in December 1619, when the two companies decided to abandon the merger.[41]

Such activities hardly amounted to a major commitment, though it is apparent that Sandys was showing more interest in East India Company affairs in 1618 and 1619, even as his Virginia work was growing. Apart from the Muscovy merger, he took part, together with Lionel Cranfield, in a committee formed in April 1619 to discuss relations with a new competitor, a group seeking a patent to explore a southwest passage to the Pacific.[42] The directors obviously liked to make use of the talents of prominent gen-

[39] India Office Library, East India Company Court Book no. 2, fol. 120; no. 3, 54.

[40] Ibid., 189.

[41] Court Book no. 4, 69–70, 75, 150, 151, 483. The only evidence we have about Sandys's investment in the East India Company is his payment of £500 late in 1619 (Kingsbury, 3:225). This was clearly not his first contribution in a decade of membership, but his subsequent difficulties suggest it may have been his last. And his finances in general cannot have allowed him to repeat a subscription of this magnitude often. In 1629, according to his will, his investment amounted to £1,500 (below, chapter 14, note 2).

[42] Court Book no. 4, 157.

try members like Sandys whenever delicate public negotiations became necessary, and Sir Edwin must have seemed especially appropriate because of his dealings with trade matters at the national level. In the end he, together with Smythe, Cranfield, Digges, and a few leading merchants, drew up the company's protest to the king. They had met with the patentees, but found their experience inadequate, since new discoveries won dividends only "after much expense, and many years' patience." To maintain their monopoly, the India merchants promised to send out an expedition themselves, and with that assurance James agreed not to issue the new patent.[43]

The committee assignments were the prelude to a more ambitious undertaking. In April and May of 1619 Sandys launched his most audacious ventures in the business world: campaigns for the governorship of the Bermuda Company as well as the treasurership of the Virginia Company. He lost the first and won the second, but since in both cases the incumbent he wished to oust was Smythe, one must suspect that the disturbance at the East India Company election on July 2 (the next company election involving Smythe) also emanated from Sandys. Unfortunately, though, the suspicion cannot be confirmed, because the confrontation is very poorly documented.

All that Chamberlain heard was that "the East India Company with some difficulty have chosen Sir Thomas Smith their governor." The court records, which naturally present the official side, and play down the seriousness of the disagreement, indicate merely that, as in the Virginia Company, the basic issue was whether to appoint auditors "as a means to take away all exceptions, and to dash and quell all other plots." Presumably the demand for auditors was an attempt to impugn the honesty of Smythe's administration, and the issue was still alive six months later, at a General Court on December 29. According to the minutes, such discontent had "never [been] heard of before"; it was equally unprecedented for "many of the generality . . . [to be] desirous to have the business for the election" handled by secret ballot—again a proposal identified with the Sandys party in the Virginia and Bermuda companies. But a direct link cannot be proved. The request for a ballot box came from John Holloway, a veteran East India and Levant merchant, who had long been an associate of Smythe in both companies and also in the abortive quest for a northwest passage in 1612.[44] Yet it may be significant that he joined the Virginia

<hr />

[43] Ibid., 158–161.

[44] *Chamberlain*, 2:251; *CSP, East Indies, 1617–1621*, 282; Court Book no. 4, 378, 379, 484. According to Digges, the fight threatened to split the company in two: PRO, SP/84/94/96. Lacking a (much-needed) biography of Smythe, one cannot tell if the disputes had roots earlier than the 1619 conflicts with Sandys and the Riches; it may be that they went back to the days of the Essex conspiracy, which involved Smythe as well as Southampton.

Company the next year, during Sandys's leadership; and, though nothing more concrete can be said, the evidence leaves little doubt that Sir Edwin was a prime mover of the challenge to Smythe.

It was certainly a distinguished gathering that appeared for the election, including, in addition to Sandys, the earl of Southampton, Lord Pagett, Sir Thomas Edmondes, Sir Julius Caesar, Cranfield, Digges, and various other gentry. Forewarned by recent experiences in the Virginia and Bermuda companies' annual meetings, Smythe opened the proceedings by pointing out that they had to elect "such as shall be *fit* to manage so great business."[45] This enterprise was too important and profitable to hand over to restless but inexperienced gentry, and the merchants, united and determined, had no trouble blocking the challenge. The proposal for a secret ballot was rejected; then, in a nice piece of evasion worthy of Sandys himself, a committee was set up to investigate grievances and audit the books. Not a single gentry member was appointed to the committee, a clear indication of the merchants' victory. The final dispute was over the board of directors, the so-called "committee." Complaints were made that only half of the board was elected each year, and there was a demand that some gentry, "and not merchants only," be chosen. This assault, too, was turned back, to the accompaniment of a reminder that only merchants knew how to run the business and that only they were permanently in London, ready at all times for a board meeting. The one concession was the appointment of eight subsidiary "committees [i.e., directors] at large," including two gentry, Sandys and Digges, who could come to meetings as they pleased.[46]

This compromise has to be seen in the context of the general rebuke the company leaders dispensed to "gentlemen who, having been taken into the Company by courtesy, do aim to get all the government into their hands." Nevertheless, it indicates that Sandys did not leave the encounter entirely without spoils. Digges was a close ally of Smythe, and therefore not unwelcome to the governor.[47] But Sandys, particularly after the events of the previous weeks in other companies, must have seemed unfriendly. Whether it was merely his rhetorical skill in debate that won him enough support for the appointment—and even a detractor of his role in trading companies admitted (though not without a barb) that he was "very eloquent, and by many and himself thought eloquent" in such meetings—or whether he had organized a sufficient number of the membership in advance, we cannot tell. But it is probable that he was acting in concert with his Virginia colleague, the earl of Warwick, who was in the midst of a fierce

[45] Ibid., 378. My italics.
[46] Ibid., 380, 381.
[47] *CSP, East Indies, 1617–1621*, 330; Kiffin, "Digges," 76–77, 169–171.

quarrel with Smythe and the East India merchants.[48] Whatever its origins, however, Sandys's achievement was certainly not insignificant; given the stature of the East India Company, the appointment was a major success in his campaign to win a larger role in overseas enterprise. And it added to the qualifications that paved the way for his remarkable election as a full-fledged director four years later.

That is not to say that Sandys now plunged into East India Company business. He was much too occupied by Virginia to take this second position very seriously. As far as we know, he attended only two other meetings before his election as a director in 1623. He was the only gentleman present at a meeting in December 1619, when there was more grumbling about the auditors (perhaps a last attempt to revive that issue), and when a request for quarterly, rather than annual, General Courts (a demand that bears Sandys's stamp) was deferred. He also attended an uneventful court in March 1620, and late the following year hoped for an appointment (like Digges's) to the commission negotiating an agreement with the Dutch East India Company.[49] It is possible that he had other, less formal, involvements in proceedings, because he knew most of the leaders of the company and he was frequently in London; but he made little impact on its affairs. His contribution is best seen as further evidence of his growing interest in commerce and his extensive connections in the business world.

That this burst of activity also aroused ill feelings, however, cannot be denied. Partly this was because of the audits and because in the East India Company Sandys seemed to be seeking the finest gem in Smythe's crown. But the primary responsibility for the rise in temperature lay with the earl of Warwick, who was in the midst of an angry dispute with Smythe not only because of East India Company interference in his activities as a privateer in the Red Sea and as a promoter of Guiana, but also because Smythe had supported the imprisonment of Warwick's relative in Bermuda.[50]

Since Sandys won election in the Virginia Company with Warwick's help, he may well have been drawn into this bad feeling (which was so at odds

---

[48] Wilkinson, *Bermuda*, 145 n, quoting *Bermudaes*, 242. See, too, ibid., 120: "Sir Edwin [was] a popular man, a great speaker, and of wise estimation in [Bermuda Company] courts." For the Smythe-Warwick quarrel, see below, note 50. The East India Company tried to keep it out of the public eye, and the leadership was upset when Rich made it widely known: *CSP, East Indies, 1617–1621*, 330.

[49] Court Book no. 4, 483, 547–550; Kingsbury, 3:529.

[50] Ibid., 1:212. Craven, *Dissolution*, 83–85; *History of Bermuda*, 111–117; and Thompson, "Warwick" are the best accounts of these quarrels. The fact that Smythe's son secretly married Warwick's sister (a union that Southampton arranged) merely increased the tension. It should be noted that the member of Warwick's family in Bermuda, also called Robert Rich (a brother of Sir Nathaniel), was the manager of the family's interests on the island, and thus not an insignificant relative.

with the way he usually conducted himself). There is no other way to
explain his behavior less than two years later when, in the midst of a successful parliamentary election campaign against Smythe in Sandwich, Sir
Edwin told the voters that "the East Indies Company was a pernicious
matter to them and the whole kingdom, and he is against that."[51] At one
level this was merely a clever appeal to outport distrust of big London
monopolies; but at another level it was a shamefully hypocritical attack on
a former close associate. Smythe, for his part, apparently lost his temper in
the midst of one of the attempts to remove Daniel Tucker, his choice as
governor of the Bermuda colony: he refused to entertain the motion, denouncing its proposers "suddenly and sullenly" and "with much heat and
passion."[52] The reprimand issued after the dispute in the East India Company was similarly brusque.

Although the main stimulators of ill will were Warwick and Smythe,
Sandys was drawn into the hostilities, possibly as part of the bargain
whereby he won Warwick's support for the Virginia treasurership. Therein,
moreover, lies the principal contrast between the East India Company
clash and the Virginia and Bermuda company fights. Where the New
World was concerned, Sandys could genuinely feel that he was acting in
the public interest; for the Far East he could make no much claim, because this was already the most flourishing overseas trade in Jacobean
London. Without detracting from the idealism of Sir Edwin's concern for
the American colonies, therefore, one must admit that in the East India
conflict he became a pawn in a vendetta not of his making.

THE SANDYS ADMINISTRATION OF THE VIRGINIA COMPANY

That Sandys took command in Virginia did not mean that he ran day-to-
day affairs. These were usually dealt with by John Ferrar, though Sir Edwin must still have spent considerable time on company matters. Even
when forced by family and estate concerns to stay in Kent, he was constantly in touch with Ferrar, and one detects more than a little impatience
in his correspondence of the spring, summer, and autumn of 1620, when
he was forced to stay at Northbourne longer than expected because of the
anticipated birth of yet another child, various illnesses that afflicted his
wife, and finally a miscarriage.[53] His route to London when he could leave

---

[51] *CSP, East Indies, 1617–1621*, 410.

[52] *Bermudaes*, 116. Tucker was the man who imprisoned Robert Rich in Bermuda; he was
finally replaced by Warwick's client, Butler, at the 1619 election.

[53] Kingsbury, 3:270–271, 376, 406–407, 415–416. He was also in Kent late in 1619 ("Lord
Sackville's Papers," 498–499), though he was back in London by January 11, 1620, when he
wrote to the earl of Huntingdon (Huntington Library, HA 10673). Starting with his election
to the treasurership, he was (on average) absent from half of the company's meetings whose
minutes have survived. On the miscarriage, see above, chapter 2, note 41.

was apparently across Kent to Gravesend, and then by boat to the capital. That is how Ferrar came to him when Sandys's absence from the city threatened to make him lose touch with company activities. In addition to correspondence with his deputy, and his entertainment of Ferrar and others connected with the organization, he had official letters sent straight to his home in Kent, so that he could be kept informed despite his distance from London.[54] Yet there is no denying that his supervision of the enterprise was nowhere near as close as that of a Smythe, who was always at hand. Indeed, it became necessary in 1623 to appoint a four-man executive committee precisely because the leaders of the company, "absent in the vacation," could not be relied upon to deal with "weighty and urgent businesses."[55]

Sandys's frequent remoteness from events reinforces the impression that his prime interest was the grand strategy of creating a viable colony. As befitted a gentleman, he had little patience for detailed problems of provisioning ships or hiring sailors. Those could be left to Ferrar while Sir Edwin concentrated on the larger vision which, during these first two relatively untroubled years of his administration, focused on two overriding ambitions. The first, a sizeable increase in the population of Jamestown and its environs, so as to improve defenses and productive capacity, had been one of his main concerns since the earliest days of his serious involvement in company affairs in 1618. The second, diversification of the settlement's economy, was also a long-standing aim. Both policies seemed eminently logical in the abstract, and could boast an impeccable ancestry reaching back to Richard Hakluyt, but in practice neither fulfilled Sandys's purposes. The waves of colonists eventually caused massive problems, and

[54] On the journey: Kingsbury, 3:192. It took about a day to get from Northbourne to Rochester, and another day to reach London (ibid., 371), though it could take three days altogether (ibid., 270). Why Sir Edwin did not sail from Deal, less than three miles from his house, and thus avoid the unpleasantness of seventeenth-century road travel, we can only conjecture. Perhaps direct passage was not easily available; perhaps the seas were too often choppy; perhaps it was an unnecessary expense. But he did find land travel laborious, and from the early 1610s he was physically incapable of going on horseback, being "able to travel [only] by coach, and by easy stages" (CSP, Ireland, 1615–1625, 454). When his wife, who always insisted on accompanying him, was ill, as she was repeatedly from 1620, they had no choice but to progress by "small journeys": Kingsbury, 3:529. Yet he still managed to conduct business from afar. Some correspondence was sent via Ferrar (ibid.,) but some came directly to Sandys (ibid., 223–224). At one point he even intercepted a ship headed for Jamestown as it was passing nearby Sandwich so that he could add seven colonists to its payload (ibid., 191). He also had plenty of visitors with company connections (e.g., ibid., 216), and in at least one case Sandys's presence in Kent brought new blood into the enterprise—Sir Nicholas Tufton, a Kentish neighbor who became deeply involved in Virginia affairs, supplied colonists from his estate, and conducted business at Northbourne: ibid., 191, and Felix Hull, "The Tufton Manuscripts and the Virginia Connection," *Virginia Magazine of History and Biography* 65 (1957): 313–327, esp. 325.

[55] Kingsbury, 2:447–448. The four were all Londoners.

diversification proved to be a chimera because tobacco was the one safe and profitable guarantee of Virginia's continued existence.

In terms of sheer numbers, the shipment of new inhabitants to America was remarkably efficient. We have already seen that Sir Edwin played a considerable part in the resumption of emigration in 1618; and once he took control of the company there was a veritable flood. Most estimates revolve around a figure somewhat larger than a thousand a year; John Wroth and Nathaniel Rich, for instance, both of whom were well informed about such matters, seemed happy with the estimate "that in the years 1619, 1620, 1621 there was 3560 or 3570 persons transported to Virginia." This was a quite astonishing feat, considering the inadequacy of logistics at the time, and it was accomplished only because Sandys was so single-mindedly dedicated to this goal. Though few of the settlers were from the fringes of society, he accepted colonists from every source, including vagrant boys or Pilgrims.[56] And to give investors as much incentive as possible, he encouraged private plantations and subsidiary joint stocks, which allowed individuals to reap the substantial profits of tobacco directly, without having to wait for the company as a whole to get back on its feet. Despite the disappointments in sustaining so large a number of settlers— because of deaths and returns to England, the colony never managed to reach a total size much above two thousand, and it probably remained well below two thousand for most of Sandys's administration—one must nevertheless conclude that the influx of settlers was well-nigh essential for the survival of Jamestown.

The case is fairly straightforward. Notwithstanding some four thousand new colonists shipped to Virginia in the five years following the spring of 1619, the total population in 1624 was only a few hundred larger than it had been when Sandys assumed the treasurership.[57] An attrition rate of these proportions suggests that, without the extra inhabitants to cushion

---

[56] Ibid., 3:537, 259; Craven, *Dissolution*, 300–302; Morgan, "American Boom," 170–171, 184–185. Craven, *Company of London*, 48–49, suggests Sandys's program may have been inspired by the writings of his fellow Middle Templar Richard Hakluyt. Three documents of 1620 exemplify the emphasis on new colonists: Sir Edwin's letter to Naunton about transporting children to Virginia (PRO, SP/14/112/26); a memorandum by a close friend and associate, the "Project by Sir John Danvers for advancing the Plantation of Virginia," which examined ways of encouraging "men of extraordinary quality and good condition to go thither" (MCFP, Box 3, no. 1562); and an attempt to establish a royal plantation in the king's name (ibid., Box 4, no. 1563). Although the Pilgrims apparently headed for the Hudson, and ended up on Cape Cod, they still served Sandys's aim of ensuring the survival of English settlements by swelling their population, however scattered. For the social origins of the settlers, see below, note 61.

[57] Kingsbury, 3:259, 550–551; Carville V. Earle, "Environment, Disease, and Mortality in Early Virginia," in *The Chesapeake in the Seventeenth Century*, ed. Thad Tate and David Ammerman (New York, 1979), 96–125.

the impact of disease, accident, departures, and Indian hostility, there may not have been enough people to sustain the settlement, though it is difficult to tell, because casualties were always highest among newcomers. Nevertheless, considering that only about one fifth of the approximately five thousand English men and women who were in Virginia between 1619 and 1624 were still alive and *in situ* at the end of this period, it takes little imagination to estimate what would have happened without the emigration program. And if the basis for comparison is taken back to the beginning of 1618—before Sandys, newly devoted to the cause, helped bring about the first substantial increase in the colony's inhabitants—the importance of his policies in preventing the collapse of the venture becomes clear. It is also worth recalling that, even with a strength of perhaps two thousand, the Virginians lost nearly 350 of their number in the Indian attack of 1622; if the rate of emigration had been just half of what it was, there is a good possibility that Opachankano would have wiped out the entire settlement.[58]

This is not to deny the misguidedness of Sandys's policy when viewed from other perspectives. As early as June 1620 he was being warned by his friend Yeardley in Jamestown that the almost reckless transportation of people was having serious consequences:

I protest before God I run myself out of all the provision of Corn I have for the feeding of these people. . . . Mr. Ferrar is my worthy and loving friend, but herein I must blame him in casting up so short allowance [of food and clothes]. . . . They come very short, wheresoever the fault is I know not: it behooves him to look at it. The people are ready to mutiny for more. . . . What shall I say? All I have . . . I am willing to offer for the performing and making good your promises there [in England] made, but Sir, I beseech you, be not offended if I deal plainly respecting the honor and reputation of my friends and suffer me, I pray you, to advise you that you do not run into so great matters in speedy and hasty sending so many people over hither, and undertaking so great works, before you have acquainted me and have truly been informed by me of the state of the plantation and what may be done here. If you do not observe this rule, I shall and must fail in the executing of your projects. . . . What I can and am able to do if you will have patience I will from time to time inform you.[59]

[58] Kingsbury, 3:550–551. For similar reasons, as I argued in *Enterprise*, England's overseas expansion as a whole required years of waste, suffering, and failure before success was possible. This argument is given broader context in my "The Expansion of Europe and the Spirit of Capitalism," *Historical Journal* 17 (1974): 675–689.

[59] Kingsbury, 3:298–300. For the unfortunate consequences of the overzealous colonization see Craven, *Dissolution*, 300–303. His assessment is elaborated in Morgan, "American Boom," which stresses "the extreme demand for labor in combination with the long terms of service that were exacted for transportation" (197), though the research of the so-called Chesapeake School of historians (Lois Carr, Russell Menard, and others) has shown that oppor-

Sir Edwin took little heed of such counsels of restraint, and the result was a recklessness that imposed severe hardship on many of the colonists. A few prospered (among them Yeardley and Sir Edwin's brother George), thanks to cheap labor and lucrative tobacco, but most endured considerable misery. Moreover, the encouragement of private plantations meant that the settlers were widely dispersed and thus more vulnerable to the Indian attack (which the very demand for land may have helped provoke). Yet Sandys probably considered the sacrifices caused by his emphasis on numbers eminently worthwhile, because in the end his policy did ensure Jamestown's permanence. At a distance of three and a half centuries it is hard to deny the force of that argument, especially when the choice is seen, as it should be, in Sandys's own terms: suffering versus surrender (rather than the unwarranted juxtaposition of "patriot" libertarianism and royal repression).[60] Sir Edwin, determined that the English should remain in Virginia, saw a flow of emigrants as the only way to achieve his objective, and for that reason alone he pressed ahead regardless of consequences. It is one of the first signs of his increasing willingness to subordinate means to ends.

On diversification he was less single-minded. The effort to establish an ironworks, one of his favorite projects, was the object of heedless enthusiasm rather than the careful attention it needed, and it was quietly abandoned after the Indian attack. Similar fates befell the attempts to encourage saltworks, shipbuilding, glassworks, sawmills, silk production (patronized by the king himself), wine, and naval stores. Either the artisans died, or the climate was unfavorable, or the necessary financing was unavailable.[61] All

---

tunities in the colony were probably better than in England for members of the servant class: Tate and Ammerman, *Chesapeake*. Yeardley's letter was not the first carrier of bad tidings. A month earlier, the Company published a broadside that admitted the deaths of hundreds of the previous year's new settlers: Kingsbury, 3:275.

[60] This, of course, is how patriotic American historians like Alexander Brown have justified Sandys's conduct. Craven, *Dissolution*, 276–285, showed that only one contemporary document raised suspicions of Sir Edwin's harboring antimonarchical and "Genevan" ambitions, or using Virginia for political and religious ends. Craven's analysis totally destroyed that document's credibility, and in the perspective of Sandys's total career its accusations approach absurdity. Morgan, "American Boom," 185, argued more subtly that Sandys hoped to free the colonists from "the heavy burden of taxation" under the Stuarts. Sandys certainly contrasted Smythe's martial law with his own representative government, but it is unlikely that he had the pioneers' freedom or wealth in mind when he sent them out. His main aim was to get enough people to Virginia to assure the settlement's survival.

[61] Craven, *Dissolution*, 100, 178–180, 187–188, 195; Charles E. Hatch, "Mulberry Trees and Silkworms: Sericulture in Early Virginia," *Virginia Magazine of History and Biography* 65 (1957): 3–61. That the variety and skills of the settlers refute the myth that Sandys colonized Virginia with "the sweepings of the London streets" has been demonstrated by David R. Ransome, "'Shipt for Virginia': The Beginnings in 1619–1622 of the Great Migration to the Chesapeake," ibid., 103 (1995): 443–458. For Sandys's eventual acceptance of tobacco's importance, see above, note 28.

were well-intentioned undertakings which could have benefited the colony. But the Virginians could hardly be diverted from tobacco long enough to produce staple crops; exotica like mulberry trees were doomed from the start. And even if Sandys's policy had been successful, it would have made little difference to the settlers. His conviction that diversity would provide economic advantages—a belief he pursued both when he assumed the treasurership and two years later, when, despite a deteriorating situation, he renewed the campaign for industrial expansion—ignored the fact that tobacco was king. Fortunately, he soon realized the need for compromise: by the beginning of 1620 his friend Lionel Cranfield had secured the company's market by forbidding tobacco cultivation in England, and thereafter Sir Edwin concentrated on the profits of the company's one valuable commodity.

Between 1619 and the spring of 1621 such troubles must have seemed well within Sandys's power to contain, especially as he was already reducing the company debts that he had inherited from Smythe. It is true that he was unable to win reelection as treasurer in 1620. Both Smythe and Warwick opposed him, and may well have prevailed on the king (as Sandys suspected) to forbid his candidacy. But James had personal reasons aplenty for feeling that Sir Edwin was "his greatest enemy, and that he could hardly think well of whomsoever was his friend." One can easily understand why, "in a furious passion," James was able to give "no other answer but 'Choose the Devil if you will but not Sir Edwin Sandys.'"[62] After all, this was anything but his most amenable and respectful subject. Nevertheless, despite the pressure, Sandys's adherents did manage to avoid electing any of the four candidates the king suggested—Smythe and three of his associates—and chose instead one of their own number, the earl of Southampton. The earl, a newly appointed privy councillor, seemed an appropriate choice because he had access to James, but in fact he was merely a spokesman for Sandys. For all the fuss, therefore, Sir Edwin's supporters retained control of the company, and they added to their victories the following year when Southampton was elected governor of the Bermuda Company.[63]

At this level of political infighting, Sandys was more than a match for his opponents; nor was he bereft of powerful connections in 1620. Apart from

---

[62] Craven, *Dissolution*, 142; Kingsbury, 3:295; Brown, *First Republic*, 367.

[63] Craven, *Dissolution*, 144–145; anyone who reads the letters sent to Sandys from Virginia in mid-1621 (Kingsbury, 3:445–459) will see that his domination of the company's affairs continued. Southampton had become a privy councillor on April 30, 1619, and the king could hardly object to the earl's election, though he had specifically asked for a merchant. One must not overdo either the antagonism or the cohesiveness of the two opposing parties in the Virginia and Bermuda Company courts (see above, note 31), but one must also not attribute electoral victories to innocent accident, as did Butler, who claimed Southampton was chosen governor "contrary to his own knowledge and meaning": *Bermudaes*, 247.

his friendship with Southampton, he was close to two of the rising stars of the Jacobean court, Sir Lionel Cranfield and Sir Robert Naunton (not to mention one of its oldest lights, viscount Doncaster), and through them he had connections to the brightest star of all, the marquess of Buckingham.[64] Even though he had added to his enemies by quarreling with Warwick and pursuing the audit of Smythe—in both cases, however, in the belief that he was acting for the good of the company—his opponents cannot have had any illusions about his position.[65] He was far too strongly placed, not only among shareholders but also at Court, to be seriously vulnerable to their criticisms and attacks as long—and this was crucial—as he seemed to be running a reasonably successful enterprise.

Until the spring of 1621 the latter did not seem seriously in doubt. Unperturbed by a chronic shortage of funds, and the persistent losses of a new Magazine, the colony was growing rapidly, and glowing expectations were reported by intelligent colonists like John Pory and John Rolfe. Sandys called Pory's descriptions "panegyrics," and with Rolfe, the husband of Pocahontas and a leading promoter of tobacco, he developed a warm friendship.[66] The company felt sufficiently confident about its endeavors in 1620 to publish both an account of the thousand colonists it had sent out (accompanied by substantial supplies) during the year, and an assertive tract which trumpeted its accomplishments: *A Declaration of the State of the Colony and Affairs in Virginia*.[67] Designed as a response to doubts about Virginia's attractions, the tract was almost certainly written by Sandys; it was probably the work he referred to as "my discourse" in a letter to Ferrar. The cadences of the long sentences are strongly reminiscent of the *Relation*, and the emphasis on the reforms with which he had been associated is particularly noticeable. It is unlikely that any other leader of the company at the time would have been so careful to point out that "the laudable form of justice and government used in this realm [of

[64] Craven, *Dissolution*, 145–147, and *Company of London*, 48, analyzes Sandys's successes among company voters. He appealed to the average investor as a public-minded and persuasive reformer, and since each shareholder had a vote, regardless of the size of his holdings, Sir Edwin's support among the *menu peuple* was decisive. But his connections to the powerful were also weighty: he had met Buckingham (Kingsbury, 3:294), and he had links in 1620 with Cranfield, Southampton, Naunton, and Doncaster (above, chapter 8, notes 1–5).

[65] Warwick's piracy (which offended the king) and Smythe's unpaid debts seemed to Sandys real dangers for the company: Craven, *Dissolution*, 136–137, 106, 112–113; Thompson, "Warwick."

[66] Kingsbury, 3:241–248, 300–306, 307 ("panegyrics"), and 20, 241 (Rolfe's closeness to Sandys).

[67] Ibid., 239–241, 307–365. Sandys had the insouciance to produce these optimistic publications at the very time that a company broadside was admitting the death of hundreds of new colonists even while urging renewed building, additional clergy, and diversification of products to improve conditions in Virginia: ibid., 275–280.

England is] established [in Virginia] and followed as near as may be. The Governor is so restrained to a Council joined with him, that he can do wrong to no man, who may not have speedy remedy."[68] Characteristic, too, was the focus on diversification, on the growing population, and on the new legislation that had restructured both company and colony.

Sir Edwin clearly felt that he had ample justification for refuting Smythe's charge that he was too inexperienced to take control of a major business venture. In fact, the burden of the tract was to demonstrate his superiority to his predecessor. Putting the case bluntly in a letter to Buckingham, Sandys claimed "that more hath been done in my one year, with less than eight thousand pounds, for the advancement of that colony in people and store of commodities, than was done in Sir Thomas Smythe's twelve years, with the expense of near eighty thousand pounds."[69] Even without such exaggeration, Sir Edwin was not without grounds (particularly as regards the transportation of settlers) for feeling pleased with himself. There was new life in the colony; ambitious plans for various industries and for the founding of a college were nicely under way; and both the lottery and fresh investments were providing a good, if not totally adequate, income. Nor could Sir Edwin complain about his private interests in Bermuda and Virginia, for his plantations were benefiting from the influx of tenants to work the land. If he had reason to admit to John Ferrar in October 1620 that "this year in me doth verify the Italian proverb: Il mal non vien mai scompagnato," he was referring primarily to personal problems: to his wife's illness, to her miscarriage, and to a fire in their London house.[70] He had little cause for such regret in the year's colonial affairs. Although he cannot have been happy with James's interference in the election, with the outbreak of a dispute over fishing rights that was to pit him against Sir Ferdinando Gorges and the New England ventures, with the worsening of relations with Smythe and Warwick, or with the concomitant "mass of Malignity," he nevertheless seemed, in general, to be achieving exactly what he wanted for Virginia.[71]

If one focuses on the early months of 1621, therefore, without looking

[68] Ibid., 306, 310. The similarities among this tract, the instructions for Yeardley in 1618, the reforms of 1618, and the 1625 defense of the Sandys administration (see above, notes 26, 27, 29), in style and content, suggests that all were from the same hand: presumably Sir Edwin's.

[69] Ibid., 295.

[70] Ibid., 416. He also used the proverb five months earlier in a letter to Ferrar about his wife's illness and the beating of his coachman by a band of thieves in Sandwich: ibid., 270. On the new investments, see ibid., 59–63, 339–340, and Rabb, *Enterprise*, 90; for the college, Craven, *Dissolution*, 55, 150.

[71] Kingsbury, 3:218. On the fishing dispute, see Craven, *Dissolution*, 292 ff., and Harold A. Innis, *The Cod Fisheries: The History of an International Economy* (New Haven, Conn., 1940), esp. 64–75.

ahead to the time when overhasty settlement, financial inadequacies, and the assaults of his enemies ruined Sandys's dreams, one finds him at the pinnacle of his career. True, he was about to turn sixty, but then he had not made an early start: he was forty-two before he exerted himself in Parliament, and fifty-six when he began to take a major interest in Virginia. In both endeavors he had gained rapidly, and held successfully, a prominencee unmatched by any of his associates at the time. Although these splendid attainments were to turn sour with alarming speed, in early 1621 his public stature was at its zenith, and he seemed to be moving from triumph to triumph.

Chapter XIII

COLLAPSE IN VIRGINIA

FALTERING HOPES IN VIRGINIA

Suggestions of trouble in Virginia began to mount during 1621. Diversification continued to be Sandys's watchword, and he was doubtless glad to hear, in July 1621, that "the iron works go forward very well." But this was an illusion: ten months later, before London had heard of the Indian assault that ended the attempt to manufacture iron, the company was still hoping "that by Whitsuntide next, we may rely upon iron made by" a new ironmaster. Similarly, despite the hopes for silk, a report from the colony in May 1621 was hardly cheering: "people are now very much discouraged" as they encountered the difficulties of silk production. In the words of Sandys's correspondent, Thomas Nuce, "they thought themselves in Italy, Spain, or France: countries plentiful and populous" of entrepreneurs. He himself, he wrote, had done his best: "I would to God the seed had come safe that I might have made trial, though to my loss, so I might have given the Company satisfaction." Unfortunately, there were not too many colonists like Nuce, and unfortunately, too, he only encouraged Sandys's determination to ship people to Virginia. Most revealing, however, was Nuce's postscript, another hint of things to come: "Since I cannot write pleasing things, I have forborn to direct my letters to the Company."[1] Unrelenting in his belief that his methods were the right ones, Sandys was increasingly resorting to the concealment and deception that, to my knowledge, were first indicated by this letter. As his hopes faded, his questionable tactics multiplied, and in the end hastened the destruction of his position.

Another sign of fading hopes is the list of fifty people sent across the Atlantic in September 1620 which John Smith of Nibley annotated, apparently in the summer of 1621. By then twenty-seven had died, three had returned, and four had gone no further than Ireland. In other words, over two thirds had not become long-term colonists. And yet almost fourteen hundred new emigrants were sent out on twenty-one ships during 1621, including sixteen Italians expert in glassmaking, twenty-five boatmakers (to promote fishing), and fifty-seven "young maids," not to mention a Magazine worth £2,000. It was no wonder that over the year 1621 the company

---

[1] Kingsbury, 3:457.

went £1,400 into debt; what was remarkable was that after they heard this, on May 22, 1622, the adventurers at once approved an outlay of a further £200 for such "necessary provisions" as hatchets, axes, shovels, and spades. And they did so despite concern over improprieties in the accounts of one of the company's captains, Samuel Argall, though they agreed to "think on some course to call him to account, which if he shall refuse to do then to proceed in a legal course against him." Moreover, it was to be another year before John Ferrar's accounts, also questioned, were audited and cleared.[2] That Sir Edwin persisted in his policy of rapid population growth in the face of these fiscal uncertainties is all the more telling, because he must now have been aware of the likelihood that the losses were due, not to corruption, but to the inherent flaws in his policies.

The insistence that diversity of products and increase of population should remain the prime goals of the Virginia enterprise is everywhere apparent in the records of 1621. On July 24 Sandys and Southampton signed a long document that laid out nearly fifty instructions for the colonists, amongst which the single most frequently reiterated demand was for the encouragement of new products: among others, timber, iron, salt, pitch, tar, drugs, and "good fishing between James river and Cape Cod." The latter directly contravened the Privy Council's decision the previous month (despite a parliamentary asssault led by Sandys) to authorize Gorges' patent for fishing rights off the Atlantic coast. Since the authorization did, however, require that fishing and shore privileges be given to Jamestown for its "sustentation," this was enough of a loophole to allow the Virginians virtually carte blanche, though they never became seriously interested in a fishing industry. Yet the discouragement of tobacco continued. The supplies brought over by the Magazine were not to be paid for with smoke, and artisans were not to be allowed "to forsake their former occupations for planting tobacco or such useless commodities." To give teeth to the instructions, Sandys's youngest brother, George, was to come over to the colony as its treasurer, with authority over "staple commodities." There was also hope for an influx of inhabitants into a series of new plantations that the earl of Pembroke wanted to establish.[3]

None of these efforts were to be more successful than their predecessors. Exhortations, the dispatch of George Sandys, the replacement of Yeardley with Sir Francis Wyatt, and the attempt to streamline the colony's government and its record-keeping (part of the July 24 instructions) could not create a successful enterprise. There had apparently been some hope of drawing up a new patent early in the year, but that, too, had proved fruitless.[4]

Nor was the one staple, tobacco, quite the savior it had once seemed to be. Even though the planters ignored the company's instructions that only small amounts, of good quality, be grown, their profits were diminishing as the market became increasingly well supplied. The very "smoke" that was supposed to be sustaining the Magazine, let alone the other wants of the Virginians, was not living up to expectations. In 1619 the company had agreed to pay three shillings per pound for the best grades of the crop, but by August 1621, as the council informed the colonists, it was being "sold for less than . . . 20 pence per pound": that is, at about half the price paid in Virginia. Accordingly, they now refused to continue the set price, and asserted that henceforth they would accept no rolled tobacco, only the leaf. Moreover, they gave notice "that after this year [the company] will expect no further supply of any necessaries to be exchanged with [the colonists] for their darling tobacco."[5] Not only was the value of this one essential product declining; its sale was causing friction between the directors at home and the settlers overseas.

For all the protestations, however, the indispensability of tobacco could not be ignored. Consequently, Sandys fought for a tobacco bill in the Commons in 1621; the company continued using the Netherlands market, especially Middelburg, until forbidden to do so, because the customs duty was a halfpenny instead of twelve pennies per pound; it tried hard during October 1621 to prevent the Privy Council issuing the order that forced all Virginia tobacco to be brought to England; and it complained about its competitors, even when the new tobacco farmer, Abraham Jacob (who was granted a patent for a year in December), was forced to restrict imports from Spain to 60,000 pounds' weight.[6] These actions are much more telling than the pious statements about "darling tobacco."

As in earlier years, Sandys's involvement was from afar. After signing the

---

[4] Kingsbury, 1:438–446, passim., 3:311.

[5] Ibid., 3:162, 496. In early 1620, the company said five shillings per pound was the highest price it had ever received for tobacco, though Captain Bargrave later asserted that he was offered eight shillings in 1618: ibid., 1:291; 3:599. By June the company was trying to establish a minimum selling price of four shillings, but the very effort suggests this level was not being reached—though the price had probably not fallen below two shillings, as the company claimed it had the previous year: ibid., 2:56. All prices refer to "best grade" Virginia tobacco. Even when paying more than double customs duty, Spanish tobacco was sufficiently finer in quality to sell at a higher price and offer a better profit to all parties.

[6] Ibid., 1:422 (the Middleburg arrangement), 292 (the English customs duty), 526–532 (the arguments with the Privy Council); APC, 1621–1623, 73 (the Privy Council's order). Jacob's patent is described in W. F. Craven, *Dissolution of the Virginia Company: The Failure of a Colonial Experiment* (New York, 1932), 230, and "Lord Sackville's Papers Respecting Virginia, 1613–1631," *American Historical Review* 27 (1922): 528.

July 24 instructions, he did not appear at a company meeting until the quarterly court of January 30, 1622. In the meantime, he could rest secure in the knowledge that the Ferrars, his old friend Sir John Danvers, and colleagues like Lord Sheffield and Sir Walter Erle were attending meetings regularly. Distracted by his problems in the 1621 Parliament and his wife's continued ill health, he could barely bring himself to congratulate Ferrar on a recovery from sickness: "If my afflicted mind were capable of any joy in this world, I should greatly rejoice for your good recovery."[7] Yet the company continued his policies doggedly in his absence, and despite the relentless evidence of mounting failure. As 1621 ended, and Sir Edwin, still reeling from his imprisonment that summer, gloomily entered his sixty-first year, it had become clear that the company he directed had none of the reserves of capital, good will, or imagination that it needed to survive the devastating shocks of the next two years.

The Tobacco Contract

The first shock was not long in coming. On March 22, 1622, the Indians of Virginia, fearful of the growing intrusions of the colonists, "massacred in all parts above three hundred men, women, and children," killed cattle, burned houses, and forced the colonists to abandon "many dispersed and straggling plantations."[8] The news was sent from the colony in late April, and reached London by mid-July. Before he returned to Northbourne at the end of that month, Sandys took a large part in drafting the company's letter of reply, a document of measured cadences and points laid out one by one that bears the stamp of his methodical style. Its content, however, was anything but measured. By turns petulant and utopian, the instructions now sent to Jamestown reveal how completely the directors in England had lost touch with the settlement's needs. After berating the colonists for lack of preparation, for "enormous excesses of apparel and drinking," and for neglecting prayer, the council exhorted them to adopt a spartan existence, reliance on God, and (again) "the setting up of staple commodities." The latter demand was sweetened by the news that the company itself might obtain the monopoly of tobacco imports once Jacob's patent expired (a matter that was already under negotiation). There was also good news in that the king, shocked by the attack, had contributed arms for the colony. But finances were so grim that there was no chance of

---

[7] Kingsbury, 1:555, 556, 584; 3:509. One of the company's agents, Edward Blayney, told Sandys at this time that he prayed daily for the health of his "honored lady": ibid., 3:508. Katherine Sandys's illness of September and October 1621, and her recovery by November 5, are described in MCFP, Box 7, nos. 973, 974. In the first letter, on October 1, Sandys takes comfort, amidst his troubles, in the belief that "God will not abandon Virginia."

[8] Kingsbury, 3:612–613, 666–673, 2:93–96.

raising money for a Magazine, and so the settlers had to fend for themselves in the production of food. It almost defies belief that this catastrophic information should have been accompanied by assurances that "many hundreds of people" were on their way to swell the numbers of the shattered (and ill-supplied) population. Contemporary estimates indicate that well over a thousand were sent out in 1622, fewer only than those transported in the bumper year of 1621.[9]

Nothing in former policies was to be changed, except that settlements were to be more concentrated. The ironworks were to be resumed, and plans were to continue for the creation of a college, to be supervised by George Sandys. As for the Indians, "we must advise you to root out from being any longer a people, so cursed a nation, ungrateful to all benefits, and uncapable of all goodness." Only children were to be spared so as to "be reduced to civility, and afterwards to Christianity." As for their chief, "if any can take Opachancano himself, he shall have a great and singular reward from us." The entire dispatch, pervaded as it was by recrimination, vindictiveness, and stubborn self-righteousness, presents a depressing spectacle. Its plaintive demands for more tobacco from Virginia, coupled with its high-flown sentiments, its admission of poverty and helplessness, and its narrow concern for the company's own land, suggest an enterprise on the verge of desperation. Much the same message came forth in the council's next major letter, in October.[10] Even without the Indian attack to accentuate the company's failures, it is hard to see where Virginia was likely to find the fresh ideas or the discipline it needed.

Pouring out ever more colonists was certainly no answer. Even the king perceived "that the planters in Virginia attended more their present profit rather than their safety . . . by living so scatteringly."[11] They considered open land, fertile in tobacco, to be more important than secure and protected holdings. Neat formulas, deriving from the schoolmasterish principles of an armchair theorist like Sandys, were doomed to ineffectiveness in the frontier community of Jamestown.

One major effort by the company in 1622 did succeed, though it was a qualified success, and its provisions were to trigger a confrontation that ultimately helped destroy the organization. Bedeviled by tobacco, dismayed by its importance, but even more dismayed by the royal contracts that impeded its sale, Sandys finally realized that the only remedy was for the Virginia and Bermuda companies to seek the monopoly over imports themselves. The idea must have taken hold soon after Sir Edwin, back in

[9] Ibid., 3:537. According to a hostile analysis, 4,270 colonists were sent out between 1619 and 1622: ibid., 4:135.

[10] Ibid., 3:683–690. Contrast the assessments cited in notes 49–51, below.

[11] Kingsbury, 2:96.

London, returned to active participation in colonial affairs at the end of January 1622, not long after Jacob's patent took effect. There is no evidence of actual negotiations with the Crown until early June, but the notion must have been floating around earlier, possibly during February, when Sandys was attending all the company's meetings.

The official record during this period shows Sandys at work on the countless details of company business: much concerned about the school for Indians, the ironworks, the accounts, and the continuing dispute with Smythe. He did not appear at any meetings from March to May, not even the annual election on May 22, when Southampton and Nicholas Ferrar were easily elected treasurer and deputy.[12] But at the next session, on June 5, he reappeared with a welcome progress report on the tobacco contract.

Possibly he was keeping a low profile because of the annual election, in which James took a close interest for the third year running. The king even recommended ten prominent London merchants for the positions of treasurer and deputy, and declared himself "not well satisfied" that the company avoided all his choices.[13] But the small crisis passed, and Sandys was able to negotiate the tobacco contract without hindrance. He was joined in the discussions by Southampton and other members of the company's council, but they admitted that he was "best acquainted with the manner of it," and so he reported the developments. The initiative, he said, had come from Cranfield, lord treasurer since the previous autumn. Ever "bending his thoughts to the advancing of his Majesty's profit and revenue, and yet careful to avoid grieving of his Majesty's subjects," Cranfield had lighted upon the Virginia Company, of which he had long been a member. He had realized that the tobacco patents worked "to the discontent and perhaps detriment" of both Virginia and Bermuda, and he had concluded that the two companies might want to control the monopoly themselves. He had therefore approached Sandys (unpleasantness in Parliament notwithstanding) and urged him to seek financial advice from another longtime member, Sir Arthur Ingram, who happened also to be closely associated with the lord treasurer. Whether Ingram, a rather shady customer, helped Sandys as much as he helped Cranfield is doubtful, but Sandys had little choice, and in any case he was now ready to accept whatever hopeful prospects he could find.

The proposal the two men came up with was to offer the king a quarter

---

[12] Ibid., 1:584–611, passim; 2:29. In addition to the recriminations against Smythe, there were continuing complaints and countercomplaints involving Samuel Argall, the former governor of Virginia whose links with Warwick (as a privateer captain) were to have ill consequences for Sir Edwin. The statement of accounts presented to the company in May showed Southampton receiving and disbursing nearly £7,000 as treasurer, and Deputy John Ferrar spending £1,400 more than he received: ibid., 2:19.

[13] Ibid., 2:28, 34–35.

of the weight imported each year. Cranfield had rejected this offer as inadequate, and the company therefore appointed a committee of eight to pursue the matter further, joined by six from the Somers Islands Company, which had its meeting immediately thereafter. The membership revealed unmistakably that this was Sandys's project and his negotiating team.[14]

The discussions proceeded until Sandys returned to Northbourne around the end of July, but on June 29 a first draft of the agreement was considered at a special meeting of the company. In return for administering the monopoly, the company was asking for the end of Spanish imports and planting in England, regulation of prices, and more favorable regard by the king. Cranfield's response was as tough as his reputation. He wanted James to receive a third of the tobacco; he wanted all freight charges undertaken by the company; and he wanted to continue a set amount of Spanish tobacco imports. The adventurers took two days to consider these demands, and the full-dress debate on July 1 at which they decided their reply was heated. On point after point, however, despite widespread opposition, they came to realize the "necessity of yielding" if they were not to lose the chance at a monopoly. Sandys ran the debate as he had managed many similar confrontations on the floor of the Commons. After a while, in fact, the five peers who were present put the proceedings in Sir Edwin's hands so that they might reach some conclusion in "orderly fashion." He at once reduced the various issues to his usual numbered "heads," each to be discussed on its own. There were still moments of "long pause and much dispute," but gradually the opposition to the new terms was worn down.[15] Sandys was doubtless much helped by Southampton, Cavendish, Sir Walter Erle, the Ferrars, his brother Samuel, and other allies, but the main burden of pointing out the benefits and minimizing the disadvantages lay on his shoulders. There was no getting away from the fact that it was a one-sided arrangement, because the company, in its anxiety for the monopoly, had no bargaining counters. Unless he got excellent terms, the king could easily go elsewhere; indeed, there was never a hint, for all of Cranfield's professed good wishes and decade of commitment to Virginia, that his proposal had any purpose but revenue for the Crown.

Sandys doubtless believed that the contract would be a sure source of

---

[14] Ibid., 2:35–38. That the idea of a contract arose during a conversation between Cranfield and Sandys is plausible, because the two men were in touch at this time about personal business—on May 8 Cranfield smoothed the way for Sir Edwin to purchase timber from the king's holdings in the New Forest: Sackville MSS. ON 8247, a reference I owe to Conrad Russell. The negotiators were Sandys, Southampton, Danvers, Nicholas Ferrar, and four of their friends from the Virginia Company; and Cavendish (governor), John Barnard (governor-elect and a director of the Virginia Company), John Ferrar (the new deputy), and three of their friends from the Somers Islands Company.

[15] Kingsbury, 2:57–72.

income for a company which had exhausted every other possibility. The agreement also offered him a chance to gain some recompense after years of profitless endeavor. He presumably had some kind of salaried post for himself in mind when, at the end of the exhausting July 1 discussion, he slipped in a resolution stating that the company would retain sole jurisdiction, without royal interference, over the appointing and paying of the officers who supervised the tobacco imports.[16] That provision was to lead to salaries which, within a few months, were to give Sandys's enemies ammunition for their assault on his policies, and which, more recently, have been used by historians to question Sir Edwin's motives.

It is obvious that nobody entered the world of commerce and colonization for recreation, charity, or love of a fine cause alone. An interest in money doubtless animated Sandys no less than most human beings. Yet he had many other aims, and until 1622 personal profit seemed remarkably low among his priorities. If he now sought private gain, his actions impugn neither the sincerity of his continuing work for Virginia nor the public-mindedness of some five years of effort to create a viable colony. After all, both of the syndicates that had undertaken the tobacco contract during the previous two years had done so solely for profit, and it must have seemed likely that there would be large enough profits to support salaries for the officers who spent their time managing the monopoly. In the size of the salaries and in the politics of the arrangement, Sandys (usually so sensitive to appearances) miscalculated badly; moreover, as the company collapsed he did become deceitful and self-serving; but in the final analysis this attempt to serve his own financial interest has to be seen as a minor matter in the context of his times and his long-term efforts to build an English overseas empire.

Southampton and Sandys went to see Cranfield the day after the July 1 meeting. The following afternoon, after further complaints against Warwick's privateer captain, Samuel Argall (who was ultimately to be the cause of the fatal breach between Sandys and Warwick), the company heard Sir Edwin report the latest progress. Cranfield had pushed for better terms yet again. Whereas Virginian interests wanted Spanish imports limited to two years, he wanted three; they sought a renewable three-year contract, but he insisted on seven. Sandys might eventually have felt obliged to grant these and two other concessions, but at the time he argued against them, and Cranfield relented. He accepted two years of Spanish imports and a contract terminable after three years; he also agreed that the king could not expect a third of all the tobacco (since some was grown by individuals and private plantations in Virginia) but only a third of the company crop, though he did insist that it be a third of all imports, not a third

[16] Ibid., 2:72.

of all sales. Going through the particulars one at a time, Sandys obtained approval for each proviso, and a new text of the contract was drawn up. On July 10 a Somers Islands meeting endorsed an essentially identical document.[17]

With Sandys away in the country during the summer, the negotiations went no further until November 6, the date of the first meeting Sir Edwin attended after returning to London. The only news was that Ingram had asked John Ferrar what was happening, and had requested one further change: that the forty thousand pounds imported from Spain should be the best-quality tobacco. The adventurers agreed, though not without mutterings about the difficulty of finding that much of the finest grades. Both Sandys and Southampton then went back to see Cranfield, and everyone agreed that the time was at last approaching for the signing of the contract. The same committees representing the two companies were to prepare for the final discussion at the next quarterly meeting, on November 20; to strengthen them, seven members were added to the committee, including two peers and Samuel Wrote, a fairly new merchant member and director of the Virginia Company, who had been one of the group that had written the draft of the contract.[18]

On the afternoon of the twentieth, the revised agreement came up for consideration. The latest flurry of talks with Cranfield had three new provisions: first, if the company could not obtain eighty thousand pounds of the best Spanish tobacco before the end of two years, they could take a third year; second, the king no longer wanted prices fixed; but, third, he wanted the company to accept a maximum price in England. The first two proposals were approved after some debate, but the third was "thought to be so dangerous as the Companies might no way thereunto agree, it being conceived that . . . the damage might be so great as might utterly undo the Companies." Sandys and Southampton were therefore asked to renegotiate this provision. The rest was accepted, and to save time the adventurers resorted to a device which, by requiring that "the letter of the law might in rigor seem somewhat violated," revealed how closely the Virginia and Somers Islands enterprises were related: final ratification would take place at the junior company's quarterly meeting on November 27.[19]

In the meantime, on the twenty second, a special meeting learned that the details of the Spanish imports had been settled in a clause (whose "words were drawn up by Sir Edwin Sandys") that recognized the problems of obtaining first-rate tobacco. Nobody was enormously happy, but

---

[17] Ibid., 2:79–88, 97–98. The Somers Islanders made one small amendment that the senior company accepted.

[18] Ibid., 2:120–122, 127–129, 98.

[19] Ibid., 2:138–140.

there seemed to be no alternative. As "a noble and honorable person" put
it, they were willing to take the Crown's terms "not as good meat well
sauced but of a portion necessary for their health." Reluctantly satisfied,
the members then heard that Southampton and the directors thought that
officers should be appointed to manage the contract. Cavendish explained
that they felt it best to have a director, a deputy-cum-treasurer, and a
board of eight committeemen. To get "requisite" people to serve, the company would have to offer a "just reward" to the officers, and everyone
agreed. The nominee for director, Sandys, was then proposed. Sir Edwin
at once "very earnestly besought them to spare him, being unexperienced
in matter of merchandising and trading, of both [of] which that officer
would require exact knowledge." Besides, he could not continually reside
in town, for he had "a great family in the country, and began now as he
grew old to wax weak, and therefore proposed rather to withdraw himself
from the businesses of the world than to engage himself further." The
company refused to accept his excuses, or those of John Ferrar, nominated
for deputy, who claimed that his private affairs were suffering from inat-
tention.[20]

Thus was the scene set for the salaries which did such harm to both
Sandys and the company. His protestations against the appointment ring
true, and there is no reason to doubt that he wished to avoid the weight of
new and difficult responsibilities. On the other hand, he had taken such a
major part in the negotiation, design, and acceptance of the contract, and
his hopes for the company remained so strong, that it is easy to understand
why he could be prevailed upon to accept. The prospect of a salary may
also have been an inducement, though one cannot tell how heavily it
weighed at this stage of the proceedings.

On the twenty-seventh final approval was reached. The Somers Islands
meeting transformed itself into a Virginia Company court, and Southampton announced that he and Sandys had persuaded Cranfield to make
the adjustments about Spanish imports that had been discussed at the
previous meeting. The price maximum was not mentioned, which suggests
that at the eleventh hour the two men had managed to wring a concession
from the lord treasurer. In July they had managed to resist a few of his
demands about the length of time various arrangements were to remain in
effect, and the new compromise indicates that they had not been completely browbeaten. That they had remained defensive and subservient to
the Crown's wishes, however, nobody could fail to see. Cranfield had used
his advantages to the full, and even at the last moment had insisted on a
few minor changes of wording. Then, at last, he had signed the articles
"with his hand." The adventurers, "after some pause," made no objections

    [20] Ibid., 2:142–145.

to the document, "and the whole bargain ... was ratified and confirmed with an unanimous consent by a general erection of hands, no one dissenting."[21] It had been a long affair, whose shepherding had been, if anything, more complex than the guidance of a parliamentary bill toward passage. That the successful resolution was no small triumph for Sandys is perhaps less noteworthy than the fact that this was the last of his triumphs in his Virginian venture.

THE ASSAULT ON THE CONTRACT

Almost immediately the first signs of trouble appeared. When Southampton announced the staff that would manage the monopoly—a score of employees, whose salaries (led by Sandys with £500 and John Ferrar with £400), not to mention the premises they required, swelled total annual expenses to £2,000—he was met by "a general silence." The Virginia adventurers reacted no differently than M.P.s when unpalatable news arrived. Southampton broke the quiet by urging everyone to be candid, whereupon Robert Smith spoke up. Smith was an experienced London merchant, a member of the company since 1609 and of numerous other enterprises (including the East India Company), and a Virginia Company council member whom Sandys probably recruited, since he was nominated together with such friends of Sir Edwin as Dr. Gulston and Sir Edward Sackville. Smith voiced what must have been the feelings of many of the ordinary adventurers. In his view, "there were divers gentlemen and other sufficient men that for conscience sake would do the business for far less reward." Sackville answered that "in conscience" they ought to pay people who worked for their profit; that salaries made them more answerable; and that others who "had for conscience sake served this Company had for conscience sake undone it": a good description of Sandys, but Sackville doubtless meant it to refer to Smythe.[22]

Southampton thanked Smith for speaking his mind, and Nicholas Ferrar resumed the defense. Both the chief money earners (Sandys and John Ferrar), he said, would work far more than they would be recompensed; for the sake of conscience alone, he would neither offer nor, perhaps, would they accept the positions. Robert Barker, a Spanish merchant and a member since 1609, would have none of that. "Having followed these courts many years," he remarked, "he had never heard of so great salaries"; in fact, what he had heard was that the company had fallen *short* £500 and more, even in enterprises run by unpaid officers. Another long-time adventurer, Edward Ditchfield, who had invested in various colonial enterprises,

---

[21] Ibid., 2:147–148.

[22] Ibid., 2:148–152; for Smith's election to the council, see ibid., 1:379, 383.

including Bermuda, tried to mediate. "This was like to be a hard year," he informed the assembly, and "perhaps there would not be so great a quantity of tobacco brought in." Consequently, there would be less work, and they might reduce the salaries. Southampton squashed this idea: although "it would be a year of the least benefit," the work of setting up the mechanism would tax the officers more severely than in any succeeding year. The great man having spoken, that was the end of the debate. "After good pause" the salaries were accepted and the officers elected—Sandys by a vote of sixty-five to five, Ferrar by sixty-eight to two.[23]

But the smooth conclusion was deceiving. A week later, on December 4, a regular Virginia Company meeting exploded into an assault on the actions of the previous weeks that signified the erosion of Sandys's support among ordinary members—his mainstay for nearly four years. At the November 27 meeting it had been the quiet adventurers Smith, Barker, and Ditchfield who had raised questions. Now it was the turn of another of the new members whom Sir Edwin's administration had brought into the company: Samuel Wrote. He had joined the organization (as well as the Somers Islands Company) in 1620, and had been elected a member of the Virginia Council on the same day as Robert Smith, Sir Edward Sackville, and Dr. Gulston.[24] In other words, he seemed exactly the kind of small investor who was likely to go along with the plans of those who had brought him into the two companies in the first place. His expressions of concern revealed how distressed an average, thoughtful member was bound to become as he surveyed the failures of Sandys's hopes and policies.

The protest began as a continuation of a point that Sir Edwin himself made. He announced that the official proclamation of the contract had been delayed, and that in the meantime he and his committee had spent "many days" looking up precedents for the arrangement. Moreover, to encourage the importation of sufficient Spanish tobacco to meet their forty thousand pounds' weight quota, they had been seeking subscribers, as laid down at the quarterly court, and thus far nearly £2,500 had been raised. The purchase of the Spanish crop was being run as a separate joint-stock venture, with a requirement that anyone who was not already a member of the Virginia Company had to buy four shares of Virginia land worth £50 so as to gain the right to subscribe. Sandys regretted that so high a requirement had been set, because "he knew some worthy gentlemen [who] would willingly have underwritten" the venture if the prerequisite had

[23] Ibid., 2:153–155. As soon as the Virginia Company made its decisions, Cavendish took the chair and the Somers Islands Company came into being to approve the same provisions: ibid., 2:156–157.

[24] Ibid., 1:379, 383.

been merely two shares of land.[25] Wrote's intervention, following immediately on Sandys's speech, was at least in part an endorsement of Sir
Edwin's wish to revise the four-share proviso.

Wrote was a member of the committee elected to supervise the tobacco
contract, and he noted that he had originally proposed the four-share prerequisite. He was not committed to the idea, however, and he certainly did
not think that the orders accepted at the previous meeting should be
treated like "the laws of the Medes and Persians, never to be altered or
revoked." Indeed, he thought that this decision, as well as some of the
others that had been hastily reached at the November 27 meeting, might
be reconsidered. He was particularly concerned about the Company's having to raise a tenth of the joint stock, and about the salaries they had
agreed to pay.[26]

Once aroused, Wrote was a man of short temper, boundless self-righteousness, and an inclination toward vehement argument. Before the dispute (which dragged on for two months) was over, he had walked angrily
out of a meeting, had been rude to just about everyone who failed to agree
with him, and had asserted himself stubbornly, lengthily, and without restraint until he brought meetings to uproar. There was plenty to justify
Wrote's charges, but it was bad luck for Sandys that the man who came to
embody the opposition to the tobacco contract should have been so volatile, so unrelenting, and finally so destructive. Thoroughly outnumbered
in the company itself, Wrote had only one recourse: to make as much noise
as possible, a tactic he implemented so successfully that eventually he
brought Sandys's old enemies to the realization that they now had an issue
that could bring Sir Edwin down.

The problem Wrote was to pose was fully apparent by the end of the
December 4 meeting. Ignoring explanations, he "persisted in his former
opinion, that this business was not fairly carried, nor a fair course taken for
preparing of matters, but were hastily shuffled over." He was mildly supported by Alderman Johnson, a friend of Smythe and an old foe of Sandys
who had continued to attend occasional meetings. It may well have been
Johnson who passed the word along that a damaging confrontation was
brewing in the company, but at the meeting his remarks were brief and
limited.

The response, by Sandys and Nicholas Ferrar (Southampton was absent), defended their preparations and argued that the decisions of a quarterly court could be overturned only by another quarterly court. Wrote was
now playing the Sandys role, and he spoke in character: "he knew many

[25] Ibid., 2:162–163.
[26] Ibid., 2:163–164. Wrote's remaining remarks and the debate that followed, analyzed below, are on pp. 164–177.

eyes were upon him, and desired the speeches he had spoken might be set down." It was almost like Sir Edwin worrying about the Commons' Journal and about later retribution from the government for words he had spoken in Parliament. Indeed, Nicholas Ferrar concluded that the argument was "maintained with such violence and unorderliness" that—given Wrote's usual "great zeal" for Virginia—his actions seemed prompted by urgings "from some others who had by wrong informations and grounds persuaded him to do what he did." (This accusation of being an "undertaker" only strengthened the parallel with Sandys.) Wrote denied Ferrar's imputation, and there is in fact no reason to doubt that the tireless obstreperousness that ensued was his own doing.

The attempts to quiet Wrote finally prompted him to launch a major blast against the salaries as exactions that neither the company nor the planters could afford. Sandys himself, he noted, had opposed similar fees in the past as too burdensome for the struggling company. John Ferrar tried to stem the flow by noting that "neither was the government so tyrannical nor the Company so silly and simple men as Mr. Wrote would make them." But Wrote would not be appeased. Escalating the intemperance, he "willed Sir Edwin Sandys to keep his own laws, which he had made," and which were of no consequence to anyone else. William Lord Cavendish told him that he had now "affronted" members of the council, but Wrote insisted that his rudeness was directed only at Sandys.

Sir Edwin tried a sober reply that corrected some of his accuser's exaggerations. And Nicholas Ferrar accused Wrote of ignorance or mischief-making (Wrote's rejoinder was that he relied on conscience instead of knowledge), for the salaries had been discussed at great length at meetings which Wrote himself had attended. But Wrote, rebuffed, now sought to create any trouble he could. It was in sadness, not partisanship, that Arthur Bromfield, one of Southampton's stewards and a member since Smythe's administration, expressed "much grief for Mr. Wrote's proceedings and concluded there was much time spent to no purpose."

Despite the meeting's dwindling patience, Sir Edwin made one last effort to vindicate the company's conduct. Giving a parliamentary disquisition covering the entire history of the issue, he indicated how much they had suffered from previous contracts, and how much they had to gain from the new agreement. Even Alderman Johnson gave the proposed arrangement a degree of approval. He had heard that "it was said in the town, it was Sir Edwin Sandys's contriving"; but whether that was true or not, "for the salaries his opinion was that if the business thrived well they should well deserve them."

That was a fair judgment from a hardheaded merchant, but Wrote had further complaints to offer. Nicholas Ferrar told him to bring them to the next committee meeting, and the assembly, "much scandalized at the disorderliness used in calling in question and disputing of matters ordered in the quarter court," voted that the objections "should be silenced till the next quarter court." This was a vain gesture, because Wrote, engaged on a mission, would not hold back until he had done irreparable damage.

That December 4 meeting, followed by a directors' meeting a week later at which Wrote repeated his performance for the previously absent Southampton, was a grim ending to a bad year for Sandys. The king might be encouraging a silk industry, and Sandys might still be hoping for diversification, but after the Indian attack the grandiose policies pursued since 1618 had become an empty shell.[27] Emigration was in its last bumper year; the devastating death rate persisted; and now the one apparent success, the tobacco contract, was threatened.

This was also a difficult time in Sandys's private life. Since a miscarriage in 1620, his wife had been ill on and off, yet she accompanied him despite "tormenting pains" when Virginia business brought him to London. That distress only added to his worry at having to leave Northbourne before rents were collected, "with a multitude of workmen in all parts of my house," and while his sons were being prepared for school. As he told Ferrar, "never shall [I] leave things in greater confusion. But the torments & danger of my wife exceeds all other grief." Sandys's plantation in Bermuda seemed to be doing quite well, but this was small consolation. As he wrote Ferrar before leaving for London, "Your last close, of the desperate state of Virginia, if I knew all, does trouble me exceedingly."[28] He could hardly have guessed that, however bad prospects looked at the end of 1622, they were to worsen dramatically during 1623.

SANDYS UNDER ASSAULT

The new year began with more tantrums by Wrote. Not until the company had endured a series of drawn-out, painful sessions could it bring the mat-

---

[27] Ibid., 3:662; 2:187–195. Lest there be doubt where his sympathies lay, James intervened in June 1622 to halt a complaint by Captain Bargrave, a close associate of Sandys, against Sir Thomas Smythe.

[28] In late September Katherine Sandys was "very ill," and on October 13 she was "still worse and weaker." And yet, "though sick," she entertained various guests, including Lady Wyatt, off to join Governor Wyatt in Virginia. Sir Edwin admitted that "for her [Lady Wyatt's] sake, I would wish she stayed at home," but he realized what that would imply about the colony. Sandys's letters of September 1 and 23, and October 13, 1622 are in ibid., 3:676–677, 679–680, 690–692, and MCFP, Box 8, no. 983. The nature of Katherine's repeated ailments is unclear, though a description of a recurring fever over a number of weeks in 1625 (MCFP, letter to Ferrar of December 23, 1625) has suggested to one physician a possible case of brucellosis or malaria—a diagnosis I owe to Dr. A. V. Hoffbrand. Other symptoms at other times, however, such as a fever with an inflamed neck and throat in 1620 (Kingsbury, 3:270) point to entirely different illnesses. Katherine's toughness amidst these travails is remarkable.

ter to an end by censuring Wrote and suspending his membership on February 5.[29] But now the dispute gained new and ominous overtones. A number of members had been persuaded by Wrote's proposal for a smaller staff, costing less than £600 a year, and Sandys, forced on the defensive, resigned from his directorship of the contract. What was worse, King James (perhaps alerted by Wrote) sent a message through a courtier member of the company, Sir Henry Mildmay, to express displeasure at the suppression of free speech at meetings. And worst of all, Sir Edwin's old antagonists, emboldened by the turn of events, had reappeared. At the February 5 meeting Sir Edward Sackville (who was close to Sandys) reported Sir Thomas Smythe's renewed insistence that his financial dealings had been maligned; significantly, Warwick resumed active attendance at the same meeting, and a week later he was joined by Sir Nathaniel Rich, Argall, and other associates.[30]

It was this February 12 meeting that set the final destruction of Sandys's position implacably in motion. The Wrote affair did recede, but it had done its damage. Like Sir Edwin in Parliament, one individual, catching the right mood in the Virginia Company, had wrought havoc with a powerful position. If Sandys was usually the beneficiary of the consensual politics of Jacobean London, now he was their victim.

The attendance on February 12 was excellent (well over a hundred members) because the meeting immediately followed a Somers Islands quarterly court. Southampton used the occasion to inform the adventurers that the contract, ostensibly agreed upon months before, had only now been signed by Cranfield and passed on to him. However, after consulting the Privy Council, the lord treasurer had signified that the royal proclamation confirming the contract would not be issued for three or four months. He promised to implement all its provisions (e.g., the prohibition on domestic production of tobacco), but in the meantime the only explanation he could give for the delay was the pressure of "some important reasons of State." The one other record of these events is the order issued by the Privy Council on February 2 approving the contract, which suggests that the postponement may have been James's doing. Whatever the cause, it cannot have seemed a propitious development, and both Nicholas Ferrar and Sandys expressed worry about the future. The other members dis-

[29] Kingsbury, 2:181–259, passim.

[30] Ibid., 2:226–227, 240–243 (Wrote's proposal), 272–273 (Sandys's resignation), 214 (the king), 216 (Mildmay's report from the king), 260–261 (Smythe's complaint), 244 and 263 (Warwick, Rich, and Argall—among their aassociates was the lawyer Peter Phesaunt). For Smythe's "party" in 1623 see Robert Brenner, *Merchants and Revolution: Commercial Change, Political Conflict, and London's Overseas Traders, 1550–1653* (Cambridge, 1993), 101.

agreed, but did seek a June deadline for issuance of the proclamation. They then returned to the salaries.[31]

The ensuing discussion left no doubt that the adventurers had been swung around completely by Wrote. There was some injured defensiveness from Nicholas Ferrar, but he found no support as opposition to the salaries swept all before it. Sandys's own contribution to the debate was carefully considered. He pointed out how time-consuming the importation and sale of so much tobacco was bound to be, but he emphasized that his own interests were no longer involved. Since the previous meeting he had resigned from the directorship of the contract, and "having surrendered his place, which he very seriously protested he would not again accept," he felt that he could explain the administrative problems more objectively. But his opponents were not to be diverted. Nathaniel Rich asked for a greater say for the Bermuda adventurers, among whom Warwick, as the dominant shareholder, had far more influence, and he was supported by Alderman Johnson, Smythe's old ally who, hitherto moderate, was now resuming a hostile stance. These moves brought Rich into prominence, and he was proposed as a replacement for Sandys: a maneuver that could be interpreted as a tactic to neutralize criticism, but which seems to have been, in the context of the meeting, a spontaneous suggestion. Rich wisely declined, as did two other nominees, whereupon the company voted to refuse Sandys's resignation. He thus came out of the meeting with some of his honor salvaged, but he could have been under no illusions about the threat he now faced from powerful adversaries.[32]

That the struggle would quickly move to a wider arena, beyond Sir Edwin's control, became apparent almost at once. At a February 19 Virginia–Somers Islands court meeting which made plans to ensure that "no enemy or open hinderer of the Plantations" became a member (and excluded opponents from the planning committee), Sandys mentioned that he, Cavendish, and some others had to confer with Cranfield again, and on February 22 Southampton announced that they had been summoned by the lord treasurer. This time the reason was explicitly to adjudicate complaints made by the Warwick party. Indeed, Cranfield asked to see the minutes of the February 19 meeting, and all decisions about the contract, before he heard the two sides. Finally, on February 24, Sandys, Danvers, Southampton, Cavendish, John Ferrar, and a few of their supporters faced Warwick, Rich, Johnson, Wrote, and Wolstenholme in the presence of Cranfield.[33]

[31] Kingsbury, 2:263–266; *CSP, Colonial, 1574–1660*, 37.

[32] Kingsbury, 2:264–273; for Warwick's Bermuda holdings, see ibid., 4:20.

[33] Ibid., 2:273–295, 297.

What ensued, according to Sir Edwin, was that "much speech passed, which the Lord Treasurer heard with a great deal of patience." Warwick was joined by the customs farmers, led by Wolstenholme, who were fearful that the contract would ruin their profits, and who emphasized the interest of king and planters alike in the termination of the agreement. But at this stage Cranfield remained unmoved. The king, he said, had always tried to help the company (through the lottery and other favors) and therefore the contract ought to proceed. His one proviso was that all tobacco had to come to England to pay customs duties. Apart from this unwelcome suggestion, however, the meeting ended entirely to Sandys's satisfaction.[34]

Yet the meetings were by no means over. On March 1 the Privy Council summoned the opposing parties: Cavendish versus Warwick and Rich from Somers Islands, and Sandys and Nicholas Ferrar versus Smythe and Johnson from Virginia. To bolster themselves, Cavendish and Sandys brought Lord St. John, Lord Pagett, Sir Edward Sackville, Sir John Brooke, Sir Robert Killigrew, Danvers, and various other friends to the session three days later. The subject was to be the contract, but the proceedings were dominated by an onslaught on Southampton by a Mr. Bing. This new actor was apparently a friend of Wrote's, and also a member of the original committee that had drawn up the tobacco contract. Whether this second Wrote's appearance was planned, or merely indicated the ordinary adventurers' disaffection, there could be no mistaking Bing's vehemence as he poured out his grievances. The earl, he asserted, had shown his displeasure over the opposition to the contract by sinking into his chair, "pulling his hat over his eyes, and folding his arms across." This, and various supposedly threatening remarks, had frightened the company into submission.[35]

Warwick and Wrote were out of the room, speaking directly with the king, while Bing held forth. Had they been present, they would doubtless have attempted to restrain such absurdities, which only got Bing into trouble and certainly did their cause no good. As the council immediately reminded their impertinent witness, Southampton was "a peer of the realm and a member" of the very body before which Bing was testifying. He was

---

[34] Ibid., 2:297–298. A summary of the reasons against the award of the contract is in PRO, CO/1/3, fols. 52–55.

[35] Kingsbury, 2:98, 302–303. Bing's identity is uncertain, though he may be among the Bings in J. A. Venn, *Alumni Cantabrigienses*, vol. 1 (Cambridge, 1922), 152–153, perhaps William (153), since Kingsbury calls him W. Bing. This in turn may be the William Byng of Wrotham, Kent, admitted to Gray's Inn in 1612 (Joseph Foster, ed., *The Register of Admissions to Gray's Inn, 1521–1889*, vol. 1 [London, 1889], 131) since Venn and Foster indicate that the Bings of Wrotham were closely connected with Cambridge and Gray's Inn. I assume the friendship with Wrote because Bing delivered Wrote's contract proposals to the company in early February: Kingsbury, 2:228.

sent to prison for his misconduct, but within a year the victory of his friends over Sandys had made him a possible candidate for the commission that took over the affairs of Virginia. It took Sir Thomas Coventry himself, the attorney-general who officially sued for the dissolution of the company, to put an end to that idea: Mr. Bing, he wrote, was "a mere good fellow, of no estate."[36]

But these were the very people who were bringing Sir Edwin down. While a Warwick, a Rich, and a Wolstenholme were wielders of influence who could work within the government against Sandys's administration, they would never have gained their opportunity if the Virginia adventurers had not been rent into noisy factions by the likes of Wrote and Bing. During the two months that followed Bing's explosion in early March, the support the company's leadership had previously enjoyed from Cranfield and the Privy Council withered away. Rich, the chief organizer at Warwick's side, was to achieve his first success later in March, and by early May the tobacco contract had been nullified and the Privy Council had decided to look into the unseemly quarrels that were making Virginian affairs the talk of London.[37] The ensuing inquiry by a special commission proved fatal to Sandys's colonial venture; yet it is no small irony that the commission's disclosure of mismanagement and concealment was occasioned, not by the Indian attack or the company's near-bankruptcy, but by a sequence of events similar to those that usually worked to Sir Edwin's advantage. Now it was his turn to look like a profiteer from office, and to stand helpless against a well-orchestrated attack by clever politicians who made excellent use of the grievances of ordinary members. In this scenario, Wrote and Bing were the irate backbenchers, Rich played Sandys's character, Warwick was Southampton, and Sir Edwin and the earl themselves took on the roles of a Winwood or even a Bacon. Given the history of such encounters over the preceding twenty years, the outcome of this particular script, once the parts had been assigned, was not too hard to predict.

[36] Ibid., 2:303; Alexander Brown, *The Genesis of the United States*, 2 vols. (Boston, 1890), 2:828. Coventry explained that "for offensive behavior to Lord Southampton, [Bing] had been committed to the Marshalsea." Ibid., 828–829. Coventry kept a careful neutrality in the dispute, though he may have hoped Sandys would succeed, since he had rejoined the company in July 1622, when Sir Edwin was seeking new members. As attorney-general, Coventry acted under instructions when the company was dissolved, but his gesture in keeping Bing off the Virginia Commission may have hinted at his own allegiance.

[37] On April 19 Chamberlain noted that "there is a great faction fallen out in the Virginia Company," pitting Southampton, Cavendish, Sackville, and Sandys against Warwick, Smythe, Rich, and Johnson: N. E. McClure, ed., *The Letters of John Chamberlain*, 2 vols. (Philadelphia, 1939), 2:492.

THE COLLAPSE

The disintegration of the Virginia Company during the months that followed was swift and unrelenting. By the end of March 1623 it became clear that Cranfield would insist on the proviso he had raised a few weeks earlier: namely, that all Virginia tobacco had to pass through London to pay customs. Despite company pleas, and efforts to devise alternative schemes, the Privy Council refused to amend the requirement. Cranfield even cited Rich's opinion that it was perfectly possible for them to comply—a reference to a proposal by Sir Nathaniel that the king take over the importation of tobacco directly. That the lord treasurer was now listening more favorably to Rich became clear when the latter told a Virginia meeting on April 2 that the two of them had been speaking. What he had heard was that, if the company were to petition simply for the right to import all tobacco, including forty-thousand pounds' weight of Spanish origin, they might obtain the privilege. But this meant accepting Spanish imports, which the company rejected: a fatal misjudgement of the shifting balance at Court.[38]

Just four weeks earlier, Cranfield had rebuffed Johnson's claim that Sandys had mismanaged the company by speaking "of the good carriage of the business of the Plantation for these four years last past (whereby . . . it had thriven and prospered beyond belief and almost miraculously)." Now he was accepting suggestions from Sir Edwin's harshest opponents. And within another month he was to put Rich's scheme forward as his own proposal, while making certain that the Privy Council dissolved the still unimplemented tobacco contract. The company was being left stranded, but still it ignored the obvious political lifeline of accepting the lord treasurer's own alternative. Instead, it rejected his recommendations on April 30 without even recording the arguments put forward in a "long debate."[39]

The sudden reticence of the minutes may well have been prompted by the realization that events were beginning to swing against the company's leadership. A bitter tone had entered the proceedings. When, early in March, Cranfield's praise of the current handling of Virginian affairs (which the treasurer compared favorably with Smythe's and Johnson's misguided administration) was contradicted by Canning, who noted that Sir Edwin had been an assistant to Smythe, Sandys responded sharply: al-

---

[38] Cranfield's views were made official in a March 4 order of the Privy Council: Kingsbury, 2:321–322. The company's counterarguments, drawn up by Sandys (ibid., 2:325–327), were discussed during succeeding company meetings (ibid., 2:329 ff.). See also ibid., 2:335 (Cranfield's citation of Rich), 4:49–52 (Rich's document), and 2:342–344 (Rich's discussion with Cranfield, and the company's rejection of their proposal).

[39] Ibid., 2:319, 387–388, 392; it is almost certain that the rejection was the result of the Sandys party's continued fear of Spanish competition.

though he had given faithful advice, he said, "commonly what was then done in term times during his abode in town was for the most part undone again in the vacations when he was absent out of town." This was all very well, but not of much help when the comparison began to go against him. For no sooner had the contract been dissolved than the issue returned. "After the dissolution of the Contract," Cavendish informed the company on May 7, "the Companies supposed all things quiet"; just then, however, Johnson and other opponents of the contract "delivered unto his Majesty a very bitter and grievous petition against the Government and carriage of the Company these four last years." From this onslaught, accompanied as it was by an "unmasking" of the true condition of the colony, stemmed the investigation that was to doom the company in little more than two months.[40]

The campaign against Sandys was beautifully organized. The complaints of economic mismanagement, coming from respected London merchants, were bound to have cumulative effect, although a month earlier Cranfield had been inclined to dismiss them. Even more damaging was the carefully timed "unmasking" of the woeful situation in Jamestown. The author, Captain Nathaniel Butler, had been a protégé of Warwick even before the earl and Sandys parted company. This quarrel, never healed, had arisen in 1619 over Sir Edwin's refusal to offer a haven to a ship Warwick had sent out on a privateering mission under the command of Samuel Argall. Instead, the Virginia Company had gone to the Privy Council in 1620 to denounce Argall's expedition, on the ground that the nascent colony could not afford to give offense to the Spaniards. Butler was the governor of the Bermuda colony at the time. He did give Argall refuge, and thus placed himself irrevocably on Warwick's side of the dispute. There is good reason to suppose that, when his term as governor of Bermuda expired in 1622, Butler deliberately stopped off at Jamestown on his way back to England so that he could give first-hand information about the colony's deterioration.[41]

And there is no question that Sandys and his friends seriously mishandled their defense. They were caught completely by surprise by Johnson's and Butler's documents; as late as April 18, Cavendish was describing conversations with Cranfield in which he was unaware that the axe was about to fall. He had copies of the two damaging documents five days later, but by then they had reached the Privy Council. During the crucial week, Butler had exulted to Rich that "our petition and my declaration are as yet

---

[40] Ibid., 2:320, 392. Johnson's petition is in ibid., 2:374–375, followed by the "unmasking" that Nathaniel Butler composed after a visit to Virginia late in 1622.

[41] The story of the quarrel, and Butler's part in it from 1619 to 1623, is in Craven, *Dissolution*, 134–140, 254–258. See in general David Hebb, *Piracy and the English Government, 1616–1642* (Aldershot, Hampshire, 1994).

... unknown to them in the particulars." Throughout this period, moreover, Rich was furiously at work, gathering arguments and evidence to bolster Butler's contentions, drawing up a list of over eighty Virginia adventurers who opposed Sandys's regime, advising the commission of inquiry, and clearly working behind the scenes in exactly the fashion that Sir Edwin himself had used to such good effect in his political ventures.[42] Now the pursuer was the pursued, and he fell straight into the perfectly arranged trap.

The commission of inquiry, announced at the April 17 Privy Council meeting at which the two factions had made their opposing cases, was officially appointed on May 9. Within four days, however, the Sandys party, despite protestations welcoming the investigation, compromised itself totally in the government's eyes. For the replies it prepared to refute Johnson and Butler were intemperate and insinuating, and they were accompanied by a lengthy and ill-advised denunciation of Warwick as the conspirator behind the entire proceedings.[43] This document was quickly brought before the Privy Council, where it was judged to be an "impertinent declaration, consisting for the most part of bitter and unnecessary invectives and aspersions upon the person of the Earl of Warwick and others . . . styled his instruments and agents." As a result, Sandys, the Ferrar brothers, and Cavendish were confined to their lodgings on May 13 for having disobeyed the Council's command to cease "provocation" during the commission's inquiries.[44] Prevented from responding to the investigation in its most crucial phase, Sir Edwin faced a hopeless end game.

But there was little that he could have done to save the situation, because every one of the commissioners had some reason for resenting Sandys, or at least for favoring Warwick.[45] Moreover, not only was the com-

---

[42] Kingsbury, 2:367–368, 372 and 4:112. Ibid., 4:65–67 (marginal notes), 80–88, 92–93, 116–118, 124–126, 194–195 indicate some of Rich's activities during this period. See, too, below, note 52. The best analysis of Rich's maneuvers is Christopher Thompson's unpublished paper, "The Dissolution of the Virginia Company," an important study to which this chapter is much indebted.

[43] APC, 1621–1623, 469–470; Kingsbury, 4:575–580; 2:393–409. The company welcomed the Commission as a way to end the calumnies: ibid., 2:410–411, 429–430.

[44] APC, Colonial, 1613–1688, 64. Southampton, as a privy councillor, sensibly removed himself from prominence in Virginia affairs as the dispute unfolded: further evidence that the company was really run by Sandys and the Ferrars.

[45] The chairman, Sir Richard Jones, had been associated with Rich in 1622, investigating Irish affairs, as had Sir Nicholas Fortescue, who also—like three other members, Sir Francis Gofton, Sir Richard Sutton, and Sir William Pitt—was a commissioner for naval affairs (all four were knighted on the same day in February 1619) and was thus a colleague of Cranfield, Smythe, and Wolstenholme. Sutton came from Essex, a county dominated by Warwick. Sir Henry Spiller, another member, was the very M.P. whom Sandys's friend Heyman threatened with an investigation (during the debate over Sir Edwin's imprisonment in 1621) for having gone through Sandys's study searching for incriminating papers about extra-parliamentary

mission carefully tilted in advance, but it soon had more than enough evidence to condemn the company's administration. Just to make sure, though, the Privy Council kept Sir Edwin away. Cavendish and the Ferrars reappeared at a company meeting on May 24, newly released from confinement, but Sandys, though ostensibly freed at the same time, did not come to a meeting until April of the following year. What apparently happened was that, instead of removing all restraint, the government ordered Sir Edwin to the country. For on June 19 he wrote to Cranfield to thank him for "procuring my liberty to return to the city."[46] He had presumably just come back to London, which meant that throughout the decisive first month of the commission's inquiry he was *hors de combat*. Indeed, the commission's report, totally unfavorable to Sandys, was ready for the king only a week or so after Sir Edwin wrote his letter to Cranfield.[47] By then it was much too late to save the day, and he was already looking beyond the immediate disaster toward a possible reconciliation with the Court. If Cranfield had been kind enough to procure his liberty, might he not now put in a good word with James?

It was a foolish expectation. The attack on Warwick had been a dreadful mistake, fully exploited by his enemies, and he may soon have realized that Cranfield's supposed kindness was offered only after he had been kept away during the decisive weeks. That removal was a testimony to Sandys's skills in maneuvering, but his opponents need not have worried. Caught by surprise, he made blunder after blunder: refusing to consider Rich's alternative to the contract, rejecting Cranfield's repetition of the same scheme, and then stupidly denouncing Warwick. It may be that he was worried about the future of a Virginia deprived of the profits of a tobacco monopoly, and fearful that the colonists' desperate situation, concealed until Butler's revelations, might force the abandonment of Jamestown. His absorption in these matters, and in his wife's continuing ill health, may explain the uncharacteristic ineptness of his counterattack.[48] Yet even his mistakes and his absence were relatively trivial by comparison with the devastating and unanswerable evidence that was marshaled against him.

---

activity. The final member of the commission, Sir Henry Bourchier, was on the New England Council, and thus linked to Gorges, whose New England patent Sandys attacked in 1621. See Victor Treadwell, "The Irish Court of Wards under James I," *Irish Historical Studies* 12 (1960–61): 1–27, p. 18; and BL, Additional, 4756 (both cited in Thompson, "Dissolution of the Virginia Company"); *CSP, Ireland, 1615–1625*, 345; Wm. A. Shaw, *The Knights of England*, 2:171; *APC, 1618–1619*, 434; *CD*, 4:441; Theodore K. Rabb, *Enterprise and Empire: Merchant and Gentry Investment in the Expansion of England, 1575–1630* (Cambridge, Mass., 1967), 250.

[46] Kingsbury, 2:413–414, 434, 518, 4:239–240; *APC, Colonial, 1613–1680*, 63–64; *APC, 1621–1623*, 498.

[47] Kingsbury, 2:450; 4:215–218.

[48] Ibid., 4:239.

Johnson's petition and Butler's "unmasking" were not long documents—about six hundred and nine hundred words respectively—but they contained more than enough indictments of Sandys's administration. Johnson made four points: that a great deal of money had been lost; that the colony had been unproductive, despite a "great multitude" of emigrants; that the Indian assault had been allowed to happen; and that high-handed leadership had caused discord among adventurers who had lost money and had no recourse but an appeal to the king. Butler, speaking from first-hand experience, was even blunter. The location of Jamestown was unhealthy; its facilities were dreadful, both for shipping and for new immigrants; food shortages caused speculation and terrible hardship; living conditions were appalling; the requirements of defense had been ignored; all the company's high hopes for industry and agriculture were laughed at as tobacco alone flourished; there was little respect for law; and only two thousand of the ten thousand people transported to Virginia were still alive, "many of them also in a sickly and desperate state." If the situation were not remedied soon, then "instead of a plantation, it will shortly get the name of a slaughter house and so justly become both odious to ourselves and contemptible to all the world."[49]

The vivid image drove home Butler's critique. His assessment of the state of Jamestown has inspired analogies with the freewheeling frontier communities of the American West, though it seems fairer to see the Indian attack as a milestone in the settlers' growing autonomy and self-suffiency in face of misjudgements by the home company.[50] Sandys's pathetic rebuttals—full of excuses; promises of improvement; accusations that Butler exaggerated; and direct evasions, like the claim that the Company was "ignorant how many have been transported or are now living there"—revealed that he had no real defense once the truth was known, though he may have hinted at the colonists' rising determination to serve their own needs when he noted that the pitiful homes looked that way because "houses there were most built for use and not for ornament." Significantly, the residents of Virginia who were asked to verify his answers at the end of the document refused to acknowledge his one substantive refutation of Butler: thirteen out of the sixteen would not confirm Sandys's avowal—misinformed at best—that all the settlements were well defended with

[49] Ibid., 2:373–376.

[50] Edmund S. Morgan, "The First American Boom: Virginia 1618–1630," *William and Mary Quarterly*, 3d ser., 28 (1971); Governor Wyatt's June 21, 1622, proclamations in Kingsbury, 3:658–660. For the growing control of their own affairs by the colonists, see David Konig, "Colonization and the Common Law in Ireland and Virginia, 1569–1634," in *The Transformation of Early American History*, ed. James Henretta, Michael Kammen, and Stanley Katz (New York, 1991), 70–92—a reference I owe to Karen Kupperman.

ordnance and palisades.[51] He could reasonably argue with Johnson about the state of finances when Smythe left the governorship of the company, but he could not deny the economic shortcomings of his schemes for mass migration; on all other major issues, including the disastrous condition of the colony, he had no case at all.

Under these circumstances, it was merely bad luck that proof of the extent to which the hardship had been concealed arrived in the form of a letter from an unimpeachable sourse: Sir Edwin's own brother, George. That tireless traveler, who had already journeyed through Europe to Constantinople and the Holy Land, had gone to Jamestown as treasurer of the colony the previous year. Only John Smith had come to Virginia with as much experience of foreign lands, and it was certainly not because of an inability to come to terms with unfamiliar conditions that he reacted with such dismay to what he found. The ill luck that intervened, as far as Sir Edwin was concerned, was that George was unaware of Wrote's campaign of the previous winter when, on March 28, 1623, he wrote about the state of the colony to a man who had been both a friend and a colleague of his brother's in the company, and whom he could not have suspected of ill will, namely, Samuel Wrote. The letter immediately found its way into Sir Nathaniel Rich's hands, its choicer parts emphasized by marginal comments.[52]

It was not as if the letter had malicious intent. George was in fact trying to improve the level of information available to his *friends*. He wrote at the same time to Ferrar with a similar story. What particularly upset him was that the directors of the company in London were berating the leadership in the colony, and had been ever since the Indian attack, for failing to carry out impossible demands. Indeed, he told Ferrar that he was writing directly to him, and not to the company at large, because their previous irritation convinced him that they would "both judge and condemn whatsoever succeeds not to their desires, without either inquiry of the truth or necessity of our actions." And this would be especially true now because the tobacco crop had been poor, a shipbuilding scheme had "failed with the rest in this general decay," a storm and an angry Italian glassworker had sabotaged the glass works, the mulberry trees and vines were still in the planning stage, and the company had sent instructions whose consequences were a further "straggling" of the settlements. George was convinced that the ignorance about Virginia was appalling, and he advised Ferrar to "adventure not too much in joint stocks" because fevers were so common and so high that no project could be completed.[53]

---

[51] Kingsbury, 2:381–386.

[52] Ibid., 4:64–69; see also above, note 42.

[53] Kingsbury, 4:22–26. George wrote to the same effect to his brothers Miles and Samuel,

Ferrar had had such information earlier. The previous autumn he had sent a letter to Sir Edwin Sandys in Kent about "the desperate state of Virginia". Moreover, the councillors in Jamestown had sent the company a gloomy letter in January 1623, deploring the blame that had been placed on them, which "added sorrow to affliction," and stressing how hard the road to success would be.[54] George Sandys must therefore have assumed that his letters would come as no surprise; he was seeking help when he told Wrote that supplies were inadequate, sickness and mortality were horrendous, and the company's instructions had been ill-advised. The council in Virginia had already complained about the London directors urging the colonists to fraternize with the Indians (a fatal mistake), and George explicitly condemned the policy that spread plantations (contrary to local wishes) far beyond a defensible perimeter—presumably so as to increase the land available for tobacco. He could hardly have been more pessimistic; nor could his testimony have been better designed to seal the case against his brother's administration. Indeed, his letter was quoted (doubtless at Rich's instigation) when the commission of inquiry justified its condemnation of Sir Edwin.[55]

The letter's most crippling revelation, as it wound its way toward the commission, was the extent to which the company had hidden the truth from public view. The angry responses to Johnson and Butler had been almost entirely hypocritical, and the attacks on Warwick and Smythe had been both gratuitous and diversionary. There were already grounds for suspicion when the company sought to avoid telling the colonists that the tobacco contract had failed, and now the untrustworthiness was confirmed.[56]

The strategy of Sandys and his colleagues was thus not only underhanded but self-defeating; their own testimony condemned them as mismanaging and devious defenders of a ruined cause. The endless stream of settlers may have kept the colony manned, but it caused much hardship, and Sandys's chimeric schemes for diversity in manufactures and agriculture had contributed to the disorder, suffering, and death. For all the high ideals of his earliest colonial activities, their impracticality had at last overwhelmed him. Refusing to admit error, even in the wake of the Indian

---

and these letters, together with one to Sir Edwin that has not survived, fell into the hands of Sir Nathaniel Rich when the contents of the ships that brought them were inspected for the commission of inquiry in May and June 1623: ibid., 4:158–161, 228–239. The two dozen letters Rich obtained all told the same story.

[54] Ferrar's letter was probably sent in September, because the quotation comes from Sandys's reply, dated from Northbourne October 13, 1622: ibid., 3:692. For the councillors' letter, see ibid., 4:9–17.

[55] Ibid., 4:10, 64–68, 216.

[56] Ibid., 2:372.

attack, he had antagonized the settlers, refused to change course, and sought self-justification at the expense of truth. As soon as the facts were revealed, his downfall was inescapable.

Compared to the disaster which intensified so rapidly in the spring of 1623, the factions in company meetings that Sir Edwin had feared the previous year, and the petitions organized by Sir Thomas Smythe, were of small account.[57] The fatal blows were the deterioration in Virginia and his own stupidity in trying to bluff his way through criticism. It was extraordinary misjudgement for a man normally so clear-headed and so adept at political maneuvering. Why his good sense failed him at this juncture is difficult to say. Perhaps Nicholas Ferrar, in charge of day-to-day company affairs, became more influential because Sandys was often absent. Perhaps the illness of Sir Edwin's wife distracted him. Or perhaps (and most likely) the actual situation in Virginia was so grave that he saw no alternative but a bold front. He may have felt that the crisis would pass, that in the interim he ought to defend himself with every conceivable means, and that if these tactics failed then at least he was no worse off than if he admitted his failures at the outset.

Seen in this light, his actions may not have been devoid of calculation. That the odds were against him was clear, but he may have thought he had no choice if he was to try to retain control of the company. Admittedly, he might have salvaged more of his reputation if he had acknowledged early in 1623 how seriously his policies had been mistaken, and offered to withdraw from company affairs. But no Jacobean gentleman would have accepted such humiliation lightly, and Sandys could have convinced himself that, without his enthusiasm, Virginia would not survive. By accepting defeat, might he not be suggesting it was not worth the effort to settle a land as forbidding as the New World? Sir Edwin was of course proved wrong on all counts, yet it would be unfair to represent him as purely self-serving during the agonizing last months of the Virginia Company. Mistaken he may have been, but as he watched the organization disintegrate he refused to abandon the commitments that had motivated him, six years before, to seek new glory for England overseas.

THE COMPANY DISSOLVED

The denouement was as rapid as it was relentless. In March 1623 Rich had made his first dent in Cranfield's support of Sandys's administration. By June the commission of inquiry had concluded that the colony was "in a very poor and almost desperate estate," "reduced into great extremities" for lack of food, defense, and order, and that only direct action from the

---

[57] Ibid., 3:680, 616; the "Sir T.S." on the latter page was undoubtedly Smythe.

king himself could relieve "the most calamitous and distressed estate" and "extreme miseries" of the settlers. Before June was over, the company's annual election had been stopped by the king and the Privy Council had accepted the commission's conclusions; then, in July, James suggested, and the attorney-general and solicitor-general formally reported, that the Virginia patent was flawed and could be revoked. All that remained was to institute the legal proceedings that dissolved the company.[58]

The law moved more slowly; it took another ten months, until May 1624, before the company was formally dissolved and the king officially resumed direct control of the colony.[59] But the fate of the Sandys administration had been decided between late March, when Rich's activities began to gather momentum, and late June, when the commission reached its conclusions. At the earliest, the start of the downfall could be dated back to Wrote's first outburst in December: a debacle so swift that Sir Edwin seemed to have been tossed aside almost casually.

That Jamestown was not, in actuality, on the point of collapse was soon discovered, and was confirmed by its prosperity over ensuing years—a prosperity that was made possible by the very measure for which Sandys had fought so desperately in 1622, a proclamation forbidding the importation of all but Virginian and Bermudan tobacco, which James finally issued in March 1625.[60] And it could also be argued that, had Sandys not relentlessly poured settlers into Jamestown, the colony would indeed have disappeared. The hardships he caused are clear, but one can ask how even a minimum settlement could have been maintained, given the death rates and other losses, if the stream of immigrants had not averted the danger of total depopulation—hastened by the Indian attack—during the early 1620s. Sandys may not have been Virginia's wisest or most comprehending

[58] Ibid., 2:451, 459, 4:216–218, 244, 255–256. A more detailed analysis of the events of 1623 and their consequences, of the issues that Sandys and his opponents disputed, and of the condition of Virginia, is in Craven's *Dissolution*, chaps. 9 and 10—repeated here only in outline. On Sir Edwin's brief confinement to his house because of his dispute with Warwick, see PRO, PC 2-31, fol. 699. The futility of the counterattack is evident in the manuscript edited by David Ransome: Nicholas Ferrar's *Sir Thomas Smith's Mismanagement of the Virginia Company* (Cambridge, 1990). By claiming that (unlike Smythe's arbitrary government) they had promoted constitutional politics (7), the Sandys group was drawing a contrast that, considering Cavendish's prominence (xi), may have amused Cavendish's secretary Thomas Hobbes.

[59] Craven, *Dissolution*, 318.

[60] Ibid., 325–326. The April 1624 letter to Rich from John Harvey, the leader of the investigation in Virginia, admitted: we "do find the persons here more in number, and provisions of victuals to be more plentiful than we expected." Kingsbury, 4:476. James's proclamation is in James F. Larkin and Paul L. Hughes, eds., *Stuart Royal Proclamations*, vol. 1 (Oxford, 1973), 626–632.

leader, but there is little question that, without him, the colony would not have survived.

But Sir Edwin failed miserably in the propaganda war; and if his administrative failures were not quite as catastrophic as the commission believed, they were still serious enough to merit his removal from a position of power. Thus the triumph of his opponents was complete. They dominated the commission set up in 1624 to run Virginia; Warwick took over the tobacco contract; and his and Smythe's friends regained control of Bermuda.[61] There was even an attempt to smear Sandys's good name by suggesting that he had "republican" ambitions and hated monarchy. Rich gathered some evidence on this subject, not from Sir Edwin's speeches and writings, where he might have found some suggestive nuggets, but from Captain John Bargrave, a Kentish neighbor of Sir Edwin who seems to have been hopelessly confused, and whose concern about antimonarchical sentiments was apparently a private obsession, to which he gave voice not only in secret with Rich, but also in a formal letter to Cranfield.[62]

A FINAL FLOURISH

None of this did any real harm to Sandys himself. The English "Establishment" could divide and reunite with consumate ease, and the loss of Virginia did not affect any of his other activities. Indeed, it was apparent to those who knew him that his standing in the second major forum in which he operated, Parliament, would be undiminished. That is doubtless why the Privy Council, probably urged by Cranfield, tried in December 1623 to send Sir Edwin as a sheriff to Ireland, where he would have been prevented from sitting in the Commons.[63] But he did return to the House in 1624, he did reassert his claim to influence, and he did gain a good measure of revenge on his enemies. Nor did his trading interests come to an end: the East India Company was going through hard times in the 1620s, but it was still very much alive, and a continuing focus of Sandys's attention.

[61] Kingsbury, 4:490–497; BL, Additional, 12,496, fols. 440–446, a reference I owe to Christopher Thompson; Craven, *Dissolution*, 332.

[62] Kingsbury, 4:194–195, 223–224. The real meaning of Bargrave's famous testimony is lucidly exposed in Craven, *Dissolution*, 278–283.

[63] *APC, 1623–1625*, 157–158; *CSP, Domestic, 1623–1625*, 134, 144. Symptomatic of the cohesion of the "Establishment" was the reported offer by Southampton of a marriage alliance with Cranfield in the summer of 1623, as the Virginia Company was collapsing. That the offer was accompanied by the prophetic warning that the lord treasurer needed all the friends he could get only accentuates the ability of England's elite to transcend personal slights: BL, Harleian, 1581, fol. 370, a reference I owe to Christopher Thompson.

Despite his differences with Sir Thomas Smythe, Sir Edwin was a member of the committee, or directors, of the company in 1622–23, though he was much distracted at the time with the last struggles of the Virginia Company. He had subscribed to the second East India joint stock, and took some dividends in pepper in 1624. Then, in May 1625, he became more closely involved in company matters. A disgruntled member, Anthony Withers, accused the company before the Privy Council of abandoning the trade with Persia. It was true that this particular connection was not faring well, and at one meeting of the committee the members had been warned to stop making "unfitting speeches" about the business because they might cause trouble. What came as a shock to the leadership when they appeared before the Privy Council was that Sandys was in attendance, standing on the other side from themselves, and (as they subsequently discovered) that he had seen the text of Withers' complaint in advance. But Sir Edwin was quick to reassure them. He stood on the other side, he told them, only because he had been called over by a lord who wanted to discuss a different matter. Neither he nor any other gentleman had any interest in the case, and certainly did not support Withers. The merchants, relieved that the "scandal" was getting no encouragement from a powerful quarter, threatened to sue Withers, and "rested confident" that Sir Edwin remained loyal—as indeed he did. When he complained the following May that a clerk had not been willing to pay him his dividend and had been rude, the leadership reprimanded the foolish man.[64]

The issue that drew Sandys more closely into company affairs, and in fact prompted his last public service, was the winding up of the second joint stock. It had become clear to the directors by 1627 that the adventurers in that joint stock were no longer capable of raising the funds they needed to keep the enterprise going. They had received good dividends, and now the issue had to be faced: either end all trading, or float a new joint stock offering. At a meeting of the committee on July 4, 1627, it was decided to acquaint a specially convened General Court with what was intended, and to suggest the formation of a joint committee of directors and adventurers to decide future action. At the General Court that afternoon, Sir Edwin headed the list of those elected to the joint committee, and he was present at its first meeting, on July 20, though not thereafter. Still, this initial appearance proved important in the long process of winding up the second joint stock, which was not completed until 1631, after Sandys's death.[65]

---

[64] India Office Library, East India Company Court Books B/10, 35–39, 60, 393.

[65] Ibid., B/11, 582; B/12, 11. The best account of the company's finances is K. N. Chaudhuri, *The English East India Company: The Study of an Early Joint-Stock Company 1600–1640* (London, 1965), 56–58, 64–69, 209–221.

One thing had to be established at once. Technically, only adventurers in the amount of £4,000 could be part of the joint committee (which excluded Sir Edwin), so that rule had to be waived. The governor of the Company, Maurice Abbot, then explained why all trading had been suspended. The profits were not sufficient, the rivalry of the Dutch too potent, and the investments too few. What could be done? Sandys was not sure, but in a long speech he made clear that the suspension would somehow have to be lifted. He was apologetic about the fact "that, being no merchant, he should adventure to speak in things unknown to him." Yet, as he pointed out (in characteristic vein), matters were "to be argued in point of reason and judgment," and here he felt qualified. The numbered list came next: the four points that required debate. First, could they continue as they were? The answer was no, because one could not trade without profit. Second, could it be made profitable? In the face of Dutch competition, that seemed unlikely. And that led to the third question, the causes, to which there were two answers: the Dutch, and the lack of investment. There was no real remedy for the first, he said, because although the English king could control his subjects, in the Netherlands a "popular" government, the Estates General, could not control its citizens. There was little point even in asking for royal help. Finally, therefore, the question arose: what was to be done? The only chance was to raise more funds, either through a new stock offering or by canceling dividends for two to three years. Which alternative was best he left to the merchants to decide. And their response, for the time being, was to continue the suspension until the future became clearer, though they did resume the Persian trade while the second joint stock was being settled.[66]

Sir Edwin remained in touch with the discussions that continued during the next two years. The situation was complicated in 1628 by a new attack on the leadership of the company, this time by Thomas Smethwick, another disgruntled adventurer, who was not silenced until 1635. The day his criticisms first became public, May 20, 1628, was also the day that Sandys became more deeply involved in East India affairs, as the newly appointed head of a committee of adventurers specifically instructed to work out ways of winding up the second joint stock. As a result of this assignment, he remained busy during the next few weeks, attending meetings on June 5 and 25, when a new joint stock was finally agreed upon.[67]

It may have been this activity that led to Sir Edwin's nomination, along with five others, for election to the governorship of the company on July 2, 1628. He withdrew his name, but it was a signal honor—a remarkable testimony to his contribution to Jacobean commerce. And he was still at

---

[66] Court Books, B/12, 20–25.
[67] Ibid., B/12, 366–377, 394, 395, 398, 410, 413.

work on July 16, when a number of privy councillors, including Buckingham and Pembroke, came to offer the company help against the Dutch.
Sandys complained that the Dutch would not honor their promises, but
the councillors disagreed and promised to do all they could. Sir Edwin also
argued that day for a continuation of the old joint stock. It was "against
justice," he said, to float a new one just when trade might be improving
and the king was showing signs of wanting to help. Now, he believed, "the
question is to be decided not by reason but by experience"—that is, the
adventurers deserved another chance to raise the capital. And he kept up
the plea two weeks later, at a meeting on July 30 which agreed that, although a new stock would have to be raised for one specific voyage for the
honor of company, nation, and king, the rights of the old adventurers
would continue in force for another year to allow them time to subscribe
the funds the company needed. As in many a parliamentary session,
Sandys's speech determined the outcome and concluded the meeting.[68]

Within a few months, though, it became clear that Sandys's rearguard
action could not be sustained. On February 20, 1629, a few months before
his death, the question of the joint stock came up again. The funds had not
been raised, and time was running out. Sir Edwin therefore suggested
calling a meeting of the old adventurers to decide how to proceed. With
his own failing health much on his mind, he made the obvious analogy:
"Like a dying man who desired and would be glad to die with the least
pain, so this dying stock might be ended with as little loss and disadvantage
as may be."[69]

The motion was highly complimented, and the meeting was called. Ten
days later, on March 2, Sandys addressed the gathering, which included
such notable old stockholders as the earl of Warwick and Lord Saye and
Sele. He told them that the trade had to continue, but the old stock had to
be wound up—though the adventurers were naturally welcome to continue their investment in the company. "The reputation of the kingdom"
required this course of action. Despite Saye and Sele's objections, Sandys—
"a courtly knight," in the words of the clerk keeping the minutes—proposed that the old adventurers forgo their last dividends for the good of
the company. The reason, he told Saye, was quite simply the lack of cash
on hand.[70]

Sir Edwin then delivered his formal report. It gave him "heart's grief" to
see the old adventure come to an end, but four considerations softened the
blow: first, the old adventurers could subscribe to the new stock; second,
the honor of the company was at stake; third, this solution would keep the

[68] Ibid., B/13, 7, 29–31, 42–46.
[69] Ibid., B/13, 300, 322.
[70] Ibid., B/13, 323, 337, 339, 341, 342.

trade going; and fourth, continued ventures were essential for the reputation of the kingdom. The old joint stock could be saved, he said, if the adventurers put up enough money, but their record was dismal, and there was no money to be had. In his conclusion he virtually wrote his own epitaph—a fitting touch, because this was the last speech of which we have any record in a lifetime of speeches. His death was much on his mind, but his hopes for his nation, and for England's commerce, did not flag: "For his own part, because he was dying to the world, and the world unto him, he was so indifferent that he cared not whither way it were concluded, yet for the honor of the Trade, and perpetuating the same to posterity, he should be glad to see the Trade go forward to the comfort of the Adventurers."[71] And Sir Edwin put his money behind his words. His last business venture was an investment in the company's new voyage, with the dividends left in his will to three of his daughters. Sandys remained the resolute supporter of England's overseas enterprises to the very last.

[71] Ibid., B/13, 339–340.

PART FOUR

Jacobean Gentleman

Chapter XIV

THE MEASURE OF THE MAN

Last Days

Less than six months after his last recorded public appearance, at the March 2 East India Company meeting, Sandys completed his will. It is dated August 25, 1629, and was probated on October 30. Death came in the second half of October, because on the sixteenth Katherine, writing to John Ferrar to congratulate him on the pregnancy of his wife, mentioned that after weeks of sickness, brought on by "Over Study," Sir Edwin had "mended again." To the end, his "Little Gidding friends" were apparently much on his mind and in his prayers.[1]

Sandys's will is in large part a standard legalistic document. But its opening bestowal of the soul into God's hands contrasts sharply with the businesslike dispositions that follow, and marks him as the traditional, High Church Anglican that he was. He looked to God, "the great father and lord of spirits," to redeem his soul, and allow it access to his heavenly kingdom, "there with angels and saints to enjoy the happy vision of the most glorious deity." It is a moving passage, infused with the devotional spirit one often senses behind the high moral tone, the orderliness, the sobriety of his public statements.

Sir Edwin's main concern was the distribution of his property, constrained though it had become. He left his estate first to his wife, and then in order to his sons. One of his houses, at Stoneham, needed £200 in repairs, and the land was mortgaged. But the Yorkshire property he had received from his father was still substantial. Sandys himself had valued one possession, the prebendry of Wetwang, at £380 a year, a tidy sum, though he had added that he cleared only £220. The lands in Bermuda and Virginia, and the estate at Northbourne, were also solid bequests. There was still a Sandys at Northbourne in 1798, fifty years after the Jacobean house had been pulled down; and Sir Edwin's oldest son, Henry, renewed the lease on the Aldersgate house in 1639. Of the other property, however, we have no further record, perhaps because Sandys left his family in less than solid financial condition. It has been estimated that someone in his position, who paid a subsidy assessment of more than £20, was probably

---

[1] MCFP, Box 14, no. 991; the probated copy of the will, described below, is in PRO, Prob. 11/156/84.

receiving an income of some £1,000 a year. That was a considerable sum, but it must have been heavily encumbered, for it is noteworthy that, although he left £1,500 to Oxford and £1,000 to Cambridge, to found chairs of metaphysical philosophy (the first sign of Sandys's interest in the subject), there is no record of any monies being paid. Presumably the executors and the widow simply did not have the necessary cash, and one can assume that the building of Northbourne, not to mention the investments in Virginia, had been a sufficiently heavy drain to affect his finances even after his death.[2]

The executors were old friends: Sir Robert Naunton, Gabriel Barbour, and John Ferrar; the two sons-in-law Richard Spencer and Sir Thomas Wilford; and two London business colleagues, Thomas Keightley and Richard Casewell. About the latter two we have no other information that links them especially with Sandys; nor about the man for whom Sir Edwin wished to name his chairs of philosophy, Francis Mecham, who had given his estate "considerable advancement." Keightley and Casewell were East India and Virginia colleagues, but Mecham had no such connection. The executors may have had a hard time fulfilling all the obligations. They were told, for example, to raise £1,500 by 1633 so that each of Sandy's three daughters could be guaranteed one-third of that amount if his three £500 investments in the East India Company failed—though in this case his fears were not realized, and the executors were relieved of a weighty responsibility. They had less of a problem in finding £12 to maintain a "singing man" at the Church of St. Peter in York—another indication of Sir Edwin's musical and religious commitments, consonant with his publication of hymns fifteen years before.

What Sandys thought of the stirring events in the Commons during his

[2] Ibid.; Charterhouse Muniments, L3/66; *Archaeologia Cantiana* 24 (1900): 107. Henry Sandys's renewal of the lease on the Aldersgate house in 1639 (Guildhall Record Office, City Lands Grant Book 2, 81) was for thirty-one years, but it is not clear how long the family held it after Henry died in 1644. The use of subsidy payments (see above, chapter 11, note 25) to estimate income derives from Terence Hartley, "The Sheriffs of the County of Kent, c. 1580–c. 1625," (Ph.D. diss., London University, 1970), 77–78, 88, 92. Sir Edwin's widow Katherine survived until 1640 (BL, Additional, 33,920, fol. 45), and she vigorously pursued family business, often with help from the Ferrars. There is evidence as early as 1608 and again in 1623 of her involvement in her husband's financial affairs (see above, chapter 2, note 39, and MCFP, Box 10, nos. 984, 992). After his death she completed her childrens' education (a new school, for example, had to be found for Tom, who was unhappy at Westminster); worried about Richard, off at the wars in the Netherlands; helped daughters to settle down; and fought successfully for resources both with her brother-in-law George (to whom Sir Edwin had owed money) and in a court case (which eventually involved the archbishop of York, the bishop of London, and the attorney-general) to keep the Wetwang living: ibid., Box 10, no. 992; Box 14, nos. 989, 993; Box 15, nos. 1532, 1620A; Box 16, no. 1532B; and Box 17, nos. 990, 994, 995.

last months we do not know. He was in London while the 1628–29 Parliament was sitting, and he would certainly have had first-hand reports of the Petition of Right, the explosive dissolution, and much else besides. Always a voice of moderation, he must have found the emotion and violence distressing. It may in fact have been a blessing that he died before the full consequences of the upheavals of the 1620s could be foreseen.

Torn between his wish for order and his deep concern for England's welfare, Sir Edwin might have had a hard time choosing sides in the 1630s and 1640s, though his dislike of the Puritans would probably have inclined him toward the Royalists in the end. Still, the ambiguity of his inclinations remained visible, by reflection, even after he died, in the Civil War record of his own family. Two sons, Edwin and Richard, became colonels in the Parliamentary army—the first killed at Worcester, and the second notorious for his dictatorial ways in Kent. A third son, Robert, lost an arm on the other side, fighting both Scots and Irish in the king's service; he claimed to have been in Charles's Privy Chamber. Charles II ordered him paid £1,000 for his services, and eventually Robert settled in County Roscommon, on an estate named Sandifled, as the respectable son-in-law of an Irish viscount.[3] His brother-in-law, Richard Spencer, was a well-known Arminian, and another confirmed Royalist. The four most prominent members of the next generation, in other words, were neatly divided: two in leading roles for Parliament, two for the king. The spectrum was complete within the family circle, as indeed it had been within the striving and embracing mind of Sir Edwin himself.

REPUTATION

After the dramatic events of the generation following Sir Edwin's death, the period he had lived through was assigned, by comparison, a sedate though still vital place in his country's history. Apart from its extraordinary status in literature, and its major importance in intellectual and artistic developments, the England of the late Elizabethans and the Jacobeans came to be seen as the birthplace of two of the nation's most distinctive achievements: its constitutional structure, and its empire. As these became matters of growing interest, particularly in the nineteenth century, so Sandys's role as a father of both these progeny became established. It is therefore not inappropriate that the chief significance of his career should derive from his contribution to these early ferments of political change and

[3] Sandys, *Family of Sandys*, pt. 2, pedigree D, and pt. 1, 240. Sir Edwin's oldest son, Henry, described as "Captain" when he renewed the lease on the Aldersgate house, died young (about thirty-eight) in 1644, during the civil wars. This suggests he was a soldier, but if so his allegiance is unknown.

overseas activity. And yet we must be more cautious than some of our Whig ancestors when we put his life into the perspective of his times and the larger movements of English history.

Perhaps the sharpest statement of the Whig view came from Alexander Brown, the historian of early American colonization. Starting with Hume's opinion that, in James I's reign, "men of genius and enlarged minds had adopted the principles of liberty which were, as yet, pretty much unknown to the generality of the people," Brown addressed Sandys's activities both in the Commons and in Virginia, where the House of Burgesses began meeting during Sandys's leadership of the company. After adding the sponsorship of the Pilgrims (whose principles Sir Edwin deplored, but whose eagerness to settle across the Atlantic he desperately needed) Brown concluded that "something was in the air." The apostle of freedom and of America was one and the same man, after all. What, then, was more natural than the conclusion, framed as a rhetorical question, "Was the seed of our Revolution planted with the colonies?"[4]

Sandys as the beacon of liberty, both in Parliament and in America, was an image that satisfied Virginian patriotism as well as romantic republicanism. The juxtaposition seems particularly appealing because it makes the early colonies participants in the great constitutional struggles of the day— secret outposts of resistance to Stuart tyranny. None of these rose-colored views, however, not even the more modest assessment that Sir Edwin was a liberal "in political sympathy" with the Puritans, and "an almost ideal administrator" of Virginia, has survived the scholarship of the past fifty years. Starting with Craven's study of the Virginia Company, a rethinking has begun that perhaps enables us to see Sandys in terms that he himself might have understood.[5]

Craven's great contribution (and this biography, started under his direction, is in many ways an elaboration of his work) was to put Sir Edwin's leadership of the Virginia enterprise into context. Gone was the heroic idealist, the revolutionary pioneer, and even the good administrator. Instead, there was a member of the gentry with an unusually intense interest in trade and colonization, who used his political adroitness to take over the company, but then mismanaged it sufficiently to lose control. I have argued that, despite the mismanagement, Sandys's regime may well have ensured the survival of the colony, but in all essential respects Craven's

[4] Alexander Brown, *The Genesis of the United States*, 2 vols. (Boston, 1890), 2:992–993.

[5] Herbert L. Osgood, *The American Colonies in the Seventeenth Century*, vol. 1 (New York, 1904), 80–81, 131; W. F. Craven, *Dissolution of the Virginia Company: The Failure of a Colonial Experiment* (New York, 1932); for other works, see the notes to chapters 12 and 13, passim.

portrait of a well-intentioned landed gentleman out of his depth remains convincing.[6]

The parliamentary career alone had never been subject to the same degree of romanticization. Even in the Whig literature, Sir Edwin's feet remain fairly well planted on the ground. Gardiner attributed to him three major characteristics: first, a demeanor that ensured he "enjoyed the confidence of the House"; second, "a large fund of common sense"; and third, a willingness "to raise his voice for the toleration of those with whom he did not wholly agree." It would be hard to quarrel with any of those impressions, and they have been confirmed again and again in these pages. One might add other dimensions to the man, but it was entirely appropriate that Gardiner returned to "common sense" as Sir Edwin's identifying trait when he described the end of his long parliamentary career. Together with his tolerance and his ability to sway his colleagues, this feature of Sandys's speeches remains the bedrock of any interpretation. The larger claims that were made for his activities by Notestein and other successors of the Whigs, and the useful correctives that have been offered by recent revisions of the traditional account, have not reduced the appropriateness of Gardiner's judgment.[7] If Sir Edwin is to be seen in the round—as writer, as M.P., as colonizer, as landed gentleman, indeed as an essential Jacobean type—then we can do no better than to start with the man who, among his many appearances in the long historiography of his age, emerges most convincingly from the pages of Gardiner and Craven.

For a start, why did Sir Edwin elicit such respect in the Commons? He was no powerful presence. Even his portrait seems to emphasize his typicality, the small beard making his face seem pointed, in the Jacobean fashion. Nor is there other evidence that he stood out from his colleagues. That he carried weight was due to the substance of what he said, not the sparkle of his delivery. He was certainly a shrewd political maneuverer, and he also understood how advantageous it was to be thought of as commonsensical, logical, and lucid; but it was the matter rather than the manner that sustained his dominance of the House. Even the compliments he received for his speeches seem to have been prompted by his ideas, his well-shaped arguments, and his clarity, rather than his oratory.

His persuasiveness stemmed, first, from who he was: a well-known and eminently respectable member of the landed establishment, familiar in

---

[6] Craven, *Dissolution*; I was most fortunate to have had Craven's invaluable comments on early drafts of chapters 12 and 13 of this book before he died in 1981.

[7] S. R. Gardiner, *History of England . . . 1603–1642*, 10 vols. (London, 1883–84), 1:165 and 5:362. For more recent work, see my "Revisionism Revised: Two Perspectives on Early Stuart Parliamentary History," *Past & Present*, no. 92 (1981): 55–99, and the literature cited there.

Yorkshire and Kent as well as London, always thoughtful and willing to concern himself with the issues of the day, and inherently worth hearing both because of his learning (gained through an unusually long education) and because of his experience. By the time he assumed a prominent role in the Commons, he was in his forties, well traveled, and a twenty-year veteran of the House. In addition, he must have seemed reassuringly trust-worthy to the profoundly conservative gentry M.P.s. Not only was he who he was—one of them—but his middle-of-the-road, traditional stance in religious affairs, as a disciple of Hooker, must have removed all suspicion of radical intent. Even his boldest utterances could be tempered by his reputation for orthodoxy.

And what Sandys said confirmed the expectation. This was the second and most important source of his success. Pragmatic country gentlemen wanted to hear ideas that sounded reasonable, logical, and sensible, espe-cially in the areas that were Sandys's principal concerns, the economic well being and the reputation of his country. It was appropriate that he re-garded disturbance as anathema, and that he was particularly anxious to keep religious innovations within bounds. The very word "innovation" re-mained pejorative, even to so inventive a mind as Bacon's.[8] Particularly appealing, therefore, were Sir Edwin's insistence on tolerance and his reg-ular reliance on the force of common sense. That he made economic mat-ters his specialty allowed him to address the House's central worry, the country's and the king's lack of funds, on many fronts. That he urged mod-eration, in constitutional as well as religious disputes, placed him in that middle of the road where his colleagues felt most comfortable. And that he delivered speeches that were wonderfully easy to follow, with their clear outlines and numbered heads, endeared him to an educated class that increasingly appreciated the merits of plain speech, and was delighted when it could follow every argument (which was not often the case with major parliamentary speeches, as diarists and journal keepers reveal).[9] Sandys had the knack of appearing to be the reasonable party, regardless of the proposal he was making or the cause he was disputing.

Sir Edwin was helped, too, by his ability to sense the frustrations and ambitions of his fellow gentry. He became a spokesman and a guide be-cause he understood the feelings of his audience. As the activities and powers of royal government increased, despite inadequate resources, so the great questions of finance, prerogative, and subjects' rights arose. On

[8] See my "Francis Bacon and the Reform of Society" in *Action and Conviction in Early Modern Europe*, ed. Theodore K. Rabb and Jerrold E. Seigel (Princeton, N.J., 1969), 169–193.

[9] On plain speech, see Barbara Shapiro, *Probability and Certainty in Seventeenth-Century England: A Study of Relationships between Natural Science, Religion, History, Law, and Literature* (Princeton, 1983).

each of these questions it was natural for the landed class, growing in wealth, responsibilities, and education, to wax suspicious about policies or demands that it interpreted as infringing on traditional privileges or that it regarded as mistaken for the nation. It was more willing to reach its own conclusions about what was best for England, and less hesitant to express itself. Those were the very feelings Sir Edwin tapped. In straightforward and moderate tones, he portrayed the actions he opposed, from the Union with Scotland to a message threatening dissolution of Parliament, as unreasonable, as against custom, or as contrary to law. He, like his gentry colleagues, knew what was right for them and for the country. They knew about economic problems; they knew about religious passions; they knew about Catholic threats; and they were not to be ignored on these and similar issues. It was not that they (or Sandys) had a program, a vision to compare with Cecil's, but they did perceive *alternatives*. What Sir Edwin was able repeatedly to persuade the House was that his alternative was the one that made the most sense. Infused with Hookerian tolerance and a magisterial comprehensiveness, the ideal of mixed government and broad consultation that he articulated, colored as it was by an aversion to disorder, won instant assent. And with his colleagues behind him, Sandys was able to forge a new and unique role for himself, and for the independent gentry at large, as partners with the government in shaping public policy.

Occasionally, the tack the Commons took was self-serving; sometimes, it was merely obstructionist. But on the whole Sandys and those who followed his lead were both responsible and high-minded. To dismiss him, and the many who agreed with him, as mere clients of powerful courtiers, or as selfish office-seekers making trouble so as to be bought off, is to demean public figures of notable substance. The emphasis on private agendas reduces a thoughtful and largely responsible body of legislators, let alone the individuals among them, to a swarm of opportunists driven solely by ambition and greed. Sandys would probably have accepted office if it had come his way, but the surviving evidence suggests that he neither sought it nor drew his motives from the search. He had other ways of making his presence felt. The cynical view of his actions, and of the behavior of his fellow M.P.s, is mainly an argument from silence, which implies that a few conspicuous cases explain every case. Yet even those who did gain office, such as Digges and Wentworth, let alone Coke, are dismissed too easily if one assumes they spoke as they did only, or even mainly, in hope of advancement.

It seems far more plausible to start from the simple truth that there was plenty of room for honest disagreement on most of the matters Parliament discussed. Again and again when he disagreed with an official line, one can see in Sir Edwin a consistent wish for fewer government demands and lower taxes, for political, legal, and religious restraint, for the redress of grievances, and for economic prosperity—a program that reflected the deepest yearnings of generations of country gentry. To say that such views amounted to a "Country" or "patriot" vision of England's best interests is not to claim that they were held by a definable "opposition" group, but rather that they represented the general outlook of many M.P.s, an outlook that Sandys shared and advanced so effectively that he gained the leadership as well as the confidence of the Commons.

If, in Parliament, Sir Edwin embodied the growing willingness of the rulers of England's localities to assert their views about the nation's best interests, in the Virginia Company his activism set him apart. The gentry's enthusiasm for overseas ventures, their hope to emulate and outdo the hated Spaniard, cannot be doubted. Nevertheless, although hundreds of them were persuaded to invest their funds, offer their moral support, and attend the meetings that were essential to the new effort of colonization and trade, those who were prepared to board the ships or administer the enterprises in London were but a handful. Sandys was among that few, willing to take his belief in a great patriotic cause to the level of fervent participation. Yet even in this side of his career one can see that he captured the mood of his contemporaries; as in Parliament, he took the lead because he was not content to be an applauding bystander. Here, once again, his skills as a political maneuverer were apparent, particularly during the crisis periods when he deposed Smythe (another vote-gathering campaign, with no holds barred) and when the company came under the final assault. Still, his underlying commitment to the promotion of England's welfare never wavered, and this was the basic impetus for his overseas involvements. He may have been far more active than most, but he was essentially putting into practice, making effective, what his fellow gentry felt.

Sir Edwin's contribution to the intellectual life of his time may also seem out of the ordinary at first. Publishing a best-selling book that drew attention from the most famous scholars in Europe was not exactly usual for a country gentleman. Nor was it common, as yet, to have a town house in the capital and an Italianate villa in the country, or to mix with scientific and literary circles (if Sandys's contacts with the Wizard Earl and John Donne are any indication) as well as the commercial, legal, and aristocratic leaders of London society. Much of this aspect of Sandys's career has to remain speculative, because to be a good friend of Southampton's was no guarantee of acquaintance with Shakespeare, let alone patronage of the theatre. That Sir Edwin's relationships went in many directions through the culture of the age (via the Ferrars, for example, to Little Gidding and its unique spiritual and literary atmosphere) does not tell us much about his own preferences. For that we have only his book, his hymns, and the indications of the conservative Anglicanism that he inherited from his aging father and nurtured in the company of Hooker. But his religious stance was probably, once again, representative of the views of the large majority of the gentry. Certainly Sandys's instinct for tolerance and moderation epitomized the pragmatic faith that, for most of the members of his class, had the virtue of emphasizing order rather than passion. In other words, although in this respect, too, he was more active than was common for gentlemen, and perhaps closer than most to a scholarly and literary milieu, the opinions he expressed on the central issues of religious faith were largely conventional and widely accepted among the gentry of his day.

Born as he was just three years into Elizabeth's long reign, Sir Edwin carried with him many of the concerns of that age, even though in his last months the Petition of Right and the creation of the Massachusetts Bay Company marked the beginning of a new political and colonial world, which the M.P.s and colonizers of his early public years, in the 1580s and 1590s, would have been hard put to recognize. Physical confrontation in the Commons, and a colony that not only governed itself in America, without oversight from London, but spawned other colonies that did not even bother to seek royal charters—these were signs of a society more willing to come to the point of rupture. That Sandys would have found such developments profoundly distasteful suggests how deeply he was rooted in a previous age, despite his large responsibility, in the two central arenas of Parliament and empire, for the emergence of the very transformations that he might have disowned in 1629. In that respect, therefore, he was a quintessential Jacobean: a sometimes reluctant instrument of change, who exemplified a brief but crucial era that took for granted the necessity of a search for new solutions to growing political and financial problems; accepted the differences this search might provoke; and yet expected agreement and common ground always to crystalize and to preserve the harmony of the state. One finds that fine balance neither under Elizabeth nor under Charles, and it would be difficult to name a contemporary who was more closely identified with this attitude toward politics, finance, religion, and empire than Sandys, or whose active career coincided so closely with the critical reign of James I.

As the last few pages have argued, Sir Edwin embodied the attitudes of his class in many respects. Indeed, his success in both Parliament and Virginia can be attributed to this representativeness: his ability to express his colleagues' feelings, and to guide them in directions they wanted to go. Although his personal views may occasionally have strayed into an acerbity that was not publicly acceptable, on the whole he stood where they stood, he knew how to be their spokesman, and he exhibited the qualities and the anxieties that induced them to follow his lead.

Inexorably, however, they were all changing. In the Commons, each dispute, each new suspicion, moved attitudes one notch away from the deferential harmony that had dominated Elizabeth's reign. A respectable body of opinion, embracing more than the dismissible Puritans, was coming to proclaim a vision of England's interests rather different from the one that the king and his ministers (however divided) seemed to prefer. Sandys was perhaps the archetype of that shift, as he was of the struggle to secure the first ever permanent English colony overseas. Therein, in his typicality, lay the source of his power to persuade, to become the leader of his colleagues. This gentleman of unblemished orthodoxy—conservative, tolerant, paterfamilias to a large brood, the very emblem of reasonableness—was being driven by hope, by ideals, by a larger ambition for the good of his country, to become the hesitant promoter of new directions for the realm. The groundwork for vast changes in English society, and even for dramatic events, was laid by his generation. To the degree that Sir Edwin was instinctively traditional, yet willing to act forthrightly to lead his contemporaries toward what he saw as a better and a stronger nation, he helped in no small measure to shape the period in which he lived, and thus to win a place in history as the epitome of the Jacobean age.

INDEX

Note: Throughout, the abbreviation "ES" is used for Sir Edwin Sandys.

About the Author

THEODORE K. RABB is Professor of History at Princeton University. He is the author of *Renaissance Lives, The Struggle for Stability in Early Modern Europe,* and *Enterprise and Empire.* He coedited (with Robert I. Rotberg) *Climate and History* and *The New History* (Princeton).